Webster's
New Spanish
Notebook Dictionary

Wiley Publishing, Inc.

Webster's New Spanish Notebook Dictionary

Published by:
Wiley Publishing, Inc.
111 River Street
Hoboken, NJ 07030-5774
www.wiley.com

Published by Wiley, Hoboken, NJ
Published simultaneously in Canada

For general information on our other products and services or to obtain technical support, please contact our Customer Care Department within the U.S. at 800-762-2974, outside the U.S. at 317-572-3993 or fax 317-572-4002.

Wiley also publishes its books in a variety of electronic formats. Some content that appears in print may not be available in electronic books.

ISBN 978-0-470-37332-3

Designed and typeset by Chambers Harrap Publishers Ltd., Edinburgh.

Manufactured in the United States of America

10 9 8 7 6 5 4 3 2 1

Contents

Preface   iv

Guide to the pronunciation of Spanish   v

Abbreviations/Abreviaturas   vii

SPANISH–ENGLISH DICTIONARY/   1-60
DICCIONARIO ESPAÑOL–INGLÉS

ENGLISH–SPANISH DICTIONARY/   1-60
DICCIONARIO INGLÉS–ESPAÑOL

Preface

This handy dictionary is an accurate, reliable tool for learners of Spanish. With more than 25,000 words and expressions, it provides a wide-ranging selection of the most useful and up-to-date vocabulary of both Spanish (in its different regional varieties) and English.

The dictionary is designed to be easily read and used, with bold headwords and a compact, time-saving format.

Phrasal verbs are indicated by a bullet point and are listed after the verb on which they are based (e.g., see entry for **get**).

Numbers are used to divide grammatical categories of headwords with a solid block ▪ denoting meaning categories with longer entries (e.g., see entry for **do**).

An asterisk against an English verb denotes that it is irregular. A double asterisk against a Spanish noun, however, means that the feminine noun takes the masculine definite article **el** (e.g., **el agua**). The plural form is **las**.

The new system for Spanish alphabetical order has been adopted. In this system, **ch** and **ll** are no longer considered as separate letters of the alphabet, but each is incorporated at its respective position under **c** and **l**.

Finally, the syllabification of all English headwords has been included in this edition, providing the user with extra help.

Guide to the pronunciation of Spanish

Table of phonetic symbols

Letter	Phonetic symbol	Examples	Approximate English equivalent
Vowels:			
a	[a]	gato, amar, mesa	as in f*a*ther, but shorter
e	[e]	estrella, vez, firme	as in l*a*bor
i	[i]	inicio, iris	as in s*ee*, but shorter
o	[o]	bolo, cómodo, oso	between l*o*t and t*au*ght
u	[u]	turista, puro, tribu	as in f*oo*d, but shorter, but u in -que- or -qui- and -gue- or -gui- is silent (unless -güe- or -güi-)
Diphthongs:			
ai, ay	[ai]	b*ai*le, h*ay*	as in l*i*fe, *ai*sle
au	[au]	f*au*na	as in f*ow*l, h*ou*se
ei, ey	[ei]	p*ei*ne, l*ey*	as in h*a*te, f*eig*n
eu	[eu]	f*eu*do	pronounce each vowel separately
oi, oy	[oi]	b*oi*na, h*oy*	as in b*oy*
Semi-consonants:			
u	[w]	b*u*ey, c*u*ando, f*u*iste	as in *w*ait
i	[j]	v*i*ernes, vic*i*o, c*i*udad, f*i*arse	as in *y*es
Consonants:			
b	[b]	**b**oda, **b**urro, am**b**os	as in *b*e
	[β]	ha**b**a, tra**b**ar	a very light b
c	[k]	**c**abeza, **c**u**c**u, a**c**oso, fra**c**	as in *c*ar, *k*eep
	[s]	co**c**er, **c**ielo	as s in *s*illy, but in parts of Spain as in *th*ing
ch	[tʃ]	**ch**epa, o**ch**o	as in *ch*amber
d	[d]	de**d**o, an**d**ar	as in *d*ay
	[ð]	**d**e**d**o, aca**d**emia, aba**d**	as in *th*is (often omitted in spoken Spanish when at the end of a word)
f	[f]	**f**iesta, a**f**ición	as in *f*or
g	[g]	**g**as, ran**g**o, **g**ula	as in *g*et
	[ɣ]	a**g**ua, a**g**osto, la**g**arto	a very light g
g	[χ]	**g**enio, le**g**ión	similar to Scottish [χ] in lo*ch*

h		**h**ambre, a**h**ínco	Spanish h is silent
j	[χ]	**j**abón, a**j**o, relo**j**	similar to Scottish [χ] in lo**ch**
k	[k]	**k**ilo, **k**imono	as in *car*, *k*eep
l	[l]	**l**abio, hábi**l**, e**l**egante	as in *l*aw
ll	[j]	**ll**uvia, ca**ll**e	similar to the sound in *y*ellow
m	[m]	**m**ano, a**m**igo, ha**m**bre	as in *m*an
n	[n]	**n**ata, rató**n**, a**n**tes, e**n**emigo	as in *n*ight
ñ	[ɲ]	a**ñ**o, **ñ**o**ñ**o	similar to the sound in o*ni*on
p	[p]	**p**i**p**a, **p**elo	as in *p*oint
q	[k]	**q**uiosco, **q**uerer, tabi**q**ue	as in *c*ar
r(r̄)	[r]	pe**r**o, co**r**rer, pad**r**e	always pronounced, rolled as in Scots
	[rr]	**r**eír, hon**r**ado, pe**rr**o	rr is a lengthened r sound
s	[s]	**s**auna, a**s**ado, corté**s**	similar to the s in hi*ss*ing
t	[t]	**t**eja, es**t**én, a**t**raco	as in *t*ime
v	[b]	**v**erbena, **v**ena	as in *b*e
	[β]	a**v**e, vi**v**o	a very light b
x	[ks]	é**x**ito, e**x**amen	as in e*x*ercise
	[s]	e**x**tensión	as in e*s*tate
y	[j]	**y**erno, a**y**er, re**y**	as in *y*es
	[i]	**y**	as in s*ee*, but shorter
z	[s]	**z**orro, a**z**ul, ca**z**a, soe**z**	as in *s*illy, but in parts of Spain as in *th*ing

Stress rules

If a word ends in a vowel, **-n** or **-s**, the stress falls on the second last syllable:
m**a**no, ex**a**men, bocad**i**llos

If a word has any other ending, the stress falls on the last syllable:
habl**a**, Madr**i**d, ay**e**r

Exceptions to these rules carry a written accent on the stressed syllable:
c**ó**modo, legi**ó**n, h**á**bil

Abbreviations / Abbreviaturas

abbreviation	*abbr, abr*	abreviatura
adjective	*adj*	adjetivo
adverb	*adv*	adverbio
somebody, someone	*algn*	alguien
Latin America	*Am*	Hispanoamérica
Argentina	*Arg*	Argentina
article	*art*	artículo
Bolivia	*Bol*	Bolivia
Central America	*CAm*	Centroamérica
Caribe	*Carib*	Caribe
Colombia	*Col*	Colombia conjunction
conj	conjunción	
Southern Cone region (Argentina, Uruguay, Paraguay, Chile)	*CSur*	Cono Sur (Argentina, Uruguay, Paraguay, Chile)
definite	*def*	definido
demonstrative	*dem*	demostrativo
Ecuador	*Ecuad*	Ecuador
Spain	*Esp*	España
feminine	*f*	femenino
familiar	*fam*	familiar
figurative use	*fig*	uso figurado
feminine plural	*fpl*	femenino plural
future	*fut*	futuro
impersonal	*impers*	impersonal
indefinite	*indef*	indefinido
indeterminate	*indet*	indeterminado
indicative	*indic*	indicativo
interjection	*interj*	interjección
interrogative	*interr*	interrogativo
invariable	*inv*	invariable
irregular	*irreg*	irregular
masculine	*m*	masculino
Mexico	*Méx*	México
masculine plural	*mpl*	masculino plural
noun	*n*	nombre
Panama	*Pan*	Panamá
personal	*pers*	personal
plural	*pl*	plural
possessive	*poss, pos*	posesivo
past participle	*pp*	participio pasado
preposition	*prep*	preposición
present	*pres*	presente
preterite	*pret*	pretérito
pronoun	*pron*	pronombre
past tense	*pt*	pretérito
relative	*rel*	relativo
somebody, someone	*sb*	alguien
singular	*sing*	singular
something	*sth*	algo
subjunctive	*subj*	subjuntivo
auxiliary verb	*v aux*	verbo auxiliar
Venezuela	*Ven*	Venezuela
intransitive verb	*vi*	verbo intransitivo
impersonal verb	*v impers*	verbo impersonal
reflexive verb	*vr*	verbo reflexivo
transitive verb	*vt*	verbo transitivo
cultural equivalent	≃	equivalente cultural

A

a *prep (dirección)* to; **llegar a Valencia** to arrive in Valencia; **subir al tren** to get on the train. ▪ *(lugar)* at, on; **a la derecha** on the right; **a lo lejos** in the distance; **a mi lado** next to me; **al sol** in the sun. ▪ *(tiempo)* at; **a las doce** at twelve o'clock; **a los tres meses/la media hora** three months/half an hour later; **al final** in the end; **al principio** at first. ▪ *(distancia)* **a cien kilómetros de aquí** a hundred kilometers from here. ▪ *(manera)* **a mano** by hand. ▪ *(proporción)* **a 90 kilómetros por hora** at 90 kilometers an hour; **a 30 pesos el kilo** thirty pesos a kilo; **tres veces a la semana** three times a week. ▪ **ganar cuatro a dos** to win four (to) two. ▪ *(complemento)* to; *(procedencia)* from; **díselo a Javier** tell Javier; **te lo di a ti** I gave it to you; **comprarle algo a algn** to buy sth from sb; *(para algn)* to buy sth for sb; **saludé a tu tía** I said hello to your aunt. ▪ *fam* **ir a por algn/algo** to go and get sb/sth. ▪ *(verbo + a + infinitivo)* to; **aprender a nadar** to learn (how) to swim. ▪ **a decir verdad** to tell (you) the truth; **a no ser que** unless; **a ver** let's see; **¡a comer!** food's ready!; **¡a dormir!** bedtime!; **¿a que no lo haces?** *(desafío)* I bet you don't do it!
abajeño, -a *mf Am* lowlander.
abajo 1 *adv (en una casa)* downstairs; *(dirección)* down; **el piso de a.** the apartment downstairs; **ahí/aquí a.** down there/here; **la parte de a.** the bottom (part); **más a.** further down; **hacia a.** down; **venirse a.** *(edificio)* to fall down. **2** *interj* **¡a. la censura!** down with censorship!
abalanzarse *vr* **a. sobre/contra** to rush towards.
abalear *vt Andes, CAm, Ven* to shoot at.
abandonar *vt (lugar)* to leave; *(persona, cosa)* to abandon; *(proyecto, plan)* to give up.
abanico *m* fan; *(gama)* range.
abarcar *vt (incluir)* to cover.
abarrotado, -a *adj* crammed (**de** with).
abarrote *m Andes, CAm, Méx* grocer's shop, grocery store; **abarrotes** groceries; **tienda de abarrotes** grocer's (shop), grocery store.
abastecer 1 *vt* to supply. **2 abastecerse** *vr* to stock up (**de** *o* **con** with).
abatible *adj* folding; **asiento a.** folding seat.
abatido, -a *adj* downcast.
abatir 1 *vt (derribar)* to knock down; *(desanimar)* to depress. **2 abatirse** *vr (desanimarse)* to become depressed.
abdicar *vti* to abdicate.
abdominales *mpl* sit-ups.
abecedario *m* alphabet.
abedul *m* birch.
abeja *f* bee; **a. reina** queen bee.
abejorro *m* bumblebee.
abertura *f (hueco)* opening; *(grieta)* crack.
abeto *m* fir (tree).
abierto, -a *adj* open; *(grifo)* (turned) on; *(persona)* open-minded.
abismo *m* abyss.
ablandar 1 *vt* to soften. **2 ablandarse** *vr* to go soft; *fig (persona)* to mellow.
abnegado, -a *adj* selfless.
abogado, -a *mf* lawyer; *(en tribunal supremo)* attorney; **a. defensor** counsel for the defense.
abolir *vt defectivo* to abolish.
abollar *vt* to dent.
abonado, -a *mf* subscriber.
abonar 1 *vt (tierra)* to fertilize; *(pagar)* to pay (for); *(subscribir)* to subscribe. **2 abonarse** *vr* to subscribe (**a** to).
abono *m (producto)* fertilizer; *(estiércol)* manure; *(pago)* payment; *(billete)* season ticket; *(a revista etc)* subscription.
abordar *vt (persona)* to approach; *(barco)* to board; **a. un asunto** to tackle a subject.
aborrecer *vt* to detest.
abortar 1 *vi (involuntariamente)* to miscarry, to have a miscarriage; *(intencionadamente)* to abort, to have an abortion. **2** *vt* to abort.
aborto *m* miscarriage; *(provocado)* abortion.
abrasar 1 *vti* to scorch. **2 abrasarse** *vr* to burn.
abrazadera *f* clamp.
abrazar 1 *vt* to embrace. **2 abrazarse** *vr* **abrazarse a algn** to embrace sb; **se abrazaron** they embraced each other.
abrazo *m* hug.
abrelatas *m inv* can opener.
abreviar 1 *vt* to shorten; *(texto)* to abridge; *(palabra)* to abbreviate. **2** *vi* to be quick *o* brief; **para a.** to cut a long story short.
abreviatura *f* abbreviation.
abridor *m (de latas, botellas)* opener.
abrigado, -a *adj* wrapped up.
abrigar 1 *vt* to keep warm; *(esperanza)* to cherish; *(duda)* to harbor. **2** *vi* **esta chaqueta abriga mucho** this cardigan is very warm.
abrigo *m (prenda)* coat; **ropa de a.** warm clothes *pl.*
abril *m* April.
abrir[1] *m* **en un a. y cerrar de ojos** in the twinkling of an eye.
abrir[2] *(pp* **abierto***)* **1** *vi* to open. **2** *vt* to open; *(cremallera)* to undo; *(gas, grifo)* to turn on. **3 abrirse** *vr* to open; **abrirse paso** to make one's way.
abrochar *vt*, **abrocharse** *vr (botones)* to do up; *(camisa)* to button (up); *(cinturón)* to fasten; *(zapatos)* to tie up; *(cremallera)* to do up.
abrumar *vt* to overwhelm.
abrupto, -a *adj (terreno)* steep.
absceso *m* abscess.
absolutamente *adv* absolutely.
absoluto, -a *adj* absolute; **en a.** not at all.
absolver *(pp* **absuelto***)* *vt* to acquit.
absorbente *adj (papel)* absorbent; *(fascinante)* engrossing.
absorber *vt* to absorb.
absorto, -a *adj* engrossed (**en** in).
abstenerse *vr* to abstain (**de** from); *(privarse)* to refrain (**de** from).
abstracto, -a *adj* abstract.
abstraído, -a *adj (ensimismado)* engrossed (**en** in).
absuelto, -a *adj pp de* **absolver.**
absurdo, -a *adj* absurd.
abuchear *vt* to boo.
abuela *f* grandmother; *fam* grandma, granny.
abuelo *m* grandfather; *fam* grandad, grandpa; **abuelos** grandparents.
abultado, -a *adj* bulky.
abundancia *f* abundance; **... en a.** plenty of ...
abundante *adj* abundant.
aburrido, -a *adj* **ser a.** to be boring; **estar a.** to be bored; *(harto)* to be tired (**de** of).
aburrimiento *m* boredom; **¡qué a.!** what a bore!
aburrir 1 *vt* to bore. **2 aburrirse** *vr* to get bored.
abusar *vi (propasarse)* to go too far; **a. de** *(situación, persona)* to take (unfair) advantage of; *(poder, amabilidad)* to abuse; **a. de la bebida/del tabaco** to drink/smoke too much *o* to excess.
abuso *m* abuse.
a. C. *abr de* **antes de Cristo** before Christ, BC.
acá *adv (lugar)* over here; **más a.** nearer; **¡ven a.!** come here!
acabar 1 *vt* to finish (off); *(completar)* to complete. **2** *vi* to finish; **a. de ...** to have just ...; **acaba de entrar** he has just come in; **acabaron casándose** *o* **por casarse** they ended up getting married. **3 acabarse** *vr* to finish; **se nos acabó la gasolina** we ran out of gas.
acacia *f* acacia.
academia *f* academy; **a. de idiomas** language school.
académico, -a *adj & mf* academic.
acalorado, -a *adj* hot; *(debate etc)* heated.
acampar *vi* to camp.
acantilado *m* cliff.
acaparar *vt (productos)* to hoard; *(mercado)* to corner.
acápite *m Am (párrafo)* paragraph.
acariciar *vt* to caress; *(pelo, animal)* to stroke.
acarrear *vt (transportar)* to transport; *(conllevar)* to entail.
acaso *adv* perhaps, maybe; **por si a.** just in case; **si a. viene ...** if he should come ....
acatar *vt* to comply with.
acatarrado, -a *adj* **estar a.** to have a cold.
acatarrarse *vr* to catch a cold.
acceder *vi* **a. a** *(consentir)* to consent to.
accesible *adj* accessible; *(persona)* approachable.
acceso *m (entrada)* access; *(en carretera)* approach; **a. a Internet** Internet access.
accesorio, -a *adj (terreno)* uneven; *(viaje, vida)* eventful. **2** *mf* casualty.
accidental *adj* accidental; **un encuentro a.** a chance meeting.
accidente *m* accident; **a. laboral** industrial accident.
acción *f* action; *(acto)* act; *(en la bolsa)* share; **poner en a.** to put into action; **película de a.** adventure film.
accionar *vt* to drive.
accionista *mf* shareholder.
acechar *vt* to lie in wait for.
aceite *m* oil; **a. de girasol/maíz/oliva** sunflower/corn/olive oil.
aceituna *f* olive; **a. rellena** stuffed olive.
acelerador *m* accelerator.
acelerar *vti* to accelerate.
acento *m* accent; *(énfasis)* stress.
acentuar 1 *vt* to stress. **2 acentuarse** *vr* to become more pronounced.
aceptar *vt* to accept.
acequia *f* irrigation ditch *o* channel.
acera *f* sidewalk.
acerca *adv* **a. de** about.
acercar 1 *vt* to bring (over). **2 acercarse** *vr* to approach (**a** -); *(ir)* to go; *(venir)* to come.
acero *m* steel; **a. inoxidable** stainless steel.
acérrimo, -a *adj (partidario)* staunch; *(enemigo)* bitter.
acertado, -a *adj (solución)* correct; *(decisión)* wise.
acertar 1 *vt (pregunta)* to get right; *(adivinar)* to guess correctly. **2** *vi* to be right.
acertijo *m* riddle.
achacar *vt (atribuir)* to attribute.
achaque *m* ailment.
achicharrar *vt* to burn to a crisp.
acholado, -a *adj Andes* mixed.
achuchar *vt (empujar)* to shove.
aciago, -a *adj* ill-fated.
acicalarse *vr* to dress up.
acidez *f (de sabor)* sharpness; **a. de estómago** heartburn.
ácido, -a 1 *adj (sabor)* sharp. **2** *m* acid.
acierto *m (buena decisión)* good choice.
aclamar *vt* to acclaim.
aclaración *f* explanation.
aclarado *m* rinse.
aclarar 1 *vt (explicar)* to explain; *(color)* to make lighter; *(enjuagar)* to rinse. **2** *v impers (tiempo)* to clear (up). **3 aclararse** *vr* **aclararse la voz** to clear one's throat.
aclimatarse *vr* **a. algo** to get used to sth.
acné *m* acne.
acobardarse *vr* to get frightened.
acogedor, -a *adj (habitación)* cozy.
acoger 1 *vt (recibir)* to receive; *(persona desvalida)* to take in. **2 acogerse** *vr* **acogerse a** to take refuge in; **acogerse a la ley** to have recourse to the law.
acogida *f* reception, welcome.
acometer *vt (emprender)* to undertake; *(atacar)* to attack.
acomodado, -a *adj* well-off.
acomodador, -a *mf* usher.
acomodar 1 *vt (alojar)* to accommodate; *(en cine etc)* to find a place for. **2 acomodarse** *vr (instalarse)* to make oneself comfortable; *(adaptarse)* to adapt.
acompañante 1 *mf* companion. **2** *adj* accompanying.
acompañar *vt* to accompany; **¿te acompaño a casa?** can I walk you home?; *(en funeral)* **le acompaño en el sentimiento** my condolences.
acomplejado, -a *adj* **estar a.** to have a complex (**por** about).
acomplejar 1 *vt* to give a complex. **2 acomplejarse** *vr* **acomplejarse por** to develop a complex about.
acondicionado, -a *adj* **aire a.** air conditioning.
acondicionador *m* conditioner.
acondicionar *vt* to prepare, to set up; *(mejorar)* to improve; *(cabello)* to condition.
aconsejable *adj* advisable.
aconsejar *vt* to advise.
acontecimiento *m* event.
acopio *m* **hacer a. de** to store.
acordar 1 *vt* to agree; *(decidir)* to decide. **2 acordarse** *vr* to remember.
acordeón *m* accordion.
acordonar *vt (zona)* to cordon off.
acorralar *vt* to corner.
acortar *vt* to shorten.
acosar *vt* to harass; *fig* **a. a algn a preguntas** to bombard sb with questions.
acoso *m* harassment; **a. sexual** sexual harassment.
acostar 1 *vt* to put to bed. **2 acostarse** *vr* to go to bed.
acostumbrado, -a *adj* usual; **es lo a.** it is the custom; **a. al frío/calor** used to the cold/heat.
acostumbrar 1 *vi* **a. a** *(soler)* to be in the habit of. **2** *vt* **a. a algn a algo** *(habituar)* to get sb used to sth. **3 acostumbrarse** *vr* to get used (**a** to).
acotamiento *m Méx (de autopista)* shoulder.
acre *m (medida)* acre.
acreditar *vt* to be a credit to; *(probar)* to prove.

acreedor, -a *mf* creditor.
acrílico, -a *adj* acrylic.
acriollarse *vr Am* to adopt native ways.
acrobacia *f* acrobatics *sing.*
acta *f (de reunión)* minutes *pl*; *(certificado)* certificate.
actitud *f* attitude.
activar *vt* to activate; *(avivar)* to liven up.
actividad *f* activity.
activo, -a *adj* active.
acto *m* act; *(ceremonia)* ceremony; *(de teatro)* act; **en el a.** at once; **a. seguido** immediately afterwards.
actor *m* actor.
actriz *f* actress.
actuación *f* performance; *(intervención)* intervention.
actual *adj* current, present.
actualidad *f* present time; *(hechos)* current affairs *pl*; **en la a.** at present.
actualizar *vt (software, hardware)* to upgrade.
actualmente *adv (hoy en día)* nowadays.
actuar *vi* to act.
acuarela *f* watercolor.
acuario *m* aquarium.
acuciante *adj* urgent.
acudir *vi (ir)* to go; *(venir)* to come.
acuerdo *m* agreement; **¡de a.!** all right!, OK!; **de a. con** in accordance with; **ponerse de a.** to agree.
acumular *vt*, **acumularse** *vr* to accumulate.
acuñar *vt (moneda)* to mint; *(frase)* to coin.
acurrucarse *vr* to curl up.
acusación *f* accusation; *(en juicio)* charge.
acusado, -a 1 *mf* accused. **2** *adj (marcado)* marked.
acusar 1 *vt* to accuse (**de** of); *(en juicio)* to charge (**de** with). **2 acusarse** *vr (acentuarse)* to become more pronounced.
acústica *f* acoustics *sing.*
acústico, -a *adj* acoustic.
adaptador *m* adapter.
adaptar 1 *vt* to adapt; *(ajustar)* to adjust. **2 adaptarse** *vr* to adapt (oneself) (**a** to).
adecuado, -a *adj* appropriate.
a. de J. C. *abr de* **antes de Jesucristo** before Christ, BC.
adelantado, -a *adj* advanced; *(desarrollado)* developed; *(reloj)* fast; **pagar por a.** to pay in advance.
adelantamiento *m* overtaking.
adelantar 1 *vt* to move forward; *(reloj)* to put forward; *(en carretera)* to overtake; *(fecha)* to move forward. **2** *vi* to advance; *(progresar)* to make progress; *(reloj)* to be fast. **3 adelantarse** *vr (ir delante)* to go ahead; *(reloj)* to be fast.
adelante 1 *adv* forward; **más a.** *(lugar)* further on; *(tiempo)* later. **2** *interj* **¡a.!** *(pase)* come in!
adelanto *m* advance; *(progreso)* progress; **el reloj lleva diez minutos de a.** the watch is ten minutes fast.
adelgazar *vi* to slim.
ademán *m* gesture.
además *adv* moreover, furthermore; **a. de él** besides him.
adentro 1 *adv (dentro)* inside; **mar a.** out to sea; **tierra a.** inland. **2** *mpl* **decir algo para sus adentros** to say sth to oneself.
adherir 1 *vt* to stick on. **2 adherirse** *vr* **adherirse a** to adhere to.
adhesión *f* adhesion.
adhesivo, -a *adj & m* adhesive.
adicción *f* addiction.
adicto, -a 1 *mf* addict. **2** *adj* addicted (**a** to).
adiestrar *vt* to train.
adinerado, -a *adj* wealthy.
adiós *(pl* **adioses)** *interj* goodbye; *fam* bye-bye; *(al cruzarse)* hello.
aditivo, -a *adj & m* additive.
adivinanza *f* riddle.
adivinar *vt* to guess.
adjetivo *m* adjective.
adjudicar 1 *vt (premio, contrato)* to award; *(en subasta)* to sell. **2 adjudicarse** *vr* to appropriate.
adjuntar *vt* to enclose.
adjunto, -a 1 *adj* enclosed, attached. **2** *mf (profesor)* assistant teacher.
administración *f (gobierno)* authorities *pl*; *(de empresa)* management; *(oficina)* (branch) office; **a. central** *(gobierno)* central government; **a. pública** civil service.
administrador, -a 1 *mf* administrator. **2** *adj* administrating.
administrar *vt* to administer; *(dirigir)* to run.
administrativo, -a 1 *adj* administrative. **2** *mf (funcionario)* official.
admiración *f* admiration; *(ortográfica)* exclamation mark.
admirar 1 *vt* to admire; *(sorprender)* to amaze. **2 admirarse** *vr* to be amazed.
admisión *f* admission.
admitir *vt* to let in; *(aceptar)* to accept; *(permitir)* to allow; *(reconocer)* to acknowledge.
ADN *m abr de* **ácido desoxirribonucleico** deoxyribonucleic acid, DNA.
adobe *m* adobe.
adobo *m* marinade.
adolescencia *f* adolescence.
adolescente *adj & mf* adolescent.
adónde *adv* where (to)?
adonde *adv* where.
adondequiera *adv* where.
adopción *f* adoption.
adoptar *vt* to adopt.
adoptivo, -a *adj (hijo)* adopted; *(padres)* adoptive.
adorar *vt* to worship.
adormecer 1 *vt* to make sleepy. **2 adormecerse** *vr (dormirse)* to doze off; *(brazo etc)* to go numb.
adormilarse *vr* to doze, to drowse.
adornar *vt* to adorn.
adorno *m* decoration; **de a.** decorative.
adosado, -a *adj* adjacent; *(casa)* semidetached.
adquirir *vt* to acquire; *(comprar)* to purchase.
adquisición *f* acquisition; *(compra)* purchase.
adrede *adv* deliberately, on purpose.
aduana *f* customs *pl.*
aduanero, -a *mf* customs officer.
aducir *vt* to adduce.
adueñarse *vr* **a. de** to take over.
aduje *pt indef de* **aducir.**
adular *vt* to adulate.

adulterar *vt* to adulterate.
adulterio *m* adultery.
adulto, -a *adj & mf* adult.
aduzco *indic pres de* **aducir.**
adverbio *m* adverb.
adversario, -a 1 *mf* opponent. **2** *adj* opposing.
adversidad *f* adversity; *(revés)* setback.
adverso, -a *adj* adverse.
advertencia *f* warning.
advertir *vt* to warn; *(informar)* to advise; *(notar)* to notice.
adviento *m* Advent.
adyacente *adj* adjacent.
aéreo, -a *adj* aerial; *(correo, transporte)* air; **por vía aerea** by air.
aerodinámico, -a *adj* aerodynamic; **de línea aerodinámica** streamlined.
aeromoza *f Am* flight attendant.
aeronáutico, -a *adj* **la industria aeronáutica** the aeronautics industry.
aeroplano *m* light airplane.
aeropuerto *m* airport.
aerosol *m* aerosol.
afable *adj* affable.
afán *m (pl* **afanes)** *(esfuerzo)* effort; *(celo)* zeal.
afanarse *vr* **a. por conseguir algo** to do one's best to achieve sth.
afección *f* disease.
afectar *vt* **a.** to affect; **le afectó mucho** she was deeply affected.
afecto *m* affection; **tomarle a. a algn** to become fond of sb.
afectuoso, -a *adj* affectionate.
afeitar *vt*, **afeitarse** *vr* to shave.
afeminado, -a *adj* effeminate.
aferrarse *vr* to cling (**a** to).
afianzar *vt* to strengthen.
afiche *m Am* poster.
afición *f* liking; **tiene a. por la música** he is fond of music; *(de deporte)* **la a.** the fans *pl.*
aficionado, -a 1 *mf* enthusiast; *(no profesional)* amateur. **2** *adj* keen; *(no profesional)* amateur; **ser a. a algo** to be fond of sth.
aficionarse *vr* to take a liking (**a** to).
afilado, -a *adj* sharp.
afiliarse *vr* **a. a** to join, to become a member of.
afinar *vt (puntería)* to sharpen; *(instrumento)* to tune.
afinidad *f* affinity.
afirmación *f* statement.
afirmar *vt (aseverar)* to state; *(afianzar)* to strengthen.
afligir 1 *vt* to afflict. **2 afligirse** *vr* to be distressed.
aflojar 1 *vt* to loosen. **2 aflojarse** *vr (rueda)* to work loose.
afluencia *f* influx; **gran a. de público** great numbers of people.
afluente *m* tributary.
afónico, -a *adj* **estar a.** to have lost one's voice.
afortunado, -a *adj* lucky, fortunate.
afrontar *vt* to confront; **a. las consecuencias** to face the consequences.
afuera *adv* outside; **la parte de a.** the outside; **más a.** further out. **2 afueras** *fpl* outskirts.
agachar 1 *vt* to lower. **2 agacharse** *vr* to duck.
agarrado, -a *adj fam (tacaño)* stingy, tight; **baile a.** cheek-to-cheek dancing.
agarrar 1 *vt* to grasp; *Am (tomar)* to take; **agárralo fuerte** hold it tight; **a. un taxi** to take a taxi. **2 agarrarse** *vr* to hold on.
agasajar *vt* to smother with attentions.
agazaparse *vr* to crouch (down).
agencia *f* agency; *(sucursal)* branch; **a. de viajes** travel agency; **a. de seguros** insurance agency; **a. inmobiliaria** estate agency.
agenda *f* diary.
agente *mf* agent; **a. de policía** *(hombre)* policeman; *(mujer)* policewoman; **a. de seguros** insurance broker.
ágil *adj* agile.
agilidad *f* agility.
agilizar *vt (trámites)* to speed up.
agitación *f* agitation; *(inquietud)* restlessness.
agitado, -a *adj* agitated; *(persona)* anxious; *(mar)* rough.
agitar 1 *vt (botella)* to shake. **2 agitarse** *vr (persona)* to become agitated.
aglomeración *f (de gente)* crowd.
agobiado, -a *adj* **a. de problemas** snowed under with problems; **a. de trabajo** up to one's eyes in work.
agobiante *adj (trabajo)* overwhelming; *(lugar)* claustrophobic; *(calor)* oppressive; *(persona)* tiresome.
agobiar 1 *vt* to overwhelm. **2 agobiarse** *vr (angustiarse)* to worry too much.
agobio *m (angustia)* anxiety; *(sofoco)* suffocation.
agolparse *vr* to crowd.
agonía *f* agony, last days.
agonizar *vi* to be dying.
agosto *m* August.
agotado, -a *adj (cansado)* exhausted; *(existencias)* sold out; *(provisiones)* exhausted; *(libro)* out of print.
agotador, -a *adj* exhausting.
agotamiento *m* exhaustion.
agotar 1 *vt (cansar)* to exhaust; *(acabar)* to use up (completely). **2 agotarse** *vr (acabarse)* to run out; *(producto)* to be sold out; *(persona)* to become exhausted o tired out.
agradable *adj* pleasant.
agradar *vti* to please; **no me agrada** I don't like it.
agradecer *vt (dar las gracias)* to thank for; *(estar agradecido)* to be grateful to; **te lo agradezco mucho** thank you very much.
agradecido, -a *adj* grateful; **le estoy muy a.** I am very grateful to you.
agradecimiento *m* gratitude.
agrado *m* pleasure; **no es de su a.** it isn't to his liking.
agrandar 1 *vt* to enlarge. **2 agrandarse** *vr* to become larger.
agrario, -a *adj* agrarian.
agravar 1 *vt* to aggravate. **2 agravarse** *vr* to get worse.
agredir *vt defectivo* to assault.
agregado, -a *adj* **profesor a.** *(de escuela)* secondary school teacher; *(de universidad)* teaching assistant.
agregar *vt (añadir)* to add.
agresión *f* aggression.
agresivo, -a *adj* aggressive.
agrícola *adj* agricultural.
agricultor, -a *mf* farmer.
agricultura *f* agriculture.
agridulce *adj* bittersweet.
agrietar 1 *vt* to crack; *(piel, labios)* to chap. **2 agrietarse** *vr* to crack; *(piel)* to get chapped.

agringarse *vr Am* to behave like a gringo.
agrio, -a *adj* sour.
agropecuario, -a *adj* agricultural.
agrupación *f* association.
agua**** *f* water; **a. potable** drinking water; **a. corriente/del grifo** running/tap water; **a. dulce/salada** fresh/salt water; **a. mineral sin/con gas** still/fizzy mineral water.
aguacate *m (fruto)* avocado (pear).
aguacero *m* downpour.
aguafiestas *mf inv* spoilsport, wet blanket.
aguafuerte *m* etching.
aguanieve *f* sleet.
aguantar 1 *vt (soportar)* to tolerate; *(sostener)* to support; **no lo aguanto más** I can't stand it any longer; **aguanta la respiración** hold your breath. **2 aguantarse** *vr (contenerse)* to keep back; *(resignarse)* to resign oneself; **no pude aguantarme la risa** I couldn't help laughing.
aguardar 1 *vt* to await. **2** *vi* to wait.
aguardiente *m* brandy.
aguarrás *m* turpentine.
aguatero, -a *mf Am* water-carrier *o* seller.
agudizar *vt*, **agudizarse** *vr* to intensify.
agudo, -a *adj (dolor)* acute; *(voz)* high-pitched; *(sonido)* high.
aguijón *m* sting.
águila**** *f* eagle.
aguja *f* needle; *(de reloj)* hand; *(de tocadiscos)* stylus.
agujerear *vt* to make holes in.
agujero *m* hole; **a. negro** black hole.
agujetas *fpl* **tener a.** to be stiff.
aguzar *vt* **a. el oído** to prick up one's ears; **a. la vista** to look attentively.
ahí *adv* there; **a. está** there he/she/it is; **por a.** *(en esa dirección)* that way; *(aproximadamente)* over there.
ahijado, -a *mf* godchild; *(niño)* godson; *(niña)* goddaughter; **ahijados** godchildren.
ahínco *m* **con a.** eagerly.
ahogado, -a 1 *adj (en líquido)* drowned; *(asfixiado)* suffocated; **morir a.** to drown. **2** *mf* drowned person.
ahogar *vt*, **ahogarse** *vr (en líquido)* to drown; *(asfixiar)* to suffocate; *(motor)* to flood.
ahondar 1 *vt* to deepen. **2** *vi* to go deep; *fig* **a. en un problema** to go into a problem in depth.
ahora 1 *adv* now; **a. mismo** right now; **de a. en adelante** from now on; **por a.** for the time being; **a. voy** I'm coming; **hasta a.** *(hasta el momento)* until now, so far; *(hasta luego)* see you later. **2** *conj* **a. bien** *(sin embargo)* however.
ahorcar 1 *vt* to hang. **2 ahorcarse** *vr* to hang oneself.
ahorita, ahoritica *adv Andes, CAm, Carib, Méx fam (en el presente)* (right) now; **a. voy** I'm just coming; *(pronto)* in a second; *(hace poco)* just now, a few minutes ago.
ahorrar *vt* to save.
ahorrativo, -a *adj* thrifty.
ahorros *mpl* savings; **caja de a.** savings bank.
ahuevado, -a *adj Andes, CAm fam* stupid.
ahumado, -a *adj* smoked; *(bacon)* smoky.
ahuyentar *vt* to scare away.
aindiado, -a *adj Am* Indian-like.
airado, -a *adj* angry.
aire *m* air; *(de automóvil)* choke; *(viento)* wind; *(aspecto)* appearance; **a. acondicionado** air conditioning; **al a.** *(al descubierto)* uncovered; **al a. libre** in the open air; **en el a.** *(pendiente)* in the air; **tomar el a.** to get some fresh air; **cambiar de aires** to change one's surroundings; **darse aires** to put on airs.
aislado, -a *adj* isolated; *(cable)* insulated.
aislante 1 *adj* **cinta a.** insulating tape. **2** *m* insulator.
aislar *vt* to isolate; *(cable)* to insulate.
ajedrez *m (juego)* chess; *(piezas y tablero)* chess set.
ajeno, -a *adj* belonging to other people; **por causas ajenas a nuestra voluntad** for reasons beyond our control.
ajetreado, -a *adj* hectic.
ajetreo *m* activity, hard work, bustle.
ajo *m* garlic; **cabeza/diente de a.** head/clove of garlic.
ajustado, -a *adj* tight.
ajustar *vt* to adjust; *(apretar)* to tighten.
ajuste *m* adjustment; *(de precio)* fixing; *(de cuenta)* settlement; **a. de cuentas** settling of scores.
ajusticiar *vt* to execute.
al *(contracción de a & el) ver* a; *(al + infinitivo)* **al salir** on leaving.
ala *f* wing; *(de sombrero)* brim.
alabar *vt* to praise.
alabastro *m* alabaster.
alacena *f (food)* cupboard.
alambrada *f*, **alambrado** *m* barbed wire fence.
alambre *m* wire; **a. de púas** barbed wire.
alameda *f* poplar grove; *(paseo)* avenue, boulevard.
álamo *m* poplar.
alarde *m (ostentación)* bragging; **hacer a. de** to show off.
alardear *vi* to brag.
alargadera *f (cable)* extension.
alargado, -a *adj* elongated.
alargar 1 *vt* to lengthen; *(estirar)* to stretch; *(prolongar)* to prolong; *(dar)* to pass. **2 alargarse** *vr* to get longer; *(prolongarse)* to go on.
alarido *m* shriek; **dar un a.** to howl.
alarma *f* alarm; **falsa a.** false alarm; **señal de a.** alarm (signal).
alarmante *adj* alarming.
alarmar 1 *vt* to alarm. **2 alarmarse** *vr* to be alarmed.
alba**** *f* dawn.
albañil *m* bricklayer; *(obrero)* building worker.
albaricoque *m (fruta)* apricot; *(árbol)* apricot tree.
alberca *f (depósito)* water tank; *Méx (para nadar)* swimming pool.
albergar 1 *vt (alojar)* to house. **2 albergarse** *vr* to stay.
albergue *m (lugar)* hostel; *(refugio)* refuge; **a. juvenil** youth hostel.
albino, -a *adj & mf* albino.
albóndiga *f* meatball.
albornoz *m* bathrobe.
alborotar 1 *vt (desordenar)* to turn upside down. **2** *vi* to make a racket. **3 alborotarse** *vr* to get excited; *(mar)* to get rough.
alboroto *m (jaleo)* din, racket; *(desorden)* disturbance, uproar.
albufera *f* lagoon.
álbum *m* album.
alcachofa *f* artichoke.
alcalde *m* mayor.
alcaldesa *f* mayoress.
alcaldía *f (cargo)* mayorship; *(oficina)* mayor's office.

alcance *m* reach; **dar a. a** to catch up with; **fuera del a. de los niños** out of the reach of children.
alcantarilla *f* sewer; *(boca)* drain.
alcanzar 1 *vt* to reach; *(persona)* to catch up with; *(conseguir)* to achieve. **2** *vi (ser suficiente)* to be sufficient.
alcaparra *f (fruto)* caper.
alcayata *f* hook.
alcazaba *f* citadel.
alcázar *m (fortaleza)* fortress; *(castillo)* castle.
alcoba *f* bedroom.
alcohol *m* alcohol.
alcoholemia *f* **prueba de a.** breath test.
alcohólico, -a *adj & mf* alcoholic.
alcoholímetro *m* Breathalyzer®.
alcornoque *m* cork oak.
alcurnia *f* ancestry.
aldea *f* village.
aleccionador, -a *adj (ejemplar)* exemplary.
alegar *vt (aducir)* to claim.
alegrar 1 *vt (complacer)* to make glad; **me alegra que se lo hayas dicho** I am glad you told her. **2 alegrarse** *vr* to be glad; **me alegro de verte** I am pleased to see you.
alegre *adj (contento)* glad; *(color)* bright; *(música)* lively.
alegría *f* happiness.
alejado, -a *adj* remote.
alejar 1 *vt* to move further away. **2 alejarse** *vr* to go away.
alemán, -ana 1 *adj & mf* German. **2** *m (idioma)* German.
alentar *vt* to encourage.
alergia *f* allergy.
alérgico, -a *adj* allergic.
alerta *f & adj* alert.
aleta *f (de pez)* fin; *(de foca, de nadador)* flipper.
aletargar 1 *vt* to make lethargic. **2 aletargarse** *vr* to become lethargic.
aletear *vi* to flutter *o* flap its wings.
alfabetización *f* **campaña de a.** literacy campaign.
alfabeto *m* alphabet.
alfalfa *f* alfalfa grass.
alfarería *f* pottery.
alféizar *m* windowsill.
alférez *m* second lieutenant.
alfil *m (en ajedrez)* bishop.
alfiler *m* pin; *Andes, RP, Ven* **a. de gancho** *(imperdible)* safety pin.
alfombra *f* rug; *(moqueta)* carpet.
alga *f (marina)* seaweed.
álgebra**** *f* algebra.
álgido, -a *adj* **el punto a.** the climax.
algo 1 *pron indef (afirmativo)* something; *(interrogativo)* anything; *(cantidad indeterminada)* some; **a. así** something like that; **¿a. más?** anything else?; **¿queda a. de pastel?** is there any cake left? **2** *adv (un poco)* somewhat; **está a. mejor** she's feeling a bit better.
algodón *m* cotton.
alguacil *m* bailiff.
alguien *pron indef (afirmativo)* somebody, someone; *(interrogativo)* anybody, anyone.
algún *adj (delante de nombres masculinos en singular) ver* **alguno**.
alguno, -a 1 *adj (delante de nombre) (afirmativo)* some; *(interrogativo)* any; **alguna que otra vez** now and then; **¿le has visto alguna vez?** have you ever seen him?; **no vino persona alguna** nobody came. **2** *pron indef (afirmativo)* someone, somebody; *(interrogativo)* anyone, anybody; **algunos, -as** some (people).
alhaja *f* jewel.
alhelí *m (pl* alhelíes*)* wallflower.
aliado, -a *adj* allied.
alianza *f (pacto)* alliance; *(anillo)* wedding ring.
aliarse *vr* to ally, to become allies.
alicates *mpl* pliers *pl*.
aliciente *m (atractivo)* charm; *(incentivo)* incentive.
aliento *m* breath; **sin a.** breathless.
aligerar 1 *vt (carga)* to lighten; *(acelerar)* to speed up; **a. el paso** to quicken one's pace. **2** *vi fam* **¡aligera!** hurry up!
alijo *m* haul; **un a. de drogas** a consignment of drugs.
alimaña *f* vermin.
alimentación *f (comida)* food; *(acción)* feeding.
alimentar 1 *vt (dar alimento)* to feed; *(ser nutritivo para)* to be nutritious for. **2 alimentarse** *vr* **alimentarse con** *o* **de** to live on.
alimenticio, -a *adj* nutritious; **valor a.** nutritional value.
alimento *m* food.
alinear 1 *vt* to align. **2 alinearse** *vr* to line up.
aliñar *vt (ensalada)* to dress.
aliño *m (de ensalada)* dressing.
alistar 1 *vt (en el ejército)* to enlist. **2 alistarse** *vr (en el ejército)* to enlist; *Am (prepararse)* to get ready.
aliviar 1 *vt (dolor)* to relieve; *(carga)* to lighten. **2 aliviarse** *vr (dolor)* to diminish.
alivio *m* relief.
allá *adv (lugar alejado)* over there; **a. abajo/arriba** down/up there; **más a.** further on; **más a. de** beyond; **a. tú** that's your problem.
allí *adv* there; **a. abajo/arriba** down/up there; **por a.** *(movimiento)* that way; *(posición)* over there.
alma**** *f* soul.
almacén *m (local)* warehouse; **grandes almacenes** department store.
almacenar *vt* to store.
almanaque *m* calendar.
almeja *f* clam.
almendra *f* almond.
almendro *m* almond tree.
almíbar *m* syrup.
almirante *m* admiral.
almizcle *m* musk.
almohada *f* pillow.
almohadilla *f (small)* cushion.
almohadón *m* large pillow.
almorrana *f fam* pile.
almorzar 1 *vi* to have lunch. **2** *vt* to have for lunch.
almuerzo *m* lunch.
aló *interj Andes, Carib (al teléfono)* hello.
alojamiento *m* accommodations; **dar a.** to accommodate.
alojar *vt* to accommodate. **2 alojarse** *vr* to stay.
alondra *f* lark.

alpargata *f* canvas sandal.
alpinismo *m* mountaineering.
alpinista *mf* mountaineer.
alquilar *vt* to hire; *(pisos, casas)* to rent; **'se alquila'** 'to let', 'for rent'.
alquiler *m (acción)* hiring; *(de pisos, casas)* letting; *(precio)* rental; *(de pisos, casas)* rent; **a. de coches** car rental; **de a.** *(pisos, casas)* to let; *(coche)* for hire; **en una casa de a.** in a rented house.
alquitrán *m* tar.
alrededor 1 *adv (lugar)* round. **2** *prep* **a. de** round; **a. de quince** about fifteen. **3 alrededores** *mpl* surrounding area *sing.*
alta *f* dar de o el a. *(a un enfermo)* to discharge from hospital.
altamente *adv* extremely.
altanero, -a *adj* arrogant.
altar *m* altar.
altavoz *m* loudspeaker.
alteración *f (cambio)* alteration; *(alboroto)* quarrel; *(excitación)* agitation.
alterar 1 *vt* to alter. **2 alterarse** *vr (inquietarse)* to be upset.
altercado *m* argument.
alternar 1 *vt* to alternate. **2** *vi (relacionarse)* to socialize. **3 alternarse** *vr* to alternate.
alternativa *f* alternative.
alterno, -a *adj* alternate.
altibajos *mpl* ups and downs.
altiplano *m* high plateau.
altitud *f* altitude.
altivez *f* arrogance.
alto¹ *m (interrupción)* stop; **dar el a. a algn** to tell sb to stop; **un a. el fuego** a cease-fire.
alto, -a² *adj (persona, árbol, edificio)* tall; *(montaña, techo, presión)* high; *(sonido)* loud; *(precio, tecnología)* high; *(agudo)* high; **en lo a.** at the top; **clase alta** upper class; **en voz alta** aloud; **a altas horas de la noche** late at night. **2** *adv* high; *(fuerte)* loud; **¡habla más a.!** speak up. **3** *m (altura)* height; **¿cuánto tiene de a.?** how tall/high is it?
altoparlante *m Am* loudspeaker.
altura *f* height; *(nivel)* level; **de diez metros de a.** ten meters high; **estar a la a. de las circunstancias** to meet the challenge; *fig* **a estas alturas** by now.
alubia *f* bean.
alucinar 1 *vt* to hallucinate; *fig (encantar)* to fascinate. **2** *vi fam* to be amazed.
alud *m* avalanche.
aludir *vi* to allude.
alumbrar *vt (iluminar)* to illuminate; *(parir)* to give birth to.
aluminio *m* aluminum.
alumno, -a *mf (de colegio)* pupil; *(de Universidad)* student.
alusión *f* allusion.
alverja, alverjana *f Am* pea.
alza *f* rise; **en a.** rising.
alzamiento *m (rebelión)* uprising.
alzar 1 *vt* to raise; **a. los ojos/la vista** to look up. **2 alzarse** *vr (levantarse)* to rise; *(rebelarse)* to rebel.
ama *f (dueña)* owner; **a. de casa** housewife.
amabilidad *f* kindness; **tenga la a. de esperar** would you be so kind as to wait.
amable *adj* kind, nice.
amaestrar *vt (animal)* to train; *(domar)* to tame.
amainar *vi (viento etc)* to die down.
amamantar *vt* to breast-feed; *(entre animales)* to suckle.
amanecer 1 *v impers* **¿a qué hora amanece?** when does it get light?; **amaneció lluvioso** it was rainy at daybreak. **2** *vi* **amanecimos en Finlandia** we were in Finland at daybreak; **amaneció muy enfermo** he woke up feeling very ill. **3** *m* dawn; **al a.** at dawn.
amanerado, -a *adj* affected.
amante *mf* lover.
amapola *f* poppy.
amar 1 *vt* to love. **2 amarse** *vr* to love each other.
amargar 1 *vt* to make bitter; *(relación)* to embitter. **2 amargarse** *vr* to become embittered.
amargo, -a *adj* bitter.
amargor *m*, **amargura** *f* bitterness.
amarillento, -a *adj* yellowish.
amarillo, -a *adj & m* yellow.
amarilloso, -a *adj Ven* yellowish.
amarrar *vt (atar)* to tie (up).
amasar *vt* to knead.
amateur *adj & mf* amateur.
ámbar *m* amber.
ambición *f* ambition.
ambicionar *vt* to have as an ambition; **ambiciona ser presidente** his ambition is to become president.
ambicioso, -a 1 *adj* ambitious. **2** *mf* ambitious person.
ambientador *m* air freshener.
ambiental *adj* environmental.
ambiente 1 *m* environment; *Andes, RP (habitación)* room. **2** *adj* environmental; **temperatura a.** room temperature.
ambiguo, -a *adj* ambiguous.
ámbito *m* field.
ambos, -as *adj & pron pl* both.
ambulancia *f* ambulance.
ambulatorio *m* surgery.
amedrentar *vt* to frighten.
amenaza *f* threat.
amenazador, -a, amenazante *adj* threatening.
amenazar *vt* to threaten.
ameno, -a *adj* entertaining.
americana *f (prenda)* jacket.
americano, -a *adj & mf* American.
ametralladora *f* machine gun.
amigable *adj* friendly.
amígdala *f* tonsil.
amigdalitis *f* tonsillitis.
amigo, -a *mf* friend; **hacerse amigos** to become friends; **son muy amigos** they are very good friends.
aminorar *vt* to reduce; **a. el paso** to slow down.
amistad *f* friendship; **amistades** friends.
amistoso, -a *adj* friendly.
amnistía *f* amnesty.
amo *m (dueño)* owner.
amodorrarse *vr* to become sleepy.
amoldar *vt*, **amoldarse** *vr* to adapt.
amonestación *f* reprimand.
amontonar 1 *vt* to pile up. **2 amontonarse** *vr* to pile up; *(gente)* to crowd together.

amor *m* love; **hacer el a.** to make love; **a. proprio** self-esteem.
amoratado, -a *adj (frío)* blue with cold; *(de un golpe)* black and blue.
amordazar *vt (a una persona)* to gag.
amoroso, -a *adj* loving.
amortiguador *m (de vehículo)* shock absorber.
amortiguar *vt (golpe)* to cushion; *(ruido)* to muffle.
amortizar *vt* to pay off.
amotinar 1 *vt* to incite to riot. **2 amotinarse** *vr* to rise up.
amparar 1 *vt* to protect. **2 ampararse** *vr* to seek refuge.
ampliación *f* enlargement; *(de plazo, casa)* extension.
ampliar *vt* to enlarge; *(casa, plazo)* to extend.
amplificador *m* amplifier.
amplio, -a *adj* large; *(ancho)* broad.
ampolla *f (vejiga)* blister; *(de medicina)* ampule.
amputar *vt* to amputate.
amueblar *vt* to furnish.
amuleto *m* amulet.
anaconda *f* anaconda.
anacronismo *m* anachronism.
anales *mpl* annals.
analfabeto, -a *mf* illiterate.
analgésico, -a *adj & m* analgesic.
análisis *m inv* analysis; **a. de sangre** blood test.
analizar *vt* to analyze.
analogía *f* analogy.
análogo, -a *adj* analogous.
ananá *m (pl ananaes)*, **ananás** *m (pl ananases) Am* pineapple.
anarquista *adj & mf* anarchist.
anatomía *f* anatomy.
ancho, -a 1 *adj* wide, broad; **a lo a.** breadthwise; **te está muy a.** it's too big for you. **2** *m (anchura)* width, breadth; **dos metros de a.** two meters wide; **¿qué a. tiene?** how wide is it?
anchoa *f* anchovy.
anchura *f* width, breadth.
anciano, -a 1 *adj* very old. **2** *mf* old person.
ancla** *f* anchor.
ándale *interj CAm, Méx fam* come on!
andaluz, -a *adj & mf* Andalusian.
andamiaje *m* scaffolding.
andamio *m* scaffold.
andar¹ *m*, **andares** *mpl* gait *sing.*
andar² 1 *vi* to walk; *(coche etc)* to move; *(funcionar)* to work; *fam* **anda por los cuarenta** he's about forty; **¿cómo andamos de tiempo?** how are we on time?; **tu bolso debe de a. por ahí** your bag must be over there somewhere. **2** *vt (recorrer)* to walk.
andariego, -a *adj* fond of walking.
andén *m (en estación)* platform; *Andes, CAm (acera)* sidewalk.
andinismo *m Am* mountaineering.
andino, -a *adj & mf* Andean.
andrajo *m* rag.
anécdota *f* anecdote.
anegar *vt*, **anegarse** *vr* to flood.
anejo, -a *adj* attached (**a** to).
anemia *f* anemia.
anestesia *f* anesthesia.
anexión *f* annexation.
anexionar *vt* to annex.
anexo, -a 1 *adj* attached (**a** to). **2** *m* appendix.
anfitrión, -ona *mf (hombre)* host; *(mujer)* hostess.
ángel *m* angel; *Am (micrófono)* hand microphone.
angina *f* **tener anginas** to have tonsillitis; **a. de pecho** angina pectoris.
anglosajón, -ona *adj & mf* Anglo-Saxon.
angosto, -a *adj* narrow.
anguila *f* eel.
angula *f* elver.
ángulo *m* angle.
angustia *f* anguish.
anhelar *vt* to long for, to yearn for.
anhídrido *m* **a. carbónico** carbon dioxide.
anilla *f* ring.
anillo *m* ring.
animado, -a *adj (fiesta etc)* lively.
animadversión *f* animosity.
animal 1 *m* animal; *fig (basto)* brute. **2** *adj* animal.
animar 1 *vt (alentar)* to encourage; *(alegrar) (persona)* to cheer up; *(fiesta, bar)* to liven up. **2 animarse** *vr (persona)* to cheer up; *(fiesta, reunión)* to brighten up.
ánimo *m (valor, coraje)* courage; **estado de á.** state of mind; **con á. de** with the intention of; **¡á.!** cheer up!
aniñado, -a *adj (gesto)* childlike; *(comportamiento)* childish.
aniquilar *vt* to annihilate.
anís *m (bebida)* anisette.
aniversario *m* anniversary.
anoche *adv* last night; *(por la tarde)* yesterday evening; **antes de a.** the night before last.
anochecer 1 *v impers* to get dark. **2** *m* nightfall.
anodino, -a *adj (insustancial)* insubstantial; *(soso)* insipid.
anómalo, -a *adj* anomalous.
anonadado, -a *adj* **me quedé/me dejó a.** I was astonished.
anónimo, -a 1 *adj (desconocido)* anonymous; **sociedad anónima** corporation. **2** *m (carta)* anonymous letter.
anorak *m (pl anoraks)* anorak.
anormal *adj* abnormal; *(inusual)* unusual.
anotar *vt (apuntar)* to note.
anquilosarse *vr* to stagnate.
ansiar *vt* to long for.
ansiedad *f* anxiety; **con a.** anxiously.
ansioso, -a *adj (deseoso)* eager (**por** for); *(avaricioso)* greedy.
antagonismo *m* antagonism.
antaño *adv* in the past.
antártico, -a 1 *adj* Antarctic. **2** *m* **el A.** the Antarctic.
ante¹ *m (piel)* suede.
ante² ** *prep (delante de)* in the presence of; *(en vista de)* faced with; **a. todo most of all.
anteanoche *adv* the night before last.
anteayer *adv* the day before yesterday.
antecedente 1 *adj* previous. **2 antecedentes** *mpl (historial)* record *sing*; **antecedentes penales** criminal record *sing.*
antecesor, -a *mf (en un cargo)* predecessor.

antelación *f* **con un mes de a.** a month beforehand.
antemano *adv* **de a.** beforehand, in advance.
antena *f (de radio, televisión, animal)* antenna; **a. parabólica** satellite dish; **en a.** on the air.
anteojos *mpl (binoculares)* binoculars; *Am (gafas)* glasses, spectacles.
antepecho *m (de ventana)* sill.
antepenúltimo, -a *adj* **el capítulo a.** the last chapter but two.
anteproyecto *m* draft; **a. de ley** draft bill.
antepuesto, -a *pp de* **anteponer**.
antepuse *pt indef de* **anteponer**.
anterior *adj* previous; *(delantero)* front.
anteriormente *adv* previously.
antes 1 *adv* before; *(antaño)* in the past; **mucho a.** long before; **cuanto a.** as soon as possible; **a. prefiero hacerlo yo** I'd rather do it myself; **a. (bien)** on the contrary. **2** *prep* **a. de** before.
antiadherente *adj* nonstick.
antibiótico, -a *adj & m* antibiotic.
anticaspa *adj* anti-dandruff.
anticipar 1 *vt (acontecimiento)* to bring forward; *(dinero)* to pay in advance. **2 anticiparse** *vr (llegar pronto)* to arrive early; **él se me anticipó** he beat me to it.
anticonceptivo, -a *adj & m* contraceptive.
anticongelante *adj & m (de radiador)* antifreeze; *(de parabrisas)* de-icer.
anticonstitucional *adj* unconstitutional.
anticuado, -a *adj* antiquated.
anticuario, -a *mf* antique dealer.
anticuerpo *m* antibody.
antídoto *m* antidote.
antier *adv Am fam* the day before yesterday.
antifaz *m* mask.
antigüedad *f (período histórico)* antiquity; *(en cargo)* seniority; **tienda de antigüedades** antique shop.
antiguo, -a *adj* old; *(pasado de moda)* old-fashioned; *(anterior)* former.
antihistamínico *m* antihistamine.
antiniebla *adj inv* **luces a.** foglights.
antipático, -a *adj* unpleasant.
antirrobo 1 *adj inv* **alarma a.** burglar alarm; *(para coche)* car alarm. **2** *m* burglar alarm; *(para coche)* car alarm.
antiséptico, -a *adj & m* antiseptic.
antivirus *m inv* antivirus system.
antojarse *vr* **cuando se me antoja** when I feel like it; **se le antojó un helado** he wanted an ice-cream.
antojo *m (capricho)* whim; *(de embarazada)* craving.
antorcha *f* torch.
antropología *f* anthropology.
anual *adj* annual.
anudar *vt (atar)* to knot.
anular *vt (matrimonio)* to annul; *(ley)* to repeal.
anunciar *vt (producto etc)* to advertise; *(avisar)* to announce.
anuncio *m (comercial)* advertisement; *(aviso)* announcement; *(cartel)* notice.
anzuelo *m (fish)hook.*
añadir *vt* to add (**a** to).
añejo, -a *adj (vino, queso)* mature.
añicos *mpl* smithereens; **hacer a.** to smash to smithereens.
año *m* year; **el a. pasado** last year; **el a. que viene** next year; **hace años** a long time ago; **los años noventa** the nineties; **todo el a.** all the year (round); **¿cuántos años tienes?** how old are you?; **tiene seis años** he's six years old.
añorar *vt* to long for.
apacible *adj* mild.
apagado, -a *adj (luz, cigarro)* out; *(color)* dull; *(voz)* sad; *(mirada)* expressionless, lifeless; *(carácter, persona)* spiritless.
apagar *vt (fuego)* to put out; *(luz, tele etc)* to switch off.
apagón *m* power cut.
apaisado, -a *adj (papel)* landscape.
aparador *m (mueble)* sideboard.
aparato *m (dispositivo)* device; *(instrumento)* instrument; **a. de radio/televisión** radio/television set; **a. digestivo** digestive system.
aparatoso, -a *adj (pomposo)* ostentatious, showy; *(espectacular)* spectacular; *(grande)* bulky.
aparcamiento *m (en la calle)* parking place; *(parking)* parking lot.
aparcar *vti* to park.
aparecer 1 *vi* to appear; **no aparece en mi lista** he is not on my list; *(en un sitio)* to turn up; **¿apareció el dinero?** did the money turn up?; **no apareció nadie** nobody turned up. **2 aparecerse** *vr* to appear.
aparejador, -a *mf* quantity surveyor.
aparejo *m (equipo)* equipment.
aparentar 1 *vt (simular)* to affect; *(tener aspecto)* **no aparenta esa edad** she doesn't look that age. **2** *vi* to show off.
apariencia *f* appearance; **en a.** apparently; **guardar las apariencias** to keep up appearances.
apartamento *m* apartment.
apartar 1 *vt (alejar)* to remove; *(guardar)* to put aside. **2** *vi* **¡aparta!** move out of the way! **3 apartarse** *vr (alejarse)* to move away.
aparte 1 *adv* aside; **modestia/bromas a.** modesty/joking apart; **eso hay que pagarlo a.** *(separadamente)* you have to pay for it separately; **punto y a.** full stop, new paragraph. **2** *prep* **a. de eso** *(además)* besides that; *(excepto)* apart from that.
apasionado, -a *adj* passionate.
apasionante *adj* exciting.
apasionar *vt* to excite.
apático, -a 1 *adj* apathetic. **2** *mf* apathetic person.
apearse *vi (de un autobús, tren)* to get off; *(de un coche)* to get out.
apedrear *vt* to throw stones at.
apelar *vi (sentencia)* to appeal; *(recurrir)* to resort (**a** to).
apellidarse *vr* to have as a surname, to be called.
apellido *m* surname; **a. de soltera** maiden name.
apenar 1 *vt* to grieve. **2 apenarse** *vr* to be grieved; *Andes, CAm, Carib, Méx (avergonzarse)* to be ashamed.
apenas *adv (casi no)* hardly, scarcely; **a. (si) hay nieve** there is hardly any snow; **a. llegó, sonó el teléfono** he hardly had arrived when the phone rang.
apéndice *m* appendix.
apendicitis *f* appendicitis.
aperitivo *m (bebida)* apéritif; *(comida)* appetizer.
apertura *f (comienzo)* opening.
apestar *vi* to stink (**a** of).
apetecer *vi* **¿qué te apetece para cenar?** what would you like for supper?; **¿te apetece ir al cine?** do you want to go to the movie theater?
apetito *m* appetite; **tengo mucho apetito** I'm really hungry.
apetitoso, -a *adj* appetizing, tempting; *(comida)* delicious, tasty.

apiadarse *vr* to take pity (**de** on).
apilar *vt*, **apilarse** *vr* to pile up.
apiñarse *vr* to crowd together.
apio *m* celery.
apisonadora *f* steamroller.
aplacar *vt*, **aplacarse** *vr* to calm down.
aplanar *vt* to level.
aplastar *vt* to squash.
aplaudir *vt* to applaud.
aplauso *m* applause.
aplazamiento *m* postponement.
aplazar *vt* to postpone.
aplicado, -a *adj* hard-working.
aplicar 1 *vt* to apply. **2 aplicarse** *vr (esforzarse)* to apply oneself; *(usar)* to apply.
aplique *m* wall lamp.
aplomo *m* aplomb.
apocado, -a *adj* shy, timid.
apoderado, -a *mf* representative.
apoderarse *vr* **a. de** to take possession of.
apodo *m* nickname.
apogeo *m* **estar en pleno a.** *(fama etc)* to be at its height.
apoplejía *f* apoplexy.
aporrear *vt* to beat; *(puerta)* to bang.
aportar *vt* to contribute.
aposento *m (cuarto)* room.
aposta *adv* on purpose.
apostar *vti*, **apostarse** *vr* to bet (**por** on).
apoyacabezas *m* headrest.
apoyar 1 *vt* to lean; *(causa)* to support. **2 apoyarse** *vr* **apoyarse en** to lean on; *(basarse)* to be based on.
apoyo *m* support.
apreciar 1 *vt* to appreciate; *(percibir)* to see. **2 apreciarse** *vr (notarse)* to be noticeable.
aprecio *m* regard; **tener a. a algn** to be fond of sb.
aprender *vt* to learn.
aprendiz, -a *mf* apprentice.
aprensivo, -a 1 *adj* apprehensive. **2** *mf* apprehensive person.
apresar *vt* to capture.
apresurar 1 *vt (paso etc)* to speed up. **2 apresurarse** *vr* to hurry up.
apretado, -a *adj (ropa, cordón)* tight; **íbamos todos apretados en el coche** we were all squashed together in the car.
apretar 1 *vt (botón)* to press; *(nudo, tornillo)* to tighten; **me aprietan las botas** these boots are too tight for me. **2 apretarse** *vr* to squeeze together.
apretón *m* squeeze; **a. de manos** handshake.
apretujar 1 *vt* to squeeze, to crush. **2 apretujarse** *vr* to squeeze together, to cram together.
aprieto *m* tight spot; **poner a algn en un a.** to put sb in an awkward position.
aprisa *adv* quickly.
aprisionar *vt* to trap.
aprobación *f* approval.
aprobado *m (nota)* pass.
aprobar *vt (autorizar)* to approve; *(estar de acuerdo con)* to approve of; *(examen)* to pass; *(ley)* to pass.
apropiado, -a *adj* suitable.
apropiarse *vr* **a. de** to appropriate.
aprovechado, -a *adj (egoísta)* self-seeking; *(espacio)* well-planned; **bien a.** put to good use; **mal a.** *(recurso, tiempo)* wasted.
aprovechamiento *m* use.
aprovechar 1 *vt* to make good use of; *(recursos etc)* to take advantage of. **2** *vi* **¡que aproveche!** enjoy your meal! **3 aprovecharse** *vr* **aprovecharse de algo/algn** to take advantage of sth/sb.
aproximadamente *adv* approximately.
aproximado, -a *adj* approximate.
aproximar 1 *vt* to bring nearer. **2 aproximarse** *vr* to approach (**a** -).
aptitud *f* aptitude; **prueba de a.** aptitude test.
apto, -a *adj (apropiado)* suitable; *(capacitado)* capable; *(examen)* passed.
apuesta *f* bet.
apuesto, -a *adj* handsome.
apuntador, -a *mf (en el teatro)* prompter.
apuntalar *vt* to prop up.
apuntar 1 *vt (con arma)* to aim; *(anotar)* to note; *(indicar)* to suggest. **2 apuntarse** *vr (en una lista)* to put one's name down; *fam* to take part (**a** in).
apuntes *mpl* notes; **tomar apuntes** to take notes
apuñalar *vt* to stab.
apurar 1 *vt (terminar)* to finish off; *(preocupar)* to worry. **2 apurarse** *vr (preocuparse)* to worry; *(darse prisa)* to hurry.
apuro *m (situación difícil)* tight spot; *(escasez de dinero)* hardship; *(vergüenza)* embarrassment; **pasar apuros** to be hard up; **¡qué a.!** how embarrassing!
aquel, -ella *adj dem* that; **a. niño** that boy; **aquellos, -as** those; **aquellas niñas** those girls.
aquél, -élla *pron dem mf* that one; *(el anterior)* the former; **todo a. que** anyone who; **aquéllos, -as** those; *(los anteriores)* the former.
aquella *adj dem f ver* **aquel**.
aquélla *pron dem f ver* **aquél**.
aquello *pron dem neutro* that, it.
aquellos, -as *adj dem pl ver* **aquel**.
aquéllos, -as *pron dem mfpl ver* **aquél**.
aquí *adv (lugar)* here; **a. arriba/fuera** up/out here; **a. mismo** right here; **de a. para allá** up and down, to and fro; **hasta a.** this far; **por a., por favor** this way please; **está por a.** it's around here somewhere; *(tiempo)* **de a. en adelante** from now on.
árabe 1 *adj & mf* Arab. **2** *m (idioma)* Arabic.
arado *m* plow.
aragonés, -esa *adj & mf* Aragonese.
arancel *m* customs duty.
arandela *f* washer.
araña *f* spider.
arañar *vt* to scratch.
arañazo *m* scratch.
arar *vti* to plow.
arbitrario, -a *adj* arbitrary.
árbitro, -a *mf* referee; *(de tenis)* umpire; *(mediador)* arbitrator.
árbol *m* tree; **á. genealógico** family tree.
arbusto *m* bush.
arcada *f (de puente)* arch; *(náusea)* retching.
arcén *m* verge; *(de autopista)* hard shoulder.
archipiélago *m* archipelago.
archivador *m* filing cabinet.
archivar *vt (documento etc)* to file (away); *(caso, asunto)* to shelve.

archivo *m* file; *(archivador)* filing cabinet; **archivos** archives; **a. adjunto** *(en email)* attachment.

arcilla *f* clay.

arco *m (de edificio etc)* arch; *(de violín, para flechas)* bow; **a. iris** rainbow.

arder *vi* to burn.

ardiente *adj (encendido)* burning; *fig (fervoroso)* eager; **capilla a.** chapel of rest.

ardilla *f* squirrel.

ardor *m* fervor; **a. de estómago** heartburn.

área *f* area; *(medida)* are (100 square meters).

arena *f* sand; *(en plaza de toros)* bullring; **playa de a.** sandy beach.

arenisca *f* sandstone.

arenque *m* herring.

arete *m Andes, Méx* earring.

argelino, -a *adj & mf* Algerian.

argentino, -a *adj & mf* Argentinian, Argentine.

argolla *f (aro)* (large) ring; *Andes, Méx (alianza)* wedding ring.

argot *m (popular)* slang; *(técnico)* jargon.

argüir *vt* to argue.

argumentar *vt* to argue.

argumento *m (trama)* plot; *(razonamiento)* argument.

árido, -a *adj* arid.

arisco, -a *adj (persona)* unfriendly; *(áspero)* gruff; *(animal)* unfriendly.

aristócrata *mf* aristocrat.

aritmética *f* arithmetic.

arma *f* weapon; **a. de fuego** firearm; **a. nuclear** nuclear weapon.

armada *f* navy.

armado, -a *adj* armed; **ir a.** to be armed; **lucha armada** armed struggle.

armador, -a *mf* shipowner.

armadura *f (armazón)* frame.

armamento *m (armas)* armaments; **a. nuclear** nuclear weapons.

armar 1 *vt (tropa, soldado)* to arm; *(montar)* to assemble. **2 armarse** *vr* to arm oneself; **armarse de paciencia** to summon up one's patience; **armarse de valor** to pluck up courage.

armario *m (para ropa)* wardrobe; *(de cocina)* cupboard; **a. empotrado** built-in wardrobe/cupboard.

armazón *m* frame; *(de madera)* timberwork.

armisticio *m* armistice.

armonioso, -a *adj* harmonious.

aro *m* hoop; *(servilletero)* napkin ring.

aroma *m* aroma; *(de vino)* bouquet.

arpa** *f* harp.

arpón *m* harpoon.

arqueología *f* archaeology.

arquitectura *f* architecture.

arrabales *mpl* slums.

arraigado, -a *adj* deeply rooted.

arrancar 1 *vt (planta)* to uproot; *(diente, pelo)* to pull out; *(coche, motor)* to start; **a. de raíz** to uproot. **2** *vi (coche, motor)* to start; *(empezar)* to begin.

arrasar *vt* to devastate.

arrastrar 1 *vt* to drag (along); **lo arrastró la corriente** he was swept away by the current. **2 arrastrarse** *vr* to drag oneself.

arrebatar 1 *vt (coger)* to seize. **2 arrebatarse** *vr (enfurecerse)* to become furious; *(exaltarse)* to get carried away.

arrebato *m* outburst.

arreciar *vi (viento, tormenta)* to get worse.

arrecife *m* reef.

arreglado, -a *adj (reparado)* repaired; *(solucionado)* settled; *(habitación)* tidy; *(persona)* smart.

arreglar 1 *vt* to arrange; *(problema)* to sort out; *(habitación)* to tidy; *(papeles)* to put in order; *(reparar)* to repair. **2 arreglarse** *vr (vestirse)* to get ready; *fam* **arreglárselas** to manage.

arreglo *m* arrangement; *(acuerdo)* compromise; *(reparación)* repair; **no tiene a.** it is beyond repair; **con a. a** in accordance with.

arremangarse *vr* to roll one's sleeves/trousers up.

arrendar *vt (piso)* to rent; *(dar en arriendo)* to lease; *(tomar en arriendo)* to take on a lease.

arrepentido, -a *adj* regretful.

arrepentirse *vr* **a. de** to regret; *(en confesión)* to repent.

arrestar *vt* to arrest; *(encarcelar)* to put in prison.

arriba 1 *adv* up; *(encima)* on the top; *(en casa)* upstairs; **ahí a.** up there; **de a. abajo** from top to bottom; **mirar a algn de a. abajo** to look sb up and down; **desde a.** from above; **hacia a.** upwards; **más a.** further up; **la parte de a.** the top (part); **vive a.** he lives upstairs; **véase más a.** see above. **2** *interj* up you go!; **¡a. la República!** long live the Republic!; **¡a. las manos!** hands up! **3** *prep Am* **a. (de)** on top of.

arribeño, -a *Am* **1** *adj* highland. **2** *mf* highlander.

arriendo *m* lease.

arriesgado, -a *adj (peligroso)* risky; *(persona)* daring.

arriesgar *vt*, **arriesgarse** *vr* to risk.

arrimar 1 *vt* to move closer; *fam* **a. el hombro** to lend a hand. **2 arrimarse** *vr* to move nearer.

arrinconar *vt (poner en un rincón)* to put in a corner; *(acorralar)* to corner.

arrodillarse *vr* to kneel down.

arrogante *adj* arrogant.

arrojar 1 *vt (tirar)* to throw. **2 arrojarse** *vr* to throw oneself.

arrollador, -a *adj* overwhelming; *(éxito)* resounding; *(personalidad)* captivating.

arrollar 1 *vt (atropellar)* to run over, to knock down. **2** *vi* to win easily.

arropar 1 *vt* to wrap up; *(en cama)* to tuck in. **2 arroparse** *vr* to wrap oneself up.

arroyo *m* stream.

arroz *m* rice; **a. con leche** rice pudding.

arruga *f (en piel)* wrinkle; *(en ropa)* crease.

arrugar 1 *vt (piel)* to wrinkle; *(ropa)* to crease; *(papel)* to crumple (up). **2 arrugarse** *vr (piel)* to wrinkle; *(ropa)* to crease.

arruinar 1 *vt* to ruin. **2 arruinarse** *vr* to be ruined.

arsenal *m* arsenal.

arte *m o f* art; *(habilidad)* skill; **bellas artes** fine arts.

artefacto *m* device.

arteria *f* artery.

artesanal *adj* handmade.

artesanía *f* craftsmanship; *(objetos)* crafts *pl.*

ártico, -a 1 *adj* arctic; **el océano a.** the Arctic Ocean. **2** *m* **el A.** the Arctic.

articulación *f (de huesos)* joint.

artículo *m* article.

artificial *adj* artificial; *(sintético)* man-made, synthetic.

artillería *f* artillery.

artista *mf* artist; **a. de cine** film star.

artritis *f* arthritis.

arveja *f Am* pea.

as *m* ace.

asa** *f* handle.

asado, -a 1 *adj* roast; **pollo a.** roast chicken. **2** *m* roast.

asaltar *vt* to assault, to attack; *(banco)* to rob; *fig* to assail.

asamblea *f* meeting; **a. general** general meeting.

asar 1 *vt* to roast. **2 asarse** *vr fig* to be roasting.

ascender 1 *vt (en un cargo)* to promote. **2** *vi* move upward; *(temperatura etc)* to rise; **a. de categoría** to be promoted; **la factura asciende a …** the bill adds up to ….

ascenso *m* promotion; *(subida)* rise.

ascensor *m* elevator.

asco *m* disgust; **me da a.** it makes me (feel) sick; **¡qué a.!** how disgusting!

ascua** *f* live coal, ember.

aseado, -a *adj* tidy, neat.

asear 1 *vt* to tidy up. **2 asearse** *vr* to wash.

asedio *m* siege.

asegurador, -a 1 *adj* insurance. **2** *mf* insurer.

asegurar 1 *vt* to insure; *(garantizar)* to assure; *(cuerda)* to fasten. **2 asegurarse** *vr* to insure oneself; **asegurarse de que …** to make sure that ….

asemejarse *vr* **a. a** to look like.

asentamiento *m* settlement.

asentir *vi* to agree; **a. con la cabeza** to nod.

aseo *m (limpieza)* tidiness; *(cuarto de baño)* toilet.

asequible *adj* affordable; *(alcanzable)* attainable.

aserrín *m* sawdust.

asesinar *vt* to murder; *(rey, ministro)* to assassinate.

asesinato *m* murder; *(de rey, ministro)* assassination.

asesino, -a 1 *adj* murderous. **2** *mf (hombre)* murderer; *(mujer)* murderess; *(de político)* assassin.

asesor, -a 1 *mf* advisor; **a. fiscal** tax advisor. **2** *adj* advisory.

asesorar *vt* to advise.

asesoría *f* consultancy.

asfalto *m* asphalt.

asfixiar *vt*, **asfixiarse** *vr* to asphyxiate.

así 1 *adv (de esta manera)* like this o that, this way; **ponlo a.** put it this way; **a. de grande/alto** this big/tall; **algo a.** something like this o that; **¿no es a.?** isn't that so o right?; *Am* **a. no más** o **nomás** just like that; **a. las seis o a.** around six o'clock; **a. como** as well as; **aun a.** and despite that. **2** *conj* **a. pues …** so …; **a. que …** so …

asiático, -a *adj & mf* Asian.

asiduo, -a 1 *adj* assiduous. **2** *mf* regular customer.

asiento *m* seat; **a. trasero/delantero** back/front seat; **tome a.** take a seat.

asignar *vt* to allocate; *(nombrar)* to appoint.

asignatura *f* subject.

asilo *m* asylum; **a. de ancianos** old people's home.

asimismo *adv* also, as well.

asir *vt* to grasp, to seize.

asistencia *f (presencia)* attendance; *(público)* audience; **falta de a.** absence; **a. médica/técnica** medical/technical assistance.

asistenta *f* cleaning lady.

asistente 1 *adj* **el público a.** the audience; *(en estadio)* the spectators *pl.* **2** *mf (ayudante)* assistant; **a. social** social worker; **los asistentes** the audience; *(en estadio)* the spectators.

asistir 1 *vt* to assist. **2** *vi* to attend **(a -).**

asma *f* asthma.

asno *m* donkey.

asociación *f* association.

asociar 1 *vt* to associate. **2 asociarse** *vr* to be associated.

asomar 1 *vt* to stick out; **asomó la cabeza por la ventana** he put his head out the window. **2** *vi* to appear. **3 asomarse** *vr* to lean out; **asomarse a la ventana** to lean out of the window.

asombrar 1 *vt* to astonish. **2 asombrarse** *vr* to be astonished; **asombrarse de algo** to be amazed at sth.

asombro *m* astonishment.

asombroso, -a *adj* astonishing.

asorocharse *vr Andes* to suffer from altitude sickness.

aspa *f (de molino)* arm; *(de ventilador)* blade; *(cruz)* cross.

aspecto *m* look; *(de un asunto)* aspect.

áspero, -a *adj* rough; *(carácter)* surly.

aspersor *m* sprinkler.

aspiradora *f* vacuum cleaner.

aspirante *mf* candidate.

aspirar *vt (respirar)* to inhale.

aspirina *f* aspirin.

asquerosidad *f* filthy o revolting thing; **¡que a.!** how revolting!

asqueroso, -a 1 *adj (sucio)* filthy; *(desagradable)* disgusting. **2** *mf* filthy o revolting person.

asterisco *m* asterisk.

astilla *f* splinter.

astillero *m* shipyard.

astringente *adj & m* astringent.

astro *m* star.

astrología *f* astrology.

astronauta *mf* astronaut.

astronave *f* spaceship.

astronomía *f* astronomy.

asturiano, -a *adj & mf* Asturian.

astuto, -a *adj* astute.

asumir *vt* to assume.

asunto *m* subject; **no es a. tuyo** it's none of your business.

asustar 1 *vt* to frighten. **2 asustarse** *vr* to be frightened.

atacar *vt* to attack.

atajar *vi* to take a shortcut **(por** across o through).

atajo *m* shortcut.

atañer *vi* to concern.

ataque *m* attack; *(nervios, tos)* fit; **a. cardíaco** o **al corazón** heart attack.

atar 1 *vt (ligar)* to tie; **a. cabos** to put two and two together; *fam* **loco de a.** as mad as a hatter. **2 atarse** *vr fig* to get tied up; **átate los zapatos** do your shoes up.

atardecer 1 *v impers* to get dark. **2** *m* evening.

atareado, -a *adj* busy.

atascar 1 *vt (bloquear)* to block. **2 atascarse** *vr (bloquearse)* to become blocked.

atasco *m* traffic jam.

ataúd *m* coffin.

atemorizar *vt* to frighten.

atención 1 *f* attention; **llamar la a.** to attract attention; **prestar/poner a.** to pay attention **(a** to). **2** *interj* attention!; *(cuidado)* watch out!

atender 1 *vt* to attend to. **2** *vi (alumno)* to pay attention **(a** to).

atenerse *vr* **a. a** *(reglas)* to abide by; **a. a las consecuencias** to bear the consequences; **me atengo a sus palabras** I'm going by what he said; **no saber a qué a.** not to know what to expect.

atentado *m* attack.

atentamente *adv (con atención)* attentively; **le saluda a.** *(en carta)* yours sincerely.

atentar *vi* **a. a** *o* **contra** to commit a crime against; **a. contra la vida de algn** to make an attempt on sb's life.

atento, -a *adj* attentive; *(amable)* thoughtful; **estar a. a** to be aware of.

ateo, -a 1 *adj* atheistic. **2** *mf* atheist.

aterrador, -a *adj* terrifying.

aterrar 1 *vt* to terrify. **2 aterrarse** *vr* to be terrified.

aterrizaje *m* landing.

aterrizar *vi* to land.

aterrorizar 1 *vt* to terrify. **2 aterrorizarse** *vr* to be terrified.

ático *m* attic; *(vivienda)* attic apartment.

atingencia *f Am* connection.

atizar *vt (fuego)* to poke.

atlas *m inv* atlas.

atleta *mf* athlete.

atletismo *m* athletics *sing*.

atmósfera *f* atmosphere.

atolondrado, -a *adj* stunned; *(atontado)* stupid.

atómico, -a *adj* atomic.

átomo *m* atom.

atónito, -a *adj* astonished.

atontado, -a *adj (tonto)* silly; *(aturdido)* bewildered.

atorarse *vr* to get stuck.

atormentar 1 *vt* to torment. **2 atormentarse** *vr* to torment oneself.

atornillar *vt* to screw on.

atracar 1 *vt* to hold up; *(persona)* to rob. **2** *vi (barco)* to come alongside. **3 atracarse** *vr (de comida)* to stuff oneself **(de** with).

atracción *f* attraction; **parque de atracciones** amusement park.

atraco *m* hold-up; **a. a mano armada** armed robbery.

atracón *m fam* binge.

atractivo, -a 1 *adj* attractive. **2** *m* attraction.

atraer *vt* to attract.

atragantarse *vr* to choke **(con** on).

atraigo *indic pres de* **atraer**.

atraje *pt indef de* **atraer**.

atrancar 1 *vt (puerta)* to bolt. **2 atrancarse** *vr* to get stuck.

atrapar *vt* to catch.

atrás *adv (lugar)* at the back, behind; **hacia/para a.** backwards; **puerta de a.** back *o* rear door; **echarse a.** to back out; **venir de muy a.** to go back a long time.

atrasado, -a *adj* late; *(pago)* overdue; *(reloj)* slow; *(país)* backward.

atrasar 1 *vt* to put back. **2** *vi (reloj)* to be slow. **3 atrasarse** *vr* to lag behind; *(tren)* to be late.

atraso *m* delay; *(de país)* backwardness; **atrasos** *(en pago)* arrears.

atravesado, -a *adj (cruzado)* lying crosswise; *(persona)* difficult; **lo tengo a.** I can't stand him.

atravesar 1 *vt (cruzar)* to cross; *(traspasar)* to go through; *(poner a través)* to put across. **2 atravesarse** *vr* to get in the way.

atreverse *vr* to dare; **a. a hacer algo** to dare to do sth.

atrevido, -a *adj (osado)* daring; *(insolente)* insolent; *(ropa etc)* daring.

atributo *m* attribute.

atrochar *vi* to take a short cut.

atropellar *vt* to knock down.

atroz *adj (bárbaro)* atrocious; *fam (hambre, frío)* tremendous.

ATS *mf abr de* **ayudante técnico sanitario** nurse.

atuendo *m* attire.

atún *m* tuna.

aturdido, -a *adj* stunned.

aturdir *vt (con un golpe)* to stun; *(confundir)* to bewilder.

audaz *adj* audacious.

audición *f* hearing; *(en el teatro)* audition.

audiencia *f (público)* audience; *(entrevista)* audience; *(tribunal)* high court.

audiovisual *adj* audio-visual.

auditor, -a *mf* auditor.

auge *m* peak; *(económico)* boom; **estar en a.** to be booming.

aula ****** *f (en colegio)* classroom; *(en universidad)* lecture room.

aulaga *f* gorse.

aullido *m* howl.

aumentar 1 *vt* to increase; *(precios)* to put up; *(producción)* to step up; *(imagen)* to magnify. **2** *vi (precios)* to go up; *(valor)* to appreciate.

aumento *m* increase; *(de imagen)* magnification; **ir en a.** to be on the increase.

aun *adv* even; **a. así** even so.

aún *adv* still; *(en negativas)* yet; **a. está aquí** he's still here; **ella no ha venido a.** she hasn't come yet; **a. más** even more.

aunque *conj* although, though; *(enfático)* even if, even though.

aureola *f* halo.

auricular *m (del teléfono)* receiver; **auriculares** headphones.

aurora *f* dawn.

auscultar *vt* to sound (with a stethoscope).

ausencia *f* absence.

ausentarse *vr (irse)* to go away.

ausente 1 *adj* absent. **2** *mf* absentee.

austero, -a *adj* austere.

australiano, -a *adj & mf* Australian.

austríaco, -a *adj & mf* Austrian.

auténtico, -a *adj* authentic.

autista 1 *adj* autistic. **2** *mf* autistic person.

auto¹ *m RP* car.

auto² *m (sentencia)* writ; **autos** *(pleito)* documents.

autoadhesivo, -a *adj* self-adhesive.

autobiografía *f* autobiography.

autobiográfico, -a *adj* autobiographical.

autobús *m* bus.

autocar *m* coach.

autóctono, -a *adj* indigenous.

autodefensa *f* self-defense.

autoescuela *f* driving school.

autogobierno *m* self-government.

autógrafo *m* autograph.

automático, -a *adj* automatic.

automotor *m* diesel train.

automóvil *m* car.

automovilista *mf* motorist.

automovilístico, -a *adj* car.

autonomía *f* autonomy; *(región)* autonomous region.

autonómico, -a *adj* autonomous.

autopista *f* highway; **autopista(s) de la información** information superhighway.

autopsia *f* autopsy.

autor, -a *mf* author; *(de crimen)* perpetrator.

autoridad *f* authority.

autoritario, -a *adj* authoritarian.

autorizar *vt* to authorize.

autoservicio *m* self-service; *(tienda)* supermarket.

autostop *m* hitch-hiking; **hacer a.** to hitch-hike.

autostopista *mf* hitch-hiker.

autosuficiencia *f* self-sufficiency.

auxiliar 1 *adj & mf* auxiliary. **2** *vt* to assist.

auxilio *m* assistance; **primeros auxilios** first aid *sing*.

avalancha *f* avalanche.

avalar *vt* to guarantee, to endorse.

avance *m* advance.

avanzado, -a *adj* advanced; **de avanzada edad** advanced in years.

avanzar *vt* to advance.

avaricia *f* avarice.

avaricioso, -a *adj* greedy.

avaro, -a 1 *adj* miserly. **2** *mf* miser.

avasallar *vt* to subdue.

ave** *f* bird.

avellana *f* hazelnut.

avellano *m* hazelnut tree.

avena *f* oats *pl*.

avenida *f* avenue.

avenido, -a *adj* **bien/mal avenidos** on good/bad terms.

aventajar *vt (ir por delante de)* to be ahead, be in front **(a** of); *(superar)* to outdo.

aventar *vt Andes, CAm, Méx (tirar)* to throw; *CAm, Méx, Perú (empujar)* to push, to shove. **2 aventarse** *vr Méx (tirarse)* to throw oneself; *(atreverse)* **aventarse a hacer algo** to dare to do sthg.

aventura *f* adventure; *(amorosa)* (love) affair.

aventurarse *vr* to venture.

aventurero, -a 1 *adj* adventurous. **2** *mf* adventurous person.

avergonzado, -a *adj* ashamed.

avergonzar 1 *vt* to shame. **2 avergonzarse** *vr* to be ashamed **(de** of).

avería *f* breakdown.

averiar 1 *vt* to break. **2 averiarse** *vr (estropearse)* to malfunction; *(coche)* to break down.

averiguar *vt* to find out.

aversión *f* aversion.

avestruz *m* ostrich.

aviación *f* aviation; *(militar)* air force; **accidente de a.** plane crash.

aviador, -a *mf* aviator; *(piloto militar)* air force pilot.

ávido, -a *adj* avid; **a. de** eager for.

avión *m* airplane; **por a.** *(en carta)* airmail.

avioneta *f* light aircraft.

avisar *vt (informar)* to inform; *(advertir)* to warn; *(llamar)* to call for.

aviso *m* notice; *(advertencia)* warning; *(nota)* note; *Am (anuncio)* advertisement; **sin previo a.** without notice.

avispa *f* wasp.

avivar *vt (fuego)* to stoke (up); *(paso)* to quicken.

axila *f* armpit.

ay *interj (dolor)* ouch!

ayer *adv* yesterday; **a. por la mañana/por la tarde** yesterday morning/afternoon; **a. por la noche** last night; **antes de a.** the day before yesterday.

ayuda *f* help.

ayudante *mf* assistant.

ayudar 1 *vt* to help. **2 ayudarse** *vr (unos a otros)* to help; **ayudarse de** to make use of.

ayunas en a. without having eaten breakfast.

ayuntamiento *m (institución)* town council; *(edificio)* town hall.

azafata *f (de avión)* flight attendant; *(de congresos)* stewardess; *(de concurso)* hostess.

azafrán *m* saffron.

azahar *m (del naranjo)* orange blossom.

azar *m* chance; **al a.** at random.

azorado, -a *adj* embarrassed.

azorar 1 *vt* to embarrass. **2 azorarse** *vr* to be embarrassed.

azotar *vt* to beat; *(lluvia)* to beat down on; *(con látigo)* to whip.

azotea *f* flat roof.

azteca *adj & mf* Aztec.

azúcar *m o f* sugar; **a. blanco** refined sugar; **a. moreno** brown sugar.

azucarado, -a *adj* sweetened.

azucarero, -a 1 *m* sugar bowl. **2** *adj* sugar.

azucena *f* lily.

azul *adj & m* blue; **a. celeste** sky blue; **a. marino** navy blue.

azulejo *m (glazed)* tile.

B

baba *f* dribble.

babero *m* bib.

babor *m* port.

babosa *f* slug.

baboso, -a *adj fam* slimy; *Am (tonto)* stupid.

babucha *f* slipper.

baca *f* roof rack.

bacalao *m* cod.

bache *m (en carretera)* pot hole; *(mal momento)* bad patch.

bachillerato *m* high school diploma.

bacon *m* bacon.

bacteriológico, -a *adj* bacteriological; **guerra bacteriológica** germ warfare.

baden *m (en carretera)* bump.

bádminton *m* badminton.

bafle *m* loudspeaker.

bahía *f* bay.

bailar *vti* to dance.

bailarín, -ina *mf* dancer.

baile *m (danza)* dance; *(formal)* ball.

baja f *(disminución)* drop; *(en batalla)* loss; **dar de b. a algn** *(despedir)* to lay sb off; **darse de b.** *(por enfermedad)* to take sick leave.

bajada f *(descenso)* descent; *(señal)* way down; *(cuesta)* slope.

bajar 1 *vt* to come/go down; *(descender)* to get down; *(volumen)* to turn down; *(voz, telón)* to lower; *(precios etc)* to cut; *(cabeza)* to lower; **b. la escalera** to come/go downstairs. **2** *vi* to come/go down; *(apearse)* to get off; *(de un coche)* to get out (**de** of); *(disminuir)* to fall. **3 bajarse** *vr* to come/go down; *(apearse)* to get off; *(de un coche)* to get out (**de** of).

bajinis: por lo bajinis *adv fam* on the sly.

bajío m *Am* lowland.

bajo, -a 1 *adj* low; *(persona)* short; *(sonido)* faint; **en voz baja** in a low voice; **planta baja** ground floor; **de baja calidad** of poor quality. **2** *adv* low; **hablar b.** to speak quietly. **3** *prep (lugar)* under, underneath; **b. tierra** underground; **b. cero** below zero; **b. juramento** under oath; **b. fianza** on bail.

bajón m *(bajada)* sharp fall.

bala f bullet; **como una b.** like a shot.

balance m balance; *(declaración)* balance sheet.

balanza f scales pl; **b. comercial** balance of trade; **b. de pagos** balance of payments.

balazo m *(disparo)* shot; *(herida)* bullet wound; **matar a algn de un b.** to shoot sb dead.

balbucear, balbucir *vi (adulto)* to stutter, stammer; *(niño)* to babble.

balcón m balcony.

balde m **de b.** free; **en b.** in vain.

baldosa f *(ceramic)* floor tile.

balear *vt Am* to shoot.

baleo m *Am* shootout.

baliza f *(boya)* buoy; *(en aviación)* beacon.

ballena f whale.

ballet m ballet.

balneario m health resort.

balón m ball.

baloncesto m basketball.

balonmano m handball.

balonvolea m volleyball.

balsa f raft.

bálsamo m balm.

balsero, -a mf *(de Cuba)* = refugee fleeing Cuba on a raft.

bambú m *(pl* **bambúes)** bamboo.

banana f banana.

banano m *(árbol)* banana tree; *Col (fruto)* banana.

banca f *(asiento)* bench; **la b.** (the) banks; **b. electrónica** electronic banking.

bancarrota f bankruptcy.

banco m bank; *(asiento)* bench.

banda f *(de música)* band; *(cinta)* sash; **b. sonora** sound track; **(línea de) b.** touchline; **saque de b.** throw-in.

bandada f flock.

bandeja f tray.

bandera f flag.

bandido m bandit.

bando m side.

bandolero m bandit.

banquero, -a mf banker.

banqueta f stool.

banquete m banquet; **b. de bodas** wedding reception.

bañador m *(de mujer)* swimming suit; *(de hombre)* swimming trunks pl.

bañar 1 *vt* to bath. **2 bañarse** *vr (en baño)* to have a bath; *(en mar, piscina)* to go for a swim; *Am (ducharse)* to have a shower.

bañera f bath.

bañista mf swimmer.

baño m bath; *(de chocolate etc)* coating; *(cuarto de baño)* bathroom; *(lavabo)* toilet; **tomar un b.** to take a bath.

bar m bar, pub.

baraja f pack, deck.

barajar *vt (cartas)* to shuffle; *fig (nombres, cifras)* to juggle with.

baranda, barandilla f *(de escalera)* banister; *(de balcón)* handrail.

baratija f knick-knack.

barato, -a 1 *adj* cheap. **2** *adv* cheaply.

barba f *(pelo)* beard.

barbacoa f barbecue.

barbaridad f atrocity; *(disparate)* piece of nonsense; **una b.** a lot.

bárbaro, -a 1 *adj (germano)* barbarian; *(cruel)* barbaric, barbarous; *fam (enorme)* massive; *RP fam (estupendo)* tremendous, terrific. **2** mf barbarian.

barbería f barber's (shop).

barbero m barber.

barbilla f chin.

barbo m barbel.

barbudo, -a *adj* with a heavy beard.

barca f small boat.

barcaza f lighter.

barco m ship; **b. de vapor** steamer.

barlovento m windward.

barman m barman.

barniz m *(en madera)* varnish; *(en cerámica)* glaze.

barómetro m barometer.

barquillo m wafer.

barra f bar; **b. de pan** French loaf; **b. de labios** lipstick; *Andes, RP fam (grupo de amigos)* gang, group of friends; **b. brava** = group of violent soccer fans.

barraca f *(caseta)* hut; *(en Valencia y Murcia)* thatched farmhouse.

barranco m *(despeñadero)* cliff; *(torrentera)* ravine.

barrendero, -a mf *(street)* sweeper.

barreno m *(taladro)* large drill; *(explosivo)* charge.

barreño m tub.

barrer *vt* to sweep.

barrera f barrier.

barriada f *Am (de chabolas)* shanty town.

barricada f barricade.

barriga f belly, *fam* tummy.

barril m barrel; **cerveza de b.** draft beer.

barrio m district; **del b.** local; **b. chino** red-light district; **barrios bajos** slums.

barro m *(lodo)* mud; *(arcilla)* clay; **objetos de b.** earthenware *sing*.

bártulos mpl *fam* bits and pieces.

barullo m *(alboroto)* row; *(confusión)* confusion.

basar 1 *vt* to base (**en** on). **2 basarse** *vr (teoría, película)* to be based (**en** on).

báscula f scales pl.

base f base; *(de argumento, teoría)* basis; *(de partido)* grass roots; **sueldo b.** minimum wage; **b. de datos** database; **a b. de estudiar** by studying; **a b. de productos naturales** using natural products.

básico, -a *adj* basic.

básquet m basketball.

bastante 1 *adj (suficiente)* enough; **b. tiempo/comida** enough time/food; *(abundante)* quite a lot of; **hace b. calor/frío** it's quite hot/cold; **bastantes amigos** quite a lot of friends. **2** *adv (suficiente)* enough; *(considerablemente)* fairly, quite; **con esto hay b.** that is enough; **no soy lo b. rico (como) para …** I am not rich enough to …; **me gusta b.** I quite like it; **vamos b. al cine** we go to the cinema quite often.

bastar *vi* to be sufficient o enough; **basta con tres** three will be enough; **¡basta (ya)!** that's enough!

bastardo, -a *adj & mf* bastard.

basto, -a *adj (cosa)* rough; *(persona)* coarse.

bastón m stick.

bastos mpl *(in Spanish pack of cards)* ≃ clubs.

basura f trash.

basurero m *(persona)* garbage collector; *(lugar)* garbage dump.

bata f *(para casa)* dressing gown; *(de médico etc)* white coat.

batalla f battle.

batata f sweet potato.

bate m *(de béisbol)* bat.

batería 1 f battery; *(percusión)* drums pl; **b. de cocina** set of pans. **2** mf drummer.

batida f *(de la policía)* raid.

batido, -a 1 *adj (huevo, crema)* whipped. **2** m milk shake.

batidora f mixer.

batir *vt* to beat; *(huevo)* to beat; *(nata)* to whip; *(récord)* to break.

baudio m baud.

baúl m *(caja)* trunk; *Am (de vehículo)* trunk.

bautizar *vt* to baptize, christen.

bautizo m baptism.

baya f berry.

bayeta f floorcloth.

bazar m bazaar.

bazo m spleen.

bazofia f *fam* garbage.

be f *(letra)* b; *Am* **be baja** o **corta** v *(to distinguish from "b")*; *Am* **be alta** o **grande** o **larga** b *(to distinguish from "v")*.

beato, -a *adj peyorativo* sanctimonious.

bebé m baby.

beber *vti* to drink.

bebida f drink.

bebido, -a *adj* drunk.

beca f grant.

becario, -a mf grant holder.

becerro m calf.

bechamel f bechamel; **salsa b.** white sauce.

bedel m janitor.

beige *adj & m inv* beige.

béisbol m baseball.

belga *adj & mf* Belgian.

bélico, -a *adj* warlike; *(preparativos etc)* war.

belleza f beauty.

bello, -a *adj* beautiful.

bellota f acorn.

bencina f *Chile* gas.

bencinera f *Chile* gas station.

bendición f blessing.

bendito, -a *adj* blessed.

beneficencia f charity.

beneficiar 1 *vt* to benefit. **2 beneficiarse** *vr* **beneficiarse de** o **con algo** to profit from sth.

beneficio m profit; *(bien)* benefit; **en b. propio** in one's own interest; **un concierto a b. de …** a concert in aid of ….

beneficioso, -a *adj* beneficial.

benevolencia f benevolence.

bengala f flare.

benigno, -a *adj (persona)* gentle.

benjamín, -ina mf youngest child.

berberecho m *(common)* cockle.

berbiquí m drill.

berenjena f eggplant.

Bermudas 1 fpl las (Islas) B. Bermuda *sing*. **2** mpl o fpl bermudas *(prenda)* Bermuda shorts.

berrear *vi* to bellow.

berrinche m *fam* tantrum.

berro m watercress.

berza f cabbage.

besar *vt*, **besarse** *vr* to kiss.

beso m kiss.

bestia 1 f beast. **2** mf *fam* brute. **3** *adj fig* brutish.

besugo m *(pez)* sea bream.

betún m *(para el calzado)* shoe polish.

biberón m baby's bottle.

Biblia f Bible.

bibliografía f bibliography.

biblioteca f *(edificio)* library; *(estantería)* bookcase.

bicarbonato m bicarbonate; **b. sódico** bicarbonate of soda.

bíceps m inv biceps.

bicho m bug.

bici f *fam* bike.

bicicleta f bicycle; **montar en b.** to ride a bicycle.

bidé m bidet.

bidón m drum.

bien¹ 1 *adv (correctamente)* well; **responder b.** to answer correctly; **hiciste b. en decírmelo** you were right to tell me; **las cosas le van b.** things are going well for him; **¡b.!** good!, great!; **¡muy b.!** excellent!; **¡qué b.!** great!; **vivir b.** to live comfortably; **¡está b.!** *(de acuerdo!)* fine!, all right!; **¡ya está b.!** that's (quite) enough!; **esta falda te está b.** this skirt suits you; **ese libro está muy b.** that book is very good. • *(intensificador)* very; **b. temprano** nice and early; **b. caliente** pretty hot; **más b.** rather. **2** *conj* **o b.** or else; **b. … o b. …** either … or …; **no b. llegó … no** sooner had she arrived than …; **si b.** although.

bien² m *(bondad)* good; **el b. y el mal** good and evil; **por el b. de** for the good of; **lo hace por tu b.** he does it for your sake; **bienes** goods; **bienes inmuebles** real estate; **bienes de consumo** consumer goods.

bienestar m well-being.

bienvenida f welcome; **dar la b. a algn** to welcome sb.

bienvenido, -a *adj* welcome.

bifurcación f *(de la carretera)* fork.

bigote m *(de persona)* mustache; **bigotes** *(de animal)* whiskers pl.

bilateral *adj* bilateral.
bilingüe *adj* bilingual.
bilis *f* bile.
billar *m (juego)* billiards *sing*; *(mesa)* billiard table; **b. americano** pool; **b. ruso** snooker.
billete *m* ticket; *(de banco)* bill; **b. de ida y vuelta** round-trip ticket; **b. sencillo** *o* **de ida** one-way (ticket); **un b. de mil pesos** a thousand peso note.
billetera *f*, **billetero** *m* wallet.
billón *m* thousand billion.
bingo *m (juego)* bingo; *(sala)* bingo hall.
biografía *f* biography.
biología *f* biology.
biombo *m* (folding) screen.
biopsia *f* biopsy.
bioquímica *f* biochemistry.
bióxido *m* **b. de carbono** carbon dioxide.
biquini *m* bikini.
birria *f fam* garbage.
bisabuela *f* great-grandmother.
bisabuelo *m* great-grandfather; **bisabuelos** great-grandparents.
bisagra *f* hinge.
bisiesto *adj* **año b.** leap year.
bisnieto, -a *m (niño)* great-grandson; *(niña)* great-granddaughter; **mis bisnietos** my great-grandchildren.
bisonte *m* bison.
bisté, bistec *m* steak.
bisturí *m* scalpel.
bisutería *f* imitation jewelry.
bizco, -a 1 *adj* cross-eyed. **2** *mf* cross-eyed person.
bizcocho *m* sponge cake.
biznieto, -a *mf* = **bisnieto**.
blanco, -a¹ *adj* white; *(tez)* fair. **2** *mf (hombre)* white man; *(mujer)* white woman; **los blancos** whites.
blanco² *m (color)* white; *(hueco)* blank; *(diana)* target; **pasar la noche en b.** to have a sleepless night; **me quedé en b.** my mind went blank; **ser el b. de todas las miradas** to be the center of attention.
blancura *f* whiteness.
blando, -a *adj* soft.
blanquear *vt (encalar)* to whitewash.
blasfemar *vi* to blaspheme (**contra** against).
blindado, -a *adj (carro)* armored; *(antibalas)* bullet-proof; **coche b.** bullet-proof car; **puerta blindada** reinforced door.
bloc *m* pad; **b. de notas** notepad.
bloque *m* block; **b. de pisos** block (of apartments).
bloquear *vt* to block; *(sitiar)* to blockade.
blusa *f* blouse.
blusón *m* loose blouse.
bobada *f* nonsense; **decir bobadas** to talk nonsense.
bobina *f* reel.
bobo, -a 1 *adj (tonto)* stupid, silly; *(ingenu)* naïve. **2** *mf* fool.
boca *f* mouth; **b. abajo** face downward; **b. arriba** face upward; *fam* **¡cierra la b.!** shut up!; **con la b. abierta** open-mouthed; **se le hizo la b. agua** his mouth watered; **la b. del metro** the entrance to the subway station.
bocacalle *f* entrance to a street.
bocadillo *m* sandwich; **un b. de jamón/tortilla** a ham/omelette sandwich.
bocado *m* bite.
bocanada *f (de humo)* puff; **una b. de viento** a gust of wind.
bocata *m fam* sandwich.
bocazas *mf inv fam* bigmouth.
boceto *m (de cuadro etc)* sketch; *(esquema)* outline.
bochinche *m fam* uproar; **armar un b.** to kick up a row.
bochorno *m (tiempo)* sultry weather; *(calor sofocante)* stifling heat; *(vergüenza)* embarrassment.
bochornoso, -a *adj (tiempo)* sultry, close, muggy; *(calor)* stifling; *fig (vergonzoso)* shameful, embarrassing.
bocina *f* horn; **tocar la b.** to sound one's horn.
boda *f* marriage; **bodas de plata** silver wedding *sing*.
bodega *f (en casa)* wine cellar; *(tienda)* wine shop; *Am* grocery store, grocer's.
body *m* bodystocking.
bofetada *f*, **bofetón** *m* slap on the face; **dar una b./un b. a algn** to slap sb's face.
bohío *m Am* hut.
boicotear *vt* to boycott.
boina *f* beret.
bol *m* bowl.
bola *f* ball; *(canica)* marble; **b. de nieve** snowball; **no dar pie con b.** to be unable to do anything right.
bolera *f* bowling alley.
boletería *f Am (de estadio, estación)* ticket office; *(de teatro)* box office.
boletero, -a *mf Am* box office attendant.
boletín *m* bulletin.
boleto *m Am* ticket.
boli *m* biro®.
boliche *m (juego)* bowling; *(bola)* jack; *(lugar)* bowling alley; *CSur fam (bar)* small bar.
bólido *m (coche)* racing car.
bolígrafo *m* ballpoint (pen).
boliviano, -a *adj & mf* Bolivian.
bollo *m (de pan)* roll; *(abolladura)* dent.
bolo *m* skittle; **bolos** *(juego)* skittles.
bolsa¹ *f* bag; **b. de deportes** sports bag; **b. de la compra** shopping bag; **b. de viaje** travel bag.
bolsa² *f (de valores)* Stock Exchange.
bolsillo *m (prenda)* pocket; **de b.** pocket; **libro de b.** paperback.
bolso *m* purse.
boludo, -a *mf RP fam (estúpido)* idiot, twit.
bomba¹ *f* pump; **b. de incendios** fire engine; *Andes, Ven* **b. (de gasolina)** *(surtidor)* gas pump.
bomba² *f (explosivo)* bomb; **b. atómica/de hidrógeno/de neutrones** atom/hydrogen/neutron bomb; **b. de relojería** time bomb; *fam* **pasarlo b.** to have a great time.
bombardear *vt* to bomb.
bombazo *m* bomb blast.
bombero, -a *mf (hombre)* fireman; *(mujer)* firewoman; *(ambos sexos)* firefighter; **cuerpo de bomberos** fire brigade; **parque de bomberos** fire station.
bombilla *f* (light) bulb.
bombillo *m CAm, Carib, Col, Méx* light bulb.
bombín *m* bowler hat.
bombo *m (de percusión)* bass drum; *(de sorteo)* lottery drum; *(de lavadora)* drum.
bombón *m* chocolate.

bombona *f* cylinder.
bonachón, -ona *adj* good-natured.
bonanza *f (tiempo)* fair weather; *(prosperidad)* prosperity.
bondadoso, -a *adj* good-natured.
boniato *m* sweet potato.
bonificación *f* bonus.
bonito, -a¹ *adj* pretty, nice.
bonito² *m* tuna.
bono *m (vale)* voucher; *(título)* bond.
bono-bus *m* bus pass.
boquerón *m* anchovy.
boquete *m* hole.
boquiabierto, -a *adj* open-mouthed; **se quedó b.** he was flabbergasted.
boquilla *f (de cigarro)* tip; *(de pipa)* mouthpiece.
borda *f* gunwale; **arrojar** *o* **echar por la b.** to throw overboard; **un fuera b.** *(motor)* an outboard motor.
bordado, -a 1 *adj* embroidered. **2** *m* embroidery.
bordar *vt* to embroider.
borde *m (de mesa, camino)* edge; *(de prenda)* hem; *(de vasija)* rim; **al b. del mar** at the seaside.
bordear *vt* to skirt.
bordillo *m* curb.
bordo *m* **a b.** on board; **subir a b.** to go on board.
borrachera *f (embriaguez)* drunkenness; *(curda)* binge; **coger** *o* **pillar una b.** to get drunk.
borracho, -a 1 *adj (bebido)* drunk; *(bizcocho)* with rum; **estar b.** to be drunk. **2** *mf* drunk.
borrador *m (escrito)* rough copy; *(de pizarra)* duster.
borrar *vt (con goma)* to rub out; *(pizarra)* to clean; *(en pantalla)* to delete.
borrasca *f* area of low pressure.
borrego, -a *mf* yearling lamb; *(persona)* sheep.
borrico *m* ass, donkey; *fam fig* ass, dimwit.
borroso, -a *adj* blurred; **veo b.** I can't see clearly.
bosque *m* wood.
bosquejo *m (de dibujo)* sketch; *(de plan)* draft.
bostezar *vi* to yawn.
bostezo *m* yawn.
bota *f* boot; *(de vino)* wineskin.
botana *f Méx* snack.
botánico, -a *adj* botanic; **jardín b.** botanic gardens *pl*.
botar 1 *vi (saltar)* to jump; *(pelota)* to bounce. **2** *vt (barco)* to launch; *(pelota)* to bounce; *Am (arrojar)* to throw out.
bote¹ *m* jump; *(de pelota)* bounce.
bote² *m (lata)* can, tin; *(para propinas)* jar *o* box for tips.
bote³ *m (lancha)* boat; **b. salvavidas** lifeboat.
botella *f* bottle.
botellín *m* small bottle.
botijo *m* earthenware pitcher (with spout and handle).
botín *m (de un robo)* loot.
botiquín *m* medicine cabinet; *(portátil)* first aid kit; *(enfermería)* first aid post.
botón *m* button.
botones *m inv (en hotel)* bellboy, bellhop; *(recadero)* errand boy.
boutique *f* boutique.
boxeador *m* boxer.
boxeo *m* boxing.
boya *f (baliza)* buoy; *(corcho)* float.
boy-scout *m* boy scout.
bozal *m* muzzle.
bracear *vi (nadar)* to swim.
bragas *fpl* panties *pl*, knickers *pl*.
braguiceta *f (de pantalón)* fly, flies *pl*.
braille *m* Braille.
bramido *m* bellowing.
brandy *m* brandy.
brasa *f* ember; **chuletas a la b.** barbecued chops.
brasero *m* brazier.
brasileño, -a, *RP* **brasilero, -a** *adj & mf* Brazilian.
bravo, -a 1 *adj (valiente)* brave; **un toro b.** a fighting bull. **2** *interj* **¡b.!** well done!
braza *f* breast stroke; **nadar a b.** to do the breast stroke.
brazada *f* stroke.
brazalete *m (pulsera)* bracelet; *(insignia)* armband.
brazo *m* arm; **en brazos** in one's arms; **ir del b.** to walk arm in arm; **con los brazos abiertos** with open arms.
brecha *f (en muro)* gap; *(herida)* wound.
brécol *m* broccoli.
breva *f (higo)* early fig; *fam* **¡no caerá esa b.!** no such luck!
breve *adj* brief; **en b., en breves momentos** shortly, soon.
brezo *m* heather.
bribón, -ona 1 *adj* roguish. **2** *mf* rogue.
bricolaje *m* do-it-yourself, DIY.
bridge *m* bridge.
brigada *f* brigade; *(de policías)* squad.
brillante 1 *adj* brilliant. **2** *m* diamond.
brillantina *f* brilliantine.
brillar *vi (resplandecer)* to shine; *(ojos, joyas)* to sparkle; *(lentejuelas etc)* to glitter.
brillo *m (resplandor)* shine; *(del sol, de la luna)* brightness; *(de lentejuelas etc)* glittering; *(del cabello, de tela)* sheen; *(de zapatos)* shine; **sacar b. a** to polish.
brincar *vi* to skip.
brindar 1 *vi* to drink a toast; **b. por algn/algo** drink to sb/sth. **2 brindarse** *vr* to volunteer (**a** to).
brindis *m* toast.
brío *m* energy.
brisa *f* breeze; **b. marina** sea breeze.
británico, -a 1 *adj* British; **las Islas Británicas** the British Isles. **2** *mf* Briton; **los británicos** the British.
brocha *f (para pintar)* paintbrush; *(de afeitar)* shaving brush.
broche *m (joya)* brooch; *(de vestido)* fastener.
bróculi *m* broccoli.
broma *f (chiste)* joke; **en b.** as a joke; **¡ni en b.!** not on your life!; **b. pesada** practical joke; **gastar una b.** to play a joke.
bromear *vi* to joke.
bromista 1 *adj* fond of joking *o* playing jokes. **2** *mf* joker, prankster.
bronca *f (riña)* row; **echar una b. a algn** to bawl sb out.
bronce *m* bronze.
bronceado, -a 1 *adj* (sun)tanned. **2** *m* (sun)tan.
bronceador, -a 1 *adj* **leche bronceadora** suntan lotion. **2** *m* suntan lotion.
broncearse *vr* to get a tan *o* a suntan.

bronquitis *f inv* bronchitis.
brotar *vi (planta)* to sprout; *(agua)* to gush; *(epidemia)* to break out.
bruces: de bruces *adv* face downwards; **se cayó de b.** he fell flat on his face.
bruja *f* witch.
brújula *f* compass.
bruma *f* mist.
brusco, -a *adj (persona)* brusque; *(repentino)* sudden.
bruto, -a 1 *adj (necio)* stupid; *(grosero)* coarse; *(no neto)* gross; **un diamante en b.** an uncut diamond. **2** *mf* blockhead.
bucear *vi* to swim under water.
bucle *m* curl.
budín *m* pudding.
budista *adj* Buddhist.
buen *adj (delante de un nombre masculino singular)* good; **¡b. viaje!** have a good trip!; *ver* **bueno**.
buenamente *adv* **haz lo que b. puedas** just do what you can; **si b. puedes** if you possibly can.
bueno, -a 1 *adj* good; *(amable)* *(con ser)* good, kind; *(sano)* *(con estar)* well, in good health; **un alumno muy b.** a very good pupil; **lo b.** the good thing; **hoy hace buen tiempo** it's fine today; **un buen número de** a good number of; **una buena cantidad** a considerable amount; **un buen trozo de pastel** a nice *o* good big piece of cake; **¡en buen lío te has metido!** that's a fine mess you've got yourself into!; **¡buenas!** *(saludos)* hello!; **buenas tardes** *(desde mediodía hasta las cinco)* good afternoon; *(desde las cinco)* good evening; **buenas noches** *(al llegar)* good evening; *(al irse)* good night; **buenos días** good morning; **de buenas a primeras** all at once; **por las buenas** willingly; **por las buenas o por las malas** willy-nilly; **¡buena la has hecho!** that's done it!; **¡estaría b.!** I should hope not!; **librarse de una buena** to get off scot free. **2** *interj* **¡b.!** *(de acuerdo)* all right, OK; *Col, Méx (al teléfono)* hello.
buey *m* ox.
búfalo, -a *mf* buffalo.
bufanda *f* scarf.
bufete *m (despacho de abogado)* lawyer's office.
buhardilla *f* attic.
búho *m* owl.
buitre *m* vulture.
bujía *f (de coche)* spark plug.
bulbo *m* bulb.
bulla *f (ruido)* noise; **armar b.** to make a lot of noise.
bullicio *m* noise.
bulto *m (cosa indistinta)* shape; *(maleta, caja)* piece of luggage; *(hinchazón)* lump; **hacer mucho b.** to be very bulky.
búnker *m* bunker.
buñuelo *m* doughnut.
buque *m* ship; **b. de guerra** warship; **b. de pasajeros** passenger ship.
burbuja *f* bubble.
burdel *m* brothel.
burguesía *f* bourgeoisie.
burla *f* gibe, jeer; **hacer b. de algo** *o* **algn** to make fun of sth *o* sb; **hacer b. a algn** to stick one's tongue out at sb.
burladero *m* refuge in bullring.
burlarse *vr* to make fun (**de** of).
burlón, -ona *adj* mocking.
burocracia *f* bureaucracy.
burocrático, -a *adj* bureaucratic.
burro, -a 1 *mf* donkey; *fam (estúpido)* blockhead. **2** *adj fam (necio)* stupid; *(obstinado)* stubborn.
bursátil *adj* stock market.
busca *f* search; **ir en b. de** to go in search of.
buscar 1 *vt* to look *o* search for; **ir a b.** to go and get sth; **fue a buscarme a la estación** she picked me up at the station. **2 buscarse** *vr fam* **buscarse la vida** to try and earn one's living; **se busca** wanted.
búsqueda *f* search.
busto *m* bust.
butaca *f (sillón)* armchair; *(de teatro, cine)* seat; **b. de platea** *o* **patio** seat in the stalls.
butano *m* **(gas) b.** butane gas.
buzo *m* diver.
buzón *m* mailbox; **echar una carta al b.** to mail a letter.

C

cabalgar *vti* to ride.
caballa *f* mackerel.
caballería *f (cuerpo)* cavalry; *(cabalgadura)* mount, steed.
caballero *m* gentleman; **ropa de c.** menswear; **caballeros** *(en letrero)* gents.
caballeroso, -a *adj* gentlemanly.
caballo *m* horse; *(de ajedrez)* knight; *(de naipes)* queen; **a c.** on horseback; **montar a c.** to ride; *fig* **a c. entre ...** halfway between ....
cabaña *f (choza)* cabin.
cabaret *m (pl cabarets)* cabaret.
cabecera *f* top, head.
cabecilla *mf* leader.
cabello *m* hair.
caber *vi* to fit; **cabe en el maletero** it fits in the boot; **en este coche/jarro caben ...** this car/jug holds ...; **no cabe duda** there is no doubt; **cabe la posibilidad de que ...** there is a possibility that ...; **no está mal dentro de lo que cabe** it isn't bad, under the circumstances.
cabestrillo *m* sling.
cabeza 1 *f* head; **en c.** in the lead; **por c.** a head, per person; **a la c. de** at the head of; **estar mal de la c.** to be a mental case. **2** *mf* **el** *o* **la c. de familia** the head of the family.
cabezota *fam* **1** *adj* pigheaded. **2** *mf* pigheaded person.
cabida *f* capacity.
cabina *f* cabin; **c. telefónica** telephone booth.
cable *m* cable.
cabo *m (extremo)* end; *(rango)* corporal; *(policía)* sergeant; *(de barco)* rope, cable; *(geográfico)* cape; **al c. de** after; **atar cabos** to put two and two together.
cabra *f* goat.
cabré *indic fut de* **caber**.
cabriola *f* skip.
cacahuete *m* peanut.
cacao *m* cacao; *(polvo, bebida)* cocoa.

cacatúa *f* cockatoo.
cacería *f (actividad)* hunting; *(partida)* hunt.
cacerola *f* saucepan.
cacharro *m* earthenware pot *o* jar; *fam (cosa)* thing, piece of junk; **cacharros** *(de cocina)* pots and pans.
cachear *vt* to frisk, search.
cachetada *f Am* slap.
cachete *m (bofetada)* slap; *Am (mejilla)* cheek.
cachimba *f* pipe.
cachivache *m fam* thing, knick-knack.
cacho[1] *m fam (pedazo)* bit, piece.
cacho[2] *m Andes, Ven (cuerno)* horn.
cachondeo *m fam* laugh; **tomar algo a c.** to take sth as a joke.
cachorro, -a *mf (de perro)* pup, puppy; *(de gato)* kitten; *(de otros animales)* cub, baby.
cacique *m (jefe)* local boss.
caco *m fam* thief.
cacto *m*, **catus** *m inv* cactus.
cada *adj (de dos)* each, every; *(de varios)* each, every; **c. día** every day; **c. dos días** every second day; **c. vez más** more and more; **¿c. cuánto?** how often?; **cuatro de c. diez** four out of (every) ten.
cadáver *m (de persona)* corpse, body; *(de animal)* body, carcass.
cadena *f* chain; *(correa de perro)* lead, leash; *(canal)* channel; *(de montañas)* range; **trabajo en c.** assembly line work; **c. perpetua** life imprisonment; *(para ruedas)* **cadenas** tire chains.
cadera *f* hip.
caducar *vi* to expire.
caducidad *f* expiration; **fecha de c.** *(en alimentos)* ≃ sell-by date; *(en medicinas)* to be used before.
caer 1 *vi* to fall; *(entender)* to understand, to see; *(hallarse)* to be; **dejar c.** to drop; **ya caigo** I get it; **cae por Granada** it is somewhere near Granada; **me cae bien/mal** I like/don't like her. **2 caerse** *vr* to fall (down); **me caí de la moto** I fell off the motorbike; **se le cayó el pañuelo** she dropped her handkerchief.
café *m* coffee; *(cafetería)* café; **c. solo/con leche** black/white coffee.
cafeína *f* caffeine.
cafetera *f (para hacerlo)* coffee-maker; *(para servirlo)* coffeepot.
cafetería *f* snack bar, coffee bar; *(en tren)* buffet car.
caída *f* fall; *(de pelo, diente)* loss; *(de gobierno)* downfall, collapse.
caigo *indic pres de* **caer**.
caimán *m* cayman, alligator.
caja *f* box; *(de embalaje)* crate, case; *(en tienda)* cash desk; *(en banco)* cashier's desk; *(féretro)* coffin, casket; **c. fuerte** safe; **c. de cerveza** case of beer; **c. de cambios** gearbox; **c. de ahorros** *o* **de pensiones** savings bank.
cajero, -a *mf* cashier; **c. automático** automatic teller machine (ATM).
cajetilla *f* packet, pack.
cajón *m (en un mueble)* drawer; *(caja grande)* crate, chest.
cal *f* lime; **a c. y canto** hermetically.
calabacín *m (pequeño)* zucchini; *(grande)* squash.
calabaza *f* pumpkin, gourd.
calabozo *m (prisión)* jail, prison; *(celda)* cell.
calado, -a *adj (mojado)* soaked.
calamar *m* squid *inv*; **calamares a la romana** squid fried in batter.
calambre *m (descarga)* electric shock; *(en músculo)* cramp; **ese cable da c.** that wire is live.
calamidad *f* calamity.
calar 1 *vt (mojar)* to soak, to drench. **2** *vi (prenda)* to let in water. **3 calarse** *vr (prenda, techo)* to let in water; *(mojarse)* to get soaked; *(coche)* to stall; **calarse el sombrero** to pull one's hat down.
calavera *f* skull.
calcar *vt (dibujo)* to trace; *(imitar)* to copy, to imitate.
calcetín *m* sock.
calcio *m* calcium.
calco *m* tracing; **papel de c.** carbon paper.
calculadora *f* calculator.
calcular *vt* to calculate; *(evaluar)* to (make an) estimate; *(suponer)* to guess.
cálculo *m* calculation; *(matemático)* calculus.
caldera *f* boiler.
caldo *m* stock, broth; **c. de cultivo** breeding ground.
calefacción *f* heating; **c. central** central heating.
calendario *m* calendar.
calentador *m* heater.
calentar 1 *vt (agua, horno)* to heat; *(comida, habitación)* to warm up. **2 calentarse** *vr* to get hot, heat up.
calentura *f* fever, temperature.
calidad *f* quality; **de primera c.** first-class; **vino de c.** good-quality wine.
cálido, -a *adj* warm.
caliente *adj* hot; *(debate)* heated.
calificar *vt* to describe (**de** as); *(examen)* to mark, grade.
caligrafía *f* calligraphy; *(modo de escribir)* handwriting.
caliza *f* limestone.
callado, -a *adj* quiet; **te lo tenías muy c.** you were keeping that quiet.
callar 1 *vi (dejar de hablar)* to stop talking; *(no hablar)* to keep quiet, to say nothing; **¡calla!** be quiet!, shut up! **2** *vt (noticia)* not to mention, to keep to oneself. **3 callarse** *vr* to be quiet, to shut up; **¡cállate!** shut up!
calle *f* street, road; *(de piscina, pista)* lane; **c. de dirección única** one-way street.
callejón *m* back alley, back street; **c. sin salida** cul-de-sac, dead end.
callejuela *f* narrow street, lane.
callista *mf* chiropodist.
callo *m* callus, corn; **callos** tripe *sing.*
calma *f* calm; **¡c.!** calm down!; **en c.** calm; **tómalo con c.** take it easy.
calmante *m* painkiller; *(relajante)* tranquillizer.
calmar 1 *vt (persona)* to calm (down); *(dolor)* to soothe, to relieve. **2 calmarse** *vr (persona)* to calm down; *(dolor, viento)* to ease off.
calor *m* heat; *(entusiasmo)* warmth; **hace c.** it's hot; **tengo c.** I'm hot; **entrar en c.** to warm up.
caloría *f* calorie.
calumnia *f* slander.
caluroso, -a *adj* hot; *(acogida etc)* warm.
calvicie *f* baldness.
calvo, -a 1 *adj* bald. **2** *m* bald man.
calzada *f* road.
calzado *m* shoes *pl.*
calzador *m* shoehorn.
calzar 1 *vt (poner calzado)* to put shoes on; *(mueble)* to wedge; **¿qué número calzas?** what size shoe do you wear? **2 calzarse** *vr* **calzarse los zapatos** to put on one's shoes.
calzoncillos *mpl* briefs, underpants.
calzones *mpl* trousers.
cama *f* bed; **estar en** *o* **guardar c.** to be confined to bed; **hacer la c.** to make the bed; **irse a la c.** to go to bed; **c. doble/sencilla** double/single bed.
cámara 1 *f (aparato)* camera; *(de rueda)* inner tube; **a c. lenta** in slow motion; **c. frigorífica**

cold-storage room. **2** *mf (hombre)* cameraman; *(mujer)* camerawoman.
camarada *mf* comrade.
camarera *f (de hotel)* (chamber)-maid.
camarero, -a *mf (de restaurante) (hombre)* waiter; *(mujer)* waitress; *(tras la barra)* bartender.
camarón *m* prawn.
camarote *m* cabin.
cambiar 1 *vt* to change; *(intercambiar)* to swap, to exchange; **c. algo de sitio** to move sth. **2** *vi* to change; **c. de casa** to move (house); **c. de idea** to change one's mind. **3 cambiarse** *vr (de ropa)* to change (clothes); *(de casa)* to move (house).
cambio *m* change; *(de impresiones)* exchange; *(de divisas)* exchange; **c. de marcha** gear change; **a c. de** in exchange for; **en c.** on the other hand; **¿tienes c. de mil pesos?** have you got change for a thousand pesos?
camello, -a *mf* camel.
camilla *f* stretcher.
caminar 1 *vi* to walk. **2** *vt* to walk; **caminaron diez kilómetros** they walked (for) ten kilometers.
camino *m (ruta)* route, way; *(vía)* path, track; **ponerse en c.** to set off; **abrirse c.** to break through; **a medio c.** half-way; **estar en c.** to be on the way; **nos coge** *o* **pilla de c.** it is on the way.
camión *m* truck; *CAm, Méx (autobús)* bus; **c. cisterna** tanker; **c. de la basura** garbage truck; **c. frigorífico** refrigerated truck.
camionero, -a *mf* truck driver.
camioneta *f* van.
camisa *f* shirt; **en mangas de c.** in one's shirtsleeves; **c. de fuerza** straightjacket.
camiseta *f (de uso interior)* undershirt; *(de uso exterior)* T-shirt; *(de deporte)* shirt.
camisón *m* nightgown.
camote *m Andes, CAm, Méx* sweet potato.
campamento *m* camp.
campana *f* bell.
campanada *f* peal of a bell.
campanario *m* belfry, bell tower.
campanilla *f* small bell.
campaña *f* campaign; **c. electoral** election campaign; **c. publicitaria** advertising campaign.
campeón, -ona *mf* champion; **c. mundial** world champion.
campeonato *m* championship.
campesino, -a *mf (hombre)* countryman; *(mujer)* countrywoman.
camping *m* campsite; **hacer** *o* **ir de c.** to go camping.
campiña *f* open country.
campista *mf* camper.
campo *m* country, countryside; *(de fútbol)* pitch; *(de tenis)* court; *(de golf)* course; *(parcela, ámbito)* field; **a c. traviesa** *o* **través** cross-country; **c. de batalla** battlefield; **c. de concentración** concentration camp; **c. de trabajo** work camp.
camposanto *m* cemetery.
cana *f (gris)* gray hair; *(blanco)* white hair; **tener canas** to have gray hair.
canal *m (artificial)* canal; *(natural, de televisión)* channel; **C. de la Mancha** English Channel.
canalla *mf* swine, rotter.
canalón *m* gutter
canapé *m* canapé; *(sofá)* couch, sofa.
canario, -a 1 *adj & mf* Canarian; **Islas Canarias** Canary Islands, Canaries. **2** *m (pájaro)* canary.
canasta *f* basket.
cancela *f* wrought-iron gate.
cancelar *vt* to cancel; *(deuda)* to pay off; *Chile, Ven (compra)* to pay for.
cáncer *m* cancer; **c. de pulmón/mama** lung/breast cancer.
cancerígeno, -a *adj* carcinogenic.
canceroso, -a *adj* cancerous.
cancha *f* ground; *(de tenis, baloncesto)* court.
canciller *mf* chancellor
cancillería *f Am* foreign ministry.
canción *f* song.
candado *m* padlock.
candela *f Carib* fire.
candelabro *m* candelabra.
candidato, -a *mf* candidate; *(a un puesto)* applicant.
candidatura *f (lista)* list of candidates.
cándido, -a *adj* candid.
candoroso, -a *adj* innocent, pure.
canela *f* cinnamon.
canelones *mpl (pasta)* cannelloni.
cangrejo *m (de mar)* crab; *(de río)* freshwater crayfish.
canguro 1 *m* kangaroo. **2** *mf fam* baby-sitter.
caníbal *adj & mf* cannibal.
canica *f* marble.
caniche *m* poodle.
canícula *f* dog days, midsummer heat.
canillera *f Am (cobardía)* cowardice; *(miedo)* fear.
canillita *m Andes, RP* newspaper boy.
canino, -a 1 *adj* canine. **2** *m (colmillo)* canine.
canoa *f* canoe.
canoso, -a *adj (de pelo blanco)* white-haired; *(de pelo gris)* gray-haired; *(pelo)* white; gray.
cansado, -a *adj (agotado)* tired, weary.
cansancio *m* tiredness, weariness.
cansar 1 *vt* to tire. **2** *vi* to be tiring. **3 cansarse** *vr* to get tired; **se cansó de esperar** he got tired of waiting, he got fed up (with) waiting.
cantaleta *f Am* **la misma c.** the same old story.
cantante 1 *mf* singer. **2** *adj* singing.
cantaor, -a *mf* flamenco singer.
cantar *vti* to sing.
cántaro *m* pitcher; **llover a cántaros** to rain cats and dogs.
cante *m (canto)* singing; **c. hondo, c. jondo** flamenco.
cantera *f (de piedra)* quarry; *(de equipo)* young players *pl.*
cantidad *f* quantity; *(de dinero)* sum; *fam* **c. de gente** thousands of people.
cantina *f* canteen.
cantinero, -a *mf* bar attendant.
canto¹ *m (arte)* singing; *(canción)* song.
canto² *m (borde)* edge; **de c.** on its side.
canturrear *vi* to hum, croon.
caña *f (de cerveza)* draft beer; *(tallo)* cane, stem; *(de pescar)* rod; *Andes, Cuba, RP (aguardiente)* cane spirit, cheap rum; **c. de azúcar** sugar cane.
cañada *f (barranco)* gully, ravine.
cañería *f (piece of)* piping; **cañerías** plumbing *sing.*
caño *m (tubería)* pipe; *(tubo)* tube; *(chorro)* spout.
cañón *m* cannon; *(de fusil)* barrel; *(garganta)* canyon.
cañonazo *m* gunshot.
caoba *f* mahogany.
caos *m* chaos.

caótico, -a *adj* chaotic.
capa *f (prenda)* cloak, cape; *(de pintura)* layer, coat.
capacidad *f* capacity.
caparazón *m* shell.
capataz *mf (hombre)* foreman; *(mujer)* forewoman.
capaz *adj* capable, able; **ser c. de hacer algo** *(tener la habilidad de)* to be able to do sth; *(atreverse a)* to dare to do sth; *Am* **es c. que** it is likely that.
capicúa *adj* **número c.** reversible number; **palabra c.** palindrome.
capilla *f* chapel.
capital 1 *f* capital. **2** *m (dinero)* capital. **3** *adj* capital, main; **pena c.** capital punishment.
capitalismo *m* capitalism.
capitalista *adj & mf* capitalist.
capitán, -ana *mf* captain.
capitulación *f* agreement; *(pacto)* capitulation.
capítulo *m (de libro)* chapter; *(tema)* subject.
capó *m (de coche)* hood.
capota *f (de coche)* convertible top.
capote *m (de torero)* cape.
capricho *m (antojo)* whim, caprice.
caprichoso, -a *adj* whimsical.
cápsula *f* capsule.
captar *vt (ondas)* to receive, to pick up; *(comprender)* to understand, to grasp; *(interés etc)* to attract.
captura *f* capture.
capturar *vt (criminal)* to capture; *(cazar, pescar)* to catch.
capucha *f* hood.
capullo *m (de insecto)* cocoon; *(de flor)* bud.
caqui 1 *adj (color)* khaki. **2** *m (fruto)* persimmon.
cara 1 *f* face; *(lado)* side; *(de moneda)* right side; *fam (desfachatez)* cheek, nerve; **c. a c.** face to face; **tener buena/mala c.** to look good/bad; **(de) c.** with a view to; **echarle a algn algo en c.** to reproach sb for sth; **¿c. o cruz?** heads or tails?; **echar algo a c. o cruz** to flip (a coin) for sth; **¡qué c. (más dura) tienes!** you've got a lot of nerve! **2** *m fam (desvergonzado)* bold person.
caracol *m (animal)* snail; *(cubierta)* shell.
caracola *f* conch.
carácter *m (pl caracteres)* character; *(índole)* nature; **tener buen/mal c.** to be good-natured/bad-tempered.
característica *f* characteristic.
característico, -a *adj* characteristic.
caradura *mf fam* cheeky devil; **¡qué c. eres!** you're so cheeky!
caramba *interj (sorpresa)* good grief!; *(enfado)* damn it!
carámbano *m* icicle.
caramelo *m (dulce)* candy; *(azúcar quemado)* caramel.
caravana *f* caravan; *(cola)* hatchback.
carbón *m* coal; **c. vegetal** charcoal; **c. mineral** coal.
carbonizar *vt*, **carbonizarse** *vr* to char.
carbono *m* carbon.
carburador *m* carburetor.
carburante *m* fuel.
carcajada *f* guffaw.
cárcel *f* prison, jail.
carcelero, -a *mf* warden.
cardenal *m* cardinal; *(en la piel)* bruise.
cardiaco, -a, cardíaco, -a *adj* cardiac, heart; **ataque c.** heart attack.
cardinal *adj* cardinal; **punto/número c.** cardinal point/number.
cardiólogo, -a *mf* cardiologist.
cardo *m (con espinas)* thistle.
carecer *vi* **c. de** to lack.
carencia *f* lack (**de** of).
careta *f* mask; **c. antigás** gas mask.
carezco *indic pres de* **carecer**.
carga *f (acción)* loading; *(cosa cargada)* load; *(de avión, barco)* cargo, freight; *(explosiva, eléctrica)* charge; *(obligación)* burden.
cargado, -a *adj (cargado)* loaded; *(bebida)* strong; **un café c.** a strong coffee; **atmósfera cargada** stuffy atmosphere; **c. de deudas** full of debt.
cargamento *m (carga)* load; *(mercancías)* cargo, freight.
cargar *vt* to load; *(mechero, pluma)* to fill; *(batería)* to charge; **cárguelo a mi cuenta** charge it to my account. **2** *vi* **c. con** *(llevar)* to carry; **c. con las consecuencias** to suffer the consequences. **3 cargarse** *vr* to load oneself with; *fam (estropear)* to smash, to ruin; *fam (matar)* to kill, to bump off.
cargo *m (puesto)* post, position; *(persona)* top person; *(débito)* charge, debit; *(acusación)* charge, accusation; **alto c.** *(puesto)* top job; **estar al c. de** to be in charge of; **correr a c. de** *(gastos)* to be met by; **hacerse c. de** to take charge of; **hazte c. de mi situación** please try to understand my situation; **con c. a mi cuenta** charged to my account.
cargoso, -a *adj CSur* annoying.
caricatura *f* caricature.
caricia *f* caress, stroke.
caridad *f* charity.
caries *f inv* decay, caries.
cariño *m (amor)* affection; *(querido)* darling; **coger/tener c. a algo/algn** to grow/to be fond of sth/sb; **con c.** *(en carta)* love.
cariñoso, -a *adj* loving, affectionate.
caritativo, -a *adj* charitable.
cariz *m* look.
carmín *m (de color)* **c.** carmine; **c. (de labios)** lipstick.
carnaval *m* carnival.
carne *f* flesh; *(alimento)* meat; **ser de c. y hueso** to be only flesh and blood; **c. de gallina** goose pimples; **c. de cerdo/cordero/ternera/vaca** pork/lamb/veal/beef.
carné, carnet *m* card; **c. de conducir** driver's license; **c. de identidad** identity card.
carnero *m* ram; *(carne)* mutton.
carnicería *f* butcher's (shop).
caro, -a 1 *adj (precios)* expensive; *(querido)* dear. **2** *adv* **salir c.** to cost a lot; **te costará c.** *(amenaza)* you'll pay dearly for this.
carpa *f (pez)* carp; *(de circo)* big top, marquee; *Am (de camping)* tent.
carpeta *f* folder.
carpintería *f (oficio)* carpentry; *(taller)* carpenter's (shop).
carpintero, -a *mf* carpenter.
carraspear *vi* to clear one's throat.
carrera *f* run; *(de media)* run, ladder; *(competición)* race; *(estudios)* degree; *(profesión)* career, profession; **c. de coches** rally, meeting; **echar una c. a algn** to race sb.
carrerilla *f* **tomar c.** to take a run; **de c.** parrot fashion.
carreta *f* cart.
carrete *m (de hilo)* reel; *(de película)* spool.
carretera *f* road; **c. de circunvalación** bypass; **c. de acceso** access road; *Méx* **c. de cuota** toll road.

carretilla f wheelbarrow.
carril m (de trenes) rail; (de carretera) lane.
carrillo m cheek.
carriola f Méx (de bebé) baby carriage.
carro m (carreta) cart; (de máquina de escribir) carriage; Andes, CAm, Carib, Méx car; **c. de combate** tank.
carrocería f bodywork.
carta f letter; (menú) menu; (de baraja) card; **c. certificada/urgente** registered/express letter; **a la c.** à la carte; **c. de vinos** wine list; **tomar cartas en un asunto** to take part in an affair.
cartel m poster.
cartera f (de bolsillo) wallet; (para documentos) briefcase; (de colegial) satchel, schoolbag; Andes, RP (de mujer) purse.
cartero, -a mf (hombre) postman; (mujer) postwoman.
cartilla f (libreta) book; (para leer) first reader; **c. de ahorros** savings book.
cartón m (material) card, cardboard; (de cigarrillos) carton.
cartucho m cartridge; (de papel) cone.
cartulina f card.
casa f (edificio) house; (hogar) home; (empresa) company, firm; **c. de huéspedes** boarding house; **c. de socorro** first aid post.
casado, -a 1 adj married. **2** mf married person; **los recién casados** the newlyweds.
casamiento m marriage; (boda) wedding.
casar 1 vt to marry. **2 casarse** vr to marry, to get married.
cascabel m bell.
cascada f waterfall, cascade.
cascanueces m inv nutcracker.
cascar vt, **cascarse** vr to crack.
cáscara f shell; (de fruta) skin, peel; (de grano) husk.
cascarón m eggshell.
casco m helmet; (de caballo) hoof; (envase) empty bottle; (de barco) hull; **c. urbano** city center; **cascos** (auriculares) headphones.
casero, -a 1 adj (hecho en casa) home-made; (persona) home-loving. **2** mf (dueño) (hombre) landlord; (mujer) landlady.
caseta f hut, booth; (de feria, exposición) stand, stall.
casete 1 m (magnetófono) cassette player o recorder. **2** f (cinta) cassette (tape).
casi adv almost, nearly; **c. nunca** hardly ever; **c. nadie** hardly anyone; **c. me caigo** I almost fell.
casino m casino.
caso m case; **el c. es que …** the thing is that …; **el c.** Mattei the Mattei affair; **(en) c. contrario** otherwise; **en c. de necesidad** if need be; **en cualquier c.** in any case; **en el mejor/peor de los casos** at best/worst; **en ese c.** in such a case; **en todo c.** in any case; **hacer c. a** o **de algn** to pay attention to sb; **no venir al c.** to be beside the point; **pongamos por c.** let's say.
caspa f dandruff.
cassette m o f = **casete**.
castaña f chestnut.
castaño, -a 1 adj chestnut-brown; (pelo, ojos) brown, dark. **2** m (árbol) chestnut.
castellano, -a 1 adj Castilian. **2** mf (persona) Castilian. **3** m (idioma) Spanish, Castilian.
castigar vt to punish; (penalizar) to penalize.
castigo m punishment; (pena) penalty.
castillo m castle.
casual adj accidental, chance.
casualidad f chance, coincidence; **de** o **por c.** by chance; **dio la c. de que …** it so happened that …; **¿tienes un lápiz, por c.?** do you happen to have a pencil?; **¡que c.!** what a coincidence!
casualmente adv by chance.
cataclismo m cataclysm.
catalejo m telescope.
catalogar vt to catalog; (clasificar) to classify.
catálogo m catalog.
catapulta f catapult.
catarata f waterfall; (enfermedad) cataract.
catarro m (common) cold.
catástrofe f catastrophe.
catecismo m catechism.
cátedra f (universidad) chair.
catedral f cathedral.
catedrático, -a mf (de universidad) professor; (de instituto) head of department.
categoría f category; **de c.** (persona) important.
cateto, -a mf (paleto) yokel, bumpkin.
católico, -a adj & mf Catholic.
catorce adj & m inv fourteen.
cauce m (de un río) bed; fig channel.
caucho m rubber; Am (cubierta) tire.
caudal m (de un río) flow; (riqueza) wealth.
caudillo m leader, head.
causa f cause; **a** o **por c. de** because of.
causante 1 adj causal. **2** mf **el c. del incendio** the person who caused the fire.
causar vt to cause; **c. buena/mala impresión** to make a good/bad impression.
cautela f caution.
cautivar vt to capture, to take prisoner.
cautiverio m, **cautividad** f captivity.
cautivo, -a adj & mf captive.
cava 1 f (bodega) wine cellar. **2** m (vino espumoso) champagne.
cavar vt to dig.
caverna f cave.
caviar m caviar.
cavidad f cavity.
cavilar vt to ponder.
cayado m (de pastor) crook.
caza f hunting; (animales) game; (persecución) hunt; **ir de c.** to go hunting; **c. furtiva** poaching; **c. mayor/menor** big/small game.
cazador, -a mf hunter.
cazadora f (waist-length) jacket.
cazar vt to hunt.
cazo m (cacerola) saucepan; (cucharón) ladle.
cazuela f saucepan; (guiso) casserole, stew; **a la c.** stewed.
cebada f barley.
cebo m bait.
cebolla f onion.
cebolleta f spring onion.
cebra f zebra; **paso de c.** cross-walk.
cecear vi to lisp.
ceder 1 vt to give, to hand over; **c. el paso** to give way. **2** vi (cuerda, cable) to give way; (consentir) to give in.
cédula f document, certificate; **c. de identidad** identity card.
cegar vt to blind; (puerta, ventana) to wall up.
ceguera f blindness.

ceja f eyebrow.
celador, -a mf attendant; (de cárcel) warder.
celda f cell.
celebración f (festejo) celebration; (de juicio etc) holding.
celebrar 1 vt to celebrate; (reunión, juicio, elecciones) to hold. **2 celebrarse** vr to take place, be held.
célebre adj famous, well-known.
celeste 1 adj (de cielo) celestial; (color) sky-blue. **2** m sky blue.
celibato m celibacy.
celo m zeal; **en c.** (macho) in rut; (hembra) in heat; **celos** jealousy sing; **tener celos (de algn)** to be jealous (of sb).
celo® m Scotch tape®.
celofán m cellophane.
celoso, -a adj jealous.
célula f cell.
celular 1 adj cellular; **coche c.** police van; Am **teléfono c.** cellphone, mobile phone. **2** m Am cellphone, mobile.
celulitis f inv cellulite.
cementerio m cemetery.
cemento m cement; (hormigón) concrete.
cena f dinner.
cenar 1 vi to have dinner. **2** vt to have for dinner.
cenicero m ashtray.
cenit m zenith.
ceniza f ash.
censo m census; **c. electoral** electoral roll.
censura f censorship; **moción de c.** vote of no confidence.
censurar vt (libro, película) to censor.
centavo m Am cent.
centellear vi to flash, sparkle.
centena f, **centenar** m hundred.
centenario m centenary.
centeno m rye.
centésimo, -a adj & mf hundredth.
centígrado, -a adj centigrade.
centilitro m centiliter.
centímetro m centimeter.
céntimo m cent.
centinela m sentry.
centollo m spider crab.
central 1 adj central. **2** f (oficina principal) head office; **c. nuclear/térmica** nuclear/coal-fired power station.
centralismo m centralism.
centralita f switchboard.
centralizar vt to centralize.
centrar vt to center; (esfuerzos, atención) to concentrate, to center (**en** on). **2 centrarse** vr to be centered o based; (concentrarse) to concentrate (**en** on).
céntrico, -a adj centrally situated.
centrifugar vt (ropa) to spin-dry.
centro m center; **c. de la ciudad** city center; **c. comercial** shopping center, mall.
ceñido, -a adj tight-fitting, clinging.
ceñirse vr (prenda) to cling (**a** to); (atenerse, limitarse) to limit oneself (**a** to); **c. al tema** to keep to the subject.
cepillar vt, **cepillarse** vr to brush.
cepillo m brush; (en carpintería) plane; **c. de dientes** toothbrush; **c. del pelo** hairbrush.
cera f wax; (de abeja) beeswax.
cerámica f ceramics sing.
cerca¹ 1 adv near, close; **de c.** closely. **2** prep **c. de** (al lado de) near, close to; (casi) nearly, around; **el colegio está c. de mi casa** the school is near my house; **c. de cien personas** about one hundred people.
cerca² f enclosure.
cercanía f proximity, nearness; **cercanías** outskirts, suburbs; **(tren de) c.** suburban train.
cercano, -a adj nearby; **el C. Oriente** the Near East.
cercar vt (tapiar) to fence, enclose; (rodear) to surround.
cerdo m pig; (carne) pork.
cereal m cereal.
cerebro m brain; (inteligencia) brains pl.
ceremonia f ceremony.
cereza f cherry.
cerezo m cherry tree.
cerilla f match.
cero m zero; (en resultado) nil; **ser un c. a la izquierda** to be useless.
cerrado, -a adj closed, shut; (intransigente) uncompromising; (acento) broad; (curva) sharp.
cerradura f flock.
cerrar 1 vt to shut, to close; (grifo, gas) to turn off; (cremallera) to do up; (negocio) to close down; (cuenta) to close; (sobre) to seal; **c. con llave** to lock; **c. el paso a algn** to block sb's way. **2** vi to close, to shut. **3 cerrarse** vr to close, to shut.
cerril adj (obstinado) pig-headed, headstrong.
cerro m hill.
cerrojo m bolt; **echar el c.** (de una puerta) to bolt (a door).
certamen m competition, contest.
certeza, certidumbre f certainty; **tener la c. de que …** to be certain that ….
certificado, -a 1 adj certified; (correo) registered. **2** m certificate; **c. médico** medical certificate.
cervecería f (bar) pub, bar; (fábrica) brewery.
cerveza f beer; **c. de barril** draft beer; **c. negra** stout.
cesar 1 vi to stop, cease (**de** -); **sin c.** incessantly. **2** vt (empleado) to dismiss.
cese m cessation, suspension; (despido) dismissal.
césped m lawn, grass.
cesta f basket.
cesto m basket.
ceviche m = raw fish marinated in lemon and garlic.
chabola f shack.
chacal m jackal.
chacinería f pork butcher's shop.
chacra f Andes, RP small farm.
chafar vt fam (plan etc) to ruin; (aplastar) to squash.
chal m shawl.
chalado, -a adj fam crazy, nuts (**por** about).
chalé m (pl chalés) villa.
chaleco m vest; (de punto) sleeveless pullover; **c. salvavidas** life jacket.
chalet m villa.
chalupa f (embarcación) boat, launch; Méx (torta) = small tortilla with a raised rim to contain a filling.

chamaco, -a *mf Méx fam* kid.
champán, champaña *m* champagne.
champiñón *m* mushroom.
champú *m* shampoo.
chamuscar *vt* to singe, scorch.
chancaca *f CAm* syrup cake.
chance *m Am* opportunity.
chancear *vi* to joke, horse around.
chanchada *f Am fam* dirty trick.
chancho, -a *mf Am* pig.
chancla *f* flipflop.
chándal *m* track suit, jogging suit.
chantaje *m* blackmail; **hacer c. a algn** to blackmail sb.
chantajear *vt* to blackmail.
chantajista *mf* blackmailer.
chapa *f (de metal)* sheet; *(tapón)* bottle top, cap; *(de adorno)* badge; *Col (cerradura)* lock.
chapado, -a *adj (metal)* plated; **c. en oro** gold-plated.
chaparrón *m* downpour, heavy shower.
chapotear *vi* to splash about, to paddle.
chapucero, -a *adj fam (trabajo)* slapdash, shoddy; *(persona)* bungling.
chapurrear *vt (idioma)* to speak badly.
chapuza *f fam (trabajo mal hecho)* shoddy piece of work; *(trabajo ocasional)* odd job.
chapuzón *m (baño corto)* dip; **darse un c.** to have a dip.
chaqueta *f* jacket.
charca *f* pond, pool.
charco *m* puddle.
charcutería *f* delicatessen.
charla *f (conversación)* talk, chat; *(conferencia)* informal lecture.
charlar *vi* to talk, to chat.
charlatán, -ana **1** *adj (parlanchín)* talkative. **2** *mf (parlanchín)* chatterbox; *(embaucador)* charlatan.
charol *m* patent leather.
chárter *adj inv* **vuelo c.** charter flight.
chasca *f Andes (cabellera)* mop of hair, tangled hair.
chasco *m fam (decepción)* disappointment; **llevarse un c.** to be disappointed.
chasis *m inv* chassis.
chasqui *m Am* messenger, courier.
chasquido *m (de la lengua)* click; *(de los dedos)* snap; *(de látigo, madera)* crack.
chatarra *f* scrap (metal), scrap iron; *(cosa inservible)* junk.
chato, -a *adj (nariz)* snub; *(persona)* snub-nosed.
chauvinista *adj & mf* chauvinist.
chaval, -a *mf (chico)* boy, lad; *(chica)* girl, lass.
chavo, -a *fam* **1** *mf Méx (chico)* guy; *(chica)* girl. **2** *m (dinero)* **no tener un c.** to be broke.
chepa *f* hump.
cheque *m* check; **c. de viaje** traveler's check.
chequeo *m* checkup.
chévere *adj Andes, CAm, Carib, Méx fam* great, fantastic.
chicano, -a *adj & mf* chicano.
chicha *f Andes* maize liquor.
chícharo *m CAm, Méx* pea.
chicharra *f* cicada.
chichón *m* bump, lump.
chicle *m* chewing gum.
chico, -a **1** *mf (muchacho)* boy, lad; *(muchacha)* girl, lass. **2** *adj (pequeño)* small, little.
chicote *m Am* whip.
chiflado, -a *adj fam* mad, crazy (**por** about).
chiflar *vt (silbar)* to hiss (at), to boo (at); *fam* **le chiflan las motos** he's really into motorbikes.
chiflido *m* whistle, whistling.
chillar *vi (persona)* to scream, to shriek; *(ratón)* to squeak.
chillido *m (de persona)* scream, shriek; *(de ratón)* squeak.
chillón, -ona *adj (voz)* shrill, high-pitched; *(sonido)* harsh; *(color)* loud.
chimenea *f* fireplace, hearth; *(conducto)* chimney.
chincheta *f* thumbtack.
chinchín *interj* **¡c.!** cheers!, (to) your (good) health!
chingana *f Perú fam* bar.
chip *m (pl chips)* chip.
chipirón *m* baby squid.
chiquillo, -a *mf* kid, youngster.
chirimoya *f* custard apple.
chiringuito *m (en playa etc)* refreshment stall; *(en carretera)* roadside snack bar.
chirriar *vi (puerta)* to creak; *(frenos)* to screech.
chirrido *m (de puerta)* creak, creaking; *(de frenos)* screech.
chisme *m (habladuría)* piece of gossip; *fam (trasto)* knick-knack; *(cosa)* thing.
chismear *vi* to gossip.
chismoso, -a **1** *adj (murmurador)* gossipy. **2** *mf* gossip.
chispa *f* spark.
chispear *vi* to spark; *(lloviznar)* to spit.
chiste *m* joke; **contar un c.** to tell a joke.
chistoso, -a *adj (persona)* funny, witty; *(anécdota)* funny, amusing.
chivatazo *m fam (soplo)* tip-off; **dar el c.** to squeal.
chivato, -a *mf fam (acusica)* tell-tale; *(delator)* grass.
chivo, -a *mf (animal)* kid, young goat; *fig* **c. expiatorio** scapegoat.
chocante *adj (sorprendente)* surprising; *(raro)* strange.
chocar **1** *vi (topar)* to crash, to collide; *(pelota)* to hit, to strike; **c. con** o **contra** to run into, to collide with. **2** *vt* to knock; *(sorprender)* to surprise.
chochear *vi (viejo)* to be senile.
chocolate *m* chocolate.
chocolatina *f* bar of chocolate, chocolate bar.
chófer *m (pl chóferes)*, *Am* **chofer** *m (pl choferes)* driver; *(particular)* chauffeur.
chollo *m fam* bargain, snip.
chomba *f Arg* jumper, pullover.
chonta *f Am* palm tree.
chopo *m* poplar.
choque *m* impact; *(de coches etc)* crash, collision.
chorizo *m* highly-seasoned pork sausage.
choro *m Andes* mussel.
chorrear *vi* to gush, to spurt; *(gotear)* to drip, to trickle; *fam* **estoy chorreando** I am soaking wet.
chorro *m (de agua etc)* spurt; *(muy fino)* trickle; **salir a chorros** to gush forth.
chovinista **1** *adj* chauvinistic. **2** *mf* chauvinist.
choza *f* hut, shack.
chubasco *m* heavy shower, downpour.
chubasquero *m* raincoat.
chuchería *f fam* candy.

chuleta *f* chop, cutlet; **c. de cerdo** pork chop.
chulo, -a *fam* **1** *mf* show-off. **2** *adj (bonito)* smashing.
chupachup® *m* lollipop.
chupar **1** *vt* to suck; *(lamer)* to lick; *(absorber)* to soak up, to absorb. **2** *vi* to suck. **3** **chuparse** *vr* **está para chuparse los dedos** it's really mouthwatering.
chupete *m* pacifier.
churrasco *m* barbecued meat.
churrete *m* dirty mark, grease spot.
churro *m* cruller.
chutar *vi (a gol)* to shoot.
cicatriz *f* scar.
cicatrizar *vti* to heal.
ciclismo *m* cycling.
ciclista **1** *adj* cycling. **2** *mf* cyclist.
ciclo *m* cycle; *(de conferencias etc)* series.
ciclomotor *m* moped.
ciclón *m* cyclone.
ciego, -a **1** *adj* blind; **a ciegas** blindly. **2** *mf* blind person; **los ciegos** the blind *pl.*
cielo *m* sky; *(gloria)* heaven; *(de la boca)* roof.
ciempiés *m inv* centipede.
cien *adj & m inv* hundred; **c. libras** a o one hundred pounds; **c. por c.** one hundred per cent.
ciencia *f* science; **saber algo a c. cierta** to know something for certain; **c. ficción** science fiction.
cieno *m* mud.
científico, -a **1** *adj* scientific. **2** *mf* scientist.
ciento *adj* hundred; **c. tres** one hundred and three; **por c.** per cent.
cierre *m (acción)* closing, shutting; *(de fábrica)* shutdown; *(de emisión)* close-down; *(de bolso)* clasp; *(de puerta)* catch; *Am* **c. relámpago** zipper.
cierto, -a **1** *adj* certain; *(verdadero)* true; **lo c. es que ...** the fact is that ...; **por c.** by the way. **2** *adv* certainly.
ciervo, -a *mf* deer; *(macho)* stag; *(hembra)* doe, hind.
cifra *f (número)* figure, number; *(suma)* amount.
cigala *f* Norway lobster.
cigarra *f* cicada.
cigarrillo *m* cigarette.
cigarro *m (cigarrillo)* cigarette; *(puro)* cigar.
cigüeña *f* stork.
cilindro *m* cylinder.
cima *f* summit.
cimientos *mpl* foundations.
cinco *adj & m inv* five.
cincuenta *adj & m inv* fifty.
cine *m* movie theater; *(arte)* cinema.
cinematográfico, -a *adj* cinematographic; **la industria cinematográfica** the movie industry.
cínico, -a **1** *adj* shameless. **2** *mf* shameless person.
cinismo *m* shamelessness.
cinta *f (tira)* band, strip; *(para adornar)* ribbon; *(película)* film; **c. adhesiva/aislante** adhesive/insulating tape; **c. de vídeo** video tape; **c. transportadora** conveyor belt.
cintura *f* waist.
cinturón *m* belt; **c. de seguridad** safety belt.
ciprés *m* cypress.
circo *m* circus.
circuito *m* circuit.
circulación *f* circulation; *(tráfico)* traffic.
circular **1** *adj & f* circular. **2** *vi (moverse)* to circulate; *(líquido)* to flow; *(tren, autobús)* to run; *(rumor)* to go round.
círculo *m* circle.
circuncisión *f* circumcision.
circundante *adj* surrounding.
circunferencia *f* circumference.
circunscripción *f* district.
circunstancia *f* circumstance.
cirio *m* wax candle.
ciruela *f* plum; **c. claudia** greengage; **c. pasa** prune.
ciruelo *m* plum tree.
cirugía *f* surgery; **c. estética** o **plástica** plastic surgery.
cirujano, -a *mf* surgeon.
cisne *m* swan.
cisterna *f* cistern, tank.
cita *f* appointment; *(amorosa)* date; *(mención)* quotation.
citar *vt (mencionar)* to quote; **me ha citado el dentista** I have an appointment with the dentist.
cítrico, -a **1** *adj* citric, citrus. **2** **cítricos** *mpl* citrus fruits.
ciudad *f* town; *(grande)* city.
ciudadano, -a **1** *mf* citizen. **2** *adj* civic.
cívico, -a *adj* civic.
civil *adj* civil; *(no militar)* civilian; **matrimonio c.** civil marriage.
civilización *f* civilization.
civilizado, -a *adj* civilized.
civismo *m* civility.
clamoroso, -a *adj* resounding.
clan *m* clan.
clandestino, -a *adj* clandestine.
clara *f (de huevo)* white.
claraboya *f* skylight.
clarear *vi (amanecer)* to dawn; *(despejar)* to clear up.
clarete *adj & m* claret.
claridad *f (luz)* brightness; *(inteligibilidad)* clarity; **con c.** clearly.
clarificar *vt* to clarify.
clarinete *m* clarinet.
claro, -a **1** *adj* clear; *(líquido, salsa)* thin; *(color)* light. **2** *interj* of course!; **¡c. que no!** of course not!; **¡c. que sí!** certainly! **3** *m (en un bosque)* clearing; *(tiempo despejado)* bright spell. **4** *adv* clearly.
clase *f* class; *(tipo)* kind, sort; *(curso)* class; *(aula)* classroom; **c. alta/media** upper/middle class; **primera/segunda c.** first/second class; **toda c. de ...** all kinds of ....
clásico, -a **1** *adj* classical; *(típico, en el vestir)* classic. **2** *m* classic.
clasificación *f* classification; *(para campeonato, concurso)* qualification.
clasificar **1** *vt* to classify, to class. **2** **clasificarse** *vr* to qualify.
claustrofobia *f* claustrophobia.
cláusula *f* clause.
clausura *f (cierre)* closure.
clausurar *vt* to close.
clavar **1** *vt* to nail; *(clavo)* to hammer in; *(estaca)* to drive in. **2** **clavarse** *vr* **clavarse una astilla** to get a splinter.

clave f key; **la palabra c.** the key word.
clavel m carnation.
clavícula f collarbone.
clavo m nail; fig **dar en el c.** to hit the nail on the head; (especia) clove.
claxon m (pl cláxones) horn; **tocar el c.** to sound the horn.
clemencia f mercy, clemency.
clementina f clementine.
clérigo m priest.
clero m clergy.
cliché m (tópico) cliché; (negativo) negative.
cliente mf customer, client.
clima m climate.
climatizado, -a adj air-conditioned.
climatizar vt to air-condition.
clínica f clinic.
clip m (para papel) clip.
cloaca f sewer, drain.
cloro m chlorine.
cloroformo m chloroform.
club m (pl clubs o clubes) club; **c. náutico** yacht club.
coacción f coercion.
coalición f coalition.
coartada f alibi.
cobarde 1 adj cowardly. **2** mf coward.
cobaya f guinea pig.
cobertizo m shed, shack.
cobertor m bedspread.
cobija f Am blanket.
cobijar vt, **cobijarse** vr to shelter.
cobra f cobra.
cobrador, -a mf (de autobús) (hombre) conductor; (mujer) conductress; (de luz, agua etc) collector.
cobrar vt (dinero) to charge; (cheque) to cash; (salario) to earn; **c. importancia** to become important.
cobre m (metal) copper; Am (moneda) copper cent.
cobro m (pago) collecting; (de cheque) cashing; **llamada a c. revertido** collect call.
coca f coca.
cocaína f cocaine.
cocción f cooking; (en agua) boiling; (en horno) baking.
cocer vt, **cocerse** vr (comida) to cook; (hervir) to boil; (en horno) to bake.
cochambroso, -a adj squalid.
coche m car; **en c.** by car; **c. de bomberos** fire engine; (vagón) carriage, coach; **c. cama** sleeper.
cochecito m (de niño) baby carriage.
cochera f garage; (de autobuses) depot.
cochino, -a 1 mf (macho) pig; (hembra) sow; fig (persona) pig. **2** adj (sucio) filthy.
cocido m stew.
cocina f kitchen; (aparato) cooker; (arte) cooking; **c. eléctrica/de gas** electric/gas cooker; **c. casera** home cooking.
cocinar vti to cook.
cocinero, -a mf cook.
coco m coconut.
cocodrilo m crocodile.
cocotero m coconut palm.
cóctel m cocktail.
codazo m (señal) nudge with one's elbow; (golpe) blow with one's elbow.
codicia f greed.
codicioso, -a 1 adj covetous. **2** mf greedy person.
código m code.
codo m elbow; fam **hablar por los codos** to talk nonstop.
coeficiente m **c. intelectual** IQ.
coetáneo, -a adj & mf contemporary.
coexistir vi to coexist.
cofre m trunk, chest.
coger 1 vt to take; (del suelo) to pick (up); (fruta, flores) to pick; (asir) to seize, to take hold of; (coche, bus) to take, to catch; (pelota, ladrón, resfriado) to catch; (atropellar) to run over. **2 cogerse** vr (agarrarse) to hold on.
cogote m back of the neck.
cohabitar vi to live together, to cohabit.
coherente adj coherent.
cohete m rocket.
cohibido, -a adj inhibited.
cohibir 1 vt to inhibit. **2 cohibirse** vr to feel inhibited.
coincidencia f coincidence.
coincidir vi to coincide; (concordar) to agree; (encontrarse) to meet by chance.
cojear vi (persona) to limp; (mesa etc) to wobble.
cojín m cushion.
cojinete m bearing.
cojo, -a 1 adj (persona) lame; (mueble) rickety. **2** mf lame person.
col f cabbage; **c. de Bruselas** Brussels sprout.
cola¹ f tail; (de vestido) train; (de pelo) ponytail; (fila) line; **a la c.** at the back; **hacer c.** stand in line.
cola² f glue.
colaboración f collaboration.
colaborador, -a 1 mf collaborator. **2** adj collaborating.
colaborar vi to collaborate.
colada f wash, laundry; **hacer la c.** to do the washing.
colador m colander, sieve; (de té, café) strainer.
colapso m collapse; **c. circulatorio** traffic jam.
colar 1 vt (líquido) to strain. **2 colarse** vr to slip in; (a fiesta) to gatecrash; (en una cola) to cut in line.
colcha f bedspread.
colchón m mattress.
colchoneta f air bed.
colección f collection.
coleccionar vt to collect.
colecta f collection.
colectivo, -a 1 adj collective. **2** m (asociación) association; Andes (taxi) long-distance taxi; Arg (autobús) bus.
colega mf colleague.
colegial, -a 1 adj (escolar) school. **2** mf (alumno) schoolboy; (alumna) schoolgirl; **los colegiales** the schoolchildren.
colegio m (escuela) school; **c. mayor o universitario** (residencia) residence hall.
cólera¹ f anger, rage.

cólera² m (enfermedad) cholera.
colesterol m cholesterol.
colgante 1 m (joya) pendant. **2** adj hanging.
colgar 1 vt to hang (up); (colada) to hang (out); (ahorcar) to hang. **2** vi to hang (de from); (teléfono) to hang up. **3 colgarse** vr (ahorcarse) to hang oneself.
cólico m colic.
coliflor f cauliflower.
colilla f cigarette end.
colina f hill.
colindante adj adjoining, adjacent.
colirio m eyedrops.
colisión f collision, crash.
collar m (adorno) necklace; (de perro) collar.
colmado, -a adj full, filled; (cucharada) heaped.
colmena f beehive.
colmillo m eye tooth; (de carnívoro) fang; (de jabalí, elefante) tusk.
colmo m ¡eso es el c.! that's the last straw!; **para c.** to top it all off.
colocación f (acto) positioning; (situación) situation; (empleo) job.
colocar vt to place, to put; (emplear) to give work to. **2 colocarse** vr (situarse) to put oneself; (emplearse) to take a job (de as).
Colón n Columbus.
colonia¹ f colony; (campamento) summer camp; Méx (barrio) district.
colonia² f (agua de colonia) cologne.
colonial adj colonial.
colonizar vt to colonize.
coloquio m discussion.
color m color; **de colores** multi-colored.
colorado, -a 1 adj red; **ponerse c.** to blush. **2** m red.
colorante m coloring.
colorear vt to color.
colorete m rouge.
colorido m color.
columna f column; **c. vertebral** spinal column.
columpio m swing.
coma¹ f (ortográfica) comma.
coma² m (estado) coma.
comadrona f midwife.
comandante m commander, commanding officer; (de avión) captain.
comarca f region.
combate m combat; (de boxeo) fight; (batalla) battle; **fuera de c.** out for the count.
combatir vti to fight.
combinación f combination; (prenda) slip.
combinar vt, **combinarse** vr to combine.
combustible 1 m fuel. **2** adj combustible.
comedia f comedy.
comedido, -a adj self-restrained, reserved.
comedor m dining room.
comentar vt (escribir) to comment on; (discutir) to discuss.
comentario m comment; **sin c.** no comment.
comentarista mf commentator.
comenzar vti to begin, to start; **comenzó a llover** it started raining o to rain; **comenzó diciendo que ...** he started by saying that ….
comer 1 vti to eat; **dar de c. a algn** to feed sb. **2 comerse** vr to eat.
comercial adj commercial.
comercializar vt to market.
comerciante mf merchant.
comerciar vi to trade; **comercia con oro** he trades in gold.
comercio m commerce, trade; (tienda) shop.
comestible 1 adj edible. **2** mpl **comestibles** food sing.
cometa 1 m comet. **2** f (juguete) kite.
cometer vt (error, falta) to make; (delito, crimen) to commit.
cometido m (tarea) task, assignment; (deber) duty; **cumplir su c.** to do one's duty.
comezón m itch.
comicios mpl elections.
cómico, -a 1 adj (divertido) comical, funny; **actor c.** comedian. **2** mf comic; (hombre) comedian; (mujer) comedienne.
comida f (alimento) food; (almuerzo, cena) meal.
comienzo m beginning, start; **dar c. (a algo)** to start (sth).
comillas fpl inverted commas; **entre c.** in inverted commas.
comilón, -ona 1 adj greedy. **2** mf big eater.
comilona f fam big meal, feast.
comisaría f police station.
comisión f (retribución) commission; (comité) committee.
como 1 adv (manera) as; **hazlo c. quieras** do it however you like. ▪ (comparación) as; **blanco c. la nieve** as white as snow; **habla c. su padre** he talks like his father. ▪ (según) as; **c. decíamos ayer** as we were saying yesterday. ▪ (en calidad de) as; **lo compré c. recuerdo** I bought it as a souvenir. ▪ (aproximadamente) about; **c. unos diez** about ten. **2** conj **c. + subj** (si) if; **c. no estudies vas a suspender** if you don't study hard, you'll fail. ▪ (porque) as, since; **c. no venías me marché** as you didn't come I left. ▪ **c. si** as if; **c. si nada** o **tal cosa** as if nothing had happened.
cómo 1 adv ¿c.? (¿perdón?) what? ▪ (interrogativo) how; **¿c. estás?** how are you?; **¿a c. están los tomates?** (a cuánto) how much are the tomatoes?; (por qué) **¿c. es eso?** how come?; **¿c. fue que no viniste a la fiesta?** how come you didn't come to the party? ▪ (exclamativo) how; **¡c. has crecido!** you've really grown a lot!; **¡c. no!** but of course!
cómoda f chest of drawers.
comodidad f comfort; (conveniencia) convenience.
comodín m joker.
cómodo, -a adj comfortable; (útil) handy, convenient.
compacto, -a adj compact; **disco c.** compact disc.
compadecer 1 vt to feel sorry for, to pity. **2 compadecerse** vr to take pity (de on).
compadre m (padrino) godfather; Am fam (amigo) friend, mate.
compañero, -a mf companion; **c. de piso** roommate.
compañía f company; **hacer c. a algn** to keep sb company.
comparación f comparison; **en c.** comparatively; **en c. con** compared to; **sin c.** beyond compare.
comparar vt to compare (con with).
compartimento, compartimiento m compartment.
compartir vt to share.
compás m (pair of) compasses; (brújula) compass; (ritmo) rhythm; **al c. de** in time to.
compasión f compassion, pity; **tener c. de algn** to feel sorry for sb.
compasivo, -a adj compassionate.
compatible adj compatible.
compatriota mf compatriot; (hombre) fellow countryman; (mujer) fellow countrywoman.
compensar 1 vt (pérdida, error) to make up for; (indemnizar) to compensate (for). **2** vi to be worthwhile.

competencia *f (rivalidad, empresas rivales)* competition; *(capacidad)* competence; *(incumbencia)* field.
competente *adj* competent.
competición *f* competition.
competir *vi* to compete.
competitivo, -a *adj* competitive.
compinche *mf (cómplice)* accomplice.
complacer *vt* to please.
complejo, -a *adj & m* complex.
complemento *m* complement; *(objeto)* object.
completamente *adv* completely.
completar *vt* to complete.
completo, -a *adj (terminado)* complete; *(lleno)* full; **por c.** completely.
complicado, -a *adj (complejo)* complicated; *(implicado)* involved.
complicar 1 *vt* to complicate; *(involucrar)* to involve (**en** in). **2 complicarse** *vr* to get complicated.
cómplice *mf* accomplice.
complot *m* (*pl* **complots**) conspiracy, plot.
componer (*pp* **compuesto**) **1** *vt* to compose; *(reparar)* to mend, repair. **2 componerse** *vr (consistir)* to be made up (**de** of), consist (**de** of).
comportamiento *m* behavior.
composición *f* composition.
compota *f* compote.
compra *f (acción)* buying; *(cosa comprada)* purchase, buy; **ir de compras** to go shopping.
comprar *vt* to buy.
comprender *vt (entender)* to understand; *(contener)* to comprise, to include.
comprensión *f* understanding.
comprensivo, -a *adj* understanding.
compresa *f (para mujer)* sanitary napkin.
comprimido, -a 1 *m* tablet. **2** *adj* compressed.
comprobante *m (de compra)* voucher, receipt.
comprobar *vt* to check.
comprometer 1 *vt (arriesgar)* to compromise; *(obligar)* to compel. **2 comprometerse** *vr (involucrarse)* to involve oneself; *(novios)* to become engaged; **comprometerse a hacer algo** to undertake to do sth.
compromiso *m (obligación)* obligation, commitment; *(acuerdo)* agreement; **por c.** out of a sense of duty; **poner a algn en un c.** to put sb in a difficult situation.
compuesto, -a 1 *adj* compound; **c. de** composed of. **2** *m* compound.
compuse *pt indef de* **componer**.
computadora *f* computer.
comulgar *vi* to receive Holy Communion; *fig* **no comulgo con sus ideas** I don't share his ideas.
común *adj* common; *(compartido)* shared; **poco c.** unusual; **por lo c.** generally.
comuna *f Am (municipalidad)* municipality.
comunicación *f* communication; *(oficial)* communiqué; *(telefónica)* connection; *(unión)* link, connection.
comunicar 1 *vt* to communicate; **comuníquenoslo lo antes posible** let us know as soon as possible. **2** *vi* to communicate; *(teléfono)* to be engaged. **3 comunicarse** *vr* to communicate.
comunidad *f* community; **C. Europea** European Community.
comunión *f* communion.
con *prep* with; **c. ese frío/niebla** in that cold/fog; **estar c. (la) gripe** to have the flu; **una bolsa c. dinero** a bag (full) of money; **habló c. todos** he spoke to everybody. ▪ *(con infinitivo)* **c. llamar será suficiente** it will be enough just to phone. ▪ (**con que** + *subj*) **bastará c. que lo esboces** a general idea will do; **c. tal (de) que ...** provided that ....
concebir 1 *vt (plan, hijo)* to conceive; *(entender)* to understand. **2** *vi (mujer)* to conceive.
conceder *vt* to grant; *(premio)* to award; *(admitir)* to concede.
concejal, -a *mf* town councilor.
concentración *f* concentration; *(de manifestantes)* gathering.
concentrado *m* concentrate.
concentrar *vt*, **concentrarse** *vr* to concentrate (**en** on).
concepción *f* conception.
concepto *m* concept; **bajo/por ningún c.** under no circumstances.
concerniente *adj* concerning, regarding (**a** -); *fml* **en lo c. a** with regard to.
concernir *v impers (afectar)* to concern; *(corresponder)* to be up to; **en lo que a mí concierne** as far as I am concerned; **en lo que concierne a** with regard/respect to.
concesión *f* concession; *(de premio, contrato)* awarding.
concha *f (caparazón)* shell; *(carey)* tortoiseshell.
conciencia *f* conscience; *(conocimiento)* consciousness, awareness; **a c.** conscientiously.
concienzudo, -a *adj* conscientious.
concierto *m* concert; *(composición)* concerto; *(acuerdo)* agreement.
conciso, -a *adj* concise.
concluir *vt* to conclude.
conclusión *f* conclusion; **sacar una c.** to draw a conclusion.
concretamente *adv* specifically.
concretar *vt (precisar)* to specify, to state explicitly; *(fecha, hora)* to fix.
concreto, -a 1 *adj (preciso, real)* concrete; *(particular)* specific; **en c.** specifically. **2** *m Am* concrete.
concurrido, -a *adj* crowded, busy.
concursante *mf* contestant, competitor.
concursar *vi* to compete, to take part.
concurso *m (competición)* competition; *(de belleza etc)* contest; *(televisivo)* quiz show.
condecorar *vt* to decorate.
condena *f* sentence; *(desaprobación)* condemnation, disapproval.
condenado, -a 1 *adj* convicted; **c. a muerte** condemned to death. **2** *mf* convicted person; *(a muerte)* condemned person.
condenar *vt* to convict, find guilty; *(desaprobar)* to condemn.
condensado, -a *adj* condensed; **leche condensada** condensed milk.
condensar *vt*, **condensarse** *vr* to condense.
condición *f* condition; **en buenas/malas condiciones** in good/bad condition; **con la c. de que ...** on condition that ....
condimentar *vt* to season, to flavor.
condimento *m* seasoning, flavoring.
condominio *m Am (edificio)* condominium.
condón *m* condom.
conducir 1 *vt (coche)* to drive; *(electricidad)* to conduct. **2** *vi* to drive; *(llevar)* to lead; **permiso de c.** driver's license.
conducta *f* behavior, conduct.
conducto *m (tubería)* pipe.
conductor, -a *mf* driver.
conectar *vt* to connect up; *(enchufar)* to plug in, to switch on.
conejillo *m* **c. de Indias** guinea pig.
conejo *m* rabbit.
conexión *f* connection.
confección *f* dressmaking; *(de ropa masculina)* tailoring; *(de plan)* making.
conferencia *f* lecture; *(telefónica)* long-distance call.
confesar 1 *vti* to confess. **2 confesarse** *vr* to confess; *(de pecados)* to go to confession; **confesarse culpable** to admit one's guilt.
confiado, -a *adj (seguro)* self-confident; *(crédulo)* gullible, unsuspecting.
confianza *f (seguridad)* confidence; **tener c. en uno mismo** to be self-confident; **de c.** reliable; **tener c. con algn** to be on intimate terms with sb.
confiar 1 *vt (entregar)* to entrust; *(información, secreto)* to confide. **2** *vi* **c. en** to trust; **no confíes en su ayuda** don't count on his help. **3 confiarse** *vr* to confide (**en, a** in).
confidencia *f* confidence.
confidencial *adj* confidential.
confidente, -a *mf (hombre)* confidant; *(mujer)* confidante; *(de la policía)* informer.
confirmar *vt* to confirm.
confiscar *vt* to confiscate.
confitería *f* candy store; *CSur* café.
confitura *f* preserve, jam.
conflicto *m* conflict.
conformarse *vr* **tendrás que conformarte (con esto)** you will have to be content with that.
conforme 1 *adj (satisfecho)* satisfied; **no estoy c.** I don't agree. **2** *conj* as. **3** *prep* **c. a** in accordance with.
confort *m* (*pl* **conforts**) comfort.
confortable *adj* comfortable.
confrontación *f* confrontation.
confrontar *vt* to confront; *(comparar)* to compare, to collate.
confundir 1 *vt* to confuse (**con** with); *(engañar)* to mislead; **c. a una persona con otra** to mistake somebody for somebody else. **2 confundirse** *vr (equivocarse)* to be mistaken; *(mezclarse)* to mingle; *(colores, formas)* to blend.
confusión *f* confusion.
confuso, -a *adj* confused; *(formas, recuerdo)* vague.
congelado, -a 1 *adj* frozen. **2** *mpl* **congelados** frozen food *sing.*
congelador *m* freezer.
congelar 1 *vt* to freeze. **2 congelarse** *vr* to freeze.
congoja *f* sorrow, grief.
congreso *m* congress, conference; **c. de los Diputados** ≃ Congress.
congrio *m* conger eel.
conjugación *f* conjugation.
conjunción *f* conjunction.
conjunto, -a 1 *m (grupo)* collection, group; *(todo)* whole; *(pop)* group, band; *(prenda)* outfit; **de c.** overall; **en c.** on the whole. **2** *adj* joint.
conllevar *vt* to entail.
conmemoración *f* commemoration.
conmigo *pron pers* with me; **él habló c.** he talked to me.
conmoción *f* commotion, shock; **c. cerebral** concussion.
conmovedor, -a *adj* touching.
conmover *vt* to touch, to move.
conmutador *m* switch; *Am* switchboard.
cono *m* cone.
conocedor, -a *adj & mf* expert; *(de vino, arte etc)* connoisseur.
conocer 1 *vt* to know; *(por primera vez)* to meet; *(reconocer)* to recognize; **dar (algo/algn) a c.** to make (sth/sb) known. **2 conocerse** *vr (dos personas)* to know each other; *(por primera vez)* to meet.
conocido, -a 1 *adj* known; *(famoso)* well-known. **2** *mf* acquaintance.
conocimiento *m* knowledge; *(conciencia)* consciousness; **perder/ recobrar el c.** to lose/regain consciousness; **conocimientos** knowledge.
conquista *f* conquest.
conquistador, -a *mf* conqueror.
conquistar *vt (país, ciudad)* to conquer; **c. a algn** to make a conquest of sb.
consabido, -a *adj (bien conocido)* well-known; *(usual)* familiar, usual.
consagrar 1 *vt (artista)* to establish; *(vida, tiempo)* to devote. **2 consagrarse** *vr (dedicarse)* to devote oneself (**a** to); *(lograr fama)* to establish oneself.
consciente *adj* conscious.
consecuencia *f* consequence; *(coherencia)* consistency; **a** *o* **como c. de** as a consequence of; **en c.** therefore.
consecuente *adj* consistent.
consecutivo, -a *adj* consecutive; **tres días consecutivos** three days in a row.
conseguir *vt* to get, to obtain; *(objetivo)* to achieve; *(lograr)* to manage.
consejero, -a *mf (asesor)* adviser; *(ministro)* regional minister.
consejo *m (recomendación)* advice; *(junta)* council; *(reunión)* cabinet meeting; **un c.** a piece of advice; **c. de ministros** cabinet; **c. de administración** board of directors.
consentido, -a *adj* spoiled.
consentimiento *m* consent.
consentir 1 *vt (tolerar)* to allow, to permit; *(mimar)* to spoil; **no consientas que haga eso** don't allow him to do that. **2** *vi* to consent; **c. en** to agree to.
conserje *m (bedel)* janitor.
conserva *f* tinned *o* canned food.
conservador, -a *adj & mf* conservative; *(derechista)* Conservative.
conservante *m* preservative.
conservar 1 *vt* to conserve, to preserve; *(mantener)* to keep up; *(alimentos)* to preserve. **2 conservarse** *vr (tradición etc)* to survive.
conservatorio *m* conservatory.
considerado, -a *adj (atento)* considerate, thoughtful.
considerar *vt* to consider; **lo considero imposible** I think it's impossible.
consigna *f (para maletas)* checkroom.
consigo[1] *pron pers (tercera persona) (hombre)* with him; *(mujer)* with her; *(cosa, animal)* with it; *(plural)* with them; *(usted)* with you; **hablar c. mismo** to speak to oneself.
consigo[2] *indic pres de* **conseguir**.
consiguiente *adj* consequent; **por c.** therefore, consequently.
consistente *adj (firme)* firm, solid.
consistir *vi* to consist (**en** of).
consola *f* console.
consolar 1 *vt* to console, to comfort. **2 consolarse** *vr* to console oneself.
consomé *m* clear soup, consommé.
consonante *adj & f* consonant.
consorte *mf (cónyuge)* partner, spouse.
conspiración *f* conspiracy, plot.
conspirar *vi* to conspire, to plot.
constancia *f* perseverance; *(testimonio)* proof, evidence.
constante 1 *adj* constant; *(persona)* steadfast. **2** *f* constant feature.
constantemente *adv* constantly.
constar *vi (figurar)* to figure in, be included (in); **me consta que ...** I am absolutely certain that ...; **c. de** *(consistir)* to consist of.
constatar *vt* to state; *(comprobar)* to check.
constipado, -a 1 *adj* **estar c.** to have a cold. **2** *m* cold.
constiparse *vr* to catch a cold.
constitución *f* constitution.
constituir 1 *vt (formar)* to constitute; *(suponer)* to represent; *(fundar)* to constitute, to set up;

estar constituido por to consist of. **2 constituirse** *vr* to set oneself up (**en** as).
construcción *f* construction; *(sector)* building industry.
constructor, -a 1 *mf* builder. **2** *adj* **empresa constructora** builders *pl*, construction company.
construir *vt* to construct, to build.
consuelo *m* consolation.
cónsul *mf* consul.
consulado *m* consulate.
consulta *f* consultation; *(médica)* surgery; *(despacho)* consulting room; **horas de c.** surgery hours.
consultar *vt* to consult.
consultivo, -a *adj* consultative, advisory.
consultorio *m (médico)* medical center.
consumidor, -a 1 *mf* consumer. **2** *adj* consuming.
consumir 1 *vt* to consume. **2 consumirse** *vr (agua, jugo)* to boil away.
consumo *m* consumption; **bienes de c.** consumer goods; **sociedad de c.** consumer society.
contabilidad *f (profesión)* accountancy; *(de empresa, sociedad)* accounting.
contabilizar *vt (en contabilidad)* to enter in the books; *(en partido)* to score.
contable *mf* accountant.
contactar *vi* **c. con** to contact.
contacto *m* contact; *(en coche)* ignition; **ponerse en c.** to get in touch.
contado, -a 1 *adj (pocos)* few and far between; **contadas veces** very seldom. **2** *m* **pagar al c.** to pay cash.
contador *m* meter.
contagiar 1 *vt (enfermedad)* to pass on. **2 contagiarse** *vr (enfermar)* to get infected; *(transmitirse)* to be contagious.
contagio *m* contagion.
contagioso, -a *adj* contagious; *(risa)* infectious.
contaminación *f* contamination; *(del aire)* pollution.
contar 1 *vt (sumar)* to count; *(narrar)* to tell. **2** *vi* to count; **c. con** *(confiar en)* to count on; *(tener)* to have.
contemplar *vt* to contemplate; *(considerar)* to consider.
contemporáneo, -a *adj & mf* contemporary.
contenedor *m* container.
contener 1 *vt* to contain; *(reprimir)* to restrain, to hold back. **2 contenerse** *vr* to control oneself, to hold (oneself) back.
contenido *m* content, contents *pl*.
contentar 1 *vt (satisfacer)* to please; *(alegrar)* to cheer up. **2 contentarse** *vr (conformarse)* to make do, to be satisfied (**con** with).
contento, -a *adj* happy, pleased (**con** with).
contestación *f* answer.
contestador *m* **c. automático** answering machine.
contestar *vt* to answer.
contienda *f* struggle.
contigo *pron pers* with you.
contiguo, -a *adj* adjoining.
continente *m* continent.
continuación *f* continuation; **a c.** next.
continuamente *adv* continuously.
continuar *vti* to continue.
continuo, -a *adj* continuous; *(reiterado)* continual, constant.
contra 1 *prep* against; **en c. de** against. **2** *mpl* **los pros y los contras** the pros and cons.
contrabajo *m* double bass.
contrabandista *mf* smuggler; **c. de armas** gunrunner.
contrabando *m* smuggling; **pasar algo de c.** to smuggle sth in.
contracción *f* contraction.
contracepción *f* contraception.
contracorriente 1 *f* crosscurrent. **2** *adv* **ir (a) c.** to go against the tide.
contradecir *(pp contradicho)* *vt* to contradict.
contradicción *f* contradiction.
contraer 1 *vt* to contract; **c. matrimonio** to get married. **2 contraerse** *vr* to contract.
contraigo *indic pres de* **contraer**.
contraje *pt indef de* **contraer**.
contramano: a contramano *adv* in the wrong direction, the wrong way.
contrapeso *m* counterweight.
contraproducente *adj* counterproductive.
contrariamente *adv* **c. a ...** contrary to ....
contrariar *vt (oponerse a)* to oppose, to go against; *(disgustar)* to upset.
contrariedad *f (contratiempo)* obstacle, setback; *(decepción)* annoyance.
contrario, -a 1 *adj* opposite; **en el lado/sentido c.** on the other side/in the other direction; **al c., por el c.** on the contrary; **de lo c.** otherwise; **todo lo c.** quite the opposite. **2** *mf* opponent, rival. **3** **llevar la contraria** to be contrary.
contrarrestar *vt* to offset, to counteract.
contraseña *f* password.
contrastar *vt* to contrast (**con** with).
contraste *m* contrast.
contratar *vt (empleado)* to hire, to engage.
contratiempo *m* setback, hitch.
contratista *mf* contractor.
contrato *m* contract.
contraventana *f* shutter.
contribución *f* contribution; *(impuesto)* tax.
contribuir *vti* to contribute (**a** to).
contribuyente *mf* taxpayer.
contrincante *mf* rival, opponent.
control *m* control; *(inspección)* check; *(de policía etc)* checkpoint; **c. remoto** remote control.
controlador, -a *mf* **c. (aéreo)** air traffic controller.
controlar 1 *vt* to control. **2 controlarse** *vr* to control oneself.
controversia *f* controversy.
contundente *adj (arma)* blunt; *(argumento)* forceful, convincing.
contusión *f* contusion, bruise.
convalecencia *f* convalescence.
convalidar *vt* to validate; *(documento)* to ratify.
convencer *vt* to convince; **c. a algn de algo** to convince sb about sth.
convencional *adj* conventional.
conveniencia *f (provecho)* convenience; **conveniencias sociales** social proprieties.
conveniente *adj (oportuno)* convenient; *(aconsejable)* advisable; *(precio)* good, fair.
convenio *m* agreement.
convenir *vti (acordar)* to agree; *(ser oportuno)* to suit, to be good for; **c. en** to agree on; **conviene recordar que** it's as well to remember that.
convento *m (de monjas)* convent.
conversación *f* conversation.
conversar *vi* to converse, to talk.
conversión *f* conversion.
convertir 1 *vt* to change, to convert. **2 convertirse** *vr* **convertirse en** to turn into, to become.

convicción *f* conviction.
convidado, -a *adj & mf* guest.
convidar *vt* to invite.
convivencia *f* life together.
convivir *vi* to live together.
convocar *vt* to summon; *(reunión, elecciones)* to call.
convocatoria *f (a huelga etc)* call.
convulsión *f* convulsion.
conyugal *adj* conjugal; **vida c.** married life.
cónyuge *mf* spouse; **cónyuges** married couple *sing*, husband and wife.
coñac *m* brandy, cognac.
cooperación *f* co-operation.
cooperar *vi* to co-operate (**a, en** in; **con** with).
cooperativa *f* co-operative.
coordenada *f* co-ordinate.
coordinar *vt* to co-ordinate.
copa *f* glass; *(de árbol)* top; *(premio)* cup; **tomar una c.** to have a drink.
copia *f* copy; **c. de seguridad** *(archivo)* backup; **hacer una c. de seguridad de algo** to back up sth.
copiar *vt* to copy.
copla *f* verse, couplet.
copo *m* flake; **c. de nieve** snowflake; **copos de maíz** cornflakes.
coquetear *vi* to flirt.
coqueto, -a *adj* coquettish.
coraje *m (valor)* courage; *(ira)* anger, annoyance.
coral¹ *m* coral.
coral² *f (composición)* choral, chorale.
Corán *m* Koran.
coraza *f* armor.
corazón *m* heart; *(de fruta)* core; **tener buen c.** to be kind-hearted.
corazonada *f* hunch, feeling.
corbata *f* necktie.
corcho *m* cork; *(de pesca)* float.
cordel *m* rope, cord.
cordero, -a *mf* lamb.
cordial *adj* cordial, warm.
cordillera *f* mountain range.
cordón *m* string; *(de zapatos)* shoelace.
cordura *f* common sense.
cornada *f (de toro)* goring.
córner *m* corner (kick).
corneta *f* bugle.
cornisa *f* cornice.
coro *m (musical)* choir; *(en tragedia)* chorus; **a c.** all together.
corona *f* crown; *(de flores etc)* wreath, garland.
coronación *f* coronation.
coronel *m* colonel.
coronilla *f* crown of the head; *fam* **estar hasta la c.** to be fed up (**de** with).
corporación *f* corporation.
corporal *adj* corporal; **olor c.** body odor, BO.
corpulento, -a *adj* corpulent, stout.
corral *m* corral.
correa *f (tira)* strap; *(de pantalón)* belt; *(de perro)* lead, leash; *(de motor)* belt.
corrección *f (rectificación)* correction; *(educación)* courtesy, politeness.
correcto, -a *adj (sin errores)* correct; *(educado)* polite, courteous (**con** to); *(conducta)* proper.
corredizo, -a *adj (puerta etc)* sliding; **nudo c.** slipknot.
corredor, -a *mf (deportista)* runner; *(balconada)* gallery.
corregir 1 *vt* to correct. **2 corregirse** *vr (persona)* to mend one's ways.
correo *m* post, mail; **echar al c.** to post; **por c.** by post; **correos** *(edificio)* post office *sing*; **c. aéreo** airmail; **c. certificado** registered post; **c. electrónico** electronic mail, e-mail; **me envió un c. (electrónico)** *(un mensaje)* she e-mailed me, she sent me an e-mail.
correr 1 *vi* to run; *(coche)* to go fast; *(conductor)* to drive fast; *(viento)* to blow; **c. prisa** to be urgent. **2** *vt (cortina)* to draw; *(cerrojo)* to close; *(mover)* to pull up, to draw up; **c. el riesgo** to run the risk. **2 correrse** *vr (moverse)* to move over.
correspondencia *f* correspondence.
corresponder 1 *vi* to correspond (**a** to; **con** with); *(ajustarse)* to go (**con** with); *(incumbir)* to concern; *(pertenecer)* to be one's due; **me dieron lo que me correspondía** they gave me my share. **2 corresponderse** *vr (ajustarse)* to correspond; *(dos cosas)* to tally; **no se corresponde con la descripción** it does not match the description.
correspondiente *adj* corresponding (**a** to).
corresponsal *mf* correspondent.
corrida *f* **c. (de toros)** bullfight.
corriente 1 *adj (común)* common; *(agua)* running; *(mes, año)* current, present; *(cuenta)* current; **estar al c.** to be up to date. **2** *f* current, stream; *(de aire)* draft; *(tendencia)* trend, current; *fam* **seguirle** o **llevarle la c. a algn** to humor sb; **c. (eléctrica)** (electric) current.
corrijo *indic pres de* **corregir**.
corro *m* circle, ring; *(juego)* ring-a-ring-a-roses.
corroborar *vt* to corroborate.
corromper 1 *vt* to rot. **2 corromperse** *vr* to go bad, to rot.
corrosivo, -a *adj (sustancia)* corrosive; *fig (comentario)* caustic.
corrupción *f* corruption.
corrupto, -a *adj* corrupt.
cortacésped *m o f* lawnmower.
cortado, -a 1 *adj* cut (up); *(leche)* sour; *(labios)* chapped; *fam (tímido)* shy. **2** *m* small coffee with a dash of milk.
cortar 1 *vt* to cut; *(carne)* to carve; *(árbol)* to cut down; *(piel)* to chap, to crack; *(luz, teléfono)* to cut off; *(paso, carretera)* to block. **2 cortarse** *vr (herirse)* to cut oneself; *(leche etc)* to curdle; **cortarse el pelo** to have one's hair cut; **se cortó la comunicación** we were cut off.
corte *m* cut; *(sección)* section; **c. de pelo** haircut.
cortés *adj* courteous, polite.
cortesía *f* courtesy, politeness.
corteza *f (de árbol)* bark; *(de queso)* rind; *(de pan)* crust.
cortijo *m* Andalusian farmhouse.
cortina *f* curtain.
corto, -a *adj (distancia, tiempo)* short; **c. de vista** short-sighted; **luz corta** dipped headlights *pl*; **quedarse c.** *(calcular mal)* to underestimate.
cortocircuito *m* short circuit.
cosa *f* thing; *(asunto)* matter, business; **eso es c. tuya** that's your business; **eso es otra c.** that's different; **hace c. de una hora** about an hour ago.
coscorrón *m* knock on the head.
cosecha *f* harvest, crop; *(año del vino)* vintage.
coser *vt* to sew.
cosmético, -a *adj & m* cosmetic.
cosmonauta *mf* cosmonaut.

coso *m (taurino)* bullring; *CSur fam (objeto)* whatnot, thing.
cosquillas *fpl* **hacer c. a algn** to tickle sb; **tener c.** to be ticklish.
costa *f* coast; *(litoral)* coastline; *(playa)* beach, seaside.
costado *m (lado)* side; **de c.** sideways.
costar *vi* to cost; **¿cuánto cuesta?** how much is it?; **c. barato/caro** to be cheap/expensive; **c. trabajo** o **mucho** to be hard; **me cuesta hablar francés** I find it hard to speak French.
coste *m* cost; **c. de la vida** cost of living.
costear 1 *vt* to afford, to pay for. **2 costearse** *vr* to pay for.
costilla *f (hueso)* rib; *(chuleta)* cutlet.
costo *m* cost.
costoso, -a *adj* costly, expensive.
costra *f* crust; *(de herida)* scab.
costumbre *f (hábito)* habit; *(tradición)* custom; **como de c.** as usual; **tengo la c. de levantarme temprano** I usually get up early; **tenía la c. de ...** he used to ....
costura *f* sewing; *(confección)* dressmaking; *(línea de puntadas)* seam; **alta c.** haute couture.
costurero *m* sewing basket.
cotidiano, -a *adj* daily.
cotilla *mf fam* busybody, gossip.
cotillear *vi fam* to gossip (**de** about).
cotilleo *m fam* gossip.
cotización *f (market)* price, quotation.
coto *m* enclosure; **c. de caza** game reserve.
cotorra *f* parrot; *(persona)* chatterbox.
coz *f* kick.
cráneo *m* cranium, skull.
cráter *m* crater.
creación *f* creation.
crear *vt* to create.
creativo, -a *adj* creative.
crecer *vi* to grow.
crecimiento *m* growth.
credencial *adj* credential; **cartas credenciales** credentials.
crédito *m* credit; **dar c. a** to believe.
creencia *f* belief.
creer 1 *vt* to believe; *(pensar)* to think; **creo que no** I don't think so; **creo que sí** I think so; **ya lo creo** I should think so. **2** *vi* to believe. **3 creerse** *vr* **se cree guapo** he thinks he's good-looking.
creíble *adj* credible, believable.
crema *f* cream.
cremallera *f* zipper.
crematorio *m* crematory.
cremoso, -a *adj* creamy.
crepe *f* pancake.
crepúsculo *m* twilight.
cresta *f* crest; *(de gallo)* comb.
cretino, -a 1 *adj* stupid, cretinous. **2** *mf* cretin.
creyente *mf* believer.
crezco *indic pres de* **crecer**.
cría *f (cachorro)* young; *(crianza)* breeding.
criada *f* maid.
criado, -a 1 *adj* **mal c.** spoiled. **2** *mf* servant.
criar *vt (animales)* to breed; *(niños)* to bring up.
criatura *f (living)* creature; *(crío)* baby, child.
criba *f* sieve.
crimen *m (pl crímenes)* crime.
criminal *adj & mf* criminal.
crin *f*, **crines** *fpl* mane *sing*.
crío, -a *mf* kid.
criollo, -a *adj & mf* Creole.
crisis *f inv* crisis; **c. nerviosa** nervous breakdown.
crispar *vt* to make tense; **me crispa los nervios** it makes me nervous.
cristal *m* crystal; *(vidrio)* glass; *(de gafas)* lens; *(de ventana)* (window) pane.
cristiano, -a *adj & mf* Christian.
Cristo *m* Christ.
criterio *m (pauta)* criterion; *(opinión)* opinion.
crítica *f* criticism; *(reseña)* review.
criticar 1 *vt* to criticize. **2** *vi (murmurar)* to gossip.
crítico, -a 1 *adj* critical. **2** *mf* critic.
croissant *m* croissant.
crol *m (en natación)* crawl.
cromo *m (metal)* chromium, chrome; *(estampa)* picture card.
cromosoma *m* chromosome.
crónica *f* feature.
crónico, -a *adj* chronic.
cronológico, -a *adj* chronological.
cronometrar *vt* to time.
cronómetro *m* stopwatch.
croqueta *f* croquette.
croquis *m inv* sketch.
cruce *m* crossing; *(de carreteras)* crossroads.
crucero *m (viaje)* cruise; *(barco)* cruiser.
crucifijo *m* crucifix.
crucigrama *m* crossword (puzzle).
crudo, -a 1 *adj (natural)* raw; *(comida)* underdone; *(color)* cream. **2** *m (petróleo)* crude.
cruel *adj* cruel.
crueldad *f* cruelty.
crujiente *adj* crunchy.
crujir *vi (madera)* to creak; *(comida)* to crunch; *(hueso)* to crack.
cruz *f* cross; **C. Roja** Red Cross; **¿cara o c.?** ≃ heads or tails?
cruzado, -a *adj* crossed; *(atravesado)* lying across; **con los brazos cruzados** arms folded.
cruzar 1 *vt* to cross; *(palabra, mirada)* to exchange. **2** *vi (atravesar)* to cross. **2 cruzarse** *vr* to cross; **cruzarse con algn** to pass sb.
cuaderno *m* notebook.
cuadra *f (establo)* stable; *Am* block (of houses).
cuadrado, -a *adj & m* square; **elevar (un número) al c.** to square (a number).
cuadriculado, -a *adj* **papel c.** squared paper.
cuadro *m* square; *(gráfico)* chart, graph; *(pintura)* painting, picture; **tela a cuadros** checked cloth; **c. de mandos** control panel.
cual *pron rel* **el/la c.** *(persona)* who; *(cosa)* which; **con el/la c.** with whom/which; **lo c.** which.
cuál 1 *pron interr* which (one)?; **¿c. quieres?** which one do you want? **2** *adj interr* which.
cualidad *f* quality.
cualquier *adj indef* any; **c. cosa** anything; **en c. momento** at any moment.
cualquiera *(pl cualesquiera)* **1** *adj indef (indefinido)* any; *(corriente)* ordinary. **2** *pron indef (persona)* anybody, anyone; *(cosa, animal)* any one; **c. que sea** whatever it is.

cuando *adv & conj* when; **de c. en c., de vez en c.** from time to time; **c. quieras** whenever you want; **c. vengas** when you come; **(aun) c.** even if.
cuándo *adv interr* when; **¿desde c.?** since when?; **¿para c. lo quieres?** when do you want it for?
cuanto, -a 1 *adj* **toma cuantos caramelos quieras** take all the sweets you want; **unas cuantas niñas** a few girls. **2** *pron rel* as much as; **coma (todo) c. quiera** eat as much as you want. **3** *pron indef pl* **unos cuantos** a few. **4** *adv (tiempo)* **c. antes** as soon as possible; **en c.** as soon as; **c. más ... más** the more ... the more; **en c. a** with respect to, regarding.
cuánto, -a 1 *adj & pron interr* how much; **¿cuántas veces?** how many times?; **¿c. es?** how much is it? **2** *adv* how, how much; **¡cuánta gente hay!** what a lot of people there are!
cuarenta *adj & m inv* forty.
cuaresma *f* Lent.
cuartel *m (militar)* barracks *pl*; **c. general** headquarters.
cuartilla *f* sheet of paper.
cuarto, -a 1 *m (habitación)* room; *(cuarta parte)* quarter; **c. de baño** bathroom; **c. de estar** living room; **c. de hora** quarter of an hour. **2** *adj & mf* fourth.
cuate *mf Méx fam* pal, buddy.
cuatro *adj & m inv* four.
cuatrocientos, -as *adj & mf* four hundred.
cubalibre *m* rum o gin and coke.
cubano, -a *adj & mf* Cuban.
cubata *m fam* cubalibre.
cubierta *f* cover; *(de rueda)* tire; *(de barco)* deck.
cubierto, -a 1 *adj* covered; *(piscina etc)* indoor; *(cielo)* overcast. **2** *mpl* **cubiertos** cutlery *sing*.
cubo *m* bucket; *(en matemática)* cube; **c. de la basura** trash bin.
cubrecama *m* bedspread.
cubrir *(pp cubierto)* **1** *vt* to cover. **2 cubrirse** *vr (cielo)* to become overcast.
cucaracha *f* cockroach.
cuchara *f* spoon.
cucharada *f* spoonful.
cucharilla *f* teaspoon; **c. de café** coffee spoon.
cucharón *m* ladle.
cuchichear *vi* to whisper.
cuchilla *f* blade; **c. de afeitar** razor blade.
cuchillo *m* knife.
cuchitril *m fam* hovel, hole.
cuco *m* cuckoo.
cucurucho *m (de helado)* cornet; *(envoltorio)* paper cone.
cuello *m* neck; *(de camisa etc)* collar.
cuenco *m* bowl.
cuenta *f (factura)* check; *(de banco)* account; *(cálculo)* count; *(de collar)* bead; **c. corriente** current account; **caer en la c., darse c.** to realize; **tener en c.** to take into account; **traer c.** to be worthwhile; **en resumidas cuentas** in short; **trabajar por c. propia** to be self-employed.
cuentakilómetros *m inv (distancia)* ≃ milometer; *(velocidad)* speedometer.
cuento *m* story; **contar un c.** to tell a story; **c. de hadas** fairy story.
cuerda *f (cordel)* rope; *(de instrumento)* string; *(del reloj)* spring; **dar c. al reloj** to wind up a watch.
cuerdo, -a *adj* sane.
cuerno *m* horn; *(de ciervo)* antler; *fam* **¡vete al c.!** get lost!
cuero *m* leather; **chaqueta de c.** leather jacket; **c. cabelludo** scalp.
cuerpo *m* body; *(cadáver)* corpse; **c. de bomberos** fire brigade; **c. diplomático** diplomatic corps; **c. de policía** police force.
cuervo *m* raven.
cuesta 1 *f* slope; **c. abajo** downhill; **c. arriba** uphill. **2 a cuestas** *adv* on one's back.
cuestión *f (asunto)* matter, question; *(pregunta)* question; **en c. de unas horas** in just a few hours.
cuestionario *m* questionnaire.
cueva *f* cave.
cuezo *indic pres de* **cocer**.
cuidado, -a 1 *adj* careful. **2** *m* care; **con c.** carefully; **tener c.** to be careful; **estar al c. de** to be in charge of; *(persona)* to look after; **me trae sin c.** I couldn't care less; **cuidados intensivos** intensive care *sing*. **3** *interj* **¡c.!** look out!
cuidadoso, -a *adj* careful.
cuidar 1 *vt* to care for, to look after. **2 cuidarse** *vr* **cuídate** take care of yourself.
culebra *f* snake.
culebrón *m* soap opera.
culo *m fam (trasero)* backside; *(de recipiente)* bottom.
culpa *f* blame; *(culpabilidad)* guilt; **echar la c. a algn** to put the blame on sb; **fue c. mía** it was my fault; **por tu c.** because of you.
culpable 1 *adj* guilty; **declararse c.** to plead guilty. **2** *mf* offender, culprit.
culpar *vt* to blame; **c. a algn de un delito** to accuse sb of an offence.
cultivar *vt* to cultivate.
culto, -a 1 *adj* educated; *(palabra)* learned. **2** *m (devoción)* worship; *(religión)* cult.
cultura *f* culture.
culturismo *m* body building.
cumbre *f (de montaña)* summit, top; **(conferencia) c.** summit conference.
cumpleaños *m inv* birthday; **¡feliz c.!** happy birthday!
cumplir 1 *vt* to carry out; *(deseo)* to fulfil; *(promesa)* to keep; **ayer cumplí veinte años** I was twenty (years old) yesterday. **2** *vi (plazo)* to expire, end; **c. con el deber** to do one's duty. **3 cumplirse** *vr (deseo)* to come true; *(plazo)* to expire.
cuna *f* cot.
cundir *vi (extenderse)* to spread; **cundió el pánico** panic spread; **cundió la voz de que ...** rumor had it that ...; **me cunde mucho el trabajo** o **el tiempo** I seem to get a lot done.
cuneta *f (de la carretera)* gutter.
cuñado, -a *mf (hombre)* brother-in-law; *(mujer)* sister-in-law.
cuota *f (de club etc)* membership fees *pl*; *(porción)* quota, share; *Méx* **carretera de c.** toll road.
cupe *pt indef de* **caber**.
cupiera *subj imperfecto de* **caber**.
cupón *m* coupon, voucher.
cura 1 *m (religioso)* priest. **2** *f (de enfermedad)* cure.
curación *f* cure, treatment.
curandero, -a *mf* quack.
curar 1 *vt* to cure; *(herida)* to dress; *(enfermedad)* to treat. **2** *vi*, **curarse** *vr (sanar)* to recover, to get well; *(herida)* to heal up.
curiosidad *f* curiosity.
curioso, -a 1 *adj (extraño)* strange, odd; *(indiscreto)* curious, inquisitive. **2** *mf (mirón)* onlooker.
currículum *m* **c. vitae** curriculum vitae.
cursi *adj* posh.
cursillo *m* short course; **c. de reciclaje** refresher course.
curso *m (año académico)* year; *(clase)* class; *(de acontecimientos, río)* course; **en el c. de** in the course of; **moneda de c. legal** legal tender.

cursor *m* cursor.
curtir *vt (cuero)* to tan; *(endurecer)* to harden.
curva *f* curve; *(en carretera)* bend; **c. cerrada** sharp bend.
cutis *m* complexion.
cuyo, -a *pron rel & pos (persona)* whose; *(de cosa)* of which; **en c. caso** in which case.

D

D. *abr de* **don** Mister, Mr.
D.ª *abr de* **doña** Mrs; *(señorita)* Miss.
dactilar *adj* **huellas dactilares** fingerprints.
dado *m* dice.
dálmata *mf* Dalmatian.
dama *f (señora)* lady; **damas** *(juego)* checkers.
danés, -esa 1 *adj* Danish. **2** *mf (persona)* Dane. **3** *m (idiom)* Danish; **gran d.** *(perro)* Great Dane.
danza *f* dancing; *(baile)* dance.
dañar *vt (cosa)* to damage; *(persona)* to hurt, to harm.
dañino, -a *adj* harmful, damaging (**para** to).
daño *m (a cosa)* damage; *(a persona) (físico)* hurt; *(perjuicio)* harm.
dar 1 *vt* to give; *(noticia)* to tell; *(mano de pintura, cera)* to apply; *(fruto, flores)* to bear; *(beneficio, interés)* to yield; *(hora)* to strike; **dale a la luz** switch the light on; **d. la mano a algn** *(saludo)* to shake hands with sb; **d. los buenos días/las buenas noches a algn** to say good morning/good evening to sb; **me da lo mismo** *or* **me da igual** it's all the same to me; **¿qué más da?** what difference does it make?; **d. de comer** to feed; **d. a conocer** *(noticia)* to release; **d. a entender que ...** to imply that ...; **d. por** *(considerar)* to consider; **d. por descontado/sabido** to take for granted. **2** *vi* **me dio un ataque de tos/risa** I had a coughing fit/an attack of the giggles; **d. a** *(ventana, habitación)* to overlook; *(puerta)* to open onto; **d. con la solución** to hit upon the solution; **d. de sí** *(ropa)* to stretch; **el presupuesto no da para más** the budget will not stretch any further; **d. que hablar** to get people talking. **3 darse** *vr* **se dio la circunstancia de que** it happened that; **se dio a la bebida** he started drinking; **darse con** *o* **contra** to bump into; **darse por satisfecho** to feel satisfied; **darse por vencido** to give in; **se le da bien/mal el francés** she's good/bad at French.
dardo *m* dart.
dársena *f* dock.
dátil *m* date.
dato *m* piece of information; **datos** *(de ordenador)* data.
d.C. *abr de* **después de Cristo** Anno Domini, AD.
dcha. *abr de* **derecha** right.
de *prep (pertenencia)* of; **el título de la novela** the title of the novel; **el coche/hermano de Sofía** Sofia's car/brother. ▪ *(procedencia)* from; **vino de Madrid** he came from Madrid. ▪ *(descripción)* **el niño de ojos azules** the boy with blue eyes; **una avenida de quince kilómetros** an avenue fifteen kilometers long; **una botella de litro** a liter bottle; **el señor de la chaqueta** the man in the jacket; **un reloj de oro** a gold watch. ▪ *(contenido)* of; **un saco de patatas** a sack of potatoes. ▪ *(oficio)* by, as; **trabaja de secretaria** she's working as a secretary. ▪ *(acerca de)* about; **curso de informática** computer course. ▪ *(tiempo)* **a las tres de la tarde** at three in the afternoon; **de día** by day; **de noche** at night; **de lunes a jueves** from Monday to Thursday; **de pequeño** as a child. ▪ *(con superlativo)* in; **el más largo de España** the longest in Spain. ▪ *(causa)* with, because of; **llorar de alegría** to cry with joy; **morir de hambre** to die of hunger. ▪ **de cuatro en cuatro** four at a time; **de semana en semana** every week.
debajo 1 *adv* underneath, below. **2** *prep* **d. de** under(neath); **por d. de lo normal** below normal.
debate *m* debate.
debatir 1 *vt* to debate. **2 debatirse** *vr* to struggle.
deber¹ *m* duty; *(en el colegio)* **deberes** homework *sing.*
deber² 1 *vt (dinero, explicación)* to owe. **2** *vi* **debe irse ahora** she has to leave now; **la factura debe pagarse mañana** the bill must be paid tomorrow; **deberías vistar a tus padres** you ought to visit your parents; **debería haber ido ayer** I should have gone yesterday; **no debiste hacerlo** you shouldn't have done it; **deben de estar fuera** they must be out. **3 deberse** *vr* **deberse a** to be due to.
debidamente *adv* duly.
debido, -a *adj* **d. a** due to.
débil *adj* weak; *(luz)* dim; **punto d.** weak spot.
debilitar 1 *vt* to weaken. **2 debilitarse** *vr* to weaken, to grow weak.
debutar *vi* to make one's debut.
década *f* **en la d. de los noventa** during the nineties.
decadencia *f* decadence.
decaer *vi* to deteriorate.
decano, -a *mf* dean.
decena *f* (about) ten; **una d. de veces** (about) ten times; **por decenas** in tens.
decenio *m* decade.
decente *adj* decent; *(decoroso)* modest.
decepción *f* disappointment.
decepcionante *adj* disappointing.
decepcionar *vt* to disappoint.
decidido, -a *adj* determined.
decidir 1 *vti* to decide. **2 decidirse** *vr* **decidirse (a hacer algo)** to make up one's mind (to do sth); **decidirse por algo** to decide on sth.
décima *f* tenth.
decimal *adj & m* decimal.
décimo, -a 1 *adj & mf* tenth. **2** *m (parte)* tenth.
decir *(pp* **dicho**) **1** *vt* to say; **d. una mentira/la verdad** to tell a lie/the truth; **dígame** *(al teléfono)* hello; **esta película no me dice nada** this film doesn't appeal to me; **querer d.** to mean; *(locuciones)* **es d.** that is (to say); **por así decirlo** so to speak; **digamos** let's say; **digo yo** in my opinion; **ni que d. tiene** needless to say; **¡no me digas!** really! **2 decirse** *vr* **¿cómo se dice 'mesa' en inglés?** how do you say 'mesa' in English?; **se dice que ...** they say that ....
decisión *f* decision; *(resolución)* determination; **tomar una d.** to make a decision; **con d.** decisively.
decisivo, -a *adj* decisive.
declaración *f* declaration; **d. de (la) renta** tax return; *(afirmación)* statement; **hacer declaraciones** to comment.
declarar 1 *vt* to declare; *(afirmar)* to state; **d. la guerra a** to declare war on. **2** *vi (en juicio)* to testify. **3 declararse** *vr (guerra, incendio)* to break out; **declararse a favor/en contra de** to declare oneself in favor of/against; **declararse en huelga** to go on strike; **declararse a algn** to declare one's love for sb.
decoración *f* decoration.
decorador, -a *mf* decorator; *(en teatro)* set designer.
decorar *vt* to decorate.
decorativo, -a *adj* decorative.
decretar *vt* to decree.
decreto *m* decree.
decreto-ley *m* decree.
dedal *m* thimble.
dedicar 1 *vt* to dedicate; *(tiempo, esfuerzos)* to devote (**a** to). **2 dedicarse** *vr* **¿a qué se dedica Vd.?** what do you do for a living?; **los fines de semana ella se dedica a pescar** on weekends she spends her time fishing.
dedicatoria *f* dedication.
dedo *m (de la mano)* finger; *(del pie)* toe; **d. anular/corazón/indice/meñique** ring/middle/index/little finger; **d. pulgar, d. gordo** thumb.
deducir 1 *vt* to deduce. **2 deducirse** *vr* **de aquí se deduce que ...** from this it follows that ....
defecar *vi* to defecate.
defecto *m* defect.
defectuoso, -a *adj* defective.
defender 1 *vt* to defend (**contra** against; **de** from). **2 defenderse** *vr* to defend oneself.
defensa 1 *f* defense; **en d. propia, en legítima d.** in self-defense. **2** *m (en equipo)* defender.
defensor, -a *mf* defender; **abogado d.** counsel for the defense; **el defensor del pueblo** the ombudsman.
deficiente 1 *adj* deficient. **2** *m (nota)* fail.
definición *f* definition.
definir *vt* to define.
definitivamente *adv (para siempre)* for good, once and for all; *(con toda seguridad)* definitely.
definitivo, -a *adj* definitive; **en definitiva** in short.
deformar 1 *vt* to deform; *(cara)* to disfigure; *(la verdad, una imagen)* to distort. **2 deformarse** *vr* to become distorted.
deforme *adj* deformed; *(objeto)* misshapen.
defraudar *vt* to disappoint; **d. a Hacienda** to evade taxes.
defunción *f* demise.
degenerado, -a *adj & mf* degenerate.
degenerar *vi* to degenerate.
degollar *vt* to behead.
degradante *adj* degrading.
degradar *vt* to degrade.
degustación *f* tasting.
dejar 1 *vt* to leave; *(prestar)* to lend; *(abandonar)* to give up; *(permitir)* to let, to allow; **déjame en paz** leave me alone; **dejé el tabaco y la bebida** I gave up smoking and drinking; **d. caer** to drop; **d. entrar/salir** to let in/out; **d. triste** to make sad; **d. preocupado/sorprendido** to worry/surprise. **2** *v aux* **d. de** + *inf* to stop; *(renunciar)* to give up; **no deja de llamarme** she's always calling me. **3 dejarse** *vr* **me he dejado las llaves dentro** I've left the keys inside; **dejarse barba** to grow a beard; **dejarse llevar por** to be influenced by.
del *(contracción de* **de** + **el**) *ver* **de**.
delantal *m* apron.
delante 1 *adv* in front; **la entrada de d.** the front entrance; **por d.** in front; **se lo lleva todo por d.** he destroys everything in his path; **tiene toda la vida por d.** he has his whole life ahead of him. **2** *prep* **d. de** in front of; *(en serie)* ahead of.
delantero, -a 1 *adj* front. **2** *m (en fútbol)* forward; **d. centro** center forward.
delatar *vt* to inform against.
delegación *f (acto, delegados)* delegation; *(oficina)* local office.
delegado, -a *mf* delegate.
delegar *vt* to delegate (**en** to).
deletrear *vt* to spell (out).
delfín *m* dolphin.
delgado, -a *adj* slim; *(capa)* fine.
deliberado, -a *adj* deliberate.
deliberar *vi* to deliberate (on).
delicadeza *f (finura)* daintiness; *(tacto)* tactfulness; **falta de d.** tactlessness.
delicado, -a *adj* delicate.
delicioso, -a *adj (comida)* delicious; *(agradable)* delightful.
delimitar *vt* to delimit.
delincuencia *f* crime.
delincuente *mf* criminal.
delineante *mf (hombre)* draftsman; *(mujer)* draftswoman.
delinquir *vi* to break the law, to commit an offense.
delirar *vi* to be delirious.
delirio *m* delirium.
delito *m* crime.
delta *m* delta.
demacrado, -a *adj* emaciated.
demanda *f (judicial)* lawsuit.
demandar *vt* to sue.
demás 1 *adj* **los/las d.** the rest of. **2** *pron* **lo/los/las d.** the rest; **por lo d.** otherwise, apart from that.
demasiado, -a 1 *adj (singular)* too much; *(plural)* too many. **2** *adv* too (much); **es d. grande/caro** it is too big/dear; **fumas/trabajas d.** you smoke/work too much.
demencia *f* insanity.
democracia *f* democracy.
demócrata 1 *adj* democratic. **2** *mf* democrat.
democrático, -a *adj* democratic.
demográfico, -a *adj* demographic; **crecimiento d.** population growth.
demoledor, -a *adj* devastating.
demonio *m* devil.
demora *f* delay.
demorar 1 *vt* to delay, to hold up. **2 demorarse** *vr (retrasarse)* to be delayed, to be held up.
demostrar *vt (mostrar)* to show; *(evidenciar)* to prove.
denegar *vt* to refuse.
denigrante *adj* humiliating.
denominación *f* denomination.
denominar *vt* to name.
denotar *vt* to denote.
densidad *f* density.
denso, -a *adj* dense.
dentadura *f* teeth; **d. postiza** false teeth *pl*, dentures *pl*.
dental *adj* dental.
dentera *f* **me da d.** it sets my teeth on edge.
dentífrico, -a 1 *adj* **pasta/crema dentífrica** toothpaste. **2** *m* toothpaste.
dentista *mf* dentist.
dentro 1 *adv (en el interior)* inside; **aquí d.** in here; **por d.** (on the) inside. **2** *prep* **d. de** *(lugar)* inside; **d. de poco** shortly, soon; **d. de un mes** in a month's time.
denuncia *f (a la policía)* report; *(crítica)* denunciation.
denunciar *vt (delito)* to report (**a** to).
departamento *m* department; *(territorial)* province; *Am (piso)* apartment.
depender *vi* to depend (**de** on); *(económicamente)* to be dependent (**de** on).

dependienta *f* shop assistant.
dependiente 1 *adj* dependent (**de** on). **2** *m* shop assistant.
depilación *f* depilation.
depilar *vt* to remove the hair from; *(cejas)* to pluck.
depilatorio, -a *adj & m* depilatory; **crema depilatoria** hair-remover.
deportar *vt* to deport.
deporte *m* sport; **hacer d.** to go out for sports.
deportista *mf (hombre)* sportsman; *(mujer)* sportswoman. **2** *adj* sporty.
deportivo, -a 1 *adj* sports; **club d./chaqueta deportiva** sports club/jacket. **2** *m (coche)* sports car.
depositar 1 *vt (colocar)* to put. **2 depositarse** *vr* to settle.
depósito *m (dinero)* deposit; *(de agua, gasolina)* tank.
depresión *f* depression.
deprimente *adj* depressing.
deprimir 1 *vt* to depress. **2 deprimirse** *vr* to get depressed.
deprisa *adv* quickly.
depuradora *f* purifier.
derecha *f (mano)* right hand; *(lugar)* right, right-hand side; **a la d.** on the right, on the right-hand side; *(en política)* **la d.** the right.
derecho, -a 1 *adj (de la derecha)* right; *(recto)* straight. **2** *m (privilegio)* right; *(carrera)* law; **derechos civiles/humanos** civil/human rights; **tener d. a** to be entitled to; **no hay d.** it's not fair. **3** *adv* **siga todo d.** go straight ahead.
derivar 1 *vi* to drift; **d. de** to derive from. **2 derivarse** *vr* to stem (**de** from).
dermatólogo, -a *mf* dermatologist.
derramar 1 *vt* to spill; *(lágrimas)* to shed. **2 derramarse** *vr* to spill.
derrapar *vi* to skid.
derretir *vt*, **derretirse** *vr* to melt; *(hielo, nieve)* to thaw.
derribar *vt (demoler)* to knock down; *(gobierno)* to bring down.
derrochar *vt* to waste.
derroche *m* waste.
derrota *f* defeat.
derrotar *vt* to defeat.
derruir *vt* to demolish.
derrumbar *vt (edificio)* to knock down. **2 derrumbarse** *vr* to collapse; *(techo)* to fall in.
desabrido, -a *adj (tono)* harsh; *(persona)* irritable.
desabrochar 1 *vt* to undo. **2 desabrocharse** *vr (prenda)* to come undone; **desabróchate la camisa** undo your shirt.
desacertado, -a *adj* unwise.
desaconsejar *vt* to advise against.
desacreditar *vt (desprestigiar)* to discredit; *(criticar)* to disparage.
desactivar *vt (bomba)* to defuse.
desacuerdo *m* disagreement.
desafiante *adj* defiant.
desafiar *vt* to challenge.
desafinado, -a *adj* out of tune.
desafinar 1 *vi* to sing out of tune; *(instrumento)* to play out of tune. **2 desafinarse** *vr* to go out of tune.
desafío *m* challenge.
desafortunado, -a *adj* unfortunate.
desagradable *adj* unpleasant.
desagradar *vt* to displease.
desagradecido, -a 1 *adj* ungrateful. **2** *mf* ungrateful person.
desagrado *m* displeasure.
desagüe *m (cañería)* drainpipe; *(vaciado)* drain.
desaguisado *m* mess.
desahogado, -a *adj (acomodado)* well-off; *(espacioso)* spacious.
desahogarse *vr* to let off steam.
desahuciar *vt (desalojar)* to evict; *(enfermo)* to deprive of all hope.
desairar *vt* to slight.
desajuste *m* disorder, imbalance.
desalentar 1 *vt* to dishearten. **2 desalentarse** *vr* to get discouraged.
desaliento *m* discouragement.
desaliñado, -a *adj* untidy.
desalmado, -a *adj* heartless.
desalojar *vt (inquilino)* to evict; *(público)* to move on; *(lugar)* to evacuate; *(abandonar)* to abandon.
desamparado, -a *adj (persona)* helpless.
desangrarse *vr* to lose (a lot of) blood.
desanimado, -a *adj (persona)* downhearted; *(fiesta etc)* dull.
desanimar 1 *vt* to dishearten. **2 desanimarse** *vr* to lose heart.
desánimo *m* dejection.
desapacible *adj* unpleasant.
desaparecer *vi* to disappear.
desaparición *f* disappearance.
desapercibido, -a *adj* **pasar d.** to go unnoticed.
desaprovechar *vt (dinero, tiempo)* to waste.
desarmar *vt (desmontar)* to dismantle; *(ejército)* to disarm.
desarme *m* disarmament; **d. nuclear** nuclear disarmament.
desarraigado, -a *adj* rootless.
desarreglar *vt* to mess up.
desarrollado, -a *adj* developed.
desarrollar 1 *vt* to develop. **2 desarrollarse** *vr (persona, enfermedad)* to develop; *(tener lugar)* to take place.
desarrollo *m* development; **países en vías de d.** developing countries.
desarticular *vt* to dismantle.
desasir 1 *vt* to release. **2 desasirse** *vr* to get loose; **desasirse de** to free oneself of.
desasosiego *m* uneasiness.
desastrado, -a *adj* scruffy.
desastre *m* disaster.
desastroso, -a *adj* disastrous.
desatar *vt* to untie, undo. **2 desatarse** *vr (zapato, cordón)* to come undone.
desatascar *vt* to clear.
desatornillar *vt* to unscrew.
desatrancar *vt* to unblock; *(puerta)* to unbolt.
desautorizar *vt* to disallow; *(huelga etc)* to ban.
desavenencia *f* disagreement.
desayunar *vi* to have breakfast. **2** *vt* to have for breakfast.
desayuno *m* breakfast.
desbarajuste *m* confusion.
desbaratar *vt* to ruin.
desbordar 1 *vt* to overflow. **2** *vi* to overflow (**de** with). **3 desbordarse** *vr* to overflow.
descabellado, -a *adj* crazy.
descafeinado, -a *adj* decaffeinated.
descalabro *m* misfortune.

descalificar *vt* to disqualify.
descalzarse *vr* to take one's shoes off.
descalzo, -a *adj* barefoot.
descaminado, -a *adj fig* **ir d.** to be on the wrong track.
descampado *m* garbage dump.
descansado, -a *adj (persona)* rested; *(vida, trabajo)* restful.
descansar *vi* to rest, to have a rest; *(poco tiempo)* to take a break.
descansillo *m* landing.
descanso *m* rest; *(en teatro, cine)* interval; *(en deporte)* half-time; **un día de d.** a day off.
descapotable *adj & m* convertible.
descarado, -a 1 *adj (insolente)* rude; *(desvergonzado)* shameless. **2** *mf* rude person.
descarga *f* unloading; *(eléctrica, explosiva)* discharge.
descargar 1 *vt* to unload; *(golpe)* to deal. **2** *vi (tormenta)* to burst. **3 descargarse** *vr* to go flat.
descaro *m* cheek.
descarrilar *vi* to be derailed.
descartar *vt* to rule out.
descato *m* lack of respect (**a** for).
descender 1 *vi (temperatura, nivel)* to fall; **d. de** to descend from. **2** *vt* to lower.
descendiente *mf* descendant.
descenso *m* descent; *(de temperatura)* fall.
descifrar *vt* to decipher; *(mensaje)* to decode; *(misterio)* to solve.
descolgar *vt (el teléfono)* to pick up; *(cuadro, cortinas)* to take down.
descolorido, -a *adj* faded.
descomponer *(pp* **descompuesto** *)* **1** *vt* to break down; *(corromper)* to decompose. **2 descomponerse** *vr (corromperse)* to decompose; *(ponerse nervioso)* to lose one's cool.
descomposición *f (de carne)* decomposition.
descompuse *pt indef de* **descomponer**.
descomunal *adj* massive.
desconcertar 1 *vt* to disconcert. **2 desconcertarse** *vr* to be bewildered.
desconcierto *m* chaos, confusion.
desconectar *vt* to disconnect.
desconfiado, -a *adj* distrustful.
desconfiar *vi* to distrust (**de** -).
descongelar *vt* to defrost.
desconocer *vt* not to know.
desconocido, -a 1 *adj* unknown; *(irreconocible)* unrecognizable. **2** *m* **lo d.** the unknown. **3** *mf* stranger.
desconsiderado, -a 1 *adj* inconsiderate, thoughtless. **2** *mf* inconsiderate *o* thoughtless person.
desconsolado, -a *adj* disconsolate.
descontado, -a *adj fam* **dar por d.** to take for granted; **por d.** needless to say, of course.
descontar *vt* to deduct.
descontento, -a 1 *adj* unhappy. **2** *m* dissatisfaction.
descontrolarse *vr* to lose control.
desconvocar *vt* to call off.
descorchar *vt* to uncork.
descorrer *vt* to draw back.
descortés *adj* impolite, discourteous.
descoser *vt* to unpick.
descoyuntar *vt* to dislocate.
descrédito *m* disrepute.
descremado, -a *adj* skimmed.
describir *(pp* **descrito** *)* *vt* to describe.
descripción *f* description.
descuartizar *vt* to cut into pieces.
descubierto, -a 1 *adj* open. **2** *m* **al d.** in the open; **poner al d.** to bring out into the open.
descubrimiento *m* discovery.
descubrir *(pp* **descubierto** *)* *vt* to discover; *(conspiración)* to uncover; *(placa)* to unveil.
descuento *m* discount.
descuidado, -a *adj (negligente)* careless; *(desaseado)* untidy; *(desprevenido)* off one's guard.
descuidar 1 *vt* to neglect, to overlook. **2** *vi* **descuida, voy yo** don't worry, I'll go. **3 descuidarse** *vr (despistarse)* to be careless; **como te descuides, llegarás tarde** if you don't watch out, you'll be late.
descuido *m* oversight; *(negligencia)* carelessness; **por d.** inadvertently.
desde *adv (tiempo)* since; *(lugar)* from; **no lo he visto d. hace un año** I haven't seen him for a year; **d. siempre** always; **d. luego** of course; **d. que** ever since.
desdén *m* disdain.
desdeñar *vt* to disdain.
desdichado, -a 1 *adj* unfortunate. **2** *mf* poor devil.
desdoblar *vt* to unfold.
desear *vt* to desire; *(querer)* to want; **¿qué desea?** can I help you?; **estoy deseando que vengas** I'm looking forward to your coming; **te deseo buena suerte/feliz Navidad** I wish you good luck/a Merry Christmas.
desechable *adj* disposable.
desechar *vt (tirar)* to discard; *(idea, proyecto)* to drop.
desembalar *vt* to unpack.
desembarcar 1 *vt (mercancías)* to unload; *(personas)* to disembark. **2** *vi* to disembark.
desembarco, desembarque *m (de mercancías)* unloading; *(de personas)* disembarkation.
desembocadura *f* mouth.
desembocar *vi (río)* to flow (**en** into); *(calle, situación)* to lead (**en** to).
desembolsar *vt* to pay out.
desembolso *m* expenditure.
desembrollar *vt fam (aclarar)* to clear up; *(desenredar)* to disentangle.
desempaquetar *vt* to unpack.
desempatar *vi* to break the deadlock.
desempate *m* play-off.
desempeñar *vt (cargo)* to hold; *(función)* to fulfill; *(papel)* to play.
desempleado, -a 1 *adj* unemployed, out of work. **2** *mf* unemployed person; **los desempleados** the unemployed.
desempleo *m* unemployment; **cobrar el d.** to be on welfare.
desencadenar 1 *vt (provocar)* to unleash. **2 desencadenarse** *vr (viento, pasión)* to rage; *(conflicto)* to break out.
desencaminado, -a *adj* **= descaminado.**
desencanto *m* disillusion.
desenchufar *vt* to unplug.
desenfadado, -a *adj* free and easy.
desenfocado, -a *adj* out of focus.
desenfrenado, -a *adj* frantic, uncontrolled; *(vicio, pasión)* unbridled.
desenganchar *vt* to unhook; *(vagón)* to uncouple.
desengañar 1 *vt* **d. a algn** to open sb's eyes. **2 desengañarse** *vr* to be disappointed; *fam* **¡desengáñate!** get real!
desengaño *m* disappointment.
desengrasar *vt* to remove the grease from.
desenlace *m* outcome; *(de historia)* ending.

desenmascarar *vt* to unmask.
desenredar *vt* to disentangle.
desenrollar *vt* to unroll; *(cable)* to unwind.
desenroscar *vt* to unscrew.
desentenderse *vr* **se desentendió de mi problema** he didn't want to have anything to do with my problem.
desentonar *vi* to be out of tune; *(colores etc)* not to match; *(persona, comentario)* to be out of place.
desentrañar *vt* to unravel.
desentrenado, -a *adj* out of training.
desenvolver *(pp* **desenvuelto) 1** *vt* to unwrap. **2 desenvolverse** *vr (persona)* to manage.
desenvuelto, -a *adj* relaxed.
deseo *m* wish; *(sexual)* desire.
deseoso, -a *adj* eager; **estar d. de** be eager to.
desequilibrado, -a 1 *adj* unbalanced. **2** *mf* unbalanced person.
desértico, -a *adj* desert.
desertor, -a *mf* deserter.
desesperado, -a *adj (sin esperanza)* desperate; *(exasperado)* exasperated.
desesperante *adj* exasperating.
desesperar 1 *vt* to drive to despair; *(exasperar)* to exasperate. **2 desesperarse** *vr* to despair.
desestabilizar *vt* to destabilize.
desestimar *vt* to reject.
desfachatez *f* cheek.
desfallecer *vi (debilitarse)* to feel faint; *(desmayarse)* to faint.
desfasado, -a *adj* outdated; *(persona)* old-fashioned, behind the times.
desfavorable *adj* unfavorable.
desfigurar *vt (cara)* to disfigure.
desfiladero *m* narrow pass.
desfilar *vi* to march in single file; *(soldados)* to march past.
desfile *m (militar)* parade; **d. de modas** fashion show.
desganado, -a *adj (apático)* apathetic; **estar d.** *(inapetente)* to have no appetite.
desgarbado, -a *adj* ungraceful, ungainly.
desgarrador, -a *adj* bloodcurdling.
desgarrar *vt* to tear.
desgastar *vt*, **desgastarse** *vr* to wear away.
desgaste *m* wear.
desgracia *f* misfortune; **por d.** unfortunately.
desgraciadamente *adv* unfortunately.
desgraciado, -a 1 *adj* unfortunate; *(infeliz)* unhappy. **2** *mf* unfortunate person.
desgravación *f* deduction; **d. fiscal** tax deduction.
desgravar *vt* to deduct.
deshabitado, -a *adj* uninhabited.
deshacer *(pp* **deshecho) 1** *vt (paquete)* to undo; *(maleta)* to unpack; *(destruir)* to destroy; *(disolver)* to dissolve; *(derretir)* to melt. **2 deshacerse** *vr* to come undone; **deshacerse de algn/algo** to get rid of sb/sth; *(disolverse)* to dissolve; *(derretirse)* to melt.
deshidratar *vt* to dehydrate.
deshielo *m* thaw.
deshonesto, -a *adj* dishonest; *(indecente)* indecent.
deshonrar *vt* to dishonor; *(a la familia etc)* to bring disgrace on.
deshora a d. *adv* at an inconvenient time; **comer a d.** to eat at odd times.
deshuesar *vt (carne)* to bone; *(fruta)* to stone.
desierto, -a 1 *m (deshabitado)* uninhabited; *(vacío)* deserted. **2** *m* desert.
designar *vt* to designate; *(fecha, lugar)* to fix.
desigual *adj* uneven.
desigualdad *f* inequality; *(del terreno)* unevenness.
desilusión *f* disappointment.
desilusionar *vt* to disappoint.
desinfectante *adj* & *m* disinfectant.
desinfectar *vt* to disinfect.
desinflar 1 *vt* to deflate; *(rueda)* to let down. **2 desinflarse** *vr* to go flat.
desintegrar *vt*, **desintegrarse** *vr* to disintegrate.
desinterés *m (indiferencia)* lack of interest, apathy; *(generosidad)* unselfishness.
desinteresado, -a *adj* selfless.
desintoxicar 1 *vt* to detoxicate; *(de alcohol)* to dry out. **2 desintoxicarse** *vr* to detoxicate oneself; *(de alcohol)* to dry out.
desistir *vi* to desist.
deslenguado, -a *adj (insolente)* insolent.
desliz *m* slip.
deslizar 1 *vi* to slide. **2 deslizarse** *vr (patinar)* to slide; *(bajar)* to slide down.
deslumbrador, -a, **deslumbrante** *adj* dazzling; *fig* stunning.
deslumbrar *vt* to dazzle.
desmadrarse *vr fam* to go wild.
desmandarse *vr* to get out of hand.
desmano: a desmano *adv* out of the way; **me coge a d.** it is out of my way.
desmantelar *vt* to dismantle.
desmaquillador, -a 1 *m* make-up remover. **2** *adj* **leche desmaquilladora** cleansing cream.
desmaquillarse *vr* to remove one's make-up.
desmayarse *vr* to faint.
desmayo *m* fainting fit; **tener un d.** to faint.
desmedido, -a *adj* out of proportion.
desmejorar(se) *vi* & *vr* to deteriorate.
desmemoriado, -a *adj* forgetful.
desmentir *vt* to deny.
desmenuzar *vt* to crumble.
desmesurado, -a *adj* excessive.
desmontable *adj* that can be taken apart.
desmontar *vt* to dismantle.
desmoralizar *vt* to demoralize.
desmoronarse *vr* to crumble.
desnatado, -a *adj (leche)* skim milk.
desnivel *m* drop.
desnudar *vt*, **desnudarse** *vr* to undress.
desnudista *adj* & *mf* nudist.
desnudo, -a *adj* naked.
desnutrido, -a *adj* undernourished.
desobedecer *vt* to disobey.
desobediente 1 *adj* disobedient. **2** *mf* disobedient person.
desocupado, -a *adj (vacío)* empty; *(ocioso)* free.
desocupar *vt* to empty, to vacate.
desodorante *adj* & *m* deodorant.
desolar *vt* to devastate.
desollar 1 *vt* to skin. **2 desollarse** *vr* to scrape; **me desollé el brazo** I scraped my arm.
desorbitado, -a *adj (precio)* exorbitant.
desorden *m* mess; **d. público** civil disorder.

desordenado, -a *adj* untidy.
desordenar *vt* to make untidy, to mess up.
desorganizar *vt* to disorganize, to disrupt.
desorientar 1 *vt* to disorientate. **2 desorientarse** *vr* to lose one's bearings.
despabilado, -a *adj (sin sueño)* wide awake; *(listo)* quick.
despachar *vt (asunto)* to get through; *(en tienda)* to serve.
despacho *m (oficina)* office; *(en casa)* study.
despacio *adv (lentamente)* slowly.
desparramar *vt*, **desparramarse** *vr* to scatter; *(líquido)* to spill.
despavorido, -a *adj* terrified.
despectivo, -a *adj* derogatory.
despedida *f* goodbye.
despedir 1 *vt (empleado)* to sack; *(decir adiós a)* to say goodbye to; *(olor, humo etc)* to give off. **2 despedirse** *vr (decir adiós)* to say goodbye (**de** to).
despegado, -a *adj* unstuck; *(persona)* couldn't-care-less.
despegar 1 *vt* to detach. **2** *vi (avión)* to take off. **3 despegarse** *vr* to come unstuck.
despegue *m* takeoff.
despeinado, -a *adj* dishevelled.
despejado, -a *adj* clear; *(cielo)* cloudless.
despejar 1 *vt* to clear. **2 despejarse** *vr (cielo)* to clear; *(persona)* to clear one's head.
despeje *m (de balón)* clearance.
despensa *f* pantry.
despeñarse *vr* to go over a cliff.
desperdiciar *vt* to waste; *(oportunidad)* to throw away.
desperdicio *m* waste; **desperdicios** *(basura)* trash *sing, (desechos)* leftovers.
desperdigar *vt*, **desperdigarse** *vr* to scatter.
desperezarse *vr* to stretch (oneself).
desperfecto *m (defecto)* flaw; *(daño)* damage.
despertador *m* alarm clock.
despertar *vt*, **despertarse** *vr* to wake (up).
despiadado, -a *adj* merciless.
despido *m* dismissal.
despierto, -a *adj (desvelado)* awake; *(listo)* quick.
despilfarrar *vt* to squander.
despilfarro *m* squandering.
despistado, -a 1 *adj* scatterbrained. **2** *mf* scatterbrain.
despistar 1 *vt (hacer perder la pista a)* to lose. **2 despistarse** *vr (perderse)* to get lost; *(distraerse)* to switch off.
desplazamiento *m (viaje)* journey.
desplazar 1 *vt* to displace. **2 desplazarse** *vr* to travel.
despojar *vt* to strip (**de** of); *fig* to deprive (**de** of).
desposar *vt* to marry.
déspota *mf* despot, tyrant.
despreciar *vt (desdeñar)* to scorn; *(rechazar)* to reject.
desprecio *m (desdén)* scorn, disdain; *(desaire)* slight, snub.
desprender 1 *vt (separar)* to remove; *(olor, humo etc)* to give off. **2 desprenderse** *vr (soltarse)* to come off; **desprenderse de** to rid oneself (**de** of).
despreocupado, -a *adj (tranquilo)* unconcerned; *(descuidado)* careless; *(estilo)* casual.
despreocuparse *vr (tranquilizarse)* to stop worrying; *(desentenderse)* to be unconcerned, to be indifferent (**de** to).
desprestigiar *vt* to discredit.
desprestigio *m* discredit, loss of reputation; **campaña de d.** smear campaign.
desprevenido, -a *adj* unprepared; **coger** o **pillar a algn d.** to catch sb unawares.
desproporcionado, -a *adj* disproportionate.
desprovisto, -a *adj* lacking (**de** -).
después 1 *adv* afterwards, later; *(entonces)* then; *(seguidamente, lugar)* next; **poco d.** soon after. **2** *prep* **d. de** after. **3** *conj* **d. de que** after.
destacar 1 *vt* to stress. **2 destacar(se)** *vi* & *vr* to stand out.
destapador *m Am* bottle opener.
destapar 1 *vt* to take the lid off; *(botella)* to open. **2 destaparse** *vr* to get uncovered.
destartalado, -a *adj* rambling; *(desvencijado)* ramshackle.
destello *m* sparkle.
desteñir 1 *vti* to discolor. **2 desteñirse** *vr* to fade.
desternillarse *vi* **d. (de risa)** to split one's sides laughing.
desterrar *vt* to exile.
destiempo: a destiempo *adv* at the wrong time o moment.
destierro *m* exile.
destilería *f* distillery.
destinar *vt (dinero etc)* to assign; *(empleado)* to appoint.
destino *m (rumbo)* destination; *(sino)* fate; *(de empleo)* post; **el avión con d. a Bilbao** the plane to Bilbao.
destituir *vt* to remove from office.
destornillador *m* screwdriver.
destreza *f* skill.
destrozar *vt (destruir)* to destroy; *(abatir)* to shatter.
destrozo *m* destruction; **destrozos** damage.
destrucción *f* destruction.
destructivo, -a *adj* destructive.
destruir *vt* to destroy.
desuso *m* disuse; **caer en d.** to fall into disuse.
desvalijar *vt (robar)* to rob; *(casa, tienda)* to burgle.
desván *m* loft.
desvanecerse *vr (disiparse)* to vanish; *(desmayarse)* to faint.
desvariar *vi* to talk nonsense.
desvelar 1 *vt* to keep awake. **2 desvelarse** *vr* to make every effort.
desvencijarse *vr* to fall apart.
desventaja *f* disadvantage; *(inconveniente)* drawback; **estar en d.** to be at a disadvantage.
desvergonzado, -a 1 *adj (indecente)* shameless; *(descarado)* insolent. **2** *mf (sinvergüenza)* shameless person; *(fresco)* insolent person.
desvergüenza *f (indecencia)* shamelessness; *(atrevimiento)* insolence; *(acto impertinente)* insolent o rude remark; **tuvo la d. de negarlo** he had the cheek to deny it.
desvestir *vt*, **desvestirse** *vr* to undress.
desviar 1 *vt (río, carretera)* to divert; *(golpe, conversación)* to deflect. **2 desviarse** *vr* to go off course; *(coche)* to turn off.
desvío *m* diversion.
detallado, -a *adj* detailed.
detallar *vt* to give the details of.
detalle *m* detail; *(delicadeza)* nice thought.
detallista *adj* perfectionist.
detectar *vt* to detect.
detective *mf* detective; **d. privado** private detective.
detener 1 *vt* to stop; *(arrestar)* to arrest. **2 detenerse** *vr* to stop.
detenidamente *adv* carefully.
detenido, -a 1 *adj (parado)* stopped; *(arrestado)* detained; *(minucioso)* thorough. **2** *mf* detainee.

detenimiento *m* **con d.** carefully, thoroughly.
detergente *adj & m* detergent.
deteriorar 1 *vt* to spoil. **2 deteriorarse** *vr (estropearse)* to get damaged.
determinado, -a *adj (preciso)* definite; *(resuelto)* resolute.
determinar 1 *vt (fecha etc)* to set; *(decidir)* to decide on. **2 determinarse** *vr* **determinarse a** to make up one's mind to.
detestar *vt* to hate.
detrás 1 *adv* behind. **2** *prep* **d. de** behind.
detuve *pt indef de* **detener**.
deuda *f* debt; **d. pública** national debt.
deudor, -a *mf* debtor.
devaluar *vt* to devalue.
devastador, -a *adj* devastating.
devastar *vt* to devastate, to ravage.
devoción *f* devoutness; *(al trabajo etc)* devotion.
devolución *f* return; *(de dinero)* refund.
devolver *(pp* devuelto*)* **1** *vt* to give back; *(dinero)* to refund. **2** *vi (vomitar)* to vomit. **3 devolverse** *vr Am* to go/come back.
devorar *vt* to devour.
devoto, -a 1 *adj* devout. **2** *mf* pious person; *(seguidor)* devotee.
devuelto, -a *pp de* **devolver**.
DF *m abr de* **Distrito Federal** *(en México)* Mexico City.
di *pt indef de* **dar**; *imperativo de* **decir**.
día *m* day; **¿qué d. es hoy?** what's the date today?; **d. a d.** day by day; **de d.** by day; **durante el d.** during the daytime; **un d. sí y otro no** every other day; **pan del d.** fresh bread; **hoy (en) d.** nowadays; **el d. de mañana** in the future; **d. festivo** holiday; **d. laborable** working day; **d. libre** day off; **es de d.** it is daylight; **hace buen/mal d.** it's a nice/rotten day.
diabético, -a *adj & mf* diabetic.
diablo *m* devil.
diadema *f* tiara.
diagnosticar *vt* to diagnose.
diagnóstico *m* diagnosis.
diagonal *adj & f* diagonal; **en d.** diagonally.
dial *m* dial.
dialogar *vi* to have a conversation; *(para negociar)* to talk.
diálogo *m* dialog.
diamante *m* diamond.
diámetro *m* diameter.
diana *f (blanco)* bull's eye.
diapositiva *f* slide.
diariamente *adv* daily.
diario, -a 1 *adj* daily; **a d.** daily. **2** *m* (daily) newspaper; *(memorias)* diary.
diarrea *f* diarrhea.
dibujante *mf* drawer; *(de cómic)* cartoonist; *(delineante) (hombre)* draftsman; *(mujer)* draftswoman.
dibujar *vt* to draw.
dibujo *m* drawing; **dibujos animados** cartoons.
diccionario *m* dictionary.
dicho, -a *adj* said; **mejor d.** or rather; **d. y hecho** no sooner said than done; **dicha persona** the above-mentioned person.
dichoso, -a *adj (feliz)* happy; *fam (maldito)* damned.
diciembre *m* December.
dictado *m* dictation.
dictadura *f* dictatorship.
dictáfono® *m* Dictaphone®.
dictar *vt* to dictate; *(ley)* to enact.
didáctico, -a *adj* didactic.
diecinueve *adj & m inv* nineteen.
dieciocho *adj & m inv* eighteen.
dieciséis *adj & m inv* sixteen.
diecisiete *adj & m inv* seventeen.
diente *m* tooth; **d. de ajo** clove of garlic; **d. de leche** milk tooth; **dientes postizos** false teeth.
diera *subj imperfecto de* **dar**.
diesel *adj & m* diesel.
diestro, -a 1 *adj (hábil)* skilful. **2** *m* bullfighter.
dieta *f (paga)* diet; **estar a d.** to be on a diet; **dietas** expenses.
diez *adj & m inv* ten.
diferencia *f* difference; **a d. de** unlike.
diferenciar 1 *vt* to differentiate *(* **entre** between*)*. **2 diferenciarse** *vr* to differ *(* **de** from*)*.
diferente 1 *adj* different *(* **de** than*)*. **2** *adv* differently.
diferido, -a *adj* **en d.** recorded.
difícil *adj* difficult; **d. de creer/hacer** difficult to believe/do; **es d. que venga** it is unlikely that she'll come.
dificultad *f* difficulty; *(aprieto)* problem.
dificultar *vt* to make difficult.
dificultoso, -a *adj* difficult, hard.
difundir *vt*, **difundirse** *vr* to spread.
difunto, -a *mf* deceased.
digerir *vt* to digest; *fig* to assimilate.
digestión *f* digestion.
digestivo, -a *adj* easy to digest.
digital *adj* digital; **huellas digitales** fingerprints.
dígito *m* digit.
dignarse *vr* to deign *(* **a** to*)*, to condescend *(* **a** to*)*.
dignidad *f* dignity.
digno, -a *adj (merecedor)* worthy; *(decoroso)* decent.
digo *indic pres de* **decir**.
dije *pt indef de* **decir**.
dilatar *vt*, **dilatarse** *vr* to expand.
dilema *m* dilemma.
diluir *vt*, **diluirse** *vr* to dilute.
diluyo *indic pres de* **diluir**.
dimensión *m* dimension; **de grandes dimensiones** very large.
dimisión *f* resignation; **presentar la d.** to hand in one's resignation.
dimitir *vi* to resign *(* **de** from*)*.
dinámico, -a *adj* dynamic.
dinamita *f* dynamite.
dínamo *f*, **dínamo** *f* dynamo.
dinastía *f* dynasty.
dinero *m* money; **d. efectivo** *o* **en metálico** cash.
dinosaurio *m* dinosaur.
dios *m* god; **¡D. mío!** my God!; **¡por D.!** for goodness sake!
diploma *m* diploma.
diplomacia *f* diplomacy.

diplomarse *vr* to graduate.
diplomático, -a 1 *adj* diplomatic. **2** *mf* diplomat.
diptongo *m* diphthong.
diputación *f* **d. provincial** ≃ county council.
diputado, -a *mf & (hombre)* Congressman; *(mujer)* Congresswoman; **Congreso de los Diputados** ≃ Congress.
dique *m* dike.
diré *fut de* **decir**.
dirección *f* direction; *(señas)* address; *(destino)* destination; *(de vehículo)* steering; *(dirigentes)* management; *(cargo)* directorship; *(de un partido)* leadership; **d. prohibida** no entry; **calle de d. única** one-way street.
directa *f (marcha)* top gear.
directamente *adv* directly.
directiva *f* board of directors.
directo, -a *adj* direct; **en d.** live.
director, -a *mf* director; *(de colegio) (hombre)* headmaster; *(mujer)* headmistress; *(de periódico)* editor; **d. de cine** (film) director; **d. de orquesta** conductor; **d. gerente** managing director.
dirigir 1 *vt* to direct; *(empresa)* to manage; *(negocio, colegio)* to run; *(orquesta)* to conduct; *(partido)* to lead; *(periódico)* to edit; **d. la palabra a algn** to speak to sb. **2 dirigirse** *vr* **dirigirse a o hacia** *(ir)* to make one's way towards; *(hablar)* to speak to.
discapacidad *f* disability.
discernir *vt* to discern.
disciplina *f* discipline.
discípulo, -a *mf* disciple.
disco *m* disk; *(de música)* record; **d. compacto** compact disk; **d. duro** hard disk; **d. óptico** optical disk.
discontinuo, -a *adj* discontinuous; **línea discontinua** *(en carretera)* broken line.
discoteca *f* discotheque.
discrepar *vi (disentir)* to disagree *(* **de** with; **en** on*)*.
discreto, -a *adj* discreet.
discriminación *f* discrimination.
disculpa *f* excuse; **dar disculpas** to make excuses; **pedir disculpas a algn** to apologize to sb *(* **por** for*)*.
discurrir *vi* to think.
discurso *m* speech; **dar** *o* **pronunciar un d.** to make a speech.
discusión *f* argument.
discutir 1 *vi* to argue *(* **de** about*)*. **2** *vt* to discuss.
diseñar *vt* to design.
diseño *m* design.
disfrazar 1 *vt* to disguise. **2 disfrazarse** *vr* to disguise oneself.
disfrutar 1 *vi (gozar)* to enjoy oneself; *(poseer)* to enjoy *(* **de** -*)*. **2** *vt* to enjoy.
disgustado, -a *adj* upset, displeased.
disgustar 1 *vt* to upset. **2 disgustarse** *vr (molestarse)* to get upset; *(dos amigos)* to quarrel.
disgusto *m (preocupación)* upset; *(desgracia)* trouble; **llevarse un d.** to get upset; **dar un d. a algn** to upset sb; **a d.** unwillingly.
disimular *vt* to conceal.
disimulo *m* pretense.
disipar 1 *vt (niebla)* to drive away; *(temor, duda)* to dispel. **2 disiparse** *vr (niebla, temor etc)* to disappear.
disketera *f* disk drive.
dislocar *vt* to dislocate.
disminuir 1 *vt* to reduce. **2** *vi* to diminish.
disolvente *adj & m* solvent.
disolver *(pp* disuelto*)* *vt* to dissolve.
disparar 1 *vt (pistola etc)* to fire; *(flecha, balón)* to shoot. **2 dispararse** *vr (arma)* to go off; *(precios)* to rocket.
disparate *m (dicho)* nonsense; **decir disparates** to talk nonsense; *(acto)* foolish act.
disparo *m* shot.
dispersar *vt*, **dispersarse** *vr* to disperse.
disponer *(pp* dispuesto*)* **1** *vt (arreglar)* to arrange; *(ordenar)* to order. **2** *vi* **d. de** to have at one's disposal. **3 disponerse** *vr* to get ready.
disponible *adj* available.
disposición *f (colocación)* layout; *(orden)* law; **a su d.** at your service.
dispositivo *m* device.
disputa *f (discusión)* argument; *(contienda)* contest.
disputar 1 *vt (premio)* to compete for; *(partido)* to play. **2 disputarse** *vr (premio)* to compete for.
disquete *m* diskette, floppy disk.
disquetera *f* disk drive.
distancia *f* distance.
distante *adj* distant.
distinguir 1 *vt (diferenciar)* to distinguish; *(reconocer)* to recognize. **2** *vi (diferenciar)* to discriminate. **3 distinguirse** *vr* to distinguish oneself.
distintivo, -a 1 *adj* distinctive. **2** *m* distinctive mark.
distinto, -a *adj* different.
distracción *f* entertainment; *(pasatiempo)* pastime; *(descuido)* absent-mindedness.
distraer 1 *vt (atención)* to distract; *(divertir)* to entertain. **2 distraerse** *vr (divertirse)* to amuse oneself; *(abstraerse)* to let one's mind wander.
distraído, -a *adj* entertaining; *(abstraído)* absent-minded.
distribuidor, -a 1 *adj* distributing. **2** *mf* distributor.
distribuir *vt* to distribute; *(trabajo)* to share out.
distrito *m* district; **d. postal** postal district.
disturbio *m* riot.
disuadir *vt* to dissuade.
disuelto, -a *pp de* **disolver**.
divagar *vi* to digress, to wander.
diván *m* couch.
diversión *f* fun.
diverso, -a *adj* different; **diversos** various.
divertido, -a *adj* funny.
divertir 1 *vt* to amuse. **2 divertirse** *vr* to enjoy oneself.
dividir *vt*, **dividirse** *vr* to divide *(* **en** into*)*.
divino, -a *adj* divine.
divisa *f* foreign currency.
división *f* division.
divorciado, -a 1 *adj* divorced. **2** *mf (hombre)* divorcé; *(mujer)* divorcée.
divorciarse *vr* to get divorced.
divorcio *m* divorce.
divulgación *f (de ciencia)* popularization.
divulgar *vt (noticia)* to spread; *(ciencia)* to popularize.
DNI *m abr de* **Documento Nacional de Identidad** Identity Card, ID card.
dóberman *m* Doberman (pinscher).
dobladillo *m* hem.

doblar 1 *vt* to double; *(plegar)* to fold up; *(torcer)* to bend; *(la esquina)* to go round. **2** *vi (girar)* to turn. **3 doblarse** *vr (plegarse)* to fold; *(torcerse)* to bend.

doble 1 *adj* double. **2** *m* double; **gana el d. que tú** she earns twice as much as you do.

doce *adj & m inv* twelve.

docena *f* dozen.

docente *adj* teaching; **centro d.** educational center.

dócil *adj* docile.

doctor, -a *mf* doctor.

doctorado *m* doctorate, PhD.

documentación *f* documentation; *(DNI, de conducir etc)* papers *pl.*

documental *adj & m* documentary.

documento *m* document; **d. nacional de identidad** identity card.

dogo *m* bulldog.

dólar *m* dollar.

doler *vi* to ache; **me duele la cabeza** I've got a headache.

dolor *m* pain; *(pena)* grief; **d. de cabeza** headache; **d. de muelas** toothache.

domar *vt* to tame; *(caballo)* to break in.

doméstico, -a *adj* domestic; **animal d.** pet.

domicilio *m* residence; *(señas)* address.

dominante *adj* dominant; *(déspota)* domineering.

dominar 1 *vt* to dominate; *(situación)* to control; *(idioma)* to speak very well. **2** *vi* to dominate; *(resaltar)* to stand out. **3 dominarse** *vr* to control oneself.

domingo *m* Sunday; **D. de Resurrección** *o* **Pascua** Easter Sunday.

dominical 1 *adj* Sunday. **2** *m (suplemento)* Sunday supplement.

dominicano, -a *adj & mf* Dominican; **República Dominicana** Dominican Republic.

dominio *m (poder)* control; *(de un idioma)* command; *(territorio)* dominion.

dominó, dómino *m* dominoes *pl.*

don¹ *m (habilidad)* gift; **tener el d. de** to have a knack for.

don² *m* Señor D. José García Mr José Garcia; **D. Fulano de Tal** Mr So-and-So.

donante *mf* donor; **d. de sangre** blood donor.

donar *vt (sangre etc)* to donate.

donativo *m* donation.

dónde *adv* where *(in questions)*; **¿por d. se va a la playa?** which way is it to the beach?

donde *adv rel* where; **a** *o* **en d.** where; **de** *o* **desde d.** from where.

doña *f* Señora D. Leonor Benítez Mrs Leonor Benítez.

dorada *f (pez)* gilthead bream.

dorado, -a *adj* golden.

dormido, -a *adj* asleep; **quedarse d.** to fall asleep; *(no despertarse)* to oversleep.

dormilón, -ona *fam* **1** *adj* sleepy-headed. **2** *mf* sleepyhead.

dormir 1 *vi* to sleep. **2** *vt* **d. la siesta** to have an afternoon nap. **2 dormirse** *vr* to fall asleep; **se me ha dormido el brazo** my arm has gone to sleep.

dormitorio *m (de una casa)* bedroom; *(de colegio, residencia)* dormitory.

dorsal 1 *adj* **espina d.** spine. **2** *m (de camiseta)* number.

dorso *m* back; **instrucciones al d.** instructions over; **véase al d.** see overleaf.

dos 1 *adj* two. **2** *m inv* two; **los d.** both; **nosotros/vosotros d.** both of us/you.

doscientos, -as *adj & mf* two hundred.

dosis *f inv* dose.

dotar *vt* **d. de** to provide with.

doy *indic pres de* **dar**.

Dr. *abr de* **doctor** doctor, Dr.

Dra. *abr de* **doctora** doctor, Dr.

dragón *m* dragon.

drama *m* drama.

dramático, -a *adj* dramatic.

drástico, -a *adj* drastic.

droga *f* drug; **d. blanda/dura** soft/hard drug.

drogadicto, -a *mf* drug addict.

drogar 1 *vt* to drug. **2 drogarse** *vr* to take drugs.

droguería *f* hardware and household goods shop.

ducha *f* shower; **darse/tomar una d.** to take/have a shower.

ducharse *vr* to take a shower.

duda *f* doubt; **sin d.** without a doubt; **no cabe d.** (there is) no doubt.

dudar 1 *vi* to doubt; *(vacilar)* to hesitate (**en** to). **2** *vt* to doubt.

dudoso, -a *adj (poco honrado)* dubious; **ser d.** *(incierto)* to be uncertain *o* doubtful; **estar d.** *(indeciso)* to be undecided.

dueña *f* owner; *(de pensión)* landlady.

dueño *m* owner; *(de casa etc)* landlord.

dulce 1 *adj (sabor)* sweet; *(carácter, voz)* gentle; *(agua)* fresh. **2** *m (pastel)* cake; *(caramelo)* candy.

duna *f* dune.

duodécimo, -a *adj & mf* twelfth.

duplicar 1 *vt* to duplicate; *(cifras)* to double. **2 duplicarse** *vr* to double.

duración *f* duration.

duradero, -a *adj* durable, lasting.

durante *prep* during.

durar *vi* to last.

durazno *m Am (fruto)* peach; *(árbol)* peach tree.

dureza *f* hardness; *(severidad)* severity; *(callosidad)* corn.

duro, -a 1 *adj* hard; *(resistente)* tough. **2** *adv* hard.

E

e *conj (before words beginning with* **i** *or* **hi***)* and.

ébano *m* ebony.

echar 1 *vt* to throw; *(carta)* to post; *(vino, agua)* to pour; *(expulsar)* to throw out; *(despedir)* to sack; *(humo, olor etc)* to give off; **e. una mano** to give a hand; **e. una mirada/una ojeada** to have a look/a quick look; **e. gasolina al coche** to put gas in the car; **e. de menos** *o* **en falta** to miss. **2** *vi* (**+ a +** *infinitivo) (empezar)* to begin to; **echó a correr** he ran off. **3 echarse** *vr (tumbarse)* to lie down; *(lanzarse)* to throw oneself; (**+ a +** *infinitivo) (empezar)* to begin to; *fig* **echarse atrás** to get cold feet; **echarse a llorar** to burst into tears; **echarse a perder** *(comida)* to go bad.

eclesiástico, -a 1 *adj* ecclesiastical. **2** *m* clergyman.

eclipse *m* eclipse.

eco *m* echo.

ecológico, -a *adj* ecological.

ecologista 1 *adj* ecological. **2** *mf* ecologist.

economía *f* economy; *(ciencia)* economics *sing.*

económico, -a *adj* economic; *(barato)* economical.

economizar *vti* to economize.

ecuación *f* equation.

ecuador *m* equator.

ecuánime *adj (temperamento)* even-tempered; *(juicio)* impartial.

ecuatoriano, -a *adj & mf* Ecuadorian.

ecuestre *adj* equestrian.

edad *f* age; **¿qué e. tienes?** how old are you?; **E. Media** Middle Ages *pl.*

edición *f (publicación)* publication; *(conjunto de ejemplares)* edition.

edicto *m* edict.

edificar *vt* to build.

edificio *m* building.

edil, -a *mf* town councilor.

editar *vt (libro, periódico)* to publish; *(disco)* to release; *(en ordenador)* to edit.

editor, -a 1 *adj* publishing. **2** *mf* publisher. **3** *m* **e. de textos** text editor.

editorial 1 *adj* publishing. **2** *f* publishing house. **3** *m* editorial.

edredón *m* duvet, eiderdown.

educación *f* education; *(formación)* upbringing; **buena/mala e.** *(modales)* good/bad manners; **falta de e.** bad manners.

educado, -a *adj* polite.

educar *vt (hijos)* to raise.

educativo, -a *adj* educational.

edulcorante *m* sweetener.

efectivamente *adv* yes indeed!

efectivo, -a 1 *adj* effective; **hacer e. un cheque** to cash a check. **2** *m* **en e.** in cash.

efecto *m (resultado)* effect; *(impresión)* impression; **efectos personales** personal belongings; **en e.** yes indeed!

efectuar *vt* to carry out; *(viaje)* to make; *(pedido)* to place.

efervescente *adj* effervescent; **aspirina e.** soluble aspirin.

eficacia *f (de persona)* efficiency; *(de remedio, medida)* effectiveness.

eficaz *adj (persona)* efficient; *(remedio, medida)* effective.

eficiencia *f* efficiency.

eficiente *adj* efficient.

efusivo, -a *adj* effusive.

egipcio, -a *adj & mf* Egyptian.

egoísmo *m* egoism.

egoísta 1 *adj* selfish. **2** *mf* ego(t)ist.

egresar *vi Am* to leave school; to graduate.

ej. *abr de* **ejemplo** example.

eje *m (de rueda)* axle; *(de máquina)* shaft.

ejecutar *vt (ajusticiar)* to execute; *(sinfonía)* to perform.

ejecutiva *f (gobierno)* executive.

ejecutivo, -a 1 *adj* executive; **el poder e.** the government. **2** *mf* executive.

ejemplar 1 *m (de libro)* copy; *(de revista, periódico)* issue; *(especimen)* specimen. **2** *adj* exemplary.

ejemplo *m* example; **por e.** for example; **dar e.** to set an example.

ejercer *vt (profesión etc)* to practice; *(influencia)* to exert.

ejercicio *m* exercise; *(de profesión)* practice; **hacer e.** to take exercise.

ejercitar *vt* to practice.

ejército *m* army.

el 1 *art def m* the; **el Sr. García** Mr. Garcia. ▪ *(no se traduce)* **el hambre/destino** hunger/fate. ▪ *(con partes del cuerpo, prendas de vestir)* **me he cortado el dedo** I've cut my finger; **métetelo en el bolsillo** put it in your pocket. ▪ *(con días de la semana)* **el lunes** on Monday. **2** *pron* the one; **el de las once** the eleven o'clock one; **el que tienes en la mano** the one you've got in your hand; **el que quieras** whichever one you want; **el de tu amigo** your friend's.

él *pron pers (sujeto) (persona)* he; *(animal, cosa)* it; *(complemento) (persona)* him; *(animal, cosa)* it.

elaboración *f (de un producto)* production.

elaborar *vt (producto)* to produce.

elasticidad *f* elasticity; *fig* flexibility.

elástico, -a *adj & m* elastic.

elección *f* choice; *(votación)* election.

electorado *m* electorate *pl.*

electoral *adj* electoral; **campaña e.** election campaign; **colegio e.** polling station.

electricidad *f* electricity.

electricista *mf* electrician.

eléctrico, -a *adj* electric.

electrocutar *vt* to electrocute.

electrodoméstico *m* (domestic) electrical appliance.

electrónico, -a *adj* electronic.

elefante *m* elephant.

elegancia *f* elegance.

elegante *adj* elegant.

elegir *vt* to choose; *(en votación)* to elect.

elemental *adj (fundamental)* basic; *(simple)* elementary.

elemento *m* element; *(componente)* component.

elepé *m* LP (record).

elevación *f* elevation; *(de precios)* rise.

elevado, -a *adj* high; *(edificio)* tall.

elevalunas *m inv* **e. eléctrico** electric windows *pl.*

elevar 1 *vt* to raise. **2 elevarse** *vr (subir)* to rise; **elevarse a** *(cantidad)* to come to.

elijo *indic pres de* **elegir**.

eliminar *vt* to eliminate.

eliminatoria *f* heat, qualifying round.

eliminatorio, -a *adj* qualifying.

ella *pron pers f (sujeto)* she; *(animal, cosa)* it, she; *(complemento)* her; *(animal, cosa)* it, her.

ellas *pron pers fpl (sujeto)* they; *(complemento)* them.

ello *pron pers neutro* it; **por e.** for that reason.

ellos *pron pers mpl (sujeto)* they; *(complemento)* them.

elocuente *adj* eloquent.

elogiar *vt* to praise.

elote *m CAm, Méx* tender corncob.

eludir *vt* to avoid.

embajada *f* embassy.

embajador, -a *mf* ambassador.

embalaje *m* packing.

embalse *m* reservoir; *(presa)* dam.

embarazada 1 *adj* pregnant. **2** *f* pregnant woman.

embarazo *m (preñez)* pregnancy; *(turbación)* embarrassment.

embarazoso, -a *adj* embarrassing.

embarcación *f* boat.

embarcadero *m* quay.

embarcar 1 *vt* to ship. **2** *vi* to go on board. **3 embarcarse** *vr* to go on board (**en** -); *(en avión)* to board (**en** -).

embargar *vt (bienes)* to seize, to impound; *fig* **le embarga la emoción** he's overwhelmed with joy.

embarque *m (de persona)* boarding; *(de mercancías)* loading; **tarjeta de e.** boarding card.
embellecer *vt* to embellish.
embestida *f* onslaught; *(de toro)* charge.
embestir *vt (a torero)* to charge; *(atacar)* to attack.
emblema *m* emblem.
embobado, -a *adj* fascinated.
embobarse *vr* to be fascinated *o* besotted (**con, de** by).
émbolo *m* piston.
embolsar *vt*, **embolsarse** *vr* to pocket.
emborrachar *vt*, **emborracharse** *vr* to get drunk.
emboscada *f* ambush.
embotellamiento *m* traffic jam.
embotellar *vt* to bottle; *(tráfico)* to block.
embrague *m* clutch.
embriagar 1 *vt* to intoxicate. **2 embriagarse** *vr* to get drunk.
embriaguez *f* intoxication.
embrollar 1 *vt* to confuse. **2 embrollarse** *vr* to get confused.
embrujado, -a *adj (sitio)* haunted.
embudo *m* funnel.
embuste *m* lie.
embustero, -a *mf* cheat.
embutido *m* sausage.
emergencia *f* emergency; **salida de e.** emergency exit; **en caso de e.** in an emergency.
emigración *f* emigration.
emigrante *adj & mf* emigrant.
emigrar *vi* to emigrate.
emisión *f* emission; *(de radio, TV)* broadcasting.
emisora *f (de radio)* radio station; *(de televisión)* television station.
emitir *vt* to emit; *(luz, calor)* to give off; *(opinión, juicio)* to express; *(programa)* to transmit.
emoción *f* emotion; *(excitación)* excitement; **¡qué e.!** how exciting!
emocionado, -a *adj* deeply moved *o* touched.
emocionante *adj (conmovedor)* moving; *(excitante)* exciting.
emocionar 1 *vt (conmover)* to move; *(excitar)* to thrill. **2 emocionarse** *vr (conmoverse)* to be moved; *(excitarse)* to get excited.
emotivo, -a *adj* emotional.
empacar *vt Am (mercancías)* to pack.
empacho *m (de comida)* indigestion.
empalagoso, -a *adj (dulce)* sickly sweet.
empalizada *f* fence.
empalmar 1 *vt (unir)* to join; *(cuerdas, cables)* to splice. **2** *vi* to converge; *(trenes)* to connect.
empanada *f* pie.
empanadilla *f* pastry.
empañar *vt*, **empañarse** *vr (cristales)* to steam up.
empapar 1 *vt (mojar)* to soak; *(absorber)* to soak up. **2 empaparse** *vr (persona)* to get soaked; *fam fig* to take in (**de -**).
empapelar *vt* to wallpaper.
empaquetar *vt* to pack.
emparedado *m* sandwich.
empastar *vt (diente)* to fill.
empaste *m (de diente)* filling.
empatar *vi* to draw; *Am (unir)* to join.
empate *m* draw.
empedrado, -a 1 *adj* cobbled. **2** *m (adoquines)* cobblestones *pl.*
empeine *m (de pie, de zapato)* instep.
empellón *m* shove.
empeñar 1 *vt* to pawn. **2 empeñarse** *vr (insistir)* to insist (**en** on); *(endeudarse)* to get into debt.
empeño *m (insistencia)* insistence; *(deuda)* pledge.
empeoramiento *m* deterioration, worsening.
empeorar 1 *vi* to deteriorate. **2** *vt* to make worse. **3 empeorarse** *vr* to deteriorate.
emperador *m* emperor.
empezar *vti* to begin, start (**a hacer algo** to do sth).
empinado, -a *adj (cuesta)* steep.
empinar 1 *vt* to raise. **2 empinarse** *vr (persona)* to stand on tiptoe.
emplazamiento *m (colocación)* location.
empleado, -a *mf* employee; *(de oficina, banco)* clerk.
emplear *vt (usar)* to use; *(contratar)* to employ; *(dinero, tiempo)* to spend.
empleo *m* employment; *(oficio)* job; *(uso)* use; **modo de e.** instructions for use.
emplomar *vt Am (diente)* to fill.
empobrecer 1 *vt* to impoverish. **2 empobrecerse** *vr* to become impoverished.
empobrecimiento *m* impoverishment.
empollón, -ona *mf fam* grind.
emporio *m Am* department store.
empotrado, -a *adj* fitted.
emprendedor, -a *adj* enterprising.
emprender *vt* to undertake; *fam* **emprenderla con algn** to pick on sb.
empresa *f* firm; *(tarea)* undertaking.
empresarial *adj (de empresa)* business; *(espíritu)* entrepreneurial; **(ciencias) empresariales** business studies.
empresario, -a *mf (hombre)* businessman; *(mujer)* businesswoman; *(patrón)* employer.
empujar *vt* to push, to shove.
empujón *m* push, shove.
emulsión *f* emulsion.
en *prep (posición)* in; at; *(sobre)* on; **en Madrid/Bolivia** in Madrid/Bolivia; **en casa/el trabajo** at home/work; **en la mesa** on the table. ▪ *(movimiento)* into; **entrar en la casa** to go into the house. ▪ *(tiempo)* in; on; at; **en 1940** in 1940; *Am* **en la mañana** in the morning; **cae en martes** it falls on a Tuesday; **en ese momento** at that moment. ▪ *(transporte)* by; **en coche/tren** by car/train. ▪ *(modo)* **en español** in Spanish; **en broma** jokingly; **en serio** seriously. ▪ *(reducción, aumento)* by; **los precios aumentaron en un diez por ciento** the prices went up by ten percent. ▪ *(tema, materia)* at, in; **bueno en deportes** good at sports; **experto en política** expert in politics. ▪ *(división, separación)* in; **lo dividió en tres partes** he divided it in three. ▪ *(con infinitivo)* **fue rápido en responder** he was quick to answer.
enaguas *fpl* petticoat *sing.*
enamorado, -a 1 *adj* in love. **2** *mf* person in love.
enamorar 1 *vt* to win the heart of. **2 enamorarse** *vr* to fall in love (**de** with).
enano, -a *adj & mf* dwarf.
encabezamiento *m (de carta)* heading; *(de periódico)* headline.
encabezar *vt (carta, lista)* to head; *(periódico)* to lead; *(rebelión, carrera, movimiento)* to lead.
encajar 1 *vt (ajustar)* to insert; **e. un golpe a algn** to land sb a blow. **2** *vi (ajustarse)* to fit; **e.** to fit (in) with.
encaje *m* lace.
encallar *vi* to run aground.
encantado, -a *adj (contento)* delighted; *(embrujado)* enchanted; **e. de conocerle** pleased to meet you.

encantador, -a *adj* charming.
encantar *vt (hechizar)* to cast a spell on; **me encanta nadar** I love swimming.
encanto *m* charm; **ser un e.** to be charming.
encapricharse *vr* to set one's mind (**con** on).
encaramarse *vr* to climb up.
encarar 1 *vt* to face. **2 encararse** *vr* **encararse con** to face up to.
encarcelar *vt* to imprison.
encarecer 1 *vt* to put up the price of. **2 encarecerse** *vr* to go up (in price).
encarecidamente *adv* earnestly, insistently.
encargado, -a 1 *mf* manager; *(responsable)* person in charge. **2** *adj* in charge.
encargar 1 *vt* to entrust with; *(mercancías)* to order. **2 encargarse** *vr* **encargarse de** to see to.
encargo *m* order; *(recado)* errand; *(tarea)* job.
encariñarse *vr* to become fond (**con** of).
encarnado, -a *adj (rojo)* red.
encarnizado, -a *adj* fierce.
encauzar *vt* to channel.
encendedor *m* lighter.
encender 1 *vt (luz, radio, tele)* to switch on, to put on; *(cigarro, vela, fuego)* to light; *(cerilla)* to strike. **2 encenderse** *vr (fuego)* to catch; *(lámpara etc)* to go *o* come on.
encendido *m* ignition.
encerado *m (pizarra)* blackboard.
encerrar 1 *vt* to shut in; *(con llave)* to lock in. **2 encerrarse** *vr* to shut oneself in; *(con llave)* lock oneself in.
enchaquetado, -a *adj* smartly dressed.
encharcar *vt*, **encharcarse** *vr* to flood.
enchufado, -a 1 *adj fig fam* **estar e.** to have good connections. **2** *mf (favorito)* pet.
enchufar *vt* to plug in; *(unir)* to join.
enchufe *m (hembra)* socket; *(macho)* plug; *fam* contact.
encía *f* gum.
enciclopedia *f* encyclopedia.
encima 1 *adv* on top; *(arriba)* above; *(en el aire)* overhead; *(además)* besides. **2** *prep* **e. de** *(sobre)* on; *(además)* besides; **ahí e.** up there; **por e.** above; **leer un libro por e.** to skim through a book.
encina *f* holm oak.
encinta *adj* pregnant.
enclenque *adj (débil)* puny; *(enfermizo)* sickly.
encoger 1 *vti* to contract; *(prenda)* to shrink. **2 encogerse** *vr (contraerse)* to contract; *(prenda)* to shrink; **encogerse de hombros** to shrug (one's shoulders).
encolar *vt (papel)* to paste; *(madera)* to glue.
encolerizar 1 *vt* to infuriate. **2 encolerizarse** *vr* to become furious.
encono *m* spitefulness.
encontrar 1 *vt (hallar)* to find; *(a persona)* to meet; *(problema)* to come up against. **2 encontrarse** *vr (sentirse)* to feel, to be; *(estar)* to be; **encontrarse a gusto** to feel comfortable; **encontrarse con algn** to meet sb.
encontronazo *m (choque)* clash.
encorvarse *vr* to bend (over).
encrucijada *f* crossroads.
encuadernar *vt* to bind.
encubrir *vt* to conceal.
encuentro *m* meeting; *(deportivo)* match.
encuesta *f (sondeo)* (opinion) poll; *(investigación)* investigation.
encuestar *vt* to poll.
endeble *adj* weak.
endémico, -a *adj* endemic.
enderezar 1 *vt (poner derecho)* to straighten out; *(poner vertical)* to set upright. **2 enderezarse** *vr* to straighten up.
endeudarse *vr* to get into debt.
endiablado, -a *adj* mischievous.
endibia *f* endive.
endosar *vt (cheque)* to endorse; *fam (tarea)* to lumber with.
endulzar *vt* to sweeten.
endurecer *vt*, **endurecerse** *vr* to harden.
enemigo, -a *adj & mf* enemy.
enemistad *f* hostility, enmity.
enemistar 1 *vt* to set at odds. **2 enemistarse** *vr* to become enemies; **enemistarse con algn** to fall out with sb.
energético, -a *adj* energy.
energía *f* energy; **e. nuclear** nuclear power; **e. vital** vitality.
enérgico, -a *adj* energetic; *(tono)* emphatic.
enero *m* January.
enfadado, -a *adj* angry.
enfadar 1 *vt* to make angry. **2 enfadarse** *vr* to get angry (**con** with); *(dos personas)* to fall out.
enfado *m* anger.
énfasis *m inv* emphasis.
enfático, -a *adj* emphatic.
enfatizar *vt* to emphasize, to stress.
enfermar *vi*, **enfermarse** *vr Am* to fall ill.
enfermedad *f* illness; *(contagiosa)* disease.
enfermería *f* infirmary.
enfermero, -a *mf (mujer)* nurse; *(hombre)* male nurse.
enfermizo, -a *adj* unhealthy.
enfermo, -a 1 *adj* ill. **2** *mf* ill person; *(paciente)* patient.
enfocar *vt (imagen)* to focus; *(tema)* to approach; *(con linterna)* to shine a light on.
enfrentamiento *m* clash.
enfrentar 1 *vt (situación, peligro)* to confront; *(enemistar)* to set at odds. **2 enfrentarse** *vr* **enfrentarse con** *o* **a** *(encararse)* to confront.
enfrente *adv* opposite; **la casa de e.** the house opposite. **2** *prep* **e. de** opposite.
enfriamiento *m (proceso)* cooling; *(catarro)* chill.
enfriar 1 *vt* to cool (down). **2 enfriarse** *vr* to get cold; *(resfriarse)* to catch a cold.
enfurecer 1 *vt* to enrage. **2 enfurecerse** *vr* to get furious.
engalanar 1 *vt* to deck out, to adorn. **2 engalanarse** *vr* to dress up, to get dressed up.
enganchar 1 *vt* to hook. **2 engancharse** *vr (ropa)* to get caught; *(persona)* to get hooked.
engañar 1 *vt* to deceive; *(estafar)* to cheat; *(mentir a)* to lie to; *(al marido, mujer)* to be unfaithful to. **2 engañarse** *vr* to deceive oneself.
engaño *m* deceit; *(estafa)* fraud; *(mentira)* lie.
engañoso, -a *adj (palabras)* deceitful; *(apariencias)* deceptive.
engarzar *vt (unir)* to link; *(engastar)* to mount.
engatusar *vt fam* to coax; **e. a algn para que haga algo** to coax sb into doing sth.
engendrar *vt fig* to engender.
englobar *vt* to include.
engordar 1 *vt* to make fat. **2** *vi* to put on weight; *(comida, bebida)* to be fattening.
engorro *m* nuisance.
engranaje *m* gearing.
engrasar *vt (lubricar)* to lubricate; *(manchar)* to make greasy.

engreído, -a *adj* conceited.
engrudo *m* paste.
engullir *vt* to gobble up.
enharinar *vt* to cover with flour.
enhebrar *vt* to thread.
enhorabuena *f* congratulations *pl*; **dar la e. a algn** to congratulate sb.
enigma *m* enigma.
enjabonar *vt* to soap.
enjambre *m* swarm.
enjaular *vt (animal)* to cage.
enjuagar *vt* to rinse.
enjugar *vt,* **enjugarse** *vr (secar)* to mop up; *(lágrimas)* to wipe away.
enjuiciar *vt (criminal)* to prosecute.
enjuto, -a *adj* lean, skinny.
enlace *m* connection; *(casamiento)* marriage.
enlatado, -a *adj* canned.
enlatar *vt* to can.
enlazar *vti* to connect (**con** with).
enloquecedor, -a *adj* maddening.
enloquecer 1 *vi* to go mad. **2** *vt* to drive mad. **3 enloquecerse** *vr* to go mad.
enmarañar 1 *vt (pelo)* to tangle; *(complicar)* to complicate. **2 enmarañarse** *vr (pelo)* to get tangled.
enmarcar *vt* to frame.
enmascarar *vt (problema, la verdad)* to disguise.
enmendar 1 *vt (corregir)* to put right. **2 enmendarse** *vr (persona)* to mend one's ways.
enmienda *f* correction; *(de ley)* amendment.
enmohecerse *vr (metal)* to rust; *(comida)* to get moldy.
enmoquetar *vt* to carpet.
enmudecer *vi* to fall silent; *(por sorpresa etc)* to be dumbstruck.
ennegrecer *vt,* **ennegrecerse** *vr* to turn black.
enojado, -a *adj* angry.
enojar 1 *vt* to anger. **2 enojarse** *vr* to get angry.
enojo *m* anger, annoyance.
enorgullecer 1 *vt* to fill with pride. **2 enorgullecerse** *vr* to be proud (**de** of).
enorme *adj* enormous.
enraizado, -a *adj* rooted.
enraizar *vi,* **enraizarse** *vr (planta, costumbre)* to take root.
enrarecerse *vr (aire)* to become rarefied.
enredadera *f* climbing plant.
enredar 1 *vt (enmarañar)* to entangle; *fig (implicar)* to involve (**en** in). **2 enredarse** *vr (enmarañarse)* to get tangled up; *fig (involucrarse)* to get involved, to get entangled (**con** with).
enredo *m (maraña)* tangle; *fig (lío)* muddle, mess.
enrejado *m (de ventana)* lattice.
enrevesado, -a *adj* complicated, difficult.
enriquecer 1 *vt* to make rich; *fig* to enrich. **2 enriquecerse** *vr* to become rich; *fig* to become enriched.
enrojecer 1 *vt* to redden, to turn red. **2** *vi (ruborizarse)* to blush.
enrollado, -a *adj* rolled up.
enrollar 1 *vt* to roll up; *(cable)* to coil; *(hilo)* to wind up. **2 enrollarse** *vr fam (hablar)* to go on and on.
enroscar 1 *vt* to coil (round); *(tornillo)* to screw in; *(tapón)* to screw on. **2 enroscarse** *vr* to coil.
ensaimada *f* kind of spiral pastry from Majorca.
ensalada *f* salad.
ensaladera *f* salad bowl.
ensaladilla rusa *f* Russian salad.
ensamblaje *m* assembly.
ensamblar *vt* to assemble.
ensanchar 1 *vt* to widen; *(ropa)* to let out. **2 ensancharse** *vr* to widen.
ensangrentado, -a *adj* blood-stained.
ensañarse *vr* to be brutal (**con** with); *(cebarse)* to delight in tormenting (**con** -).
ensayar *vt* to try out; *(obra, canción)* to rehearse.
ensayo *m* trial; *(de obra)* rehearsal; **e. general** dress rehearsal.
enseguida, en seguida *adv (inmediatamente)* at once, straight away; *(poco después)* in a minute, soon.
ensenada *f* inlet.
enseñanza *f (educación)* education; *(de idioma etc)* teaching.
enseñar *vt* to teach; *(mostrar)* to show; *(señalar)* to point out; **e. a algn a hacer algo** to teach sb how to do sth.
ensimismado, -a *adj (absorbido)* engrossed; *(abstraído)* lost in thought.
ensimismarse *vr (absorberse)* to become engrossed; *(abstraerse)* to be lost in thought.
ensombrecer 1 *vt* to cast a shadow over. **2 ensombrecerse** *vr* to darken.
ensopar *vt Am* to soak.
ensordecedor, -a *adj* deafening.
ensuciar *vt,* **ensuciarse** *vr* to get dirty.
ensueño *m* dream.
entablar *vt (conversación)* to begin; *(amistad)* to strike up.
entallado, -a *adj (vestido)* close-fitting; *(camisa)* fitted.
entender 1 *vt (comprender)* to understand; **dar a algn a e. que ...** to give sb to understand that .... **2** *vi (comprender)* to understand; **e. de** *(saber)* to know about. **3 entenderse** *vr (comprenderse)* to be understood.
entendimiento *m* understanding.
enteramente *adv* entirely.
enterarse *vr* to find out; **me he enterado de que ...** I understand ...; **ni me enteré** I didn't even realize it.
entereza *f* strength of character.
enternecedor, -a *adj* moving.
enternecer 1 *vt* to move. **2 enternecerse** *vr* to be moved.
entero, -a *adj (completo)* entire, whole.
enterrador *nm* gravedigger.
enterrar *vt* to bury.
entidad *f* organization, entity.
entierro *m* burial; *(ceremonia)* funeral.
entonar *vt (canción)* to intone, to sing.
entonces *adv* then; **por aquel e.** at that time.
entornar *vt (ojos etc)* to half-close; *(puerta)* to leave ajar.
entorno *m* environment.
entorpecer *vt (obstaculizar)* to hinder.
entrada *f* entrance; *(billete)* ticket; *(recaudación)* takings *pl*; *(plato)* starter; **entradas** *(en la frente)* receding hairline.
entrañable *adj (lugar)* intimate, close; *(persona)* affectionate, warm-hearted.
entrar *vi* to enter; *(venir dentro)* to come in; *(ir dentro)* to go in; *(encajar)* to fit; **me entró dolor de cabeza** I got a headache; **me entraron ganas de reír** I felt like laughing. **2** *vt (datos)* to enter.
entre *prep (dos)* between; *(más de dos)* among(st).
entreabierto, -a *adj (ojos etc)* half-open; *(puerta)* ajar.

entreacto *m* interval.
entrecejo *m* space between the eyebrows.
entrecortado, -a *adj (voz)* faltering.
entrecot *m* fillet steak.
entredicho *m* **estar en e.** to be suspect; **poner algo en e.** to bring sth into question.
entrega *f (de productos)* delivery; *(de premios)* presentation; *(devoción)* selflessness.
entregar 1 *vt (dar)* to hand over; *(deberes etc)* to hand in; *(mercancía)* to deliver. **2 entregarse** *vr (rendirse)* to give in; **entregarse a** to devote oneself to.
entrelazar *vt,* **entrelazarse** *vr* to entwine.
entremedias *adv* in between.
entremés *m* hors d'oeuvres.
entremeterse *vr* = **entrometerse**.
entremezclarse *vr* to mix, to mingle.
entrenador, -a *mf* trainer.
entrenamiento *m* training.
entrenar *vi,* **entrenarse** *vr* to train.
entresuelo *m* mezzanine.
entretanto *adv* meanwhile.
entretención *f Am* entertainment.
entretener 1 *vt (divertir)* to entertain; *(retrasar)* to delay; *(detener)* to detain. **2 entretenerse** *vr (distraerse)* to amuse oneself; *(retrasarse)* to be held up.
entretenido, -a *adj* entertaining.
entretenimiento *m* entertainment.
entretiempo *adj* **ropa de e.** lightweight clothing.
entrever *vt* to glimpse, to catch sight of; *fig* **dejó e. que ...** she hinted that ...
entrevista *f* interview.
entrevistador, -a *mf* interviewer.
entrevistar 1 *vt* to interview. **2 entrevistarse** *vr* **entrevistarse con algn** to have an interview with sb.
entristecer 1 *vt* to sadden. **2 entristecerse** *vr* to be sad (**por** about).
entrometerse *vr* to meddle (**en** in, with).
entumecerse *vr* to go numb.
enturbiar 1 *vt* to make cloudy. **2 enturbiarse** *vr* to become cloudy.
entusiasmar 1 *vt* to fill with enthusiasm. **2 entusiasmarse** *vr* to get enthusiastic (**con** about).
entusiasmo *m* enthusiasm; **con e.** enthusiastically.
enumerar *vt* to enumerate.
envasar *vt (embotellar)* to bottle; *(empaquetar)* to pack; *(enlatar)* to can, to tin.
envase *m (recipiente)* container; *(botella vacía)* empty.
envejecer *vti* to age.
envejecimiento *m* aging.
envenenar *vt* to poison.
envergadura *f* **de gran e.** large-scale.
enviar *vt* to send.
envidia *f* envy; **tener e. de algn** to envy sb.
envidiable *adj* enviable.
envidiar *vt* to envy.
envidioso, -a *adj* envious.
envío *m* sending; *(remesa)* consignment; *(paquete)* parcel; **gastos de e.** postage and packing.
enviudar *vi (hombre)* to become a widower; *(mujer)* to become a widow.
envoltorio *m,* **envoltura** *f* wrapping.
envolver *(pp* **envuelto)** **1** *vt (con papel)* to wrap; *(en complot etc)* to involve (**en** in). **2 envolverse** *vr* to wrap oneself up (**en** in).
enyesar *vt* to put in plaster.
epidemia *f* epidemic.
episodio *m* episode.
época *f* time; *(periodo)* period.
equilibrar *vt* to balance.
equilibrio *m* balance.
equilibrista *mf* tightrope walker; *Am* opportunist.
equipaje *m* luggage; **hacer el e.** to pack.
equipar *vt* to equip (**con, de** with).
equiparar *vt* to compare (**con** with).
equipo *m (de expertos, jugadores)* team; *(aparatos)* equipment; *(ropas)* outfit; **e. de alta fidelidad** hi-fi stereo system.
equitación *f* horseriding.
equitativo, -a *adj* equitable.
equivalente *adj* equivalent.
equivaler *vi* to be equivalent (**to** a).
equivocación *f* error.
equivocado, -a *adj* mistaken.
equivocar 1 *vt* to mix up. **2 equivocarse** *vr* to make a mistake.
equívoco, -a *adj* misleading.
era *pt imperfecto de* **ser**.
eras *pt imperfecto de* **ser**.
eres *indic pres de* **ser**.
erguir *vt* to erect.
erizarse *vr* to stand on end.
erizo *m* hedgehog; **e. de mar, e. marino** sea urchin.
ermita *f* shrine.
erosión *f* erosion.
erosionar *vt* to erode.
erótico, -a *adj* erotic.
erradicar *vt* to eradicate.
errante *adj* wandering.
errar 1 *vt* to miss, to get wrong. **2** *vi (vagar)* to wander, to roam; *(fallar)* to err.
errata *f* misprint.
erróneo, -a *adj* erroneous.
error *m* mistake.
eructar *vi* to belch.
eructo *m* belch, burp.
erudito, -a 1 *adj* erudite. **2** *mf* scholar.
erupción *f (de volcán)* eruption; *(en la piel)* rash.
es *indic pres de* **ser**.
esa *adj dem* that.
ésa *pron dem ver* **ése**.
esbelto, -a *adj* slender.
esbozar *vt* to sketch, to outline.
escabeche *m* brine.
escabullirse *vr* to scurry off.
escala *f* scale; *(parada) (de barco)* port of call; *(escalera)* ladder; **a gran e.** on a large scale; **hacer e. en** to stop over in.
escalada *f* climb.
escalador, -a *mf* climber.
escalar *vt* to climb.

escaldar *vt* to scald.
escalera *f* stair; *(escala)* ladder; **e. de incendios** fire escape; **e. mecánica** escalator.
escalerilla *f* steps *pl.*
escalfar *vt* to poach.
escalinata *f* stoop.
escalofriante *adj* hair-raising, bloodcurdling.
escalofrío *m* shiver.
escalón *m* step; **e. lateral** *(en letrero)* ramp.
escalonar *vt* to space out.
escama *f (de animal)* scale; *(de jabón)* flake.
escamotear *vt* to cheat out of.
escampar *vi* to clear up.
escandalizar **1** *vt* to scandalize. **2 escandalizarse** *vr* to be shocked (**de** at, by).
escándalo *m (alboroto)* racket; *(desvergüenza)* scandal; **armar un e.** to kick up a fuss.
escandaloso, -a *adj (ruidoso)* noisy, rowdy; *(ofensivo)* scandalous.
escanear *vt* to scan.
escáner *m* scanner.
escaño *m (parlamentario)* seat.
escapada *f (de prisión)* escape.
escapar **1** *vi* to escape. **2 escaparse** *vr* to escape; *(gas etc)* to leak.
escaparate *m* shop window.
escapatoria *f* escape; **no tener e.** to have no way out.
escape *m (huida)* escape; *(de gas etc)* leak; **tubo de e.** exhaust (pipe).
escarabajo *m* beetle.
escarbar *vt (suelo)* to scratch.
escarcha *f* frost.
escarlata *adj* scarlet.
escarlatina *f* scarlet fever.
escarmentar *vi* to learn one's lesson.
escarmiento *m* lesson.
escarola *f* escarole.
escarpado, -a *adj (paisaje)* craggy.
escasear *vi* to be scarce.
escasez *f* scarcity.
escaso, -a *adj* scarce; *(dinero)* tight; *(conocimientos)* scant.
escatimar *vt* to skimp on; **no escatimó esfuerzos para ...** he spared no efforts to ...
escayola *f* plaster of Paris; *(para brazo etc)* plaster.
escayolar *vt (brazo etc)* to put in plaster.
escena *f* scene; *(escenario)* stage.
escenario *m (en teatro)* stage; *(de película)* setting.
escéptico, -a *adj & mf* sceptic.
esclarecer *vt* to shed light on.
esclavo, -a *adj & mf* slave.
esclusa *f* lock.
escoba *f* brush.
escocer *vi* to sting.
escocés, -a **1** *adj* Scottish, Scots; **falda escocesa** kilt. **2** *mf* Scot.
escoger *vt* to choose.
escolar **1** *adj (curso, año)* school. **2** *mf (niño)* schoolboy; *(niña)* schoolgirl.
escollo *m* reef; *(obstáculo)* pitfall.
escolta *f* escort.
escoltar *vt* to escort.
escombros *mpl* debris *sing.*
esconder *vt,* **esconderse** *vr* to hide (**de** from).
escondidas: a escondidas *adv* secretly.
escondite *m (lugar)* hiding place; *(juego)* hide-and-seek.
escondrijo *m* hiding place.
escopeta *f* shotgun; **e. de aire comprimido** air gun.
escotado, -a *adj* low-cut.
escote *m* low neckline.
escotilla *f* hatch.
escozor *m* stinging.
escribir *(pp* escrito*)* **1** *vt* to write; **e. a máquina** to type. **2 escribirse** *vr (dos personas)* to write to each other.
escrito, -a **1** *adj* written; **por e.** in writing. **2** *m (documento)* document.
escritor, -a *mf* writer.
escritorio *m (mueble)* writing desk; *(en computadora)* desktop.
escritura *f (documento)* document.
escrúpulo *m (recelo)* scruple; **una persona sin escrúpulos** an unscrupulous person.
escrupuloso, -a *adj* squeamish; *(honesto)* scrupulous; *(meticuloso)* painstaking.
escrutinio *m (de votos)* count.
escuadra *f (instrumento)* square; *(militar)* squad; *(de barcos)* squadron.
escuálido, -a *adj* emaciated.
escuchar **1** *vt* to listen to; *(oír)* to hear. **2** *vi* to listen.
escudarse *vr fig* **e. en algo** to hide behind sth.
escudo *m (arma defensiva)* shield; *(blasón)* coat of arms.
escuela *f* school; **e. de idiomas** language school.
escueto, -a *adj* plain.
escuezo *indic pres de* **escocer**.
esculcar *vt Am (registrar)* to search.
escultor, -a *mf (hombre)* sculptor; *(mujer)* sculptress; *(de madera)* woodcarver.
escultura *f* sculpture.
escupidera *f (recipiente)* spittoon, cuspidor; *(orinal)* chamberpot.
escupir **1** *vi* to spit. **2** *vt* to spit out.
escurreplatos *m inv* dish rack.
escurridizo, -a *adj* slippery.
escurridor *m* colander; *(escurreplatos)* dish rack.
escurrir **1** *vt (plato, vaso)* to drain; *(ropa)* to wring out; **e. el bulto** to wriggle out. **2 escurrirse** *vr (resbalarse)* to slip.
ese, -a *adj dem* that; **esos, -as** those.
ése, -a *pron dem mf* that one; **ésos, -as** those (ones); *fam* **¡ni por ésas!** no way!
esencia *f* essence.
esencial *adj* essential; **lo e.** the main thing.
esencialmente *adv* essentially.
esfera *f* sphere; *(de reloj de pulsera)* dial; *(de reloj de pared)* face.
esforzarse *vr* to endeavor (**por** to).
esfuerzo *m* effort.
esfumarse *vr fam* to beat it.
esgrima *f* fencing.
esgrimir *vt* to wield.
esguince *m* sprain.
eslabón *m* link.
eslogan *m (pl* eslóganes*)* slogan.

esmalte *m* enamel; *(de uñas)* nail polish.
esmeralda *f* emerald.
esmerarse *vr* to be careful; *(esforzarse)* to go to great lengths.
esmero *m* great care.
esmoquin *m (pl* esmóquines*)* tuxedo.
esnob *(pl* esnobs*)* **1** *adj (persona)* snobbish; *(restaurante etc)* posh. **2** *mf* snob.
eso *pron dem neutro* that; **¡e. es!** that's it!; **por e.** that's why; **a e. de las diez** around ten.
esos, -as *adj dem pl* those.
ésos, -as *pron dem mfpl* those.
espabilado, -a *adj (despierto)* wide awake; *(listo)* clever.
espabilar *vt,* **espabilarse** *vr* to wake up.
espacial *adj* spatial; **nave e.** spaceship.
espacio *m* space; *(de tiempo)* length; *(programa)* program.
espacioso, -a *adj* spacious.
espada *f* sword; **pez e.** swordfish.
espaguetis *mpl* spaghetti *sing.*
espalda *f* back; *(en natación)* backstroke; **espaldas** back *sing;* **a espaldas de algn** behind sb's back; **por la e.** from behind; **volver la e. a algn** to turn one's back on sb.
espantajo *m (muñeco)* scarecrow.
espantapájaros *m inv* scarecrow.
espantar **1** *vt (asustar)* to frighten; *(ahuyentar)* to frighten away. **2 espantarse** *vr* to become frightened (**de** of).
espantoso, -a *adj* dreadful.
español, -a **1** *adj* Spanish. **2** *mf* Spaniard; **los españoles** the Spanish. **3** *m (idioma)* Spanish.
esparadrapo *m* sticking plaster.
esparcir **1** *vt (papeles, semillas)* to scatter; *(rumor)* to spread. **2 esparcirse** *vr* to be scattered.
espárrago *m* asparagus.
espátula *f* spatula.
especia *f* spice.
especial *adj* special; **en e.** especially.
especialidad *f* specialty.
especialista *mf* specialist.
especializarse *vr* to specialize (**en** in).
especialmente *adv (exclusivamente)* specially; *(muy)* especially.
especie *f* species *inv;* *(clase)* kind.
específicamente *adv* specifically.
especificar *vt* to specify.
específico, -a *adj* specific.
espectacular *adj* spectacular.
espectáculo *m* show.
espectador, -a *mf* spectator; *(en teatro, cine)* member of the audience; **los espectadores** the audience *sing; (de televisión)* viewers.
especulación *f* speculation.
espejismo *m* mirage.
espejo *m* mirror; **e. retrovisor** rear-view mirror.
espeluznante *adj* horrifying.
espera *f* wait; **en e. de** waiting for; **a la e. de** expecting; **sala de e.** waiting room.
esperanza *f* hope; **e. de vida** life expectancy.
esperanzador, -a *adj* encouraging.
esperar **1** *vi (aguardar)* to wait; *(tener esperanza)* to hope. **2** *vt (aguardar)* to wait for; *(tener esperanza)* to hope for; *(estar a la espera de, bebé)* to expect; **espero que sí** I hope so; **espero que vengas** I hope you'll come.
esperma *m* sperm; *Am (vela)* candle.
espesar *vt,* **espesarse** *vr* to thicken.
espeso, -a *adj (bosque, niebla)* dense; *(líquido)* thick; *(masa)* stiff.
espesor *m* thickness; **tres metros de e.** three meters thick.
espía *mf* spy.
espiar **1** *vi* to spy. **2** *vt* to spy on.
espiga *f (de trigo)* ear.
espigado, -a *adj* slender.
espina *f (de planta)* thorn; *(de pescado)* bone; **e. dorsal** spine.
espinaca *f* spinach.
espinazo *m* spine.
espinilla *f* shin; *(en la piel)* spot.
espionaje *m* spying.
espiral *adj & f* spiral.
espirar *vi* to breathe out.
espíritu *m* spirit; *(alma)* soul.
espiritual *adj* spiritual.
espléndido, -a *adj (magnífico)* splendid; *(generoso)* lavish.
esplendor *m* splendor.
espliego *m* lavender.
esponja *f* sponge.
espontáneo, -a *adj* spontaneous.
esposado, -a *adj (con esposas)* handcuffed.
esposas *fpl* handcuffs.
esposo, -a *mf* spouse; *(hombre)* husband; *(mujer)* wife.
esprint *m* sprint.
espuela *f* spur.
espuma *f* foam; *(de cerveza)* head; *(de jabón)* lather; **e. de afeitar** shaving foam.
espumoso, -a *adj* frothy; *(vino)* sparkling.
esqueleto *m* skeleton.
esquema *m* diagram.
esquemático, -a *adj (escueto)* schematic; *(con diagramas)* diagrammatic.
esquí *m (objeto)* ski; *(deporte)* skiing; **e. acuático** water-skiing.
esquiador, -a *mf* skier.
esquiar *vi* to ski.
esquimal *adj & mf* Eskimo.
esquina *f* corner.
esquivar *vt (a una persona)* to avoid; *(un golpe)* to dodge.
esta *adj dem* this.
está *indic pres de* **estar**.
ésta *pron dem f* this (one).
estabilidad *f* stability.
estable *adj* stable.
establecer **1** *vt* to establish; *(récord)* to set. **2 establecerse** *vr (instalarse)* to settle.
establecimiento *m* establishment.
establo *m* cow shed.
estaca *f* stake; *(de tienda de campaña)* peg.
estación *f* station; *(del año)* season; **e. de servicio** service station; **e. de esquí** ski resort; **e. de trabajo** work station.
estacionamiento *m (acción)* parking.
estacionar *vt,* **estacionarse** *vr* to park.
estacionario, -a *adj* stationary.

estada *f,* **estadía** *f Am* stay.
estadio *m (deportivo)* stadium; *(fase)* stage.
estadística *f* statistics *sing;* **una e.** a statistic.
estado *m* state; **e. civil** marital status; **e. de cuentas** statement of account.
estadounidense 1 *adj* United States, American. **2** *mf* United States citizen.
estafa *f* swindle.
estafar *vt* to swindle.
estafeta *f* **e. de Correos** sub post office.
estallar *vi* to burst; *(bomba)* to explode; *(guerra)* to break out.
estallido *m* explosion; *(de guerra)* outbreak.
estampa *f* illustration.
estampado, -a 1 *adj (tela)* printed. **2** *m (de tela)* print.
estampilla *f Am (postage)* stamp.
estancar 1 *vt (agua)* to hold back; *(paralizar)* to block; *(negociaciones)* to bring to a standstill. **2 estancarse** *vr* to stagnate.
estancia *f (permanencia)* stay; *(habitación)* room; *Am (hacienda)* ranch.
estanco *m* tobacconist's.
estándar *(pl* **estándares)** *adj & m* standard.
estanque *m* pond.
estante *m* shelf; *(para libros)* bookcase.
estantería *f* shelves.
estaño *m* tin.
estar 1 *vi* to be; **¿está tu madre?** is your mother in?; **¿cómo estás?** how are you?; **está escribiendo** she is writing; **estamos a 2 de noviembre** it is the 2nd of November; **están a 20 pesos el kilo** they're 20 pesos a kilo; **¿estamos?** OK?; **e. de más** not to be needed. ▪ **(+ para) estará para las seis** it will be finished by six; **hoy no estoy para bromas** I'm in no mood for jokes today; **el tren está para salir** the train is just about to leave. ▪ **(+ por) está por hacer** it has still to be done; **eso está por ver** it remains to be seen. ▪ **(+ con)** to have; **e. con la gripe** to have the flu. ▪ **(+ sin)** to have no. **2 estarse** *vr* **¡estáte quieto!** keep still!
estatal *adj* state.
estatua *f* statue.
estatura *f* height.
estatuto *m* statute; *(de empresa etc)* rules *pl.*
este 1 *adj* eastern; *(dirección)* easterly. **2** *m* east; **al e. de** to the east of.
esté *subj pres de* **estar**.
este, -a *adj dem* this; **estos, -as** these.
éste, -a *pron dem mf* this one; **aquél … é.** the former … the latter; **éstos, -as** these (ones); **aquéllos … éstos** the former … the latter.
estela *f (de barco)* wake; *(de avión)* vapor trail.
estepa *f* steppe.
estera *f* rush mat.
estercolero *m* dunghill.
estéreo *adj & m* stereo.
estereofónico, -a *adj* stereophonic.
estereotipo *m* stereotype.
estéril *adj* sterile.
esterilla *f* small mat.
esterlina *adj* **libra e.** pound (sterling).
esternón *m* breastbone.
estero *m Am* marsh.
esteticienne, esteticista *f* beautician.
estético, -a *adj* aesthetic; **cirugía estética** plastic surgery.
estiércol *m* manure.
estilarse *vr* to be in vogue.
estilo *m* style; *(modo)* manner; *(en natación)* stroke.
estilográfica *f (pluma)* **e.** fountain pen.
estima *f* esteem.
estimación *f (estima)* esteem; *(valoración)* evaluation; *(cálculo aproximado)* estimate.
estimado, -a *adj* respected; **E. Señor** *(en carta)* Dear Sir.
estimar *vt (apreciar)* to esteem; *(considerar)* to think; *(valuar)* to value.
estimativo, -a *adj* approximate, estimated.
estimulante 1 *adj* stimulating. **2** *m* stimulant.
estimular *vt* to stimulate.
estímulo *m* stimulus.
estirar *vt,* **estirarse** *vr* to stretch.
estival *adj* summer.
esto *pron dem (esta cosa)* this, this thing; *(este asunto)* this matter.
estocada *f* stab.
estofado *m* stew.
estómago *m* stomach; **dolor de e.** stomach ache.
estoque *m* sword.
estorbar 1 *vt (dificultar)* to hinder. **2** *vi* to be in the way.
estorbo *m (obstáculo)* obstacle.
estornudar *vi* to sneeze.
estornudo *m* sneeze.
estos, -as *adj dem pl* these.
éstos, -as *pron dem mfpl* these.
estoy *indic pres de* **estar**.
estragos *mpl* **hacer e. en** to wreak havoc with o on.
estrangular *vt* to strangle.
estraperlo *m* black market.
estratagema *f* ruse.
estratégico, -a *adj* strategic.
estrechamente *adv (íntimamente)* closely.
estrechamiento *m* narrowing; **'e. de calzada'** *(en letrero)* 'road narrows'.
estrechar 1 *vt* to make narrow; **e. la mano a algn** to shake sb's hand; *(lazos de amistad)* to tighten. **2 estrecharse** *vr* to narrow.
estrechez *f* narrowness; **pasar estrecheces** to be hard up.
estrecho, -a 1 *adj* narrow; *(ropa, zapato)* tight; *(amistad, relación)* close. **2** *m* strait.
estrella *f* star; **e. de cine** film star; **e. de mar** starfish; **e. fugaz** shooting star.
estrellado, -a *adj (en forma de estrella)* star-shaped; *(cielo)* starry; *(huevos)* scrambled.
estrellar 1 *vt fam* to smash. **2 estrellarse** *vr (chocar)* to crash (**contra** into).
estremecedor, -a *adj* bloodcurdling.
estremecer *vt,* **estremecerse** *vr* to shake.
estrenar *vt* to use for the first time; *(ropa)* to wear for the first time; *(obra, película)* to premiere.
estreno *m (teatral)* first performance; *(de película)* premiere.
estreñido, -a *adj* constipated.
estreñimiento *m* constipation.
estrépito *m* din.
estrepitoso, -a *adj (fracaso)* spectacular.
estrés *m* stress.
estresante *adj* stressful.
estribillo *m (en canción)* chorus; *(en poema)* refrain.
estribo *m* stirrup; *fig* **perder los estribos** to fly off the handle.

estribor *m* starboard.
estricto, -a *adj* strict.
estropajo *m* scourer.
estropear 1 *vt (máquina, cosecha)* to damage; *(fiesta, plan)* to spoil; *(pelo, manos)* to ruin. **2 estropearse** *vr* to be ruined; *(máquina)* to break down.
estropicio *m fam (destrozo)* damage; *(ruido)* crash, clatter.
estructura *f* structure; *(armazón)* framework.
estruendo *m* roar.
estrujar *vt (limón etc)* to squeeze; *(apretar)* to crush.
estuche *m* case.
estudiante *mf* student.
estudiantil *adj* student.
estudiar *vti* to study.
estudio *m* study; *(encuesta)* survey; *(sala)* studio; *(apartamento)* studio (apartment).
estudioso, -a 1 *adj* studious. **2** *mf* specialist.
estufa *f* heater.
estupefaciente *m* drug.
estupefacto, -a *adj* astounded.
estupendamente *adv* marvelously.
estupendo, -a *adj* marvelous; **¡e.!** great!
estupidez *f* stupidity.
estúpido, -a 1 *adj* stupid. **2** *mf* idiot.
estuve *pt indef de* **estar**.
ETA *f abr de* **Euzkadi Ta Askatasuna** *(Patria Vasca y Libertad)* ETA.
etapa *f* stage.
etcétera *adv* etcetera.
eterno, -a *adj* eternal.
ético, -a *adj* ethical.
etílico, -a *adj* alcohol **e.** ethyl alcohol.
etiqueta *f (de producto)* label; *(ceremonia)* etiquette; **de e.** formal.
étnico, -a *adj* ethnic.
EU *f abr de* **Unión Europea** European Union, EU.
eucalipto *m* eucalyptus.
eufórico, -a *adj* euphoric.
euro *m* euro.
europeo, -a *adj & mf* European.
euskera *m* Basque.
eutanasia *f* euthanasia.
evacuación *f* evacuation.
evacuar *vt* to evacuate.
evadir 1 *vt (respuesta, peligro, impuestos)* to avoid; *(responsabilidad)* to shirk. **2 evadirse** *vr* to escape.
evaluación *f* evaluation; *(en colegio)* assessment.
evaluar *vt* to evaluate, to assess.
evangelio *m* gospel.
evaporación *f* evaporation.
evaporar *vt,* **evaporarse** *vr* to evaporate.
evasión *f (fuga)* escape; *(escapismo)* escapism; **e. de capitales** flight of capital.
evasiva *f* evasive answer.
evasivo, -a *adj* evasive.
evento *m (acontecimiento)* event; *(incidente)* unforeseen event.
eventual *adj (posible)* possible; *(trabajo, obrero)* casual.
evidencia *f* obviousness; **poner a algn en e.** to show sb up.
evidenciar *vt* to show, to demonstrate.
evidente *adj* obvious.
evidentemente *adv* obviously.
evitar *vt* to avoid; *(problema futuro)* to prevent; *(desastre)* to avert.
evocar *vt (traer a la memoria)* to evoke.
evolución *f* evolution; *(desarrollo)* development.
evolucionar *vi* to develop; *(especies)* to evolve.
ex *prefijo* former, ex-; **ex alumno** former pupil; **ex marido** ex-husband; *fam* **mi ex** my ex.
exabrupto *m* sharp comment.
exacerbar 1 *vt (agravar)* to exacerbate. **2 exacerbarse** *vr (irritarse)* to feel exasperated.
exactamente *adv* exactly.
exactitud *f* accuracy; **con e.** precisely.
exacto, -a *adj* exact; **¡e.!** precisely!
exageración *f* exaggeration.
exagerado, -a *adj* exaggerated; *(excesivo)* excessive.
exagerar *vti* to exaggerate.
exaltarse *vr (acalorarse)* to get carried away.
examen *m* examination, exam; **e. de conducir** driving test.
examinador, -a *mf* examiner.
examinar 1 *vt* to examine. **2 examinarse** *vr* to sit for an examination.
exasperante *adj* exasperating.
exasperar 1 *vt* to exasperate. **2 exasperarse** *vr* to become exasperated.
excavación *f* excavation; *(en arqueología)* dig.
excavadora *f* digger.
excavar *vt* to excavate, to dig.
excedencia *f (de empleado)* leave (of absence); *(de profesor)* sabbatical.
excedente *adj & m* surplus.
exceder 1 *vt* to exceed. **2 excederse** *vr* to go too far.
excelencia *f* excellence.
excelente *adj* excellent.
excéntrico, -a *adj* eccentric.
excepción *f* exception; **a e. de** except for.
excepcional *adj* exceptional.
excepto *adv* except (for).
exceptuar *vt* to except.
excesivo, -a *adj* excessive.
exceso *m* excess; **e. de velocidad** speeding.
excitación *f (sentimiento)* excitement; *(acción)* excitation.
excitante *adj* exciting.
excitar 1 *vt* to excite. **2 excitarse** *vr* to get excited.
exclamación *f* exclamation.
exclamar *vti* to exclaim.
excluir *vt* to exclude.
exclusive *adv (en fechas)* exclusive.
exclusivo, -a *adj* exclusive.
excremento *m* excrement.
exculpar *vt* to exonerate.
excursión *f* excursion.
excursionista *mf* tripper; *(a pie)* hiker.
excusa *f (pretexto)* excuse; *(disculpa)* apology.
excusado *m (retrete)* toilet.

excusar 1 *vt (justificar)* to excuse; *(eximir)* to exempt (**de** from). **2 excusarse** *vr (disculparse)* to apologize.
exención *f* exemption.
exento, -a *adj* exempt (**de** from).
exhalar *vt* to breathe out.
exhaustivo, -a *adj* exhaustive.
exhausto, -a *adj* exhausted.
exhibición *f* exhibition.
exhibir 1 *vt (mostrar)* to exhibit; *(lucir)* to show off. **2 exhibirse** *vr* to show off.
exigencia *f* demand; *(requisito)* requirement.
exigente *adj* demanding.
exigir *vt* to demand.
exilado, -a 1 *adj* exiled. **2** *mf* exile.
exilar 1 *vt* to exile. **2 exilarse** *vr* to go into exile.
exiliado, -a *adj & mf* = **exilado**.
exiliar *vt* = **exilar**.
exilio *m* exile.
existencia *f (vida)* existence; **existencias** stocks.
existente *adj* existing.
existir *vi* to exist.
éxito *m* success; **con é.** successfully; **tener é.** to be successful.
exitoso, -a *adj* successful.
éxodo *m* exodus.
exorbitante *adj* exorbitant.
exótico, -a *adj* exotic.
expandir *vt*, **expandirse** *vr* to expand.
expansión *f* expansion; *(de noticia)* spreading; *(diversión)* relaxation.
expatriar 1 *vt* to exile, to banish. **2 expatriarse** *vr* to leave one's country.
expectación *f (interés)* excitement.
expectativa *f* expectancy.
expedición *f* expedition.
expediente *m (informe)* record; *(ficha)* file; **e. académico** student's record.
expedir *vt (pasaporte etc)* to issue.
expendeduría *f* tobacconist's.
expensas *fpl* **a e. de** at the expense of.
experiencia *f* experience; *(experimento)* experiment.
experimentado, -a *adj* experienced.
experimental *adj* experimental.
experimentar 1 *vi* to experiment. **2** *vt* to undergo; *(aumento)* to show; *(pérdida)* to suffer; *(sensación)* to experience.
experimento *m* experiment.
experto, -a *adj & mf* expert.
expirar *vi* to expire.
explanada *f* esplanade.
explicación *f* explanation.
explicar 1 *vt* to explain. **2 explicarse** *vr (persona)* to explain (oneself); **no me lo explico** I can't understand it.
exploración *f* exploration.
explorador, -a *mf* explorer.
explorar *vt* to explore.
explosión *f* explosion; **hacer e.** to explode.
explosionar *vti* to explode, to blow up.
explosivo, -a *adj & m* explosive.
explotación *f* exploitation.
explotar 1 *vi (bomba)* to explode, to go off. **2** *vt* to exploit.
exponer *(pp* **expuesto) 1** *vt (mostrar)* to exhibit; *(presentar)* to put forward; *(arriesgar)* to expose. **2 exponerse** *vr* to expose oneself (**a** to).
exportación *f* export.
exportar *vt* to export.
exposición *f* exhibition.
exprés *adj* express; **olla e.** pressure cooker; **café e.** espresso (coffee).
expresamente *adv* expressly.
expresar 1 *vt* to express; *(manifestar)* to state. **2 expresarse** *vr* to express oneself.
expresión *f* expression.
expresivo, -a *adj* expressive.
expreso, -a 1 *adj* express. **2** *m* express (train). **3** *adv* on purpose.
exprimidor *m* juicer.
exprimir *vt (limón)* to squeeze; *(zumo)* to squeeze out.
expulsar *vt* to expel; *(jugador)* to send off.
expuse *pt indef de* **exponer**.
exquisito, -a *adj* exquisite; *(comida)* delicious; *(gusto)* refined.
extender 1 *vt* to extend; *(agrandar)* to enlarge; *(mantel, mapa)* to spread (out); *(mano, brazo)* to stretch (out); *(crema, mantequilla)* to spread. **2 extenderse** *vr (en el tiempo)* to last; *(en el espacio)* to stretch; *(rumor, noticia)* to spread.
extendido, -a *adj* extended; *(mapa, plano)* open; *(mano, brazo)* outstretched; *(costumbre, rumor)* widespread.
extensión *f (de libro etc)* length; *(de terreno)* expanse.
extenso, -a *adj (terreno)* extensive; *(libro, película)* long.
extenuar 1 *vt* to exhaust. **2 extenuarse** *vr* to exhaust oneself.
exterior 1 *adj (de fuera)* outer; *(puerta)* outside; *(política, deuda)* foreign; **Ministerio de Asuntos Exteriores** State Department. **2** *m (parte de fuera)* outside; *(extranjero)* abroad.
exteriormente *adv* outwardly.
exterminar *vt* to exterminate.
externo, -a *adj* external.
extinguir 1 *vt (fuego)* to extinguish; *(raza)* to wipe out. **2 extinguirse** *vr (fuego)* to go out; *(especie)* to become extinct.
extintor *m* fire extinguisher.
extirpar *vt (tumor)* to remove; *fig* to eradicate, to stamp out.
extorsión *f* extortion.
extorsionar *vt* to extort.
extra 1 *adj* extra; *(superior)* top quality; **horas e.** overtime; **paga e.** bonus. **2** *mf* extra.
extracto *m* extract; **e. de cuenta** statement of account.
extraer *vt* to extract.
extranjero, -a 1 *adj* foreign. **2** *mf* foreigner. **3** *m* abroad; **en el e.** abroad.
extrañar 1 *vt (sorprender)* to surprise; *Am (echar de menos)* to miss. **2 extrañarse** *vr* **extrañarse de** *(sorprenderse)* to be surprised at.
extrañeza *f (sorpresa)* surprise; *(singularidad)* strangeness.
extraño, -a 1 *adj* strange. **2** *mf* stranger.
extraoficial *adj* unofficial.
extraordinario, -a *adj* extraordinary.
extrarradio *m* suburbs *pl*.
extraterrestre *mf* alien.
extravagante *adj* outlandish.
extravertido, -a *adj & mf* = **extrovertido**.

extraviar 1 *vt* to mislay. **2 extraviarse** *vr* to be missing.
extremeño, -a *adj & mf* Estremaduran.
extremidad *f (extremo)* tip; *(miembro)* limb.
extremo, -a 1 *m (de calle, cable)* end; *(máximo)* extreme; **en último e.** as a last resort; *f* **e. derecha/ izquierda** outside-right/-left. **2** *adj* extreme; **E. Oriente** Far East.
extrovertido, -a *adj & mf* extrovert.
exuberante *adj* exuberant; *(vegetación)* lush.

F

fabada *f* stew of beans, pork sausage and bacon.
fábrica *f* factory.
fabricación *f* manufacture.
fabricante *mf* manufacturer.
fabricar *vt* to manufacture.
fabuloso, -a *adj* fabulous.
facción *f* faction; **facciones** *(rasgos)* features.
facha *f fam* look.
fachada *f* façade.
facial *adj* facial.
fácil *adj* easy; **es f. que ...** it's (quite) likely that ....
facilidad *f (sencillez)* easiness; *(soltura)* ease; **facilidades de pago** easy terms.
facilitar *vt (simplificar)* to make easy *o* easier; **f. algo a algn** to provide sb with sth.
fácilmente *adv* easily.
facsímil, facsímile *m* facsimile.
factible *adj* feasible.
factor *m* factor.
factoría *f* factory.
factura *f* invoice.
facturación *f (en aeropuerto)* check-in; *(en estación)* registration.
facturar *vt (en aeropuerto)* to check in; *(en estación)* to register.
facultad *f* faculty.
faena *f (tarea)* task; *(en corrida)* performance.
faisán *m* pheasant.
faja *f (corsé)* corset.
fajo *m (de billetes)* wad.
falda *f (prenda)* skirt; *(de montaña)* slope; **f. pantalón** culottes *pl*.
falla *f Am (defecto)* fault.
fallar *vi* to fail; **le falló la puntería** he missed his target. **2** *vt* to miss.
fallecer *vi* to pass away, die.
fallecimiento *m* demise.
fallo *m (error)* mistake; *(del corazón, de los frenos)* failure.
falsear *vt (hechos, la verdad)* to distort.
falsificar *vt* to falsify; *(cuadro, firma, moneda)* to forge.
falso, -a *adj* false; *(persona)* insincere.
falta *f (carencia)* lack; *(escasez)* shortage; *(ausencia)* absence; *(error)* mistake; *(defecto)* fault, defect; *(fútbol)* foul; *(tenis)* fault; **sin f.** without fail; **echar algo/a algn en f.** to miss sth/sb; **f. de ortografía** spelling mistake; **hacer f.** to be necessary; **(nos) hace f. una escalera** we need a ladder; **harán f. dos personas para mover el piano** it'll take two people to move the piano; **no hace f. que ...** there is no need for ....
faltar *vi (no estar)* to be missing; *(escasear)* to be lacking *o* needed; *(quedar)* to be left; **¿quién falta?** who is missing?; **le falta confianza en sí mismo** he lacks confidence in himself; **¡lo que me faltaba!** that's all I needed!; **¡no faltaría o faltaba más!** *(por supuesto)* (but) of course!; **¿cuántos kilómetros faltan para Managua?** how many kilometers is it to Managua?; **ya falta poco para las vacaciones** it won't be long now until the holidays; **f. a la verdad** not to tell the truth.
fama *f* fame; *(reputación)* reputation.
familia *f* family.
familiar 1 *adj (de la familia)* family; *(conocido)* familiar. **2** *mf* relation, relative.
familiarizarse *vr* to familiarize oneself (**con** with).
famoso, -a *adj* famous.
fan *mf* fan.
fanático, -a 1 *adj* fanatical. **2** *mf* fanatic.
fanfarrón, -ona 1 *adj* boastful. **2** *mf* show-off.
fango *m (barro)* mud.
fantasía *f* fantasy.
fantasma *m* ghost.
fantástico, -a *adj* fantastic.
fardo *m* bundle.
farmacéutico, -a 1 *adj* pharmaceutical. **2** *mf* pharmacist.
farmacia *f* pharmacy.
fármaco *m* medicine, medication.
faro *m (torre)* lighthouse; *(de coche)* headlight.
farol *m (luz)* lantern; *(en la calle)* streetlight, streetlamp.
farola *f* streetlight, streetlamp.
farsante *mf* fake, impostor.
fascículo *m* installment.
fascinar *vt* to fascinate.
fascista *adj & mf* fascist.
fase *f* phase, stage.
fastidiar 1 *vt (molestar)* to annoy, to bother. **2 fastidiarse** *vr (aguantarse)* to put up with it; **que se fastidie** that's his tough luck; **fastidiarse el brazo** to hurt one's arm.
fastidio *m* nuisance.
fastuoso, -a *adj (acto)* splendid, lavish.
fatal 1 *adj (muy malo)* awful; *(mortal)* fatal. **2** *adv* awfully; **lo pasó f.** he had a rotten time.
fatiga *f (cansancio)* fatigue.
fatigar *vt*, **fatigarse** *vr* to tire.
fauna *f* fauna.
favor *m* favor; **¿puedes hacerme un f.?** can you do me a favor?; **estar a f. de** to be in favor of; **por f.** please; **haga el f. de sentarse** please sit down.
favorable *adj* favorable.
favorecedor, -a *adj* flattering.
favorecer *vt* to favor; *(sentar bien)* to flatter.
favorito, -a *adj & mf* favorite.
fe *f* faith; **fe de bautismo/matrimonio** baptism/marriage certificate.
fealdad *f* ugliness.
febrero *m* February.
fecha *f* date; **f. de caducidad** sell-by date; **hasta la f.** so far.

fechar *vt* to date.
fecundación *f* fertilization.
federación *f* federation.
felicidad *f* happiness; **(muchas) felicidades** *(en cumpleaños)* many happy returns.
felicitación *f* **tarjeta de f.** greeting card.
felicitar *vt* to congratulate (**por** on); **¡te felicito!** congratulations!
feligrés, -a *mf* parishioner.
feliz *adj (contento)* happy; **¡felices Navidades!** Merry Christmas!
felpa *f (tela)* plush; **oso** o **osito de f.** teddy bear.
felpudo *m* mat.
femenino, -a *adj* feminine; *(equipo, ropa)* women's; **sexo f.** female sex.
feminista *adj & mf* feminist.
fémur *m* femur.
fenomenal 1 *adj* phenomenal; *fam (fantástico)* great. **2** *adv fam* wonderfully.
fenómeno *m* phenomenon; *(prodigio)* genius; *(monstruo)* freak.
feo, -a *adj* ugly.
féretro *m* coffin.
feria *f* fair; **f. de muestras/del libro** trade/book fair.
feriado, -a *Am* **1** *adj* **día f.** (public) holiday. **2** *m* (public) holiday.
fermentar *vi* to ferment.
feroz *adj* fierce, ferocious.
ferretería *f* hardware store.
ferrocarril *m* railroad.
ferroviario, -a *adj* railway, rail.
ferry *m* ferry.
fértil *adj* fertile.
fertilizante *m* fertilizer.
fertilizar *vt* to fertilize.
fervor *m* fervor.
festejar *vt* to celebrate.
festín *m* feast.
festival *m* festival.
festividad *f* festivity.
festivo, -a **1** *adj (ambiente etc)* festive; **día f.** holiday. **2** *m* holiday.
feto *m* fetus.
fiable *adj* reliable, trustworthy.
fiador, -a *mf* guarantor.
fiambre *m* cold meat.
fiambrera *f* lunch box.
fianza *f (depósito)* deposit; *(jurídica)* bail.
fiarse *vr* to trust (**de** -).
fibra *f* fibre.
ficción *f* fiction.
ficha *f (de archivo)* filing card; *(en juegos)* counter; *(de ajedrez)* piece.
fichaje *m* signing.
fichar **1** *vt* to put on file; *(deportista)* to sign up. **2** *vi (en el trabajo) (al entrar)* to clock in; *(al salir)* to clock out; *(deportista)* to sign.
fichero *m* card index; *(de ordenador)* file.
ficticio, -a *adj* fictitious.
fidelidad *f* faithfulness; **alta f.** high fidelity, hi-fi.
fideo *m* noodle.
fiebre *f* fever; **tener f.** to have a temperature.
fiel 1 *adj (leal)* faithful, loyal. **2** *mpl* **los fieles** the congregation.
fieltro *m* felt.
fiera *f* wild animal.
fierro *m Am (hierro)* iron; *(navaja)* knife.
fiesta *f (entre amigos)* party; *(vacaciones)* holiday; *(festividad)* celebration.
figura *f* figure.
figurar **1** *vi (aparecer)* to figure. **2 figurarse** *vr* to imagine; **ya me lo figuraba** I thought as much; **¡figúrate, figúrese!** just imagine!
fijador *m (gomina)* gel.
fijamente *adv* **mirar f.** to stare.
fijar **1** *vt* to fix. **2 fijarse** *vr (darse cuenta)* to notice; *(poner atención)* to pay attention, to watch.
fijo, -a *adj* fixed; *(trabajo)* steady.
fila *f* file; *(de cine, teatro)* row; **en f. india** in single file.
filántropo, -a *mf* philanthropist.
filarmónico, -a *adj* philharmonic.
filatelia *f* stamp collecting, philately.
filete *m* fillet.
filial 1 *adj (de hijos)* filial. **2** *f (empresa)* subsidiary.
filmar *vt* to film.
film(e) *m* film.
filo *m* edge.
filosofía *f* philosophy.
filosófico, -a *adj* philosophical.
filósofo, -a *mf* philosopher.
filtración *f* filtration; *(de noticia)* leak(ing).
filtrar **1** *vt* to filter; *(noticia)* to leak. **2 filtrarse** *vr (líquido)* to seep; *(noticia)* to leak out.
filtro *m* filter.
fin *m (final)* end; *(objetivo)* purpose, aim; **dar** o **poner f. a** to put an end to; **en f.** anyway; **¡por** o **al f.!** at last!; **f. de semana** weekend; **al f. y al cabo** when all's said and done; **a f. de** in order to, so as to.
final 1 *adj* final. **2** *m* end; **al f.** in the end; **a finales de octubre** at the end of October. **3** *f (de campeonato)* final.
finalizar *vti* to end, to finish.
finalmente *adv* finally.
financiación *f* financing.
financiar *vt* to finance.
financiero, -a *adj* financial.
financista *mf Am* financier.
finanzas *fpl* finances.
finca *f (de campo)* country house.
fingir **1** *vt* to feign. **2** *vi* to pretend.
fino, -a *adj (hilo, capa)* fine; *(flaco)* thin; *(educado)* refined, polite; *(oído)* sharp, acute. **2** *m (vino)* type of dry sherry.
firma *f* signature; *(empresa)* firm.
firmar *vt* to sign.
firme 1 *adj* firm; **tierra f.** terra firma. **2** *adv* hard.
firmemente *adv* firmly.
fiscal 1 *adj* fiscal, tax. **2** *mf* district attorney.
fisco *m* treasury.
fisgar *vi fam* to snoop, to pry.
fisgón, -ona *mf* snooper.
física *f* physics *sing*.

físico, -a *adj* physical.
fisioterapia *f* physiotherapy.
flaco, -a *adj (delgado)* skinny.
flamante *adj (nuevo)* brand-new; *(vistoso)* splendid, brilliant.
flamenco, -a 1 *adj (música)* flamenco; *(de Flandes)* Flemish. **2** *m (música)* flamenco.
flan *m* caramel custard.
flanco *m* flank, side.
flaquear *vi (fuerzas, piernas)* to weaken, to give way.
flaqueza *f* weakness.
flash *m* flash.
flauta *f* flute.
flecha *f* arrow.
flechazo *m (enamoramiento)* love at first sight.
fleco *m* fringe.
flema *f* phlegm.
flemático, -a *adj* phlegmatic.
flemón *m* gumboil.
flequillo *m* bangs *pl*.
fletar *vt* to charter.
flexible *adj* flexible.
flexión *f* flexion.
flexionar *vt* to bend; *(músculo)* to flex.
flexo *m* reading lamp.
flirtear *vi* to flirt.
flojear *vi (ventas etc)* to fall off, to go down; *(piernas)* to weaken, to grow weak; *(memoria)* to fail; *Andes fam (holgazanear)* to laze around o about.
flojera *f fam* weakness, faintness.
flojo, -a *adj (tornillo, cuerda etc)* loose, slack; *(perezoso)* lazy, idle.
flor *f* flower.
flora *f* flora.
floreado, -a *adj* flowery.
florecer *vi (plantas)* to flower; *(negocio)* to flourish, to thrive.
floreciente *adj* flourishing, prosperous.
florero *m* vase.
floristería *f* florist's (shop).
flota *f* fleet.
flotador *m (para nadar)* rubber ring.
flotar *vi* to float.
flote *m* **a f.** afloat.
flotilla *f* flotilla.
fluctuar *vi* to fluctuate.
fluidez *f* fluency.
fluido, -a 1 *adj (líquido)* fluid; *(estilo etc)* fluent. **2** *m* liquid.
fluir *vi* to flow.
flujo *m* flow; *(de la marea)* rising tide.
flúor *m* fluorine.
fluorescente *adj* fluorescent.
fluvial *adj* river.
FMI *m abr de* **Fondo Monetario Internacional** International Monetary Fund, IMF.
fobia *f* phobia (**a** of).
foca *f* seal.
foco *m (lámpara)* spotlight, floodlight; *Andes, Méx (bombilla)* (electric light) bulb; *Am (de coche)* (car) headlight; *Am (farola)* street light.
fofo, -a *adj* soft; *(persona)* flabby.
fogata *f* bonfire.
fogón *m (de cocina)* ring.
folio *m* sheet of paper.
folklórico, -a *adj* **música folklórica** folk music.
follaje *m* foliage.
folletín *m (relato)* newspaper serial.
folleto *m* leaflet; *(turístico)* brochure.
follón *m fam (alboroto)* ruckus; *(enredo, confusión)* mess.
fomentar *vt* to promote.
fomento *m* promotion.
fonda *f* inn.
fondear *vi* to anchor.
fondista *mf (corredor)* long-distance runner.
fondo¹ *m (parte más baja)* bottom; *(de habitación)* back; *(de pasillo)* end; *(segundo término)* background; **a f.** thoroughly; **al f. de la calle** at the end of the street; **en el f. es bueno** deep down he's kind; **música de f.** background music.
fondo² *m (dinero)* fund; **cheque sin fondos** bad check.
fonético, -a *adj* phonetic.
fontanero, -a *mf* plumber.
footing *m* jogging; **hacer f.** to go jogging.
forastero, -a *mf* outsider.
forcejear *vi* to wrestle.
forense 1 *adj* forensic. **2** *mf (médico)* **f.** forensic surgeon.
forestal *adj* forest; **repoblación f.** re-afforestation.
forjar *vt* to forge.
forma *f* form, shape; *(manera)* way; **¿qué f. tiene?** what shape is it?; **de esta f.** in this way; **de f. que** so that; **de todas formas** anyway, in any case; **estar en f.** to be in shape; **estar en baja f.** be out of shape.
formación *f* formation; *(enseñanza)* training; **f. profesional** vocational training.
formal *adj* formal; *(serio)* serious; *(fiable)* reliable.
formalizar *vt (hacer formal)* to formalize; *(contrato)* to legalize.
formar 1 *vt* to form; **f. parte de algo** to be a part of sth; *(enseñar)* to educate, to train. **2 formarse** *vr* to be formed, to form.
formatear *vt* to format.
formato *m* format; *(del papel)* size.
formidable *adj (estupendo)* terrific.
fórmula *f* formula.
formular *vt (quejas, peticiones)* to make; *(deseo)* to express; *(pregunta)* to ask; *(una teoría)* to formulate.
formulario *m* form.
forrar *vt (por dentro)* to line; *(por fuera)* to cover.
forro *m (por dentro)* lining; *(por fuera)* cover.
fortalecer *vt* to fortify, to strengthen.
fortificar *vt* to fortify.
fortísimo, -a *adj* very strong.
fortuito, -a *adj* fortuitous.
fortuna *f (suerte)* luck; *(capital)* fortune; **por f.** fortunately.
forzado, -a *adj* forced; **trabajos forzados** hard labor.
forzar *vt* to force.
forzosamente *adv* necessarily.

forzoso, -a *adj* obligatory, compulsory.
fosa *f (sepultura)* grave; *(hoyo)* pit.
fósforo *m (cerilla)* match.
fósil *adj & m* fossil.
foso *m (hoyo)* pit.
foto *f* photo.
fotocopia *f* photocopy.
fotocopiadora *f* photocopier.
fotocopiar *vt* to photocopy.
fotografía *f* photograph; **hacer fotografías** to take photographs.
fotografiar *vt* to photograph, to take a photograph of.
fotógrafo, -a *mf* photographer.
FP *f abr de* **Formación Profesional** vocational training.
frac *m (pl* **fracs** *o* **fraques** *)* dress coat, tails *pl.*
fracasar *vi* to fail.
fracaso *m* failure.
fraccionar *vt,* **fraccionarse** *vr* to break up.
fractura *f* fracture.
fragancia *f* fragrance.
frágil *adj (quebradizo)* fragile; *(débil)* frail.
fragmento *m* fragment; *(de novela etc)* passage.
fraile *m* friar, monk.
frambuesa *f* raspberry.
francamente *adv* frankly.
francés, -esa 1 *adj* French. **2** *mf (hombre)* Frenchman; *(mujer)* Frenchwoman. **3** *m (idioma)* French.
franco, -a[1] *adj (persona)* frank; **puerto f.** free port.
franco[2] *m (moneda)* franc.
franela *f* flannel.
franja *f (de terreno)* strip; *(de bandera)* stripe.
franqueo *m* postage.
frasco *m* small bottle, flask.
frase *f (oración)* sentence; *(expresión)* phrase.
fraterno, -a *adj* fraternal, brotherly.
fraude *m* fraud.
frazada *f Am* blanket.
frecuencia *f* frequency; **con f.** frequently.
frecuentar *vt* to frequent.
frecuente *adj* frequent.
frecuentemente *adv* frequently, often.
fregadero *m (kitchen)* sink.
fregar *vt (lavar)* to wash; *(suelo)* to mop; *Am* to annoy.
fregón, -ona *adj Am* annoying.
fregona *f* mop.
freidora *f (deep)* fryer.
freír *(pp* **frito)** *vt* to fry.
frenar *vti* to brake.
frenazo *m* sudden braking.
frenético, -a *adj* frantic.
freno *m* brake; **pisar/soltar el f.** to press/release the brake; **f. de mano** handbrake.
frente 1 *m* front; **chocar de f.** to crash head on; **hacer f. a algo** to face up to sth. **2** *f (de la cara)* forehead; **f. a f.** face to face. **3** *prep* **f. a** opposite.
fresa *f* strawberry.
fresco, -a 1 *adj (frío)* cool; *(comida, fruta)* fresh; *(descarado)* rude. **2** *m (frescor)* fresh air; *(caradura)* cheek; **hace f.** it's chilly.
frescor *m* freshness.
frescura *f* freshness; *(desvergüenza)* nerve.
fresón *m (large)* strawberry.
fríamente *adv* coolly.
fricción *f* friction.
friegaplatos *mf inv (persona)* dishwasher.
frígido, -a *adj* frigid.
frigorífico *m* refrigerator, fridge.
frijol, fríjol *m* kidney bean.
frío, -a 1 *adj* cold; *(indiferente)* cold, cool. **2** *m* cold; **hace f.** it's cold.
friolento, -a *adj Am* sensitive to the cold.
friolero, -a *adj* sensitive to the cold, chilly.
frívolo, -a *adj* frivolous.
frontera *f* frontier.
fronterizo, -a *adj* frontier, border; **países fronterizos** neighboring countries.
frontón *m* pelota.
frotar 1 *vt* to rub. **2 frotarse** *vr* **f. las manos** to rub one's hands together.
fruncir *vt* **f. el ceño** to frown.
frustrar 1 *vt* to frustrate. **2 frustrarse** *vr (esperanza)* to fail; *(persona)* to be frustrated *o* disappointed.
fruta *f* fruit; **f. del tiempo** fresh fruit.
frutería *f* fruit shop.
frutero *m* fruit dish *o* bowl.
frutilla *f Bol, CSur, Ecuad* strawberry.
fruto *m* fruit; **frutos secos** nuts.
fucsia *f* fuchsia.
fuego *m* fire; *(lumbre)* light; **fuegos artificiales** fireworks; **¿me da f., por favor?** have you got a light, please?
fuel, fuel-oil *m* diesel.
fuente *f (artificial)* fountain; *(recipiente)* dish; *(origen)* source; *(de caracteres)* font.
fuera[1] **1** *adv* outside; **desde f.** from (the) outside; **por f.** on the outside; **la puerta de f.** the outer door. **2** *prep* **f. de** out of; **f. de serie** extraordinary.
fuera[2] **1** *subj imperfecto de* **ir**. **2** *subj imperfecto de* **ser**.
fuerte 1 *adj* strong; *(dolor)* severe; *(sonido)* loud; *(comida)* heavy. **2** *m (fortaleza)* fort. **3** *adv* **¡abrázame f.!** hold me tight!; **¡habla más f.!** speak up!; **¡pégale f.!** hit him hard!
fuerza *f (fortaleza)* strength; *(cuerpo)* force; **a la f.** *(por obligación)* of necessity; *(con violencia)* by force; **por f.** of necessity; **Fuerzas Armadas** Armed Forces.
fuese 1 *subj imperfecto de* **ir**. **2** *subj imperfecto de* **ser**.
fuete *m Am* whip.
fuga *f (huida)* escape; *(de gas etc)* leak.
fugarse *vr* to escape.
fui 1 *pt indef de de* **ir**. **2** *pt indef de* **ser**.
fulano, -a *mf* so-and-so; *(hombre)* what's his name; *(mujer)* what's her name; **Doña Fulana de tal** Mrs So-and-so.
fullería *f* cheating; **hacer fullerías** to cheat.
fullero, -a 1 *adj* cheating. **2** *mf* cheat.
fulminante *adj (muerte, enfermedad)* sudden; *(mirada)* withering.
fumador, -a *mf* smoker; **los no fumadores** non-smokers.
fumar 1 *vti* to smoke; **no f.** *(en letrero)* no smoking. **2 fumarse** *vr* **f. un cigarro** to smoke a cigarette.

función *f* function; *(cargo)* duties *pl*; *(de teatro, cine)* performance.
funcionamiento *m* operation; **poner/entrar en f.** to put/come into operation.
funcionar *vi* to work; **no funciona** *(en letrero)* out of order.
funcionario, -a *mf* civil servant.
funda *f* cover; *(de gafas etc)* case; **f. de almohada** pillowcase.
fundación *f* foundation.
fundamental *adj* fundamental.
fundamento *m* basis, grounds *pl*; **sin f.** unfounded.
fundar 1 *vt (crear)* to found. **2 fundarse** *vr (empresa)* to be founded; *(teoría, afirmación)* to be based.
fundir *vt,* **fundirse** *vr (derretirse)* to melt; *(bombilla, plomos)* to blow; *(unirse)* to merge.
fúnebre *adj (mortuorio)* funeral; **coche f.** hearse.
funeral *m* funeral.
funeraria *f* funeral parlor.
fungir *vi Am* to act *(* **de** *as)*.
funicular *m* funicular *(railway)*.
furgoneta *f* van.
furia *f* fury.
furioso, -a *adj* furious.
furor *m* fury.
furtivo, -a *adj* furtive; **cazador/pescador f.** poacher.
furúnculo *m* boil.
fusible *m* fuse.
fusil *m* gun, rifle.
fusilar *vt* to shoot, to execute.
fusión *f (de metales)* fusion; *(del hielo)* thawing, melting; *(de empresas)* merger.
fusionar *vt,* **fusionarse** *vr (metales)* to fuse; *(empresas)* to merge.
fútbol *m* soccer; **f. americano** football.
futbolín *m* table football.
futbolista *mf* football/soccer player.
futuro, -a 1 *adj* future. **2** *m* future.

G

gabardina *f (prenda)* raincoat.
gabinete *m (despacho)* study; *(de gobierno)* cabinet.
gacho, -a *adj* **con la cabeza gacha** hanging one's head.
gafas *fpl* glasses, spectacles; **g. de sol** sunglasses.
gafe *m* **ser (un) g.** to be a jinx.
gaita *f* bagpipes *pl.*
gajes *mpl fam irón* **g. del oficio** occupational hazards.
gajo *m (de naranja, pomelo etc)* segment.
gala *f (espectáculo)* gala; **de g.** dressed up; *(ciudad)* decked out.
galán *m* handsome young man; *(personaje)* leading man.
galante *adj* gallant.
galápago *m* turtle.
galardón *m* prize.
galardonar *vt* to award a prize to.
galería *f (corredor)* covered balcony; *(museo)* art gallery.
Gales *m* **(el país de) G.** Wales.
galés, -esa 1 *adj* Welsh. **2** *mf (hombre)* Welshman; *(mujer)* Welshwoman; **los galeses** the Welsh. **3** *m (idioma)* Welsh.
galgo *m* greyhound.
Galicia *f* Galicia.
galimatías *m inv* gibberish.
gallego, -a 1 *adj* Galician; *Am* Spanish. **2** *mf* Galician; *Am* Spaniard. **3** *m (idioma)* Galician.
galleta *f* cracker.
gallina *f* hen.
gallinero *m* henhouse.
gallo *m* cock.
galopante *adj (inflación etc)* galloping.
galopar *vi* to gallop.
galope *m* gallop; **a g. tendido** flat out.
gama *f* range.
gamba *f* prawn.
gamberro, -a 1 *mf* hooligan. **2** *adj* uncouth.
gamo *m* fallow deer.
gamuza *f (trapo)* chamois *o* shammy leather.
gana *f (deseo)* wish *(* **de** *for)*; *(apetito)* appetite; **de buena g.** willingly; **de mala g.** reluctantly; **tener ganas de (hacer) algo** to feel like (doing) sth.
ganadero, -a *mf* livestock farmer.
ganado *m* livestock.
ganador, -a 1 *adj* winning. **2** *mf* winner.
ganancia *f* profit.
ganar 1 *vt (sueldo)* to earn; *(premio)* to win; *(aventajar)* to beat. **2 ganarse** *vr* to earn.
ganchillo *m* crochet work.
gancho *m* hook; *Am (para el pelo)* hairpin; *Andes, CAm, Méx, Ven (para la ropa)* hanger.
ganga *f* bargain.
ganso, -a *mf* goose; *(macho)* gander; *fam* dolt.
garabato *m* scrawl.
garaje *m* garage.
garantía *f* guarantee.
garantizar *vt (cosa)* to guarantee; *(a persona)* to assure.
garbanzo *m* chickpea.
garfio *m* hook.
garganta *f* throat; *(desfiladero)* narrow pass.
gargantilla *f* short necklace.
gárgara *f Am (elixir)* gargling solution; **gárgaras** gargling *sing*; **hacer gárgaras** to gargle.
garra *f* claw; *(de ave)* talon; *fig* **tener g.** to be compelling.
garrafa *f* carafe.
garrafal *adj* monumental.
garrapata *f* tick.
garrote *m (porra)* club.
gas *m* gas; *(en bebida)* fizz; **g. ciudad** town gas; **gases (nocivos)** fumes; **g. de escape** exhaust fumes; **agua con g.** fizzy water.
gasa *f* gauze.
gaseosa *f* lemonade.
gasoducto *m* gas pipeline.

gasoil, gasóleo *m* diesel oil.
gasolina *f* gasoline.
gasolinera *f* gas station.
gastar 1 *vt (consumir) (dinero, tiempo)* to spend; *(gasolina, electricidad)* to consume; *(malgastar)* to waste; *(ropa)* to wear; **g. una broma a algn** to play a practical joke on sb. **2 gastarse** *vr (zapatos etc)* to wear out.
gasto *m* expenditure; **gastos** expenses.
gatas: a gatas *adv* on all fours.
gatear *vi* to crawl.
gatillo *m (de armas)* trigger.
gato *m* cat; *(de coche)* jack.
gauchada *f CSur* favor.
gaucho, -a 1 *adj RP fam (servicial)* helpful, obliging. **2** *mf* gaucho.
gaveta *f (cajón)* drawer; *Am (guantera)* glove compartment.
gaviota *f* seagull.
gay *adj inv & m (pl* **gays***)* gay.
gazpacho *m* gazpacho.
gel *m* gel; **g. (de ducha)** shower gel.
gelatina *f (ingrediente)* gelatin; *(para postre)* jelly.
gema *f* gem.
gemelo, -a 1 *adj & mf* (identical) twin. **2** *mpl* **gemelos** *(de camisa)* cufflinks; *(anteojos)* binoculars.
gemido *m* groan.
gemir *vi* to groan.
generación *f* generation.
general *adj* general; **por lo** *o* **en g.** in general.
generalizar 1 *vt* to generalize. **2 generalizarse** *vr* to become widespread *o* common.
generalmente *adv* generally.
generar *vt* to generate.
género *m (clase)* kind, sort; *(mercancía)* article; *(gramatical)* gender.
generoso, -a *adj* generous (**con, para** to).
genético, -a *adj* genetic.
genial *adj* brilliant.
genio *m f inv* genius; *(mal carácter)* temper; **estar de mal g.** to be in a bad mood.
genocidio *m* genocide.
gente *f* people *pl*; *Am* respectable people.
gentuza *f* riffraff.
genuino, -a *adj (puro)* genuine; *(verdadero)* authentic.
geografía *f* geography.
geología *f* geology.
geometría *f* geometry.
geranio *m* geranium.
gerente *mf* manager.
gérmen *m* germ.
gerundio *m* gerund.
gestación *f* gestation.
gesticular *vi* to gesticulate.
gestión *f (administración)* management; **gestiones** *(negociaciones)* negotiations; *(trámites)* formalities.
gestionar *vt* to take steps to acquire *o* obtain; *(negociar)* to negotiate.
gesto *m (mueca)* face; *(con las manos)* gesture.
gestor, -a *mf* ≃ solicitor.
gigante *adj & m* giant.
gigantesco, -a *adj* gigantic.
gil, -ila *mf CSur fam* twit, idiot.
gimnasia *f* gymnastics *pl*.
gimnasio *m* gym, gymnasium.
gimotear *vi* to whine.
ginebra *f (bebida)* gin.
ginecólogo, -a *mf* gynecologist.
gira *f (musical, teatral)* tour.
girar *vi (dar vueltas)* to spin; **g. a la derecha/izquierda** to turn right/left.
girasol *m* sunflower.
giratorio, -a *adj* revolving.
giro *m (vuelta)* turn; *(frase)* turn of phrase; *(libranza)* draft; **g. telegráfico** giro *o* money order; **g. postal** postal *o* money order.
gitano, -a *adj & mf* gypsy.
glaciar *m* glacier.
glándula *f* gland.
global *adj* comprehensive.
globo *m* balloon; *(esfera)* globe.
gloria *f (fama)* glory; *(cielo)* heaven.
glorieta *f (plazoleta)* small square; *(encrucijada de calles)* roundabout, traffic circle.
glosario *m* glossary.
glotón, -ona 1 *adj* greedy. **2** *mf* glutton.
glucosa *f* glucose.
gobernación *f* government; **Ministerio de la Gobernación** ≃ Department of the Interior.
gobernador, -a *mf* governor.
gobernante 1 *adj* ruling. **2** *mpl* **los gobernantes** the rulers.
gobernar *vt* to govern; *(un país)* to rule.
gobierno *m* government; *(mando)* running.
gofio *m (en América y Canarias)* roasted maize meal.
gol *m* goal.
golf *m* golf; **palo de g.** golf club.
golfo, -a¹ *mf* good for nothing.
golfo² *m* gulf.
golondrina *f* swallow.
golosina *f* candy.
goloso, -a *adj* sweet-toothed.
golpe *m* blow; *(llamada)* knock; *(puñetazo)* punch; *(choque)* bump; *(desgracia)* blow; **de g.** all of a sudden; **g. de estado** coup d'état.
golpear *vt* to hit; *(con el puño)* to punch; *(puerta, cabeza)* to bang.
goma *f* rubber; *(elástica)* rubber band; *Cuba, CSur (para ruedas)* tire; **g. de borrar** eraser.
gomal *m Am* rubber plantation.
gomero *m Am* gum tree; *(recolector)* rubber collector.
gordo, -a 1 *adj (carnoso)* fat; *(grueso)* thick. **2** *mf* fat person, *fam* fatty; *Am fam (como apelativo)* **¿cómo estás, gorda?** hey, how are you doing? **3** *m* **el g.** *(de lotería)* first prize.
gorila *m* gorilla.
gorra *f* cap.
gorrión *m* sparrow.
gorro *m* cap.
gota *f* drop; **g. a g.** drop by drop; **ni g.** not a bit.
gotear *v impers* to drip; **el techo gotea** there's a leak in the ceiling.
gotera *f* leak.

gozar 1 *vt* to enjoy. **2** *vi (disfrutar)* to enjoy (**de** -).
gozne *m* hinge.
grabación *f* recording.
grabado *m (arte)* engraving; *(dibujo)* drawing.
grabadora *f* tape recorder.
grabar *vt (sonidos, imágenes)* to record; *(en ordenador)* to save.
gracia *f (chiste)* joke; *(indulto)* pardon; **hacer** *o* **tener g.** to be funny.
gracias *fpl* thanks; **muchas** *o* **muchísimas g.** thank you very much.
gracioso, -a 1 *adj (divertido)* funny. **2** *mf (personaje)* comic character.
grada *f (peldaño)* step; **gradas** *(estadio)* terracing.
grado *m* degree; **de buen g.** willingly.
gradual *adj* gradual.
gradualmente *adv* gradually.
graduar 1 *vt (regular)* to regulate. **2 graduarse** *vr (soldado, alumno)* to graduate; **g. la vista** to have one's eyes tested.
gráfico, -a 1 *adj* graphic. **2** *mf* graph; **gráficos** *(de ordenador)* graphics.
gragea *f* pill.
gral. *abr de* **General** Gen.
gramática *f* grammar.
gramo *m* gram.
gran *adj ver* **grande**.
granada *f (fruto)* pomegranate; *(explosivo)* grenade.
granate 1 *adj inv* maroon. **2** *m* maroon.
grande *adj (before singular noun* **gran** *is used) (tamaño)* big, large; *fig (persona)* great; *(cantidad)* large; **pasarlo en g.** to have a great time.
granel: a granel *adv* loose.
granero *m* granary.
granito *m* granite.
granizada *f*, **granizado** *m* iced drink.
granizo *m* hail.
granja *f* farm.
granjear(se) *vt & vr* to gain.
granjero, -a *mf* farmer.
grano *m* grain; *(de café)* bean; *(espinilla)* spot.
granuja *m* **1** *(pilluelo)* rascal. **2** *(estafador)* con-man.
grapa *f* staple.
grapadora *f* stapler.
grasa *f* grease.
grasiento, -a *adj* greasy.
graso, -a *adj (pelo)* greasy; *(materia)* fatty.
gratis *adv* free.
gratitud *f* gratitude.
gratuito, -a *adj (de balde)* free (of charge); *(arbitrario)* gratuitous.
grava *f (guijas)* gravel; *(en carretera)* gravel *pl*.
gravar *vt (impuestos)* to tax.
grave *adj (importante)* serious; *(muy enfermo)* seriously ill; *(voz, nota)* low.
gravedad *f* seriousness; *(fuerza)* gravity.
gravilla *f (en carretera)* gravel *pl*.
griego, -a 1 *adj & mf* Greek. **2** *m (idioma)* Greek.
grieta *f* crack; *(en la piel)* chap.
grifo *m* faucet.
grillo *m* cricket.
gringo, -a *adj & mf* gringo, yankee.
gripe *f* flu.
gris *adj & m* gray.
grisáceo, -a *adj* grayish.
gritar *vti* to shout.
grito *m* shout.
grosella *f (fruto)* redcurrant; **g. negra** blackcurrant; **g. silvestre** gooseberry.
grosería *f (ordinariez)* rude word *o* expression.
grosero, -a *adj (tosco)* coarse; *(maleducado)* rude.
grosor *m* thickness.
grotesco, -a *adj* grotesque.
grúa *f (en construcción)* crane; *(para coches)* tow truck.
grueso, -a 1 *adj* thick; *(persona)* stout. **2** *m (parte principal)* bulk.
grumo *m* lump.
gruñido *m* grunt.
gruñir *vi* to grunt.
gruñón, -ona *adj* grumpy.
grupo *m* group.
gruta *f* cave.
guacamol, guacamole *m Am* avocado sauce.
guachafita *f Am* uproar.
guacho, -a *adj & mf Am* orphan.
guagua¹ *f (en Canarias y Cuba)* bus.
guagua² *Am* baby.
guajiro, -a *mf Cuba fam (campesino)* peasant.
guante *m* glove.
guantera *f (en coche)* glove compartment.
guapo, -a 1 *adj* good-looking; *(mujer)* beautiful, pretty; *(hombre)* handsome. **2** *m Am (matón)* bully.
guaraca *f Am* sling.
guarango, -a *adj Am* rude.
guarda *mf* guard; **g. jurado** security guard.
guardacoches *mf inv* parking attendant.
guardacostas *m inv (persona)* coastguard; *(embarcación)* coastguard vessel.
guardaespaldas *mf inv* bodyguard.
guardameta *mf* goalkeeper.
guardar *vt (conservar, reservar)* to keep; *(un secreto)* to keep; *(poner en un sitio)* to put away; *(en ordenador)* to save.
guardarropa *m (cuarto)* cloakroom; *(armario)* wardrobe.
guardería infantil *f* nursery (school).
guardia 1 *f (vigilancia)* watch; *(turno de servicio)* duty; **la g. civil** the civil guard. **2** *mf (hombre)* policeman; *(mujer)* policewoman.
guardián, -ana *mf (hombre)* watchman; *(mujer)* watchwoman.
guarecerse *vr* to take shelter *o* refuge (**de** from).
guarro, -a 1 *adj* filthy. **2** *m* pig.
guaso, -a *adj Am* peasant.
guasón, -ona 1 *adj* humorous. **2** *mf* joker.
guata *f (relleno)* padding; *Am (barriga)* paunch.
guayabera *f CAm, Carib, Col* short jacket.
guayabo, -a *mf Am (chica bonita)* pretty young girl; *(chico guapo)* good-looking boy.
güero, -a *adj Méx fam* blond, blonde.
guerra *f* war; **g. civil/fría/mundial/nuclear** civil/cold/world/nuclear war.

guerrilla *f (partida armada)* guerrilla force o band; *(lucha)* guerrilla warfare.

guía 1 *mf (persona)* guide. **2** *f (libro)* guide; **la g. de teléfonos** the telephone directory.

guiar 1 *vt (indicar el camino)* to guide; *(automóvil)* to drive. **2 guiarse** *vr* to be guided **(por** by).

guijarro *m* pebble.

guindilla *f* chili.

guiñapo *m (andrajo)* rag.

guiñar *vti* to wink.

guiño *m* wink.

guión *m (de cine, televisión)* script; *(ortográfico)* hyphen; *(esquema)* sketch.

guirnalda *f* garland.

guisante *m* pea.

guisar *vt* to cook.

guiso *m* dish; *(guisado)* stew.

guita *f* rope.

guitarra 1 *f* guitar. **2** *mf* guitarist.

gula *f* gluttony.

gusano *m* worm; *(oruga)* caterpillar.

gustar 1 *vt* **me gusta el vino** I like wine; **me gustaban los caramelos** I used to like sweets; **me gusta nadar** I like swimming; **me gustaría ir** I would like to go. **2** *vi* **g. de** to enjoy.

gusto *m* taste; **con (mucho) g.** with (great) pleasure; **tanto g.** pleased to meet you; **estar a g.** to feel comfortable o at ease; **ser de buen/mal g.** to be in good/bad taste; **tener buen/mal g.** to have good/bad taste.

H

ha *indic pres de* **haber**.

haba *f* broad bean.

habano *m* Havana (cigar).

haber 1 *v aux (en tiempos compuestos)* to have; **lo he visto** I have seen it; **ya lo había hecho** he had already done it. ▪ **h. de** + *infinitivo (obligación)* to have to; **has de ser bueno** you must be good. **2** *v impers (special form of present tense: **hay**) (existir, estar) (singular used also with plural nouns)* **hay** there is o are; **había** there was o were; **habrá una fiesta** there will be a party; **había una vez ...** once upon a time ...; **no hay de qué** you're welcome; **¿qué hay?** how are things? ▪ **hay que** + *infinitivo* it is necessary to.

habichuela *f* kidney bean.

hábil *adj (diestro)* skillful; **días hábiles** working days.

habitación *f (cuarto)* room; *(dormitorio)* bedroom; **h. individual/doble** single/double room.

habitante *mf* inhabitant.

hábito *m (costumbre)* habit; *(de monje)* habit.

habitual *adj* usual, habitual.

habituar 1 *vt* to accustom (**a** to). **2 habituarse** *vr* to get used (**a** to), to become accustomed (**a** to).

hablador, -a *adj (parlanchín)* talkative.

hablar 1 *vi* to speak, to talk; **h. con algn** to speak to sb; **¡ni h.!** no way!; *fam* **¡quién fue a h.!** look who's talking! **2** *vt (idioma)* to speak. **3 hablarse** *vr* to speak o talk to one another; **'se habla español'** 'Spanish spoken'.

habré *indic fut de* **haber**.

hacer 1 *vt* to do; *(crear, fabricar)* to make; **hazme un favor** do me a favor; **¿qué haces?** *(en este momento)* what are you doing?; *(para vivir)* what do you do (for a living)?; **tengo mucho que h.** I have a lot to do; **lo hizo con sus propias manos** he made it with his own hands; **h. la cama** to make the bed; **h. la cena** to make dinner; **el negro le hace más delgado** black makes him look slimmer; **ya no puedo leer como solía hacerlo** I can't read as well as I used to; **¡bien hecho!** well done! **2** *vi (actuar)* to play; **hizo de Desdémona** she played Desdemona; **h. por** o **para** + *infinitivo* to try to; **haz por venir** try and come. **3** *v impers* **hace calor/frío** it's hot/cold; **hace mucho (tiempo)** a long time ago; **hace dos días que no lo veo** I haven't seen him for two days; **hace dos años que vivo en Chicago** I've been living in Chicago for two years. **4 hacerse** *vr (volverse)* to become, to grow; *(simular)* to pretend; **hacerse el dormido** to pretend to be sleeping; **hacerse con** *(apropiarse)* to get hold of; **hacerse a** *(habituarse)* to get used to.

hacha *f (herramienta)* ax.

hachís *m* hashish.

hacia *prep (dirección)* towards, to; *(aproximadamente)* at about, at around; **h. abajo** down, downwards; **h. adelante** forwards; **h. arriba** up, upwards; **h. atrás** back, backwards.

hacienda *f* ranch.

hada *f* fairy; **cuento de hadas** fairy tale.

hago *indic pres de* **hacer**.

halagar *vt* to flatter.

halago *m* flattery.

halcón *m* falcon.

hallar 1 *vt (encontrar)* to find; *(descubrir)* to discover. **2 hallarse** *vr (estar)* to be, to find oneself; *(estar situado)* to be situated.

hallazgo *m (descubrimiento)* discovery; *(cosa encontrada)* find.

hamaca *f* hammock.

hambre *f (apetito)* hunger; *(inanición)* starvation; *(catástrofe)* famine; **tener h.** to be hungry.

hambriento, -a *adj* starving.

hamburguesa *f* hamburger.

han *indic pres de* **haber**.

haré *indic fut de* **hacer**.

harina *f* flour.

hartar 1 *vt (cansar, fastidiar)* to annoy; *(atiborrar)* to satiate. **2 hartarse** *vr (saciar el apetito)* to eat one's fill; *(cansarse)* to get fed up (**de** with).

harto, -a *adj (lleno)* full; *(cansado)* fed up; **estoy h. de trabajar** I'm fed up with working.

has *indic pres de* **haber**.

hasta 1 *prep (lugar)* up to, as far as; *(tiempo)* until, up to; *(con cantidad)* up to, as many as; *(incluso)* even; **h. la fecha** up to now; **h. luego** see you later. **2** *conj* **h. que** until.

hay *indic pres de* **haber**.

haya *subj pres de* **haber**.

haz *imperativo de* **hacer**.

hazmerreír *m* laughing stock.

he *indic pres de* **haber**.

hebilla *f* buckle.

hebra *f* thread.

hebreo, -a 1 *adj* Hebrew. **2** *mf* Hebrew.

hechizo *m (embrujo)* spell.

hecho, -a 1 *adj* made, done; *(carne)* done; *(ropa)* ready-made. **2** *m (realidad)* fact; *(acto)* act, deed; *(suceso)* event, incident; **de h.** in fact.

hectárea *f* hectare.

heder *vi* to stink, to smell foul.

hedor *m* stink, stench.

helada *f* frost.

heladería *f* ice-cream parlor.

helado, -a 1 *m* ice cream. **2** *adj (muy frío)* freezing cold; *fig* **quedarse h.** *(atónito)* to be flabbergasted.

helar 1 *vt (congelar)* to freeze. **2** *v impers* to freeze; **anoche heló** there was a frost last night. **3 helarse** *vr (congelarse)* to freeze.

helecho *m* fern.

hélice *f (de avión, barco)* propeller.

helicóptero *m* helicopter.

hembra *f (animal, planta)* female; *(mujer)* woman.

hemorragia *f* hemorrhage.

hemos *indic pres de* **haber**.

hendidura *f* crack.

heno *m* hay.

herbolario *m (tienda)* herbalist's (shop).

heredar *vt* to inherit.

heredero, -a *mf (hombre)* heir; *(mujer)* heiress.

herencia *f* inheritance, legacy; *(biológica)* heredity.

herida *f (lesión)* injury; *(corte)* wound.

herido, -a 1 *adj* injured, hurt. **2** *mf* injured person.

herir 1 *vt (físicamente) (lesionar)* to injure; *(cortar)* to wound. **2 herirse** *vr* to injure o hurt oneself.

hermana *f* sister.

hermanastro, -a *mf (hombre)* stepbrother; *(mujer)* stepsister.

hermano *m* brother; **primo h.** first cousin; **hermanos** brothers and sisters.

herméticamente *adv* **h. cerrado** hermetically sealed.

hermético, -a *adj (cierre)* hermetic, airtight; *fig (grupo)* secretive.

hermoso, -a *adj* beautiful, lovely; *(grandioso)* fine.

hermosura *f* beauty.

héroe *m* hero.

heroína *f (mujer)* heroine; *(droga)* heroin.

herradura *f* horseshoe.

herramienta *f* tool.

hervir *vt (hacer bullir)* to boil. **2** *vi (bullir)* to boil.

heterogéneo, -a *adj* heterogeneous.

hice *pt indef de* **hacer**.

hiciste *pt indef de* **hacer**.

hidratante *adj* moisturizing; **crema/leche h.** moisturizing cream/lotion.

hidráulico, -a *adj* hydraulic.

hidroavión *m* hydroplane.

hiedra *f* ivy.

hielo *m* ice.

hiena *f* hyena.

hierba *f* grass; **mala h.** weed.

hierbabuena *f* mint.

hierro *m* iron.

hígado *m* liver.

higiene *f* hygiene.

higiénico, -a *adj* hygienic; **papel h.** toilet paper.

higo *m* fig; *fam fig* **hecho un h.** wizened, crumpled.

hija *f* daughter.

hijastro, -a *mf (hombre)* stepson; *(mujer)* stepdaughter.

hijo *m* son; **hijos** children.

hilera *f* line, row.

hilo *m* thread; *(grueso)* yarn; *(fibra)* linen; **perder el h.** to lose the thread; **h. musical** background music.

himno *m* hymn; **h. nacional** national anthem.

hincapié *m* **hacer h. en** *(insistir)* to insist on; *(subrayar)* to emphasize.

hincar 1 *vt (clavar)* to drive (in). **2 hincarse** *vr* **hincarse de rodillas** to kneel (down).

hincha 1 *mf (de equipo)* fan, supporter. **2** *f (antipatía)* grudge, dislike.

hinchado, -a *adj* swollen.

hinchar 1 *vt (inflar)* to inflate, to blow up. **2 hincharse** *vr* to swell (up); *fam (hartarse)* to stuff oneself.

hindú *adj & mf* Hindu.

hipermercado *m* hypermarket.

hípico, -a *adj* horse.

hipnotizar *vt* to hypnotize.

hipo *m* **tener h.** to have the hiccups.

hipócrita 1 *adj* hypocritical. **2** *mf* hypocrite.

hipopótamo *m* hippopotamus.

hipoteca *f* mortgage.

hipótesis *f inv* hypothesis.

hispánico, -a *adj* Hispanic.

hispano, -a 1 *adj* Hispanic. **2** *mf* Spanish American, Hispanic.

hispanohablante 1 *adj* Spanish-speaking. **2** *mf* Spanish speaker.

histérico, -a *adj* hysterical.

historia *f (estudio del pasado)* history; *(narración)* story.

historial *m* record; *(antecedentes)* background.

histórico, -a *adj* historical; *(de gran importancia)* historic, memorable.

historieta *f (tira cómica)* comic strip.

hizo *indic indef de* **hacer**.

hocico *m (de animal)* snout.

hogar *m (casa)* home; *(de la chimenea)* hearth.

hoguera *f* bonfire.

hoja *f* leaf; *(de papel)* sheet; *(de cuchillo, espada)* blade; *(impreso)* hand-out.

hojalata *f* tin.

hojaldre *m* puff pastry.

hojear *vt (libro)* to leaf through.

hola *interj* hello!

holgado, -a *adj (ropa)* loose, baggy; *(económicamente)* comfortable; *(espacio)* roomy.

holgazán, -ana 1 *adj* lazy. **2** *mf* lazybones *inv*.

hollín *m* soot.

hombre 1 *m* man; **h. de negocios** businessman. **2** *interj (saludo)* hey!; **¡sí h.!, ¡h. claro!** *(enfático)* sure!, you bet!

hombrera *f* shoulder pad.

hombro *m* shoulder; **a hombros** on one's shoulders; **encogerse de hombros** to shrug one's shoulders; **mirar a algn por encima del h.** to look down one's nose at sb.

homenaje *m* homage, tribute.

homicida 1 *mf (hombre)* murderer; *(mujer)* murderess. **2** *adj* homicidal.

homicidio *m* homicide.

homogéneo, -a *adj* homogeneous, uniform.

homosexual *adj & mf* homosexual.

hondo, -a *adj* deep; **plato h.** soup dish.

honesto, -a *adj (honrado)* honest; *(recatado)* modest.

hongo *m* fungus; *(sombrero)* derby (hat); **h. venenoso** toadstool.
honor *m* honor; **palabra de h.** word of honor.
honorario, -a 1 *adj* honorary. **2** *mpl* **honorarios** fees.
honra *f (dignidad)* dignity; *(honor)* honor; **¡a mucha h.!** and proud of it!
honradez *f* honesty.
honrado, -a *adj (de fiar)* honest.
honrar *vt (respetar)* to honor; *(enaltecer)* to be a credit to.
honroso, -a *adj (loable)* honorable.
hora *f* hour; *(cita)* appointment; **media h.** half an hour; **h. punta** rush hour; **horas extra** overtime (hours); **¿qué h. es?** what time is it?; **a última h.** at the last moment; **pedir h.** *(al médico etc)* to ask for an appointment.
horario *m* schedule.
horca *f* gallows *pl*.
horchata *f* sweet milky drink made from chufa nuts.
horizonte *m* horizon.
hormiga *f* ant.
hormigón *m* concrete.
hormigueo *m* pins and needles *pl*, tingling *o* itching sensation.
hormiguero *m* anthill.
hormona *f* hormone.
horno *m (de cocina)* oven; *(para metales)* furnace; *(para cerámica etc)* kiln; **pescado al h.** baked fish.
horóscopo *m* horoscope.
horquilla *f (del pelo)* hair-grip.
horrendo, -a *adj* horrifying, horrible.
horrible *adj* horrible.
horror *m* horror; **¡qué h.!** how awful!; *fam* **tengo h. a las motos** I hate motorbikes.
horrorizar *vt* to horrify; *(dar miedo)* to terrify.
horroroso, -a *adj* horrifying; *(que da miedo)* terrifying; *fam (muy feo)* hideous; *fam (malísimo)* awful.
hortaliza *f* vegetable.
hortera *adj fam (persona)* flashy; *(cosa)* tacky.
hospedaje *m* lodgings *pl*, accommodations.
hospedar 1 *vt* to put up. **2 hospedarse** *vr* to stay (**en** at).
hospicio *m (para huérfanos)* orphanage.
hospital *m* hospital.
hospitalizar *vt* to send into hospital, to hospitalize.
hostal *m* guest house.
hostelería *f (negocio)* catering business; *(estudios)* hotel management.
hostería *f Am* hostel, inn.
hostil *adj* hostile.
hotel *m* hotel.
hoy *adv (día)* today; **h. (en) día** nowadays.
hoyo *m* hole.
hube *pt indef de* **haber**.
hubiera *subj imperfecto de* **haber**.
hucha *f* piggy bank.
hueco, -a 1 *adj (vacío)* empty, hollow; *(sonido)* resonant. **2** *m (cavidad)* hollow, hole; *(sitio no ocupado)* empty space.
huele *indic pres de* **oler**.
huelga *f* strike; **estar en** *o* **de h.** to be on strike; **hacer h.** to go on strike.
huella *f (del pie)* footprint; *(coche)* track; **h. dactilar** fingerprint; *fig (vestigio)* trace.
huérfano, -a *adj & mf* orphan.
huerta *f (parcela)* truck garden; *(región)* irrigated area used for cultivation.
huerto *m (de verduras)* vegetable garden; *(de frutales)* orchard.
hueso *m (del cuerpo)* bone; *(de fruto)* pit; *Am (enchufe)* contact.
huésped, -a *mf* guest; **casa de huéspedes** guesthouse.
huevo *m* egg; **h. duro** hard-boiled egg; **h. frito** fried egg; **h. pasado por agua,** *Am* **h. tibio** soft-boiled egg; **huevos revueltos** scrambled eggs.
huevón, -ona *muy fam mf Andes, Arg, Ven* dork.
huida *f* flight, escape.
huir *vi (escaparse)* to run away (**de** from); *(evadirse)* to escape (**de** from).
hule *m (tela impermeable)* oilcloth; *(de mesa)* tablecloth; *Am* rubber.
humanitario, -a *adj* humanitarian.
humano, -a 1 *adj (relativo al hombre)* human; *(compasivo)* humane; **ser h.** human being. **2** *m* human (being).
humeante *adj (chimenea)* smoky, smoking.
humedad *f (atmosférica)* humidity; *(de lugar)* dampness.
humedecer 1 *vt* to moisten, to dampen. **2 humedecerse** *vr* to become damp *o* moist.
húmedo, -a *adj (casa, ropa)* damp; *(clima)* humid, damp.
humildad *f (de persona)* humility; *(de cosa)* humbleness.
humilde *adj* humble; *(familia)* poor.
humillante *adj* humiliating.
humillar 1 *vt* to humiliate. **2 humillarse** *vr* **humillarse ante algn** to humble oneself before sb.
humo *m* smoke; *(gas)* fumes *pl*; *(vapor)* vapor, steam.
humor *m (genio)* mood; *(gracia)* humor; **estar de buen** *o* **mal h.** to be in a good *o* bad mood; **sentido del h.** sense of humor.
hundimiento *m (de edificio)* collapse; *(de barco)* sinking; *(de tierra)* subsidence; *(ruina)* downfall.
hundir 1 *vt (barco)* to sink; *(derrumbar)* to bring *o* knock down. **2 hundirse** *vr (barco)* to sink; *(edificio, empresa)* to collapse.
huracán *m* hurricane.
huraño, -a *adj* unsociable.
hurgar 1 *vi (fisgar)* to poke one's nose (**en** in). **2** *vt (fuego etc)* to poke.
hurto *m* petty theft.
huyo *indic pres de* **huir**.

I

ibérico, -a *adj* Iberian.
iberoamericano, -a *adj & mf* Latin American.
iceberg *m (pl* icebergs*)* iceberg.
icono *m* icon.
ida *f* billete de i. y vuelta round trip ticket.
idea *f* idea; **hacerse a la i. de** to get used to the idea of; **ni i.** no idea; **cambiar de i.** to change one's mind.
ideal *adj & m* ideal.
idear *vt (inventar)* to devise; *(concebir)* to think up.

idéntico, -a *adj* identical.
identidad *f* identity; **carnet de i.** identity card.
identificación *f* identification.
identificar 1 *vt* to identify. **2 identificarse** *vr* to identify oneself; *(simpatizar)* to identify (**con** with).
idilio *m (romance)* romance.
idioma *m* language.
idiota 1 *adj* stupid. **2** *mf* idiot.
idiotez *f* decir/hacer una i. to say/to do something stupid.
ídolo *m* idol.
idóneo, -a *adj* suitable.
iglesia *f (edificio)* church; **la I.** the Church.
ignorante 1 *adj (sin instrucción)* ignorant; *(no informado)* unaware (**de** of). **2** *mf* ignoramus.
ignorar 1 *vt (algo)* not to know; *(algn)* to ignore. **2 ignorarse** *vr* to be unknown.
igual 1 *adj (lo mismo)* the same; *(equivalente)* equal; **i. que** the same as; **a partes iguales** fifty-fifty; **al i. que** just like; **por i.** equally; **6 más 7 i. a 13** 6 plus 7 equals 13. **2** *m* equal. **3** *adv* **lo haces i. que yo** you do it the same way I do; **es i.** it doesn't matter.
igualar *vt* to make equal; *(nivelar)* to level.
igualdad *f* equality; *(identidad)* sameness; **en i. de condiciones** on equal terms.
igualmente *adv* equally; *(también)* also, likewise; **¡gracias! — ¡i.!** thank you! — the same to you!
ilegal *adj* illegal.
ilegalmente *adv* illegally.
ilegible *adj* illegible, unreadable.
ilegítimo, -a *adj* illegitimate.
ileso, -a *adj* unharmed.
ilícito, -a *adj* unlawful.
ilimitado, -a *adj* unlimited.
iluminación *f (alumbrado)* illumination.
iluminar *vt* to illuminate.
ilusión *f (esperanza)* hope; *(esperanza vana)* illusion; *(emoción)* excitement; **hacerse ilusiones** to build up one's hopes; **me hace i. verla** I'm looking forward to seeing her; **¡qué i.!** how exciting!
ilusionar 1 *vt (esperanzar)* **i. a algn** to build up sb's hopes; *(entusiasmar)* to excite. **2 ilusionarse** *vr (esperanzarse)* to build up one's hopes; *(entusiasmarse)* to be excited (**con** about).
ilustración *f (grabado)* illustration; *(erudición)* learning.
ilustrar *vt* to illustrate.
ilustre *adj* distinguished.
imagen *f* image; *(de televisión)* picture.
imaginación *f* imagination.
imaginar 1 *vt* to imagine. **2 imaginarse** *vr* to imagine; **me imagino que sí** I suppose so.
imaginario, -a *adj* imaginary.
imán *m* magnet.
imbatible *adj* unbeatable.
imbécil 1 *adj* stupid. **2** *mf* imbecile.
imitar *vt* to imitate; *(gestos)* to mimic.
impacientar 1 *vt* **i. a algn** to exasperate sb. **2 impacientarse** *vr* to get impatient (**por** at).
impaciente *adj (deseoso)* impatient; *(intranquilo)* anxious.
impactar *vt* to shock, to stun.
impactante *adj* **una noticia i.** a sensational piece of news.
impacto *m* impact.
impar *adj* odd.
imparable *adj* unstoppable.
imparcial *adj* impartial.
impartir *vt (clases)* to give.
impasible *adj* impassive.
impecable *adj* impeccable.
impedimento *m* impediment; *(obstáculo)* hindrance.
impedir *vt (obstaculizar)* to impede; *(imposibilitar)* to prevent, to stop.
impenetrable *adj* impenetrable.
impensable *adj* unthinkable.
imperante *adj (gobernante)* ruling; *(predominante)* prevailing.
imperativo, -a 1 *adj* imperative. **2** *m* imperative.
imperdible *m* safety pin.
imperdonable *adj* unforgivable, inexcusable.
imperfecto, -a *adj* imperfect; *(defectuoso)* defective; *(tiempo verbal)* imperfect.
imperio *m* empire.
impermeable 1 *adj* impervious; *(ropa)* waterproof. **2** *m* raincoat.
impertinente *adj (insolente)* impertinent; *(inoportuno)* irrelevant.
impetuoso, -a *adj (violento)* violent; *(fogoso)* impetuous.
implacable *adj* implacable.
implicar *vt (involucrar)* to involve (**en** in); *(conllevar)* to imply.
implícito, -a *adj* implicit.
implorar *vt* to implore.
imponente *adj (impresionante)* imposing; *(sobrecogedor)* stunning.
imponer *(pp impuesto)* **1** *vt* to impose; *(impresionar)* to be impressive; **i. respeto** to inspire respect. **2 imponerse** *vr (prevalecer)* to prevail; *(ser necesario)* to be necessary.
importación *f (mercancía)* import; *(acción)* importing; **artículos de i.** imported goods.
importancia *f* importance; *(tamaño)* size.
importante *adj* important; *(grande)* significant.
importar¹ 1 *vi (tener importancia)* to be important; **no importa** it doesn't matter; **eso no te importa a tí** that doesn't concern you; **¿te importa si fumo?** do you mind if I smoke? **2** *vt (valer)* to amount to.
importar² *vt* to import.
importe *m* amount.
importunar *vt* to bother, to pester.
imposibilitar *vt (impedir)* to make impossible; *(incapacitar)* to disable.
imposible *adj* impossible; **me es i. hacerlo** I can't (possibly) do it.
impostor, -a *mf* impostor.
impotencia *f* powerlessness.
imprenta *f (taller)* printer's; *(aparato)* printing press.
imprescindible *adj* essential.
impresentable *adj* unpresentable.
impresión *f (efecto, opinión)* impression; *(acto, de revista etc)* printing; *(edición)* edition.
impresionante *adj* impressive.
impresionar *vt (causar admiración)* to impress; *(sorprender)* to stun.
impresionismo *m* impressionism.
impreso, -a 1 *adj* printed. **2** *m (papel, folleto)* printed matter; *(formulario)* form; **i. de solicitud** application form.
impresora *f* printer; **i. de chorro de tinta** ink-jet (printer); **i. láser** laser (printer); **i. matricial** dot matrix (printer).
imprevisible *adj* unforeseeable.
imprevisto, -a 1 *adj* unforeseen. **2** *m* unforeseen event.
imprimir *(pp impreso)* *vt* to print.

impropio, -a *adj (inadecuado)* inappropriate.
improvisado, -a *adj (espontáneo)* improvised; *(provisional)* makeshift.
improvisar *vt* to improvise.
imprudencia *f* rashness; *(indiscreción)* indiscretion.
imprudente *adj* imprudent, unwise; *(indiscreto)* indiscreet.
impuesto *m* tax; **i. sobre la renta** income tax; **libre de impuestos** tax-free.
impulsar *vt* to drive.
impulso *m* impulse.
impunemente *adv* with impunity.
impureza *f* impurity.
impuse *pt indef de* **imponer**.
inacabable *adj* endless.
inaccesible *adj* inaccessible.
inaceptable *adj* unacceptable.
inadaptado, -a 1 *adj* maladjusted. **2** *mf* misfit.
inadecuado, -a *adj* unsuitable.
inadmisible *adj* inadmissible.
inadvertido, -a *adj* unnoticed; **pasar i.** to escape notice, to pass unnoticed.
inagotable *adj (recursos etc)* inexhaustible; *(persona)* tireless.
inaguantable *adj* unbearable.
inalcanzable *adj* unattainable, unachievable.
inapreciable *adj (valioso)* invaluable; *(insignificante)* insignificant.
inasequible *adj (producto)* unaffordable; *(meta)* unattainable; *(persona)* unapproachable.
inaudito, -a *adj* unprecedented.
inauguración *f* inauguration.
inaugurar *vt* to inaugurate.
inca *adj & mf* Inca.
incalculable *adj* incalculable.
incandescente *adj* white hot.
incansable *adj* tireless.
incapacidad *f* inability; *(incompetencia)* incompetence.
incapacitar *vt* to incapacitate; *(inhabilitar)* to disqualify.
incapaz *adj* incapable (**de** of).
incendiar 1 *vt* to set fire to. **2 incendiarse** *vr* to catch fire.
incendio *m* fire; **i. forestal** forest fire.
incentivo *m* incentive.
incertidumbre *f* uncertainty.
incidente *m* incident.
incierto, -a *adj* uncertain.
incinerar *vt (basura)* to incinerate; *(cadáveres)* to cremate.
incipiente *adj* incipient.
incitar *vt* to incite.
inclinación *f (de terreno)* slope; *(del cuerpo)* stoop; *(reverencia)* bow.
inclinar 1 *vt* to incline; *(cabeza)* to nod. **2 inclinarse** *vr* to lean; *(al saludar)* to bow; *(optar)* **inclinarse a** to be inclined to.
incluir *vt* to include; *(contener)* to contain; *(adjuntar)* to enclose.
inclusive *adv (incluido)* inclusive; *(incluso)* even; **hasta la lección ocho i.** up to and including lesson eight.
incluso *adv* even.
incógnita *f (misterio)* mystery.
incoherente *adj* incoherent.
incoloro, -a *adj* colorless.
incombustible *adj* incombustible.
incomodar 1 *vt (causar molestia)* to inconvenience, to put out; *(fastidiar)* to bother, to annoy. **2 incomodarse** *vr (tomarse molestias)* to put oneself out, to go out of one's way; *(disgustarse)* to get annoyed o angry.
incomodidad *f* discomfort; *(molestia)* inconvenience.
incómodo, -a *adj* uncomfortable.
incompatible *adj* incompatible.
incompetencia *f* incompetence.
incompetente 1 *adj* incompetent. **2** *mf* incompetent person.
incompleto, -a *adj* incomplete; *(inacabado)* unfinished.
incomprensible *adj* incomprehensible.
incomunicado, -a *adj (aislado)* isolated; *(en la cárcel)* in solitary confinement; **el pueblo se quedó i.** the town was cut off.
inconcebible *adj* inconceivable.
incondicional *adj* unconditional; *(apoyo)* wholehearted; *(amigo)* faithful; *(partidario)* staunch.
inconexo, -a *adj (incoherente)* incoherent, confused.
inconfundible *adj* unmistakable.
incongruente *adj* incongruous.
inconsciencia *f* unconsciousness; *(irresponsabilidad)* irresponsibility.
inconsciente 1 *adj (con estar)* *(desmayado)* unconscious; *(con ser)* *(despreocupado)* unaware (**de** of); *(irreflexivo)* thoughtless.
inconsistente *adj (argumento)* weak.
inconstante *adj* fickle.
incontrolable *adj* uncontrollable.
inconveniencia *f* inconvenience; *(impropiedad)* unsuitability.
inconveniente 1 *adj* inconvenient; *(inapropiado)* unsuitable. **2** *m (objeción)* objection; *(desventaja)* disadvantage; *(problema)* difficulty.
incordiar *vt fam* to bother, to pester.
incordio *m fam* nuisance, pain.
incorporación *f* incorporation.
incorporar 1 *vt* to incorporate (**en** into); *(levantar)* to help to sit up. **2 incorporarse** *vr (en la cama)* to sit up; **incorporarse a** *(sociedad)* to join; *(trabajo)* to start.
incorrecto, -a *adj (equivocado)* incorrect.
incorregible *adj* incorrigible.
incrédulo, -a 1 *adj* incredulous. **2** *mf* disbeliever.
increíble *adj* incredible.
incrementar 1 *vt* to increase. **2 incrementarse** *vr* to increase.
inculto, -a 1 *adj* uneducated. **2** *mf* ignoramus.
incultura *f* ignorance, lack of culture.
incumplimiento *m (de un deber)* non-fulfillment; *(de una orden)* failure to execute.
incumplir *vt* not to fulfill; *(deber)* to fail to fulfill; *(promesa, contrato)* to break; *(orden)* to fail to carry out.
incurrir *vi* to fall (**en** into).
indagar *vt* to investigate.
indebido, -a *adj (desconsiderado)* undue; *(ilegal)* unlawful.
indecente *adj* indecent.
indeciso, -a 1 *adj* hesitant. **2** *m (en encuesta)* don't know.
indefenso, -a *adj* defenseless.
indefinidamente *adv* indefinitely.
indefinido, -a *adj (indeterminado)* indefinite; *(impreciso)* vague; *(tiempo verbal)* indefinite.
indemnización *f (acto)* indemnification; *(compensación)* compensation.

indemnizar *vt* to compensate (**por** for).
independencia *f* independence.
independiente *adj (libre)* independent; *(individualista)* self-reliant.
independientemente *adv* independently (**de** of); *(aparte de)* irrespective (**de** of).
indescriptible *adj* indescribable.
indeseable *adj & mf* undesirable.
indeterminado, -a *adj* indefinite; *(impreciso)* vague; *(artículo)* indefinite.
indicación *f (señal)* indication; *(instrucción)* instruction.
indicador *m* indicator.
indicar *vt* to indicate.
indicativo, -a *adj* indicative (**de** of); **(modo) i.** indicative (mode).
índice *m (de libro)* index; *(relación)* rate; **i. de natalidad/mortalidad** birth/death rate; **(dedo) í.** index finger.
indicio *m* indication (**de** of).
índico, -a *adj* Indian; **Océano I.** Indian Ocean.
indiferente *adj* indifferent; **me es i.** it makes no difference to me.
indígena 1 *adj* indigenous (**de** to). **2** *mf* native (**de** of).
indigestión *f* indigestion.
indignación *f* indignation.
indignar 1 *vt* to infuriate. **2 indignarse** *vr* to be indignant (**por** at, about).
indigno, -a *adj* unworthy (**de** of); *(despreciable)* wretched, dreadful.
indio, -a *adj & mf* Indian.
indirecta *f fam* insinuation.
indirecto, -a *adj* indirect.
indiscreto, -a *adj* indiscreet.
indiscutible *adj* indisputable.
indispensable *adj* indispensable.
indisponer *(pp indispuesto)* **1** *vt* to make ill. **2 indisponerse** *vr* to become ill.
indispuse *pt indef de* **indisponer**.
indistintamente *adv* **pueden escribir en inglés o en español i.** you can write in English or Spanish, it doesn't matter which.
individual *adj* individual; **habitación i.** single room.
individuo *m* individual.
índole *f (carácter)* character; *(clase, tipo)* kind.
inducir *vt* to lead.
indudable *adj* indubitable; **es i. que** there is no doubt that.
induje *pt indef de* **inducir**.
indultar *vt* to pardon.
indumentaria *f* clothing.
industria *f* industry.
industrial 1 *adj* industrial. **2** *mf* manufacturer.
industrialización *f* industrialization.
induzco *indic pres de* **inducir**.
ineficacia *f (ineptitud)* inefficiency; *(inutilidad)* ineffectiveness.
ineficaz *adj (inepto)* inefficient; *(inefectivo)* ineffective.
ineludible *adj* inescapable, unavoidable.
ineptitud *f* ineptitude, incompetence.
inepto, -a 1 *adj* inept. **2** *mf* incompetent person.
inequívoco, -a *adj* unmistakable, unequivocal.
inerte *adj (inanimado)* inert; *(inmóvil)* motionless.
inesperado, -a *adj (fortuito)* unexpected; *(imprevisto)* sudden.
inestabilidad *f* instability.
inevitable *adj* inevitable.
inexistente *adj* non-existent.
inexperiencia *f* lack of experience.
inexplicable *adj* inexplicable.
infalible *adj* infallible.
infame *adj (vil)* infamous, vile; *(despreciable)* dreadful, awful.
infancia *f* childhood.
infantería *f* infantry.
infantil *adj* **literatura i.** *(para niños)* children's literature. **2** *(aniñado)* childlike; *(peyorativo)* childish.
infarto *m* **i. (de miocardio)** heart attack.
infección *f* infection.
infectar 1 *vt* to infect. **2 infectarse** *vr* to become infected (**de** with).
infeliz 1 *adj* unhappy; *(desdichado)* unfortunate. **2** *mf fam* simpleton.
inferior 1 *adj (más bajo)* lower; *(calidad)* inferior; *(cantidad)* lower. **2** *mf (persona)* subordinate.
infestado, -a *adj* **i. de** infested with; **i. de turistas** swarming with tourists.
infidelidad *f* unfaithfulness.
infierno *m* hell; *(horno)* inferno; *fam* **¡vete al i.!** go to hell!
infinidad *f* infinity; *(sinfín)* great number; **en i. de ocasiones** on countless occasions.
infinitivo, -a *adj & m* infinitive.
infinito, -a 1 *adj* infinite. **2** *m* infinity.
inflable *adj* inflatable.
inflación *f* inflation.
inflamable *adj* flammable.
inflamación *f* inflammation.
inflamar 1 *vt* to inflame; *(encender)* to set on fire. **2 inflamarse** *vr* to become inflamed; *(incendiarse)* to catch fire.
inflar 1 *vt* to inflate. **2 inflarse** *vr* to inflate.
inflexible *adj* inflexible.
influencia *f* influence; **ejercer o tener i. sobre algn** to have an influence on sb.
influir 1 *vt* to influence. **2** *vi* to have influence; **i. en o sobre** to influence.
información *f* information; *(servicio telefónico)* directory enquiries *pl*.
informal *adj (reunión, cena)* informal; *(comportamiento)* casual; *(persona)* unreliable.
informar 1 *vt (enterar)* to inform (**de** of); *(dar informes)* to report. **2 informarse** *vr (procurarse noticias)* to find out (**de** about); *(enterarse)* to inquire (**de** about).
informática *f* information technology, IT.
informático, -a 1 *adj* computer, computing. **2** *mf* (computer) technician.
informe *m* report; **informes** references.
infracción *f* infringement.
infraestructura *f* infrastructure.
infringir *vt* **i. una ley** to break a law.
infundir *vt* to infuse; *(idea etc)* to instil.
infusión *f* infusion.
ingeniero, -a *mf* engineer; **i. de caminos** civil engineer; **i. técnico** technician.
ingenio *m (talento)* talent; *(inventiva)* inventiveness; *(agudeza)* wit.
ingenioso, -a *adj* ingenious; *(vivaz)* witty.
ingenuo, -a 1 *adj* naïve. **2** *mf* naïve person.
ingerir *vt (comida)* to ingest, to consume; *(líquidos, alcohol)* to drink, to consume.
ingle *f* groin.
inglés, -esa 1 *adj* English. **2** *mf (hombre)* Englishman; *(mujer)* Englishwoman; **los ingleses** the English. **3** *m (idioma)* English.

ingratitud *f* ingratitude.
ingrediente *m* ingredient.
ingresar 1 *vt (dinero)* to pay in; *(enfermo)* to admit; **la ingresaron en el hospital** she was admitted to the hospital. **2** *vi* to enter.
ingreso *m (dinero)* deposit; *(entrada)* entry (**en** into); *(admisión)* admission (**en** to); **ingresos** *(sueldo, renta)* income *sing*; *(beneficios)* revenue *sing*.
inhalador *m* inhaler.
inhalar *vt* to inhale.
inhumano, -a *adj* inhumane; *(cruel)* inhuman.
inicial *adj & f* initial.
iniciar 1 *vt (empezar)* to begin, to start; *(discusión)* to initiate; *(una cosa nueva)* to pioneer. **2 iniciarse** *vr* to begin, to start.
iniciativa *f* initiative; **por i. propia** on one's own initiative.
inicio *m* beginning, start.
ininterrumpido, -a *adj* uninterrupted.
injerirse *vr* to interfere (**en** in).
injuria *f* insult.
injusticia *f* injustice.
injustificado, -a *adj* unjustified.
injusto, -a *adj* unjust.
inmaduro, -a *adj* immature.
inmediaciones *fpl* neighborhood *sing*.
inmediatamente *adv* immediately, at once.
inmediato, -a *adj (en el tiempo)* immediate; *(en el espacio)* next (**a** to); **de i.** at once.
inmejorable *adj (trabajo)* excellent; *(precio)* unbeatable.
inmenso, -a *adj* immense.
inmigración *f* immigration.
inmigrante *adj & mf* immigrant.
inminente *adj* imminent.
inmiscuirse *vr* to interfere (**en** in).
inmobiliaria *f* real estate company.
inmoral *adj* immoral.
inmortal *adj & mf* immortal.
inmóvil *adj* motionless.
inmovilizar *vt* to immobilize.
inmueble *m* building.
inmune *adj* immune (**a** to).
inmunidad *f* immunity (**contra** to).
inmunizar *vt* to immunize (**contra** against).
inmutarse *vr* **ni se inmutó** he didn't turn a hair.
innato, -a *adj* innate.
innecesario, -a *adj* unnecessary.
innegable *adj* undeniable.
innovación *f* innovation.
innumerable *adj* countless.
inocencia *f* innocence; *(ingenuidad)* naïvety.
inocentada *f* ≃ April Fools' joke.
inocente 1 *adj* innocent. **2** *mf* innocent (person).
inocuo, -a *adj* innocuous.
inofensivo, -a *adj* harmless.
inolvidable *adj* unforgettable.
inoportuno, -a *adj* inappropriate.
inoxidable *adj* **acero i.** stainless steel.
inquietante *adj* worrying.
inquietar 1 *vt* to worry. **2 inquietarse** *vr* to worry (**por** about).
inquieto, -a *adj (preocupado)* worried (**por** about); *(intranquilo)* restless.
inquietud *f (preocupación)* worry; *(agitación)* restlessness.
inquilino, -a *mf* tenant.
insaciable *adj* insatiable.
insatisfecho, -a *adj* dissatisfied.
inscribir *(pp* **inscrito) 1** *vt (registrar)* to register; *(matricular)* to enroll; *(grabar)* to inscribe. **2 inscribirse** *vr (registrarse)* to register; *(hacerse miembro)* to join; *(matricularse)* to enroll; **inscribirse en un club** to join a club.
inscripción *f (matriculación)* enrollment; *(escrito etc)* inscription.
insecticida *m* insecticide.
insecto *m* insect.
inseguridad *f (falta de confianza)* insecurity; *(duda)* uncertainty; *(peligro)* lack of safety.
inseguro, -a *adj (poco confiado)* insecure; *(dubitativo)* uncertain; *(peligroso)* unsafe.
insensato, -a 1 *adj* foolish. **2** *mf* fool.
insensible *adj (indiferente)* unfeeling; *(imperceptible)* imperceptible; *(miembro)* numb.
inseparable *adj* inseparable.
insertar *vt* to insert.
inservible *adj* useless.
insignia *f* badge.
insignificante *adj* insignificant.
insinuar *vt* to insinuate.
insistir *vi* to insist (**en** on).
insolación *f* sunstroke.
insolente *adj* insolent.
insólito, -a *adj (poco usual)* unusual; *(extraño)* strange, odd.
insomnio *m* insomnia.
insoportable *adj* unbearable.
insospechado, -a *adj* unsuspected.
insostenible *adj* untenable.
inspección *f* inspection.
inspeccionar *vt* to inspect.
inspector, -a *mf* inspector; **i. de Hacienda** tax inspector.
inspiración *f* inspiration; *(inhalación)* inhalation.
inspirar 1 *vt* to inspire; *(inhalar)* to inhale. **2 inspirarse** *vr* **inspirarse en** to be inspired by.
instalación *f* installation; **instalaciones deportivas** sports facilities.
instalar 1 *vt* to install; *(erigir)* to set up. **2 instalarse** *vr* to settle (down).
instancia *f (solicitud)* request; **a instancia(s) de** at the request of; **en última i.** as a last resort.
instantáneamente *adv* instantly.
instantáneo, -a *adj* instantaneous; **café i.** instant coffee.
instante *m* instant; **a cada i.** constantly; **al i.** immediately.
instaurar *vt* to found.
instigar *vt* to instigate.
instintivo, -a *adj* instinctive.
instinto *m* instinct; **por i.** instinctively.
institución *f* institution.
instituto *m* institute; *(colegio)* high school.
institutriz *f* governess.
instrucción *f (educación)* education; **instrucciones para el** *o* **de uso** instructions *o* directions for use.

instructivo, -a *adj* instructive.
instruir *vt* to instruct; *(enseñar)* to educate.
instrumento *m* instrument.
insubordinarse *vr* to rebel (**contra** against).
insuficiente 1 *adj* insufficient. **2** *m (nota)* fail.
insulso, -a *adj* insipid.
insultar *vt* to insult.
insulto *m* insult.
insuperable *adj (inmejorable)* unsurpassable; *(problema)* insurmountable.
insurrección *f* insurrection.
intacto, -a *adj* intact.
integral *adj* integral; **pan i.** wholewheat bread.
integrante 1 *adj* integral; **ser parte i. de** to be an integral part of. **2** *mf* member.
integrar 1 *vt* to integrate; *(formar)* to compose. **2 integrarse** *vr* to integrate (**en** with).
integridad *f* integrity.
íntegro, -a *adj (entero)* whole; *(honrado)* upright; **versión íntegra** unabridged version.
intelectual *adj & mf* intellectual.
inteligencia *f* intelligence.
inteligente *adj* intelligent.
inteligible *adj* intelligible.
intemperie *f* **a la i.** in the open (air).
intención *f* intention; **con i.** deliberately; **tener la i. de hacer algo** to intend to do sth.
intencionadamente *adv* on purpose.
intencionado, -a *adj* deliberate.
intensidad *f* intensity; *(del viento)* force.
intensificar *vt*, **intensificarse** *vr* to intensify; *(relación)* to strengthen.
intenso, -a *adj* intense.
intentar *vt* to try.
intento *m* attempt; **i. de suicidio** attempted suicide.
intercambiar *vt* to exchange.
interceder *vi* to intercede.
interceptar *vt (detener)* to intercept; *(carretera)* to block; *(tráfico)* to hold up.
interés *m* interest; *(provecho personal)* self-interest; **tener i. en** *o* **por** to be interested in; **tipos de i.** interest rates.
interesante *adj* interesting.
interesar 1 *vt (tener interés)* to interest; *(concernir)* to concern. **2** *vi (ser importante)* to be of interest. **2 interesarse** *vr* **interesarse por** *o* **en** to be interested in.
interferencia *f* interference; *(en radio, televisión)* jamming.
interfono *m* intercom.
interior 1 *adj* inner; **ropa i.** underwear; *(política, vuelo)* domestic; *(región)* inland. **2** *m* inside; *(de un país)* interior; **Ministerio del I.** Department of the Interior.
interjección *f* interjection.
interlocutor, -a *mf* speaker.
intermediario, -a *mf* intermediary, middleman.
intermedio, -a 1 *adj* intermediate. **2** *m (en televisión)* break.
interminable *adj* endless.
intermitente 1 *adj* intermittent. **2** *m (de automóvil)* indicator.
internacional *adj* international.
internado *m (colegio)* boarding school.
internauta *mf* Net user.
Internet *f* Internet; **está en I.** it's on the Internet.
interno, -a 1 *adj* internal; *(política)* domestic. **2** *mf (alumno)* boarder.
interpretación *f* interpretation.
interpretar *vt* to interpret; *(papel)* to play; *(obra)* to perform; *(concierto)* to perform; *(canción)* to sing.
intérprete *mf (traductor)* interpreter; *(actor, músico)* performer; *(cantante)* singer.
interrogación *f* interrogation; **(signo de) i.** question mark.
interrogante *f fig* question mark.
interrogar *vt* to question; *(con amenazas)* to interrogate.
interrogatorio *m* interrogation.
interrumpir *vt* to interrupt; *(tráfico)* to block.
interruptor *m* switch.
interurbano, -a *adj* intercity; **conferencia interurbana** long-distance call.
intervalo *m* interval.
intervenir 1 *vi (mediar)* to intervene (**en** in); *(participar)* take part (**en** in). **2** *vt (teléfono)* tap.
interviú *m (pl* **interviús)** interview.
intestino *m* intestine.
intimidar *vt* to intimidate.
íntimo, -a *adj* intimate; *(vida)* private; *(amigo)* close.
intolerante 1 *adj* intolerant. **2** *mf* intolerant person.
intoxicación *f* poisoning; **i. alimenticia** food poisoning.
intranquilizarse *vr* to get worried.
intranquilo, -a *adj (preocupado)* worried; *(agitado)* restless.
intransigente *adj* intransigent.
intransitivo, -a *adj* intransitive.
intriga *f* intrigue; *(trama)* plot.
intrigar 1 *vt (interesar)* to intrigue. **2** *vi (maquinar)* to plot.
intrínseco, -a *adj* intrinsic.
introducir *vt* to introduce; *(meter)* to insert.
introvertido, -a 1 *adj* introverted. **2** *mf* introvert.
intruso, -a *mf* intruder.
intuición *f* intuition.
intuir *vt* to know by intuition.
inundación *f* flood.
inusitado, -a *adj* unusual.
inútil 1 *adj* useless; *(esfuerzo, intento)* pointless. **2** *mf fam* good-for-nothing.
inutilizar *vt* to make useless.
invadir *vt* to invade; **los estudiantes invadieron la calle** students poured out onto the street.
inválido, -a 1 *adj (nulo)* invalid; *(minusválido)* disabled. **2** *mf* disabled person.
invariable *adj* invariable.
invasión *f* invasion.
invencible *adj (enemigo)* invincible; *(obstáculo)* insurmountable.
invención *f (invento)* invention; *(mentira)* fabrication.
inventar *vt (crear)* to invent; *(excusa, mentira)* to concoct.
inventario *m* inventory.
invento *m* invention.
invernadero *m* greenhouse.
invernal *adj* winter.
inversión *f* inversion; *(de dinero)* investment.
inverso, -a *adj* **en sentido i.** in the opposite direction; **en orden i.** in reverse order.
invertir *vt (orden)* to invert; *(dinero)* to invest (**en** in); *(tiempo)* to spend (**en** on).
investigación *f (policial etc)* investigation; *(científica)* research.
investigar *vt (indagar)* to investigate; *(científicamente)* to research.

invierno *m* winter.
invisible *adj* invisible.
invitado, -a 1 *adj* invited. **2** *mf* guest.
invitar *vt* to invite; **me invitó a una copa** he treated me to a drink.
involucrarse *vr* to get involved (**en** in).
involuntario, -a *adj* involuntary; *(impremeditado)* unintentional.
inyección *f* injection; **poner una i.** to give an injection.
inyectar *vt* to inject (**en** into); **i. algo a algn** to inject sb with sth.
ir 1 *vi* to go; **¡vamos!** let's go!; **¡ya voy!** (I'm) coming!; **¿cómo le va el nuevo trabajo?** how is he doing in his new job?; **el negro no te va** black doesn't suit you; **ir con falda** to wear a skirt; **ir de blanco/de uniforme** to be dressed in white/in uniform; **va para abogado** he's studying to be a lawyer; **ir por la derecha** to keep (to the) right; **ve (a) por agua** go and fetch some water; **voy por la página noventa** I've got as far as page ninety; **en lo que va de año** so far this year; **ir a parar** to end up; **¡qué va!** of course not!; **va a lo suyo** he looks after his own interests; **¡vamos a ver!** let's see!; **¡vaya!** fancy that; **¡vaya moto!** what a bike! **2** *v aux* **ir andando** to go on foot; **va mejorando** she's improving; **ya van rotos tres** three (of them) have already been broken; **iba a decir que ...** I was going to say that ...; **va a llover** it's going to rain. **3** *irse* *vr* *(marcharse)* to go away; **me voy** I'm off; **¡vámonos!** let's go!; **¡vete!** go away!; **¡vete a casa!** go home!; **¿por dónde se va a ...?** which is the way to ...?
ira *f* rage.
iraní *adj & mf* (*pl* **iraníes**) Iranian.
iraquí *adj & mf* (*pl* **iraquíes**) Iraqi.
irascible *adj* irascible.
iris *m inv* **arco i.** rainbow.
irlandés, -esa 1 *adj* Irish. **2** *mf* *(hombre)* Irishman; *(mujer)* Irishwoman; **los irlandeses** the Irish. **3** *m* *(idioma)* Irish.
ironía *f* irony.
irónico, -a *adj* ironic.
irracional *adj* irrational.
irreal *adj* unreal.
irregular *adj* irregular.
irremediable *adj* incurable.
irresistible *adj* *(impulso, persona)* irresistible; *(insoportable)* unbearable.
irresponsable *adj* irresponsible.
irrisorio, -a *adj* derisory, ridiculous.
irritación *f* irritation.
irritante *adj* irritating.
irritar 1 *vt* to irritate. **2 irritarse** *vr* to become irritated.
irrompible *adj* unbreakable.
irrumpir *vi* to burst (**en** into).
isla *f* island.
islámico, -a *adj* Islamic.
israelí *adj & mf* (*pl* **israelíes**) Israeli.
italiano, -a 1 *adj* Italian. **2** *mf* *(persona)* Italian. **3** *m* *(idioma)* Italian.
itinerario *m* itinerary.
IVA *m abr de* **impuesto sobre el valor añadido** value-added tax, VAT.
izqda., izqdª *abr de* **izquierda** left.
izqdo., izqdº *abr de* **izquierdo** left.
izquierda *f* left; *(mano)* left hand; **a la i.** on the left; **girar a la i.** to turn left.
izquierdo, -a *adj* left.

J

jabalí *m* (*pl* **jabalíes**) wild boar.
jabalina *f* javelin.
jabón *m* soap; **j. de afeitar/tocador** shaving/toilet soap.
jabonera *f* soap dish.
jaca *f* gelding.
jacaré *m Am* caiman.
jacinto *m* hyacinth.
jactarse *vr* to boast (**de** about).
jadear *vi* to pant.
jalar 1 *vt Andes, CAm, Carib, Méx (tirar)* to pull; *fam (comer)* to wolf down. **2 jalarse** *vr fam (comerse)* to wolf down, to scoff.
jalea *f* jelly.
jaleo *m* *(alboroto)* ruckus; *(confusión)* muddle.
jalón *m Am* lift.
jamás *adv* never; **j. he estado allí** I have never been there; **el mejor libro que j. se ha escrito** the best book ever written; **nunca j.** never again.
jamón *m* ham; **j. de York/serrano** boiled/cured ham.
japonés, -esa *adj & mf* Japanese; **los japoneses** the Japanese.
jaque *m* check; **j. mate** checkmate; **j. al rey** check.
jaqueca *f* migraine.
jarabe *m* syrup; **j. para la tos** cough mixture.
jardín *m* garden; **j. botánico** botanical garden; **j. de infancia** nursery school.
jardinero, -a *mf* gardener.
jarra *f* pitcher.
jarro *m* *(recipiente)* jug; *(contenido)* jugful.
jarrón *m* vase.
jaula *f* cage.
jazmín *m* jasmine.
J.C. *abr de* **Jesucristo** Jesus Christ, J.C.
jeep *m* jeep.
jefa *f* manager.
jefatura *f* *(cargo, dirección)* leadership; *(sede)* central office.
jefe *m* head; *(de empresa)* manager; *(de partido)* leader; **J. de Estado** Head of State.
jengibre *m* ginger.
jerarquía *f* hierarchy; *(categoría)* rank.
jerez *m* sherry.
jerga *f* *(técnica)* jargon; *(vulgar)* slang.
jeringa *f* syringe.
jeringuilla *f* (hypodermic) syringe.
jeroglífico *m* hieroglyphic; *(juego)* rebus.
jersey *m* (*pl* **jerseis**) pullover.
Jesucristo *m* Jesus Christ.
Jesús 1 *m* Jesus. **2** *interj (al estornudar)* bless you!
jíbaro, -a *mf Am* peasant.
jícara *f Am* gourd.

jilguero *m* goldfinch.
jinete *m* horseman, rider.
jirafa *f* giraffe.
jirón *m* *(trozo desgarrado)* strip; *(pedazo suelto)* scrap; **hecho jirones** in tatters.
JJOO *mpl abr de* **Juegos Olímpicos** Olympic Games.
jornada *f* **j. (laboral)** *(día de trabajo)* working day; **trabajo de media j./j. completa** part-time/full-time work.
jornal *m* day's wage.
jornalero, -a *mf* day laborer.
joroba *f* hump.
jorobado, -a 1 *adj* hunchbacked. **2** *mf* hunchback.
joven 1 *adj* young; **de aspecto j.** young-looking. **2** *mf* *(hombre)* young man; *(mujer)* young woman; **de j.** as a young man/woman; **los jóvenes** young people.
joya *f* jewel; **ser una j.** *(persona)* to be a gem.
joyería *f* *(tienda)* jewelry shop.
joyero, -a 1 *mf* jeweler. **2** *m* jewel case.
jubilado, -a 1 *adj* retired. **2** *mf* retired person; **los jubilados** retired people.
judía *f* bean; **j. verde** green bean.
judío, -a 1 *adj* Jewish. **2** *m* Jew.
judo *m* judo.
juego *m* game; *(conjunto de piezas)* set; *(apuestas)* gambling; **j. de azar** game of chance; **j. de cartas** card game; **Juegos Olímpicos** Olympic Games; **terreno de j.** field; **fuera de j.** offside; **j. de café/té** coffee/tea service; **ir a j. con** to match.
juerga *f fam* rave-up; **ir de j.** to go on a binge.
jueves *m inv* Thursday; **J. Santo** Holy Thursday.
juez, -a *mf* judge; **j. de línea** linesman.
jugada *f* move; *fam* dirty trick.
jugador, -a *mf* player; *(apostador)* gambler.
jugar 1 *vi* to play; **j. a(l) fútbol** to play football; **j. sucio** to play dirty. **2** *vt* to play; *(apostar)* to bet. **3 jugarse** *vr (arriesgar)* to risk; *(apostar)* to bet.
jugo *m* juice.
juguete *m* toy; **pistola de j.** toy gun.
juicio *m* *(facultad mental)* judgement; *(sensatez)* reason; *(opinión)* opinion; *(en tribunal)* trial; **a j. de** in the opinion of; **a mi j.** in my opinion; **perder el j.** to go mad.
julio *m* July.
junco *m* rush.
jungla *f* jungle.
junio *m* June.
júnior *adj* junior.
junta *f* *(reunión)* meeting; *(dirección)* board; *(gobierno militar)* junta.
juntar 1 *vt (unir)* to join; *(piezas)* to assemble; *(dinero)* to raise. **2 juntarse** *vr (unirse)* to join; *(ríos, caminos)* to meet; *(personas)* to gather.
junto, -a 1 *adj* together. **2** *adv* **j. con** together with; **j. a** next to.
jurado *m* jury.
juramento *m* oath; **bajo j.** under oath.
jurar 1 *vi* to swear. **2** *vt* to swear; **j. el cargo** to take the oath of office.
jurídico, -a *adj* legal.
justamente *adv* **¡j.!** precisely!; **j. detrás de** right behind.
justicia *f* justice; **tomarse la j. por su mano** to take the law into one's own hands.
justificado, -a *adj* justified.
justificante *m* written proof.
justificar 1 *vt* to justify. **2 justificarse** *vr* to justify oneself.
justo, -a 1 *adj* just; *(apretado) (ropa)* tight; *(exacto)* accurate; **un trato j.** a fair deal; **estamos justos de tiempo** we're pressed for time; **llegamos en el momento j. en que salían** we arrived just as they were leaving; **lo j.** just enough. **2** *adv (exactamente)* precisely; **j. al lado de** right beside.
juvenil *adj* young; **ropa j.** *(de joven)* young people's clothes; **delincuencia j.** juvenile delinquency.
juventud *f* *(edad)* youth; *(jóvenes)* young people.
juzgado *m* court.
juzgar *vt* to judge; **a j. por ...** judging by ....

K

kárate *m* karate.
kilo *m* *(medida)* kilo.
kilogramo *m* kilogram.
kilometraje *m* ≃ mileage.
kilómetro *m* kilometer.
kiosco *m* kiosk.
kiwi *m* *(fruto)* kiwi (fruit).
kleenex® *m* tissue.

L

la¹ 1 *art def f* the. **2** *pron dem* the one; **la del vestido azul** the one in the blue dress.
la² *pron pers f* *(persona)* her; *(usted)* you; *(cosa)* it; **la invitaré I'll invite her along; **ya la avisaremos, señora** we'll let you know, madam; **no la dejes abierta** don't leave it open.
labio *m* lip.
labor *f* job; *(de costura)* needlework.
laborable *adj* **día l.** working day.
laboral *adj* industrial; **accidente l.** industrial accident; **jornada l.** working day.
laboratorio *m* laboratory.
labrar 1 *vt (tierra)* to till; *(madera)* to carve; *(piedra)* to cut; *(metal)* to work. **2 labrarse** *vr fig* **labrarse un porvenir** to build a future for oneself.
laca *f* hairspray; **l. de uñas** nail polish.
ladear 1 *vt (inclinar)* to tilt; *(cabeza)* to lean. **2 ladearse** *vr (inclinarse)* to lean, to tilt; *(desviarse)* to go off to one side.
ladera *f* slope.
ladino, -a 1 *adj (astuto)* crafty; *CAm, Méx, Ven (no blanco)* non-white. **2** *mf CAm, Méx, Ven (no blanco)* = non-white Spanish-speaking person.
lado *m* side; **a un l.** aside; **al l.** close by, nearby; **al l. de** next to; **ponte de l.** stand sideways; **por todos lados** on all sides; **por otro l.** *(además)* moreover; **por un l. ..., pro otro l. ...** on the one hand ..., on the other hand ....

ladrar *vi* to bark.
ladrillo *m* brick.
ladrón, -ona *mf* thief.
lagartija *f* small lizard.
lagarto *m* lizard.
lago *m* lake.
lágrima *f* tear.
laguna *f* small lake.
lamentar 1 *vt* to regret; **lo lamento** I'm sorry. **2 lamentarse** *vr* to complain.
lamer *vt* to lick.
lámina *f* sheet.
lámpara *f* lamp; *(bombilla)* bulb.
lana *f* wool; *Andes, Méx fam (dinero)* dough, cash.
lancha *f* motorboat; **l. motora** speedboat; **l. neumática** rubber dinghy; **l. salvavidas** lifeboat.
langosta *f* lobster; *(insecto)* locust.
langostino *m* king prawn.
lanza *f* spear.
lanzar 1 *vt (arrojar)* to throw; *(grito)* to let out; *(ataque, producto)* to launch. **2 lanzarse** *vr* to throw oneself.
lapicera *f CSur* ballpoint (pen); **l. fuente** fountain pen.
lápiz *m* pencil; **l. de labios** lipstick; **l. de ojos** eyeliner.
largo, -a 1 *adj* long; **a lo l. de** *(espacio)* along; *(tiempo)* through; **a la larga** in the long run. **2** *m (longitud)* length; **¿cuánto tiene de l.?** fam how long is it?; *fam* **esto va para l.** this is going to last a long time. **3** *adv fam* **¡l. (de aquí)!** clear off!
largometraje *m* feature film.
las¹ *art def fpl* the. **2** *pron dem* **l. que** *(personas)* those who; *(objetos)* those that; **toma l. que quieras** take whichever ones you want.
las² *pron pers fpl (ellas)* them; *(ustedes)* you; **no l. rompas** don't break them; **l. llamaré mañana** *(a ustedes)* I'll call you tomorrow.
láser *m inv* laser.
lástima *f* pity; **¡qué l.!** what a pity!; **es una l. que ...** it's a pity (that) ....
lata¹ *f (envase)* tin, can; *(hojalata)* tin(plate); **en l.** tinned, canned.
lata² *f fam* drag; **dar la l.** to be a nuisance.
lateral *adj* side; **escalón l.** *(en letrero)* ramp.
latido *m* beat.
látigo *m* whip.
latín *m* Latin.
latinomericano, -a *adj & mf* Latin American.
latir *vi* to beat.
latón *m* brass.
laucha *f Am* mouse.
laurel *m* bay leaf.
lava *f* lava.
lavable *adj* washable.
lavabo *m (pila)* washbasin; *(cuarto de aseo)* washroom; *(retrete)* toilet.
lavadero *m (de coches)* carwash.
lavado *m* washing; **l. en seco** dry-cleaning.
lavadora *f* washing machine.
lavanda *f* lavender.
lavandería *f* laundromat; *(atendida por personal)* laundry.
lavaplatos *m inv* dishwasher.
lavar *vt* to wash.
lavavajillas *m inv* dishwasher.
laxante *adj & m* laxative.
lazo *m (adorno)* bow; *(nudo)* knot; **lazos** *(vínculo)* links.
le 1 *pron pers mf (objeto indirecto)* (a él) (to/for) him; *(a ella)* (to/for) her; *(a cosa)* (to/for) it; *(a usted)* (to/for) you; **lávale la cara** wash his face; **le compraré uno** I'll buy one for her; **¿qué le pasa (a usted)?** what's the matter with you? **2** *pron pers m (objeto directo)* (él) him; *(usted)* you; **no le oigo** I can't hear him; **no quiero molestarle** I don't wish to disturb you.
leal *adj* faithful.
lección *f* lesson.
leche *f* milk; **dientes de l.** milk teeth; **l. descremada** *o* **desnatada** skim milk.
lechuga *f* lettuce.
lechuza *f* owl.
lector, -a *mf (persona)* reader; *(de colegio)* (language) assistant.
lectura *f* reading.
leer *vt* to read.
legal *adj* legal.
legalizar *vt* to legalize; *(documento)* to authenticate.
legislación *f* legislation.
legítimo, -a *adj* legitimate; *(auténtico)* real; **en legítima defensa** in self-defense; **oro l.** pure gold.
legumbres *fpl* pulses.
lejano, -a *adj* far-off.
lejía *f* bleach.
lejos *adv* far (away); **a lo l.** in the distance; **de l.** from a distance; *fig* **sin ir más l.** to take an obvious example.
lema *m* motto.
lencería *f (prendas)* lingerie; *(ropa blanca)* linen (goods *pl*).
lengua *f (tongue)*; *(idioma)* language; **l. materna** mother tongue.
lenguado *f* sole.
lenguaje *m* language; **l. corporal** body language.
lente 1 *f* lens; **lentes de contacto** contact lenses. **2** *mpl* **lentes** *Am* glasses, spectacles; **lentes de contacto** contact lenses.
lenteja *f* lentil.
lentejuela *f* sequin.
lentilla *f* contact lens.
lento, -a *adj* slow; **a fuego l.** on a low heat.
leña *f* firewood.
leño *m* log.
león *m* lion.
leopardo *m* leopard.
leotardos *mpl* thick tights.
les *pron pers mfpl (a ellos/ellas)* them; *(a ustedes)* you; **dales el dinero** give them the money; **l. he comprado un regalo** I've bought you/them a present; **l. esperaré** I shall wait for you/them; **no quiero molestarles** I don't wish to disturb you/them.
lesión *f (física)* injury.
lesionar *vt* to injure.
letal *adj* lethal.
letargo *m* lethargy.
letra *f* letter; *(escritura)* (hand)writing; *(de canción)* lyrics *pl*; **l. de imprenta** block capitals; **l. mayúscula** capital letter; **l. minúscula** small letter; **l. (de cambio)** bill of exchange; *(carrera)* **letras** arts.
letrero *m (aviso)* notice; *(cartel)* poster.

levadura *f* yeast; **l. en polvo** baking powder.
levantamiento *m* lifting; *(insurrección)* uprising; **l. de pesos** weightlifting.
levantar 1 *vt* to lift; *(mano, voz)* to raise; *(edificio)* to erect; *(ánimos)* to raise. **2 levantarse** *vr* to get up; *(ponerse de pie)* to stand up.
levante *m* **(el) L.** Levante, the regions of Valencia and Murcia.
leve *adj (ligero)* light; *(de poca importancia)* slight.
levemente *adv* slightly.
ley *f* law; **aprobar una l.** to pass a bill; **oro de l.** pure gold; **plata de l.** sterling silver.
leyenda *f (relato)* legend; *(bajo ilustración)* caption.
liar 1 *vt (envolver)* to wrap up; *(cigarrillo)* to roll; *(enredar)* to muddle up; *(confundir)* to confuse. **2 liarse** *vr (embarullarse)* to get muddled up.
liberal 1 *adj* liberal; *(generoso)* generous; *(carácter)* open-minded; **profesión l.** profession. **2** *mf* liberal.
liberalizar *vt* to liberalize.
liberar *vt (país)* to liberate; *(prisionero)* to release.
libertad *f* freedom; **(en) l. bajo palabra/fianza** (on) parole/bail; **(en) l. condicional** (on) parole.
libio, -a *adj & mf* Libyan.
libra *f* pound; **l. esterlina** pound sterling.
librar 1 *vt* to free; *(preso)* to release. **2 librarse** *vr* to escape; **librarse de algn** to get rid of sb.
libre *adj* free; *(sin restricción)* open to the public; **entrada l.** admission free; **l. de impuestos** tax-free.
librería *f (tienda)* bookstore; *(estante)* bookcase.
libreta *f* notebook.
libro *m* book; **l. de texto** textbook.
licencia *f (permiso)* permission; *(documentos)* licence; *Am* driver's license.
licenciado, -a *mf* graduate; *Am* lawyer; **l. en Ciencias** Bachelor of Science.
licenciar 1 *vt (soldado)* to discharge; *(estudiante)* to confer a degree on. **2 licenciarse** *vr (estudiante)* to graduate.
licenciatura *f (título)* (bachelor's) degree (course); *(carrera)* degree (course).
licor *m* liquor.
licuadora *f* liquidizer.
líder *mf* leader.
liderar *vt* to lead, to head.
liderato, liderazgo *m* leadership; *(en deportes)* top *o* first position.
lidia *f* bullfighting.
lidiar *vt* to fight.
liebre *f* hare.
liga *f* league.
ligar 1 *vt* to join. **2** *vi fam* **l. con una chica** to flirt with a girl.
ligeramente *adv (levemente)* lightly; *(un poco)* slightly.
ligereza *f* lightness; *(frivolidad)* flippancy; *(acto)* indiscretion; *(rapidez)* speed.
ligero, -a 1 *adj (peso)* light; *(veloz)* quick; *(leve)* slight; **l. de ropa** lightly clad; **brisa/comida ligera** light breeze/meal. **2** *adv* **ligero** *(rápido)* fast.
liguero *m* garter belt.
lija *f* sandpaper; **papel de l.** sandpaper.
lima *f (herramienta)* file; **l. de uñas** nailfile.
limar *vt* to file.
limitar 1 *vt* to restrict. **2** *vi* **l. con** to border on.
límite *m* limit; *(de país)* border; **fecha l.** deadline; **velocidad l.** maximum speed.
limón *m* lemon.
limonada *f* lemon squash.
limonero *m* lemon tree.
limosna *f* alms; **pedir l.** to beg.
limpiabotas *m inv* bootblack, shoeshine.
limpiaparabrisas *m inv* windshield wiper.
limpiar *vt* to clean; *(con un trapo)* to wipe; *(zapatos)* to polish.
limpieza *f (calidad)* cleanliness; *(acción)* cleaning.
limpio, -a 1 *adj (aseado)* clean; *(neto)* net; **juego l.** fair play. **2** *adv* **limpio** fairly; **jugar l.** to play fair.
lindar *vi* **l. con** to border on.
lindo, -a 1 *adj (bonito)* pretty; **de lo l.** a great deal. **2** *adv Am (bien)* nicely.
línea *f* line; **l. aérea** airline; **en líneas generales** roughly speaking; **guardar la l.** to watch one's figure.
lino *m (fibra)* linen.
linterna *f* torch.
lío *m (paquete)* bundle; *(embrollo)* mess; **hacerse un l.** to get mixed up; **meterse en líos** to get into trouble.
lipotimia *f* fainting fit.
liquidación *f (saldo)* clearance sale; *(de deuda, cuenta)* settling.
liquidar 1 *vt (deuda, cuenta)* to settle; *(mercancías)* to sell off. **2** *vr* **liquidarse a algn** *(matar)* to bump sb off.
líquido, -a 1 *adj* liquid; *(cantidad)* net. **2** *m* liquid.
lirio *m* iris.
lisiado, -a 1 *adj* crippled. **2** *mf* cripple.
liso, -a *adj (superficie)* smooth; *(pelo, falda)* straight; *(tela)* self-colored; *Am (desvergonzado)* rude.
lista *f (relación)* list; *(franja)* stripe; **l. de espera** waiting list; *(en avión)* standby; **pasar l.** to call the register; **de/a listas** striped.
listín *m* **l. telefónico** telephone directory.
listo, -a *adj* **ser l.** to be clever; **estar l.** to be ready.
litera *f (cama)* bunk bed; *(en tren)* couchette.
literatura *f* literature.
litigio *m* lawsuit.
litoral 1 *m* coast. **2** *adj* coastal.
litro *m* liter.
llaga *f* sore; *(herida)* wound.
llama *f* flame; **en llamas** in flames.
llamada *f* call; **l. interurbana** long-distance call.
llamado, -a 1 *adj* so-called. **2** *m Am (telefónico)* call; *(a la puerta)* knock; *(con timbre)* ring; *(llamamiento)* appeal, call; **hacer un l.** to make a phone call.
llamamiento *m* appeal.
llamar 1 *vt* to call; **l. (por teléfono)** to call; **l. la atención** to attract attention. **2** *vi (a la puerta)* to knock. **3 llamarse** *vr* to be called; **¿cómo te llamas?** what's your name?
llano, -a 1 *adj (superficie)* level. **2** *m* plain.
llanta *f (de rueda)* wheel rim; *Am* tire.
llanto *m* crying.
llanura *f* plain.
llave *f* key; *(interruptor)* switch; *(herramienta)* spanner; **cerrar con l.** to lock; *(de coche)* **l. de contacto** ignition key; **l. inglesa** adjustable spanner; **l. de paso** stopcock.
llavero *m* key ring.
llegada *f* arrival; *(meta)* finish.
llegar *vi* to arrive; **l. a Madrid** to arrive in Madrid; **¿llegas al techo?** can you reach the ceiling?; **l. a + infinitivo** to go so far as to; **l. a ser** to become.

llenar 1 vt to fill; (satisfacer) to satisfy. **2** vi (comida) to be filling. **3 llenarse** vr to fill (up).

lleno, -a adj full (up).

llevar 1 vt to take; (hacia el oyente) to bring; (transportar) to carry; (prenda) to wear; (negocio) to be in charge of; **llevo dos años aquí** I've been here for two years; **esto lleva mucho tiempo** this takes a long time. **2** v aux **l.** + gerundio to have been + present participle; **llevo dos años estudiando español** I've been studying Spanish for two years. ▪ **l.** + participio pasado to have + past participle; **llevaba escritas seis cartas** I had written six letters. **3 llevarse** vr to take away; (premio) to win; (estar de moda) to be fashionable; **llevarse bien con algn** to get along well with sb.

llorar vi to cry.

lloriquear vi to whimper, to snivel.

llover v impers to rain.

llovizna f drizzle.

lloviznar v impers to drizzle.

lluvia f rain.

lluvioso, -a adj rainy.

lo¹ art def neutro the; **lo mismo** the same thing; **lo mío** mine; **lo tuyo** yours.

lo² pron pers m & neutro (cosa) it; **debes hacerlo** you must do it; (no se traduce) **no se lo dije** I didn't tell her; **lo que ...** what ...; **lo cual ...** which ...; **lo de ...** the business of ...; **cuéntame lo del juicio** tell me about the trial.

lobo m wolf; **como boca de l.** pitch-dark.

local 1 adj local. **2** m (recinto) premises pl.

localidad f (pueblo) locality; (asiento) seat.

localizar vt (encontrar) to find; (fuego, dolor) to localize.

loción f lotion.

loco, -a 1 adj mad; **a lo l.** crazily; **l. por** crazy about; **volverse l.** to go mad. **2** mf (hombre) madman; (mujer) madwoman.

locomotora f locomotive.

locura f madness.

locutor, -a mf presenter.

locutorio m telephone booth.

lodo m mud.

lógico, -a adj logical; **era l. que ocurriera** it was bound to happen.

lograr vt to get, to obtain; (premio) to win; (meta) to achieve; **l. hacer algo** to manage to do something.

lombriz f earthworm.

lomo m back; (para filete) loin.

lona f canvas.

loncha f slice.

lonchería f Méx snack bar.

longaniza f spicy (pork) sausage.

longitud f length; **dos metros de l.** two meters long; **salto de l.** long jump.

lonja f market.

loquería f Am mental hospital.

lord m (pl lores) lord.

loro m parrot.

los¹ 1 art def mpl the. **2** pron **l. que** (personas) those who; (cosas) the ones (that); **toma l. que quieras** take whichever ones you want; **esos son l. míos/tuyos** these are mine/yours.

los² pron pers mpl them; **¿l. has visto?** have you seen them?

losa f slab.

lote m (de productos) lot; Am (terreno) plot (of land).

lotería f lottery; **tocarle la l. a algn** to win a prize in the lottery.

loza f (material) earthenware; (vajilla) crockery.

lubricante m lubricant.

lucha f fight; (deporte) wrestling; **l. libre** free-style o all-in wrestling.

luchar vi to fight; (como deporte) to wrestle.

lucir 1 vi (brillar) to shine. **2** vt (ropa) to sport. **3 lucirse** vr (hacer buen papel) to do very well; (pavonearse) to show off.

luego 1 adv (después) then, next; (más tarde) later (on); **¡hasta l.!** so long!; Am **l. de** after; **desde l.** of course. **2** conj therefore.

lugar m place; **en primer l.** in the first place; **en l. de** instead of; **sin l. a dudas** without a doubt; **tener l.** to take place; **dar l. a** to give rise to.

lujo m luxury.

lujoso, -a adj luxurious.

lujuria f lust.

lumbre f fire.

luminoso, -a adj luminous; fig bright.

luna f moon; (espejo) mirror; fig **estar en la l.** to have one's head in the clouds; **l. llena** full moon; **l. de miel** honeymoon.

lunar m (en la ropa) dot; (en la piel) mole.

lunes m inv Monday.

lupa f magnifying glass.

lustre m shine.

luto m mourning.

luz f light; **apagar la l.** to put out the light; **dar a l.** (parir) to give birth to; **luces de cruce** dipped headlights; **luces de posición** sidelights; **luces largas** headlights; **traje de luces** bullfighter's costume.

luzco indic pres de **lucir**.

M

macabro, -a adj macabre.

macana f Am (palo) club; (trasto) rubbish.

macanear vt Am to make up.

macarrones mpl macaroni sing.

macedonia f fruit salad.

maceta f flowerpot.

machacar vt to crush.

machista adj & m male chauvinist.

macho 1 adj male; fam (viril) manly. **2** m male; fam (hombre viril) macho.

machote m Am rough draft.

macizo, -a 1 adj solid. **2** m massif.

macuto m haversack.

madeja f hank.

madera f wood; (de construcción) lumber; **de m.** wooden.

madrastra f stepmother.

madre 1 f mother; **m. de familia** housewife; **m. política** mother-in-law; **m. soltera** unmarried mother. **2** interj **¡m. mía!** good heavens!

madrina f (de bautizo) godmother; (de boda) ≃ bridesmaid.

madrugada f small hours pl; **de m.** in the small hours; **las tres de la m.** three o'clock in the morning.

madrugador, -a 1 adj early rising. **2** mf early riser.

madrugar vi to get up early.

madurar vi (persona) to mature; (fruta) to ripen.

madurez f maturity; (de fruta) ripeness.

maduro, -a adj mature; (fruta) ripe; **de edad madura** middle-aged.

maestro, -a 1 mf teacher; (especialista) master; (músico) maestro. **2** adj **obra maestra** masterpiece.

magdalena f bun.

magia f magic; **por arte de m.** as if by magic.

magnetofón, magnetófono m tape recorder.

magnífico, -a adj magnificent.

mago, -a mf wizard; **los (tres) Reyes Magos** the Three Wise Men, the Three Kings.

magro, -a 1 m (de cerdo) lean meat. **2** adj (sin grasa) lean.

magullar 1 vt to bruise. **2 magullarse** vr to get bruised.

mahonesa f mayonnaise.

maíz m corn.

majestad f majesty.

majo, -a adj (bonito) pretty, nice; fam (simpático) nice.

mal 1 m evil; (daño) harm; (enfermedad) illness. **2** adj bad; **un m. año** a bad year; ver **malo**. **3** adv badly; **menos m. que ...** it's a good job (that) ...; **no está (nada) m.** it is not bad (at all); **te oigo/veo (muy) m.** I can hardly hear/see you.

malabarista mf juggler.

malcriado, -a adj spoiled.

malcriar vt to spoil.

maldad f badness; (acción perversa) evil thing.

maldecir vti to curse.

maldición 1 f curse. **2** interj damnation!

maldito, -a adj fam (molesto) damned; **¡maldita sea!** damn it!

maleducado, -a 1 adj bad-mannered. **2** mf bad-mannered person.

malentendido m misunderstanding.

malestar m (molestia) discomfort; (inquietud) uneasiness.

maleta f suitcase; **hacer la m.** to pack one's case.

maletero m (de coche) trunk.

maletín m briefcase.

maleza f (arbustos) undergrowth; (malas hierbas) weeds pl.

malgastar vt to waste.

malhablado, -a 1 adj foul-mouthed. **2** mf foul-mouthed person.

malhechor, -a mf wrongdoer.

malhumor m bad mood; **de m.** in a bad mood.

malicia f (mala intención) malice; (astucia) cunning; (maldad) badness.

malintencionado, -a 1 adj ill-intentioned. **2** mf ill-intentioned person.

malla f (red) mesh; Am (bañador) swimsuit; (mallas) leotard.

malo, -a adj bad; (persona) (malvado) wicked; (travieso) naughty; (enfermo) ill; (cosa) bad; (perjudicial) harmful; **por las malas** by force; **lo m. es que ...** the problem is that ....

maloliente adj foul-smelling.

malpensado, -a 1 adj nasty-minded. **2** mf nasty-minded person.

malta f malt.

maltratado, -a adj battered.

maltratar vt to ill-treat.

malvado, -a 1 adj evil, wicked. **2** mf villain, evil person.

malvender vt to sell at a loss.

malvivir vi to live badly.

mama f (de mujer) breast; (de animal) teat; (mamá) mum.

mamá f fam mum, mummy.

mamadera f Am feeding bottle.

mamar vt to suck.

mamífero, -a mf mammal.

mampara f screen.

manada f (de vacas, elefantes) herd; (de ovejas) flock; (de lobos, perros) pack; (de leones) pride.

manantial m spring.

mancha f stain.

manchar 1 vt to stain. **2 mancharse** vr to get dirty.

manco, -a 1 adj (de un brazo) one-armed; (de una mano) one-handed. **2** mf (de un brazo) one-armed person; (de una mano) one-handed person.

mancornas fpl Am cufflinks.

mandado m (recado) errand; **hacer un m.** to run an errand.

mandar vt (ordenar) to order; (dirigir) to be in charge of; (ejército) to command; (enviar) to send; **m. (a) por** to send for; **m. algo por correo** to send sth by post.

mandarina f mandarin.

mandíbula f jaw.

mando m (autoridad) command; (control) controls pl; **cuadro o tablero de mandos** dashboard; **m. a distancia** remote control.

manecilla f (de reloj) hand.

manejar 1 vt (máquina, situación) to handle; (dirigir) to manage; Am (coche) to drive. **2 manejarse** vr to manage.

manejo m (uso) handling, use; (de un negocio) management; Am (de un coche) driving; **de fácil m.** easy-to-use.

manera f way, manner; **de cualquier m.** (mal) carelessly; (en cualquier caso) in any case; **de esta m.** in this way; **de ninguna m.** certainly not; **de todas maneras** anyway; **de m. que** so; **de tal m. que** in such a way that; **maneras** manners; **con buenas maneras** politely.

manga f sleeve; (de riego) hose; (vuelta) leg; (en tenis) set; **m. corta/larga** short-/long-sleeved; **sin mangas** sleeveless; fig **sacarse algo de la m.** to pull sth out of one's hat.

mango m handle.

manguera f hose.

maní m (pl manises) Am peanut.

maniático, -a 1 adj fussy. **2** mf fusspot.

manicomio m mental hospital.

manifestación f demonstration; (expresión) expression.

manifestante mf demonstrator.

manifestar 1 vt (declarar) to state; (mostrar) to show. **2 manifestarse** vr (por la calle) to demonstrate.

manilla f (de reloj) hand; Am (palanca) lever.

manillar m handlebar.

maniobra f maneuver.

manipular vt to manipulate; (máquina) to handle.

maniquí m dummy.

manivela f crank.

manjar m delicacy, dish.

mano f hand; **a m.** (sin máquina) by hand; (asequible) at hand; **escrito a m.** hand-written; **hecho a m.** hand-made; **estrechar la m. a algn** to shake hands with sb; **de segunda m.** se-

cond-hand; **¡manos a la obra!** hands on the wheel!; **equipaje de m.** hand luggage; **a m. derecha/izquierda** on the right/left(-hand side); **m. de pintura** coat of paint; **m. de obra** labor (force).
manojo m bunch.
manopla f mitten.
manso, -a adj (animal) tame.
manta f blanket.
manteca f fat; **m. de cacao/cacahuete** cocoa/peanut butter.
mantecado m shortcake.
mantel m tablecloth.
mantener 1 vt (conservar) to keep; (entrevista, reunión) to have; (familia) to support; (sostener) to hold up; **m. la línea** to keep in trim. **2 mantenerse** vr (sostenerse) to stand; (sustentarse) to live (**de** on); **mantenerse firme** (perseverar) to hold one's ground.
mantenimiento m (de máquina) maintenance; (alimento) sustenance.
mantequilla f butter.
manto m cloak.
mantón m shawl.
mantuve pt indef de **mantener**.
manual 1 adj manual; **trabajos manuales** handicrafts. **2** m (libro) manual.
manufactura f manufacture.
manzana f apple; (de edificios) block.
manzanilla f (infusión) camomile tea; (vino) manzanilla.
maña f (astucia) cunning; (habilidad) skill.
mañana 1 f (parte de día) morning; **de m.** early in the morning; **por la m.** in the morning. **2** m el m. tomorrow. **3** adv tomorrow; **¡hasta m.!** see you tomorow!; **m. por la m.** tomorrow morning; **pasado m.** the day after tomorrow.
mañoso, -a adj skillful.
mapa m map.
maquillaje m make-up.
maquillar 1 vt to make up. **2 maquillarse** vr (ponerse maquillaje) to put one's make-up on; (usar maquillaje) to wear make-up.
máquina f machine; **escrito a m.** typewritten; **hecho a m.** machine-made; **m. de afeitar (eléctrica)** (electric) shaver; **m. de coser** sewing machine; **m. de escribir** typewriter; **m. fotográfica** o **de fotos** camera.
maquinaria f machinery; (mecanismo) mechanism.
maquinilla f m. de afeitar safety razor.
mar m o f sea; **en alta m.** on the high seas; fam **está la m. de guapa** she's looking really beautiful; **llover a mares** to rain cats and dogs.
maratón m o f marathon.
maravilla f marvel; **de m.** wonderfully; **¡qué m. de película!** what a wonderful film!
maravilloso, -a adj wonderful, marvellous.
marca f mark; (de producto) brand; (récord) record; **m. registrada** registered trademark.
marcador m (tablero) scoreboard; (persona) scorer; Am (rotulador) felt-tip pen; Méx (fluorescente) highlighter pen.
marcar vt to mark; (número) to dial; (indicar) to indicate; (gol, puntos) to score; (cabello) to set.
marcha f march; (de coche) gear; **hacer algo sobre la m.** to do sth as one goes along; **estar en m.** (vehículo) to be in motion; (máquina) to be working; **poner en m.** to start; **m. atrás** reverse (gear).
marchar 1 vi (ir) to walk; (aparato) to be on; **m. bien** (negocio) to be going well. **2 marcharse** to leave, to go away.
marchitar vt, **marchitarse** vr to shrivel, to wither.
marco m (de cuadro etc) frame; (moneda) mark.
marea f tide; **m. alta/baja** high/low tide; **m. negra** oil slick.
marear 1 vt to make sick; (en el mar) to make seasick; (en un avión) to make airsick; (en un coche) to make carsick; (aturdir) to make dizzy; fam (fastidiar) to annoy. **2 marearse** vr to get sick/seasick/airsick/carsick; (quedar aturdido) to get dizzy.
marejada f swell.
mareo m (náusea) sickness; (en el mar) seasickness; (en un avión) airsickness; (en un coche) carsickness; (aturdimiento) dizziness.
marfil m ivory.
margarina f margarine.
margarita f daisy.
margen m edge; (de folio) margin; fig **mantenerse al m.** not to get involved.
marginado, -a 1 adj excluded. **2** mf dropout.
marginar vt (a una persona) to exclude.
marido m husband.
marihuana, marijuana, mariguana f marijuana.
marinero m sailor.
marioneta f marionette.
mariposa f butterfly.
mariquita f ladybird.
marisco m shellfish; **mariscos** seafood.
marítimo, -a adj maritime; **paseo m.** promenade.
mármol m marble.
marqués m marquis.
marrano, -a 1 adj (sucio) filthy. **2** mf (animal) pig; fam slob.
marrón adj & m brown.
marroquí adj & mf (pl marroquíes) Moroccan.
Marte m Mars.
martes m inv Tuesday.
martillo m hammer.
mártir mf martyr.
marzo m March.
más 1 adv more; **m. gente de la que esperas** more people than you're expecting; **m. de** more than, over; **cada día** o **vez m.** more and more; **es m.** what's more, furthermore; **lo m. posible** as much as possible; **m. bien** rather; **m. o menos** more or less; **m. aún** even more; **¿qué m. da?** what's the difference? • (comparativo) **es m. alta/inteligente que yo** she's taller/more intelligent than me. • (superlativo) **el m. bonito/caro** the prettiest/most expensive. • (exclamación) **¡qué casa m. bonita!** what a lovely house!; **¡está m. guapa!** she looks so beautiful! • (después de pron interr e indef) else; **¿algo m.?** anything else?; **no, nada m.** no, nothing else; **¿quién m.?** who else?; **nadie/alguien m.** nobody/somebody else. • **por m. que** (+ adj/adv +) que + subj however (much); **por m. fuerte que sea** however strong he may be. **2** m inv **los/las m.** most people. **3** prep (en sumas) plus.
masa f mass; (de cosas) bulk; (de pan etc) dough; **medios de comunicación de masas** mass media.
masaje m massage; **dar masaje(s) (a)** to massage.
mascar vti to chew.
máscara f mask; **m. de gas** gas mask.
mascarilla f mask; **m. de oxígeno** oxygen mask; (cosmética) face pack.
mascota f mascot.
masculino, -a male; (para hombre) men's; (género) masculine.
máster m master's degree.
masticar vt to chew.
mástil m mast.

mastín m mastiff.
mata f (matorral) shrub.
matador m matador, bullfighter.
matanza f slaughter.
matar vt to kill.
mate¹ adj (sin brillo) matt.
mate² m mate; **jaque m.** checkmate.
matemática f, **matemáticas** fpl mathematics sing.
materia f matter; (tema) question; (asignatura) subject; **m. prima** raw material; **índice de materias** table of contents.
material 1 adj material. **2** m material; **m. escolar/de construcción** teaching/building materials pl; **m. de oficina** office equipment.
materialmente adv physically.
maternal adj maternal.
maternidad f maternity, motherhood.
materno, -a adj maternal; **abuelo m.** maternal grandfather; **lengua materna** mother tongue.
matiz m (de color) shade.
matizar vt to clarify, to explain.
matorral m thicket.
matrero, -a mf Am (bandolero) bandit.
matrícula f registration; (de coche) (número) registration number; (placa) license plate.
matricular vt, **matricularse** vr to register.
matrimonio m marriage; (pareja casada) married couple; **m. civil/ religioso** civil/church wedding; **contraer m.** to marry; **cama de m.** double bed.
matriz f matrix; (útero) womb.
matrona f (comadrona) midwife.
maullar vi to mew.
maxilar 1 adj maxillary. **2** m jaw.
máximo, -a 1 adj maximum. **2** m maximum; **al m.** to the utmost; **como m.** (como mucho) at the most; (lo más tarde) at the latest.
mayo m May.
mayonesa f mayonnaise.
mayor adj (comparativo) (tamaño) bigger (**que** than); (edad) older, elder; (superlativo) (tamaño) biggest; (edad) oldest, eldest; (adulto) grown-up; (maduro) mature; (principal) major; **la m. parte** the majority; **la m. parte de las veces** most often; **ser m. de edad** to be of age; **al por m.** wholesale.
mayoría f majority; **la m. de los niños** most children; **m. de edad** majority.
mayorista 1 adj wholesale. **2** mf wholesaler; **precios de m.** wholesale prices.
mayoritario, -a adj majority; **un gobierno m.** a majority government.
mayúscula f capital letter.
mazapán m marzipan.
me pron pers (objeto directo) me; **no me mires** don't look at me. • (objeto indirecto) me, to me, for me; **¿me das un caramelo?** will you give me a sweet?; **me lo dio** he gave it to me. • (pron reflexivo) myself; **me he cortado** I've cut myself; **me voy/muero** (no se traduce) I'm off/dying.
mecánico, -a 1 adj mechanical. **2** mf mechanic.
mecanismo m mechanism.
mecanografía f typing.
mecanografiar vt to type.
mecanógrafo, -a mf typist.
mecedora f rocking chair.
mecer 1 vt to rock. **2 mecerse** vr to rock.
mecha f (de vela) wick; (de pelo) streak.
mechero m (cigarette) lighter.
mechón m (de pelo) lock; (de lana) tuft.
medalla f medal.
media f stocking; Am (calcetín) sock; (promedio) average; **a medias** (incompleto) unfinished; (entre dos) half and half.
medialuna f Am (pasta) croissant.
mediano, -a adj (tamaño) medium-sized.
medianoche f midnight.
mediante prep by means of.
medicación f medication.
medicamento m medicine.
medicina f medicine; **estudiante de m.** medical student.
médico, -a 1 mf doctor; **m. de cabecera** family doctor. **2** adj medical.
medida f measure; (dimensión) measurement; **a (la) m.** (ropa) made-to-measure; **a m. que avanzaba** as he advanced; **adoptar** o **tomar medidas** to take steps.
medieval adj medieval.
medio, -a 1 adj half; (intermedio) middle; (normal) average; **una hora y media** an hour and a half; **a media mañana/tarde** in the middle of the morning/afternoon; **clase media** middle class; **salario m.** average wage. **2** adv half; **está m. muerta** she is half dead. **3** m (mitad) half; (centro) middle; **en m. (de)** (en el centro) in the middle (of); (entre dos) in between; **medios de transporte** means of transport; **por m. de** by means of; **medios de comunicación** (mass) media; **m. ambiente** environment.
medioambiental adj environmental.
mediocre adj mediocre.
mediodía m (hora exacta) midday; (período aproximado) early afternoon; (sur) south.
medir 1 vt to measure. **2** vi to measure; **mide 2 metros** he is 2 meters tall; **mide dos metros de alto/ancho/largo** it is two meters high/wide/long.
médula f marrow; **m. ósea** bone marrow.
megafonía f public-address system.
mejicano, -a adj & mf Mexican.
mejilla f cheek.
mejillón m mussel.
mejor 1 adj (comparativo) better (**que** than); (superlativo) best; **tu m. amiga** your best friend; **lo m.** the best thing. **2** adv (comparativo) better (**que** than); (superlativo) best; **cada vez m.** better and better; **m. dicho** or rather; **es el que m. canta** he is the one who sings the best; **a lo m.** (quizás) perhaps; (ojalá) hopefully.
mejora f improvement.
mejorar 1 vti to improve. **2 mejorarse** vr to get better; **¡que te mejores!** get well soon!
melancolía f melancholy.
melancólico, -a adj melancholic.
melena f (head of) hair; (de león) mane.
mellado, -a adj (sin dientes) gap-toothed.
mellizo, -a adj & mf twin.
melocotón m peach.
melodía f tune.
melón m melon.
membrana f membrane.
membrillo m quince.
memoria f memory; (informe) report; **memorias** (biografía) memoirs; **aprender/saber algo de m.** to learn/know sth by heart.
memorizar vt to memorize.
mencionar vt to mention.

mendigo, -a *mf* beggar.
mendrugo *m* crust (of stale bread).
menear 1 *vt* to shake; *(cola)* to wag. **2 menearse** *vr* to shake.
menestra *f* vegetable stew.
menguar *vti* to diminish.
menopausia *f* menopause.
menor 1 *adj (comparativo) (de tamaño)* smaller (**que** than); *(de edad)* younger (**que** than); *(superlativo) (de tamaño)* smallest; *(de intensidad)* least, slightest; *(de edad)* youngest; **ser m. de edad** to be a minor, to be under age; **al por m.** retail. **2** *mf* minor.
menos 1 *adj (comparativo) (con singular)* less; *(con plural)* fewer; **m. dinero/leche/tiempo que** less money/milk/time than; **m. libros que** fewer books than; **tiene m. años de lo que parece** he's younger than he looks; *(superlativo)* **fui el que perdí m. dinero** I lost the least money. **2** *adv* **m. de** *(con singular)* less than; *(con plural)* fewer than, less than. ▪ *(superlativo) (con singular)* least; **el m. inteligente de la clase** the least intelligent boy in the class. ▪ *(con plural)* the fewest; **ayer fue cuando vinieron m. personas** yesterday was when the fewest people came. ▪ *(locuciones)* **a m. que** + *subj* unless; **al** *o* **por lo m.** at least; **echar a algn de m.** to miss sb; **¡m. mal!** just as well!; **ni mucho m.** far from it. **3** *prep* except; *(en restas)* minus.
menosprecio *m* contempt.
mensaje *m* message.
mensajero, -a *mf* messenger.
mensual *adj* monthly.
mensualidad *f (pago)* monthly payment; *(sueldo)* monthly salary *o* wage.
menta *f* mint; *(licor)* crème de menthe.
mental *adj* mental.
mentalidad *f* mentality; **de m. abierta/cerrada** open-/narrow-minded.
mentalizar 1 *vt (concienciar)* to make aware. **2 mentalizarse** *vr (concienciarse)* to become aware; *(hacerse a la idea)* to come to terms (**a** with).
mente *f* mind.
mentir *vi* to lie.
mentira *f* lie.
mentón *m* chin.
menú *m* menu.
menudo, -a 1 *adj* minute; **¡m. lío/susto!** what a mess/fright! **2** *adv* **a m.** often.
meñique *adj & m* **(dedo) m.** little finger.
mercado *m* market; **M. Común** Common Market.
mercadotecnia *f* marketing.
mercancías *fpl* goods.
mercantil *adj* commercial.
merecer *vt* **1** to deserve; *(uso impers)* **no merece la pena hacerlo** it's not worth while doing it. **2 merecerse** *vr* to deserve.
merecido, -a 1 *adj* deserved; **lo tiene m.** *(castigo)* it serves him right. **2** *m* just deserts *pl*.
merendar 1 *vt* to have for tea. **2** *vi* to have tea.
merendero *m (en el campo)* picnic spot.
merezco *indic pres de* **merecer**.
meridional *adj* southern.
merienda *f* afternoon snack.
mérito *m* merit.
merluza *f* hake.
mermelada *f* jam; *(de agrios)* marmalade; **m. de fresa** strawberry jam; **m. de naranja** orange marmalade.
mes *m* month; **el m. pasado/que viene** last/next month.
mesa *f* table; *(de despacho etc)* desk; **poner/recoger la m.** to set/clear the table.
mesada *f Am (dinero)* monthly payment; *RP (para adolescentes)* (monthly) allowance.
mesero, -a *mf CAm, Col, Méx (hombre)* waiter; *(mujer)* waitress.
meseta *f* plateau.
mesilla *f* **m. de noche** bedside table.
mesón *m* old-style tavern.
meta *f (objetivo, portería)* goal; *(de carrera)* finishing line.
metal *m* metal.
metálico, -a 1 *adj* metallic. **2** *m* **pagar en m.** to pay (in) cash.
meteorológico, -a *adj* meteorological; **parte m.** weather report.
meter 1 *vt (poner)* to put (**en** in); *(comprometer)* to involve (**en** in). **2 meterse** *vr (entrar)* to go/come in; *(entrometerse)* to meddle; *(estar)* **¿dónde te habías metido?** where have you been (all this time)?; **meterse con algn** *(en broma)* to get at sb.
método *m* method.
metralleta *f* submachine-gun.
métrico, -a *adj* metric; **sistema m.** metric system.
metro *m* meter; *(tren)* subway.
mexicano, -a *adj & mf* Mexican.
mezcla *f (producto)* mixture; *(acción)* mixing.
mezclar 1 *vt* to mix; *(involucrar)* to involve. **2 mezclarse** *vr (cosas)* to get mixed up; *(gente)* to mingle.
mezquino, -a *adj (tacaño)* mean; *(escaso)* miserable.
mezquita *f* mosque.
mi *adj* my; **mis cosas/libros** my things/books.
mí *pron pers* me; **a mí me dio tres** he gave me three; **compra otro para mí** buy one for me too; **por mí mismo** by myself.
mía *adj & pron pos f ver* **mío**.
microbús *m* minibus.
micrófono *m* microphone.
microonda *f* **un (horno) microondas** a microwave (oven).
microprocesador *m* microprocessor.
miedo *m (pavor)* fear; *(temor)* apprehension; **una película de m.** a horror film; **tener m. de algo/algn** to be afraid of sth/sb.
miedoso, -a *adj* fearful.
miel *f* honey.
miembro *m (socio)* member; *(de cuerpo)* limb.
mientras 1 *conj* while; *(cuanto)* **m. más/menos …** the more/less …. **2** *adv* **m. (tanto)** meanwhile, in the meantime.
miércoles *m inv* Wednesday; **M. de Ceniza** Ash Wednesday.
miga *f (de pan etc)* crumb.
mil *adj & m* thousand; **m. pesos** a *o* one thousand pesos.
milagro *m* miracle.
milagroso, -a *adj* miraculous.
milésimo, -a *adj & mf* thousandth.
mili *f* military service; **hacer la m.** to do one's military service.
milímetro *m* millimeter.
militar 1 *adj* military. **2** *mf* soldier.
milla *f* mile.
millar *m* thousand.
millón *m* million.
millonario, -a *adj & mf* millionaire.
mimar *vt* to spoil.
mimbre *f* wicker.

mina *f* mine; *(de lápiz)* lead.
mineral 1 *adj* mineral. **2** *m* ore.
minero, -a 1 *mf* miner. **2** *adj* mining.
miniatura *f* miniature.
minifalda *f* miniskirt.
mínimo, -a 1 *adj (muy pequeño)* minute; *(en matemáticas)* minimum. **2** *m* minimum; **como m.** at least.
ministerio *m* department.
ministro, -a *mf* minister; **primer m.** Prime Minister.
minoría *f* minority; **m. de edad** minority.
minúsculo, -a *adj* minute; **letra minúscula** small letter.
minusválido, -a 1 *adj* disabled. **2** *mf* disabled person.
minuto *m* minute.
mío, -a 1 *adj pos* of mine; **un amigo m.** a friend of mine; **no es asunto m.** it is none of my business. **2** *pron pos* mine.
miope *mf* short-sighted person.
mirada *f* look; **lanzar** *o* **echar una m. a** to glance at.
mirar 1 *vt* to look at; *(observar)* to watch; *(cuidar)* **mira que no le pase nada** see that nothing happens to him. **2** *vi* **la casa mira al norte** the house faces north.
mirlo *m* blackbird.
misa *f* mass.
miserable *adj (mezquino) (persona)* despicable; *(sueldo etc)* miserable; *(pobre)* wretched.
miseria *f (pobreza extrema)* extreme poverty; *(insignificancia)* pittance; *(tacañería)* meanness.
misión *f* mission.
mismo, -a 1 *adj* same; *(uso enfático)* **yo m.** I myself; **por eso m.** that is why; **por uno** *o* **sí m.** by oneself; **aquí m.** right here. **2** *pron* same; **es el m. de ayer** it's the same one as yesterday; **lo m.** the same (thing); **dar** *o* **ser lo m.** to make no difference. **3** *adv* **así m.** likewise.
misterio *m* mystery.
mitad *f* half; *(centro)* middle; **a m. de camino** half-way there; **a m. de precio** half price; **en la m. del primer acto** half-way through the first act.
mitote *m Am* uproar.
mixto *adj* mixed.
mobiliario *m* furniture.
moca *m* mocha.
mochila *f* rucksack.
moco *m* snot; **sonarse los mocos** to blow one's nose.
mocoso, -a *mf fam* brat.
moda *f* fashion; **a la m., de m.** in fashion; **pasado de m.** old-fashioned.
modales *mpl* manners.
modelo 1 *adj inv & m* model. **2** *mf* (fashion) model; **desfile de modelos** fashion show.
módem *m* modem.
moderado, -a *adj* moderate.
modernizar *vt*, **modernizarse** *vr* to modernize.
moderno, -a *adj* modern.
modesto, -a *adj* modest.
modificar *vt* to modify.
modisto, -a *mf* fashion designer.
modo *m (manera)* way, manner; *(en lingüística)* mood; **m. de empleo** instructions for use; **modos** manners.
mofarse *vr* to laugh (**de** at).
moflete *m* chubby cheek.
mohoso, -a *adj* moldy; *(oxidado)* rusty.
mojar 1 *vt* to wet; *(humedecer)* to dampen. **2 mojarse** *vr* to get wet.
molde *m* mold.
moldeador *m (de pelo)* wave.
mole *f* mass.
moler *vt* to grind.
molestar 1 *vt (incomodar)* to disturb; *(causar malestar)* to hurt; **¿le molestaría esperar fuera?** would you mind waiting outside? **2 molestarse** *vr (tomarse la molestia)* to bother; *(ofenderse)* to take offense.
molestia *f* bother; *(dolor)* slight pain.
molesto, -a *adj (irritante)* annoying; **estar m. con algn** *(enfadado)* to be annoyed with sb.
molino *m* mill; **m. de viento** windmill.
momentáneo, -a *adj* momentary.
momento *m (instante)* moment; *(periodo)* time; **al m.** at once; **de m.** for the time being; **en cualquier m.** at any time.
monasterio *m* monastery.
mondar 1 *vt* to peel. **2 mondarse** *vr fam* **mondarse (de risa)** to laugh one's head off.
moneda *f (pieza)* coin; *(dinero)* currency; **m. suelta** small change.
monedero *m* purse.
monetario, -a *adj* monetary.
monigote *m (persona)* wimp; *(dibujo)* rough sketch (of a person).
monitor, -a *mf* monitor; *(profesor)* instructor.
monja *f* nun.
monje *m* monk.
mono, -a 1 *m* monkey; *(prenda) (de trabajo)* overalls *pl*; *(de vestir)* catsuit. **2** *adj fam (bonito)* pretty.
monopolio *m* monopoly.
monótono, -a *adj* monotonous.
monstruo *m* monster; *(genio)* genius.
montaje *m (instalación)* fitting; *(ensamblaje)* assembling.
montaña *f* mountain; **m. rusa** big dipper.
montañismo *m* mountaineering.
montañoso, -a *adj* mountainous.
montar 1 *vi (en bici, a caballo)* to ride; *(en coche, tren)* to travel; *(subirse)* to get in. **2** *vt (colocar)* to put on; *(máquina etc)* to assemble; *(negocio)* to set up. **3 montarse** *vr (subirse)* to get on; *(en coche)* to get in.
monte *m (montaña)* mountain; *(con nombre propio)* mount.
montón *m* heap; **un m. de** a load of.
montura *f (cabalgadura)* mount; *(de gafas)* frame.
monumento *m* monument.
moño *m* bun.
moqueta *f* fitted carpet.
mora *f (zarzamora)* blackberry.
morado, -a *adj & m* purple.
moral 1 *adj* moral. **2** *f (ética)* morals *pl*; *(ánimo)* morale.
morboso, -a *adj (malsano)* morbid.
morcilla *f* black pudding.
mordaz *adj* biting.
morder *vt* to bite.
mordida *f Am (soborno)* bribe.
mordisco *m* bite.
moreno, -a 1 *adj (pelo)* dark-haired; *(piel)* dark-skinned; *(bronceado)* tanned; **ponerse m.** to

get a suntan; **pan/azúcar** m. brown bread/sugar. **2** mf (persona) (de pelo) dark-haired person; (mujer) brunette; (de piel) dark-skinned person.
morgue f Am morgue.
moribundo, -a adj moribund. **2** mf dying person.
morir 1 vi to die; **m. de frío/hambre/cáncer** to die of cold/hunger/cancer. **2 morirse** vr to die; **morirse de hambre** to starve to death; fig to be starving; **morirse de aburrimiento** to be bored to death; **morirse de risa** to die laughing.
moro, -a adj & mf Moor; fam (musulmán) Muslim; (árabe) Arab.
morocho, -a adj Am (moreno) swarthy.
morro m (hocico) snout.
mortadela f mortadella.
mortal adj mortal; (mortífero) fatal; **un accidente m.** a fatal accident.
mortalidad f mortality; **índice de m.** death rate.
mortandad f death toll.
mosca f fly; fam **estar m.** (suspicaz) to be suspicious; fam **por si las moscas** just in case.
moscardón m blowfly.
mosquitero m (red) mosquito net.
mosquito m mosquito.
mostaza f mustard.
mostrador m (de tienda) counter; (de bar) bar.
mostrar 1 vt to show. **2 mostrarse** vr to be; **se mostró muy comprensiva** she was very understanding.
mota f speck.
mote[1] m (apodo) nickname.
mote[2] m Am boiled salted corn.
motín m (amotinamiento) mutiny; (disturbio) riot.
motivo m (causa) reason; **motivos** grounds; **con m. de** on the occasion of; **sin m.** for no reason at all.
moto f motorbike.
motocicleta f motorbike.
motociclista mf motorcyclist.
motoneta f Am (motor) scooter.
motor m (grande) engine; (pequeño) motor; **m. de reacción** jet engine.
motora f motorboat.
motorista mf motorcyclist.
mover 1 vt to move; (hacer funcionar) to drive. **2 moverse** vr to move.
móvil 1 adj mobile; **teléfono m.** mobile phone; **unidad m.** (de radio, TV) outside broadcast unit. **2** m (de delito) motive; (teléfono) mobile.
movimiento m movement; (en física) motion; (actividad) activity; **(poner algo) en m.** (to set sth) in motion.
moza f young girl.
mozo m boy; (de estación) porter; (de hotel) bellboy.
mucamo, -a mf Am servant.
muchacha f girl.
muchacho m boy.
muchedumbre f crowd.
mucho, -a 1 adj sing lots of; (en frases negativas e interrogativas) much; **hay m. tonto suelto** there are lots of idiots around; **no tengo m. dinero** I don't have much money; **¿bebes m. café?** do you drink a lot of coffee?; **m. tiempo** a long time; **tengo m. sueño/mucha sed** I am very sleepy/thirsty. ▪ **muchos, -as** lots of; (en frases negativas e interrogativas) many; **no hay muchas chicas** there aren't many girls; **¿tienes muchos amigos?** do you have many friends?; **tiene muchos años** he is very old. **2** pron lots; **¿cuánta leche queda? — mucha** how much milk is there left? — a lot; **muchos, -as** lots; **¿cuántos libros tienes? — muchos** how many books have you got? — lots; **muchos creemos que …** many of us believe that …. **3** adv a lot; **lo siento m.** I'm very sorry; **como m.** at the most; **con m.** by far; **m. antes/después** long before/after; **¡ni m. menos!** no way!; **por m. (que)** + subj however much; **hace m. que no viene por aquí** he has not been to see us for a long time.
mudanza f move; **estar de m.** to be moving; **camión de m.** removal van.
mudar 1 vt (ropa) to change; (plumas, pelo) to molt; (de piel) to shed. **2 mudarse** vr **mudarse de casa/ropa** to move house/to change one's clothes.
mudo, -a 1 adj (que no habla) dumb. **2** mf mute.
mueble m piece of furniture; **muebles** furniture sing; **con/sin muebles** furnished/unfurnished.
muela f molar; **dolor de muelas** toothache; **m. del juicio** wisdom tooth.
muelle[1] m spring.
muelle[2] m (en puerto) dock.
muerte f death; **dar m. a algn** to kill sb; **odiar a algn a m.** to loathe sb; **un susto de m.** the fright of one's life.
muerto, -a 1 adj dead; **m. de hambre** starving; **m. de frío** frozen to death; **m. de miedo** scared stiff; **m. de risa** laughing one's head off; **(en) punto m.** (in) neutral. **2** mf (difunto) dead person; **hacerse el m.** to pretend to be dead.
muestra f (espécimen) sample; (modelo a copiar) model; (prueba, señal) sign; **dar muestras de** to show signs of; **m. de cariño/respeto** token of affection/respect.
mugido m (de vaca) moo; (de toro) bellow.
mugre f filth.
mugriento, -a adj filthy.
mujer f woman; (esposa) wife; **m. de la limpieza** cleaning lady; **m. de su casa** houseproud woman.
muleta f (prótesis) crutch; (de torero) muleta.
mulo, -a mf mule.
multa f fine; (de tráfico) ticket.
multicopista f duplicator.
multinacional adj & f multinational.
múltiple adj multiple.
multiplicación f multiplication.
multiplicar 1 vti to multiply (por by). **2 multiplicarse** vr to multiply.
multitud f (de personas) crowd; (de cosas) multitude.
mundial 1 adj worldwide; **campeón m.** world champion; **de fama m.** world-famous. **2** m world championship.
mundialmente adv **m. famoso** world-famous.
mundo m world; **todo el m.** everyone.
munición f ammunition.
municipal adj municipal; (policía) local.
municipio m municipality; (ayuntamiento) town council.
muñeca f wrist; (juguete, muchacha) doll.
muñeco m (juguete) (little) boy doll; **m. de trapo** rag doll; **m. de nieve** snowman.
murciélago m bat.
murmullo m murmur.
murmurar vi (criticar) to gossip; (susurrar) to whisper; (producir murmullo) to murmur.
muro m wall.
músculo m muscle.
musculoso, -a adj muscular.
museo m museum.
musgo m moss.

música f music; **m. clásica** classical music.
musical adj musical.
músico, -a mf musician.
muslo m thigh.
musulmán, -ana adj & mf Muslim.
mutilado, -a mf disabled person.
mutuo, -a adj mutual.
muy adv very; **m. bueno/malo** very good/bad; **¡m. bien!** very good!; **M. señor mío** Dear Sir; **m. de mañana/noche** very early/late.

N

nº abr de **número** number, n.
nabo m turnip.
nácar m mother-of-pearl.
nacer vi to be born; (pelo) to begin to grow; (río) to rise; **nací en Montoro** I was born in Montoro.
nacimiento m birth; (de río) source; (belén) Nativity scene; **lugar de n.** place of birth.
nación f nation; **las Naciones Unidas** the United Nations.
nacional 1 adj national; (producto, mercado, vuelo) domestic. **2** mf national.
nacionalidad f nationality.
nada 1 pron nothing; (con verbo) not … anything, nothing; **no sé n.** I don't know anything; **yo no digo n.** I'm saying nothing, I'm not saying anything; **más que n.** more than anything; **sin decir n.** without saying anything; **casi n.** hardly anything; **gracias — de n.** thanks — don't mention it; **para n.** not at all; **como si n.** just like that; **n. de eso** nothing of the kind; **n. de n.** nothing at all; **n. más verla** as soon as he saw her. **2** adv not at all; **no me gusta n.** I don't like it at all.
nadar vi to swim; **n. a braza** to do the breaststroke.
nadador, -a mf swimmer.
nadie pron no one, nobody; (con verbo) not … anyone o anybody; **no conozco a n.** I don't know anyone o anybody; **más que n.** more than anyone; **sin decírselo a n.** without telling anyone; **casi n.** hardly anyone.
nafta f Am (gasolina) gasoline.
nailon m nylon; **medias de n.** nylons.
naipe m playing card.
nalga f buttock.
nana f lullaby.
naranja 1 f orange. **2** adj & m (color) orange.
naranjada f orangeade.
naranjo m orange tree.
narcotraficante mf drug trafficker.
narcotráfico m drug trafficking.
nariz f nose; **narices** nose sing, fam **meter las narices en algo** to poke one's nose into sth.
nata f cream; (de leche hervida) skin; **n. batida/montada** whipped cream.
natación f swimming.
natal adj **mi país n.** my native country; **su pueblo n.** his home town.
natillas fpl custard sing.
nativo, -a adj & mf native.
nato, -a adj born.
natural 1 adj natural; (fruta, flor) fresh; (bebida) at room temperature; **de tamaño n.** life-size. **2** mf native.
naturaleza f nature; **en plena n.** in unspoilt countryside.
naturalidad f (sencillez) naturalness; (espontaneidad) ease; **con n.** straightforwardly.
naturalizar 1 vt to naturalize. **2 naturalizarse** vr to become naturalized.
naturalmente adv naturally; **¡n.!** of course!
naturismo m naturism.
naufragar vi (barco) to be wrecked.
naufragio m shipwreck.
náusea f nausea; **me da n.** it makes me sick; **sentir náuseas** to feel sick.
náutico, -a adj nautical.
navaja f (cuchillo) penknife; **n. de afeitar** razor.
nave f ship; (de iglesia) nave; **n. (espacial)** spaceship; **n. industrial** plant.
navegable adj navigable.
navegar vi to sail; (en avión) to navigate, to fly; **n. por Internet** to surf the Net.
Navidad(es) f(pl) Christmas; **árbol de Navidad** Christmas tree; **Feliz Navidad/Felices Navidades** Merry Christmas.
navideño, -a adj Christmas.
navío m ship.
neblina f mist.
necesario, -a adj necessary; **es n. hacerlo** it has to be done; **es n. que vayas** you must go; **no es n. que vayas** it's not necessary for you to go; **si fuera n.** if need be.
neceser m make-up bag.
necesidad f need; **por n.** of necessity; **tener n. de** to need.
necesitado, -a 1 adj (pobre) needy, poor; **n. de** in need of. **2** mpl **los necesitados** the needy.
necesitar vt to need.
necio, -a 1 adj silly. **2** mf fool.
nectarina f nectarine.
neerlandés, -esa 1 adj Dutch. **2** mf (hombre) Dutchman; (mujer) Dutchwoman; **los neerlandeses** the Dutch. **3** m (idioma) Dutch.
nefasto, -a adj (perjudicial) harmful; (funesto) ill-fated.
negación f negation; (negativa) denial; (gramatical) negative.
negar 1 vt to deny; (rechazar) to refuse; **negó haberlo robado** he denied stealing it; **le negaron la beca** they refused him the grant. **2 negarse** vr to refuse (**a** to).
negativo, -a adj & m negative.
negligencia f negligence.
negociación f negotiation.
negociante mf dealer; (hombre) businessman; (mujer) businesswoman.
negociar 1 vt to negotiate. **2** vi (comerciar) to do business.
negocio m business; (transacción) deal; (asunto) affair; **hombre de negocios** businessman; **mujer de negocios** businesswoman.
negro, -a 1 adj black; **verlo todo n.** to be very pessimistic. **2** mf (hombre) black; (mujer) black (woman); fam **trabajar como un n.** to work like a dog. **3** m (color) black.
nene, -a mf (niño) baby boy; (niña) baby girl.
neocelandés, -esa 1 adj New Zealand. **2** mf New Zealander.
neoyorkino, -a 1 adj New York. **2** mf New Yorker.
neozelandés, -esa adj & mf = **neocelandés**.
nervio m nerve; (de la carne) sinew; **nervios** nerves; **ataque de nervios** a fit of hysterics; **ser un manojo de nervios** to be a bundle of nerves.
nervioso, -a adj nervous; **poner n. a algn** to get on sb's nerves.

neto, -a *adj (peso, cantidad)* net.
neumático, -a 1 *adj* pneumatic. **2** *m* tire; **n. de recambio** spare tire.
neumonía *f* pneumonia.
neurótico, -a *adj & mf* neurotic.
neutral *adj* neutral.
neutro, -a *adj (imparcial)* neutral; *(género)* neuter.
nevada *f* snowfall.
nevar *v impers* to snow.
nevera *f (frigorífico)* fridge; *(portátil)* cool box.
ni *conj* no ... ni, **ni, ni ... ni** neither ... nor, not ... or; **ni se te ocurra** don't even think about it.
nicaragüense, nicaragüeño, -a *adj & mf* Nicaraguan.
nido *m* nest.
niebla *f* fog; **hay mucha n.** it is very foggy.
nieto, -a *mf (niño)* grandson; *(niña)* granddaughter; **mis nietos** my grandchildren.
nieve *f* snow.
nigeriano, -a *adj & mf* Nigerian.
ningún *adj (delante de m sing)* ver **ninguno**.
ninguno, -a 1 *adj (con verbo)* not ... any; **en ninguna parte** nowhere; **de ningún modo** no way. **2** *pron (persona)* nobody, no one; **n. de los dos** neither of the two; **n. de ellos** none of them; *(cosa)* not ... any of them; *(enfático)* none of them; **n. me gusta** I don't like any of them; **no vi n.** I saw none of them.
niña *f* girl; *(pupila)* pupil.
niñera *f* nanny.
niñez *f* childhood.
niño, -a *mf* child; *(bebé)* baby; *(muchacho)* (small) boy; *(muchacha)* (little) girl; **de n.** as a child; **niños** children.
nitrógeno *m* nitrogen.
nivel *m (altura)* level; *(categoría)* standard; **a n. del mar** at sea level; **n. de vida** standard of living.
no *adv* not; *(como respuesta)* no; **no vi a nadie** I did not see anyone, I didn't see anyone; **aún no** not yet; **ya no** no longer; **¿por qué no?** why not?; **no fumar/aparcar** *(en letrero)* no smoking/parking; **no sea que** + *subj* in case; **es rubia, ¿no?** she's blonde, isn't she?; **llegaron anoche, ¿no?** they arrived yesterday, didn't they?
noble 1 *adj* noble. **2** *mf (hombre)* nobleman; *(mujer)* noblewoman; **los nobles** the nobility *sing.*
noche *f* evening; *(después de las diez)* night; **de n., por la n.** at night; **esta n.** tonight; **mañana por la n.** tomorrow night/evening; **buenas noches** *(saludo)* good evening; *(despedida)* good night.
nochebuena *f* Christmas Eve.
nochevieja *f* New Year's Eve.
nocturno, -a *adj* night; **clases nocturnas** evening classes.
nombrar *vt* to name.
nombre *m* name; *(sustantivo)* noun; **n. de pila** Christian name; **n. y apellidos** full name; **n. propio** proper noun.
nordeste *adj & m* northeast.
nórdico, -a 1 *adj (del norte)* northern; *(escandinavo)* Nordic. **2** *mf* Nordic person.
noreste *adj & m* northeast.
norma *f* norm.
normal *adj* normal; **lo n.** the usual.
normalizar 1 *vt* to normalize. **2 normalizarse** *vr* to return to normal.
noroeste *adj & m* northwest.
norte *m* north; **al n. de** to the north of.
norteafricano, -a *adj & mf* North African.
norteamericano, -a *adj & mf* (North) American.
noruego, -a 1 *adj* Norwegian. **2** *mf* Norwegian. **3** *m (idioma)* Norwegian.
nos *pron pers* us; *(con verbo reflexivo)* ourselves; *(con verbo recíproco)* each other; **n. hemos divertido mucho** we enjoyed ourselves a lot; **n. queremos mucho** we love each other very much.
nosotros, -as *pron pers (sujeto)* we; *(complemento)* us; **con n.** with us.
nostalgia *f* nostalgia; *(morriña)* homesickness.
nota *f* note; *(de examen)* mark, grade; **sacar buenas notas** to get good grades.
notable 1 *adj (apreciable)* noticeable; *(digno de notar)* outstanding. **2** *m (nota)* very good.
notar 1 *vt (percibir)* to notice. **2 notarse** *vr (percibirse)* to show; **no se nota** it doesn't show.
notaría *f (despacho)* notary's office.
notario, -a *mf* notary (public).
noticia *f* news *sing*; **una n.** a piece of news; **una buena n.** (some) good news.
noticiario, *Am* **noticiero** *m* television news *sing.*
notificar *vt* to notify.
novato, -a 1 *adj (persona)* inexperienced. **2** *mf (principiante)* novice.
novecientos, -as *adj & mf* nine hundred.
novedad *f (cosa nueva)* novelty; *(cambio)* change; *(cualidad)* newness.
novela *f* novel; *(corta)* story.
novelista *mf* novelist.
noveno, -a *adj & m* ninth; **novena parte** ninth.
noventa *adj & m inv* ninety.
novia *f (amiga)* girlfriend; *(prometida)* fiancée; *(en boda)* bride.
noviembre *m* November.
novillada *f* bullfight with young bulls.
novillo, -a *mf (toro)* young bull; *(vaca)* young cow; **hacer novillos** to play hooky.
novio *m (amigo)* boyfriend; *(prometido)* fiancé; *(en boda)* bridegroom; **los novios** the bride and groom.
nube *f* cloud.
nublado, -a *adj* cloudy, overcast.
nublarse *vr* to cloud over.
nuboso, -a *adj* cloudy.
nuca *f* back of the neck.
nuclear *adj* nuclear; **central n.** nuclear power station.
núcleo *m* nucleus; *(parte central)* core.
nudillo *m* knuckle.
nudista *adj & mf* nudist.
nudo *m* knot; **hacer un n.** to tie a knot.
nuera *f* daughter-in-law.
nuestro, -a 1 *adj pos* our; **un amigo n.** a friend of ours. **2** *pron pos* ours; **este libro es n.** this book is ours.
nuevamente *adv* again.
nueve *adj & m inv* nine.
nuevo, -a *adj* new.
nuez *f* walnut; **n. (de Adán)** Adam's apple.
nulo, -a *adj (sin valor)* null and void, invalid; *(inepto)* useless; **voto n.** invalid vote; **crecimiento n.** zero growth.
numérico, -a *adj* digital.
número *m* number; *(de zapatos)* size; **n. e matrícula** license number.
numeroso, -a *adj* numerous.
nunca *adv* never; *(enfático)* not ... ever; **no he estado n. en España** I've never been to Spain; **yo no haría n. eso** I wouldn't ever do that; **casi n.** hardly ever; **más que n.** more than ever; **n. jamás** never ever; *(futuro)* never again.

nupcial *adj* wedding, nuptial; **marcha n.** wedding march.
nutrición *f* nutrition.
nutrir 1 *vt* to nourish, to feed. **2 nutrirse** *vr* to feed (**de, con** on).
nutritivo, -a *adj* nutritious; **valor n.** nutritional value.
ñame *m Am* yarn.
ñapa *f Am* bonus.
ñato, -a *adj Am* snub-nosed.
ñoño, -a 1 *adj Am (soso)* dull. **2** *mf* dullard.

O

o *conj* or; **o ... o** either ... or; **o sea** in other words.
oasis *m inv* oasis.
obedecer *vt* to obey.
obediencia *f* obedience.
obediente *adj* obedient.
obesidad *f* obesity.
obeso, -a *adj* obese.
obispo *m* bishop.
objetar 1 *vt* **no tengo nada que o.** I've got no objections. **2** *vi* to be a conscientious objector.
objetivo, -a 1 *m (fin, meta)* objective; *(de cámara)* lens. **2** *adj* objective.
objeto *m* object; *(fin)* purpose; **con o. de ...** in order to ....
obligación *f (deber)* obligation; **por o.** out of a sense of duty.
obligar *vt* to force.
obligatorio, -a *adj* obligatory.
obra *f (trabajo)* work; **o. maestra** masterpiece; *(acto)* deed; *(construcción)* building site; **'carretera en o.'** 'roadworks'.
obrar *vi (proceder)* to act; **o. bien/mal** to do the right/wrong thing.
obrero, -a 1 *mf* worker. **2** *adj* working; **clase obrera** working class.
obsceno, -a *adj* obscene.
obscuro, -a *adj* dark; *(origen, idea)* obscure.
obsequio *m* gift.
observador, -a 1 *mf* observer. **2** *adj* observant.
observar *vt (mirar)* to watch; *(notar)* to notice; *(cumplir)* to observe.
observatorio *m* observatory.
obsesión *f* obsession.
obsesionarse *vr* to get obsessed.
obsesivo, -a *adj* obsessive.
obsoleto, -a *adj* obsolete.
obstaculizar *vt* to obstruct, to get in the way of.
obstáculo *m* obstacle.
obstante: no obstante *adv* nevertheless.
obstinado, -a *adj* obstinate.
obstinarse *vr* to persist (**en** in).
obstruir 1 *vt (salida, paso)* to block. **2 obstruirse** *vr* to get blocked up.
obtener *vt (alcanzar)* to obtain, to get.
obvio, -a *adj* obvious.
oca *f* goose.
ocasión *f (momento)* occasion; *(oportunidad)* opportunity; *(saldo)* bargain; **en cierta o.** once; **aprovechar la o.** to make the most of an opportunity.
ocasional *adj (eventual)* occasional; **de forma o.** occasionally.
ocasionar *vt* to cause.
occidental *adj* western.
occidente *m* West.
océano *m* ocean.
ochenta *adj & m inv* eighty.
ocho *adj & m inv* eight.
ochocientos, -as *adj & mf* eight hundred.
ocio *m* leisure.
ocioso, -a *adj (inactivo)* idle; *(inútil)* pointless.
octavilla *f (panfleto)* hand-out, leaflet.
octavo, -a *adj & mf* eighth.
octubre *m* October.
oculista *mf* ophthalmologist.
ocultar 1 *vt* to conceal; **o. algo a algn** to hide sth from sb. **2 ocultarse** *vr* to hide.
oculto, -a *adj* concealed, hidden.
ocupación *f (tarea)* occupation.
ocupado, -a *adj (persona)* busy; *(asiento)* taken; *(aseos, teléfono)* engaged; *(puesto de trabajo)* filled.
ocupante *mf* occupant; *(ilegal)* squatter.
ocupar 1 *vt* to occupy; *(espacio, tiempo)* to take up; *(cargo)* to hold. **2 ocuparse** *vr* **ocuparse de** *(cuidar)* to look after; *(encargarse)* to see to.
ocurrencia *f (agudeza)* witty remark; *(idea)* idea.
ocurrente *adj* witty.
ocurrir 1 *v impers* to happen; **¿qué te ocurre?** what's the matter with you? **2 ocurrirse** *vr* **no se me ocurre nada** I can't think of anything.
odiar *vt* to hate.
odio *m* hatred.
odioso, -a *adj* hateful.
odontólogo, -a *mf* dental surgeon.
oeste *adj & m* west.
ofender 1 *vt* to offend. **2 ofenderse** *vr* to take offense (**con, por** at).
ofensa *f* offense.
ofensiva *f* offensive.
ofensivo, -a *adj* offensive.
oferta *f* offer; *(presupuesto)* bid.
ofertar *vt* to offer.
oficial, -a 1 *adj* official. **2** *m (rango)* officer; *(obrero)* skilled worker.
oficialismo *m Am (gobierno)* government.
oficialista *Am* **1** *adj* pro-government. **2** *mf* government supporter.
oficina *f* office; **o. de turismo** tourist office; **o. de correos** post office.
oficinista *mf* office worker.
oficio *m (ocupación)* occupation; *(profesión)* trade.
ofimática *f* office automation.
ofrecer 1 *vt* to offer; *(aspecto)* to present. **2 ofrecerse** *vr (prestarse)* to offer; *(situación)* to present itself.
ofrezco *indic pres de* **ofrecer**.
oftalmólogo, -a *mf* ophthalmologist.

oídas: de oídas *adv* by hearsay.
oído *m (sentido)* hearing; *(órgano)* ear.
oír *vt* to hear; **¡oye!** hey!; **¡oiga!** excuse me!
ojal *m* buttonhole.
ojalá 1 *interj* let's hope so! **2** *conj + subj* **¡o. sea cierto!** I hope it is true!
ojeada *f* echar una o. to have a quick look (**a** at).
ojeras *fpl* bags under the eyes.
ojo 1 *m* eye; *(de cerradura)* keyhole; **calcular a o.** to guess. **2** *interj* careful!
ojota *f Méx (sandalia)* sandal; *RP (chancleta)* thong.
ola *f* wave.
oleaje *m* swell.
óleo *m* oil; **pintura** *o* **cuadro al ó.** oil painting.
oleoducto *m* pipeline.
oler 1 *vt* to smell. **2** *vi (exhalar)* to smell; **o. a** to smell of; **o. bien/mal** to smell good/bad.
olfatear *vt (oler)* to sniff; *fig (indagar)* to pry into.
olfato *m* sense of smell.
olimpiada *f* Olympic Games *pl*; **las olimpiadas** the Olympic Games.
olímpicamente *adv* **paso o. de estudiar** I don't give a damn about studying.
olímpico, -a *adj* Olympic.
oliva *f* olive; **aceite de o.** olive oil.
olivo *m* olive (tree).
olla *f* saucepan; **o. exprés** *o* **a presión** pressure cooker.
olmo *m* elm.
olor *m* smell.
olvidadizo, -a *adj* forgetful.
olvidar 1 *vt* to forget; *(dejar)* to leave. **2 olvidarse** *vr* **olvidarse de algo** to forget sth.
olvido *m (desmemoria)* oblivion; *(lapsus)* oversight.
ombligo *m* navel.
omisión *f* omission.
omitir *vt* to omit.
omnipotente *adj* almighty.
omoplato, omóplato *m* shoulder blade.
once *adj & inv* eleven.
onda *f* wave; **o. larga/media/corta** long/medium/short wave; *fam* **¡qué buena o.!** that's cool! *Méx, RP fam* **¿qué o.?** *(¿qué tal?)* how's it going?, how are things?
ondulado, -a *adj (pelo)* wavy; *(paisaje)* rolling.
ONU *f abr de* **Organización de las Naciones Unidas** United Nations (Organization), UN(O).
opaco, -a *adj* opaque.
opcional *adj* optional.
ópera *f* opera.
operación *f* operation; *(financiera)* transaction.
operador, -a *mf* operator; *(de la cámara) (hombre)* cameraman; *(mujer)* camerawoman.
operar 1 *vt* to operate (**a** on). **2 operarse** *vr* to have an operation (**de** for); *(producirse)* to take place.
opinar *vi (pensar)* to think; *(declarar)* to give one's opinion.
opinión *f* opinion; **cambiar de o.** to change one's mind.
oponente *mf* opponent.
oponer *(pp* **opuesto)** **1** *vt (resistencia)* to offer. **2 oponerse** *vr (estar en contra)* to be against.
oporto *m (vino)* port.
oportunidad *f* opportunity.
oportuno, -a *adj* timely; *(conveniente)* appropriate.
oposición *f* opposition; *(examen)* competitive examination.
opresión *f* oppression.
oprimir *vt (pulsar)* to press; *(subyugar)* to oppress.
optar *vi (elegir)* to choose (**entre** between); *(aspirar)* to apply (**a** for); **opté por ir yo mismo** I decided to go myself; **puede o. a medalla** he's in with a chance of winning a medal.
optativo, -a *adj* optional.
óptica *f (tienda)* optician's (shop).
óptico, -a 1 *adj* optical. **2** *mf* optician.
optimista 1 *adj* optimistic. **2** *mf* optimist.
óptimo, -a *adj* excellent; *(condiciones)* optimum.
opuesto, -a *adj (contrario)* contrary; *(de enfrente)* opposite; **en direcciones opuestas** in opposite directions.
opuse *pt indef de* **oponer**.
oración *f (plegaria)* prayer.
oral *adj* oral; **por vía o.** to be taken orally.
órale *interj Méx fam (vamos)* come on!; *(de acuerdo)* right!, sure!
orar *vi* to pray.
orden 1 *m* order; **o. público** law and order; **por o. alfabético** in alphabetical order; **del o. de** in the order of. **2** *f* order; *(judicial)* warrant; **¡a la o.!** sir!
ordenado, -a *adj* tidy.
ordenador *m* computer; **o. de sobremesa** desktop (computer); **o. doméstico** home computer.
ordenanza 1 *m (empleado)* office boy. **2** *f* regulations *pl*.
ordenar *vt (organizar)* to put in order; *(habitación)* to tidy up; *(mandar)* to order; *Am (encargar)* to order.
ordeñar *vt* to milk.
ordinario, -a *adj (corriente)* ordinary; *(grosero)* common.
orégano *m* oregano.
oreja *f* ear.
orfanato, orfelinato *m* orphanage.
orgánico, -a *adj* organic.
organismo *m* organism; *(institución)* body.
organización *f* organization.
organizador, -a 1 *adj* organizing. **2** *mf* organizer.
organizar 1 *vt* to organize. **2 organizarse** *vr (armarse)* to happen.
órgano *m* organ.
orgullo *m (propia estima)* pride; *(arrogancia)* arrogance.
orgulloso, -a *adj* **estar o.** *(satisfecho)* to be proud; **ser o.** *(arrogante)* to be arrogant.
orientación *f (dirección)* orientation; *(guía)* guidance.
oriental 1 *adj* eastern. **2** *mf* Oriental.
orientar 1 *vt (indicar camino)* to give directions to; **una casa orientada al sur** a house facing south. **2 orientarse** *vr (encontrar el camino)* to get one's bearings.
oriente *m* East; **el Extremo** *o* **Lejano/Medio/Próximo O.** the Far/Middle/Near East.
orificio *m* hole; *(del cuerpo)* orifice.
origen *m* origin; **dar o. a** to give rise to.
original *adj & mf* original.
originar 1 *vt* to cause, to give rise to. **2 originarse** *vr* to originate.
orilla *f (borde)* edge; *(del río)* bank; *(del mar)* shore.
orinal *m* chamberpot; *fam* potty.
orinar 1 *vi* to urinate. **2 orinarse** *vr* to wet oneself.
oriundo, -a *adj* native of; **ser o. de** to come from.
oro *m* gold; **de o.** golden; **o. de ley** fine gold.
orquesta *f* orchestra; *(de verbena)* dance band.

ortiga *f (stinging)* nettle.
ortodoxo, -a *adj* orthodox.
ortografía *f* spelling.
ortográfico, -a *adj* spelling.
ortopédico, -a *adj* orthopedic.
oruga *f* caterpillar.
orzuelo *m* sty(e).
os *pron pers (complemento directo)* you; *(complemento indirecto)* (to) you; *(con verbo reflexivo)* yourselves; *(con verbo recíproco)* each other; **os veo mañana** I'll see you tomorrow; **os daré el dinero** I'll give you the money; **os escribiré** I'll write to you.
osadía *f (audacia)* daring; *(desvergüenza)* impudence.
osado, -a *adj (audaz)* daring; *(desvergonzado)* shameless.
osar *vi* to dare.
oscilar *vi (variar)* to fluctuate.
oscuras: a oscuras *adv* in the dark.
oscurecer 1 *vi impers* to get dark. **2** *vt (ensombrecer)* to darken. **3 oscurecerse** *vr (nublarse)* to become cloudy.
oscuridad *f* darkness; *fig* obscurity.
oscuro, -a *adj* dark; *(origen, idea)* obscure.
osito *m* **o. (de peluche)** teddy bear.
oso *m* bear; **o. polar** polar bear.
ostentación *f* ostentation.
osteópata *mf* osteopath.
ostra *f* oyster; **aburrirse como una o.** to be bored stiff.
OTAN *f abr de* **Organización del Tratado del Atlántico Norte** North Atlantic Treaty Organization, NATO.
otoño *m* autumn, fall.
otorgar *vt (premio)* to award (**a** to).
otorrinolaringólogo, -a *mf* ear, nose and throat specialist.
otro, -a 1 *adj indef* **otro/otra ...** another ...; **otros/otras ...** other ...; **el otro/la otra ...** the other ...; **otra cosa** something else; **otra vez** again. **2** *pron indef* another (one); **otros/otras** others; **el otro/la otra** the other (one); **los otros/las otras** the others.
ovacionar *vt* to give an ovation to.
oval, ovalado, -a *adj* oval.
oveja *f* sheep; *(hembra)* ewe; **la o. negra** the black sheep.
overol *m Am* overalls *pl*.
ovillo *m* ball (of wool).
OVNI *m abr de* **objeto volador no identificado** UFO.
oxidado, -a *adj* rusty.
oxidar 1 *vt (metales)* to rust. **2 oxidarse** *vr (metales)* to rust.
oxígeno *m* oxygen.
oye *indic pres & imperativo de* **oír**.
ozono *m* ozone; **capa de o.** ozone layer.

P

pabellón *m (en feria)* stand; *(bloque)* wing; **p. de deportes** sports center.
paciencia *f* patience.
paciente *adj & mf* patient.
pacificar *vt* to pacify.
pacotilla *f* **de p.** second-rate.
pactar *vt* to agree.
padecer *vti* to suffer; **padece del corazón** he suffers from heart trouble.
padrastro *m* stepfather; *(pellejo)* hangnail.
padre 1 *m* father; **padres** parents. **2** *adj Méx (genial)* great.
padrenuestro *m* Lord's Prayer.
padrino *m (de bautizo)* godfather; *(de boda)* best man; **padrinos** godparents.
padrón *m* census.
paella *f* paella (rice dish made with vegetables, meat and/or seafood).
pág *abr de* **página** page, p.
paga *f (salario)* wage; **p. extra** bonus.
pagar *vti* to pay; *(recompensar)* to repay; **p. en metálico** *o* **al contado** to pay cash.
página *f* page.
pago *m* payment; **p. adelantado** *o* **anticipado** advance payment.
paila *f Am* (frying) pan.
país *m* country; **P. Vasco** Basque Country; **P. Valenciano** Valencia.
paisaje *m* landscape.
paisano, -a 1 *adj* of the same country. **2** *mf (hombre)* fellow countryman; *(mujer)* fellow countrywoman; **en traje de p.** in plain clothes.
paja *f* straw.
pajar *m (almacén)* straw loft; *(en el exterior)* straw rick.
pajarita *f* bow tie; *(de papel)* paper bird.
pájaro *m* bird; **p. carpintero** woodpecker.
pajita, pajilla *f* (drinking) straw.
pakistaní *adj & mf (pl* **pakistaníes)** Pakistani.
pala *f* shovel; *(de jardinero)* spade; *(de ping-pong, frontón)* bat; *(de remo)* blade.
palabra *f* word; **dirigir la p. a algn** to address sb; **juego de palabras** pun; **p. de honor** word of honor.
palabrota *f* swearword.
palacio *m (grande)* palace; *(más pequeño)* mansion.
paladar *m* palate.
paladear *vt* to savor.
palanca *f* lever; *(manecilla)* handle; **p. de cambio** gearshift.
palangana *f* washbasin.
palco *m* box.
palestino, -a *adj & mf* Palestinian.
paleta *f (espátula)* slice; *(de pintor)* palette; *(de albañil)* trowel; *(de ping-pong)* bat.
paletilla *f* shoulder blade.
paleto, -a 1 *adj* boorish. **2** *mf* country bumpkin.
paliar *vt* to alleviate.
palidecer *vi (persona)* to turn pale.
palidez *f* paleness.
pálido, -a *adj* pale.
palillero *m* toothpick case.
palillo *m (mondadientes)* toothpick; **palillos chinos** chopsticks; *(de tambor)* drumstick.
paliza *f* beating; **darle a algn una p.** to give sb a thrashing.
palma *f* palm; *(árbol)* palm tree; **hacer palmas** to applaud.
palmada *f (golpe)* slap.

palmera f palm tree.
palmo m **p. a p.** inch by inch.
palo m stick; (vara) rod; (de escoba) broomstick; (golpe) blow; (madera) wood; (de portería) woodwork; (de golf) club.
paloma f pigeon; (como símbolo) dove.
palomar m pigeon house.
palomitas (de maíz) fpl popcorn sing.
palpable adj palpable.
palpar vt to feel.
palpitar vi to palpitate.
palurdo, -a adj boorish.
pamela f broad-brimmed hat.
pampa f pampa, pampas pl.
pan m bread; **p. de molde** loaf of sliced bread; **p. integral** wholemeal bread; **p. rallado** breadcrumbs pl.
pana f corduroy.
panadería f bakery.
panameño, -a adj & mf Panamanian.
pancarta f placard; (en manifestación) banner.
panda¹ f panda.
panda² f (de amigos) gang.
pandereta f tambourine.
pandilla f gang.
panecillo m bread roll.
panera f breadbasket.
panfleto m pamphlet.
pánico m panic; **sembrar el p.** to cause panic.
panorama m panorama.
pantaletas fpl Am panties.
pantalla f (monitor) screen; (de lámpara) shade.
pantalones mpl trousers pl; **p. vaqueros** jeans pl.
pantano m (natural) marsh; (artificial) reservoir.
pantera f panther.
pantorrilla f calf.
pantufla f slipper.
panty m (pair of) tights pl.
panza f fam belly.
pañal m diaper.
paño m cloth.
pañuelo m handkerchief; (pañoleta) shawl.
Papa m **el P.** the Pope.
papa f (patata) potato.
papá m fam dad, daddy.
papada f double chin.
papagayo m parrot.
papel m paper; (hoja) piece of paper; (rol) role; **papeles** (documentos) identification papers; **p. higiénico** toilet paper; **p. de aluminio** aluminum foil; **p. pintado** wallpaper.
papelera f (en despacho) wastepaper basket; (en calle) trash can.
papelería f (tienda) stationer's.
papeleta f (de rifa) ticket; (de votación) ballot.
paperas fpl mumps sing.
papilla f mush; (de niños) baby food.
paquete m packet; (postal) parcel.
paquistaní adj & mf (pl paquistaníes) Pakistani.
par 1 adj (número) even. **2** m (pareja) pair; (dos) couple; **de p. en p.** wide open.
para prep for; (finalidad) to, in order to; (tiempo) by; (a punto de) **está p. salir** it's about to leave; **p. terminar antes** (in order) to finish earlier; **p. entonces** by then; **¿p. qué?** what for?; **ir p. viejo** to be getting old; **no es p. tanto** it's not as bad as all that; **p. mí** in my opinion.
parabólico, -a adj **antena parabólica** satellite dish.
parabrisas m inv windshield.
paracaidista mf parachutist; (soldado) paratrooper.
parachoques m inv bumper, fender.
parada f stop; **p. de autobús** bus stop; **p. de taxis** taxi rank.
paradero m (lugar) whereabouts pl; (apeadero) stop.
parado, -a 1 adj stopped; (quieto) still; (fábrica) at a standstill; (desempleado) unemployed; Am (de pie) standing; fig **salir bien/mal p.** to come off well/badly. **2** mf unemployed person.
parador m roadside inn; **p. nacional** o **de turismo** luxury hotel.
paraguas m inv umbrella.
paraíso m paradise.
paraje m spot, place.
paralelo, -a adj & m parallel.
paralítico, -a adj & m paralytic.
paralizar 1 vt to paralyze; (circulación) to stop. **2 paralizarse** vr to come to a standstill.
parapente m paragliding, parapenting.
parapeto m parapet; (de defensa) barricade.
parar 1 vt to stop; (balón) to save. **2** vi to stop; **sin p.** nonstop; **fue a p. a la cárcel** he ended up in jail. **3 pararse** vr to stop; Am (ponerse en pie) to stand up.
pararrayos m inv lightning rod.
parásito, -a adj & m parasite.
parcela f plot.
parche m patch; (emplasto) plaster.
parchís m ≃ ludo.
parcial adj (partidario) biased; (no completo) partial; **a tiempo p.** part-time.
parcialmente adv partly.
pardo, -a adj (marrón) brown; (gris) dark gray.
parecer 1 vi to seem; **parece que no arranca** it looks as if it won't start; **como te parezca** whatever you like; **¿te parece?** is that okay with you?; **¿qué te parece?** what do you think of it? **2 parecerse** vr to be alike; **parecerse a** to look like.
parecido, -a 1 adj similar; **bien p.** good-looking. **2** m resemblance.
pared f wall.
pareja f pair; (hombre y mujer) couple; (de baile, juego) partner; **por parejas** in pairs; **hacen buena p.** they make a nice couple.
parentesco m relationship.
paréntesis m inv bracket; **entre p.** in brackets.
parezco indic pres de **parecer**.
pariente mf relative, relation.
parir 1 vt to give birth to. **2** vi to give birth.
parlamento m parliament.
paro m (huelga) strike; (desempleo) unemployment; **estar en p.** to be unemployed; **cobrar el p.** to be on the dole.
parpadear vi (ojos) to blink; (luz) to flicker.
párpado m eyelid.
parque m park; (de niños) playpen; **p. de atracciones** amusement park; **p. zoológico** zoo; **p. nacional/natural** national park/nature reserve.

parqueadero m Carib, Col, Pan parking lot.
parquear vti Am to park.
parquímetro m parking meter.
parra f grapevine.
párrafo m paragraph.
parranda f fam spree.
parrilla f grill; **pescado a la p.** grilled fish.
párroco m parish priest.
parroquia f parish; (iglesia) parish church.
parte 1 f (sección) part; (en una repartición) share; (lugar) place; (en juicio) party; **en** o **por todas partes** everywhere; **por mi p.** as far as I am concerned; **de p. de ...** on behalf of ...; **¿de p. de quién?** who's calling?; **en gran p.** to a large extent; **en p.** partly; **la mayor p.** the majority; **por otra p.** on the other hand. **2** m (informe) report.
participación f participation; (acción) share; (notificación) notification.
participante 1 adj participating. **2** mf participant.
participar 1 vi to take part, participate (en in). **2** vt (notificar) to notify.
participio m participle.
particular 1 adj (concreto) particular; (privado) private; (raro) peculiar. **2** mf (individuo) private individual.
partida f (salida) departure; (remesa) batch; (juego) game; (certificado) certificate; **p. de nacimiento** birth certificate.
partidario, -a 1 adj **ser/no ser p. de algo** to be for/against sth. **2** mf supporter.
partido m party; (fútbol) match, game; **sacar p. de** to profit from.
partir 1 vt to break; (dividir) to split; (cortar) to cut. **2** vi (marcharse) to leave; **a p. de** from. **3 partirse** vr to split (up); **partirse de risa** to split one's sides laughing.
partitura f score.
parto m labor, childbirth.
pasa f raisin.
pasadizo m corridor.
pasado, -a 1 adj (último) last; (anticuado) old-fashioned; (alimento) bad; (cocido) cooked; **p. (de moda)** out of date; **p. mañana** the day after tomorrow. **2** m past.
pasaje m passage; (calle) alley; (pasajeros) passengers pl; (billete) ticket.
pasajero, -a 1 adj passing. **2** mf passenger.
pasamanos m inv (barra) handrail; (de escalera) banister.
pasaporte m passport.
pasar 1 vt to pass; (página) to turn; (trasladar) to move; (tiempo) to spend, to pass; (padecer) to suffer; (cruzar) to cross; (límite) to go beyond; **p. hambre** to go hungry. **2** vi to pass; (entrar) to come in; **p. a** (continuar) to go on to; **p. de largo** to go by (without stopping). **3** v impers (suceder) to happen; **¿qué pasa aquí?** what's going on here?; **¿qué pasa?** what's the matter?; **pase lo que pase** come what may. **4 pasarse** vr (comida) to go off; (excederse) to go too far; **se me pasó la ocasión** I missed my chance; **se le pasó llamarme** he forgot to phone me; **pasarse el día haciendo algo** to spend the day doing sth; **pasárselo bien/mal** to have a good/bad time.
pasarela f (puente) footbridge; (de barco) gangway; (de moda) catwalk.
pasatiempo m pastime, hobby.
pascua f Easter; **pascuas** (Navidad) Christmas sing; **¡Felices Pascuas!** Merry Christmas!
pasear 1 vi to go for a walk. **2** vt (perro) to walk. **3 pasearse** vr to go for a walk.
paseo m walk; (en bicicleta, caballo) ride; (en coche) drive; (avenida) avenue; **dar un p.** to go for a walk/ride/drive.
pasillo m corridor.
pasión f passion.
pasivo, -a adj passive; (inactivo) inactive.
pasmado, -a adj (asombrado) astounded, amazed; (atontado) flabbergasted; **dejar p.** to astonish; **quedarse p.** to be amazed.
paso m step; (modo de andar) gait; (ruido al andar) footstep; (camino) way; (acción) passage; (de montaña) mountain pass; **abrirse p.** to force one's way through; **'ceda el p.'** 'give way'; **'prohibido el p.'** 'no entry'; **p. de peatones** pedestrian crossing, crosswalk; **el p. del tiempo** the passage of time; **estar de p.** to be just passing through.
pasta f paste; (italiana) pasta; (galleta) biscuit; fam (dinero) dough; **p. de dientes** o **dentífrica** toothpaste.
pastel m cake; (de carne, fruta) pie.
pastelería f pastry shop, bakery.
pastilla f tablet; (de jabón) bar; **pastillas para la tos** cough drops.
pastor, -a 1 mf (hombre) shepherd; (mujer) shepherdess; **p. alemán** Alsatian. **2** m (sacerdote) pastor.
pastoso, -a adj pasty; (lengua) furry.
pata f leg; **patas arriba** upside down; **mala p.** bad luck; **meter la p.** to put one's foot in it.
patada f kick; (en el suelo) stamp.
patalear vi to stamp one's feet (with rage).
patán m bumpkin.
patata f potato; **patatas fritas** French fries; (de bolsa) potato chips.
paté m pâté.
patentar vt to patent.
patente 1 f (de invención) patent; (autorización) license; CSur (matrícula) license plate. **2** adj (evidente) patent, obvious.
paternal adj paternal.
paterno, -a adj paternal.
patilla f (de gafas) leg; **patillas** (pelo) sideburns.
patín m skate; (hidropedal) pedal boat; **p. de ruedas/de hielo** roller/ice skate.
patinaje m skating; **p. artístico** figure skating; **p. sobre hielo/ruedas** ice-/roller-skating.
patinar vi to skate; (sobre ruedas) to roller-skate; (sobre hielo) to ice-skate; (deslizarse) to slide; (resbalar) to slip; (vehículo) to skid.
patinete m scooter.
patio m (de una casa) patio; (de recreo) playground; **p. de butacas** stalls.
pato m duck.
patoso, -a adj clumsy, awkward.
patria f homeland.
patrimonio m (bienes) wealth; (heredado) inheritance.
patriotismo m patriotism.
patrocinador, -a 1 adj sponsoring. **2** mf sponsor.
patrocinar vt to sponsor.
patrón, -ona 1 mf (jefe) boss; (de pensión) (hombre) landlord; (mujer) landlady. **2** m pattern.
patronal 1 adj employers'. **2** f employers' organization.
patronato, patronazgo m (institución benéfica) foundation; (protección) patronage.
patrono, -a mf boss; (empresario) employer.
patrulla f patrol.
paulatino, -a adj gradual.
pausa f pause; (musical) rest.
pauta f guidelines pl.
pavimento m (de calle) paving.
pavo m turkey.
pavor m terror.
payaso m clown.
payo, -a mf non-Gipsy.
paz f peace; (sosiego) peacefulness; **¡déjame en p.!** leave me alone!

peaje *f* toll; **autopista de p.** turnpike.
peatón *m* pedestrian.
peca *f* freckle.
pecado *m* sin.
pecador, -a *mf* sinner.
pecar *vi* to sin.
pecera *f* fishtank.
pecho *m* chest; *(de mujer, animal)* breast; **dar el p. (a un bebé)** to breast-feed (a baby).
pechuga *f (de ave)* breast.
pectoral *adj* chest.
peculiar *adj (raro)* peculiar; *(característico)* characteristic.
pedagógico, -a *adj* pedagogical.
pedal *m* pedal.
pedante 1 *adj* pedantic. **2** *mf* pedant.
pedazo *m* piece, bit; **hacer pedazos** to smash to pieces; *(papel, tela)* to tear to pieces.
pediatra *mf* pediatrician.
pedido *m (remesa)* order.
pedir *vt* to ask (for); *(en bar etc)* to order; *(mendigar)* to beg; **p. algo a algn** to ask sb for sth; **p. prestado** to borrow; **p. cuentas** to ask for an explanation.
pedrada *f (golpe)* blow from a stone; *(lanzamiento)* throw of a stone.
pega *f fam (objeción)* objection; **de p.** *(falso)* sham.
pegajoso, -a *adj (pegadizo)* sticky.
pegamento *m* glue.
pegar 1 *vt (adherir)* to stick; *(con pegamento)* to glue; *(golpear)* to hit; *fam* **no pegó ojo** he didn't sleep a wink; **p. un grito** to shout; **p. un salto** to jump. **2** *vi (adherirse)* to stick; *(armonizar)* to match; *(sol)* to beat down. **3 pegarse** *vr (adherirse)* to stick; *(pelearse)* to fight; *(comida)* to get burnt; *(arrimarse)* to get close; **pegarse un tiro** to shoot oneself; **se me ha pegado el sol** I've got a touch of the sun.
pegatina *f* sticker.
peinado *m* hairstyle, *fam* hairdo.
peinar 1 *vt (pelo)* to comb. **2 peinarse** *vr* to comb one's hair.
peine *m* comb.
pelado, -a *adj (fruta, patata)* peeled; *(cabeza)* shorn.
pelapatatas *m inv* potato peeler.
pelar 1 *vt (cortar el pelo a)* to cut the hair of; *(fruta, patata)* to peel. **2 pelarse** *vr (cortarse el pelo)* to get one's hair cut.
peldaño *m* step; *(de escalera de mano)* rung.
pelea *f* fight; *(riña)* row.
pelear 1 *vi* to fight; *(reñir)* to quarrel. **2 pelearse** *vr* to fight; *(reñir)* to quarrel; *(enemistarse)* to fall out.
peletería *f (tienda)* fur shop.
película *f* movie; *(fotográfica)* film; **p. de miedo** *o* **terror** horror movie; **p. del Oeste** Western.
peligrar *vi* to be in danger; **hacer p.** to endanger, to jeopardize.
peligro *m* danger; *(riesgo)* risk; **correr (el) p. de ...** to run the risk of ...; **poner en p.** to endanger.
peligroso, -a *adj* dangerous.
pelirrojo, -a 1 *adj* red-haired; *(anaranjado)* ginger-haired. **2** *mf* redhead.
pellejo *m (piel)* skin; **jugarse el p.** to risk one's neck.
pellizco *m* pinch.
pelma *mf*, **pelmazo, -a** *mf (persona)* bore.
pelo *m* hair; *(de animal)* coat; **cortarse el p.** *(uno mismo)* to cut one's hair; *(en la peluquería)* to have one's hair cut; **tomar el p. a algn** to pull sb's leg; **por los pelos** by the skin of one's teeth.
pelota *f* ball; **hacer la p. a algn** to suck up to sb.
pelotón *m* squad.
pelotudo, -a *adj Am* slack.
peluca *f* wig.
peluche *m* **osito de p.** teddy bear.
peludo, -a *adj* hairy.
peluquería *f* hairdresser's (shop).
peluquero, -a *mf* hairdresser.
pelusa, pelusilla *f* fluff; *(de planta)* down; *fam* jealousy (among children).
pena *f (tristeza)* sorrow; **¡qué p.!** what a pity!; **no merece** *o* **vale la p. (ir)** it's not worthwhile (going); **a duras penas** with great difficulty; **p. de muerte** *o* **capital** death penalty.
penalti *m (pl penaltis)* penalty.
pendejo *m Am* jerk.
pendiente 1 *adj (por resolver)* pending; *(colgante)* hanging (**de** from); **asignatura p.** *(en colegio)* subject not yet passed; **estar p. de** *(esperar)* to be waiting for; *(vigilar)* to be on the lookout for. **2** *m (joya)* earring. **3** *f* slope.
penetrante *adj* penetrating; *(frío, voz, mirada)* piercing.
penetrar *vt* to penetrate. **2** *vi (entrar)* to enter (**en** -).
penicilina *f* penicillin.
península *f* peninsula.
penique *m* penny, *pl* pence.
penitenciario, -a *adj* prison.
penoso, -a *adj (lamentable)* sorry, distressing; *(laborioso)* laborious, difficult; *CAm, Carib, Col, Méx (vergonzoso)* shy.
pensamiento *m* thought; *(flor)* pansy.
pensar 1 *vi* to think (**en** of, about; **sobre** about, over); **sin p.** *(con precipitación)* without thinking; *(involuntariamente)* involuntarily. **2** *vt (considerar)* to think about; *(proponerse)* to intend; *(concebir)* to make; *fam* **¡ni pensarlo!** not on your life!
pensativo, -a *adj* thoughtful.
pensión *f (residencia)* boarding house; *(hotel)* guesthouse; *(paga)* allowance; **media p.** half board; **p. completa** full board.
pensionista *mf* pensioner.
penúltimo, -a *adj & mf* penultimate.
penumbra *f* half-light.
penuria *f* scarcity, shortage.
peña *f* rock; *(de amigos)* club.
peñón *m* rock; **el P. de Gibraltar** the Rock of Gibraltar.
peón *m* unskilled laborer; *(en ajedrez)* pawn.
peor *adj & adv (comparativo)* worse; *(superlativo)* worst; **en el p. de los casos** if the worst comes to the worst.
pepinillo *m* gherkin.
pepino *m* cucumber.
pepita *f (de fruta)* pip, seed; *(de metal)* nugget.
pequeño, -a 1 *adj* small, little; *(bajo)* short. **2** *mf* child; **de p.** as a child.
pera *f* pear.
peral *m* pear tree.
percance *m* mishap.
percatarse *vr* **p. de** to realize.
percepción *f* perception.
percha *f (colgador)* (coat)hanger.
perchero *m* clothes rack.
percibir *vt (notar)* to perceive; *(cobrar)* to receive.

percusión *f* percussion.
perdedor, -a 1 *adj* losing. **2** *mf* loser.
perder 1 *vt* to lose; *(tren, autobús, oportunidad)* to miss; *(tiempo)* to waste. **2** *vi* to lose; **echar (algo) a p.** to spoil (sth); **echarse a p.** to be spoiled; **salir perdiendo** to come off worst. **3 perderse** *vr (extraviarse) (persona)* to get lost; **se me ha perdido la llave** I've lost my key.
pérdida *f* loss; *(de tiempo, esfuerzos)* waste.
perdiz *f* partridge.
perdón *m* pardon; **¡p.!** sorry!; **pedir p.** to apologize.
perdonar *vt* to forgive; *(eximir)* to pardon; **¡perdone!** sorry!; **perdonarle la vida a algn** to spare sb's life.
perecedero, -a *adj* perishable; **artículos perecederos** perishables.
perecer *vi* to perish.
peregrino, -a 1 *mf* pilgrim. **2** *adj* **ideas peregrinas** crazy ideas.
perejil *m* parsley.
perenne *adj* perennial.
pereza *f* laziness.
perezoso, -a *adj* lazy.
perfección *f* perfection; **a la p.** to perfection.
perfeccionar *vt* to perfect; *(mejorar)* to improve.
perfeccionista *adj & mf* perfectionist.
perfectamente *adv* perfectly; **¡p.!** *(de acuerdo)* agreed!, all right!
perfecto, -a *adj* perfect.
perfil *m* profile; *(contorno)* outline; **de p.** in profile.
perfilar 1 *vt (dar forma)* to shape, to outline. **2 perfilarse** *vr* to take shape.
perforar *vt* to perforate.
perfumar 1 *vti* to perfume. **2 perfumarse** *vr* to put on perfume.
perfume *m* perfume.
pericia *f* expertise.
periferia *f* periphery; *(alrededores)* outskirts *pl*.
periférico *m* peripheral.
perilla *f (barba)* goatee; *fam* **venir de perilla(s)** to be very handy, to be just the thing.
periódico, -a 1 *m* newspaper. **2** *adj* periodic.
periodista *mf* journalist.
periodo, período *m* period.
periquito *m* budgerigar, *fam* budgie.
perjudicar *vt* to harm; *(intereses)* to prejudice.
perjudicial *adj* harmful.
perjuicio *m* damage.
perla *f* pearl.
permanecer *vi* to remain, to stay.
permanente 1 *adj* permanent. **2** *f (de pelo)* perm; **hacerse la p.** to have one's hair permed.
permiso *m (autorización)* permission; *(licencia)* license; **p. de conducir** driver's license.
permitir 1 *vt* to permit, to allow. **permitirse** *vr (costearse)* to afford; **'no se permite fumar'** 'no smoking'.
pero *conj* but.
perpendicular *adj & f* perpendicular.
perpetrar *vt* to perpetrate, to commit.
perpetuo, -a *adj* perpetual; **cadena perpetua** life imprisonment.
perplejo, -a *adj* perplexed.
perra *f* bitch.
perrera *f* kennel; *(para muchos perros)* kennels *pl*.
perro *m* dog; *fam* **vida de perros** dog's life; **p. caliente** hot dog.
persecución *f* pursuit; *(represión)* persecution.
perseguir *vt* to pursue; *(seguir)* to run after; *(reprimir)* to persecute.
perseverar *vi* to persevere; *(durar)* to last.
persiana *f* blinds *pl*.
persignarse *vr* to cross oneself.
persistente *adj* persistent.
persistir *vi* to persist.
persona *f* person; *fam* **p. mayor** grown-up.
personaje *m* character; *(celebridad)* celebrity.
personal 1 *adj* personal. **2** *m (plantilla)* personnel.
personalidad *f* personality.
perspectiva *f* perspective; *(futuro)* prospect.
perspicaz *adj* perspicacious.
persuadir *vt* to persuade.
persuasión *f* persuasion.
pertenecer *vi* to belong (**a** to).
pertinaz *adj* persistent; *(obstinado)* obstinate.
perturbación *f* disturbance.
perturbado, -a *adj (mentally)* deranged *o* unbalanced.
perturbar *vt (el orden)* to disturb.
peruano, -a *adj & mf* Peruvian.
perverso, -a *adj* perverse.
pervertir *vt* to pervert.
pesa *f* weight; **levantamiento de pesas** weightlifting.
pesadez *f* heaviness; *(de estómago)* fullness; *(fastidio)* drag.
pesadilla *f* nightmare.
pesado, -a *adj* heavy; *(aburrido)* tedious.
pésame *m* **dar el p.** to offer one's condolences.
pesar 1 *vt* to weigh; *(entristecer)* to grieve. **2** *vi* to weigh; *(ser pesado)* to be heavy. **3** *m (pena)* sorrow; *(arrepentimiento)* regret; **a p. de** in spite of.
pesca *f* fishing.
pescadería *f* fish shop.
pescadilla *f* young hake.
pescado *m* fish.
pescador, -a 1 *adj* fishing. **2** *mf (hombre)* fisherman; *(mujer)* fisherwoman.
pescar *vti* to fish.
pescuezo *m fam* neck.
pese: pese a (que) *prep* in spite of (the fact that).
peseta *f* peseta.
pesimismo *m* pessimism.
pesimista 1 *adj* pessimistic. **2** *mf* pessimist.
pésimo, -a *adj* awful.
peso *m* weight; **p. bruto/neto** gross/net weight; **de p.** *(razón)* convincing.
pestaña *f* eyelash.
peste *f (hedor)* stench; *(epidemia)* plague.
pesticida *m* pesticide.
pestillo *m* bolt.
petaca *f (para cigarrillos)* cigarette case; *(para bebidas)* flask; *Am (maleta)* suitcase.
pétalo *m* petal.
petardo *m* firecracker.
petición *f* request.
petróleo *m* oil.

petrolero *m* oil tanker.
pez *m* fish.
pezón *m* nipple.
pezuña *f* hoof.
piadoso, -a *adj* (*devoto*) pious; (*compasivo*) compassionate; **mentira piadosa** white lie.
pianista *mf* pianist.
piano *m* piano.
pibe, -a *mf* Am (*niño*) kid.
picadero *m* riding school.
picado, -a 1 *adj* (*carne*) ground; (*fruta*) bad; (*diente*) decayed; (*mar*) choppy. **2** *m* **caer en p.** to plummet.
picador *m* picador.
picadora *f* mincer.
picadura *f* (*de insecto, serpiente*) bite; (*de avispa, abeja*) sting; (*en fruta*) spot.
picante *adj* hot; (*chiste etc*) risqué.
picaporte *m* (*aldaba*) door knocker; (*pomo*) door handle.
picar 1 *vt* (*insecto, serpiente*) to bite; (*avispas, abejas*) to sting; (*comer*) (*aves*) to peck (at); (*persona*) to pick at; (*anzuelo*) to bite; (*perforar*) to prick; (*carne*) to mince. **2** *vi* (*escocer*) to itch; (*herida*) to smart; (*el sol*) to burn; (*estar picante*) to be hot; (*pez*) to bite; *fig* (*dejarse engañar*) to swallow it. **3 picarse** *vr* (*fruta*) to spot; (*dientes*) to decay; (*enfadarse*) to get cross.
pícaro, -a 1 *adj* (*travieso*) mischievous; (*astuto*) crafty. **2** *mf* rogue.
pico *m* (*de ave*) beak, bill; (*punta*) corner; (*de montaña*) peak; (*herramienta*) pick; **cincuenta y p.** fifty odd; **las dos y p.** a little after two.
picor *m* tingling.
pie *m* foot; (*de instrumento*) stand; (*de copa*) stem; (*de una ilustración*) caption; **a p.** on foot; **de p.** standing up; **de pies a cabeza** from head to foot; **en p.** standing; **hacer p.** to touch the bottom; **perder p.** to get out of one's depth; **al p. de la letra** to the letter.
piedad *f* piety; (*compasión*) pity.
piedra *f* stone; (*de mechero*) flint.
piel *f* skin; (*de patata*) peel; (*cuero*) leather; (*con pelo*) fur; **p. de gallina** goose pimples *pl*.
pienso *m* fodder.
pierna *f* leg.
pieza *f* piece, part; (*habitación*) room; (*teatral*) play; **p. de recambio** spare part.
pijama *m* pajamas *pl*.
pila *f* battery; (*montón*) pile; (*de la cocina*) sink; **nombre de p.** Christian name.
píldora *f* pill.
pileta *f* (*pila*) sink; *Am* (*piscina*) swimming pool.
pillar 1 *vt* (*coger*) to catch; (*alcanzar*) to catch up with; **lo pilló un coche** he was run over by a car. **2 pillarse** *vr* to catch; **pillarse un dedo/una mano** to catch one's finger/hand.
pillo, -a 1 *adj* (*travieso*) naughty; (*astuto*) cunning. **2** *mf* rogue.
piloto 1 *mf* (*de avión, barco*) pilot; (*de coche*) driver; (*de moto*) rider **2** *m* (*luz*) pilot lamp **3** *adj inv* **piso p.** show apartment.
pimentón *m* red pepper.
pimienta *f* pepper.
pimiento *m* (*fruto*) pepper; (*planta*) pimiento.
pinar *m* pine wood.
pincel *m* paintbrush.
pinchadiscos *mf inv* disc jockey, DJ.
pinchar 1 *vt* (*punzar*) to jag; (*balón, globo*) to burst; (*rueda*) to puncture. **2** *vi* (*coche*) to get a puncture.
pinchazo *m* (*punzadura*) prick; (*de rueda*) puncture; (*de dolor*) sharp pain.
pincho *m* (*púa*) barb; **p. moruno** shish kebab.
ping-pong *m* table tennis.
pingüino *m* penguin.
pino *m* pine; *fig* **hacer el p.** to do a handstand.
pinole *m* Am corn drink.
pinta *f* (*medida*) pint; *fam* (*aspecto*) look.
pintada *f* graffiti.
pintar 1 *vt* (*dar color*) to paint; (*dibujar*) to draw. **2 pintarse** *vr* (*maquillarse*) to put make-up on.
pintor, -a *mf* painter.
pintoresco, -a *adj* (*lugar*) picturesque; (*persona*) eccentric.
pintura *f* painting; (*materia*) paint.
pinza *f* (*para depilar*) tweezers *pl*; (*para tender*) clothes pin; (*de animal*) pincer.
piña *f* (*de pino*) pine cone; (*ananás*) pineapple.
piñón *m* pine seed.
piojo *m* louse.
pipa *f* (*de fumar*) pipe; (*de fruta*) seed; (*de girasol*) sunflower seed.
pipí *m* *fam* pee, wee-wee; **hacer p.** to pee, to wee-wee.
piragua *f* canoe.
piragüismo *m* canoeing.
pirámide *f* pyramid.
piraña *f* piranha.
pirata *adj & mf* pirate.
piratear *vt* to pirate.
piropo *m* **echar un p.** to pay a compliment.
pis *m* *fam* wee-wee, pee; **hacer p.** to wee-wee, to have a pee.
pisada *f* footstep; (*huella*) footprint.
pisapapeles *m inv* paperweight.
pisar *vt* to step on.
piscifactoría *f* fish farm.
piscina *f* swimming pool.
piscolabis *m inv fam* snack.
piso *m* apartment; (*planta*) floor; (*de carretera*) surface.
pisotear *vt* (*aplastar*) to stamp on; (*pisar*) to trample on.
pisotón *m* **me dio un p.** he stood on my foot.
pista *f* track; (*rastro*) trail; (*indicio*) clue; **p. de baile** dance floor; **p. de esquí** ski slope; **p. de patinaje** ice rink; **p. de tenis** tennis court; **p. de aterrizaje** landing strip; **p. de despegue** runway.
pistacho *m* pistachio (nut).
pistola *f* pistol.
pitar 1 *vt* (*silbato*) to blow. **2** *vi* to whistle; (*coche*) to toot one's horn.
pitido *m* whistle.
pitillo *m* cigarette.
pito *m* whistle; (*de vehículo*) horn.
pizarra *f* (*encerado*) blackboard; (*piedra*) slate.
pizarrón *m* Am blackboard.
pizca *f* little bit; **ni p.** not a bit.
placa *f* plate; (*conmemorativa*) plaque.
placentero, -a *adj* pleasant, agreeable.
placer *m* pleasure; **tengo el p. de ...** it gives me great pleasure to ....
plácido, -a *adj* placid, easy-going.
plaga *f* plague.
plagiar *vt* (*copiar*) to plagiarize; *Andes, CAm, Méx* (*secuestrar*) to kidnap.
plagiario, -a *mf* Am (*secuestrador*) kidnapper.

plagio *m* plagiarism.
plan *m* (*proyecto*) plan; (*programa*) program; **p. de estudios** syllabus; **estar a p.** to be on a diet.
plana *f* page; **primera p.** front page.
plancha *f* iron; (*de metal*) plate; (*de cocina*) hotplate; **sardinas a la p.** grilled sardines.
planchar *vt* to iron.
planeta *m* planet.
planificación *f* planning.
planificar *vt* to plan.
planilla *f* Am application form.
plano, -a 1 *m* (*de ciudad*) map; (*proyecto*) plan. **2** *adj* flat.
planta *f* plant; (*del pie*) sole; (*piso*) floor, story; **p. baja** first floor.
plantado, -a *adj fam* **dejar a algn p.** to stand sb up.
plantar 1 *vt* (*árboles, campo*) to plant; (*poner*) to put, to place. **2 plantarse** *vr* to stand; (*llegar*) to arrive.
planteamiento *m* approach.
plantear 1 *vt* (*problema*) to raise; (*proponer*) to put forward; (*exponer*) to present. **2 plantearse** *vr* (*considerar*) to consider; (*problema*) to arise.
plantilla *f* (*personal*) staff; (*de zapato*) insole.
plantón *m* *fam* **dar un p. a algn** to stand sb up.
plasmar 1 *vt* (*reproducir*) to capture; (*expresar*) to express. **2 plasmarse** *vr* **plasmarse en** to take the shape of.
plástico, -a *adj & m* plastic.
plastificar *vt* to coat o cover with plastic.
plastilina® *f* Plasticine®.
plata *f* silver; (*objetos de plata*) silverware; *Am* money; **p. de ley** sterling silver.
plataforma *f* platform.
plátano *m* (*fruta*) banana; (*árbol*) plane tree.
plática *f* CAm, Méx chat, talk.
platicar *vi* CAm, Méx to chat, to talk.
platillo *m* saucer; **p. volante** flying saucer.
platina *f* (*de tocadiscos*) deck.
plato *m* plate, dish; (*parte de una comida*) course; (*guiso*) dish; (*de balanza*) tray; (*de tocadiscos*) turntable; **de primer p.** for starters; **p. combinado** one-course meal.
playa *f* beach; (*costa*) seaside; *Am* **p. de estacionamiento** parking lot.
playera *f* sneaker; *Am* (*camiseta*) teeshirt.
plaza *f* square; (*mercado*) marketplace; (*de vehículo*) seat; (*laboral*) post; **p. de toros** bullring.
plazo *m* (*periodo*) period; (*término*) deadline; **a corto/largo p.** in the short term/in the long run; **comprar a plazos** buy on an installment plan.
plegable *adj* folding.
plegar *vt* to fold.
plegaria *f* prayer.
pleito *m* lawsuit; **poner un p. (a algn)** to sue (sb).
pleno, -a 1 *adj* full. **2** *m* plenary meeting.
pliego *m* sheet of paper.
pliegue *m* fold; (*de vestido*) pleat.
plomero *m* Am plumber.
plomo *m* (*metal*) lead; (*fusible*) fuse.
pluma *f* feather; (*de escribir*) fountain pen.
plumero *m* feather duster.
plumier *m* pencil box.
plural *adj & m* plural.
pluriempleo *m* moonlighting.
población *f* (*ciudad*) town; (*pueblo*) village; (*habitantes*) population.
poblado, -a 1 *adj* populated. **2** *m* village.
pobre 1 *adj* poor; **¡p.!** poor thing! **2** *mf* poor person; **los pobres** the poor.
pobreza *f* (*indigencia*) poverty; (*escasez*) scarcity.
pocho, -a *adj* (*fruta*) overripe.
pocillo *m* Am cup.
poco, -a 1 *m* **un p.** a little; **un p. de azúcar** a little sugar. **2** *adj* not much, little; **p. sitio/tiempo** not much space/time, little space/time; **pocos, -as** not many, few; **pocas personas** not many people, few people; **unos, -as pocos, -as** a few. **3** *pron* not much; **pocos, -as** few, not many; **queda p.** there isn't much left. **4** *adv* (*con verbo*) not (very) much, little; (*con adj*) not very; **p. generoso** not very generous; **un p. tarde/frío** a little late/cold; **dentro de p.** soon; **p. a p.** little by little; **p. antes/después** shortly before/afterwards; **por p.** almost.
poder¹ *m* power.
poder² 1 *vt* to be able to; **no puede hablar** she can't speak; **no podré llamar** I won't be able to phone. ▪ (*permiso*) may, can; **¿se puede (entrar)?** may o can I (come in)?; **aquí no se puede fumar** you can't smoke here. ▪ (*posibilidad*) may, might; **puede que no lo sepan** they may o might not know; **no puede ser** that's impossible; **puede (ser) (que sí)** maybe, perhaps. ▪ (*deber*) **podrías haberme advertido** you might have warned me. **2** *vi* to cope (**con** with).
poderoso, -a *adj* powerful.
podré *indic fut de* **poder**.
podrido, -a *adj* rotten.
podrir *vt defectivo de* **pudrir**.
poesía *f* (*género*) poetry; (*poema*) poem.
poeta *mf* poet.
póker *m* poker.
polaco, -a 1 *adj* Polish. **2** *mf* Pole. **3** *m* (*idioma*) Polish.
polea *f* pulley.
polémica *f* controversy.
polémico, -a *adj* controversial.
polen *m* pollen.
policía 1 *f* police(force). **2** *mf* (*hombre*) policeman; (*mujer*) policewoman.
policíaco, -a, policiaco, -a, policial *adj* police; **novela/película policíaca** detective story/film.
polideportivo *m* sports center.
poliéster *m* polyester.
polietileno *m* polyethylene.
polígono *m* polygon; **p. industrial** industrial estate.
polilla *f* moth.
politécnico, -a *adj & m* polytechnic.
política *f* politics *sing*; (*estrategia*) policy.
político, -a 1 *adj* political; (*pariente*) in-law; **su familia política** her in-laws. **2** *mf* politician.
póliza *f* (*sello*) stamp; **p. de seguros** insurance policy.
pollera *f* RP (*occidental*) skirt; *Andes* (*indígena*) = long skirt worn by Indian women.
polo *m* pole; (*helado*) Popsicle®; (*deporte*) polo; **P. Norte/Sur** North/South Pole.
polución *f* pollution.
polvera *f* powder compact.
polvo *m* dust; **limpiar** o **quitar el p.** to dust; **en p.** powdered; **polvo(s) de talco** talcum powder; *fam* **estar hecho p.** (*deprimido*) to be depressed.
pólvora *f* gunpowder.
polvoriento, -a *adj* dusty.
polvorón *m* sweet pastry.
pollo *m* chicken.

pomada f ointment.
pomelo m (fruto) grapefruit; (árbol) grapefruit tree.
pómez adj inv **piedra p.** pumice (stone).
pomo m (de puerta) knob.
pómulo m cheekbone.
ponche m punch.
poncho m poncho.
pondré indic fut de **poner**.
poner (pp **puesto**) **1** vt to put; (mesa, huevo) to lay; (gesto) to make; (multa) to impose; (telegrama) to send; (negocio) to set up; (encender) to switch on; (película) to put on; (+ adjetivo) to make; **p. triste a algn** to make sb sad; **¿qué llevaba puesto?** what was he wearing?; (decir) **¿qué pone aquí?** what does it say here? **2 ponerse** vr to put oneself; (vestirse) to put on; (+ adjetivo) to become; (sol) to set; **ponerse al teléfono** to answer the phone; **ponerse a** to start to; **ponerse a trabajar** to get down to work.
poney m pony.
pongo indic pres de **poner**.
poniente m (occidente) West.
popa f stern.
popular adj (música, costumbre) folk; (famoso) popular.
popularidad f popularity.
póquer m poker.
por prep (agente) by; **pintado p.** Picasso painted by Picasso; **p. qué** why. ▪ (causa) because of; **p. necesidad/amor** out of need/love. ▪ (tiempo) **p. la mañana/noche** in the morning/at night; **p. ahora** for the time being. ▪ (en favor de) for; **lo hago p. mi hermano** I'm doing it for my brother('s sake). ▪ (lugar) **pasamos p. Córdoba** we went through Cordoba; **p. ahí** over there; **¿p. dónde vamos?** which way are we taking?; **mirar p. la ventana** to look out of the window; **entrar p. la ventana** to get in through the window. ▪ (medio) by **p. avión/correo** by plane/post. ▪ (a cambio de) for; **cambiar algo p. algo** to exchange sth for sth. ▪ (distributivo) **p. cabeza** per person; **p. hora/mes** per hour/month. ▪ (multiplicación) **dos p. tres, seis** two times three is six; **un diez p. ciento** ten percent. ▪ (con infinitivo) in order to. ▪ **p. más/muy … que sea** no matter how … he/she is; **p. mí** as far as I'm concerned.
porcelana f porcelain.
porcentaje m percentage.
porche m porch.
porción f portion.
pormenor m detail; **venta al p.** retail.
porno adj inv porn.
pornográfico, -a adj pornographic.
poro m pore.
porque conj because; **¡p. no!** just because!
porqué m reason.
porquería f (suciedad) dirt; (birria) garbage.
porra f (de policía) nightstick; fam **¡vete a la p.!** get lost!
porrazo m thump.
porrón m glass bottle with a spout coming out of its base, used for drinking wine.
portada f (de libro etc) cover; (de periódico) front page; (de disco) sleeve; (fachada) facade.
portaequipajes m inv (maletero) trunk; (baca) roof rack.
portal m entrance hall; (porche) porch; (puerta de la calle) main door.
portaminas m inv propelling pencil.
portamonedas m inv purse.
portarse vr to behave.
portátil adj portable.
portazo m slam of a door; **dar un p.** to slam the door.
portento m (cosa) marvel; (persona) genius.
portería f porter's lodge; (de fútbol) goal.
portero, -a 1 mf (de vivienda) caretaker; (guardameta) goalkeeper **2** m **p. automático** entryphone.
portorriqueño, -a adj & mf Puerto Rican.
portugués, -a adj & mf Portuguese.
porvenir m future.
posada f inn.
posar 1 vi (para retrato etc) to pose. **2** vt to put down. **3 posarse** vr to settle.
posdata f postscript.
poseer vt to possess.
posibilidad f possibility; (oportunidad) chance.
posible adj possible; **de ser p.** if possible; **lo antes p.** as soon as possible; **es p. que venga** he might come.
posición f position.
positivo, -a adj positive.
posponer vt (aplazar) to postpone; (relegar) to relegate.
postal 1 adj postal. **2** f postcard.
poste m (de portería) post.
póster m poster.
posterior adj (lugar) rear; (tiempo) subsequent (**a** to).
posteriormente adv subsequently.
postgraduado, -a adj & mf postgraduate.
postigo m (de puerta) wicket; (de ventana) shutter.
postizo, -a adj false; **dentadura postiza** dentures pl.
postre m dessert.
póstumo, -a adj posthumous.
postura f position.
potable adj drinkable; **agua p./no p.** drinking water/not drinking water.
potaje m hotpot.
potencia f power; **en p.** potential.
potencial adj & m potential.
potenciar vt to promote, to strengthen.
potente adj powerful.
potro m colt; (de gimnasia) horse.
poyo m stone bench.
pozo m well; (minero) shaft.
práctica f practice; **en la p.** in practice.
practicante 1 adj (de religión) practicing. **2** mf medical assistant.
practicar vti to practice; (operación) to carry out.
práctico, -a adj practical; (útil) handy.
pradera f, **prado** m meadow.
pragmático, -a 1 adj pragmatic. **2** mf pragmatist.
preámbulo m (introducción) preamble; (rodeo) circumlocution.
precalentamiento m warm-up.
precario, -a adj precarious.
precaución f (cautela) caution; (medida) precaution; **con p.** cautiously.
precaver 1 vt to guard against. **2 precaverse** vr to take precautions (**de**, **contra** against).
precavido, -a adj cautious.
precedente 1 adj preceding. **2** m precedent; **sin p.** unprecedented.
preceder vt to precede.

precepto m precept.
precintar vt to seal off.
precinto m seal.
precio m price.
preciosidad f (cosa) lovely thing; (persona) darling.
precioso, -a adj (hermoso) lovely, beautiful; (valioso) precious.
precipicio m precipice.
precipitación f (prisa) haste; (lluvia) rainfall.
precipitado, -a adj (apresurado) hurried; (irreflexivo) rash.
precipitar 1 vt (acelerar) to hurry; (arrojar) to hurl down. **2 precipitarse** vr (persona) to hurl oneself; (acontecimientos) to gather speed; (actuar irreflexivamente) to rush.
precisamente adv (con precisión) precisely; (exactamente) exactly.
precisar vt (especificar) to specify; (necesitar) to require.
precisión f (exactitud) precision; (aclaración) clarification; **con p.** precisely.
preciso, -a adj (necesario) necessary; (exacto) accurate; (claro) clear.
precoz adj (persona) precocious.
predecesor, -a mf predecessor.
predecir (pp **predicho**) vt to predict.
predicado m predicate.
predicar vt to preach.
predicción f prediction.
predigo indic pres de **predecir**.
predije pt indef de **predecir**.
predilecto, -a adj favorite.
predisponer (pp **predispuesto**) vt to predispose.
predominante adj predominant.
predominar vi to predominate.
predominio m predominance.
preescolar adj preschool.
preferencia f preference.
preferible adj preferable; **es p. que no vengas** you'd better not come.
preferido, -a adj & mf favorite.
preferir vt to prefer.
prefijo m (telefónico) area code; (gramatical) prefix.
pregunta f question; **hacer una p.** to ask a question.
preguntar 1 vti to ask; **p. algo a algn** to ask sb sth; **p. por algn** to ask about sb. **2 preguntarse** vr to wonder.
prehistórico, -a adj prehistoric.
prejuicio m prejudice.
preliminar adj & m preliminary.
prematuro, -a adj premature.
premeditado, -a adj premeditated.
premiar vt to award a prize (**a** to); (recompensar) to reward.
premio m prize; (recompensa) reward.
prenatal adj prenatal.
prenda f garment.
prender 1 vt (sujetar) to fasten; (con alfileres) to pin; **p. fuego a** to set fire to. **2** vi (fuego) to catch; (madera) to catch fire. **2 prenderse** vr to catch fire.
prensa f press.
prensar vt to press.
preñado, -a adj pregnant.
preocupación f worry.
preocupado, -a adj worried.
preocupar 1 vt to worry. **2 preocuparse** vr to worry (**por** about); **no te preocupes** don't worry.
preparación f preparation; (formación) training.
preparado, -a 1 adj (dispuesto) ready, prepared; (capacitado) trained, qualified; **comidas preparadas** ready-cooked meals. **2** m preparation.
preparar 1 vt to prepare. **2 prepararse** vr to get ready.
preparativo m preparation.
preposición f preposition.
presa f prey; (embalse) dam; fig **ser p. de** to be a victim of.
presagiar vt to predict.
presagio m (señal) omen; (premonición) premonition.
prescindir vi **p. de** to do without.
presencia f presence; **p. de ánimo** presence of mind.
presenciar vt to witness.
presentación f presentation; (de personas) introduction.
presentador, -a mf presenter.
presentar 1 vt to present; (una persona a otra) to introduce. **2 presentarse** vr (comparecer) to present oneself; (inesperadamente) to turn up; (ocasión, oportunidad) to arise; (candidato) to stand; (darse a conocer) to introduce oneself (**a** to).
presente 1 adj present; **tener p.** (tener en cuenta) to bear in mind. **2** m present.
presentimiento m premonition.
preservar vt to preserve (**de** from; **contra** against).
preservativo m condom.
presidente, -a mf president; (de una reunión) chairperson.
presidiario, -a mf prisoner.
presidio m prison.
presidir vt to head; (reunión) to chair.
presión f pressure; **a** o **bajo p.** under pressure.
presionar vt to press; fig to pressurize.
préstamo m loan.
prestar 1 vt to lend, to loan; **¿me prestas tu pluma?** can I borrow your pen?; (atención) to pay; (ayuda) to give; (servicio) to do. **2 prestarse** vr (ofrecerse) to offer oneself (**a** to); **prestarse a** (dar motivo) to cause; **se presta a (crear) malentendidos** it makes for misunderstandings.
prestidigitador, -a mf conjuror.
prestigio m prestige.
presumido, -a 1 adj conceited. **2** mf vain person.
presumir 1 vt (suponer) to presume. **2** vi (ser vanidoso) to show off.
presunto, -a adj supposed; (culpable) alleged.
presuntuoso, -a adj (vanidoso) conceited; (pretencioso) pretentious.
presuponer (pp **presupuesto**) vt to presuppose.
presupuesto m budget; (cálculo) estimate.
pretender vt (intentar) to try; (aspirar a) to try for; (cortejar) to court.
pretendiente, -a mf (al trono) pretender **2** m (amante) suitor.
pretérito m preterite.
pretexto m pretext.
prevenir vt (precaver) to prevent; (evitar) to avoid; (advertir) to warn.
prever (pp **previsto**) vt to forecast.
previo, -a adj prior; **sin p. aviso** without notice.
previsible adj predictable.
previsión f (predicción) forecast; (precaución) precaution; **p. del tiempo** weather forecast; **en p. de** as a precaution against; Andes, RP **p. social** social security.
previsto, -a adj forecast.

primario, -a *adj* primary.
primavera *f* spring.
primer *adj (delante de m)* first.
primera *f (en tren)* first class; *(marcha)* first (gear).
primero, -a 1 *adj* first; **de primera necesidad** basic. **2** *mf* first; **a primero(s) de mes** at the beginning of the month. **3** *adv* first.
primitivo, -a *adj* primitive; *(tosco)* rough.
primo, -a 1 *mf* cousin; **p. hermano** first cousin. **2** *adj* **materia prima** raw material.
primogénito, -a *adj & mf* first-born.
primoroso, -a *adj* exquisite.
princesa *f* princess.
principal *adj* main, principal; **puerta p.** front door.
príncipe *m* prince.
principiante 1 *adj* novice. **2** *mf* beginner.
principio *m* beginning, start; *(fundamento)* principle; **a principio(s) de** at the beginning of; **al p., en un p.** at first; **en p.** in principle; **principios** basics.
pringar 1 *vt (ensuciar)* to make greasy. **2 pringarse** *vr (ensuciarse)* to get greasy.
pringoso, -a *adj (grasiento)* greasy.
prioridad *f* priority.
prisa *f* hurry; **date p.** hurry up; **tener p.** to be in a hurry; **de** *o* **a p.** in a hurry.
prisión *f* prison.
prisionero, -a *mf* prisoner.
prismáticos *mpl* binoculars.
privado, -a *adj* private.
privar 1 *vt (despojar)* to deprive (**de** of). **2 privarse** *vr (abstenerse)* to go without.
privilegio *m* privilege.
pro 1 *m* advantage; **los pros y los contras** the pros and cons. **2** *prep* in favor of.
proa *f* prow.
probable *adj* probable, likely; **es p. que llueva** it'll probably rain.
probador *m* fitting room.
probar 1 *vt* to try; *(comprobar)* to check; *(demostrar)* to prove. **2** *vi* to try. **3 probarse** *vr (ropa)* to try on.
probeta *f* test tube.
problema *m* problem.
procedente *adj (adecuado)* appropriate; *(en juicio)* proper; **p. de** coming from.
proceder 1 *vi (actuar)* to act; *(ser oportuno)* to be advisable; **p. de** *(provenir)* to come from; **p. a** *(continuar)* to go on to. **2** *m (comportamiento)* behavior.
procedimiento *m* procedure.
procesador *m* processor; **p. de textos** word processor.
procesar *vt* to prosecute; *(información)* to process.
procesión *f* procession.
proceso *m* process; *(juicios)* trial; **p. de datos** data processing.
proclamar *vt* to proclaim.
procurar *vt (intentar)* to attempt; *(proporcionar)* (to manage) to get; **procura que no te vean** make sure they don't see you.
prodigio *m* prodigy, miracle; **hacer prodigios** to work wonders; **niño p.** child prodigy.
prodigioso, -a *adj (sobrenatural)* prodigious; *(maravilloso)* wonderful.
producción *f (acción)* production; *(producto)* product; **p. en cadena/serie** assembly-line/mass production.
producir 1 *vt* to produce; *(fruto, cosecha, rendir)* to yield; *(originar)* to bring about. **2 producirse** *vr* to take place.
productivo, -a *adj* productive; *(beneficioso)* profitable.
producto *m* product; *(producción)* produce.
productor, -a 1 *adj* producing. **2** *mf* producer.
profesión *f* profession.
profesional *adj & mf* professional.
profesor, -a *mf* teacher; *(de universidad)* lecturer.
profesorado *m (grupo de profesores)* staff.
profetizar *vt* to prophesy.
prófugo, -a *adj & mf* fugitive.
profundidad *f* depth; **un metro de p.** one meter deep.
profundizar *vt (cavar)* to deepen; *fig (examinar)* to study in depth.
profundo, -a *adj* deep; *(idea, sentimiento)* profound.
progenitor, -a *mf* **progenitores** *(padres)* parents.
programa *m* program; *(informático)* program; *(de estudios)* syllabus.
programación *f* programming.
programar *vt* to program; *(para ordenador)* to program.
progresar *vi* to make progress.
progresista *adj & mf* progressive.
progresivamente *adv* progressively.
progresivo, -a *adj* progressive.
progreso *m* progress.
prohibido, -a *adj* forbidden; **'prohibida la entrada'** 'no admittance'; **p. aparcar/fumar** no parking/smoking.
prohibir *vt* to forbid.
prójimo, -a *mf* one's fellow man.
proliferar *vi* to proliferate.
prólogo *m* prologue.
prolongar 1 *vt (alargar)* to extend. **2 prolongarse** *vr (continuar)* to carry on.
promedio *m* average.
promesa *f* promise.
prometedor, -a *adj* promising.
prometer 1 *vt* to promise. **2** *vi* to be promising. **3 prometerse** *vr* to get engaged.
prometido, -a 1 *adj* promised. **2** *mf (hombre)* fiancé; *(mujer)* fiancée.
promocionar *vt* to promote.
promover *vt (cosas, personas)* to promote; *(juicio, querella)* to initiate; *(causar)* to cause, to give rise to.
pronombre *m* pronoun.
pronosticar *vt* to forecast.
pronóstico *m (del tiempo)* forecast; *(médico)* prognosis.
pronto, -a 1 *adj* quick, prompt. **2** *adv (deprisa)* quickly; *(temprano)* early; **de p.** suddenly; **por de** *o* **lo p.** *(para empezar)* to start with; **¡hasta p.!** see you soon!
pronunciación *f* pronunciation.
pronunciar *vt* to pronounce; *(discurso)* to deliver.
propaganda *f (política)* propaganda; *(comercial)* advertising.
propagar 1 *vt* to spread. **2 propagarse** *vr* to spread.
propiamente *adv* **p. dicho** strictly speaking.
propiedad *f (posesión)* ownership; *(cosa poseída)* property; **con p.** properly.
propietario, -a *mf* owner.
propina *f* tip.
propio, -a *adj (de uno)* own; *(correcto)* suitable; *(característico)* typical; *(mismo) (hombre)* himself; *(mujer)* herself; *(animal, cosa)* itself; **el p. autor** the author himself; **propios, -as** themselves.
proponer *(pp propuesto)* **1** *vt* to propose. **2 proponerse** *vr* to intend.

proporción *f* proportion; **proporciones** *(tamaño)* size *sing.*
proporcional *adj* proportional.
proporcionar *vt (dar)* to give; *(suministrar)* to supply.
proposición *f (propuesta)* proposal.
propósito *m (intención)* intention; **a p.** *(por cierto)* by the way; *(adrede)* on purpose.
propuesta *f* suggestion.
propuse *pt indef de* **proponer**.
prórroga *f (prolongación)* extension; *(en partido)* overtime; *(aplazamiento)* postponement.
prorrogar *vt (prolongar)* to extend; *(aplazar)* to postpone.
prosa *f* prose.
proseguir *vti* to carry on.
prospecto *m* leaflet.
prosperar *vi (negocio, país)* to prosper; *(propuesta)* to be accepted.
próspero, -a *adj* prosperous.
prostitución *f* prostitution.
prostituta *f* prostitute.
protagonista *mf* main character.
protección *f* protection; **p. de escritura** write protection.
protector, -a 1 *adj* protective. **2** *mf* protector.
proteger *vt* to protect.
protesta *f* protest.
protestante *adj & mf* Protestant.
protestar *vi* to protest; *(quejarse)* to complain.
protocolo *m* protocol.
protuberante *adj* bulging.
provecho *m* benefit; **¡buen p.!** enjoy your meal!; **sacar p. de algo** to benefit from sth.
proveedor, -a *mf* supplier; **p. de acceso (a Internet)** Internet access provider.
proveer *(pp provisto)* *vt* to supply.
provenir *vi* **p. de** to come from.
proverbio *m* proverb.
provincia *f* province.
provisional *adj* provisional.
provisto, -a *adj* **p. de** equipped with.
provocación *f* provocation.
provocador, -a 1 *mf* instigator. **2** *adj* provocative.
provocar *vt (causar)* to cause; *(instigar)* to provoke; *Am* **si no le provoca** if he doesn't feel like it.
provocativo, -a *adj* provocative.
próximamente *adv* soon.
proximidad *f* closeness; **en las proximidades de** in the vicinity of.
próximo, -a *adj (cercano)* near, close; *(siguiente)* next.
proyección *f* projection; *(de película)* showing.
proyectar *vt (luz)* to project; *(planear)* to plan; *(película)* to show.
proyectil *m* projectile.
proyecto *m* project.
proyector *m* projector.
prudencia *f* prudence; *(moderación)* care.
prudente *adj* prudent; *(conductor)* careful.
prueba *f (argumento)* proof; *(examen etc)* test; **a p. de agua/balas** waterproof/bullet-proof.
psicoanálisis *m inv* psychoanalysis.
psicología *f* psychology.
psicológico, -a *adj* psychological.
psicólogo, -a *mf* psychologist.
psicópata *mf* psychopath.
psiquiatra *mf* psychiatrist.
psiquiátrico, -a 1 *adj* psychiatric. **2** *m* mental hospital.
psíquico, -a *adj* psychic.
pta(s)., pts *abr de* **peseta(s)** peseta(s).
púa *f (de planta)* thorn; *(de animal)* spine; *(de peine)* tooth.
pub *m (pl* **pubs, pubes)** pub.
publicación *f* publication.
publicar *vt* to publish; *(divulgar)* to publicize.
publicidad *f* advertising; *(conocimiento público)* publicity.
público, -a 1 *adj* public. **2** *m* public; *(de teatro)* audience; *(de estadio)* spectators *pl.*
puchero *m (olla)* cooking pot; *(cocido)* stew; **hacer pucheros** to pout.
pucho *m Am* dog-end.
pude *pt indef de* **poder**.
pudiente *adj* rich, wealthy.
pudor *m* modesty.
pudoroso, -a *adj* modest.
pudrir *vt defective*, **pudrirse** *vr* to rot.
pueblo *m* village; *(small)* town; *(gente)* people.
puente *m* bridge; **p. aéreo** *(civil)* air shuttle service.
puerco, -a 1 *adj* filthy. **2** *m* pig; *f* sow.
puericultura *f* pediatrics *sing.*
pueril *adj* childish.
puerro *m* leek.
puerta *f* door; *(verja)* gate.
puerto *m (de mar, ordenador)* port; *(de montaña)* (mountain) pass; **p. deportivo** marina.
puertorriqueño, -a *adj & mf* Puerto Rican.
pues *conj (puesto que)* as, since; *(por lo tanto)* therefore; *(entonces)* so; *(para reforzar)* **¡p. claro que sí!** but of course!; **p. como iba diciendo** well, as I was saying; **¡p. no!** certainly not!
puestero, -a *mf Am* stallholder.
puesto, -a 1 *conj* **p. que** since, as. **2** *m (lugar)* place; *(empleo)* post; *(tienda)* stall; **p. de trabajo** job. **3** *adj (colocado)* put; **llevar p.** *(ropa)* to have on, to wear.
pugna *f* fight.
pulcro, -a *adj (extremely)* neat.
pulga *f* flea.
pulgada *f* inch.
pulgar *m* thumb.
pulir *vt (metal, madera)* to polish.
pulmón *m* lung.
pulpería *f Am* store.
pulpo *m* octopus.
pulsación *f* pulsation; *(en mecanografía)* keystroke.
pulsar *vt (timbre, botón)* to press; *(tecla)* to hit.
pulsera *f (aro)* bracelet; **reloj de p.** wristwatch.
pulso *m* pulse; *(mano firme)* steady hand; **echarse un p.** to arm-wrestle.
pulverizador *m* spray, atomizer.
puma *m* puma.
puna *f Am* high moor; *(mal)* mountain sickness.
punta *f (extremo)* tip; *(extremo afilado)* point; *(de cabello)* end; **sacar p. a un lápiz** to sharpen a pencil; **tecnología p.** state-of-the-art technology; **hora p.** rush hour.

puntapié *m* kick.
puntería *f* aim; **tener buena/mala p.** to be a good/bad shot.
puntiagudo, -a *adj* sharp.
puntilla *f (encaje)* lace; **dar la p.** to finish (the bull) off; **de puntillas** on tiptoe.
punto *m* point; *(marca)* dot; *(lugar)* point; *(de costura, sutura)* stitch; **a p.** ready; **a p. de** on the point of; **hasta cierto p.** to a certain extent; **p. muerto** neutral; **p. de vista** point of view; **p. y seguido** period; **p. y coma** semicolon; **dos puntos** colon; **p. y aparte** full stop, new paragraph; **las ocho en p.** eight o'clock sharp; **hacer p.** to knit.
puntuación *f (ortográfica)* punctuation; *(deportiva)* score; *(nota)* mark.
puntual 1 *adj* punctual. **2** *adv* punctually.
puntualidad *f* punctuality.
puntualizar *vt* to make it clear.
puntuar 1 *vt (al escribir)* to punctuate; *(calificar)* to mark. **2** *vi (marcar)* to score; *(ser puntuable)* to count.
punzante *adj (objeto)* sharp; *(dolor)* acute, piercing.
puñado *m* handful.
puñal *m* dagger.
puñalada *f* stab.
puñetazo *m* punch.
puño *m* fist; *(de camisa etc)* cuff; *(de herramienta)* handle.
pupa *f (herida)* sore.
pupila *f* pupil.
pupitre *m* desk.
puré *m* purée; **p. de patata** mashed potatoes *pl.*
pureza *f* purity.
purificar *vt* to purify.
puritano, -a 1 *adj* puritanical. **2** *mf* puritan.
puro, -a 1 *adj (sin mezclas)* pure; *(mero)* sheer; **aire p.** fresh air; **la pura verdad** the plain truth. **2** *m (cigarro)* cigar.
púrpura *adj inv* purple.
puse *pt indef de* **poner**.
puzzle *m* jigsaw puzzle.
P.V.P. *m abr de* **precio de venta al público** recommended retail price.
Pza., Plza. *abr de* **plaza** square, Sq.

Q

que¹ *pron rel (sujeto, persona)* who, that; *(cosa)* that, which. ▪ *(complemento, persona)* no se traduce o that; *(cosa)* no se traduce o that, which; **la chica q. conocí** the girl (that) I met; **el coche q. compré** the car (that o which) I bought. ▪ **lo q.** what. ▪ *(con infinitivo)* **hay mucho q. hacer** there's a lot to do.
que² *conj* no se traduce o that; **dijo que llamaría** he said (that) he would call. ▪ *(consecutivo)* no se traduce o that; **habla tan bajo q. no se le oye** he speaks so quietly (that) he can't be heard. ▪ *(en comparativas)* than; **mejor q. tú** better than you. ▪ *(causal)* because; **date prisa q. no tenemos mucho tiempo** hurry up, because we haven't got much time. ▪ *(enfático)* **¡q. no!** no! ▪ *(deseo, mandato)* (+ *subj*) **¡q. te diviertas!** enjoy yourself! ▪ *(final)* so that; **ven q. te dé un beso** come and let me give you a kiss. ▪ *(disyuntivo)* whether; **me da igual q. suba o no** I couldn't care whether he comes up or not. ▪ *(locuciones)* **q. yo sepa** as far as I know; **yo q. tú** if I were you.
qué 1 *pron interr* what; **¿q. quieres?** what do you want? ▪ *(exclamativo)* (+ *adj*) how; (+ *n*) what a; **¡q. bonito!** how pretty!; **¡q. lástima!** what a pity! **2** *adj interr* which; **¿q. libro quieres?** which book do you want?
quebrada *f Am* stream.
quebrar 1 *vt (romper)* to break. **2** *vi (empresa)* to go bankrupt. **2 quebrarse** *vr* to break.
quedar 1 *vi (restar)* to be left; *(con amigo)* to arrange to meet; *(acordar)* to agree (**en** to); *(estar situado)* to be; **quedan dos** there are two left; **quedaría muy bien allí** it would look very nice there; **q. en ridículo** to make a fool of oneself; **q. bien/mal** to make a good/bad impression. **2 quedarse** *vr (permanecer)* to stay; **quedarse sin dinero/pan** to run out of money/bread; **quedarse con hambre** to be still hungry; **quedarse (con)** *(retener)* to keep; **quédese (con) el cambio** keep the change.
quehacer *m* chore.
queja *f* complaint; *(de dolor)* groan.
quejarse *vr* to complain (**de** about).
quemadura *f* burn.
quemar 1 *vt* to burn. **2** *vi* to be burning hot. **3 quemarse** *vr fig* to burn oneself out.
quemazón *f* smarting.
quepo *indic pres de* **caber**.
querella *f* lawsuit.
querer 1 *vt* to want; *(amar)* to love; **sin q.** without meaning to; **¡por lo que más quieras!** for heaven's sake!; **¿quiere pasarme el pan?** would you pass me the bread?; **q. decir** to mean; **no quiso darme permiso** he refused me permission. **2 quererse** *vr* to love each other.
querido, -a *adj* dear.
querré *indic fut de* **querer**.
queso *m* cheese.
quicio *vt (de puerta)* doorpost; **sacar de q. (a algn)** to infuriate (sb).
quien *pron rel* **el hombre con q. vino** the man she came with; *(formal)* the man with whom she came. ▪ *(indefinido)* **q. quiera venir** whoever wants to come; **hay q. dice lo contrario** thre are some people who say the opposite.
quién *pron interr* who; **¿q. es?** who is it?; **¿para q. es?** who is it for?; **¿de q. es esa bici?** whose bike is that?
quienquiera *pron indef (pl* **quienesquiera***)* whoever.
quieto, -a *adj* still; **¡estáte q.!** keep still!
quilo *m* = **kilo**.
química *f (ciencia)* chemistry.
químico, -a 1 *adj* chemical. **2** *mf (científico)* chemist.
quince *adj & m inv* fifteen.
quiniela *f* sports lottery.
quinientos, -as *adj & mf* five hundred.
quinqué *m* oil lamp.
quintal *m (medida)* 46 kg; **q. métrico** = 100 kg.
quinto, -a *adj & mf* fifth.
quiosco *m* kiosk; **q. de periódicos** newspaper stand.
quirófano *m* operating room.
quirúrgico, -a *adj* surgical.
quise *pt de* **querer**.
quitaesmaltes *m inv* nail varnish remover.
quitamanchas *m inv* stain remover.
quitanieves *m (máquina)* **q.** snowplow.

quitar 1 *vt* to remove, to take away; *(ropa)* to take off; *(dolor)* to relieve; *(sed)* to quench; *(hambre)* to take away; *(robar)* to steal; *(tiempo)* to take up; *(asiento)* to take. **2** *vi* **¡quita!** get out of the way! **3 quitarse** *vr (apartarse)* to move away; *(mancha)* to come out; *(dolor)* to go away; *(ropa, gafas)* to take off; **quitarse de fumar** to give up smoking; **quitarse a algn de encima** to get rid of sb.
quizá(s) *adv* perhaps, maybe.

R

rábano *m* radish.
rabia *f (ira)* rage; *(enfermedad)* rabies *sing*; **¡qué r.!** how annoying!; **me da r.** it makes me mad.
rabiar *vi (enfadarse)* to rage; **hacer r. a algn** to make sb see red.
rabioso, -a *adj* rabid; *(enfadado)* furious.
rabo *m (de animal)* tail; *(de fruta)* stalk.
racha *f (período)* spell; *(de viento)* gust.
racial *adj* racial.
racimo *m* bunch.
ración *f* portion.
racionar *vt* to ration.
racismo *m* racism.
racista *adj & mf* racist.
radar *m (pl* **radares***)* radar.
radiación *f* radiation.
radiactividad *f* radioactivity.
radiactivo, -a *adj* radioactive.
radiador *m* radiator.
radiante *adj* radiant (**de** with).
radical *adj* radical.
radio¹ *f (aparato)* radio.
radio² *m (de circunferencia)* radius; *(de rueda)* spoke.
radioactividad *f* radioactivity.
radiocasete *m* radio cassette.
radiografía *f (imagen)* X-ray.
ráfaga *f (de viento)* gust; *(de disparos)* burst.
raído, -a *adj (gastado)* worn.
raíz *f (pl* **raíces***)* root; **r. cuadrada** square root; **a r. de** as a result of.
raja *f (corte)* cut; *(hendidura)* crack.
rajar 1 *vt (tela)* to tear; *(hender)* to crack. **2 rajarse** *vr (tela)* to tear; *(partirse)* to crack; *fam (echarse atrás)* to back out; *(acobardarse)* to chicken out.
rallado, -a *adj* **queso r.** grated cheese; **pan r.** breadcrumbs *pl.*
rallador *m* grater.
rallar *vt* to grate.
ralo, -a *adj* thin.
rama *f* branch.
ramillete *m (de flores)* posy.
ramo *m (de flores)* bunch; *(sector)* branch.
rampa *f* ramp.
rana *f* frog.
rancho *m (granja)* ranch.
rancio, -a *adj (comida)* stale.
rango *m* rank; *(jerarquía elevada)* high social standing.
ranura *f* slot; **r. de expansión** expansion slot.
rapar *vt* to crop.
rapaz 1 *adj* predatory; **ave r.** bird of prey. **2** *mf (muchacho)* lad; *(muchacha)* lass.
rape *m (pez)* angler fish; **cortado al r.** close-cropped.
rapidez *f* speed.
rápido, -a 1 *adj* quick, fast. **2** *adv* quickly. **3** *m (tren)* fast train.
raptar *vt* to kidnap.
rapto *m (secuestro)* kidnapping.
raqueta *f (de tenis)* racket; *(de ping-pong)* paddle.
raquítico, -a *adj (delgado)* emaciated; *fam (escaso)* meager.
raro, -a *adj* rare; *(extraño)* strange.
rascacielos *m inv* skyscraper.
rascar *vt (con las uñas)* to scratch.
rasgar *vt* to tear.
rasgo *m* feature.
rasguño *m* scratch.
raso, -a 1 *adj (llano)* flat; *(cielo)* clear. **2** *m* satin.
raspa *f (de pescado)* bone.
raspar 1 *vt (limar)* to scrape (off). **2** *vi (ropa, tela)* to chafe.
rastrear *vt (zona)* to comb.
rastrillo *m* rake; *(mercadillo)* flea market.
rastro *m* trace; *(en el suelo)* trail.
rasurar *vt,* **rasurarse** *vr* to shave.
rata *f* rat.
ratero, -a *mf* pickpocket.
ratificar *vt* to ratify.
rato *m (momento)* while; **a ratos** at times; **al poco r.** shortly after; **pasar un buen/mal r.** to have a good/bad time; **ratos libres** free time *sing.*
ratón *m (también de ordenador)* mouse.
raya *f (línea)* line; *(del pantalón)* crease; *(del pelo)* part; **camisa a rayas** striped shirt.
rayar *vt* to scratch.
rayo *m* ray; *(relámpago)* (flash of) lightning.
raza *f (humana)* race; *(de animal)* breed.
razón *f* reason; *(proporción)* rate; **uso de r.** power of reasoning; **dar la r. a algn** to say that sb is right; **tener r.** to be right.
razonable *adj* reasonable.
razonar 1 *vt (argumentar)* to reason out. **2** *vi (discurrir)* to reason.
reacción *f* reaction; **avión de r.** jet (plane).
reaccionar *vi* to react.
reactor *m* reactor; *(avión)* jet (plane).
reajuste *m* readjustment.
real¹ *adj (efectivo, verdadero)* real.
real² *adj (regio)* royal.
realidad *f* reality; **en r.** in fact.
realismo *m* realism.
realizador, -a *mf* producer.

realizar 1 *vt (hacer)* to carry out; *(ambición)* to achieve. **2 realizarse** *vr (persona)* to fulfill oneself; *(sueño)* to come true.
realmente *adv* really.
realzar *vt (recalcar)* to highlight; *(belleza, importancia)* to heighten.
reanimar *vt*, **reanimarse** *vr* to revive.
reanudar 1 *vt* to renew. **2 reanudarse** *vr* to resume.
rebaja *f (descuento)* reduction; **rebajas** sales.
rebajar 1 *vt (precio)* to cut; *(tanto por ciento)* to take off. **2 rebajarse** *vr (humillarse)* to humble oneself.
rebanada *f* slice.
rebaño *m* herd; *(de ovejas)* flock.
rebasar *vt (exceder)* to exceed.
rebeca *f* cardigan.
rebelarse *vr* to rebel.
rebelde 1 *mf* rebel. **2** *adj* rebellious.
rebelión *f* rebellion.
rebobinar *vt* to rewind.
rebosar *vi* to overflow.
rebotar *vi (pelota)* to bounce; *(bala)* to ricochet.
rebuznar *vi* to bray.
recado *m (mandado)* errand; *(mensaje)* message; **dejar un r.** to leave a message.
recalcar *vt* to stress.
recalentar *vt (comida)* to reheat.
recámara *f (de rueda)* tube; *(habitación)* dressing room; *CAm, Col, Méx (dormitorio)* bedroom.
recambio *m (repuesto)* spare (part); *(de pluma etc)* refill; **rueda de r.** spare wheel.
recapacitar *vt* to think over.
recargado, -a *adj (estilo)* overelaborate.
recargar *vt (batería)* to recharge; *(adornar mucho)* to overelaborate.
recatado, -a *adj (prudente)* cautious; *(modesto)* modest.
recaudador, -a *mf* tax collector.
recaudar *vt* to collect.
recelar *vi* **r. de** to distrust.
receloso, -a *adj* suspicious.
recepción *f* reception.
recepcionista *mf* receptionist.
receptor, -a 1 *mf (persona)* recipient. **2** *m (aparato)* receiver.
receta *f* recipe; **r. (médica)** prescription.
recetar *vt* to prescribe.
rechazar *vt* to reject.
rechinar *vi (metal)* to squeak; *(dientes)* to chatter.
rechoncho, -a *adj* chubby.
recibidor *m* entrance hall.
recibimiento *m* reception.
recibir 1 *vt* to receive; *(acoger)* to welcome. **2 recibirse** *vr Am* **recibirse de** to qualify as.
recibo *m (factura)* bill; *(resguardo)* receipt.
reciclar *vt* to recycle.
recién *adv* recently; *Am (hace poco)* recently. **r. casados** newlyweds; **r. nacido** newborn baby.
reciente *adj* recent.
recientemente *adv* recently.
recinto *m (cercado)* enclosure; **r. comercial** shopping precinct.
recio, -a *adj (robusto)* sturdy; *(grueso)* thick; *(voz)* loud.
recipiente *m* container.
recíproco, -a *adj* reciprocal.
recitar *vt* to recite.
reclamación *f (demanda)* claim; *(queja)* complaint.
reclamar 1 *vt* to claim. **2** *vi* to protest (**contra** against).
reclinar 1 *vt* to lean (**sobre** on). **2 reclinarse** *vr* to lean back.
recluir *vt* to shut away.
recluso, -a *mf* inmate.
recobrar 1 *vt* to recover; *(conocimiento)* to regain; **r. el aliento** to get one's breath back. **2 recobrarse** *vr* to recover.
recodo *m* bend.
recoger 1 *vt* to pick up; *(datos etc)* to collect; *(ordenar, limpiar)* to clean; *(cosecha)* to gather. **2 recogerse** *vr* **r. el pelo** to put one's hair up
recogida *f* collection; *(cosecha)* harvest.
recomendación *f* recommendation; *(para persona)* reference.
recomendar *vt* to recommend.
recompensa *f* reward.
reconciliar 1 *vt* to reconcile. **2 reconciliarse** *vr* to be reconciled.
reconfortante *adj* comforting.
reconocer *vt* to recognize; *(admitir)* to admit; *(paciente)* to examine.
reconocimiento *m* recognition; *(médico)* examination.
reconstituyente *m* tonic.
reconstruir *vt* to reconstruct.
recopilación *f* compilation.
recopilar *vt* to compile.
récord *m* record.
recordar *vti* to remember; **r. algo a algn** to remind sb of sth.
recorrer *vt (distancia)* to travel; *(país)* to tour; *(ciudad)* to walk round.
recorrido *m (trayecto)* journey; *(itinerario)* route.
recortar *vt* to cut out.
recorte *m* cutting; *(de pelo)* trim.
recostar 1 *vt* to lean. **2 recostarse** *vr (tumbarse)* to lie down.
recreo *m* recreation; *(en colegio)* break, playtime.
recriminar *vt* to recriminate; *(reprochar)* to reproach.
recrudecer *vt*, **recrudecerse** *vr* to worsen.
recta *f (de carretera)* straight stretch.
rectangular *adj* rectangular.
rectángulo *m* rectangle.
rectificar *vt* to rectify; *(corregir)* to remedy.
recto, -a 1 *adj (derecho)* straight; *(ángulo)* right. **2** *adv* straight (on).
rector, -a *mf* rector.
recuerdo *m (memoria)* memory; *(regalo etc)* souvenir; **recuerdos** regards.
recuperación *f* recovery.
recuperar 1 *vt (salud)* to recover; *(conocimiento)* to regain; *(tiempo, clases)* to make up. **2 recuperarse** *vr* to recover.
recurrir *vi (sentencia)* to appeal; **r. a** *(a algn)* to turn to; *(a algo)* to resort to.
recurso *m* resource; *(de sentencia)* appeal.
red *f* net; *(sistema)* network; **r. local** local area network, LAN.
redacción *f (escrito)* composition; *(acción)* writing.
redactar *vt* to draft.
redactor, -a *mf* editor.
redondel *m (círculo)* ring.
redondo, -a *adj* round; *(rotundo)* categorical.

reducción *f* reduction.
reducir 1 *vt (disminuir)* to reduce. **2 reducirse** *vr (disminuirse)* to diminish; *(limitarse)* to confine oneself (**a** to).
reembolso *m* reimbursement; **contra r.** cash on delivery.
reemplazar *vt* to replace (**con** with).
ref. *abr de* **referencia** reference, ref.
refaccionar *vt Am* to repair.
refectorio *m* refectory.
referencia *f* reference.
referéndum *m (pl* **referéndums)** referendum.
referente *adj* **r. a** concerning, regarding.
referir 1 *vt* to tell. **2 referirse** *vr (aludir)* to refer (**a** to).
refilón: de refilón *adv* briefly.
refinería *f* refinery.
reflector *m* spotlight.
reflejar 1 *vt* to reflect. **2 reflejarse** *vr* to be reflected (**en** in).
reflejo, -a 1 *m (imagen)* reflection; *(destello)* gleam; **reflejos** *(en el cabello)* highlights. **2** *adj (movimiento)* reflex.
reflexión *f* reflection.
reflexionar *vi* to think (**sobre** about).
reflexivo, -a *adj (persona)* thoughtful; *(verbo etc)* reflexive.
reforma *f* reform; *(reparación)* repair.
reformar *vt* to reform; *(edificio)* to renovate.
reformatorio *m* reform school.
reforzar *vt* to strengthen.
refrán *m* saying.
refregar *vt* to rub vigorously.
refrescante *adj* refreshing.
refrescar 1 *vt* to refresh. **2** *vi (bebida)* to be refreshing. **3 refrescarse** *vr* to cool down.
refresco *m* soft drink.
refrigeración *f* refrigeration; *(aire acondicionado)* air conditioning.
refrigerado, -a *adj (local)* air-conditioned.
refrigerador *m* refrigerator, fridge.
refrigerio *m* snack, refreshments *pl*.
refuerzo *m* strengthening.
refugiarse *vr* to take refuge.
refugio *m* refuge.
refunfuñar *vi* to grumble.
regadera *f* watering can.
regalar *vt (dar)* to give (as a present).
regaliz *m* licorice.
regalo *m* present.
regañadientes: a regañadientes *adv* reluctantly.
regañar 1 *vt* to tell off. **2** *vi* to nag.
regar *vt* to water.
regata *f* regatta.
regatear *vi* to haggle; *(en fútbol)* to dribble.
regazo *m* lap.
regeneración *f* regeneration.
régimen *m (pl* **regímenes)** regime; *(dieta)* diet; **estar a r.** to be on a diet.
regio, -a *adj (real)* regal; *Am (magnífico)* majestic.
región *f* region.
regional *adj* regional.
regir 1 *vt* to govern. **2** *vi* to be in force. **3 regirse** *vr* to be guided, to go (**por** by).
registrado, -a *adj* **marca registrada** registered trademark.
registrar 1 *vt (examinar)* to inspect; *(cachear)* to frisk; *(inscribir)* to register. **2 registrarse** *vr (detectarse)* to be recorded; *(inscripción)* to register.
registro *m* inspection; *(inscripción)* registration.
regla *f (norma)* rule; *(instrumento)* ruler; *(periodo)* period; **por r. general** as a (general) rule.
reglamentario, -a *adj* statutory.
reglamento *m* regulations *pl*.
regocijar *vt* to delight.
regocijo *m (placer)* delight; *(alborozo)* rejoicing.
regresar *vi* to return.
regreso *m* return.
regular 1 *vt* to regulate; *(ajustar)* to adjust. **2** *adj* regular; *(mediano)* so-so; **vuelo r.** scheduled flight. **3** *adv* so-so.
regularidad *f* regularity; **con r.** regularly.
regularizar *vt* to regularize.
rehabilitar *vt* to rehabilitate; *(edificio)* to convert.
rehacer *(pp* **rehecho) 1** *vt* to redo. **2 rehacerse** *vr (recuperarse)* to recover.
rehén *m* hostage.
rehogar *vt* to brown.
rehuir *vt* to shun.
rehusar *vt* to refuse.
reina *f* queen.
reinar *vi* to reign.
reincidir *vi* to relapse (**en** into).
reincorporarse *vr* **r. al trabajo** to return to work.
reino *m* kingdom; **el R. Unido** the United Kingdom.
reinserción *f* reintegration.
reinsertar *vt*, **reinsertarse** *vr* to reintegrate.
reír *vi*, **reírse** *vr* to laugh (**de** at).
reiterar *vt* to reiterate.
reivindicación *f* demand.
reivindicar *vt* to demand.
reja *f (de ventana)* grating.
rejilla *f* grill; *(de horno)* gridiron; *(por equipaje)* luggage rack.
rejoneador, -a *mf* bullfighter on horseback.
relación *f* relationship; *(conexión)* connection; **relaciones públicas** public relations.
relacionado, -a *adj* related (**con** to).
relacionar 1 *vt* to relate (**con** to). **2 relacionarse** *vr* to be related; *(alternar)* to get acquainted.
relajación *f* relaxation.
relajante *adj* relaxing.
relajar *vt*, **relajarse** *vr* to relax.
relamerse *vr* to lick one's lips.
relámpago *m* flash of lightning.
relatar *vt* to tell, to relate.
relativo, -a *adj* relative (**a** to).
relato *m* story.
relax *m* relaxation.
relegar *vt* to relegate.
relevante *adj* important.
relevar *vt (sustituir)* to take over from.

relevo m relief; (en carrera) relay.
religión f religion.
religioso, -a 1 adj religious. **2** mf (hombre) monk; (mujer) nun.
relinchar vi to neigh.
rellano m landing.
rellenar vt (impreso etc) to fill in; (llenar) to pack (**de** with).
relleno, -a 1 m (de aves) stuffing; (de pasteles) filling. **2** adj stuffed.
reloj m clock; (de pulsera) watch.
relojería f (tienda) watchmaker's.
reluciente adj shining.
relucir vi to shine.
reluzco indic pres de **relucir**.
remache m rivet.
remangar vt, **remangarse** vr (mangas, pantalones) to roll up; (camisa) to tuck up.
remar vi to row.
rematar vt to finish off.
remate m (final) finish; (en fútbol) shot at goal; **para r.** to crown it all; **de r.** utter.
remediar vt to remedy; (enmendar) to repair; **no pude remediarlo** I couldn't help it.
remedio m (cura) remedy; (solución) solution; **¡qué r.!** what else can I do!; **no hay más r.** there's no choice; **sin r.** without fail.
remendar vt (ropa) to patch.
remesa f (de mercancías) consignment.
remiendo m (arreglo) mend; (parche) patch.
remilgado, -a adj (melindroso) fussy.
remite m (en carta) sender's name and address.
remitente mf sender.
remitir 1 vt (enviar) to send. **2** vi (fiebre, temporal) to subside.
remo m oar.
remodelación f (modificación) reshaping; (reorganización) reorganization.
remojar vt to soak (**en** in).
remojón m fam **darse un r.** to go for a dip.
remolacha f red beet.
remolcador m tug.
remolcar vt to tow.
remolino m (de agua) whirlpool; (de aire) whirlwind.
remolón, -ona adj **hacerse el r.** to shirk, to slack.
remolonear vi to shirk, to slack.
remolque m (acción) towing; (vehículo) trailer.
remordimiento m remorse.
remoto, -a adj remote.
remover vt (tierra) to turn over; (líquido) to shake up; (comida etc) to stir.
remplazar vt = **reemplazar**.
remuneración f remuneration.
remunerar vt to remunerate.
renacer vi to be reborn; fig (revivir) to revive, to come back to life.
renacuajo m tadpole; fam (niño pequeño) shrimp.
rencor m resentment; **guardar r. a algn** to have a grudge against sb.
rencoroso, -a adj resentful.
rendido, -a adj (muy cansado) exhausted.
rendija f crack.
rendimiento m (de máquina, motor) performance.
rendir 1 vt (fruto, beneficios) to yield; (cansar) to exhaust. **2** vi (dar beneficios) to pay. **3** **rendirse** vr to surrender.
RENFE f abr de **Red Nacional de Ferrocarriles Españoles** Spanish railroad network.
renglón m line.
reno m reindeer.
renombre m renown.
renovación f (de contrato, pasaporte) renewal.
renovar vt to renew; (edificio) to renovate.
renta f (ingresos) income; (beneficio) interest; (alquiler) rent.
rentable adj profitable.
renunciar vi (dimitir) to resign; (no aceptar) to decline; **r. a** to give up.
reñido, -a adj (disputado) hard-fought.
reñir 1 vt (regañar) to tell off. **2** vi (discutir) to argue; (pelear) to fight.
reo mf (acusado) accused; (culpable) culprit.
reojo: de reojo adv **mirar algo de r.** to look at sth out of the corner of one's eye.
reparar 1 vt to repair. **2** vi **r. en** (darse cuenta de) to notice.
reparo m **no tener reparos en** not to hesitate to; **me da r.** I am embarrassed.
repartidor, -a mf distributor.
repartir vt (dividir) to share out; (regalo, premio) to give out; (correo) to deliver.
reparto m distribution; (distribución) handing out; (de mercancías) delivery; (de actores) cast.
repasar vt to revise.
repaso m revision.
repecho m short steep slope.
repeler vt (repugnar) to disgust.
repente: de repente adv suddenly.
repentino, -a adj sudden.
repercutir 1 vt (subida de precio) to pass on. **2** vi **r. en** to affect.
repertorio m repertoire.
repetición f repetition.
repetir 1 vt to repeat; (plato) to have a second helping of. **2** vi (en colegio) to repeat a year. **3** **repetirse** vr (hecho) to recur.
repicar vti (campanas) to ring.
repisa f shelf.
replegarse vr to fall back.
repleto, -a adj full (up); **r. de** packed with.
réplica f answer; (copia) replica.
replicar 1 vt (objetar) to argue. **2** vi to reply.
repoblar vt to repopulate; (bosque) to reforest.
repollo m cabbage.
reponer 1 vt to replace. **2** **reponerse** vr **reponerse de** to recover from.
reportaje m report; (noticias) news item.
reportar 1 vt (beneficios) to bring; Am (informar) to report. **2** **reportarse** vr Am (presentarse) to report (**a** to).
reportero, -a mf reporter.
reposar vti to rest (**en** on).
reposo m rest.
repostar vti (gasolina) to fill up.
repostería f confectionery.
reprender vt to reprimand.
represalia f (usu pl) reprisals pl, retaliation.
representante mf representative.
representar vt to represent; (significar) to mean; (obra) to perform.
represión f repression.

represivo, -a adj repressive.
reprimenda f reprimand.
reprimir vt to repress.
reprochar vt **r. algo a algn** to reproach sb for sth.
reproducción f reproduction.
reproducir vt, **reproducirse** vr to reproduce.
reptil m reptile.
república f republic.
repuesto m (recambio) spare (part); **rueda de r.** spare wheel.
repugnante adj disgusting.
repugnar vt to disgust.
repulsivo, -a adj repulsive.
repuse pt indef de **reponer**.
reputación f reputation.
requesón m cottage cheese.
requisar vt to requisition.
requisito m requirement.
res f animal.
resaca f hangover.
resaltar vi (sobresalir) to project; fig to stand out.
resbaladizo, -a adj slippery.
resbalar vi, **resbalarse** vr to slip.
resbalón m slip.
rescatar vt (liberar) to rescue.
rescate m rescue; (dinero pagado) ransom.
rescindir vt (contrato) to cancel.
rescoldo m embers pl.
resecarse vr to dry up, to become parched.
reseco, -a adj parched.
resentido, -a adj resentful.
resentimiento m resentment.
reserva f (de entradas etc) booking; (provisión) reserve.
reservado, -a adj reserved.
reservar vt (billetes etc) to reserve, to book; (guardar) to keep.
resfriado, -a 1 m (catarro) cold; **coger un r.** to catch (a) cold. **2** adj **estar r.** to have a cold.
resfriarse vr to catch (a) cold.
resguardo m (recibo) receipt.
residencia f residence; **r. de ancianos** old people's home.
residencial adj residential.
residente adj & mf resident.
residir vi to reside (**en** in).
resignado, -a adj resigned.
resignarse vr to resign oneself (**a** to).
resina f resin.
resistencia f resistance; (aguante) endurance; (de bombilla etc) element.
resistente adj resistant (**a** to); (fuerte) tough, hardy.
resistir 1 vi to resist; (soportar) to hold (out). **2** vt (situación, persona) to put up with; (tentación) to resist. **2** **resistirse** vr to resist; (oponerse) to offer resistance; (negarse) to refuse.
resolver (pp **resuelto**) **1** vt (solucionar) to solve; (asunto) to settle. **2** **resolverse** vr (solucionarse) to be solved.
resonar vi to resound; (tener eco) to echo.
resoplar vi (respirar) to breathe heavily; (de cansancio) to puff and pant.
resorte m (muelle) spring; (medio) means.
respaldar vt to support, to back (up).
respaldo m (de asiento) back.
respecto m **al r., a este r.** in this respect; **con r. a, r. a** with regard to.
respetable adj respectable.
respetar vt to respect.
respeto m respect.
respetuoso, -a adj respectful.
respingo m start.
respiración f (acción) breathing; (aliento) breath.
respirar vti to breathe.
resplandecer vi to shine.
resplandor m (brillo) brightness; (muy intenso) brilliance; (de fuego) blaze.
responder 1 vt to answer. **2** vi (a una carta) to reply; (reaccionar) to respond; (corresponder) to answer; (protestar) to answer back.
responsabilidad f responsibility.
responsabilizar 1 vt to make responsible (**de** for); (culpar) hold responsible (**de** for). **2** **responsabilizarse** vr to claim responsibility (**de** for).
responsable 1 adj responsible. **2** mf **el/la r.** (de robo etc) the perpetrator.
respuesta f answer, reply; (reacción) response.
resquicio m chink.
resta f subtraction.
restablecer 1 vt to re-establish; (el orden) to restore. **2** **restablecerse** vr (mejorarse) to recover.
restaguardia f rearguard.
restante adj remaining.
restar vt to subtract.
restaurante m restaurant.
restaurar vt to restore.
resto m rest; (en resta) remainder; **restos** remains; (de comida) leftovers.
restregar vt to scrub.
restricción f restriction.
restringir vt to restrict.
resucitar vti to revive.
resuello m gasp.
resultado m result; (consecuencia) outcome.
resultar vi (ser) to turn out; **me resultó fácil** it turned out to be easy for me.
resumen m summary; **en r.** in short.
resumir vt to sum up.
resurgir vi to reappear.
retahíla f series sing.
retal m (pedazo) scrap.
retar vt to challenge.
retardarse vr to be delayed.
retazo m (pedazo) scrap.
retención f retention; **r. de tráfico** (traffic) hold-up.
retener vt (conservar) to retain; (detener) to detain.
reticente adj reticent, reserved.
retirada f withdrawal.
retirar 1 vt (apartar, alejar) to take away; (dinero) to withdraw. **2** **retirarse** vr (apartarse) to withdraw; (irse, jubilarse) to retire.
retiro m (lugar tranquilo) retreat.

reto *m* challenge..

retoque *m* final touch.

retorcer 1 *vt (cuerda, hilo)* to twist; *(ropa)* to wring (out). **2 retorcerse** *vr* to become twisted.

retorcido, -a *adj fig* twisted.

retornar 1 *vt* to return, to give back. **2** *vi* to return, to come back, to go back.

retorno *m* return.

retortijón *m (dolor)* stomach cramp.

retraído, -a *adj* reserved.

retransmisión *f* broadcast.

retrasado, -a 1 *adj (tren etc)* late; *(reloj)* slow; **estar r.** *(en el colegio)* to be behind. **2** *mf* **r. (mental)** mentally retarded person.

retrasar 1 *vt (retardar)* to slow down; *(atrasar)* to postpone; *(reloj)* to put back. **2 retrasarse** *vr* to be delayed; *(reloj)* to be slow.

retraso *m (demora)* delay; **con r.** late; **una hora de r.** an hour behind schedule.

retratar 1 *vt (pintar)* to paint a portrait of; *(fotografiar)* to take a photograph of; *fig (describir)* to describe, to depict. **2 retratarse** *vr* to have one's photograph taken.

retrato *m (pintura)* portrait; *(fotografía)* photograph.

retrete *m* toilet.

retribución *f (pago)* pay; *(recompensa)* reward.

retroceder *vi* to back away.

retroceso *m (movimiento)* backward movement.

retrógrado, -a *adj & mf (reaccionario)* reactionary.

retrospectivo, -a *adj & f* retrospective.

retrovisor *m* rear-view mirror.

retumbar *vi (resonar)* to resound; *(tronar)* to thunder.

retuve *pt indef de* **retener**.

reúma, reumatismo *m* rheumatism.

reunión *f* meeting.

reunir 1 *vt* to gather together; *(dinero)* to raise; *(cualidades)* to possess; *(requisitos)* to fulfill. **2 reunirse** *vr* to meet.

revalorizar *vt*, **revalorizarse** *vr (moneda)* to revalue.

revancha *f* revenge; *(partido)* return match.

revelar *vt* to reveal; *(película)* to develop.

reventa *f (de entradas)* touting.

reventar *vti*, **reventarse** *vr* to burst.

reventón *m (de neumático)* blow-out.

reverencia *f (de hombre)* bow; *(de mujer)* curtsy.

reversible *adj* reversible.

reverso *m* back.

revés *m (reverso)* reverse; *(contrariedad)* setback; **al o del r.** *(al contrario)* the other way round; *(la parte interior en el exterior)* inside out; *(boca abajo)* upside down; *(la parte de detrás delante)* back to front.

revisar *vt* to check; *(coche)* to service.

revisión *f* checking; *(de coche)* service; **r. médica** checkup.

revisor, -a *mf* corrector, inspector.

revista *f* magazine.

revitalizar *vt* to revitalize.

revivir *vti* to revive.

revolcarse *vr* to roll about.

revoltijo, revoltillo *m* jumble.

revoltoso, -a *adj (travieso)* mischievous.

revolución *f* revolution.

revolucionar *vt* to revolutionize.

revolver *(pp revuelto)* **1** *vt (desordenar)* to mess up; **me revuelve el estómago** it turns my stomach. **2 revolverse** *vr (agitarse)* to roll; *(el mar)* to become rough.

revólver *m (pl revólveres)* revolver.

revuelo *m (agitación)* stir.

revuelta *f* revolt.

revuelto, -a *adj (desordenado)* in a mess; *(tiempo)* unsettled; *(mar)* rough; *(huevos)* scrambled.

rey *m* king; **(el día de) Reyes** Epiphany, January 6.

rezagarse *vr* to fall behind.

rezar 1 *vi (orar)* to pray. **2** *vt (oración)* to say.

rezumar *vt* to ooze.

ría *f* estuary.

riada *f* flood.

ribera *f (de río)* bank; *(zona)* riverside.

rico, -a 1 *adj* **ser r.** to be rich; **estar r.** *(delicioso)* to be delicious. **2** *mf* rich person; **los ricos** the rich.

ridiculizar *vt* to ridicule.

ridículo, -a 1 *adj* ridiculous. **2** *m* ridicule; **hacer el r., quedar en r.** to make a fool of oneself; **poner a algn en r.** to make a fool of sb.

riego *m* irrigation.

rienda *f* rein.

riesgo *m* risk; **correr el r. de** to run the risk of.

rifa *f* raffle.

rifar *vt* to raffle (off).

rifle *m* rifle.

rigidez *f* rigidity; *(severidad)* inflexibility.

rígido, -a *adj* rigid, stiff; *fig (severo)* strict, inflexible.

rigor *m* rigor; *(severidad)* severity.

rigurosamente *adv* rigorously; *(meticulosamente)* meticulously; *(severamente)* severely.

riguroso, -a *adj* rigorous; *(severo)* severe.

rimar *vti* to rhyme *(con* with*)*.

rímel *m* mascara.

rincón *m* corner.

rinoceronte *m* rhinoceros.

riña *f (pelea)* fight; *(discusión)* row.

riñón *m* kidney.

río *m* river; **r. abajo** downstream; **r. arriba** upstream.

riqueza *f* wealth.

risa *f* laugh; *(carcajadas)* laughter; **me da r.** it makes me laugh; **morirse o mondarse de r.** to die laughing.

risueño, -a *adj (sonriente)* smiling.

ritmo *m* rhythm; *(paso)* rate.

rito *m* rite; *(ritual)* ritual.

ritual *adj & m* ritual.

rival *adj & mf* rival.

rivalizar *vi* to rival *(en* in*)*.

rizado, -a *adj (pelo)* curly; *(mar)* choppy.

rizar *vt*, **rizarse** *vr (pelo)* to curl.

rizo *m (de pelo)* curl.

robar *vt (objeto)* to steal; *(banco, persona)* to rob; *(casa)* to burgle.

roble *m* oak (tree).

robo *m* robbery, theft; *(en casa)* burglary; **r. a mano armada** armed robbery.

robot *m (pl robots)* robot; **r. de cocina** food processor.

robustecer *vt* to strengthen.

robusto, -a *adj* robust.

roca *f* rock.

roce *m (fricción)* friction; *(en la piel)* chafing; *(contacto ligero)* brush.

rociar *vt* to sprinkle.

rocío *m* dew.

rocoso, -a *adj* rocky.

rodaja *f* slice.

rodaje *m* shooting.

rodar 1 *vt (película etc)* to shoot. **2** *vi* to roll.

rodear *vt* to surround. **2 rodearse** *vr* to surround oneself *(* **de** with*)*.

rodeo *m (desvío)* detour; *(al hablar)* evasiveness; rodeo; **no andarse con rodeos** to get straight to the point.

rodilla *f* knee; **de rodillas** kneeling; **hincarse o ponerse de rodillas** to kneel down.

rodillera *f (de pantalón)* knee patch; *(para la rodilla)* knee pad.

roer *vt (hueso)* to gnaw; *(galleta)* to nibble at.

rogar *vt (pedir)* to ask; *(implorar)* to beg; **hacerse de r.** to play hard to get.

roído, -a *adj* gnawed, eaten away.

rojizo, -a *adj* reddish.

rojo, -a 1 *adj* red; **estar en números rojos** to be in the red. **2** *m (color)* red.

rollizo, -a *adj* chubby.

rollo *m* roll; *fam (pesadez)* drag.

romance *m (aventura amorosa)* romance.

romántico, -a *adj & mf* romantic.

rombo *m* diamond; *(en geometría)* rhombus.

rompecabezas *m inv (juego)* (jigsaw) puzzle.

rompeolas *m inv* breakwater, jetty.

romper *(pp roto)* **1** *vt* to break; *(papel, tela)* to tear; *(vajilla, cristal)* to smash; *(pantalones)* to split; *(relaciones)* to break off. **2** *vi* to break; **r. a llorar** to burst out crying. **3 romperse** *vr* to break; *(papel, tela)* to tear; **romperse la cabeza** to rack one's brains.

ron *m* rum.

roncar *vi* to snore.

roncha *f (en la piel)* swelling.

ronco, -a *adj* hoarse; **quedarse r.** to lose one's voice.

ronda *f* round; *(patrulla)* patrol; *(carretera)* ring road; *(paseo)* avenue.

rondar *vti (merodear)* to prowl around; *(estar cerca de)* to be about.

ronquido *m* snore.

ronronear *vi* to purr.

roñoso, -a *adj (mugriento)* filthy; *(tacaño)* mean.

ropa *f* clothes *pl*, clothing; **r. interior** underwear.

ropero *m (armario)* **r.** wardrobe, closet.

rosa 1 *adj inv (color)* pink; **novela r.** romantic novel. **2** *f (flor)* rose. **3** *m (color)* pink.

rosado, -a 1 *adj (color)* pink; *(vino)* rosé. **2** *m (vino)* rosé.

rosal *m* rosebush.

rosbif *m* roast beef.

rosco *m (pastel)* ring-shaped pastry.

rosquilla *f* ring-shaped pastry; **venderse como rosquillas** to sell like hot cakes.

rostro *m (cara)* face; *fam* **tener mucho r.** to have a lot of nerve.

roto, -a 1 *adj* broken; *(papel)* torn; *(gastado)* worn out; *(ropa)* in tatters. **2** *m (agujero)* hole.

rótula *f* kneecap.

rotulador *m* felt-tip pen.

rótulo *m (letrero)* sign; *(titular)* heading.

rotundo, -a *adj* categorical; **éxito r.** resounding success.

rotura *f (ruptura)* breaking; *(de hueso)* fracture.

rozadura *f* scratch.

rozar 1 *vt* to brush against. **2** *vi* to rub. **3 rozarse** *vr* to brush *(con* against*)*.

Rte. *abr de* **remite, remitente** sender.

rubí *m (pl rubíes)* ruby.

rubio, -a 1 *adj (pelo, persona)* blond; **tabaco r.** Virginia tobacco. **2** *mf* blond; *f* blonde.

ruborizarse *vr* to blush.

rudimentario, -a *adj* rudimentary.

rudo, -a *adj* rough.

rueda *f* wheel; **r. de recambio** spare wheel; **r. de prensa** press conference.

ruedo *m* bullring.

ruego *m* request.

rugido *m (de animal)* roar.

rugir *vi* to roar.

rugoso, -a *adj* rough.

ruido *m* noise; *(sonido)* sound; **hacer r.** to make a noise.

ruidoso, -a *adj* noisy.

ruin *adj (vil)* vile; *(tacaño)* mean.

ruina *f* ruin.

ruiseñor *m* nightingale.

ruleta *f* roulette.

rulo *m (para el pelo)* roller.

rumba *f* rumba.

rumbo *m* direction; **(con) r. a** bound for.

rumor *m* rumor; *(murmullo)* murmur.

rumorearse *v impers* to be rumored.

ruptura *f* breaking; *(de relaciones)* breaking-off.

rural *adj* rural.

ruso, -a *adj & mf* Russian.

rústico, -a *adj* rustic.

ruta *f* route.

rutina *f* routine.

S

S.A. *abr de* **Sociedad Anónima** ≃ PLC, ≃ Ltd, ≃ Inc.

sábado *m* Saturday.

sábana *f* sheet; *fam* **se pegaron las sábanas** I overslept.

sabañón *m* chilblain.

sabelotodo *mf inv* know-all.

saber¹ *m* knowledge.

saber² *vt* to know; *(tener habilidad)* to be able to; *(enterarse)* to learn; **que yo sepa** as far as I know; **vete tú a s.** goodness knows; **a s.** namely; **¿sabes cocinar?** can you cook? **2** *vi (tener*

sabor) to taste (**a** of); (*soler*) to be accustomed to; **sabe a fresa** it tastes of strawberries.
sabiduría *f* wisdom.
sabiendas: a sabiendas *adv* **lo hizo a s.** he did it in the full knowledge of what he was doing; **a s. de que ...** knowing full well that ...
sabio, -a 1 *adj* (*prudente*) wise. **2** *mf* scholar.
sable *m* sabre.
sabor *m* (*gusto*) flavor; **con s. a limón** lemon-flavored.
saborear *vt* (*degustar*) to taste.
sabotaje *m* sabotage.
sabotear *vt* to sabotage.
sabré *indic fut de* **saber**.
sabroso, -a *adj* tasty; (*delicioso*) delicious.
sacacorchos *m inv* corkscrew.
sacapuntas *m inv* pencil sharpener.
sacar 1 *vt* to take out; (*con más fuerza*) to pull out; (*obtener*) to get; (*conclusiones*) to draw; (*entrada*) to buy; (*libro, disco*) to bring out; (*fotografía*) to take; **s. la lengua** to stick one's tongue out; **s. provecho de algo** to benefit from sth.
sacarina *f* saccharin.
sacerdote *m* priest.
saciar *vt* (*sed*) to quench; (*deseos, hambre*) to satisfy.
saciedad *f* satiety; **repetir algo hasta la s.** to repeat sth ad nauseam.
saco *m* sack; *Am* (*chaqueta*) jacket; **s. de dormir** sleeping bag.
sacrificar 1 *vt* to sacrifice. **2 sacrificarse** *vr* to make sacrifices.
sacrificio *m* sacrifice.
sacudida *f* shake; (*espasmo*) jolt; (*de terremoto*) tremor.
sacudir *vt* (*agitar*) to shake; (*alfombra, sábana*) to shake out; (*arena, polvo*) to shake off; (*golpear*) to beat.
sádico, -a 1 *adj* sadistic. **2** *mf* sadist.
saeta *f* (*dardo*) dart.
safari *m* (*cacería*) safari; (*parque*) safari park.
sagaz *adj* (*listo*) clever; (*astuto*) shrewd.
sagrado, -a *adj* sacred.
sal¹ *f* salt; **s. de mesa** table salt; **s. gorda** cooking salt.
sal² *imperativo de* **salir**.
sala *f* room; (*en un hospital*) ward; **s. de estar** living room; **s. de espera** waiting room; **s. de exposiciones** exhibition hall; **s. de fiestas** nightclub.
salado, -a *adj* (*con sal*) salted; (*con exceso de sal*) salty; (*infortunado*) unlucky; **agua salada** salt water.
salario *m* salary.
salchicha *f* sausage.
salchichón *m* (*salami-type*) sausage.
saldar *vt* (*cuenta*) to settle; (*deuda*) to pay off.
saldo *m* (*de cuenta*) balance; **saldos** sales.
saldré *indic fut de* **salir**.
salero *m* (*recipiente*) saltcellar.
salgo *indic pres de* **salir**.
salida *f* (*partida*) departure; (*puerta etc*) exit, way out; (*de carrera*) start; (*de un astro*) rising; (*perspectiva*) opening; (*en ordenador*) output; **callejón sin s.** dead end; **s. de emergencia** emergency exit; **te vi a la s. del cine** I saw you leaving the cinema; **s. del sol** sunrise.
salir 1 *vi* (*de un sitio, tren etc*) to leave; (*venir de dentro, revista, disco*) to come out; (*novios*) to go out; (*aparecer*) to appear; (*ley*) to come in; (*trabajo, vacante*) to come up; (*resultar*) to turn out (to be); (*problema*) to work out; **salió de la habitación** she left the room; **¿cómo te salió el examen?** how did your exam go?; **s. ganando** to come out on top; **s. barato/caro** to work out cheap/expensive; **esta cuenta no me sale** I can't work this calculation out. **2 salirse** *vr* (*líquido, gas*) to leak (out); **salirse de lo normal** to be out of the ordinary; **salirse con la suya** to get one's own way.
saliva *f* saliva.
salivar *vi* to salivate.
salmón 1 *m* (*pescado*) salmon. **2** *adj inv* (*color*) salmon pink.
salmonete *m* (*pescado*) red mullet.
salobre *adj* (*agua*) brackish; (*gusto*) salty.
salón *m* (*en una casa*) lounge; **s. de actos** assembly hall; **s. de belleza** beauty salon; **s. del automóvil** motor show.
salpicar *vt* (*rociar*) to splash; **me salpicó el abrigo de barro** he splashed mud on my coat.
salsa *f* sauce; (*de carne*) gravy.
saltamontes *m inv* grasshopper.
saltar 1 *vt* (*obstáculo, valla*) to jump (over). **2** *vi* to jump; (*romperse*) to break; (*plomos*) to blow; (*desprenderse*) to come off; **s. a la vista** to be obvious. **2 saltarse** *vr* (*omitir*) to skip; (*no hacer caso*) to ignore; **saltarse el semáforo** to run the lights; **se me saltaron las lágrimas** tears came to my eyes.
salto *m* (*acción*) jump, leap; **a saltos** in leaps and bounds; **dar** *o* **pegar un s.** to jump, to leap; **de un s.** in a flash; **s. de altura** high jump; **s. de longitud** long jump; **s. mortal** somersault.
salud *f* health; **beber a la s. de algn** to drink to sb's health; **¡s.!** cheers!
saludable *adj* (*sano*) healthy.
saludar *vt* (*decir hola a*) to say hello to; **saluda de mi parte a** give my regards to; **le saluda atentamente** (*en una carta*) yours faithfully.
saludo *m* greeting; **un s. de** best wishes from.
salvado *m* bran.
salvaguardar *vt* to safeguard (**de** from).
salvajada *f* brutal act.
salvaje *adj* (*planta, animal*) wild; (*pueblo, tribu*) savage.
salvam(i)ento *m* rescue.
salvar 1 *vt* to save (**de** from); (*obstáculo*) to clear; (*dificultad*) to overcome. **2 salvarse** *vr* (*sobrevivir*) to survive; (*escaparse*) to escape (**de** from); **¡sálvese quien pueda!** every man for himself!
salvavidas *m inv* life preserver.
salvo, -a 1 *adj* safe; **a s.** safe. **2** *adv* (*exceptuando*) except (for). **3** *conj* **s. que** unless.
san *adj* saint; *ver* **santo**.
sanar 1 *vt* (*curar*) to heal. **2** *vi* (*persona*) to recover; (*herida*) to heal.
sanción *f* sanction.
sancionar *vt* (*castigar*) to penalize.
sancochar *vt* to parboil; *Am* to boil meat in water and salt.
sandalia *f* sandal.
sándalo *m* sandalwood.
sandía *f* watermelon.
sandwich *m* sandwich.
sanear *vt* (*terrenos*) to drain; (*empresa*) to reorganize.
sangrar *vi* to bleed.
sangre *f* blood; **donar s.** to give blood; **a s. fría** in cold blood.
sangría *f* (*bebida*) sangria.
sangriento, -a *adj* (*cruel*) cruel.
sanguíneo, -a *adj* blood; **grupo s.** blood group.
sanidad *f* health; **Ministerio de S.** Department of Health.
sano, -a *adj* healthy; **s. y salvo** safe and sound.

santería *f* (*religión*) santería, = form of religion common in the Caribbean in which people allegedly have contact with the spirit world; *Am* (*tienda*) = shop selling religious mementoes such as statues of saints.
santiguarse *vr* to cross oneself.
santo, -a 1 *adj* holy. **2** *mf* saint; (*día onomástico*) saint's day; **se me fue el s. al cielo** I completely forgot; **¿a s. de qué?** why on earth?
santuario *m* shrine.
sapo *m* toad.
saque *m* (*en tenis*) service; (*en fútbol*) **s. inicial** kick-off; **s. de esquina** corner kick.
saquear *vt* (*casas y tiendas*) to loot.
sarampión *m* measles.
sarcástico, -a *adj* sarcastic.
sardina *f* sardine.
sargento *m* sergeant.
sarpullido *m* rash.
sarro *m* (*en los dientes*) tartar; (*en la lengua*) fur.
sartén *f* frying pan, skillet.
sastre *m* tailor.
satélite *m* satellite; **televisión vía s.** satellite television.
satén *m* satin.
sátira *f* satire.
satisfacción *f* satisfaction.
satisfacer (*pp* **satisfecho**) *vt* to satisfy; (*deuda*) to pay.
satisfecho, -a *adj* satisfied; **me doy por s.** that's good enough for me.
sauce *m* willow; **s. llorón** weeping willow.
sauna *f* sauna.
saxofón *m* saxophone.
sazonar *vt* to season.
se¹ *pron* (*reflexivo*) (*a él mismo*) himself; (*a ella misma*) herself; (*animal*) itself; (*a usted mismo*) yourself; (*a ellos/ellas mismos/mismas*) themselves; (*a ustedes mismos*) yourselves; **se afeitó** he shaved; **se compró un nuevo coche** he bought himself a new car. ▪ (*recíproco*) one another, each other. ▪ (*voz pasiva*) **el vino se guarda en cubas** wine is kept in casks. ▪ (*impersonal*) **nunca se sabe** you never know; **se habla inglés** English spoken; **se dice que...** it is said that...
se² *pron pers* (*a él*) (to *o* for) him; (*a ella*) (to *o* for) her; (*a usted o ustedes*) (to *o* for) you; (*a ellos*) (to *o* for) them; **se lo diré en cuanto les vea** I'll tell them as soon as I see them; **¿se lo explico?** shall I explain it to him/her *etc*?
sé¹ *indic pres de* **saber**.
sé² *imperativo de* **ser**.
sea *subj pres de* **ser**.
secador *m* dryer; **s. de pelo** hairdryer.
secadora *f* tumble dryer.
secar 1 *vt* to dry. **2 secarse** *vr* to dry; (*marchitarse*) to dry up; **secarse las manos** to dry one's hands.
sección *f* section.
seco, -a *adj* dry; (*tono*) curt; (*golpe, ruido*) sharp; **frutos secos** dried fruit; **limpieza en s.** drycleaning; **frenar en s.** to pull up sharply.
secretaría *f* (*oficina*) secretary's office.
secretario, -a *mf* secretary.
secreto, -a 1 *adj* secret; **en s.** in secret. **2** *m* secret.
secta *f* sect.
sector *m* sector; (*zona*) area.
secuencia *f* sequence.
secuestrar *vt* (*persona*) to kidnap; (*avión*) to hijack.
secuestro *m* (*de persona*) kidnapping; (*de avión*) hijacking.
secundar *vt* to back.
secundario, -a *adj* secondary.
sed *f* thirst; **tener s.** to be thirsty.
seda *f* silk.
sedal *m* fishing line.
sedante *adj & m* sedative.
sede *f* headquarters; (*de gobierno*) seat.
sedentario, -a *adj* sedentary.
sedimento *m* sediment.
sedoso, -a *adj* silky.
seducir *vt* to seduce.
seductor, -a 1 *adj* seductive. **2** *mf* seducer.
segar *vt* to cut.
seglar 1 *adj* secular. **2** *mf* lay person; *m* layman; *f* laywoman.
segmento *m* segment.
seguida: en seguida *adv* immediately, straight away.
seguido *adv* straight; *Am* (*a menudo*) often; **todo s.** straight ahead.
seguir 1 *vt* to follow; (*camino*) to continue. **2** *vi* to follow; **siguió hablando** he went on *o* kept on speaking; **sigo resfriado** I've still got the cold.
según 1 *prep* according to; (*en función de*) depending on; (*tal como*) just as; **estaba s. lo dejé** it was just as I had left it. **2** *conj* (*a medida que*) as; **s. iba leyendo** as I read. **3** *adv* **¿vendrás? — s.** are you coming? — it depends.
segundo, -a¹ *adj* second.
segundo² m (*tiempo*) second.
seguramente *adv* (*probablemente*) most probably; (*seguro*) surely.
seguridad *f* security; (*física*) safety; (*confianza*) confidence; (*certeza*) sureness; **s. en carretera** road safety; **s. en sí mismo** self-confidence; **con toda s.** most probably; **tener la s. de que** to be certain that; **S. Social** ≃ Social Security.
seguro, -a 1 *adj* (*cierto*) sure; (*libre de peligro*) safe; (*protegido*) secure; (*fiable*) reliable; (*firme*) steady; **estoy s. de que...** I am sure that...; **está segura de ella misma** she has self-confidence. **2** *m* (*de accidentes etc*) insurance; (*dispositivo*) safety device; **s. de vida** life insurance. **3** *adv* definitely.
seis *adj & m inv* six.
seiscientos, -as *adj & mf* six hundred.
seleccionador, -a *mf* selector; (*en fútbol*) manager.
seleccionar *vt* to select.
selecto, -a *adj* select.
self-service *m* self-service restaurant.
sello *m* (*de correos*) stamp; (*para documentos*) seal.
selva *f* jungle.
semáforo *m* traffic lights *pl*.
semana *f* week; **S. Santa** Holy Week.
semanal *adj & m* weekly.
semanario *m* weekly magazine.
sembrar *vt* to sow; **s. el pánico** to spread panic.
semejante 1 *adj* (*parecido*) similar. **2** *m* (*prójimo*) fellow being.
semestre *m* semester.
semifinal *f* semifinal.
semilla *f* seed.

seminario *m (en colegio)* seminar; *(para sacerdotes)* seminary.

sémola *f* semolina.

senado *m* senate.

senador, -a *mf* senator.

sencillo, -a *adj (fácil)* simple; *(natural)* unaffected; *(billete)* single; *(sin adornos)* plain.

senda *f*, **sendero** *m* path.

seno *m (pecho)* breast; *(interior)* heart.

sensación *f* sensation; **tengo la s. de que…** I have a feeling that…; **causar s.** to cause a sensation.

sensacional *adj* sensational.

sensato, -a *adj* sensible.

sensible *adj* sensitive; *(perceptible)* perceptible.

sensiblemente *adv* noticeably.

sensiblero, -a *adj* over-sentimental, mawkish.

sensualidad *f* sensuality.

sentar 1 *vt* to sit; *(establecer)* to establish. **2** *vi (color, ropa)* to suit; **el pelo corto te sienta mal** short hair doesn't suit you; **s. bien/mal a** *(comida)* to agree/disagree with; **la sopa te sentará bien** the soup will do you good. **3 sentarse** *vr* to sit (down).

sentencia *f (condena)* sentence.

sentido *m* sense; *(significado)* meaning; *(dirección)* direction; *(conciencia)* consciousness; **s. común** common sense; **no tiene s.** it doesn't make sense; **(de) s. único** one-way; **perder el s.** to faint.

sentimental 1 *adj* sentimental; **vida s.** love life. **2** *mf* sentimental person.

sentimiento *m* feeling; *(pesar)* sorrow.

sentir 1 *vt* to feel; *(lamentar)* to regret; **lo siento (mucho)** I'm very sorry; **siento molestarle** I'm sorry to bother you. **2 sentirse** *vr* to feel; **me siento mal** I feel ill.

seña *f* mark; *(gesto, indicio)* sign; **hacer señas a algn** to signal to sb; **señas** *(dirección)* address.

señal *f* sign; *(marca)* mark; *(vestigio)* trace; **s. de llamada** dial tone; **s. de tráfico** road sign.

señalar *vt (indicar)* to indicate; *(identificar, comunicar)* to point out; **s. con el dedo** to point at.

señor *m (hombre)* man; *(caballero)* gentleman; *(con apellido)* Mr; *(tratamiento de respeto)* sir; **el Sr. Gutiérrez** Mr Gutiérrez.

señora *f (mujer)* woman; *(trato formal)* lady; *(con apellido)* Mrs; *(tratamiento de respeto)* madam; *(esposa)* wife; **¡señoras y señores!** ladies and gentlemen!; **la Sra. Salinas** Mrs Salinas.

señorita *f (joven)* young woman; *(trato formal)* young lady; *(tratamiento de respeto)* Miss; **la S.** Padilla Miss Padilla.

sepa *subj pres de* **saber.**

separación *f* separation; *(espacio)* space.

separar 1 *vt* to separate; *(desunir)* to detach; *(dividir)* to divide; *(apartar)* to move away. **2 separarse** *vr* to separate; *(apartarse)* to move away (**de** from).

septentrional *adj* northern.

septiembre *m* September.

séptimo, -a *adj & mf* seventh.

sepultura *f* grave.

sequía *f* drought.

séquito *m* entourage.

ser¹ *m* being; **s. humano** human being; **s. vivo** living being.

ser² *vi* to be; **ser músico** to be a musician; **s. de** *(procedencia)* to be from; *(+ material)* to be made of; *(+ poseedor)* to belong to; **el perro es de Miguel** the dog belongs to Miguel; **hoy es dos de noviembre** today is the second of November; **son las cinco de la tarde** it's five o'clock; **¿cuántos estaremos en la fiesta?** how many of us will there be at the party?; **¿cuánto es?** how much is it?; **el estreno será mañana** tomorrow is the opening night; **es que…** it's just that…; **como sea** anyhow; **lo que sea** whatever; **o sea** that is (to say); **por si fuera poco** to top it all; **sea como sea** be that as it may; **a no s. que** unless; **de no s. por…** had it not been for…. ▪ *(auxiliar en pasiva)* to be; **fue asesinado** he was murdered.

sereno, -a *adj* calm.

serial *m* serial.

serie *f* series *sing*; **fabricación en s.** mass production.

seriedad *f (severidad)* seriousness; *(gravedad)* gravity; **falta de s.** irresponsibility.

serio, -a *adj* serious; **en s.** seriously.

sermón *m* sermon.

seropositivo, -a *adj* HIV-positive.

serpiente *f* snake; **s. de cascabel** rattlesnake; **s. pitón** python.

serrín *m* sawdust.

serrucho *m* handsaw.

servicial *adj* helpful.

servicio *m* service; *(retrete)* rest room; **s. a domicilio** delivery service; **s. militar** military service.

servidor, -a 1 *m* server. **2** *mf (criado)* servant.

servilleta *f* napkin.

servilletero *m* serviette ring, napkin ring.

servir 1 *vt* to serve. **2** *vi* to serve; *(valer)* to be suitable; **ya no sirve** it's no use; **¿para qué sirve esto?** what is this (used) for?; **s. de** to serve as. **3 servirse** *vr (comida etc)* to help oneself.

sesenta *adj & m inv* sixty.

sesión *f (reunión)* session; *(pase)* showing.

seso *m* brain.

seta *f (comestible)* mushroom; **s. venenosa** toadstool.

setecientos, -as *adj & mf* seven hundred.

setenta *adj & m inv* seventy.

setiembre *m* September.

seto *m* hedge.

seudónimo *m* pseudonym; *(de escritor)* pen name.

severidad *f* severity; *(rigurosidad)* strictness.

sexo *m* sex; *(órgano)* genitals *pl.*

sexto, -a *adj & mf* sixth.

sexual *adj* sexual; **vida s.** sex life.

si *conj* if; **como si** as if; **si no** if not; **me preguntó si me gustaba** he asked me if *o* whether I liked it.

sí¹ *pron pers (sing) (él)* himself; *(ella)* herself; *(cosa)* itself; *(pl)* themselves; *(uno mismo)* oneself; **por sí mismo** by himself.

sí² *adv* yes; **porque sí** just because; **¡que sí!** yes, I tell you!; **un día sí y otro no** every other day; *(uso enfático)* **sí que me gusta** of course I like it; **¡eso sí que no!** certainly not!

sico- = psico-.

sida *m* AIDS.

siderúrgico, -a *adj* iron and steel.

sidra *f* cider.

siempre 1 *adv* always; **como s.** as usual; **a la hora de s.** at the usual time; **para s.** forever. **2** *conj* **s. que** *(cada vez que)* whenever; *(a condición de que)* provided, as long as; **s. y cuando** provided, as long as.

sien *f* temple.

sierra *f* saw; *(montañosa)* mountain range.

siesta *f* siesta; **dormir la s.** to have a siesta.

siete *adj & m inv* seven.

sigilo *m* secrecy.

sigilosamente *adv (secretamente)* secretly.

sigiloso, -a *adj* secretive.

sigla *f* acronym.

siglo *m* century.

significado *m* meaning.

significar *vt* to mean.

significativo, -a *adj* significant; *(expresivo)* meaningful.

signo *m* sign; **s. de interrogación** question mark.

sigo *indic pres de* **seguir.**

siguiente *adj* following, next; **al día s.** the following day.

sílaba *f* syllable.

silbar *vi* to whistle.

silbato *m* whistle.

silbido *m* whistle.

silencio *m* silence.

silencioso, -a *adj (persona)* quiet; *(motor etc)* silent.

silicona *f* silicone.

silla *f* chair; *(de montura)* saddle; **s. de ruedas** wheelchair.

sillín *m* saddle.

sillón *m* armchair.

silueta *f* silhouette; *(de cuerpo)* figure.

silvestre *adj* wild.

símbolo *m* symbol.

simétrico, -a *adj* symmetrical.

simiente *f* seed.

similar *adj* similar.

similitud *f* similarity.

simio *m* monkey.

simpatía *f (de persona, lugar)* charm; **tenerle s. a algn** to like sb.

simpático, -a *adj* nice.

simpatizar *vi* to sympathize (**con** with); *(llevarse bien)* to hit it off (**con** with), to get along well (**con** with).

simple 1 *adj* simple; *(mero)* mere. **2** *m (persona)* simpleton.

simulacro *m* sham.

simular *vt* to simulate.

simultanear *vt* to combine; **simultanea el trabajo y los estudios** he's working and studying at the same time.

simultáneo, -a *adj* simultaneous.

sin *prep* without; **cerveza s.** alcohol-free beer; **s. más ni más** without further ado.

sinagoga *f* synagogue.

sinceridad *f* sincerity.

sincero, -a *adj* sincere.

sincronizar *vt* to synchronize.

sindicato *m* labor union.

sinfonía *f* symphony.

singular 1 *adj* singular; *(excepcional)* exceptional; *(raro)* odd. **2** *m (número)* singular; **en s.** in the singular.

siniestro, -a 1 *adj* sinister. **2** *m* disaster.

sino *conj* but; **nadie s. él** no one but him; **no quiero s. que me oigan** I only want them to listen (to me).

sinónimo, -a 1 *adj* synonymous. **2** *m* synonym.

sinsabor *m (usu pl)* trouble, worry.

sintético, -a *adj* synthetic.

sintetizar *vt* to synthesize.

síntoma *m* symptom.

sintonía *f (de programa)* tuning.

sintonizador *m (de radio)* tuning knob.

sintonizar *vt (radio)* to tune in.

sinuoso, -a *adj (camino)* winding.

sinvergüenza 1 *adj (desvergonzado)* shameless; *(descarado)* rude. **2** *mf (desvergonzado)* rogue; *(caradura)* cheeky devil.

siquiera *adv (por lo menos)* at least; **ni s.** not even.

sirena *f* mermaid; *(señal acústica)* siren.

sirviente, -a *mf* servant.

sistema *m* system; **por s.** as a rule; **s. nervioso** nervous system; **s. operativo** operating system.

sitio *m (lugar)* place; *(espacio)* room; **en cualquier s.** anywhere; **hacer s.** to make room.

situación *f* situation; *(ubicación)* location.

situar 1 *vt* to locate. **2 situarse** *vr* to be situated.

slogan *m* slogan.

smoking *m* tuxedo.

s/n. *abr de* **sin número.**

snob *adj & mf* = **esnob.**

sobaco *m* armpit.

soberanía *f* sovereignty.

soberano, -a *adj & mf* sovereign.

soberbia *f* pride.

soberbio, -a *adj* proud; *(magnífico)* splendid.

sobornar *vt* to bribe.

soborno *m (acción)* bribery; *(dinero etc)* bribe.

sobra *f* de s. *(no necesario)* superfluous; **tener de s.** to have plenty; **saber algo de s.** to know sth only too well; **sobras** *(restos)* leftovers.

sobrante 1 *adj* remaining. **2** *m* surplus.

sobrar *vi* to be more than enough; *(quedar)* to be left over; **sobran tres sillas** there are three chairs too many; **ha sobrado carne** there's still some meat left (over).

sobrasada *f* sausage spread.

sobre¹ *m (para carta)* envelope; *(de sopa etc)* packet.

sobre² *prep (encima)* on, on top of; *(por encima)* over, above; *(acerca de)* about, on; *(aproximadamente)* about; **s. todo** above all.

sobrecogedor, -a *adj* awesome.

sobrecoger *vt (conmover)* to shock.

sobredosis *f inv* overdose.

sobreentenderse *vr* **se sobreentiende** that goes without saying.

sobrehumano, -a *adj* superhuman.

sobrellevar *vt* to endure, to bear.

sobrenatural *adj* supernatural.

sobrenombre *m* nickname.

sobrepasar 1 *vt* to exceed. **2 sobrepasarse** *vr* to go too far.

sobreponerse *vr (superar)* to overcome; *(animarse)* to pull oneself together.

sobresaliente 1 *m (nota)* A. **2** *adj (que destaca)* excellent.

sobresalir *vi* to protrude; *fig (destacar)* to stand out.

sobresaltar 1 *vt* to startle. **2 sobresaltarse** *vr* to be startled, to start.

sobresalto *m (movimiento)* start; *(susto)* fright.

sobrevenir *vi* to happen unexpectedly.

sobreviviente 1 *adj* surviving. **2** *mf* survivor.

sobrevivir *vi* to survive.
sobrevolar *vt* to fly over.
sobrina *f* niece.
sobrino *m* nephew.
sobrio, -a *adj* sober.
socarrón, -ona *adj (sarcástico)* sarcastic.
socavón *m (bache)* pothole.
sociable *adj* sociable.
social *adj* social.
socialista *adj & mf* socialist.
sociedad *f* society; *(empresa)* company.
socio, -a *mf (miembro)* member; *(de empresa)* partner; **hacerse s. de un club** to join a club.
sociológico, -a *adj* sociological.
socorrer *vt* to assist.
socorrista *mf* lifeguard.
socorro *m* assistance; **¡s.!** help!; **puesto de s.** first-aid post.
soda *f (bebida)* soda water.
soez *adj* vulgar.
sofá *m (pl* **sofás)** sofa; **s. cama** sofa bed.
sofisticado, -a *adj* sophisticated.
sofocado, -a *adj* suffocated; **estar s.** to be out of breath; *(preocupado)* to be upset.
sofocante *adj* stifling.
sofocar 1 *vt (ahogar)* to suffocate; *(incendio)* to extinguish. **2 sofocarse** *vr (ahogarse)* to suffocate; *(irritarse)* to get upset.
sofoco *m fig (vergüenza)* embarrassment; **le dio un s.** *(disgusto)* it gave her quite a turn.
sofocón *m fam* shock; **llevarse un s.** to get upset.
soga *f* rope.
soja *f* soybean.
sol *m* sun; *(luz)* sunlight; *(luz y calor)* sunshine; **hace s.** it's sunny; **tomar el s.** to sunbathe; **al o bajo el s.** in the sun.
solamente *adv* only; **no s.** not only; **s. que** except that .
solapa *f (de chaqueta)* lapel; *(de sobre, bolsillo, libro)* flap.
solar¹ *adj* solar; **luz s.** sunlight.
solar² *m (terreno)* plot; *(en obras)* building site.
soldado *m* soldier.
soldar *vt (cable)* to solder; *(chapa)* to weld.
soleado, -a *adj* sunny.
soledad *f (estado)* solitude; *(sentimiento)* loneliness.
solemne *adj (majestuoso)* solemn.
soler *vi defectivo* to be in the habit of; **solemos ir en coche** we usually go by car; **solía pasear por aquí** he used to walk round here.
solicitar *vt (información etc)* to request; *(trabajo)* to apply for.
solicitud *f (petición)* request; *(de trabajo)* application.
solidaridad *f* solidarity.
sólido, -a *adj* solid.
solitario, -a *adj (que está solo)* solitary; *(que se siente solo)* lonely.
sollozar *vi* to sob.
sollozo *m* sob.
solo, -a 1 *adj* only; *(solitario)* lonely; **una sola vez** only once; **se enciende s.** it switches itself on automatically; **a solas** alone, by oneself. **2** *m (musical)* solo.
sólo *adv* only; **tan s.** only; **no s.... sino (también)** not only... but (also); **con s., (tan) s. con** just by.
solomillo *m* sirloin.
soltar 1 *vt (desasir)* to let go of; *(prisionero)* to release; *(humo, olor)* to give off; *(carcajada)* to let out; **¡suéltame!** let me go! **2 soltarse** *vr (desatarse)* to come loose; *(perro etc)* to get loose; *(desprenderse)* to come off.
soltero, -a 1 *adj* single. **2** *m (hombre)* bachelor. **3** *f (mujer)* single woman.
solterón, -ona 1 *m (hombre)* old bachelor. **2** *f (mujer)* old maid.
soltura *f (agilidad)* agility; *(seguridad)* confidence, assurance; **habla italiano con s.** he speaks Italian fluently.
soluble *adj* soluble; **café s.** instant coffee.
solución *f* solution.
solucionar *vt* to solve; *(arreglar)* to settle.
solvencia *f (financiera)* solvency; *(fiabilidad)* reliability; **fuentes de toda s.** completely reliable sources.
sombra *f* shade; *(silueta proyectada)* shadow; **s. de ojos** eyeshadow.
sombrero *m (prenda)* hat; **s. de copa** top hat; **s. hongo** derby hat.
sombrilla *f* sunshade.
sombrío, -a *adj (oscuro)* dark; *(tenebroso)* gloomy.
someter 1 *vt* to subject; *(rebeldes)* to put down; **s. a prueba** to put to the test. **2 someterse** *vr (subordinarse)* to submit; *(rendirse)* to surrender; **someterse a un tratamiento** to undergo treatment.
somnífero *m* sleeping pill.
somnoliento, -a *adj* sleepy.
sonar 1 *vi* to sound; *(timbre, teléfono)* to ring; **suena bien** it sounds good; **tu nombre/cara me suena** your name/face rings a bell. **2 sonarse** *vr* **sonarse (la nariz)** to blow one's nose.
sondeo *m (encuesta)* poll.
sonido *m* sound.
sonoro, -a *adj (resonante)* resounding; **banda sonora** soundtrack.
sonreír *vi,* **sonreírse** *vr* to smile; **me sonrió** he smiled at me.
sonrisa *f* smile.
sonrojarse *vr* to blush.
sonso, -a *adj Am* foolish, silly.
soñador, -a *mf* dreamer.
soñar *vti* to dream; **s. con** to dream of o about.
soñoliento, -a *adj* sleepy.
sopa *f* soup.
sopera *f* soup tureen.
sopesar *vt* to try the weight of; *fig* to weigh up.
soplar 1 *vi (viento)* to blow. **2** *vt (polvo etc)* to blow away; *(para enfriar)* to blow on; *(para apagar)* to blow out; *(para inflar)* to blow up.
soplo *m (acción)* puff; *(de viento)* gust.
soplón, -ona *mf fam (niño)* telltale; *(delator)* informer.
soportable *adj* bearable.
soportar *vt (sostener)* to support; *(tolerar)* to endure; *(aguantar)* to put up with.
soporte *m* support.
sorber *vt (beber)* to sip; *(absorber)* to soak up.
sorbete *m* sorbet.
sorbo *m* sip; *(trago)* gulp.
sórdido, -a *adj* sordid.
sordo, -a 1 *adj (persona)* deaf; *(ruido, dolor)* dull. **2** *mf* deaf person.
sordomudo, -a 1 *adj* deaf and dumb. **2** *mf* deaf and dumb person.
sorprender *vt* to surprise; *(coger desprevenido)* to take by surprise.
sorpresa *f* surprise; **coger por s.** to take by surprise.

sorpresivo, -a *adj Am* unexpected.
sortear *vt* to draw lots for; *(rifar)* to raffle (off).
sorteo *m* draw; *(rifa)* raffle.
sortija *f* ring.
sosegado, -a *adj (tranquilo)* calm, quiet; *(pacífico)* peaceful.
sosegar 1 *vt* to calm. **2 sosegarse** *vr* to calm down.
soso, -a *adj* lacking in salt; *(persona)* dull.
sospecha *f* suspicion.
sospechar 1 *vi (desconfiar)* to suspect; **s. de algn** to suspect sb. **2** *vt (pensar)* to suspect.
sospechoso, -a 1 *adj* suspicious. **2** *mf* suspect.
sostén *m (apoyo)* support; *(prenda)* bra, brassiere.
sostener 1 *vt* to hold; *(sustentar)* to hold up; **s. que...** to maintain that.... **2 sostenerse** *vr (mantenerse)* to support oneself; *(permanecer)* to remain.
sostuve *pt indef de* **sostener.**
sota *f (de baraja)* jack.
sotana *f* cassock.
sótano *m* basement.
soviético, -a *adj & mf* Soviet; **la Unión Soviética** the Soviet Union.
soy *indic pres de* **ser.**
spray *m (pl* **sprays)** spray.
Sr. *abr de* **Señor** Mister, Mr.
Sra. *abr de* **Señora** Mrs, Ms.
Srta. *abr de* **Señorita** Miss.
standard *adj & m* standard.
su *adj pos (de él)* his; *(de ella)* her; *(de usted, ustedes)* your; *(de animales o cosas)* its; *(impersonal)* one's; *(de ellos)* their.
suave *adj* smooth; *(luz, voz etc)* soft; *(templado)* mild.
suavidad *f* smoothness; *(dulzura)* softness; *(de tiempo)* mildness.
suavizante *m (para el pelo)* (hair) conditioner; *(para la ropa)* fabric softener.
suavizar *vt* to smooth (out). **2 suavizarse** *vr (temperatura)* to get milder.
subalterno, -a *adj & mf* subordinate.
subasta *f* auction.
subcampeón, -ona *mf* runner-up.
subconsciente *adj & m* subconscious.
subdesarrollado, -a *adj* underdeveloped.
subdirector, -a *mf* assistant director.
súbdito, -a *mf* subject.
subestimar *vt* to underestimate.
subir 1 *vt* to go up; *(llevar arriba)* to take up, to bring up; *(precio, salario, voz)* to raise; *(volumen)* to turn up. **2** *vi (ir arriba)* to go/come up; *(al autobús, barco etc)* to get on; *(aumentar)* to go up; **s. a** *(un coche)* to get into. **3 subirse** *vr* to climb up; *(al autobús, avión, tren, bici)* to get on; *(cremallera)* to do up; *(mangas)* to roll up; **subirse a** *(un coche)* to get into.
súbitamente *adv* suddenly.
súbito, -a *adj* sudden.
subjetivo, -a *adj* subjective.
sublevarse *vr* to rebel.
sublime *adj* sublime.
submarinismo *m* skin-diving.
submarino, -a 1 *adj* underwater. **2** *m* submarine.
subnormal 1 *adj* mentally handicapped. **2** *mf* mentally handicapped person.
subordinado, -a *adj & mf* subordinate.
subrayar *vt* to underline; *fig (recalcar)* to stress.
subscribir *(pp* **subscrito)** *vt* = **suscribir.**
subscripción *f* subscription.
subsecretario, -a *mf* undersecretary.
subsidiario, -a *adj* subsidiary.
subsidio *m* allowance; **s. de desempleo** unemployment benefit.
subsistencia *f* subsistence.
subterráneo, -a *adj* underground.
suburbio *m (barrio pobre)* slum; *(barrio periférico)* suburb.
subvención *f* subsidy.
suceder 1 *vi (ocurrir) (uso impers)* to happen; **¿qué sucede?** what's going on?; **s. a** *(seguir)* to follow. **2 sucederse** *vr* to follow one another.
sucesión *f (serie)* succession.
sucesivamente *adv* **y así s.** and so on.
sucesivo, -a *adj (siguiente)* following; **en lo s.** from now on.
suceso *m (acontecimiento)* event; *(incidente)* incident.
sucesor, -a *mf* successor.
suciedad *f* dirt; *(calidad)* dirtiness.
sucio, -a *adj* dirty.
suculento, -a *adj* succulent.
sucumbir *vi* to succumb.
sucursal *f (de banco etc)* branch.
sudadera *f* sweatshirt.
sudafricano, -a *adj & mf* South African.
sudamericano, -a *adj & mf* South American.
sudar *vti* to sweat.
sudeste *adj & m* southeast.
sudoeste *adj & m* southwest.
sudor *m* sweat.
sudoroso, -a *adj* sweaty.
sueco, -a 1 *adj* Swedish. **2** *mf (persona)* Swede. **3** *m (idioma)* Swedish.
suegra *f* mother-in-law.
suegro *m* father-in-law; **mis suegros** my in-laws.
suela *f* sole.
sueldo *m* wages *pl.*
suelo *m (superficie)* ground; *(de interior)* floor.
suelto, -a 1 *adj* loose; *(en libertad)* free; *(huido)* at large; *(desatado)* undone; **dinero s.** loose change. **2** *m (dinero)* (loose) change.
sueño *m* sleepiness; *(cosa soñada)* dream; **tener s.** to be sleepy.
suerte *f (fortuna)* luck; **por s.** fortunately; **tener s.** to be lucky; **¡que tengas s.!** good luck!
suéter *m* sweater.
suficiente 1 *adj (bastante)* sufficient, enough. **2** *m (nota)* pass.
suficientemente *adv* sufficiently; **no es lo s. rico como para...** he isn't rich enough to....
sufragar 1 *vt (gastos)* to pay, to defray. **2** *vi Am* to vote *(por* for).
sufragio *m (voto)* vote.
sufrido, -a *adj (persona)* long-suffering.
sufrimiento *m* suffering.
sufrir *vi* to suffer. **2** *vt (accidente)* to have; *(dificultades, cambios)* to experience; *(aguantar)* to put up with.
sugerencia *f* suggestion.
sugerir *vt* to suggest.
sugestión *f* suggestion.
suicida 1 *mf (persona)* suicide. **2** *adj* suicidal.

suicidarse *vr* to commit suicide.
suicidio *m* suicide.
suizo, -a 1 *adj* Swiss. **2** *mf (persona)* Swiss. **3** *m (pastel)* eclair.
sujetador *m* bra, brassiere.
sujetar 1 *vt (agarrar)* to hold; *(fijar)* to hold down; *(someter)* to restrain. **2 sujetarse** *vr (agarrarse)* to hold on.
sujeto, -a 1 *m* subject; *(individuo)* fellow. **2** *adj (atado)* secure.
suma *f (cantidad)* sum; *(cálculo)* addition.
sumamente *adv* extremely, highly.
sumar *vt (cantidades)* to add (up).
sumergir 1 *vt* to submerge; *(hundir)* to sink. **2 sumergirse** *vr* to submerge; *(hundirse)* to sink.
sumidero *m* drain.
suministrar *vt* to supply; **s. algo a algn** to supply sb with sth.
suministro *m* supply.
sumiso, -a *adj* submissive.
supe *pt indef de* **saber**.
súper *m (gasolina)* premium; *fam (supermercado)* supermarket.
superar *vt (obstáculo etc)* to overcome; *(prueba)* to pass; *(aventajar)* to surpass.
superdotado, -a 1 *adj* exceptionally gifted. **2** *mf* genius.
superficial *adj* superficial.
superficie *f* surface; *(área)* area.
superfluo, -a *adj* superfluous.
superior 1 *adj (posición)* top, upper; *(cantidad)* greater (**a** than); *(calidad)* superior; *(estudios)* higher. **2** *m (jefe)* superior.
supermercado *m* supermarket.
superponer *vt* to superimpose.
supersónico, -a *adj* supersonic.
supersticioso, -a *adj* superstitious.
supervisar *vt* to supervise.
supervivencia *f* survival.
súpito, -a *adj Am* sudden.
suplantar *vt* to supplant.
suplementario, -a *adj* supplementary.
suplemento *m* supplement.
suplente *adj & mf (sustituto)* substitute, deputy; *(jugador)* substitute.
suplicar *vt* to beg.
suplicio *m (tortura)* torture; *(tormento)* torment.
suplir *vt (reemplazar)* to replace; *(compensar)* to make up for.
suponer *(pp supuesto) vt* to suppose; *(significar)* to mean; *(implicar)* to entail; **supongo que sí** I suppose so.
supositorio *m* suppository.
supremo, -a *adj* supreme.
suprimir *vt (ley)* to abolish; *(restricción)* to lift; *(palabra)* to delete.
supuesto, -a *adj (asumido)* supposed; *(presunto)* alleged; **¡por s.!** of course!; **dar algo por s.** to take sth for granted.
supuse *pt indef de* **suponer**.
sur *adj & m* south.
suramericano, -a *adj & mf* South American.
surco *m (en tierra)* furrow; *(en disco)* groove.
sureste *adj & m* southeast.
surf(ing) *m* surfing.
surfista *mf* surfer.
surgir *vi (problema, dificultad)* to crop up; *(aparecer)* to arise.
suroeste *adj & m* southwest.
surtido, -a 1 *adj (variado)* assorted. **2** *m* selection.
surtidor *m* spout; **s. de gasolina** gas pump.
surtir *vt* to supply, to provide; **s. efecto** to have the desired effect.
susceptible *adj* susceptible; *(quisquilloso)* touchy; **s. de** *(capaz)* capable of.
suscitar *vt (provocar)* to cause; *(rebelión)* to stir up; *(interés etc)* to arouse.
suscribir *(pp suscrito)* **1** *vt* to subscribe to, to endorse; *fml (firmar)* to sign. **2 suscribirse** *vr* to subscribe (**a** to).
suscripción *f* subscription.
suspender 1 *vt (reunión)* to adjourn; *(examen)* to fail; *(colgar)* to hang; **me han suspendido** I've failed (the exam). **2** *vi (en colegio)* **he suspendido** I've failed.
suspense *m* suspense; **novela/película de s.** thriller.
suspensión *f (levantamiento)* hanging (up); *(de coche)* suspension.
suspenso *m (nota)* fail.
suspicacia *f* suspiciousness.
suspicaz *adj* suspicious; *(desconfiado)* distrustful.
suspirar *vi* to sigh.
suspiro *m* sigh.
sustancia *f* substance.
sustantivo *m* noun.
sustento *m (alimento)* sustenance.
sustituir *vt* to substitute.
sustituto, -a *mf* substitute.
susto *m* fright; **llevarse o darse un s.** to be frightened.
sustraer *vt* to subtract; *(robar)* to steal.
susurrar *vi* to whisper.
sutil *adj (diferencia, pregunta)* subtle; *(aroma)* delicate.
suyo, -a *adj & pron pos (de él)* his; *(de ella)* hers; *(de animal o cosa)* its; *(de usted, ustedes)* yours; *(de ellos, ellas)* theirs.

T

tabaco *m* tobacco; *(cigarrillos)* cigarettes *pl*; **t. rubio** Virginia tobacco.
taberna *f* bar.
tabique *m (pared)* partition (wall).
tabla *f* board; *(de vestido)* pleat; *(de sumar etc)* table; **t. de surf** surfboard; **t. de windsurf** sailboard.
tablero *m (tablón)* panel; *(en juegos)* board; **t. de mandos** *(de coche)* dash(board).
tableta *f (de chocolate)* bar.
tablón *m (plank)* plank; *(en construcción)* beam; **t. de anuncios** notice bulletin board.
taburete *m* stool.
tacaño, -a 1 *adj* mean. **2** *mf* miser.
tachar *vt* to cross out.
tacho *m Am* bucket.
taco *m (tarugo)* plug; *(de jamón, queso)* cube; *(palabrota)* swearword.

tacón *m* heel; **zapatos de t.** high-heeled shoes.
táctica *f* tactics *pl*.
táctico, -a *adj* tactical.
tacto *m (sentido)* touch; *(delicadeza)* tact.
tajada *f* slice.
tajante *adj* incisive.
tal 1 *adj (semejante)* such; *(más sustantivo singular contable)* such a; *(indeterminado)* such and such; **en tales condiciones** in such conditions; **nunca dije t. cosa** I never said such a thing; **t. vez** perhaps, maybe; **como si t. cosa** as if nothing had happened. **2** *adv* **t. (y) como** just as; **¿qué t.?** how are things?; **¿qué t. ese vino?** how do you find this wine? **3** *conj* as; **con t. (de) que + subj** so long as, provided. **4** *pron (cosa)* something; *(persona)* someone, somebody.
taladrar *vt* to drill; *(pared)* to bore through; *(papeles)* to punch.
taladro *m (herramienta)* drill.
talante *m (carácter)* disposition; **de mal t.** unwillingly.
talar *vt (árboles)* to fell.
talco *m* talc; **polvos de t.** talcum powder.
talega *f* sack.
talento *m* talent.
Talgo *m* fast passenger train.
talla *f (de prenda)* size; *(estatura)* height.
tallar *vt (madera, piedra)* to carve; *(piedras preciosas)* to cut; *(metales)* to engrave.
tallarines *mpl* noodles, tagliatelle *sing*.
talle *m (cintura)* waist.
taller *m (obrador)* workshop; **t. de reparaciones** *(garaje)* garage.
tallo *m* stem.
talón *m* heel; *(cheque)* check.
talonario *m (de cheques)* check book.
tamaño *m* size; **de gran t.** large; **del t. de** as big as.
tambalearse *vr (persona)* to stagger; *(mesa)* to wobble.
también *adv* too, also; **yo t.** me too.
tambor *m* drum.
tampoco *adv (en afirmativas)* nor, neither; *(en negativas)* not either; **no lo sé, yo t.** I don't know, neither o nor do I.
tampón *m* tampon.
tan *adv* so; **¡es t. listo!** he's so clever; **¡qué gente t. agradable!** such nice people; **¡qué vestido t. bonito!** such a beautiful dress. ▪ *(consecutivo)* so (that); **iba t. deprisa que no lo ví** he was going so fast that I couldn't see him. ▪ *(comparativo)* **t. ... como** as... as; **t. alto como tú** as tall as you (are). ▪ **t. sólo** only.
tango *m* tango.
tanque *m* tank.
tantear 1 *vt fig* **t. a algn** to sound sb out; **t. el terreno** to see how the land lies. **2** *vi* to (keep) score.
tanto, -a 1 *m (punto)* point; **un t. para cada uno** so much for each; **t. por ciento** percentage; **estar al t.** *(informado)* to be informed; *(pendiente)* to be on the lookout. **2** *adj (en singular)* so much; **tantos, -as** so many; **t. dinero** so much money; **¡ha pasado t. tiempo!** it's been so long!; **tantas manzanas** so many apples; **cincuenta y tantas personas** fifty odd people; **t. ... como** as much... as; **tantos, -as... como** as many... as. **3** *pron (en singular)* so much; **tantos, -as** so many; **otro t.** the same again; **no es o hay para t.** it's not that bad; **otros tantos** as many again; **uno de tantos** run-of-the-mill. **4** *adv (cantidad)* as much; *(tiempo)* so long; *(frecuencia)* so often; **t. mejor/peor** so much the better/worse; **t. ... como** both... and; **t. tú como yo** both you and I; **por lo t.** therefore.
tapa *f (cubierta)* lid; *(de libro)* cover; *(aperitivo)* appetizer.
tapadera *f* cover.
tapar 1 *vt* to cover; *(botella etc)* to put the lid on; *(con ropas o mantas)* to wrap up; *(ocultar)* to hide; *(vista)* to block. **2 taparse** *vr (cubrirse)* to cover oneself; *(abrigarse)* to wrap up.
tapete *m (table)* cover.
tapia *f* wall; *(cerca)* garden wall.
tapizar *vt* to upholster.
tapón *m (de lavabo etc)* plug; *(de botella)* cap; *(de tráfico)* traffic jam.
taponar 1 *vt (tubería, hueco)* to plug; *(herida)* to tampon. **2 taponarse** *vr* **se me han taponado los oídos** my ears are blocked up.
taquigrafía *f* shorthand.
taquilla *f* ticket office; *(de cine, teatro)* box-office.
tararear *vt* to hum.
tardar 1 *vt* **tardé dos horas en venir** it took me two hours to get here. **2** *vi (demorar)* to take long; **no tardes** don't be long; **a más t.** at the latest. **3 tardarse** *vr* **¿cuánto se tarda en llegar?** how long does it take to get there?
tarde 1 *f (hasta las cinco)* afternoon; *(después de las cinco)* evening. **2** *adv* late; **(más) t. o (más) temprano** sooner or later.
tarea *f* task; **tareas** *(de ama de casa)* housework *sing*; *(de estudiante)* homework *sing*.
tarifa *f (precio)* rate; *(en transportes)* fare; *(lista de precios)* price list.
tarjeta *f* card; **t. postal** postcard; **t. de crédito** credit card.
tarro *m (vasija)* jar; *Am (lata)* tin.
tarta *f* tart; *(pastel)* cake.
tartamudear *vi* to stutter, to stammer.
tartamudo, -a 1 *adj* stuttering, stammering. **2** *mf* stutterer, stammerer.
tartera *f* lunch box.
tasa *f (precio)* fee; *(impuesto)* tax; *(índice)* rate; **tasas académicas** course fees; **t. de natalidad/mortalidad** birth/death rate.
tasar *vt (valorar)* to value; *(poner precio)* to fix the price of.
tasca *f* bar.
tatarabuelo, -a *mf (hombre)* great-great-grandfather; *(mujer)* great-great-grandmother; **tatarabuelos** great-great-grandparents.
tataranieto, -a *mf (hombre)* great-great-grandson; *(mujer)* great-great-granddaughter; **tataranietos** great-great-grandchildren.
tatuaje *m* tattoo.
tatuar *vt* to tattoo.
taurino, -a *adj* bullfighting.
taxi *m* taxi.
taxista *mf* taxi driver.
taza *f* cup; **una t. de café** *(recipiente)* a coffee cup; *(contenido)* a cup of coffee.
tazón *m* bowl.
te *pron pers* **1** *(complemento directo)* you; *(complemento indirecto)* (to o for) you; *(reflexivo)* yourself; **no quiero verte** I don't want to see you; **te compraré uno** I'll buy you one; **te lo dije** I told you so; **lávate** wash yourself; **no te vayas** don't go.
té *m (pl tés)* tea.
teatro *m* theatre; **obra de t.** play.
tebeo *m* children's comic.
techo *m (de habitación)* ceiling; *(tejado)* roof.
tecla *f* key.
teclado *m* keyboard; **t. numérico** numeric keypad.
técnica *f (tecnología)* technology; *(método)* technique; *(habilidad)* skill.
técnico, -a 1 *adj* technical. **2** *mf* technician.
tecnología *f* technology.

tedio *m* tedium.
teja *f* tile.
tejado *m* roof.
tejanos *mpl* jeans.
tejer *vt (en el telar)* to weave; *(hacer punto)* to knit.
tejido *m* fabric.
tela *f* cloth; **t. de araña** cobweb; **t. metálica** gauze.
telaraña *f* spider's web.
tele *f fam* TV, telly.
telecabina *f* cable car.
telediario *m* television news bulletin.
telefax *m* fax.
teleférico *m* cable car.
telefilm(e) *m* TV film.
telefonear *vti* to telephone, to phone.
teléfono *m* telephone, phone; **t. portátil** portable telephone; **t. móvil** car phone; **te llamó por t.** she phoned you; **al t.** on the phone.
telegrama *m* telegram.
telenovela *f* television serial.
teleobjetivo *m* telephoto lens.
telescopio *m* telescope.
telesilla *m* chair lift.
telespectador, -a *mf* TV viewer.
telesquí *m* ski lift.
teletienda *f* home shopping program.
televidente *mf* TV viewer.
televisión *f* television; **t. digital** digital television; **t. por cable** cable television; **ver la t.** to watch television.
televisivo, -a *adj* television.
televisor *m* television set.
télex *m inv* telex.
telón *m* curtain.
tema *m* subject.
temblar *vi (de frío)* to shiver; *(de miedo)* to tremble (**de** with); *(voz, pulso)* to shake.
temblor *m* tremor; **t. de tierra** earth tremor.
temer 1 *vt* to fear. **2** *vi* to be afraid. **3 temerse** *vr* to fear; **¡me lo temía!** I was afraid this would happen!
temerario, -a *adj* reckless.
temible *adj* fearful, frightful.
temor *m* fear; *(recelo)* worry.
témpano *m* ice block.
temperamento *m* temperament.
temperatura *f* temperature.
tempestad *f* storm.
templado, -a *adj (agua)* lukewarm; *(clima)* mild.
templo *m* temple.
temporada *f* season; *(período)* period; **t. alta** high season; **t. baja** low season.
temporal 1 *adj* temporary. **2** *m* storm.
temprano, -a *adj & adv* early.
tenaz *adj* tenacious.
tenaza *f*, **tenazas** *fpl (herramienta)* pliers.
tendencia *f* tendency.
tender 1 *vt (extender)* to spread out; *(para secar)* to hang out; *(trampa)* to set; *(mano)* to hold out; *Am (cama)* to make; *Am (mesa)* to set, to lay. **2** *vi* **t. a** to tend to. **3 tenderse** *vr* to stretch out.
tendero *mf* shopkeeper.
tendón *m* tendon.
tenebroso, -a *adj (sombrío)* dark; *(siniestro)* sinister.
tenedor *m* fork.
tener 1 *vt* to have, to have got; **va a t. un niño** she's going to have a baby. ▪ *(sostener)* to hold; **tenme el bolso un momento** hold my bag a minute. ▪ **t. calor/frío** to be hot/cold; **t. cariño a algn** to be fond of sb; **t. miedo** to be frightened. ▪ *(edad)* to be; **tiene dieciocho (años)** he's eighteen (years old); ▪ *(medida)* **la casa tiene cien metros cuadrados** the house is 100 square meters. ▪ *(contener)* to hold. ▪ *(mantener)* to keep; **me tuvo despierto toda la noche** he kept me up all night. ▪ *(considerar)* to consider; **ten por seguro que lloverá** you can be sure it'll rain. ▪ **t. que** to have (got) to; **tengo que...** I have to…, I must…. **2 tenerse** *vr* **tenerse en pie** to stand (up).
tenga *subj pres de* **tener**.
tengo *indic pres de* **tener**.
teniente *mf* lieutenant.
tenis *m* tennis.
tenista *mf* tennis player.
tenor *m* tenor.
tensión *f* tension; *(eléctrica)* voltage; **t. arterial** blood pressure.
tenso, -a *adj (cuerda, cable)* taut; *(persona, relaciones)* tense.
tentación *f* temptation.
tentar *vt (incitar)* to tempt; *(atraer)* to attract.
tentativa *f* attempt.
tentempié *m (pl* **tentempiés)** *(comida)* snack; *(juguete)* tumbler.
tenue *adj (luz, sonido)* faint.
teñir 1 *vt (pelo etc)* to dye. **2 teñirse** *vr* **teñirse el pelo** to dye one's hair.
teoría *f* theory; **en t.** theoretically.
terapia *f* therapy.
tercer *adj* third; **el t. mundo** the third world.
tercero, -a *adj & mf* third.
tercio *m* (one) third; *(cerveza)* medium-sized bottle of beer.
terciopelo *m* velvet.
terco *adj* stubborn.
tergiversar *vt* to distort; *(declaraciones)* to twist.
terminal 1 *adj* terminal. **2** *f* terminal; *(de autobús)* terminal. **3** *m (de ordenador)* terminal.
terminar 1 *vt* to finish. **2** *vi (acabarse)* to finish; *(ir a parar)* to end up (**en** in); **terminó por comprarlo** he ended up buying it. **3 terminarse** *vr* to finish; *(vino, comida)* to run out.
término *m (final)* end; *(palabra)* term; **en términos generales** generally speaking; **por t. medio** on average.
termo *m* thermos (flask).
termómetro *m* thermometer.
termostato *m* thermostat.
ternera *f* calf; *(carne)* veal.
ternura *f* tenderness.
terraplén *m* embankment.
terremoto *m* earthquake.
terreno *m (tierra)* land; *(campo)* field; *(deportivo)* ground; *(ámbito)* field.
terrestre *adj (de la tierra)* terrestrial; *(transporte, ruta)* by land.
terrible *adj* terrible.
territorio *m* territory.

terrón *m (de azúcar)* lump.
terror *m* terror; **película de t.** horror film.
terrorismo *m* terrorism.
terrorista *adj & mf* terrorist.
terso, -a *adj (liso)* smooth.
tertulia *f* get-together.
tesis *f inv* thesis; *(opinión)* point of view.
tesoro *m* treasure.
test *m* test.
testamento *m* will; **hacer t.** to make one's will.
testarudo, -a *adj* obstinate.
testificar *vi* to testify.
testigo *mf* witness.
testimonio *m* testimony; *(prueba)* evidence.
tétano *m* tetanus.
tetera *f* teapot.
tetina *f (rubber)* teat.
texto *m* text; **libro de t.** textbook.
tez *f* complexion.
ti *pron pers* you; **es para ti** it's for you; **piensas demasiado en ti mismo** you think too much about yourself.
tía *f* aunt; *fam (mujer)* woman.
tibio, -a *adj* tepid.
tiburón *m* shark.
tic *m (pl* **tics)** twitch; **t. nervioso** nervous twitch.
tiempo *m* time; *(meteorológico)* weather; *(de partido)* half; *(verbal)* tense; **a t.** in time; **a su (debido) t.** in due course; **al mismo t.** at the same time; **al poco t.** soon afterwards; **con t.** in advance; **¿cuánto t.?** how long?; **¿cuánto t. hace?** how long ago?; **estar a t. de** to still have time to; **¿nos da t. de llegar?** have we got (enough) time to get there?; **t. libre** free time; **¿qué t. hace?** what's the weather like?; **hace buen/mal t.** the weather is good/bad.
tienda *f* store; **ir de tiendas** to go shopping; **t. (de campaña)** tent.
tienta *f* **a tientas** by touch; **andar a tientas** to feel one's way; **buscar (algo) a tientas** to grope (for sth).
tierno, -a *adj* tender; *(reciente)* fresh.
tierra *f* land; *(planeta)* earth; *(suelo)* ground; **tocar t.** to land.
tieso, -a *adj (rígido)* stiff; *(erguido)* upright.
tiesto *m* flowerpot.
tifus *m inv* typhus (fever).
tigre *m* tiger; *Am* jaguar.
tijeras *fpl* pair of scissors *sing*, scissors.
tila *f* lime tea.
timar *vt* to swindle.
timbre *m (de puerta)* bell; *(sonido)* timbre.
timidez *f* shyness.
tímido, -a *adj* shy.
timo *m* swindle.
timón *m (de barco, avión)* rudder; *(de coche)* steering wheel.
tímpano *m* eardrum.
tinieblas *fpl* darkness *sing*.
tino *m (puntería)* **tener buen t.** to be a good shot.
tinta *f* ink; **t. china** Indian ink.
tinte *m* dye.
tintero *m* inkwell.
tintinear *vi (vidrio)* to clink; *(campana)* to tinkle.
tinto 1 *adj (vino)* red. **2** *m (vino)* red.
tintorería *f* dry-cleaner's.
tío *m* uncle; *fam* guy; **mis tíos** *(tío y tía)* my uncle and aunt.
tiovivo *m* merry-go-round.
típico, -a *adj* typical; *(baile, traje)* traditional.
tipo *m (clase)* type, kind; *fam (persona)* guy; *(figura) (de hombre)* build; *(de mujer)* figure; **jugarse el t.** to risk one's neck; **t. bancario** *o* **de descuento** bank rate; **t. de cambio/interés** exchange/interest rate.
tira *f* strip.
tirabuzón *m* ringlet.
tirachinas *m inv* slingshot.
tirada *f* printrun.
tiranía *f* tyranny.
tirante 1 *adj (cable etc)* taut. **2** *m (de vestido etc)* strap; **tirantes** suspenders.
tirar 1 *vt (echar)* to throw, to fling; *(dejar caer)* to drop; *(desechar)* to throw away; *(derribar)* to knock down. **2** *vi* **t. de** *(cuerda, puerta)* to pull; *(disparar)* to shoot; **ir tirando** to get by; **tira a la izquierda** turn left. **3 tirarse** *vr (lanzarse)* to throw oneself; *(tumbarse)* to lie down; **tirarse de cabeza al agua** to dive into the water.
tirita® *f* Band-Aid®.
tiritar *vi* to shiver.
tiro *m (lanzamiento)* throw; *(disparo, ruido)* shot; *(de chimenea)* draft; **t. al blanco** target shooting; **t. al plato** clay pigeon shooting.
tirón *m* pull; *(de bolso)* snatch; *fam* **de un t.** in one go.
tiroteo *m* shooting.
titubear *vi (dudar)* to hesitate.
titulado, -a *adj (licenciado)* graduate; *(diplomado)* qualified.
titular¹ **1** *mf (persona)* holder. **2** *m (periódico)* headline.
titular² **1** *vt (poner título)* to call. **2 titularse** *vr (película etc)* to be called.
título *m* title; *(diploma)* diploma; *(titular)* headline.
tiza *f* chalk.
tiznar *vt* to blacken (with soot).
toalla *f* towel.
toallero *m* towel rail.
tobillo *m* ankle.
tobogán *m* slide; *(en piscina)* chute.
tocadiscos *m inv* record player.
tocador *m (mueble)* dressing table; *(habitación)* dressing room.
tocar *vt* to touch; *(instrumento, canción)* to play; *(timbre, campana)* to ring; *(bocina)* to blow; *(tema, asunto)* to touch on. **2** *vi (entrar en contacto)* to touch; **¿a quién le toca?** *(en juegos)* whose turn is it?; **me tocó el gordo** *(en rifa)* I won the jackpot. **3 tocarse** *vr (una cosa con otra)* to touch each other.
tocino *m* lard; **t. de cielo** sweet made with egg yolk.
tocólogo, -a *m* obstetrician.
todavía *adv (aún)* still; *(en negativas)* yet; *(para reforzar)* even, still; **t. la quiere** he still loves her; **t. no** not yet; **t. más/menos** even more/less.
todo, -a 1 *adj* all; *(cada)* every; **t. el mundo** everybody; **t. el día** all day, the whole day; **t. ciudadano de más de dieciocho años** every citizen over eighteen years of age; **todos, -as** all; **t. los niños** all the children; **t. los martes** every Tuesday. **2** *pron* all, everything; **t. aquél** *o* **el que quiera** anybody who wants (to); **todos, -as** all of them; **hablé con todos** I spoke to everybody; **todos aprobamos** we all passed; **ante t.** first of all; **del t.** completely; **después de t.** after

all; **eso es t.** that's all; **hay de t.** there are all sorts; **lo sé t.** I know all about it; **t. lo contrario** quite the opposite; **t. lo más** at the most. **3** *adv* completely; **t. sucio** all dirty.

toldo *m (cubierta)* awning; *(en la playa)* sunshade; *Am (cabaña)* tent.

tolerante *adj* tolerant.

tolerar *vt* to tolerate.

toma *f (acción)* taking; **t. de corriente** socket.

tomado, -a *adj Am (borracho)* drunk.

tomar 1 *vt* to take; *(comer, beber)* to have; **toma** here (you are); **t. el sol** to sunbathe; **t. en serio/broma** to take seriously/as a joke. **2 tomarse** *vr (comer)* to eat; *(beber)* to drink; **no te lo tomes así** don't take it like that.

tomate *m* tomato; **salsa de t.** *(de lata)* tomato sauce; *(de botella)* ketchup.

tómbola *f* tombola.

tomo *m* volume.

tonel *m* cask.

tonelada *f* ton; **t. métrica** tonne.

tónico, -a 1 *m* tonic. **2** *f (bebida)* tonic (water); **tónica general** overall trend.

tono *m* tone; **un t. alto/bajo** a high/low pitch.

tontería *f* silliness; *(dicho, hecho)* silly thing; *(insignificancia)* trifle.

tonto, -a 1 *adj* silly. **2** *mf* fool.

topacio *m* topaz.

toparse *vr* **t. con** to bump into; *(dificultades)* to run up against.

tope *m (límite)* limit; **estar hasta los topes** to be full up; **fecha t.** deadline.

tópico *m* cliché.

topo *m (animal)* mole; *(espía)* spy, inside informer.

topónimo *m* place name.

torbellino *m (de viento)* whirlwind.

torcer 1 *vt (tobillo)* to sprain; *(esquina)* to turn; *(inclinar)* to slant. **2** *vi* to turn. **3 torcerse** *vr (doblarse)* to twist; *(tobillo, mano)* to sprain; *(desviarse)* to go off to the side.

torear *vi* to fight.

torero, -a *mf* bullfighter.

tormenta *f* storm.

tormento *m (tortura)* torture; *(padecimiento)* torment.

tornillo *m* screw.

torno *m (de alfarero)* wheel; **en t. a** around.

toro *m* bull; **¿te gustan los toros?** do you like bullfighting?

toronja *f* grapefruit.

torpe *adj (sin habilidad)* clumsy; *(tonto)* thick; *(movimiento)* slow.

torre *f* tower; *(en ajedrez)* rook.

torrente *m* torrent.

tórrido, -a *adj* torrid.

torso *m* torso.

torta *f (pastel)* cake; *(golpe)* slap.

tortazo *m (bofetada)* slap.

tortícolis *f inv* crick in the neck.

tortilla *f* omelet; *Am* tortilla; **t. francesa/española** (plain)/potato omelet.

tortuga *f* turtle.

tortuoso, -a *adj* tortuous.

tortura *f* torture.

tos *f* cough; **t. ferina** whooping cough.

tosco, -a *adj (basto)* rough; *(persona)* uncouth.

toser *vi* to cough.

tostada *f* **una t.** some toast, a slice of toast.

tostador *m* toaster.

tostar *vt (pan)* to toast; *(café)* to roast.

total 1 *adj* total. **2** *m (todo)* whole; *(cantidad)* total; **en t.** in all. **3** *adv* anyway; *(para resumir)* in short.

totalidad *f* whole; **la t. de** all of; **en su t.** as a whole.

tóxico, -a 1 *adj* toxic. **2** *m* poison.

toxicómano, -a 1 *adj* addicted to drugs. **2** *mf* drug addict.

tozudo, -a *adj* stubborn.

traba *f (obstáculo)* hindrance.

trabajador, -a 1 *mf* worker. **2** *adj* hard-working.

trabajar 1 *vi* to work; **t. de camarera** to work as a waitress. **2** *vt* to work (on).

trabajo *m* work; *(esfuerzo)* effort; **un t.** a job; **t. eventual** casual labor; **trabajos manuales** arts and crafts.

trabalenguas *m inv* tongue twister.

trabar 1 *vt (conversación, amistad)* to start. **2 trabarse** *vr* **se le trabó la lengua** he got tongue-tied.

tractor *m* tractor.

tradición *f* tradition.

tradicional *adj* traditional.

traducción *f* translation.

traducir 1 *vt* to translate (**a** into). **2 traducirse** *vr* to result (**en** in).

traductor, -a *mf* translator.

traer 1 *vt* to bring; *(llevar consigo)* to carry; *(problemas)* to cause; *(noticia)* to feature; **trae** give it to me. **2 traerse** *vr (llevar consigo)* to bring along.

traficante *mf (de drogas etc)* trafficker.

traficar *vi (ilegalmente)* to traffic (**con** in).

tráfico *m* traffic; **t. de drogas** drug traffic.

tragaperras *f inv (máquina)* **t.** slot machine.

tragar *vt*, **tragarse** *vr* to swallow.

tragedia *f* tragedy.

trágico, -a *adj* tragic.

trago *m (bebida)* swig; **de un t.** in one go; **pasar un mal t.** to have a bad time.

traición *f* betrayal.

traicionar *vt* to betray.

traidor, -a 1 *adj* treacherous. **2** *mf* traitor.

traigo *indic pres de* **traer.**

traje¹ *m (de hombre)* suit; *(de mujer)* dress; **t. de baño** swimsuit; **t. de chaqueta** two-piece suit; **t. de novia** wedding dress.

traje² *pt indef de* **traer.**

trama *f* plot.

tramar *vt* to plot.

trámite *m (paso)* step; *(formalidad)* formality.

tramo *m (de carretera)* stretch; *(de escalera)* flight.

trampa *f (de caza)* trap; *(engaño)* fiddle; **hacer trampa(s)** to cheat.

trampilla *f* trap door.

trampolín *m* springboard.

tramposo, -a 1 *adj* deceitful. **2** *mf* cheat.

tranquilizante *m* tranquillizer.

tranquilizar 1 *vt* to calm down; **lo dijo para tranquilizarme** he said it to reassure me. **2 tranquilizarse** *vr (calmarse)* to calm down.

tranquilo, -a *adj (persona, lugar)* calm; *(agua)* still; *(conciencia)* clear; *(despreocupado)* placid, easy-going; *fam* **tú t.** don't you worry.

transatlántico, -a 1 *m* (ocean) liner. **2** *adj* transatlantic.

transbordador *m (car)* ferry; **t. espacial** space shuttle.

transbordo *m (de trenes)* **hacer t.** to change.

transcurrir *vi (tiempo)* to pass, to go by; *(acontecer)* to take place.

transcurso *m* **en el t. de** in the course of.

transeúnte *mf (peatón)* passer-by.

transferencia *f* transference; *(de dinero)* transfer; **t. bancaria** bank transfer.

transferir *vt* to transfer.

transformación *f* transformation.

transformador *m* transformer.

transformar 1 *vt* to transform. **2 transformarse** *vr* to turn (**en** into).

transfusión *f* transfusion.

transición *f* transition.

transistor *m* transistor.

transitado, -a *adj (carretera)* busy.

transitivo, -a *adj* transitive.

tránsito *m (tráfico)* traffic; *(movimiento)* passage; **pasajeros en t.** passengers in transit.

transitorio, -a *adj* transitory.

transmisión *f* transmission; *(emisión)* broadcast.

transmisor *m* transmitter.

transmitir *vt* to pass on; *(emitir)* to transmit.

transparentarse *vr* to be transparent; **se le transparentaban las bragas** you could see her panties.

transparente *adj* transparent.

transpiración *f* perspiration.

transplante *m* transplant.

transportar *vt* to transport; *(pasajeros)* to carry; *(mercancías)* to ship.

transporte *m* transport.

transversal *adj* cross.

tranvía *m* streetcar.

trapo *m (viejo, roto)* rag; *(bayeta)* cloth; **t. de cocina** dishcloth; **t. del polvo** duster.

tráquea *f* trachea.

tras *prep (después de)* after; *(detrás)* behind.

trascendencia *f (importancia)* significance.

trascendental, trascendente *adj* significant.

trascurrir *vi* = **transcurrir.**

trasero, -a 1 *adj* back, rear; **en la parte trasera** at the back. **2** *m fam* bottom.

trasladar 1 *vt (cosa)* to move; *(trabajador)* to transfer. **2 trasladarse** *vr* to move.

traslado *m (de casa)* move; *(de personal)* transfer.

trasmano: a trasmano *adv* out of reach; **(me) coge a t.** it's out of my way.

trasnochar *vi* to stay up (very) late.

traspapelarse *vr* to get mislaid *o* misplaced.

trasparentarse *vr* = **transparentarse.**

traspasar *vt (atravesar)* to go through; *(río)* to cross; *(negocio, local)* to transfer; **'se traspasa'** 'for sale'.

traspié *m (pl* traspiés*)* stumble; **dar un t.** to trip.

trastero *m (cuarto)* **t.** junk room.

trastienda *f* back room.

trasto *m* thing; *(cosa inservible)* piece of junk.

trastocar *vt* = **trastornar.**

trastornado, -a *adj (loco)* mad, unhinged.

trastornar 1 *vt (planes)* to disrupt; *fig (persona)* to unhinge. **2 trastornarse** *vr (enloquecer)* to go mad.

trastorno *m (molestia)* trouble; **t. mental** mental disorder.

tratado *m (pacto)* treaty; *(estudio)* treatise.

tratamiento *m* treatment; *(de textos etc)* processing.

tratar 1 *vt* to treat; *(asunto)* to discuss; *(manejar)* to handle; *(textos etc)* to process; **me trata de 'tú'** he calls me 'tu'. **2** *vi* **t. de** *(intentar)* to try to; **t. de** *o* **sobre** *o* **acerca** to be about. **3 tratarse** *vr (relacionarse)* to be on speaking terms; **se trata de** *(es cuestión de)* it's a question of; *(es)* it is.

tratativas *fpl CSur* negotiation.

trato *m (contacto)* contact; *(acuerdo)* agreement; *(comercial)* deal; **malos tratos** ill-treatment *sing*; **¡t. hecho!** it's a deal!

traumático, -a *adj* traumatic.

través 1 *prep* **a t. de** *(superficie)* across, over; *(agujero etc)* through; *(por medio de)* through; **a t. del periódico** through the newspaper. **2** *adv* **de t.** *(transversalmente)* crosswise; *(de lado)* sideways.

travesaño *m* crosspiece; *(en fútbol)* crossbar.

travesía *f (viaje)* crossing.

travestí, travesti *mf* transvestite.

travesura *f* mischief.

travieso, -a *adj* mischievous.

trayecto *m (distancia)* distance; *(recorrido)* route; *(viaje)* journey.

trazar *vt (línea)* to draw; *(plano)* to design.

trébol *m* trefoil; *(en naipes)* club.

trece *adj & m inv* thirteen.

trecho *m (distancia)* distance; *(tramo)* stretch.

tregua *f* truce.

treinta *adj & m inv* thirty.

tremendo, -a *adj (terrible)* terrible; *(muy grande)* enormous; *(excelente)* tremendous.

tren *m* train.

trenca *f (prenda)* duffle coat.

trenza *f (de pelo)* braid.

trepar *vi* to climb.

tres *adj & m inv* three; **t. en raya** tick-tack-toe.

trescientos, -as *adj & mf* three hundred.

tresillo *m* three-piece suite.

treta *f* ruse.

triángulo *m* triangle; *fig* **t. amoroso** love triangle.

tribu *f* tribe.

tribuna *f (plataforma)* dais; *(en estadio)* stand.

tribunal *m* court; *(de examen)* board of examiners; **T. Supremo** Supreme Court.

tributo *m* tribute; *(finanzas)* tax.

triciclo *m* tricycle.

trienio *m* three-year period.

trigésimo, -a *adj & mf* thirtieth; **t. primero** thirty-first.

trigo *m* wheat.

trimestral *adj* quarterly.

trimestre *m* quarter; *(escolar)* term.

trinchar *vt (carne)* to carve.

trinchera *f* trench.

trineo *m* sledge; *(grande)* sleigh.

tripa *f (intestino)* gut; *fam* tummy; **dolor de t.** stomachache.

triple *adj & m* triple.

triplicar *vt* to triple, to treble.

trípode *m* tripod.

tripulación *f* crew.

tripulante *mf* crew member.
tripular *vt* to man.
triquiñuela *f* dodge.
triste *adj (infeliz)* sad; *(sombrío)* gloomy.
tristeza *f* sadness.
triturar *vt* to grind (up).
triunfador, -a 1 *adj* winning. **2** *mf* winner.
triunfar *vi* to triumph.
triunfo *m (victoria)* triumph; *(deportiva)* win; *(éxito)* success.
trivial *adj* trivial.
triza *f* **hacer trizas** to tear to shreds.
trocar *vt* to transform, to turn (**en** into).
trocear *vt* to cut up (into pieces).
trofeo *m* trophy.
tromba *f* **t. de agua** violent downpour.
trombón *m* trombone.
trompa *f (instrumento)* horn; *(de elefante)* trunk; *fam* **estar t.** to be sloshed.
trompeta *f* trumpet.
tronchar 1 *vt (rama, tronco)* to cut down. **2 troncharse** *vr* **troncharse de risa** to split one's sides laughing.
tronco *m (torso, de árbol)* trunk; *(leño)* log.
trono *m* throne.
tropa *f* **tropas** troops.
tropel *m* **en t.** in a mad rush.
tropezar *vi (trompicar)* to stumble (**con** on); **t. con algn/dificultades** to run into sb/difficulties.
tropezón *m (traspié)* stumble; **dar un t.** to trip.
tropical *adj* tropical.
trópico *m* tropics *pl*.
tropiezo¹ *m (obstáculo)* trip.
tropiezo² *indic pres de* **tropezar**.
trotar *vi* to trot.
trote *m* trot; **al t.** at a trot.
trozo *m* piece.
trucha *f* trout.
truco *m (ardid)* trick; *(manera de hacer algo)* knack; **coger el t. (a algo)** to get the knack o hang (of sth).
trueno *m* thunder; **un t.** a thunderclap.
trufa *f* truffle.
tu *adj pos* your; **tu libro** your book; **tus libros** your books.
tú *pron pers* you.
tubería *f (de agua)* pipes *pl*; *(de gas, petróleo)* pipeline.
tubo *m* tube; *(tubería)* pipe; **t. de ensayo** test tube; **t. de escape** exhaust (pipe).
tuerca *f* nut.
tuerto, -a 1 *adj* blind in one eye. **2** *mf* person who is blind in one eye.
tuerzo *indic pres de* **torcer**.
tulipán *m* tulip.
tullido, -a *adj* crippled.
tumba *f* grave.
tumbar 1 *vt* to knock down. **2 tumbarse** *vr (acostarse)* to lie down.
tumbona *f* easy chair; *(de lona)* deckchair.
tumor *m* tumor.
tumulto *m* commotion.
túnel *m* tunnel; **el t. del Canal de la Mancha** the Channel Tunnel.
túnica *f* tunic.
tupé *m (pl tupés) (flequillo)* fringe.
tupido, -a *adj* thick.
turba *f (combustible)* peat.
turbado, -a *adj (alterado)* disturbed; *(desconcertado)* confused.
turbar 1 *vt (alterar)* to unsettle; *(desconcertar)* to baffle. **2 turbarse** *vr (preocuparse)* to become upset; *(desconcertarse)* to become confused.
turbio, -a *adj (agua)* cloudy; *(negocio etc)* dubious.
turbulencia *f* turbulence.
turco, -a 1 *adj* Turkish. **2** *mf (persona)* Turk; *fig* **cabeza de t.** scapegoat. **3** *m (idioma)* Turkish.
turismo *m* tourism; *(coche)* car; **ir de t.** to go touring.
turista *mf* tourist.
turístico, -a *adj* tourist; **de interés t.** of interest to tourists.
turnarse *vr* to take turns.
turno *m (en juegos etc)* turn; *(de trabajo)* shift; **t. de día/noche** day/night shift.
turquesa *adj & f* turquoise.
turrón *m* nougat.
tutear 1 *vt* to address as 'tú'. **2 tutearse** *vr* to call (each other) 'tú'.
tutela *f* guidance.
tutor, -a *mf (de huérfano)* guardian; *(de estudiante)* tutor.
tuve *pt indef de* **tener**.
tuyo, -a 1 *adj pos (con personas)* of yours; *(con objetos)* one of your; **¿es amigo t.?** is he a friend of yours?; **un libro t.** one of your books. **2** *pron pos* yours.

U

u *conj (before words beginning with o or ho)* or.
ubicación *f* location.
ubicar 1 *vt (situar)* to locate. **2 ubicarse** *vr (en un lugar)* to be located.
Ud. *abr de* **usted** you.
Uds. *abr de* **ustedes** you.
UE *f abr de* **Unión Europa** European Union, EU.
úlcera *f* ulcer.
últimamente *adv* recently.
ultimar *vt (terminar)* to finalize; *(matar)* to finish off.
ultimátum *m (pl ultimátums)* ultimatum.
último, -a *adj* last; *(más reciente)* latest; *(más alto)* top; *(más bajo)* lowest; *(definitivo)* final; *(más lejano)* back; **por ú.** finally; **a. últimos de mes** at the end of the month; **últimas noticias** latest news; **el u. piso** the top apartment; **el u. de la lista** the lowest on the list; **la última fila** the back row.
ultraderecha *f* extreme right.
ultramarinos *mpl* groceries; **tienda de u.** greengrocer.
ultrasónico, -a *adj* ultrasonic.
ultravioleta *adj inv* ultraviolet.
ulular *vi (viento)* to howl; *(búho)* to hoot.
umbral *m* threshold.

un, -a 1 *art indef* a, *(antes de vocal)* an; **unos, -as** some. **2** *adj (delante de m sing)* one; **un chico y dos chicas** one boy and two girls.
unánime *adj* unanimous.
unanimidad *f* unanimity; **por u.** unanimously.
undécimo, -a *adj* eleventh.
únicamente *adv* only.
único, -a *adj (solo)* only; *(extraordinario)* unique; **hijo ú.** only child; **lo ú. que quiero** the only thing I want.
unidad *f (unit); (cohesión)* unity; **u. de disquete** disk drive.
unido, -a *adj* united; **están muy unidos** they are very attached to one another; **una familia muy unida** a very close family.
unificación *f* unification.
uniforme 1 *m (prenda)* uniform. **2** *adj* uniform; *(superficie)* even.
unilateral *adj* unilateral.
unión *f* union.
unir *vt*, **unirse** *vr* to unite.
unísono *m* **al u.** in unison.
universal *adj* universal.
universidad *f* university.
universitario, -a 1 *adj* university. **2** *mf* university student.
universo *m* universe.
uno, -a 1 *m inv* one; **el u. de mayo** the first of May. **2** *f (hora)* **es la una** it's one o'clock. **3** *adj* **unos, -as** some; **unas cajas** some boxes; **debe haber unos/unas veinte** there must be around twenty. **4** *pron* one; *(persona)* someone, somebody; *(impers)* you, one; **u. (de ellos), una (de ellas)** one of them; **unos cuantos** a few; **se miraron el u. al otro** they looked at each other; **de u. en u.** one by one; **u. tras otro** one after the other; **vive con u.** she's living with some man; **u. tiene que…** you have to….
untar *vt* to smear; *(mantequilla)* to spread.
uña *f* nail; **morderse o comerse las uñas** to bite one's nails.
uperizado, -a *adj* **leche uperizada** UHT milk.
urbanismo *m* town planning.
urbanización *f (barrio)* housing estate; *(proceso)* urbanization.
urbano, -a *adj* urban.
urbe *f* large city.
urgencia *f* urgency; *(emergencia)* emergency.
urgente *adj* urgent; **correo u.** express mail.
urgir *vi* to be urgent.
urna *f (para votos)* ballot box.
urraca *f* magpie.
uruguayo, -a *adj & mf* Uruguayan.
usado, -a *adj (ropa)* second-hand.
usar 1 *vt* to use; *(prenda)* to wear. **2 usarse** *vr* to be used.
usina *f Am (central eléctrica)* power station.
uso *m* use; **u. externo** for external use only; **u. tópico** local application; **haga u. del casco** wear a helmet.
usted *(pl ustedes) pron pers* you; **¿quién es u.?, ¿quiénes son ustedes?** who are you?
usual *adj* usual.
usuario, -a *mf* user.
utensilio *m* utensil; *(herramienta)* tool.
útil *adj* useful; *(día)* working.
utilidad *f* utility; **tener u.** to be useful.
utilitario, -a 1 *m (coche)* utility vehicle. **2** *adj* utilitarian.
utilización *f* use.
utilizar *vt* to use.
utópico, -a *adj & mf* utopian.
uva *f* grape; **u. blanca** green grape.
UVI *f abr de* **unidad de vigilancia intensiva** intensive care unit.

V

vaca *f* cow; *(carne)* beef.
vacaciones *fpl* vacation; *(viaje)* holiday; **estar/irse de v.** to be/go on holiday.
vacante 1 *adj* vacant. **2** *f* vacancy.
vaciar *vt*, **vaciarse** *vr* to empty.
vacilar *vi (dudar)* to hesitate; *(voz)* to falter; **sin v.** without hesitation.
vacío, -a 1 *adj* empty; *(hueco)* hollow; *(sin ocupar)* vacant. **2** *m* void; *(hueco)* gap; *(espacio)* (empty) space.
vacuna *f* vaccine.
vacunación *f* vaccination.
vacunar 1 *vt* to vaccinate (**contra** against); *fig* to inure. **2 vacunarse** *vr* to get oneself vaccinated.
vacuno, -a *adj* bovine; **ganado v.** cattle.
vado *m (de un río)* ford; **v. permanente** keep clear.
vagabundo, -a 1 *adj (errante)* wandering. **2** *mf* wanderer; *(sin casa)* hobo.
vagar *vi* to wander about.
vago, -a 1 *adj (perezoso)* lazy; *(indefinido)* vague. **2** *mf (holgazán)* layabout.
vagón *m (para pasajeros)* car; *(para mercancías)* freight car.
vaho *m (de aliento)* breath; *(vapor)* vapor.
vaina *f (de guisante etc)* pod; *Am (molestia)* nuisance.
vainilla *f* vanilla.
vajilla *f* dishes *pl*.
valdré *indic fut de* **valer**.
vale¹ *interj* all right, OK.
vale² *m (comprobante)* voucher; *(pagaré)* IOU (I owe you).
valer 1 *vt* to be worth; *(costar)* to cost; **no vale nada** it is worthless; **no vale la pena (ir)** it's not worthwhile (going); **¿cuánto vale?** how much is it? **2** *vi (servir)* to be useful; *(ser válido)* to count; **más vale** it is better; **más vale que te vayas ya** you had better leave now. **3 valerse** *vr* **valerse por sí mismo** to be able to manage on one's own.
valgo *indic pres de* **valer**.
válido, -a *adj* valid.
valiente *adj (valeroso)* brave.
valioso, -a *adj* valuable.
valla *f (cerca)* fence; *(muro)* wall; **v. publicitaria** billboard.
valle *m* valley.
valor *m* value; *(precio)* price; *(valentía)* courage; **objetos de v.** valuables; **sin v.** worthless.
valoración *f* appraisal.
valorar *vt* to value.
vals *m* waltz.
válvula *f* valve; **v. de seguridad** safety valve.

vampiro *m* vampire.
vandalismo *m* vandalism.
vanguardia *f* vanguard; *(artística)* avant-garde.
vanidad *f* vanity.
vanidoso, -a *adj* conceited.
vano, -a *adj (vanidoso)* vain; *(esfuerzo, esperanza)* futile; **en v.** in vain.
vapor *m (de agua hirviendo)* steam; *(gas)* vapor; **al v.** steamed; **v. de agua** water vapor.
vaporizador *m* vaporizer.
vaquero, -a 1 *m* cowboy. **2** *adj* **pantalón v.** jeans *pl.* **3** *mpl* **vaqueros** *(prenda)* jeans.
vara *f* rod.
variable *adj & f* variable.
variado, -a *adj* varied.
variante *f (carretera)* detour.
variar *vti* to vary; *(con ironía)* **para v.** just for a change.
varicela *f* chickenpox.
variedad *f* variety; *(espectáculo)* **variedades** variety show.
varilla *f (vara)* rod; *(de abanico, paraguas)* rib.
varios, -as *adj* several.
variz *f* varicose vein.
varón *m (hombre)* man; *(chico)* boy.
vas *indic pres de* **ir.**
vascuence *m (idioma)* Basque.
vaselina *f* Vaseline®.
vasija *f* pot.
vaso *m (para beber)* glass.
vaticinar *vt* to predict.
vatio *m* watt.
vaya¹ *interj* **¡v. lío!** what a mess!
vaya² *subj pres de* **ir.**
Vd., Vds. *abr de* **usted, ustedes** you.
ve 1 *imperativo de* **ir. 2** *indic pres de* **ver.**
vecindad *f,* **vecindario** *m (área)* neighborhood; *(vecinos)* residents *pl.*
vecino, -a 1 *mf (persona)* neighbor; *(residente)* resident. **2** *adj* neighboring.
vega *f* fertile plain.
vegetación *f* vegetation; *(en nariz)* **vegetaciones** adenoids.
vegetal *adj & m* vegetable.
vegetariano, -a *adj & mf* vegetarian.
vehemente *adj* vehement.
vehículo *m* vehicle.
veinte *adj & m inv* twenty.
vejez *f* old age.
vejiga *f* bladder.
vela¹ *f* candle; **pasar la noche en v.** to have a sleepless night.
vela² *f (de barco)* sail.
velador *m Am (mesilla de noche)* bedside table.
velar 1 *vt (difrento)* to hold a wake; *(enfermo)* to watch over. **2** *vi (no dormir)* to stay awake. **3 velarse** *vr* to blur.
velatorio *m* vigil.
velero *m* sailing boat.
veleta *f* weather vane.
vello *m* hair.
velo *m* veil.
velocidad *f (rapidez)* speed; *(marcha)* gear; **v. máxima** speed limit.
velocímetro *m* speedometer.
veloz *adj* rapid.
vena *f* vein.
venado *m* deer; *(carne)* venison.
vencedor, -a 1 *mf* winner. **2** *adj* winning.
vencer 1 *vt* to defeat; *(dificultad)* to overcome. **2** *vi (pago, deuda)* to be payable; *(plazo)* to expire.
vencido, -a *adj (derrotado)* defeated; *(equipo etc)* beaten; **darse por v.** to give up.
venda *f* bandage.
vendaje *m* dressing.
vendar *vt* to bandage; **v. los ojos a algn** to blindfold sb.
vendaval *m* gale.
vendedor, -a *mf* seller; *(hombre)* salesman; *(mujer)* saleswoman.
vender *vt,* **venderse** *vr* to sell; **se vende** for sale.
vendimia *f* grape harvest.
vendré *indic fut de* **venir.**
veneno *m* poison; *(de serpiente)* venom.
venenoso, -a *adj* poisonous.
venéreo, -a *adj* venereal.
venezolano, -a *adj & mf* Venezuelan.
venga *subj pres de* **venir.**
venganza *f* vengeance, revenge.
vengarse *vr* to avenge oneself; **v. de algn** to take revenge on sb.
vengo *indic pres de* **venir.**
venir 1 *vi* to come; **el año que viene** next year; *fam* **¡venga ya!** *(expresa incredulidad)* come off it!; *(vamos)* come on!; **v. grande/pequeño** *(ropa)* to be too big/small; **v. mal/bien** to be inconvenient/convenient. ■ *(en pasivas)* **esto vino provocado por...** this was brought about by... ■ **esto viene ocurriendo desde hace mucho tiempo** this has been going on for a long time now. **2 venirse** *vr* **venirse abajo** to collapse.
venta *f* sale; *(posada)* country inn; **en v.** for sale; **a la v.** on sale; **v. a plazos/al contado** credit/cash sale; **v. al por mayor/al por menor** wholesale/retail.
ventaja *f* advantage; **llevar v. a** to have the advantage over.
ventana *f* window; *(de la nariz)* nostril.
ventanilla *f* window; *(de la nariz)* nostril.
ventilador *m* ventilator; *(de coche)* fan.
ventilar *vt* to ventilate.
ventisca *f* blizzard; *(de nieve)* snowstorm.
ver 1 *vt* to see; *(televisión)* to watch; **a v.** let's see; **a v. si escribes** I hope you'll write; **(ya) veremos** we'll see; **no tener nada que v. con** to have nothing to do with. **2 verse** *vr (imagen etc)* to be seen; *(encontrarse con algn)* to see each other; **¡nos vemos!** see you later!; *Am* **te ves divina** you look divine.
veraneante *mf* vacationist, tourist.
veranear *vi* to spend one's summer vacation.
veraniego, -a *adj* summer.
verano *m* summer.
veras: de veras *adv* really.
verbena *f* street *o* night party.
verbo *m* verb.
verdad *f* truth; **es v.** it is true; **¡de v!** really!; truly!; **un amigo de v.** a real friend; *(en frase afirmativa)* **está muy bien, ¿(no es) v.?** it is very good, isn't it?; *(en frase negativa)* **no te gusta, ¿v.?** you don't like it, do you?
verdaderamente *adv* truly.

verdadero, -a *adj* true.
verde 1 *adj* green; *(fruta)* unripe; *(chiste, película)* blue. **2** *m (color)* green.
verdoso, -a *adj* greenish.
verdura *f* vegetables *pl.*
vereda *f* path; *Am (acera)* sidewalk.
veredicto *m* verdict.
vergonzoso, -a *adj (penoso)* disgraceful; *(tímido)* shy.
vergüenza *f* shame; *(timidez)* shyness; **¿no te da v.?** aren't you ashamed?; **es una v.** it's a disgrace; **me da v.** I'm too embarrassed.
verificar *vt* to check.
verja *f (reja)* grating; *(cerca)* railing; *(puerta)* iron gate.
vermut, vermú *m (pl* **vermús)** vermouth.
verosímil *adj* probable, likely; *(creíble)* credible.
verruga *f* wart.
versión *f* version.
verso *m (poesía)* verse.
vertebrado, -a *adj & m* vertebrate.
vertedero *m (de basura)* tip.
verter *vt* to pour (out); *(basura)* to dump.
vertical *adj* vertical.
vertiente *f (de montaña, tejado)* slope; *Am (manantial)* spring.
vertiginoso, -a *adj (velocidad)* breakneck.
vértigo *m* vertigo; **me da v.** it makes me dizzy.
vespa® *f (motor)* scooter.
vespino® *m* moped.
vestíbulo *m (de casa)* hall; *(de edificio público)* foyer.
vestido, -a 1 *m (de mujer)* dress. **2** *adj* dressed.
vestigio *m* trace.
vestir 1 *vt (a alguien)* to dress; *(llevar puesto)* to wear. **2** *vi* to dress; **ropa de (mucho) v.** formal dress. **3 vestirse** *vr* to get dressed; **vestirse de** to wear; *(disfrazarse)* to dress up as.
vestuario *m (conjunto de vestidos)* wardrobe; *(para teatro)* costumes *pl*; *(camerino)* dressing room; *(en estadio)* changing room.
veterano, -a *adj & mf* veteran.
veterinario, -a 1 *mf* vet, veterinarian. **2** *f* veterinary medicine.
veto *m* veto.
vez *f* time; *(turno)* turn; **una v.** once; **dos veces** twice; **cinco veces** five times; **a o algunas veces** sometimes; **cada v.** each *o* every time; **cada v. más** more and more; **de v. en cuando** now and again; **¿le has visto alguna v.?** have you ever seen him?; **otra v.** again; **a la v.** at the same time; **tal v.** perhaps, maybe; **de una v.** in one go; **en v. de** instead of.
vía 1 *f (del tren)* track; *(camino)* road; **(por) v. oral** to be taken orally; **por v. aérea/marítima** by air/sea. **2** *prep (a través de)* via.
viajar *vi* to travel.
viaje *m* journey, trip; *(largo, en barco)* voyage; **¡buen v.!** have a good trip!; **estar de v.** to be away (on a trip); **v. de negocios** business trip; **v. de novios** honeymoon.
viajero, -a *mf* traveler; *(en transporte público)* passenger.
víbora *f* viper.
vibración *f* vibration.
vibrar *vti* to vibrate.
vicepresidente, -a *mf* vice president; *(de compañía, comité)* vice-chairman, vice president.
viceversa *adv* vice versa.
vicio *m* vice; *(mala costumbre)* bad habit.
vicioso, -a 1 *adj (persona)* depraved; **círculo v.** vicious circle. **2** *mf* depraved person.
víctima *f* victim.
victoria *f* victory.
vid *f* vine.
vida *f* life; **en mi v.** never in my life; **ganarse la v.** to earn one's living; **¿qué es de tu v.?** how's life?
vídeo *m* video; **grabar en v.** to video.
videocámara *f* video camera.
videoclub *m* video club.
videojuego *m* video game.
vidriera *f* stained-glass window; *Am (escaparate)* shop window.
vidrio *m* glass.
viejo, -a 1 *adj* old; **hacerse v.** to grow old; **un v. amigo** an old friend. **2** *mf (hombre)* old man; *(mujer)* old woman; **los viejos** old people; *fam* **mis viejos** my parents.
viento *m* wind; **hace** *o* **sopla mucho v.** it is very windy.
vientre *m* belly.
viernes *m inv* Friday; **V. Santo** Good Friday.
vietnamita *adj & mf* Vietnamese.
viga *f (de madera)* beam; *(de hierro)* girder.
vigencia *f* validity; **entrar en v.** to come into force.
vigésimo, -a *adj & mf* twentieth.
vigilante *m* guard; *(nocturno)* night watchman.
vigilar 1 *vt* to watch; *(lugar)* to guard. **2** *vi* to keep watch.
vigor *m* vigor; *(fuerza)* strength; **en v.** in force.
vil *adj* vile.
villa *f (población)* town; *(casa)* villa.
villancico *m (Christmas)* carol.
vinagre *m* vinegar.
vinagreras *fpl* oil and vinegar cruets.
vinagreta *f* vinaigrette.
vincha *f Am* headband.
vínculo *m* link.
vine *pt indef de* **venir.**
vino *m* wine; **v. blanco/tinto** white/red wine; **v. rosado** rosé.
viña *f* vineyard.
viñedo *m* vineyard.
viñeta *f* illustration.
violación *f (de persona)* rape; *(de ley, derecho)* violation.
violar *vt (persona)* to rape; *(ley, derecho)* to violate.
violencia *f* violence.
violento, -a *adj* violent; *(situación)* embarrassing; **sentirse v.** to feel awkward.
violeta 1 *adj* violet. **2** *m (color)* violet. **3** *f (flor)* violet.
violín *m* violin.
violonc(h)elo *m* cello.
virar *vt* to turn round.
virgen *adj (persona, selva)* virgin; *(aceite, lana)* pure; *(cinta)* blank.
viril *adj* virile.
virtud *f* virtue; *(propiedad)* ability.
virtuoso, -a *adj* virtuous; *(músico)* virtuoso.
viruela *f* smallpox.
virus *m inv* virus.
visa *f Am* visa.
visado *m* visa.
visera *f (de gorra)* peak; *(de casco)* visor.

visibilidad *f* visibility.
visible *adj* visible.
visillo *m* small net curtain.
visión *f* vision; *(vista)* sight.
visita *f* visit; *(invitado)* visitor; **hacer una v.** to pay a visit; **estar de v.** to be visiting.
visitante 1 *mf* visitor. **2** *adj (equipo)* away.
visitar *vt* to visit.
vislumbrar *vt* to glimpse.
visón *m* mink.
víspera *f (día anterior)* day before; *(de festivo)* eve.
vista *f* sight; *(panorama)* view; **a la v.** visible; **a primera** *o* **simple v.** on the face of it; **en v. de** in view of, considering; **corto de v.** short-sighted; **conocer a algn de v.** to know sb by sight; **perder de v. a** to lose sight of; **¡hasta la v.!** see you!; **con vista(s) al mar** overlooking the sea.
vistazo *m* glance; **echar un v. a algo** *(ojear)* to have a (quick) look at sth.
visto, -a 1 *adj* **está v. que** it is obvious that; **por lo v.** apparently; **estar bien v.** to be well looked upon; **estar mal v.** to be frowned upon. **2** *m* **v. bueno** approval.
vitalicio, -a *adj* lifelong.
vitalidad *f* vitality.
vitamina *f* vitamin.
viticultor, -a *mf* wine grower.
vitorear *vt* to cheer.
vitrina *f (aparador)* display cabinet; *(de exposición)* showcase; *Am (escaparate)* shop window.
viudo, -a *mf (hombre)* widower; *(mujer)* widow.
viva *interj* hurrah!
vivaracho, -a *adj* lively.
vivaz *adj* vivacious; *(perspicaz)* quick-witted.
víveres *mpl* provisions.
vivero *m (de plantas)* nursery.
vivienda *f* housing; *(casa)* house; *(piso)* apartment.
vivir 1 *vi* to live. **2** *vt (guerra, experiencia)* to live through.
vivo, -a *adj* alive; *(vivaz)* lively; *(listo)* clever; *(color)* vivid; **en v.** *(programa)* live; **al rojo v.** red-hot.
vocabulario *m* vocabulary.
vocación *f* vocation.
vocal 1 *f* vowel. **2** *m* member. **3** *adj* vocal.
voceador, -a *mf Am* vendor.
vocero, -a *mf Am* spokesperson; *(hombre)* spokesman; *(mujer)* spokeswoman.
vociferar *vi* to shout.
vodka *m* vodka.
volandas: en vandas *adv* flying through the air.
volante 1 *m* steering wheel; *(de vestido)* frill; **ir al v.** to be at the wheel. **2** *adj* flying; **platillo v.** flying saucer.
volantín *m Am (cometa)* small kite.
volar 1 *vi* to fly; *fam* **lo hizo volando** he did it in a flash. **2** *vt (explotar)* to blow up; *(caja fuerte)* to blow open; *(terreno)* to blast. **3 volarse** *vr (papel etc)* to be blown away.
volcán *m* volcano.
volcar 1 *vt (cubo etc)* to knock over; *(barco, bote)* to capsize; *(vaciar)* to empty out. **2** *vi (coche)* to turn over; *(barca)* to capsize. **3 volcarse** *vr (vaso, jarra)* to fall over; *(coche)* to turn over; *(barca)* to capsize.
voleibol *m* volleyball.
voltaje *m* voltage.
voltear 1 *vt CSur (derribar)* to knock over; *Andes, CAm, Carib, Méx (cabeza)* to turn; **v. la espalda a alguien** to turn one's back on sb. **2 voltearse** *vr Andes, CAm, Carib, Méx (volverse)* to turn around.
voltereta *f* somersault.
voltio *m* volt.
volumen *m* volume.
voluminoso, -a *adj* voluminous; *(enorme)* massive.
voluntad *f* will; **fuerza de v.** willpower; **tiene mucha v.** he is very strong-willed.
voluntario, -a 1 *adj* voluntary; **ofrecerse v.** to volunteer. **2** *mf* volunteer.
volver *(pp vuelto)* **1** *vi* to return; *(venir de vuelta)* to come back; *(ir de vuelta)* to go back; **v. en sí** to come round; **v. a hacer algo** to do sth again. **2** *vt (convertir)* to make; *(dar vuelta a)* to turn; *(boca abajo)* to turn upside down; *(de fuera adentro)* to turn inside out; *(de atrás adelante)* to turn back to front; *(cinta, disco)* to turn over; **volverle la espalda a algn** to turn one's back on sb; **al v. la esquina** on turning the corner. **3 volverse** *vr* to turn; *(venir de vuelta)* to come back; *(ir de vuelta)* to go back; *(convertirse)* to become; **volverse loco** to go mad.
vomitar 1 *vi* to vomit; **tengo ganas de v.** I feel sick. **2** *vt* to bring up.
voraz *adj* voracious.
vos *pron pers pl Am* you.
vosotros, -as *pron pers pl* you.
votación *f (voto)* vote; *(acción)* voting.
votante *mf* voter.
votar *vi* to vote; **v. a algn** to vote for sb.
voto *m* vote.
voy *indic pres de* **ir**.
voz *f* voice; *(grito)* shout; **en v. alta** aloud; **en v. baja** in a low voice; **a media v.** in a low voice; **a voces** shouting; **dar voces** to shout; **no tener ni v. ni voto** to have no say in the matter.
vuelo *m* flight; **v. chárter/regular** charter/scheduled flight; **una falda de v.** a full skirt.
vuelta *f (regreso)* return; *(viaje)* return journey; *(giro)* turn; *(en carreras)* lap; *(ciclista)* tour; *(dinero)* change; **a v. de correo** by return post; **estar de v.** to be back; **dar media v.** to turn round; **la cabeza me da vueltas** my head is spinning; **no le des más vueltas** stop worrying about it; **dar una v.** *(a pie)* to go for a walk; *(en coche)* to go for a drive.
vuelto *m Am* change.
vuestro, -a 1 *adj pos (antes del sustantivo)* your; *(después del sustantivo)* of yours. **2** *pron pos* yours; **lo v.** what is yours.
vulgar *adj* vulgar.
vulnerable *adj* vulnerable.

walkman® *m* Walkman®.
wáter *m (pl* **wáteres**) toilet.

whisky *m* whiskey.
windsurf(ing) *m* windsurfing.

xenofobia *f* xenophobia.

y *conj* and; **son las tres y cuarto** it's a quarter past three; **¿y qué?** so what?; **¿y tú?** what about you?; **¿y eso?** how come?; *ver* **e**.
ya 1 *adv* already; *(ahora mismo)* now; **ya lo sabía** I already knew; **¡hazlo ya!** do it at once!; **ya mismo** right away; **ya hablaremos luego** we'll talk about it later; **ya verás** you'll see; **ya no** no longer; **ya no viene por aquí** he doesn't come round here any more; **ya era hora** about time too; **ya lo creo** I should think so; **¡ya voy!** coming!; **¡ya está!** that's it! **2** *conj* **ya que** since.
yacaré *m Am* alligator.
yacer *vi* to lie.
yacimiento *m* deposit.
yanqui 1 *adj* Yankee. **2** *mf* Yank.
yarda *f* yard.
yate *m* yacht.
yedra *f* ivy.
yegua *f* mare.
yema *f (de huevo)* yolk; *(de planta)* bud; *(pastel)* sweet made from sugar and egg yolk; **y. del dedo** fingertip.
yendo *gerundio de* **ir**.
yerba *f* = **hierba**.
yerbatero, -a *mf Am (curandero)* witch doctor who uses herbs.
yerno *m* son-in-law.
yerro *indic pres de* **errar**.
yeso *m* plaster.
yo *pron pers* I; **entre tú y yo** between you and me; **¿quién es? — soy yo** who is it? — it's me; **yo no** not me; **yo que tú** if I were you; **yo mismo** I myself.
yoga *m* yoga.
yogur *m* yogurt.
yuca *f* yucca.
yudo *m* judo.
yugo(e)slavo, -a *adj & mf* Yugoslav, Yugoslavian.

zafarse *vr* to get away (**de** from).
zafiro *m* sapphire.
zalamero, -a 1 *mf* crawler. **2** *adj* crawling.
zamarra *f (prenda)* sheepskin jacket.
zambo, -a *adj* knock-kneed; *Am* half Indian and half Negro.
zambullirse *vr* to jump.
zanahoria *f* carrot.
zancada *f* stride.
zancadilla *f* **ponerle la z. a algn** to trip sb up.
zanco *m* stilt.
zancudo *m Am* mosquito.
zanja *f* ditch.
zapatería *f* shoe shop.
zapatero, -a *mf (vendedor)* shoe shop owner; *(fabricante)* shoemaker; *(reparador)* cobbler.
zapatilla *f* slipper; **zapatillas de deporte** trainers.
zapato *m* shoe.
zarandear *vt* to shake.
zarcillo *m (pendiente)* earring.
zarpa *f* claw.
zarpar *vi* to set sail.
zarza *f* bramble.
zarzamora *f (zarza)* blackberry bush; *(fruto)* blackberry.
zarzuela *f* Spanish operetta; **la Z.** royal residence in Madrid.
zigzag *m (pl* **zigzags** *o* **zigzagues**) zigzag.
zócalo *m (de pared)* baseboard.
zodiaco, zodíaco *m* zodiac; **signo del z.** sign of the zodiac.
zona *f* zone.
zoo *m* zoo.
zoológico, -a 1 *adj* zoological; **parque z.** zoo. **2** *m* zoo.
zopilote *m Am* buzzard.
zoquete *mf fam* blockhead.
zorra *f* vixen.
zorro *m* fox.
zueco *m* clog.
zumbar *vi* to buzz; **me zumban los oídos** my ears are buzzing.
zumbido *m* buzzing.
zumo *m* juice.
zurcir *vt* to darn.
zurdo, -a 1 *mf (persona)* left- handed person. **2** *adj* left-handed.

A

a *indef art* (*before vowel or silent h* **an**) un, una; **he has a big nose** tiene la nariz grande; **half a liter/an hour** medio litro/media hora; **he's a teacher** es profesor; **60 cents a kilo** 60 centavos el kilo; **three times a week** tres veces a la semana.
a·ban·don *vt* abandonar.
ab·bey abadía *f.*
ab·bre·vi·a·tion abreviatura *f.*
a·bil·i·ty capacidad *f.*
a·ble *adj (capable)* capaz; **to be a. to do sth** poder hacer algo.
a·ble-bod·ied *adj* sano, -a.
ab·nor·mal *adj* anormal.
ab·nor·mal·ly *adv* anormalmente.
a·board 1 *adv* a bordo; **to go a.** *(ship)* embarcarse; *(train)* subir. **2** *prep* a bordo de.
a·bol·ish *vt* abolir.
a·bor·tion aborto *m*; **to have an a.** abortar.
a·bout 1 *adv (approximately)* más o menos; **he's a. 40** tendrá unos 40 años; **it's a. time you got up** ya es hora de que te levantes. **2** *prep (concerning)* acerca de; **a program a. New York** un programa sobre Nueva York; **to speak a. sth** hablar de algo; **what's it all a.?** ¿de qué se trata?; **how a. a game of tennis?** ¿qué te parece un partido de tenis? ▪ **it's a. to start** está a punto de empezar.
a·bove 1 *adv* arriba; **the apartment a.** el piso de arriba; **a policy imposed from a.** una política impuesta desde arriba. **2** *prep (higher than)* encima de; *(greater than)* superior a; **100 meters a. sea level** 100 metros sobre el nivel del mar; **it's a. the door** está encima de la puerta; **a. all** sobre todo; **he's not a. stealing** es capaz incluso de robar.
a·bove-men·tioned *adj* susodicho, -a.
a·breast *adv* **to keep a. of things** mantenerse al día.
a·broad *adv* en el extranjero; **to go a.** irse al extranjero.
a·brupt *adj (manner)* brusco, -a; *(change)* súbito, -a.
ab·rupt·ly *adv (act)* bruscamente; *(speak)* con aspereza.
ab·scess absceso *m.*
ab·sence *(of person)* ausencia *f*; *(of thing)* falta *f.*
ab·sent *adj* ausente.
ab·sent-mind·ed *adj* distraído, -a.
ab·so·lute *adj* absoluto, -a; *(failure)* total; *(truth)* puro, -a.
ab·so·lute·ly *adv* completamente; **a. not** en absoluto; **you're a. right** tienes toda la razón; **a.!** ¡desde luego!
ab·sorb *vt (liquid)* absorber; **to be absorbed in sth** estar absorto, -a en algo.
ab·surd *adj* absurdo, -a.
a·buse 1 *n (ill-treatment)* malos tratos *mpl*; *(misuse)* abuso *m*; *(insults)* injurias *fpl.* **2** *vt (ill-treat)* maltratar; *(misuse)* abusar de; *(insult)* injuriar.
a·bu·sive *adj (insulting)* grosero, -a.
ac·a·dem·ic 1 *adj* académico, -a; *(career)* universitario, -a; **a. year** año *m* escolar. **2** *n* académico, -a *mf.*
ac·cel·er·ate *vi* acelerar.
ac·cel·er·a·tor acelerador *m.*
ac·cent acento *m.*
ac·cept *vt* aceptar; *(theory)* admitir.
ac·cept·a·ble *adj* admisible.
ac·cess acceso *m.*
ac·ces·si·ble *adj* accesible; *(person)* asequible.
ac·ces·so·ry *(to crime)* cómplice *mf*; **accessories** accesorios *mpl*; *(for outfit)* complementos *mpl.*
ac·cess time tiempo *m* de acceso.
ac·ci·dent accidente *m*; **by a.** por casualidad.
ac·ci·den·tal *adj* fortuito, -a; *(unintended)* imprevisto, -a.
ac·ci·den·tal·ly *adv (by chance)* por casualidad.
ac·com·mo·date *vt (guests)* alojar; **to a. sb's wishes** complacer a algn.
ac·com·mo·da·tion(s) alojamiento *m.*
ac·com·pa·ny *vt* acompañar.
ac·com·plish *vt (aim)* conseguir; *(task, mission)* llevar a cabo.
ac·cord **of his own a.** espontáneamente.
ac·cor·dance **in a. with** de acuerdo con.
ac·cord·ing·ly *adv* en consecuencia.
ac·cord·ing to *prep* según.
ac·cor·di·on acordeón *m.*
ac·count *(report)* informe *m*; *(at bank, in business)* cuenta *f*; **on a. of** a causa de; **to take a. of, to take into a.** tener en cuenta; **accounts department** servicio *m* de contabilidad; **current a.** cuenta *f* corriente.
▸**account for** *vt (explain)* explicar.
ac·count·ant contable *mf.*
ac·cu·mu·late 1 *vt* acumular. **2** *vi* acumularse.
ac·cu·rate *adj (number)* exacto, -a; *(answer)* correcto, -a; *(observation)* acertado, -a; *(translation)* fiel.
ac·cu·rate·ly *adv* con precisión
ac·cu·sa·tion acusación *f.*
ac·cuse *vt* acusar.
ac·cused *n* **the a.** el/la acusado(a).
ac·cus·tomed *adj* **to be a. to sth** estar acostumbrado a algo; **to get a. to sth** acostumbrarse a algo.
ace *(card & fig)* as *m*; *(in tennis)* ace *m.*
ache 1 *n* dolor *m.* **2** *vi* doler; **my back aches** me duele la espalda.
a·chieve *vt (attain)* conseguir; *(accomplish)* llevar a cabo.
a·chieve·ment *(attainment)* logro *m*; *(feat)* hazaña *f.*
a·cid 1 *adj* ácido, -a. **2** *n* ácido *m.*
a·cid rain lluvia *f* ácida.
ac·knowl·edge *vt (recognize)* reconocer; *(letter)* acusar recibo de; *(greet)* saludar.
ac·ne acné *m.*
a·corn bellota *f.*
a·cous·tics *npl* acústica *f sing.*
ac·quaint *vt* **to be acquainted with sb** conocer a algn; **to be acquainted with sth** estar al corriente de algo.
ac·quain·tance conocimiento *m*; *(person)* conocido, -a *mf*; **to make sb's a.** conocer a algn.
ac·quire *vt* adquirir.
a·cre acre *m (approx 40,47 áreas).*
ac·ro·bat·ic *adj* acrobático, -a.
a·cross 1 *adv* a través; **to go a.** atravesar; **to run a.** atravesar corriendo. **2** *prep* a través de; *(at the other side of)* al otro lado de; **they live a. the road** viven enfrente; **to go a. the street** cruzar la calle.
a·cryl·ic *adj* acrílico, -a.
act 1 *n (action)* acto *m*; *(parliamentary)* ley *f*; *(of play)* acto *m*; **a. of God** caso *m* de fuerza mayor. **2** *vt (part)* interpretar; *(character)* representar; **to a. like a fool** hacer el tonto. **3** *vi (pretend)* fingir; *(behave)* comportarse; *(take action)* actuar; *(work)* funcionar.
▸**act for** *vt* obrar en nombre de.
▸**act out** *vt* exteriorizar.
▸**act up** *vi fam (machine)* funcionar mal; *(child)* dar guerra.
ac·tion *(deed)* acción *f*; *(in war)* acción *f* de combate; **to be out of a.** *(person)* estar fuera de servicio; *(machine)* estar estropeado, -a; **to take a.** tomar medidas.
ac·ti·ve *adj* activo, -a; *(energetic)* vigoroso, -a; *(interest)* vivo, -a.
ac·tiv·i·ty actividad *f*; *(on street etc)* bullicio *m.*
ac·tor actor *m.*
ac·tress actriz *f.*
ac·tu·al *adj* verdadero, -a.
ac·tu·al·ly *adv (really)* en efecto; *(even)* incluso.
a·cute *adj* agudo, -a; *(pain)* intenso, -a; *(hearing)* muy fino, -a.
AD *abbr of* **Anno Domini** después de Cristo, d.C.
ad *fam* anuncio *m.*
a·dapt 1 *vt* adaptar (**to** a). **2** *vi* adaptarse.
a·dapt·a·ble *adj* **he's very a.** se amolda fácilmente a las circunstancias.
a·dap·ter, a·dap·tor *(plug)* ladrón *m.*
add 1 *vt (numbers)* sumar; *(one thing to another)* añadir. **2** *vi (count)* sumar.
▸**add in** *vt (include)* incluir.
▸**add to** *vt* aumentar.
▸**add together** *vt (numbers)* sumar.
▸**add up 1** *vt (numbers)* sumar. **2** *vi* **it doesn't a. up** no tiene sentido.
ad·dict adicto, -a *mf*; **drug a.** drogadicto, -a *mf*; **television a.** teleadicto, -a *mf.*
ad·dict·ed *adj* adicto, -a.
ad·dic·tion *(to gambling etc)* vicio *m*; *(to drugs)* adicción *f.*
ad·di·tion adición *f*; **in a. to** además de.
ad·di·tion·al *adj* adicional.
ad·di·tive aditivo *m.*
ad·dress 1 *n (on letter)* dirección *f*; *(speech)* discurso *m.* **2** *vt (letter)* dirigir; *(speak to)* dirigirse (**to** a).
ad·e·noids *npl* vegetaciones *fpl* (adenoideas).
ad·e·quate *adj (enough)* suficiente; *(satisfactory)* adecuado, -a.
ad·e·quate·ly *adv* suficientemente.
ad·here *vi (stick)* pegarse (**to** a).
▸**adhere to** *vt (policy)* adherirse a; *(contract)* cumplir con.
ad·he·sive 1 *adj* adhesivo, -a. **2** *n* adhesivo *m.*
ad·ja·cent *adj (building)* contiguo, -a; *(land)* colindante; **a. to** contiguo, -a a.
ad·jec·tive adjetivo *m.*
ad·just 1 *vt (machine etc)* ajustar; *(methods)* variar. **2** *vi (person)* adaptarse (**to** a).
ad·just·a·ble *adj* ajustable.
ad·just·ment *(by person)* adaptación *f*; *(change)* modificación *f.*
ad-lib *vi* improvisar.
ad·min·is·ter *vt (country)* gobernar; *(justice)* administrar.
ad·min·is·tra·tion *(of country)* gobierno *m*; *(of justice)* administración *f.*
ad·min·is·tra·tive *adj* administrativo, -a.
ad·mi·ral almirante *m.*
ad·mi·ra·tion admiración *f.*
ad·mire *vt* admirar.
ad·mis·sion *(to school etc)* ingreso *m*; *(price)* entrada *f*; *(of fact)* reconocimiento *m.*
ad·mit *vt (person)* dejar entrar; *(crime, guilt)* confesar.
ad·mit·tance *(entry)* entrada *f.*
ad·o·les·cent adolescente *mf.*
a·dopt *vt* adoptar.
a·dopt·ed *adj* **a. child** hijo, -a *mf* adoptivo, -a.
a·dop·tion adopción *f.*
a·dor·a·ble *adj* adorable.
a·dore *vt* adorar.
a·dult 1 *n (person)* adulto, -a *mf.* **2** *adj (film, education)* para adultos.
ad·vance 1 *n (movement)* avance *m*; *(progress)* progreso *m*; **in a.** de antemano. **2** *adj (before time)* adelantado, -a; **a. payment** pago *m* por adelantado. **3** *vt (troops)* avanzar; *(time, date)* adelantar; *(idea)* proponer; *(loan)* prestar. **4** *vi (move forward, make progress)* avanzar.
ad·vanced *adj (developed)* avanzado, -a; *(student)* adelantado, -a; *(course)* superior.
ad·van·tage ventaja *f*; **to take a. of sb** abusar de algn; **to take a. of sth** aprovechar algo.
ad·ven·ture aventura *f.*
ad·ven·tur·ous *adj (character)* aventurero, -a; *(bold)* atrevido, -a.
ad·verb adverbio *m.*
ad·ver·tise 1 *vt* anunciar. **2** *vi* hacer publicidad; *(in newspaper)* poner un anuncio; **to a. for sth/sb** buscar algo/a algn mediante un anuncio.
ad·ver·tise·ment anuncio *m*; **advertisements** publicidad *f sing.*
ad·vice consejos *mpl*; **a piece of a.** un consejo.
ad·vis·a·ble *adj* aconsejable.
ad·vise *vt* aconsejar; *(on business etc)* asesorar.
▸**advise against** *vt* desaconsejar.
ad·vis·er consejero, -a *mf*; *(in business etc)* asesor, -a *mf.*
ad·vo·cate 1 *n (supporter)* defensor, -a *mf.* **2** *vt* abogar por.
aer·i·al antena *f.*
aer·o·bics aerobic *m.*
aer·o·plane avión *m.*
aer·o·sol aerosol *m.*
aes·thet·ic *adj* estético, -a.
af·fair *(matter)* asunto *m*; **business affairs** negocios *mpl*; **love a.** aventura *f* amorosa.
af·fect *vt (person, health)* afectar; *(prices, future)* influir en.
af·fec·tion afecto *m.*
af·fec·tion·ate *adj* cariñoso, -a.
af·flu·ent *adj (society)* opulento, -a; *(person)* rico, -a.
af·ford *vt (be able to buy)* permitirse el lujo de.
af·ford·a·ble *adj (price etc)* asequible.
a·float *adv* **to keep a.** mantenerse a flote.
a·fraid *adj* **to be a.** tener miedo (**of sb** a algn; **of sth** de algo); **I'm a. of it** me da miedo; **I'm a. not/so** me temo que no/sí.
Af·ri·can *adj & n* africano, -a *(mf).*
af·ter 1 *adv* después; **the day a.** el día siguiente. **2** *prep (later)* después de; *(behind)* detrás de; **the day a. tomorrow** pasado mañana; **a. you!** ¡pase usted!; **they asked a. you** preguntaron por ti; **what's he a.?** ¿qué pretende?; **he takes a. his uncle** se parece a su tío. **3** *conj* después (de) que; **a. it happened** después de que ocurrió.
af·ter·ef·fects *npl* consecuencias *fpl*; *(of drug)* efectos *mpl* secundarios.
af·ter·noon tarde *f*; **good a.!** ¡buenas tardes!; **in the a.** por la tarde.
after-sales ser·vice servicio *m* posventa.
af·ter·shave loción *f* para después del afeitado.
af·ter·wards *adv* después.
a·gain *adv* otra vez; **a. and a.** repetidas veces; **to do sth a.** volver a hacer algo; **never a.!** ¡nunca más!; **now and a.** de vez en cuando.

a·gainst *prep* contra; **a. the law** ilegal.

age 1 *n* edad *f; fam (long time)* eternidad *f;* **underage** menor de edad; **old a.** vejez *f;* **the Iron A.** la Edad del Hierro. **2** *vti* envejecer.

ag·ed¹ *adj* de or a la edad de; *(old)* anciano, -a.

ag·ed² *npl* **the a.** los ancianos.

a·gen·cy agencia *f.*

a·gen·da orden *m* del día.

a·gent agente *mf; (representative)* representante *mf.*

ag·gra·vate *vt (worsen)* agravar; *(annoy)* molestar.

ag·gres·sion agresión *f.*

ag·gres·sive *adj* agresivo, -a.

ag·ile *adj* ágil.

ag·i·tat·ed *adj* inquieto, -a.

a·go *adv* **a week a.** hace una semana; **how long a.?** ¿hace cuánto tiempo?

ag·o·ny dolor *m* muy fuerte; *(mental)* angustia *f.*

a·gree *vi (be in agreement)* estar de acuerdo; *(reach agreement)* ponerse de acuerdo; **to a. to do sth** consentir en hacer algo; **onions don't a. with me** la cebolla no me sienta bien.

▶ **agree (up)on** *vt (decide)* ponerse de acuerdo en.

a·gree·a·ble *adj (pleasant)* agradable; *(person)* simpático, -a; *(in agreement)* de acuerdo.

a·greed *adj (time, place)* acordado, -a.

a·gree·ment *(arrangement)* acuerdo *m; (contract etc)* contrato *m.*

ag·ri·cul·tur·al *adj* agrícola.

ag·ri·cul·ture agricultura *f.*

a·head *adv* delante; *(early)* antes; **go a.!** ¡adelante!; **to be a.** *(in race etc)* llevar la ventaja; **to look a.** pensar en el futuro.

aid 1 *n* ayuda *f; (rescue)* auxilio *m;* **in a. of** a beneficio de. **2** *vt* ayudar.

AIDS SIDA *m.*

aim 1 *n (with weapon)* puntería *f; (objective)* propósito *m.* **2** *vti (gun)* apuntar (**at** a, hacia).

▶ **aim at** *vt (target)* apuntar a.

▶ **aim to** *vt* **to a. to do sth** tener la intención de hacer algo.

air 1 *n* aire *m;* **to travel by a.** viajar en avión; **to be on the a.** *(program)* estar emitiendo. **2** *vt (bed, clothes)* airear; *(room)* ventilar.

air-con·di·tioned *adj* climatizado, -a.

air con·di·tion·ing aire *m* acondicionado.

air·craft *inv* avión *m.*

air·craft car·ri·er portaaviones *m inv.*

air·fare precio *m* de billete de avión.

air force fuerzas *fpl* aéreas.

air fresh·en·er ambientador *m.*

air·line línea *f* aérea.

air·line tick·et billete *m* de avión.

air·mail correo *m* aéreo; **by a.** por avión.

air·plane avión *m.*

air·port aeropuerto *m.*

air raid ataque *m* aéreo.

air·sick·ness mareos *mpl* (del avión).

air·tight *adj* hermético, -a.

air traf·fic con·trol control *m* de tráfico aéreo.

air traf·fic con·trol·ler controlador *m* aéreo.

aisle *(in church)* nave *f; (in theater)* pasillo *m.*

a·jar *adj & adv* entreabierto, -a.

a·larm 1 *n* alarma *f; (fear)* inquietud *f.* **2** *vt* alarmar.

a·larm clock despertador *m.*

al·bum álbum *m.*

al·co·hol alcohol *m.*

al·co·hol·ic *adj & n* alcohólico, -a *(mf).*

a·lert 1 *adj* alerta; *(lively)* despabilado, -a. **2** *n* alerta *m.*

al·ge·bra álgebra *f.*

Al·ge·ri·an *adj & n* argelino, -a *(mf).*

a·li·as 1 *n (pl* **aliases)** alias *m.* **2** *adv* alias.

al·i·bi coartada *f.*

a·li·en *adj & n* extranjero, -a *(mf); (from space)* extraterrestre *mf.*

a·light *adj (on fire)* ardiendo, -a.

a·like 1 *adj (similar)* parecidos, -as; *(the same)* iguales. **2** *adv (in the same way)* de la misma manera, igualmente.

a·live *adj* vivo, -a; *fig (teeming)* lleno, -a (**with** de).

all 1 *adj* todo, -a, todos, -as; **a. year** *(durante)* todo el año; **a. kinds of things** todo tipo de cosas; **at a. times** siempre; **a. six of us were there** los seis estábamos allí. **2** *pron* todo, -a, todos, -as; **after a.** al fin y al cabo; **a. who saw it** todos los que lo vieron; **it's a. you can do** es lo único que puedes hacer; **I don't like it at a.** no me gusta en absoluto; **most of a., above a.** sobre todo; **once and for a.** de una vez para siempre; **thanks — not at a.** gracias — de nada; **a. in a.** en conjunto; **that's a.** ya está; **the score was one a.** empataron a uno; **it's still 3 a.** siguen empatados a tres. **3** *adv* **a. by myself** completamente solo, -a; **a. at once** *(suddenly)* de repente; *(altogether)* de una vez; **a. the better** tanto mejor; **a. the same** de todos modos; **if it's a. the same to you** si no te importa. **4** *n* **to give one's a.** darse por completo.

all-a·round *adj (athlete etc)* completo, -a.

al·le·giance lealtad *f* (**to** a).

al·ler·gic *adj* alérgico, -a (**to** a).

al·ley callejón *m.*

al·ley·way callejón *m.*

al·li·ance alianza *f.*

al·lied *adj (country)* aliado, -a; *(matters)* afín.

al·li·ga·tor caimán *m.*

al·lo·cate *vt* destinar (**to** para).

al·lot·ment *(land)* parcela *f.*

all-out *adj (effort)* supremo, -a; *(attack)* concentrado, -a.

al·low *vt (permit)* permitir; *(a request)* acceder a; *(allot) (time)* dejar; *(money)* destinar; **you're not allowed to do that** no puedes hacer eso; **I wasn't allowed to go** no me dejaron ir.

▶ **allow for** *vt* tener en cuenta.

al·low·ance *(payment)* subsidio *m; (discount)* descuento *m;* **to make allowances for sb** disculpar a algn; **travel a.** dietas *fpl* de viaje.

all-pur·pose *adj (tool)* multiuso, de uso universal.

all-right 1 *adj (okay)* bien; **thank you very much — that's a.** muchas gracias — de nada. **2** *adv (well)* bien; *(definitely)* sin duda; *(okay)* de acuerdo.

al·ly aliado, -a *mf.*

al·mond almendra *f.*

al·most *adv* casi.

a·lone 1 *adj* solo, -a; **let a.** ni mucho menos; **leave it a.!** ¡no lo toques!; **leave me a.** déjame en paz. **2** *adv* solamente.

a·long 1 *adv* **come a.!** ¡anda, ven!; **a. with** junto con. **2** *prep (the length of)* a lo largo de; **to walk a. the street** andar por la calle.

a·long·side 1 *adv* de costado. **2** *prep* al lado de.

a·loud *adv* en voz alta.

al·pha·bet alfabeto *m.*

al·pha·bet·i·cal *adj* alfabético, -a.

al·pha·bet·i·cal·ly *adv* por orden alfabético.

Alps *npl* **the A.** los Alpes.

al·read·y *adv* ya.

al·right *adj & adv* = **all right**.

al·so *adv* también.

al·tar altar *m.*

al·ter 1 *vt (plan)* cambiar; *(law, draft etc)* modificar. **2** *vi* cambiar(se).

al·ter·a·tion *(to plan)* cambio *m; (to law etc)* modificación *f; (to timetable)* revisión *f.*

al·ter·nate 1 *adj* alterno, -a; **on a. days** cada dos días. **2** *vt* alternar; **a alternates with b** a alterna con b.

al·ter·nate·ly *adv* **a. hot and cold** ahora caliente, ahora frío.

al·ter·na·tive 1 *adj* alternativo, -a. **2** *n* alternativa *f;* **I have no a.** no tengo más remedio.

al·ter·na·tive·ly *adv* o bien.

al·though *conj* aunque.

al·to·geth·er *adv (in total)* en total; *(completely)* completamente.

a·lu·mi·num aluminio *m.*

al·ways *adv* siempre.

am *1st person sing pres of* **be**.

a.m. *abbr of* ante meridiem de la mañana; **2 a.m.** las dos de la mañana.

am·a·teur 1 *n* aficionado, -a *mf.* **2** *adj* aficionado, -a; *(pejorative)* chapucero, -a.

a·maze *vt* asombrar; **to be amazed at sth** quedar pasmado, -a de algo.

a·maz·ing *adj* asombroso, -a.

am·bas·sa·dor embajador, -a *mf.*

am·ber 1 *adj (traffic light)* amarillo, -a, ámbar. **2** *n* ámbar.

am·big·u·ous *adj* ambiguo, -a.

am·bi·tion ambición *f.*

am·bi·tious *adj* ambicioso, -a.

am·bu·lance ambulancia *f;* **a. driver** ambulanciero *m.*

a·mend *vt (law)* enmendar; *(error)* subsanar.

A·mer·i·can *adj & n (of USA)* norteamericano, -a *(mf),* estadounidense *(mf); (of continent)* americano, -a *(mf).*

a·mid(st) *prep* entre, en medio de.

am·mu·ni·tion municiones *fpl.*

a·mong(st) *prep* entre.

am·o·rous *adj (person)* ligón, -ona; *(feelings, relationship)* amoroso, -a.

a·mount cantidad *f; (of money)* suma *f; (of bill)* importe *m.*

▶ **amount to** *vt* ascender a; *(be equivalent to)* equivaler a.

am·ple *adj (enough)* bastante; *(more than enough)* abundante; *(large)* amplio, -a.

am·pli·fi·er amplificador *m.*

am·pu·tate *vt* amputar.

a·muse *vt* divertir.

a·muse·ment diversión *f.*

a·muse·ment park parque *m* de atracciones.

a·mus·ing *adj* divertido, -a.

an *indef art see* **a**.

a·nal·y·sis *(pl* **analyses)** análisis *m inv.*

an·a·lyst *n* analista *mf; (psychoanalyst)* psicoanalista *mf.*

an·a·lyze *vt* analizar.

an·ar·chy anarquía *f.*

a·nat·o·my anatomía *f.*

an·ces·tor antepasado *m.*

an·chor 1 *n* ancla *f.* **2** *vt* anclar; *fig (fix securely)* sujetar.

an·cho·vy anchoa *f.*

an·cient *adj* antiguo, -a.

and *conj* y; *(before stressed i-, hi-)* e; **a hundred a. one** ciento uno; **a. so on** etcétera; **come a. see us** ven a vernos; **she cried a. cried** no paró de llorar; **try a. help me** trata de ayudarme; **wait a. see** espera a ver; **worse a. worse** cada vez peor.

an·es·thet·ic anestesia *f.*

an·gel ángel *m.*

an·ger cólera *f.*

an·gle ángulo *m; (point of view)* punto *m* de vista.

an·gler pescador, -a *mf* de caña.

an·gling pesca *f* con caña.

an·gri·ly *adv* furiosamente.

an·gry *adj* enfadado, -a; **to get a.** enfadarse.

an·i·mal *adj & n* animal *(m).*

an·kle tobillo *m;* **a. socks** calcetines *mpl* cortos.

an·nex *(building) (edificio m)* anexo *m.*

an·ni·ver·sa·ry aniversario *m.*

an·nounce *vt* anunciar; *(news)* comunicar.

an·nounce·ment anuncio *m; (news)* comunicación *f; (statement)* declaración *f.*

an·nounc·er *(on TV)* locutor, -a *mf.*

an·noy *vt* molestar; **to get annoyed** molestarse.

an·noy·ing *adj* molesto, -a.

an·nu·al 1 *adj* anual. **2** *n (book)* anuario *m.*

an·nu·al·ly *adv* anualmente.

a·non·y·mous *adj* anónimo, -a.

an·o·rak anorak *m.*

an·oth·er 1 *adj* otro, -a; **a. one** otro, -a; **a. 15** otros quince. **2** *pron* otro, -a; **to love one a.** quererse el uno al otro.

an·swer 1 *n (to letter etc)* contestación *f; (to question)* respuesta *f; (to problem)* solución *f;* **there's no a.** *(on telephone)* no contestan; *(at door)* no abren. **2** *vt* contestar a; *(problem)* resolver; *(door)* abrir; *(phone)* contestar. **3** *vi* contestar.

▶ **answer back** *vi* replicar; **don't a. back!** ¡no repliques!

▶ **answer for** *vt* responder de; **he's got a lot to a. for** es responsable de muchas cosas.

▶ **answer to** *vt (name)* responder a; *(description)* corresponder a.

an·swer·ing ma·chine contestador *m* automático.

ant hormiga *f.*

Ant·arc·tic 1 *adj* antártico, -a; **A. Ocean** océano *m* Antártico. **2** *n* **the A.** La Antártida.

an·te·lope antílope *m.*

an·ten·na *(pl* **antennae)** antena *f.*

an·them **national a.** himno *m* nacional.

an·thol·o·gy antología *f.*

an·ti·bi·ot·ic *adj & n* antibiótico, -a *(m).*

an·ti·bod·y anticuerpo *m.*

an·tic·i·pate *vt (expect)* esperar; *(problems)* anticipar.

an·tic·i·pa·tion *(excitement)* ilusión *f.*

an·tics *npl* payasadas *fpl; (naughtiness)* travesuras *fpl.*

an·ti·freeze anticongelante *m.*

an·ti·his·ta·mine *n* antihistamínico *m.*

an·tique 1 *adj* antiguo, -a. **2** *n* antigüedad *f.*

an·tique deal·er anticuario, -a *mf.*

an·tique shop tienda *f* de antigüedades.

an·ti·sep·tic *adj & n* antiséptico, -a *(m)*.
anx·i·e·ty *(concern)* inquietud *f*, *(worry)* preocupación *f*, *(eagerness)* ansia *f*.
anx·ious *adj (concerned)* inquieto, -a; *(worried)* preocupado, -a; *(fearful)* angustiado, -a; *(eager)* ansioso, -a.
anx·ious·ly *adv (to wait)* con impaciencia.
an·y 1 *adj (in questions, conditionals)* algún, -una; **are there a. seats left?** ¿quedan plazas?; **is there a. water left?** ¿queda agua?; **if you see a. blouses you like** si ves algunas blusas que te gusten. ▪ *(in negative clauses)* ningún, -una; **there aren't a. others** no hay otros. ▪ *(no matter which)* cualquier, -a; *(every)* todo, -a; **a. doctor will say the same** cualquier médico te dirá lo mismo; **at a. moment** en cualquier momento; **in a. case** de todas formas. **2** *pron (in questions, conditionals)* alguno, -a; **do they have a.?** ¿tienen alguno?; **I need some paper, do you have a.?** necesito papel, ¿tienes?; **if you see a., let me know** si ves alguno, -a, dímelo. ▪ *(in negative clauses)* ninguno, -a; **I don't want a.** no quiero ningu- no, -a. ▪ *(no matter which)* cualquiera; **a. of them will do** cualquiera vale. **3** *adv* **is there a. more?** ¿hay más?; **not a. more/longer** ya no; **is that a. better?** ¿está mejor así?
an·y·bod·y *pron (in questions, conditionals)* alguien; *(in negative clauses)* nadie; *(no matter who)* cualquiera; **bring a. you like** trae a quien quieras.
an·y·how *adv (in spite of that)* de todas formas; *(changing the subject)* bueno; *(carelessly)* de cualquier forma.
an·y·one *pron* = **anybody**.
an·y·place *adv* = **anywhere**.
an·y·thing *pron (in questions, conditionals)* algo, alguna cosa; *(in negative clauses)* nada; *(no matter what)* cualquier cosa; **a. but that** cualquier cosa menos eso; **a. else?** ¿algo más?; **hardly a.** casi nada; **to run/work like a.** correr/trabajar a más no poder.
an·y·way *adv* = **anyhow**.
an·y·where *adv (in questions, conditionals) (position)* en alguna parte; *(movement)* a alguna parte; **could it be a. else?** ¿podría estar en otro sitio? ▪ *(in negative clauses) (position)* en ninguna parte; *(movement)* a ninguna parte. ▪ *(no matter where)* en cualquier parte; **go a. you like** ve a donde quieras.
a·part *adv* **you should keep them a.** debes mantenerlos aparte; **to fall a.** deshacerse; **to take sth a.** desmontar algo; **with his feet a.** con los pies separados; **a. from** aparte de.
a·part·ment piso *m*; **a. complex** bloque *m* de pisos.
ape mono *m*.
a·pé·ri·tif aperitivo *m*.
a·pol·o·get·ic *adj* **he was very a.** pidió mil perdones.
a·pol·o·gize *vi* disculparse (**for** por).
a·pol·o·gy disculpa *f*.
a·pos·tro·phe apóstrofo *m*.
ap·pall *vt* horrorizar.
ap·pall·ing *adj (horrifying)* horroroso, -a; *(very bad)* fatal.
ap·pa·ra·tus aparato *m*; *(equipment)* equipo *m*.
ap·par·ent *adj (obvious)* evidente; *(seeming)* aparente; **to become a.** ponerse de manifiesto.
ap·par·ent·ly *adv (seemingly)* por lo visto.
ap·peal 1 *n (request)* solicitud *f*, *(plea)* súplica *f*, *(interest)* interés *m*; *(in law)* apelación *f*. **2** *vi (plead)* rogar (**to** a); **to a. for help** solicitar ayuda; **it doesn't a. to me** no me dice nada.
ap·pear *vi (become visible)* aparecer; *(publicly)* presentarse; *(seem)* parecer; **so it appears** según parece.
ap·pear·ance *(becoming visible)* aparición *f*, *(publicly)* presentación *f*, *(of book etc)* publicación *f*, *(look)* aspecto *m*; **to all appearances** al parecer.
ap·pen·di·ci·tis apendicitis *f*.
ap·pen·dix *(pl* **appendices**) apéndice *m*.
ap·pe·tite apetito *m*; *(sexual)* deseo *m*; **he's lost his a. for this sort of job** se le han quitado las ganas de un trabajo de este tipo.
ap·pe·tiz·ing *adj* apetitoso.
ap·plaud *vti* aplaudir.
ap·plause aplausos *mpl*, aplauso *m*.
ap·ple manzana *f*; **a. pie** tarta *f* de manzana; **a. tree** manzano *m*.
ap·pli·ance dispositivo *m*.
ap·pli·ca·ble *adj* aplicable (**to** a).
ap·pli·cant *(for post)* candidato, -a *mf*.
ap·pli·ca·tion *(of cream)* aplicación *f*, *(for post etc)* solicitud *f*, **a. form** solicitud *f*.
ap·ply 1 *vt* aplicar; *(brake)* echar; *(law)* recurrir a; *(force)* usar; **to a. oneself to sth** dedicarse a algo. **2** *vi (for job)* presentar una solicitud.
▸**apply for** *vt (post, information)* solicitar.
ap·point·ment *(to post)* nombramiento *m*; *(meeting)* cita *f*.
ap·prais·al evaluación *f*.
ap·pre·ci·ate 1 *vt (be thankful for)* agradecer; *(understand)* entender; *(value)* apreciar. **2** *vi (increase in value)* apreciarse.
ap·pre·ci·a·tion *(of help, advice)* agradecimiento *m*; *(of difficulty)* comprensión *f*, *(increase in value)* apreciación *f*.
ap·pren·tice aprendiz, -a *mf*.
ap·pren·tice·ship aprendizaje *m*.
ap·proach 1 *n (coming near)* acercamiento *m*; *(to town)* acceso *m*; *(to problem)* enfoque *m*. **2** *vt (come near to)* acercarse a; *(problem)* abordar. **3** *vi* acercarse.
ap·pro·pri·ate *adj (suitable)* apropiado, -a; *(convenient)* oportuno, -a.
ap·pro·pri·ate·ly *adv* adecuadamente.
ap·prov·al aprobación *f*, **on a.** sin compromiso de compra.
ap·prove *vt* aprobar.
▸**approve of** *vt (conduct, decision, idea)* aprobar.
ap·prox·i·mate *adj* aproximado, -a.
ap·prox·i·mate·ly *adv* aproximadamente.
a·pri·cot albaricoque *m*.
A·pril abril *m*; **A. Fools' Day** día *m* uno de abril, ≃ día de los Inocentes (28 de diciembre).
a·pron delantal *m*.
apt *adj (suitable)* apropiado, -a; *(description)* exacto, -a; **to be a. to do sth** *(liable)* tener tendencia a hacer algo.
ap·ti·tude capacidad *f*.
a·quar·i·um acuario *m*.
Ar·ab *adj & n* árabe *(mf)*.
A·ra·bi·an *adj* árabe.
Ar·a·bic 1 *adj* árabe; **A. numerals** numeración *f* arábiga. **2** *n (language)* árabe *m*.
ar·bi·trar·y *adj* arbitrario, -a.
arc arco *m*.
ar·cade arcada *f*, **shopping a.** galerías *fpl* (comerciales); **amusement a.** salón *m* de juegos.
arch 1 *n (of bridge etc)* arco *m*; *(roof)* bóveda *f*. **2** *vt (back)* arquear.
arch·er arquero, -a *mf*.
arch·er·y tiro *m* con arco.
ar·chi·tect arquitecto, -a *mf*.
ar·chi·tec·ture arquitectura *f*.
Arc·tic the **A.** el Ártico.
are *2nd person sing pres, 1st, 2nd, 3rd person pl pres of* **be**.
ar·e·a zona *f*, *(of surface)* superficie *f*.
ar·e·a code prefijo *m* local.
a·re·na *n (stadium)* estadio *m*; *(circus)* pista *f*.
Ar·gen·tin·i·an *adj & n* argentino, -a *(mf)*.
ar·gue 1 *vi (quarrel)* discutir; *(reason)* argumentar. **2** *vt* discutir; *(point of view)* mantener; **to a. that ...** sostener que ....
ar·gu·ment *(quarrel)* discusión *f*, disputa *f*, *(reason)* argumento *m* (**for** a favor de; **against** en contra de).
a·rise* *vi (get up)* levantarse; *(problem, need)* surgir.
a·rith·me·tic aritmética *f*.
arm 1 *n* brazo *m*; *(of garment)* manga *f*, **arms** *(weapons)* armas *fpl*. **2** *vt* armar.
arm·band brazalete *m*; *(for swimming)* manguito *m*.
arm·chair sillón *m*.
ar·mor *(of tank etc)* blindaje *m*; **(suit of) a.** armadura *f*.
ar·mored car coche *m* blindado.
arm·pit axila *f*.
ar·my ejército *m*.
a·round 1 *adv* alrededor; **all a.** por todos lados. **2** *prep* alrededor de; *(approximately)* aproximadamente; **a. the corner** a la vuelta de la esquina; **a. here** por aquí; **there's nobody a.** no hay nadie; **to rush a.** correr de un lado para otro.
a·rouse *vt* despertar; *(sexually)* excitar.
ar·range 1 *vt (order)* ordenar; *(hair, flowers)* arreglar; *(music)* adaptar; *(plan)* organizar; *(agree on)* quedar en; **to a. a time** fijar una hora. **2** *vi* **I shall a. for him to be there** lo arreglaré para que pueda asistir.
ar·range·ment *(display)* colocación *f*, *(of music)* adaptación *f*, *(agreement)* acuerdo *m*; **arrangements** *(plans)* planes *mpl*.
ar·rears *npl* atrasos *mpl*; **to be paid in a.** cobrar con retraso; **salaries are paid monthly in a.** los salarios se pagan mensualmente con un mes de retraso.
ar·rest 1 *n* detención *f*, **to be under a.** estar detenido, -a. **2** *vt (criminal)* detener.
ar·ri·val llegada *f*.
ar·rive *vi* llegar (**at, in** a).
ar·row flecha *f*.
art arte *m*; *(drawing)* dibujo *m*; **arts** *(branch of knowledge)* letras *fpl*.
ar·ter·y arteria *f*.
ar·thri·tis artritis *f*.
ar·ti·cle artículo *m*.
ar·tic·u·late[1] *adj (speech)* claro, -a; *(person)* que se expresa bien.
ar·tic·u·late[2] *vti* articular; *(words)* pronunciar.
ar·ti·fi·cial *adj* artificial.
art·ist artista *mf*, *(painter)* pintor, -a *mf*.
ar·tis·tic *adj* artístico, -a.
as *adv & conj (comparison)* **as ... as ...** tan ... como ...; **as far as** hasta; **as far as I'm concerned** por lo que a mí respecta; **as many as** tantos, -as como; **as much as** tanto, -a como; **as opposed to** a diferencia de; **as little as $5** tan sólo cinco dólares; **as soon as they arrive** en cuanto lleguen; **I'll stay as long as I can** me quedaré todo el tiempo que pueda; **just as big** igual de grande; **three times as fast** tres veces más rápido; **the same as** igual que. ▪ *(manner)* como; **as you like** como quieras; **leave it as it is** déjalo tal como está; **do as I say** haz lo que yo te digo; **it serves as a table** sirve de mesa; **she was dressed as a gypsy** iba vestida de gitana; **to act as if** actuar como si *(+ subjunctive)*. ▪ *(time)* mientras; **as a child** de niño, -a; **as I was eating** mientras comía; **as we were leaving we saw Pat** al salir vimos a Pat; **as from, as of** a partir de. ▪ *(because)* como, ya que; **as it is getting late** ya que se está haciendo tarde. ▪ *(and so)* igual que; **as I do** igual que yo; **as well** también. ▪ *(concerning)* **as for my brother** en cuanto a mi hermano.
ASAP *abbr of* **as soon as possible** lo antes posible.
as·cer·tain *vt (establish)* precisar, determinar; *(find out)* averiguar.
ash[1] *(tree)* fresno *m*.
ash[2] ceniza *f*.
a·shamed *adj* avergonzado, -a; **you ought to be a. of yourself!** ¿no te da vergüenza?
a·shore *adv* en tierra; **to go a.** desembarcar.
ash·tray cenicero *m*.
Ash Wednes·day miércoles *m inv* de ceniza.
A·sian *adj & n* asiático, -a *(mf)*.
a·side 1 *adv* aparte; **to stand a.** apartarse. **2** *prep* **a. from** *(apart from)* aparte de; *(as well as)* además de. **3** *n* aparte *m*.
ask 1 *vt* preguntar; *(request)* pedir; *(invite)* invitar; **to a. sb a question** preguntar algo a algn; **to a. sb how to do sth** preguntar a algn cómo se hace algo. **2** *vi (inquire)* preguntar; *(request)* pedir.
▸**ask after** *vt* preguntar por.
▸**ask for** *vt (help)* pedir; *(person)* preguntar por; **to a. sb for sth** pedir algo a algn.
a·sleep *adj* dormido, -a; **to fall a.** quedarse dormido, -a.
as·par·a·gus *inv* espárrago *m*.
as·pect aspecto *m*.
as·pi·rin aspirina *f*.
as·sault 1 *n* ataque *m* (**on** a); *(crime)* agresión *f*. **2** *vt* atacar; *(sexually)* violar.
as·sem·ble 1 *vt (people)* reunir; *(furniture)* montar. **2** *vi (people)* reunirse.
as·sem·bly assamblea *f*, *(of machinery etc)* montaje *m*; **morning a.** servicio *m* matinal.
as·sert *vt* afirmar; **to a. oneself** imponerse; **to a. one's rights** hacer valer sus derechos.
as·sess *vt (estimate value)* valorar; *(damages, price)* calcular; *(effect)* evaluar.
as·set ventaja *f*, **to be an a.** *(person)* ser de gran valor; **assets** activo *m*.
as·sign *vt* asignar.
as·sign·ment *(task)* tarea *f*.
as·sist *vti* ayudar.
as·sis·tance ayuda *f*.
as·sis·tant ayudante *mf*, **a. manager** subdirector, -a *mf*, **shop a.** dependiente, -a *mf*.
as·so·ci·ate[1] **1** *vt (ideas)* relacionar. **2** *vi* **to a. with** tratar con.
as·so·ci·ate[2] *(colleague)* colega *mf*, *(partner)* socio, -a *mf*, *(accomplice)* cómplice *mf*.
as·so·ci·a·tion asociación *f*, *(company)* sociedad *f*.
as·sort·ed *adj* surtido, -a.
as·sort·ment surtido *m*.
as·sume *vt (suppose)* suponer; *(power)* asumir; *(attitude, name)* adoptar.
as·sur·ance *(guarantee)* garantía *f*, *(confidence)* confianza *f*, *(insurance)* seguro *m*.
as·sure *vt* asegurar.
as·ter·isk asterisco *m*.
asth·ma asma *f*.
asth·mat·ic *adj & n* asmático, -a *(mf)*.
a·ston·ish *vt* asombrar.
a·ston·ish·ing *adj* asombroso, -a.
a·stray *adv* **to go a.** extraviarse; *fig* equivocarse.
as·trol·o·gy astrología *f*.
as·tro·naut astronauta *mf*.
as·tron·o·my astronomía *f*.
a·sy·lum *(protection)* asilo *m*; **to seek political a.** pedir asilo político; **mental a.** manicomio *m*.
at *prep (position)* en, a; **at school/work** en el colegio/trabajo; **at the window** a la ventana; **at the top** en lo alto. ▪ *(direction)* a; **to look at sth/sb** mirar algo/a algn; **to shout at sb** gritarle a algn. ▪ *(time)* a; **at Easter/Christmas** en Semana Santa/Navidad; **at six o'clock** a las seis. ▪ **at best/worst** en el mejor/peor de los casos; **not at all** en absoluto; *(don't mention it)* de nada. ▪

(rate) a; **at 100 dollars each** a 100 dólares la unidad; **two at a time** de dos en dos.

ath·lete atleta *mf.*

ath·let·ic *adj* atlético, -a; *(sporty)* deportista.

ath·let·ics *npl* atletismo *m sing.*

At·lan·tic the A. (Ocean) el (océano) Atlántico.

at·las atlas *m.*

at·mos·phere *(air)* atmósfera *f; (ambience)* ambiente *m.*

at·om átomo *m;* **a. bomb** bomba *f* atómica.

a·tom·ic *adj* atómico, -a.

at·tach *vt (stick)* pegar; *(document)* adjuntar; **to be attached to** *(be fond of)* tener cariño a.

at·ta·ché agregado, -a *mf;* **a. case** maletín *m.*

at·tack 1 *n* ataque *m.* **2** *vt (assault)* atacar; *(problem)* abordar.

at·tack·er agresor, -a *mf.*

at·tain *vt (aim)* lograr; *(rank, age)* llegar a.

at·tempt 1 *n* intento *m;* **at the second a.** a la segunda. **2** *vt* intentar.

at·tend 1 *vt (school)* frecuentar; *(meeting)* asistir a. **2** *vi (at meeting)* asistir.

▶**attend to** *vt (business)* ocuparse de; *(in shop)* atender a.

at·ten·dance asistencia *f.*

at·ten·dant *(in museum)* guía *mf; (in parking lot)* vigilante, -a *mf.*

at·ten·tion atención *f;* **for the a. of** a la atención de.

at·ten·tive *adj (listener)* atento, -a; *(helpful)* solícito, -a.

at·tic ático *m.*

at·ti·tude actitud *f; (position of body)* postura *f.*

at·tor·ney abogado, -a *mf;* **A. General** ≈ Ministro, -a *mf* de Justicia; **district a.** fiscal *mf.*

at·tract *vt* atraer; **to a. attention** llamar la atención.

at·trac·tion *(attractive thing)* atractivo *m; (charm)* encanto *m.*

at·trac·tive *adj (person)* atractivo, -a; *(idea, proposition)* atrayente.

at·trib·ute¹ *n (quality)* atributo *m.*

at·trib·ute² *vt* atribuir **(to** a).

auc·tion 1 *n* subasta *f.* **2** *vt* subastar.

auc·tion·eer subastador, -a *mf.*

au·di·ble *adj* audible.

au·di·ence *(spectators)* público *m; (at concert, conference)* auditorio *m; (television)* telespectadores *mpl; (meeting)* audiencia *f.*

au·di·o *adj* de sonido.

au·di·o·vi·su·al *adj* audiovisual.

au·dit 1 *n* revisión *f* de cuentas. **2** *vt* revisar, intervenir.

Au·gust agosto *m.*

aunt *(also fam* **auntie, aunty)** tía *f.*

au pair a. (girl) au pair *f.*

Aus·tra·lian *adj & n* australiano, -a *(mf).*

Aus·tri·an *adj & n* austríaco, -a *(mf).*

au·then·tic *adj* auténtico, -a.

au·thor autor, -a *mf.*

au·thor·i·ty autoridad *f;* **local a.** ayuntamiento *m.*

au·thor·ize *vt* autorizar; *(payment etc)* aprobar.

au·to·bi·og·ra·phy autobiografía *f.*

au·to·graph 1 *n* autógrafo *m.* **2** *vt (book, photo)* dedicar.

au·to·mat·ic 1 *adj* automático, -a. **2** *n (car)* coche *m* automático.

au·to·mat·i·cal·ly *adv* automáticamente.

au·to·mo·bile automóvil *m, Am* carro *m.*

au·ton·o·mous *adj* autónomo, -a.

au·tumn otoño *m.*

aux·il·ia·ry *adj* auxiliar.

a·vail·a·ble *adj (thing)* disponible; *(person)* libre.

av·a·lanche avalancha *f.*

av·e·nue avenida *f, fig* vía *f.*

av·er·age 1 *n* promedio *m;* **on a.** por término medio. **2** *adj* medio, -a; *(middle)* regular.

a·vi·a·tion aviación *f.*

av·o·ca·do *(also* **avocado pear)** aguacate *m.*

a·void *vt* evitar; **to a. doing sth** evitar hacer algo.

a·void·a·ble *adj* evitable.

a·wake 1 *adj* despierto, -a. **2** *vi** despertarse.

a·ward 1 *n (prize)* premio *m; (medal)* condecoración *f; (grant)* beca *f.* **2** *vt (prize)* otorgar; *(medal)* dar; *(damages)* adjudicar.

a·ware *adj (informed)* enterado, -a; **not that I'm a. of** que yo sepa no; **to become a. of sth** darse cuenta de algo.

a·way *adv* **far a.** lejos; **go a.!** ¡lárgate!; **it's 3 miles a.** está a 3 millas (de distancia); **keep a. from the fire!** ¡no te acerques al fuego!; **right a.** en seguida; **to be a.** *(absent)* estar ausente; **to go a.** irse; **to play a.** *(in sport)* jugar fuera; **to turn a.** volver la cara; **to chatter/work a.** hablar/trabajar sin parar.

aw·ful *adj* espantoso, -a; *fam* **an a. lot of work** muchísimo trabajo.

aw·ful·ly *adv fam* terriblemente.

awk·ward *adj (clumsy)* torpe; *(difficult)* pesado, -a; *(moment)* inoportuno, -a.

awn·ing *(on shop)* marquesina *f.*

ax 1 *n* hacha *f.* **2** *vt (jobs)* suprimir; *(cut back)* reducir; *(plan)* cancelar.

ax·is *(pl* **axes)** eje *m.*

ax·le eje *m.*

B

BA *abbr of* **Bachelor of Arts.**

ba·by bebé *m; (young child)* niño, -a *mf.*

ba·by car·riage cochecito *m* de niño.

ba·by·sit *vi* hacer de canguro.

ba·by·sit·ter canguro *mf.*

bach·e·lor soltero *m;* **B. of Arts/Science** licenciado, -a *mf* en Filosofía y Letras/Ciencias.

back 1 *n (of person)* espalda *f; (of chair)* respaldo *m; (of hand)* dorso *m; (of house, car)* parte *f* de atrás; *(of stage, cupboard)* fondo *m;* **b. to front** al revés. **2** *adj* trasero, -a; **b. door** puerta *f* de atrás; **b. seat** asiento *m* de detrás; **b. wheel** rueda *f* trasera; **b. number** número *m* atrasado. **3** *adv (at the rear)* atrás; *(towards the rear)* hacia atrás. **4** *vt (support)* apoyar; *(financially)* financiar; *(bet on)* apostar por.

▶**back out** *vi (withdraw)* volverse atrás.

▶**back up** *vt (support)* apoyar a.

back·ache dolor *m* de espalda.

back·fire *vi (car)* petardear.

back·ground fondo *m; (origin)* origen *m; (past)* pasado *m; (education)* formación *f; (circumstances)* antecedentes *mpl;* **b. music** hilo *m* musical.

back·ing *(support)* apoyo *m; (financial)* respaldo *m* financiero.

back·log **to have a b. of work** tener un montón de trabajo atrasado.

back·pack mochila *f.*

back·side *fam* trasero *m.*

back·stage *adv* entre bastidores.

back·up *(of disk)* copia *f* de seguridad.

back·ward 1 *adj (movement)* hacia atrás; *(child, country)* retrasado, -a. **2** *adv* (hacia) atrás.

back·wards *adv* hacia atrás; **to walk b.** andar de espaldas.

back·yard jardín *m* trasero.

ba·con tocino *m,* beicon *m.*

bac·te·ri·a *npl* bacterias *fpl.*

bad *adj* malo, -a; *(decayed)* podrido, -a; *(accident)* grave; *(headache)* fuerte; *(ill)* enfermo, -a.

badge insignia *f; (metal disc)* chapa *f.*

badg·er tejón *m.*

bad·ly *adv* mal; *(seriously)* gravemente; *(very much)* mucho; **we need it b.** nos hace mucha falta; **to be b. off** *(financially)* andar mal de dinero.

bad-man·nered *adj* maleducado.

bad·min·ton bádminton *m.*

bad-tem·pered *adj* **to be b.** *(temperament)* tener mal genio; *(temporarily)* estar de mal humor.

baf·fle *vt* desconcertar.

bag *(plastic, paper, shopping)* bolsa *f, (handbag)* bolso *m; fam* **bags of** montones de; **bags** *(under eyes)* ojeras *fpl.*

bag·gage equipaje *m.*

bag·gy *adj* holgado, -a; **b. trousers** pantalones *mpl* anchos.

bag·pipes *npl* gaita *f sing.*

bail fianza *f;* **on b.** bajo fianza.

bait cebo *m.*

bake *vt* cocer al horno.

baked *adj* al horno; **b. potato** patata *f* asada.

baked beans alubias *fpl* cocidas en salsa de tomate.

bak·er panadero, -a *mf.*

bak·er·y panadería *f.*

bal·ance 1 *n (equilibrium)* equilibrio *m; (financial)* saldo *m; (remainder)* resto *m.* **2** *vt* poner en equilibrio **(on** en); *(budget)* equilibrar. **3** *vi* guardar el equilibrio.

bal·ance sheet balance *m.*

bal·co·ny balcón *m.*

bald *adj* calvo, -a.

bald·ness calvicie *f.*

Bal·kans *npl* **the B.** los Balcanes.

ball¹ *(in baseball, tennis etc)* pelota *f, (football)* balón *m; (in billiards, golf etc)* bola *f, (of wool)* ovillo *m;* **to be on the b.** *fam* ser un espabilado.

ball² *(dance)* baile *m.*

bal·le·ri·na bailarina *f.*

bal·let ballet *m.*

bal·loon globo *m.*

bal·lot votación *f.*

ball·point (pen) bolígrafo *m.*

ball·room salón *m* de baile.

ban 1 *n* prohibición *f.* **2** *vt (prohibit)* prohibir; *(exclude)* excluir.

ba·nan·a plátano *m, Am* banana *f.*

band *(strip)* tira *f; (stripe)* raya *f; (group)* grupo *m; (of musicians)* banda *f.*

band·age 1 *n* venda *f.* **2** *vt* vendar.

Band-Aid® tirita® *f.*

bang *n (blow)* golpe *m; (noise)* ruido *m; (explosion)* estallido *m; (of gun)* estampido *m.*

▶**bang into** *vt* golpearse contra.

bang·er *fam (firework)* petardo *m;* **old b.** *(car)* coche *m* destartalado.

ban·gle brazalete *m.*

ban·is·ter(s) pasamanos *m inv.*

bank¹ *(for money)* banco *m.*

bank² *(of river)* ribera *f,* orilla *f.*

▶**bank on** *vt* contar con.

bank ac·count cuenta *f* bancaria.

bank card tarjeta *f* bancaria.

bank·er banquero, -a *mf.*

bank·ing banca *f.*

bank·rupt *adj* en quiebra; **to go b.** quebrar.

bank·rupt·cy bancarrota *f.*

ban·ner *(in demonstration)* pancarta *f.*

bar 1 *n (of gold)* barra *f; (of chocolate)* tableta *f; (of cage)* barrote *m; (pub)* bar *m; (counter)* barra *f; (of soap)* pastilla *f.* **2** *vt (door)* atrancar; *(road)* cortar; *(exclude)* excluir **(from** de); *(prohibit)* prohibir.

bar·be·cue barbacoa *f.*

barbed *adj* **b. wire** alambre *m* de espino.

bar·ber barbero, -a *mf;* **b.'s (shop)** barbería *f.*

bare *adj* desnudo, -a; *(head)* descubierto, -a; *(foot)* descalzo, -a; *(room)* sin muebles; **with his b. hands** sólo con las manos.

bare·foot *adj & adv* descalzo, -a.

bare·ly *adv* apenas.

bar·gain 1 *n (deal)* negocio *m; (cheap purchase)* ganga *f,* **b. price** precio *m* de oferta. **2** *vi* negociar.

▶**bargain for** *vt* esperar; **I hadn't bargained for this** no contaba con esto.

barge gabarra *f.*

▶**barge in** *vi (go in)* entrar sin permiso.

▶**barge into** *vt (room)* irrumpir en; *(person)* tropezar con.

bark¹ *vi (dog)* ladrar.

bark² *(of tree)* corteza *f.*

bark·ing ladridos *mpl.*

bar·ley cebada *f.*

barn granero *m.*

ba·rom·e·ter barómetro *m.*

bar·racks *npl* cuartel *m sing.*

bar·rage *(dam)* presa *f.*

bar·rel *(of wine)* tonel *m; (of beer, oil)* barril *m; (of firearm)* cañón *m.*

bar·ren *adj* estéril; *(land)* yermo, -a.

bar·rette pasador *m* (del pelo).

bar·ri·cade 1 *n* barricada *f.* **2** *vt* cerrar con barricadas.

bar·ri·er barrera *f.*

bar·tend·er camarero *m.*

base 1 *n* base *f; (foot)* pie *m; (of column)* basa *f.* **2** *vt* basar **(on** en).

base·ball béisbol *m.*

base·ment sótano *m.*

bash 1 *n (heavy blow)* golpetazo *m; (dent)* bollo *m.* **2** *vt* golpear.

▶**bash up** *vt* **to b. sb up** darle a algn una paliza.

ba·sic 1 *adj* básico, -a; **b. pay** sueldo *m* base. **2** *npl* **basics** lo fundamental.
ba·si·cal·ly *adv* fundamentalmente.
ba·sin *(washbowl)* palangana *f*, *(for washing up)* barreño *m*; *(in bathroom)* lavabo *m*.
ba·sis (*pl* **bases**) base *f*; **on the b. of** en base a.
bask *vi (in sunlight)* tostarse.
bas·ket *(big)* cesta *f*, *(small)* cesto *m*.
bass 1 *n (singer)* bajo *m*; *(notes)* graves *mpl*; **b. drum** bombo *m*; **b. guitar** bajo *m*. **2** *adj* bajo, -a.
bat[1] *(in baseball)* bate *m*.
bat[2] *(animal)* murciélago *m*.
bat[3] *vt* **without batting an eyelid** sin pestañear.
batch *(of bread)* hornada *f*, *(of goods)* lote *m*.
bath 1 *n* baño *m*; *(tub)* bañera *f*; **to have a b.** bañarse. **2** *vt* bañar.
bathe *vi* bañarse.
bath·ing baño *m*.
bath·ing suit traje *m* de baño.
bath·ing trunks *npl* bañador *m*.
bath·robe albornoz *m*.
bath·room cuarto *m* de baño.
bath·tub bañera *f*.
bat·ter 1 *n* pasta para rebozar. **2** *vt (baby)* maltratar.
▸**batter down** *vt (door)* derribar.
bat·tered *adj (car)* desvencijado, -a.
bat·ter·y *(for radio)* pila *f*; *(for car)* batería *f*.
bat·tle 1 *n* batalla *f*; *fig* lucha *f*. **2** *vi* luchar.
bat·tle·ship acorazado *m*.
baud baudio *m*.
bawl *vi* gritar.
bay bahía *f*; *(large)* golfo *m*.
BC *abbr of* **before Christ** a.C.
be* **1** *vi (permanent state)* ser; **he is very tall** es muy alto; **Washington is the capital** Washington es la capital; **sugar is sweet** el azúcar es dulce. ▪ *(temporary state, location)* estar; **how are you?** ¿cómo estás?; **this soup is cold** esta sopa está fría. ▪ *(cost)* **a return ticket is $24** un billete de ida y vuelta cuesta 24 dólares; **how much is it?** ¿cuánto es? ▪ *(weather)* **it's foggy** hay niebla; **it's cold/hot** hace frío/calor. ▪ *(time, date)* ser; **it's one o'clock** es la una; **it's four o'clock** son las cuatro; **it's the 11th/Tuesday today** hoy es 11/martes. ▪ **to be cold/afraid/hungry** tener frío/miedo/hambre; **she is thirty (years old)** tiene treinta años. **2** *v aux* estar; **he is writing a letter** está escribiendo una carta; **she was singing** cantaba; **they are leaving next week** se van la semana que viene; **we have been waiting for a long time** hace mucho que estamos esperando. ▪ *(passive)* ser; **he was murdered** fue asesinado. ▪ *(obligation)* **I am to see him this afternoon** debo verle esta tarde. ▪ **there is, there are** hay; **there was, there were** había; **there will be** habrá; **there would be** habría; **there have been a lot of complaints** ha habido muchas quejas; **there were ten of us** éramos diez. ▪ *(in tag questions)* ¿verdad?, ¿no?; **you're happy, aren't you?** estás contento, ¿verdad?
beach playa *f*.
bea·con baliza *f*; *(lighthouse)* faro *m*.
bead *(of necklace etc)* cuenta *f*; *(of liquid)* gota *f*.
beak *(of bird)* pico *m*.
beam *(in building)* viga *f*; *(of light)* rayo *m*.
beam·ing *adj (smiling)* radiante.
bean alubia *f*, judía *f*, *Am* frijol *m*; **broad b.** haba *f*; **coffee b.** grano *m* de café; **green** *or* **runner b.** judía *f* verde.
bear[1]* **1** *vt (carry)* llevar; *(endure)* soportar; **to b. in mind** tener presente. **2** *vi* **to b. left** girar a la izquierda.
▸**bear out** *vt* confirmar.
bear[2] *(animal)* oso *m*.
bear·a·ble *adj* soportable.
beard barba *f*.
beard·ed *adj* barbudo, -a.
bear·ing *(relevance)* relación *f*; **to have a b. on** estar relacionado, -a con; **to get one's bearings** orientarse.
beast bestia *f*.
beast·ly *adj fam* asqueroso, -a.
beat 1 *vt** *(hit)* pegar; *(drum)* tocar; *(in cooking)* batir; *(defeat)* vencer. **2** *vi** *(heart)* latir. **3** *n (of heart)* latido *m*; *(of policeman)* ronda *f*.
▸**beat down** *vi (sun)* caer a plomo.
▸**beat off** *vt* rechazar.
▸**beat up** *vt* dar una paliza a.
beat·ing *(thrashing)* paliza *f*; *(defeat)* derrota *f*.
beau·ti·ful *adj* hermoso, -a, bello, -a.
beau·ty belleza *f*, hermosura *f*.
beau·ty spot *(on face)* lunar *m*; *(place)* lugar *m* pintoresco.
bea·ver castor *m*.
be·cause 1 *conj* porque. **2** *prep* **b. of** a causa de.
be·come* *vi (doctor, priest)* hacerse; *(mayor, officer)* llegar a ser; *(angry, sad)* ponerse; **what has b. of him?** ¿qué ha sido de él?
bed cama *f*; **to get out of b.** levantarse de la cama; **to go to b.** acostarse; **b. and breakfast** *(service)* cama *f* y desayuno *m*; *(sign)* 'pensión'.
bed·ding ropa *f* de cama.
bed·room dormitorio *m*.
bed·side b. table mesilla *f* de noche.
bed·time hora *f* de acostarse.
bee abeja *f*.
beech haya *f*.
beef carne *f* de vaca, *Am* carne *f* de res.
been *pp of* **be**.
beep 1 *n* pitudo *m*. **2** *vi* pitar.
beep·er busca(personas) *m inv*.
beer cerveza *f*; **a glass of b.** una caña.
beet red b. remolacha *f*.
bee·tle escarabajo *m*.
be·fore 1 *conj (earlier than)* antes de que *(+ subjunctive)*, antes de *(+ infinitive)*; **b. she goes** antes de que se vaya; **b. leaving** antes de salir. **2** *prep (place)* delante de; *(in the presence of)* ante; *(order, time)* antes de. **3** *adv (time)* antes; *(place)* (por) delante; **I have met him b.** ya lo conozco; **the night b.** la noche anterior.
be·friend *vt* trabar amistad con.
beg 1 *vt (money etc)* pedir; *(beseech)* rogar. **2** *vi (solicit)* mendigar; **to b. for money** pedir limosna.
beg·gar mendigo, -a *mf*.
be·gin* *vti* empezar, comenzar; **to b. doing** *or* **to do sth** empezar a hacer algo; **to b. with ...** para empezar ...
be·gin·ner principiante *mf*.
be·gin·ning principio *m*, comienzo *m*; **at the b. of May** a principios de mayo.
be·grudge *vt* dar de mala gana; *(envy)* envidiar; **to b. sb sth** envidiarle algo a algn.
be·half nombre *m*; **on b. of, in b. of** de parte de.
be·have *vi (person)* (com)portarse; **b. yourself!** ¡pórtate bien!
be·hav·ior comportamiento *m*, conducta *f*; *(of machine)* funcionamiento *m*.
be·hind 1 *prep* detrás de. **2** *adv (in the rear)* detrás, atrás; **I've left my umbrella b.** se me ha olvidado el paraguas; **to be b. with one's payments** estar atrasado, -a en los pagos. **3** *n fam (bottom)* trasero *m*.
beige *adj & n* beige *(m)*.
belch 1 *vi* eructar. **2** *n* eructo *m*.
Bel·gian *adj & n* belga *(mf)*.
be·lief creencia *f*; *(opinion)* opinión *f*; *(faith)* fe *f*; *(confidence)* confianza *f* (**in** en).
be·liev·a·ble *adj* creíble.
be·lieve *vti* creer; **I b. so** creo que sí; **to b. in sb/sth** creer en algn/ algo.
be·liev·er *(religious)* creyente *mf*.
be·lit·tle *vt (person)* restar importancia a.
bell *(of church)* campana *f*; *(small)* campanilla *f*; *(of school, door, bicycle)* timbre *m*; *(on animal)* cencerro *m*.
bell·boy botones *m inv*.
bel·ly *(of person)* barriga *f*, tripa *f*.
bel·ly·ache *fam* dolor *m* de barriga.
be·long *vi* pertenecer (**to** a); *(be a member)* ser socio, -a (**to** de).
be·long·ings *npl* efectos *mpl* personales.
be·low 1 *prep* debajo de. **2** *adv* abajo.
belt cinturón *m*; *(in machine)* correa *f*; *(area)* zona *f*.
▸**belt along** *vi fam* ir a todo gas.
bench *(seat)* banco *m*.
bend 1 *vt** doblar; *(back)* encorvar; *(head)* inclinar. **2** *vi** doblarse; *(road)* torcerse; **to b. (over)** inclinarse. **3** *n (in river, road)* curva *f*; *(in pipe)* recodo *m*.
▸**bend down** *vi* inclinarse.
be·neath 1 *prep (below)* bajo, debajo de. **2** *adv* debajo.
ben·e·fi·cial *adj (doing good)* benéfico, -a; *(advantageous)* beneficioso, -a.
ben·e·fit 1 *vt* beneficiar. **2** *vi* sacar provecho (**from** *or* **by** de). **3** *n (advantage)* beneficio *m*; *(allowance)* subsidio *m*; **I did it for your b.** lo hice por tu bien.
bent *adj (curved)* curvado, -a; **to be b. on doing sth** *(determined)* estar empeñado, -a en hacer algo.
be·reave·ment duelo *m*.
ber·ry baya *f*.
ber·serk *adj* **to go b.** volverse loco, -a.
berth *(bed)* litera *f*.
be·side *prep (next to)* al lado de, junto a; *(compared with)* comparado con; **that's b. the point** eso no viene al caso.
be·sides 1 *prep (in addition to)* además de; *(except)* excepto. **2** *adv* además.
best 1 *adj* mejor; **the b. thing would be to phone them** lo mejor sería llamarles; **the b. part of a year** casi un año. **2** *adv* mejor; **as b. I can** lo mejor que pueda. **3** *n* lo mejor; **to do one's b.** hacer todo lo posible; **to make the b. of sth** sacar el mejor partido de algo.
best man ≃ padrino *m* de boda.
best·sell·er best-seller *m*.
bet 1 *n* apuesta *f*. **2** *vti** apostar (**on** a).
be·tray *vt* traicionar.
be·tray·al traición *f*.
bet·ter 1 *adj* mejor; **that's b.!** ¡eso es!; **to get b.** mejorar; *(healthier)* mejor; **b. off** *(richer)* más rico, -a; **the b. part of the day** la mayor parte del día. **2** *adv* mejor; **we had b. leave** más vale que nos vayamos. **3** *vt (improve)* mejorar; *(surpass)* superar.
bet·ting apuestas *fpl*.
be·tween 1 *prep* entre; **b. you and me** entre nosotros; **closed b. 1 and 3** cerrado de 1 a 3. **2** *adv* en medio; **in b.** *(position)* en medio; *(time)* mientras (tanto).
bev·er·age bebida *f*.
be·ware *vi* tener cuidado (**of** con); **b.!** ¡cuidado!
be·wil·der *vt* desconcertar.
be·yond 1 *prep* más allá de; **it is b. me why ...** no comprendo por qué ...; **this task is b. me** no puedo con esta tarea. **2** *adv* más allá.
bi·as *(tendency)* tendencia *f* (**towards** hacia); *(prejudice)* prejuicio *m*.
bi·as(s)ed *adj* parcial; **to be b. against sth/sb** tener prejuicio en contra de algo/algn.
bib *(for baby)* babero *m*.
Bi·ble Biblia *f*.
bi·cy·cle bicicleta *f*.
bid 1 *vti** *(at auction)* pujar (**for** por). **2** *n (offer)* oferta *f*; *(at auction)* puja *f*.
big *adj* grande (gran *before sing noun*); **a b. clock** un reloj grande; **a b. surprise** una gran sorpresa; **my b. brother** mi hermano mayor; *fam* **b. deal!** ¿y qué?
big·head *fam* engreído, -a *mf*.
bike *(bicycle)* bici *f*; *(motorcycle)* moto *f*.
bike path carril *m* bici.
bi·ki·ni bikini *m*.
bile bilis *f*.
bi·lin·gual *adj* bilingüe.
bill *(for gas etc)* factura *f*; *(in restaurant)* cuenta *f*; *(in Congress)* proyecto *m* de ley; *(currency)* billete *m* (de banco).
bill·board cartelera *f*.
bill·fold billetero *m*.
bil·liards billar *m*.
bil·lion *(thousand million)* mil millones *mpl*.
bin *(for storage)* cajón *m*; **(garbage) b.** cubo *m* de la basura.
bind* *vt (tie up)* atar; *(book)* encuadernar.
bind·er *(file)* carpeta *f*.
bin·go bingo *m*.
bin·oc·u·lars *npl* prismáticos *mpl*.
bi·o·log·i·cal *adj* biológico, -a.
bi·ol·o·gy biología *f*.
birch *(tree)* abedul *m*.
bird *(small)* pájaro *m*; *(large)* ave *f*.
bird's-eye view vista *f* de pájaro.
birth nacimiento *m*; **to give b. to a child** dar a luz a un niño.
birth cer·tif·i·cate partida *f* de nacimiento.
birth·day cumpleaños *m inv*.
birth·mark antojo *m*.
bis·cuit bizcocho *m*.
bish·op obispo *m*; *(chess)* alfil *m*.
bit *(small piece)* trozo *m*; *(small quantity)* poco *m*; **a b. of sugar** un poco de azúcar; **b. by b.** poco a poco; **a b.** *(slightly)* un poco.
bitch 1 *n (dog)* perra *f*; *fam (spiteful woman)* bruja *f*. **2** *vi fam* **to b. (about)** *(criticize)* criticar.
bite 1 *n (act)* mordisco *m*; *(wound)* mordedura *f*; *(mouthful, snack)* bocado *m*; **(insect) b.** picadura *f*. **2** *vti** morder; *(insect)* picar; **to b. one's nails** morderse las uñas.
bit·ter *adj* amargo, -a; *(weather)* glacial; *(wind)* cortante; *(person)* amargado, -a; *(struggle)* enconado, -a; *(hatred)* implacable.
bit·ter·ness amargura *f*; *(of weather)* crudeza *f*; *(of person)* rencor *m*.
bi·zarre *adj (odd)* extraño, -a; *(eccentric)* estrafalario, -a.

black 1 *adj (color)* negro, -a; *fig* **b. and blue** amoratado, -a. **2** *n (color)* negro *m*; *(person)* negro, -a *mf*.
▸**black out** *vi (faint)* desmayarse.
black·ber·ry zarzamora *f*.
black·bird mirlo *m*.
black·board pizarra *f*, encerado *m*.
black·cur·rant grosella *f* negra.
black eye ojo *m* amoratado.
black·list lista *f* negra.
black·mail 1 *n* chantaje *m*. **2** *vt* chantajear.
black·mail·er chantajista *mf*.
black·out *(of lights)* apagón *m*; *(fainting)* pérdida *f* de conocimiento.
blad·der vejiga *f*.
blade *(of grass)* brizna *f*; *(of knife etc)* hoja *f*.
blame 1 *n* culpa *f*. **2** *vt* echar la culpa a; **he is to b.** él tiene la culpa.
blame·less *adj (person)* inocente; *(conduct)* intachable.
bland *adj (food)* soso, -a.
blank 1 *adj (without writing)* en blanco; **b. check** cheque *m* en blanco. **2** *n (space)* espacio *m* en blanco.
blan·ket manta *f*.
blare *vi* resonar.
▸**blare out** *vt* pregonar.
blast 1 *n (of wind)* ráfaga *f*; *(of horn etc)* toque *m*; *(explosion)* explosión *f*; *(shock wave)* onda *f* de choque. **2** *vt fam* **b. (it)!** ¡maldito sea!
blast·ed *adj* maldito, -a.
blast-off despegue *m*.
blaze 1 *n (burst of flame)* llamarada *f*; *(fierce fire)* incendio *m*; *(of sun)* resplandor *m*. **2** *vi (fire)* arder; *(sun etc)* brillar.
blaz·er chaqueta *f* sport.
bleach *(household)* lejía *f*.
bleak *adj (countryside)* desolado, -a.
bleed* *vti* sangrar.
blem·ish *(flaw)* defecto *m*; *(on fruit)* maca *f*, *fig* **without b.** sin tacha.
blend 1 *n* mezcla *f*. **2** *vt (mix)* mezclar; *(match)* armonizar. **3** *vi (mix)* mezclarse.
blend·er *(for food)* licuadora *f*.
bless *vt* bendecir; **b. you!** *(after sneeze)* ¡Jesús!
bless·ing bendición *f*; *(advantage)* ventaja *f*.
blew *pt of* **blow**.
blind 1 *adj* ciego, -a; **a b. man** un ciego; **a b. woman** una ciega. **2** *n (on window)* persiana *f*, *pl* **the b.** los ciegos.
blind·fold 1 *n* venda *f*. **2** *vt* vendar los ojos a.
blind·ly *adv* a ciegas; *(love)* ciegamente.
blind·ness ceguera *f*.
blink *vi (eyes)* pestañear; *(lights)* parpadear.
bliss felicidad *f*.
blis·ter *(on skin)* ampolla *f*.
bliz·zard ventisca *f*.
blob *(drop)* gota *f*; *(spot)* mancha *f*.
block 1 *n* bloque *m*; *(of wood)* taco *m*; *(group of buildings)* manzana *f*, **a b. of apartments** un bloque de pisos. **2** *vt (obstruct)* obstruir.
▸**block up** *vt* bloquear; **to get blocked up** *(pipe)* obstruirse.
block·age bloqueo *m*.
bloke *fam* tío *m*, tipo *m*.
blond *adj & n* rubio *(m)*.
blonde *adj & n* rubia *(f)*.
blood sangre *f*; **b. donor** donante *mf* de sangre; **b. group** grupo *m* sanguíneo; **b. pressure** tensión *f* arterial; **high/low b. pressure** hipertensión *f*/hipotensión *f*.
blood·shed derramamiento *m* de sangre.
blood·shot *adj* inyectado, -a de sangre.
blood·y *adj (battle)* sangriento, -a; *(bloodstained)* manchado, -a de sangre.
bloom 1 *n (flower)* flor *f*, **in full b.** en flor. **2** *vi (blossom)* florecer.
blos·som 1 *n (flower)* flor *f*. **2** *vi* florecer.
blot *(of ink)* borrón *m*.
blotch·y *adj (skin)* enrojecido, -a; *(paint)* cubierto, -a de manchas.
blouse blusa *f*.
blow¹ *vt* golpe *m*.
blow²* 1 *vi (wind)* soplar. **2** *vt (trumpet etc)* tocar; *(smoke)* echar; *(of wind)* llevarse; **to b. one's nose** sonarse la nariz.
▸**blow away** *vt* **the wind blew it away** el viento se lo llevó.
▸**blow down** *vt* derribar.
▸**blow off 1** *vt (remove)* quitar. **2** *vi (hat)* salir volando.
▸**blow out** *vt* apagar. **2** *vi* apagarse.
▸**blow up 1** *vt (building)* volar; *(inflate)* inflar. **2** *vi (explode)* explotar.
blow dry 1 *vt* secar con secador, marcar. **2** *n* marcado *m*.
blow·torch soplete *m*.
blue 1 *adj* azul; *(sad)* triste. **2** *n* azul *m*.
blue·ber·ry arándano *m*.
blue·print proyecto *m*.
bluff 1 *n (deception)* farol *m*. **2** *vi* tirarse un farol.
blun·der 1 *n* metedura *f* de pata, *fam* patinazo *m*. **2** *vi* meter la pata.
blunt *adj (knife)* embotado, -a; *(pencil)* despuntado, -a; *(frank)* directo, -a; *(statement)* tajante.
blur 1 *n* **he was just a b.** apenas se le veía. **2** *vt (shape)* desdibujar; *(memory)* enturbiar.
blurred *adj* borroso, -a.
blush *vi* ruborizarse.
blus·ter·y *adj* borrascoso, -a.
board 1 *n (plank)* tabla *f*; *(meals)* pensión *f*; **full b.** pensión completa; **room and b.** casa *f* y comida; **b. of directors** consejo *m* de administración; **on b.** a bordo. **2** *vt (ship, plane etc)* embarcarse en.
board·er *(in boarding house)* huésped *mf*; *(at school)* interno, -a *mf*.
board·ing *(embarkation)* embarque *m*.
board·ing house pensión *f*.
board·ing pass tarjeta *f* de embarque.
board·ing school internado *m*.
boast *vi* jactarse **(about** de).
boat barco *m*; *(small)* barca *f*; *(large)* buque *m*.
bod·i·ly *adj* físico, -a.
bod·y cuerpo *m*; *(corpse)* cadáver *m*; *(organization)* organismo *m*.
bod·y·guard guardaespaldas *mf inv*.
bod·y·work carrocería *f*.
bo·gus *adj* falso, -a.
boil¹ 1 *n* **to come to a b.** empezar a hervir. **2** *vt (water, egg)* hervir; *(food)* cocer. **3** *vi* hervir.
▸**boil over** *vi (milk)* salirse.
boil² *(on skin)* furúnculo *m*.
boiled *adj* **b. egg** huevo *m* pasado por agua.

boil·er caldera *f*.
boil·ing *adj (water)* hirviente; **it's b. hot** *(food)* quema; *(weather)* hace un calor agobiante.
bold *adj (courageous)* valiente; *(dress, proposition etc)* audaz, atrevido.
bold·ness audacia *f*, descaro *m*, osadía *f*.
Bo·liv·i·an *adj & n* boliviano, -a *(mf)*.
bolt 1 *n (on door)* cerrojo *m*; *(small)* pestillo *m*; *(with nut)* tornillo *m*. **2** *vt (lock)* cerrar con cerrojo; *(food)* engullir. **3** *vi (person)* largarse; *(horse)* desbocarse.
bomb 1 *n* bomba *f*. **2** *vt (city etc)* bombardear; *(by terrorists)* volar.
bomb·er bombardero *m*.
bomb·ing bombardeo *m*.
bond *(link)* vínculo *m*; *(financial)* bono *m*.
bone hueso *m*; *(in fish)* espina *f*.
bon·fire hoguera *f*.
bon·net *(child's)* gorro *m*.
bo·nus plus *m*; *(on wages)* prima *f*; *(on shares)* dividendo *m* extraordinario.
bon·y *adj (person)* huesudo, -a; *(fish)* lleno, -a de espinas.
boo 1 *interj* ¡bu! **2** *vt* abuchear.
boo·by trap trampa *f*; *(bomb etc)* trampa *f* explosiva.
book 1 *n* libro *m*; *(of stamps)* carpeta *f*; *(in commerce)* **books** cuentas *fpl*. **2** *vt (reserve)* reservar.
book·case estantería *f*.
booked up *adj* completo, -a.
book·ing *(reservation)* reserva *f*.
book·ing of·fice taquilla *f*.
book·keep·er contable *mf*.
book·keep·ing contabilidad *f*.
book·let *(pamphlet)* folleto *m*.
book·mak·er corredor, -a *mf* de apuestas.
book·sell·er librero, -a *mf*.
book·shelf estantería *f*.
book·store librería *f*.
boom *(noise)* estampido *m*; *(sudden prosperity)* auge *m*.
boost 1 *n* estímulo *m*. **2** *vt (increase)* aumentar; *(tourism, exports)* fomentar; **to b. sb's confidence** subirle la moral a algn.
boot *n* bota *f*; *(short)* botín *m*; *fam* **she got the b.** la echaron (del trabajo).
▸**boot out** *vt fam* echar a patadas.
booth *(in language lab etc)* cabina *f*, **telephone b.** cabina *f* telefónica.
booze *fam* **1** *n* priva *f*. **2** *vi* privar.
bor·der *n* borde *m*; *(frontier)* frontera *f*.
▸**border on** *vt (country)* lindar con.
bor·der·line 1 *adj (case etc)* dudoso, -a. **2** *n* línea *f* divisoria, frontera *f*.
bore 1 *vt* aburrir. **2** *n (person)* pesado, -a *mf*; *(thing)* lata *f*, **what a b.!** ¡qué rollo!
bore·dom aburrimiento *m*.
bor·ing *adj* aburrido, -a, pesado, -a.
born *adj* nacido, -a; **to be b.** nacer; **I was b. in 1969** nací en 1969.
bor·ough municipio *m*.
bor·row *vt* pedir prestado; **can I b. your pen?** ¿me dejas tu bolígrafo?
boss *n (head)* jefe, -a *mf*; *(factory owner etc)* patrón, -ona *mf*.
▸**boss around** *vt* ser mandón, -ona con.
boss·y *adj* mandón, -ona.
botch 1 *vt* chapucear; **a botched job** una chapuza. **2** *n* chapuza *f*.
both 1 *adj* ambos, -as, los/las dos; **b. men are teachers** ambos son profesores; **hold it with b. hands** sujétalo con las dos manos. **2** *pron* **b. (of them)** ambos, -as, los/las dos; **b. of you** vosotros dos. **3** *adv* a la vez; **b. New York and Ohio are in the U.S.** tanto Nueva York como Ohio están en los Estados Unidos.
both·er 1 *vt (disturb)* molestar; *(be a nuisance to)* dar la lata a; *(worry)* preocupar; **I can't be bothered** no tengo ganas; **he didn't b. shaving** no se molestó en afeitarse. **2** *vi* **don't b.** no te molestes. **3** *n (disturbance)* molestia *f*; *(nuisance)* lata *f*, *(trouble)* problemas *mpl*. **4** *interj* ¡maldito sea!
bot·tle botella *f*; *(of perfume, ink)* frasco *m*; **baby's b.** biberón *m*.
bot·tle o·pen·er abrebotellas *m inv*.
bot·tom 1 *adj (lowest)* más bajo, -a. **2** *n* parte *f* inferior; *(of sea, garden, street, box, bottle)* fondo *m*; *(of page, hill)* pie *m*; *(buttocks)* trasero *m*; **to be at the b. of the class** ser el último/la última de la clase.
boul·der canto *m* rodado.
bounce 1 *vi (ball)* rebotar; *(check)* ser rechazado, -a (por el banco). **2** *vt (ball)* botar.
bound¹ *adj* **he's b. to know** es seguro que lo sabe; **it's b. to happen** sucederá con toda seguridad; **it was b. to fail** estaba destinado al fracaso.
bound² *adj* **to be b. for** dirigirse a.
bound·a·ry límite *m*.
bounds *npl* **the river is out of b.** está prohibido bajar al río.
bou·quet *(of flowers)* ramillete *m*.
bou·tique boutique *f*.
bow¹ 1 *vi* hacer una reverencia. **2** *n (with head, body)* reverencia *f*.
bow² *(for violin, arrows)* arco *m*; *(knot)* lazo *m*.
bow·els *npl* entrañas *fpl*.
bowl¹ *(dish)* cuenco *m*; *(for soup)* tazón *m*; *(for washing clothes, dishes)* barreño *m*.
bowl² *vi (in cricket)* lanzar la pelota.
bowl·er *(hat)* bombín *m*.
bowl·ing *(game)* bolos *mpl*.
bowl·ing alley bolera *f*.
bowl·ing pin bolo *m*.
bowls *npl* bolos *mpl*.
bow tie pajarita *f*.
box¹ caja *f*; *(large)* cajón *m*.
box² 1 *vi* boxear. **2** *vt (hit)* pegar.
▸**box in** *vt (enclose)* aprisionar.
box·er boxeador *m*; *(dog)* bóxer *m*.
box·ing boxeo *m*; **b. ring** cuadrilátero *m*.
box of·fice taquilla *f*.
boy *(child)* chico *m*; *(youth)* joven *m*.
boy·cott 1 *n* boicot *m*. **2** *vt* boicotear.
boy·friend novio *m*; *(live-in)* compañero *m*.
bra sostén *m*.
brace·let pulsera *f*.
brack·et *(round)* paréntesis *m*; *(square)* corchete *m*.
brag *vi* jactarse **(about** de).
brag·ging fanfarronería *f*.
braid 1 *vt* trenzar. **2** *n* trenza *f*.
brain cerebro *m*; **brains** inteligencia *f*, **to have brains** ser inteligente.
brain·storm *(brilliant idea)* genialidad *f*.
brain·wash *vt* lavar el cerebro a.
brain·y *adj fam* inteligente.
brake 1 *n* freno *m*. **2** *vi* frenar.
brake light luz *f* de freno.

branch 1 *n (of tree)* rama *f*; *(of road)* bifurcación *f*; **b. (office)** sucursal *f*. **2** *vi (road)* bifurcarse.
▸ **branch off** *vi* desviarse.
▸ **branch out** *vi* diversificarse.
brand marca *f*; **b. name** marca *f* de fábrica.
brand-new *adj* flamante.
bran·dy brandy *m*.
brass latón *m*.
brave *adj* valiente.
brav·er·y valentía *f*.
brawl reyerta *f*.
brawn·y *adj* fornido, -a.
Bra·zil·i·an *adj & n* brasileño, -a *(mf)*.
bread pan *m*; **b. and butter** pan con mantequilla.
bread·box panera *f*.
bread·crumb miga *f* de pan; **breadcrumbs** pan *m sing* rallado.
breadth *(width)* anchura *f*, *(extent)* amplitud *f*.
bread·win·ner cabeza *mf* de familia.
break 1 *n (of tree)* romper; *(fail to keep)* faltar a; *(destroy)* destrozar; *(financially)* arruinar; *(journey)* interrumpir; *(record)* batir; **to b. a leg** romperse la pierna; **to b. the law** violar la ley; **she broke the news to him** le comunicó la noticia. **2** *vi** romperse; *(storm)* estallar; *(story)* divulgarse. **3** *n (fracture)* rotura *f*, *(crack)* grieta *f*, *(in a relationship)* ruptura *f*, *(pause)* pausa *f*, *(at school)* recreo *m*; *fam (chance)* oportunidad *f*; **to take a b.** descansar un rato; *(holiday)* tomar unos días libres; **a lucky b.** un golpe de suerte.
▸ **break away** *vi (become separate)* desprenderse *(from de)*.
▸ **break down 1** *vt (door)* derribar; *(resistance)* acabar con. **2** *vi (in car)* tener una avería; *(weep)* ponerse a llorar.
▸ **break in** *vi (burglar)* entrar a la fuerza.
▸ **break into** *vt (house)* allanar; *(safe)* forzar.
▸ **break loose** *vi* escaparse.
▸ **break off 1** *vt (relations)* romper. **2** *vi (become detached)* desprenderse; *(talks)* interrumpirse; *(stop)* pararse.
▸ **break out** *vi (prisoners)* escaparse; *(war etc)* estallar.
▸ **break up 1** *vt (object)* romper; *(car)* desguazar; *(crowd)* disolver. **2** *vi* romperse; *(crowd)* disolverse; *(meeting)* levantarse; *(relationship)* fracasar; *(couple)* separarse; *(at end of term)* terminar.
break·down avería *f*, *(in communications)* ruptura *f*, **(nervous) b.** crisis *f* nerviosa.
break·fast desayuno *m*; **to have b.** desayunar.
break·in robo *m* (con allanamiento de morada).
break·through avance *m*.
break·up *(in marriage)* separación *f*.
breast *(chest)* pecho *m*; *(of chicken etc)* pechuga *f*.
breast·feed *vt* dar el pecho a.
breast·stroke braza *f*.
breath aliento *m*; **out of b.** sin aliento.
Breath·a·lyz·er® alcoholímetro *m*.
breathe *vti* respirar.
▸ **breathe in** *vi* aspirar.
▸ **breathe out** *vi* espirar.
breath·ing respiración *f*; **b. space** respiro *m*.
breath·tak·ing *adj* impresionante.
breed 1 *n (of animal)* raza *f*. **2** *vt** *(animals)* criar. **3** *vi** *(animals)* reproducirse.
breed·er *(person)* criador, -a *mf*.
breed·ing *(of animals)* cría *f*, *(of person)* educación *f*, **b. ground** caldo *m* de cultivo.
breeze brisa *f*.
breez·y *adj (weather)* ventoso, -a.
brew 1 *vt (beer)* elaborar; *(hot drink)* preparar. **2** *vi (tea)* reposar; **a storm is brewing** se prepara una tormenta; **something's brewing** algo se está cociendo.
brew·er·y cervecería *f*.
bribe 1 *vt* sobornar. **2** *n* soborno *m*.
brick ladrillo *m*.
brick·lay·er albañil *m*.
bride novia *f*; **the b. and groom** los novios.
bride·groom novio *m*.
brides·maid dama *f* de honor.
bridge puente *m*.
brief 1 *adj (short)* breve; *(concise)* conciso, -a. **2** *n* **briefs** *(for men)* calzoncillos *mpl*; *(for women)* bragas *fpl*. **3** *vt (inform)* informar; *(instruct)* dar instrucciones a.
brief·case cartera *f*.
brief·ing *(meeting)* reunión *f* informativa.
brief·ly *adv* brevemente.
bright *adj (light, sun, eyes)* brillante; *(color)* vivo, -a; *(day)* claro, -a; *(cheerful)* alegre; *(clever)* listo, -a.
bright·en *vi (prospects)* mejorar; *(face)* iluminarse.
▸ **brighten up 1** *vt (room etc)* hacer más alegre. **2** *vi (weather)* despejarse; *(person)* animarse.
bright·ly *adv* brillantemente.
bright·ness *(of sun)* resplandor *m*; *(of color)* viveza *f*.
bril·liance *(of light)* brillo *m*, *(of color)* viveza *f*, *(of person)* brillantez *f*.
bril·liant *adj* brillante; *(idea)* genial; *(very good)* estupendo, -a.
bring* *vt* traer; *(take to a different position)* llevar; *(cause)* provocar; **could you b. that book?** ¿podrías traerme el libro?
▸ **bring about** *vt* provocar.
▸ **bring along** *vt* traer.
▸ **bring around** *vt (revive)* hacer volver en sí; *(persuade)* convencer.
▸ **bring back** *vt (return)* devolver; *(reintroduce)* volver a introducir; *(make one remember)* traer a la memoria.
▸ **bring down** *vt (from upstairs)* bajar (algo); *(government)* derribar; *(reduce)* rebajar.
▸ **bring forward** *vt (meeting etc)* adelantar.
▸ **bring in** *vt (yield)* dar; *(show in)* hacer entrar; *(law etc)* introducir.
▸ **bring out** *vt (publish)* publicar; *(emphasize)* recalcar.
▸ **bring to** *vt* reanimar.
▸ **bring together** *vt (reconcile)* reconciliar.
▸ **bring up** *vt (educate)* educar; *(subject)* plantear; *(vomit up)* vomitar.
brink *(edge)* borde *m*.
brisk *adj* enérgico, -a; *(pace)* rápido, -a; *(trade)* activo, -a.
brisk·ly *adv (to walk)* rápidamente.
bris·tle cerda *f*.
Brit·ish 1 *adj* británico, -a; **the B. Isles** las Islas Británicas. **2** *npl* **the B.** los británicos.
Brit·on británico, -a *mf*.
brit·tle *adj* quebradizo, -a.
broad *adj (road, river)* ancho, -a; *(not detailed)* general; **in b. daylight** a plena luz del día.
broad·cast 1 *n* emisión *f*. **2** *vt** emitir.
broad·en *vt* ensanchar.
broc·co·li brécol *m*.
bro·chure folleto *m*.

broke *adj* **to be (flat) b.** estar sin blanca.
bro·ken *adj* roto, -a; *(machinery)* averiado, -a; *(leg)* fracturado, -a; **a b. home** una familia deshecha.
bro·ken-down *adj (machine)* averiado, -a.
bron·chi·tis bronquitis *f*.
bronze bronce *m*.
brooch broche *m*.
brood 1 *n (of birds)* cría *f*. **2** *vi (ponder)* rumiar; **to b. over a problem** darle vueltas a un problema.
brood·y *adj (pensive)* pensativo, -a; *(moody)* melancólico, -a; *fam (woman)* con ganas de tener hijos.
brook arroyo *m*.
broom escoba *f*; *(plant)* retama *f*.
broom·stick palo *m* de escoba.
broth·er hermano *m*; **brothers and sisters** hermanos.
broth·er-in-law cuñado *m*.
brought *pt & pp of* **bring**.
brow *(forehead)* frente *f*, *(eyebrow)* ceja *f*, *(of hill)* cima *f*.
brown 1 *adj* marrón; *(hair)* castaño, -a; *(tanned)* moreno, -a. **2** *n* marrón *m*.
browse *vi (person in shop)* mirar; *(through book)* hojear.
bruise 1 *n* morado *m*, cardenal *m*. **2** *vt* contusionar.
bruised *adj* amoratado, -a.
brunch combinación *f* de desayuno y almuerzo.
bru·nette *adj & n* morena *(f)*.
brush 1 *n (for hair, teeth)* cepillo *m*; *(artist's)* pincel *m*; *(for house-painting)* brocha *f*. **2** *vt* cepillar; **to b. one's hair/teeth** cepillarse el pelo/los dientes.
▸ **brush aside** *vt* dejar de lado.
▸ **brush off** *vt* ignorar.
▸ **brush up (on)** *vt* repasar.
bru·tal *adj* brutal, cruel.
bru·tal·i·ty brutalidad *f*.
brute *(animal)* bruto *m*; *(person)* bestia *f*.
BS *abbr of* **Bachelor of Science**.
bub·ble burbuja *f*.
▸ **bubble over** *vi* rebosar.
buck *fam* dólar *m*.
buck·et cubo *m*.
buck·le 1 *n* hebilla *f*. **2** *vt* abrochar (con hebilla). **3** *vi (wall, metal)* combarse.
▸ **buck up 1** *vt* **b. your ideas up!** ¡espabílate! **2** *vi (cheer up)* animarse.
bud 1 *n (shoot)* brote *m*; *(flower)* capullo *m*. **2** *vi* brotar.
Bud·dhist *adj & n* budista *(mf)*.
bud·dy *fam Am* compadre *m*, *Esp* colega *m*.
budge *vi (move)* moverse.
budg·er·i·gar periquito *m*.
budg·et 1 *n* presupuesto *m*; **the B.** *(of the state)* los presupuestos del Estado. **2** *vi* hacer un presupuesto **(for** para**)**.
buf·fa·lo *(pl* **buffaloes***)* búfalo *m*.
buff·er *n (device)* parachoques *m inv*; *(in computer)* memoria *f* intermedia.
buf·fet *(snack bar)* bar *m*; *(self-service meal)* bufet *m* libre.
bug 1 *n (insect)* bicho *m*; *(microbe)* microbio *m*; **I've got a b.** tengo alguna infección; *(hidden microphone)* micrófono *m* oculto; *(in computer program)* error *m*. **2** *vt fam (annoy)* fastidiar.
bug·gy *(baby's stroller)* cochecito *m* de niño.
bu·gle bugle *m*.
build 1 *vt** construir. **2** *n (physique)* físico *m*.
build·er constructor, -a *mf*; *(contractor)* contratista *mf*.
build·ing edificio *m*.
built-in *adj (cupboard)* empotrado, -a; *(incorporated)* incorporado, -a.
built-up *adj* urbanizado, -a.
bulb *(of plant)* bulbo *m*; *(lightbulb)* bombilla *f*.
Bul·gar·i·an *adj & n* búlgaro, -a *(mf)*.
bulge 1 *n* protuberancia *f*, *(in pocket)* bulto *m*. **2** *vi (swell)* hincharse; *(be full)* estar repleto, -a.
bulg·ing *adj* abultado, -a; *(eye)* saltón.
bulk *(mass)* masa *f*, volumen *m*; *(greater part)* mayor parte *f*.
bulk·y *adj* voluminoso, -a.
bull toro *m*.
bull·dog buldog *m*.
bull·doz·er bulldozer *m*.
bul·let bala *f*.
bul·le·tin boletín *m*.
bul·le·tin board tablón *m* de anuncios.
bul·let-proof *adj* a prueba de balas; **b. vest** chaleco *m* antibalas.
bull·fight corrida *f* de toros.
bull·fight·er torero, -a *mf*.
bull·fight·ing los toros *mpl*; *(art)* tauromaquia *f*.
bull·ring plaza *f* de toros.
bul·ly 1 *n* matón *m*. **2** *vt* intimidar.
bum *fam (tramp)* vagabundo *m*, *(idler)* holgazán, -ana *mf*.
▸ **bum around** *vi fam* vaguear.
bum·ble·bee abejorro *m*.
bump 1 *n (swelling)* chichón *m*; *(on road)* bache *m*, *(blow)* golpe *m*, *(jolt)* sacudida *f*. **2** *vt* golpear; **to b. one's head** darse un golpe en la cabeza.
▸ **bump into** *vt (meet)* tropezar con.
bump·er *(on vehicle)* parachoques *m inv*.
bump·y *adj (road)* con muchos baches.
bun *(bread)* panecillo *m*, *(sweet)* magdalena *f*.
bunch *(of keys)* manojo *m*; *(of flowers)* ramo *m*; *(of grapes)* racimo *m*; *(of people)* grupo *m*.
bun·dle 1 *n (of clothes)* bulto *m*; *(of papers)* fajo *m*. **2** *vt (make bundle of)* liar; *(push)* empujar.
bun·ga·low bungalow *m*.
bunk *(bed)* litera *f*.
bun·ny *fam* **b. (rabbit)** conejito *m*.
buoy boya *f*.
bur·den 1 *n* carga *f*. **2** *vt* cargar **(with** con**)**.
bu·reau *(pl* **bureaux***)* *(office)* agencia *f*, oficina *f*, *(chest of drawers)* cómoda *f*.
bu·reauc·ra·cy burocracia *f*.
bur·er *fam* hamburguesa *f*.
bur·glar ladrón, -ona *mf*.
bur·glar a·larm alarma *f* antirrobo.
bur·glar·ize *vt* robar.
bur·gla·ry robo *m* en una casa.
bur·gle *vt* robar.
bur·i·al entierro *m*.
burn 1 *n* quemadura *f*. **2** *vt** quemar. **3** *vi** *(fire)* arder; *(building, food)* quemarse; *(ointment etc)* escocer.
▸ **burn down 1** *vt* incendiar. **2** *vi* incendiarse.

burn·er *(on stove)* quemador *m.*
burn·ing *adj (on fire)* ardiendo, -a en llamas.
burp 1 *n* eructo *m.* **2** *vi* eructar.
burst 1 *n (explosion)* estallido *m; (of tire)* reventón *m;* **b. of laughter** carcajada *f.* **2** *vt* (balloon)* reventar. **3** *vi** reventarse; *(shell)* estallar.
▸ **burst into** *vi* **b. into laughter/tears** echarse a reír/llorar; **to b. into a room** irrumpir en una habitación.
▸ **burst out** *vi* **to b. out laughing** echarse a reír.
burst·ing *adj* **the bar was b. with people** el bar estaba atestado de gente.
bur·y *vt* enterrar; *(hide)* ocultar; **to be buried in thought** estar absorto en pensamientos.
bus *(pl buses or busses)* autobús *m;* **b. shelter** marquesina *f* (de autobús); **b. station** estación *f* de autobuses.
bush *(shrub)* arbusto *m.*
bush·y *adj* espeso, -a.
busi·ness *(commerce)* negocios *mpl; (firm)* empresa *f; (matter)* asunto *m;* **on b.** de negocios; **b. hours** horas *fpl* de oficina; **b. trip** viaje *m* de negocios; **it's no b. of mine** no es asunto mío; **mind your own b.** no te metas en donde no te llaman.
busi·ness·man hombre *m* de negocios.
busi·ness·wom·an mujer *f* de negocios.
bus stop parada *f* de autobús.
bust¹ *(of woman)* pecho *m; (sculpture)* busto *m.*
bust² *adj fam* **to go b.** quebrar.
bus·tle *(activity, noise)* bullicio *m.*
▸ **bustle about** *vi* ir y venir.
bus·tling *adj* bullicioso, -a.
bus·y *adj* ocupado, -a; *(life)* ajetreado, -a; *(street)* concurrido, -a; *(telephone)* ocupado, -a; **b. signal** señal *f* de comunicando.
bus·y·bod·y entrometido, -a *mf,* cotilla *mf.*
but 1 *conj* pero; *(after negative)* sino; **not two b. three** no dos sino tres. **2** *prep* menos; **everyone b. her** todos menos ella.
butch·er carnicero, -a *mf,* **b.'s (shop)** carnicería *f.*
but·ler mayordomo *m.*
butt *(of cigarette)* colilla *f, fam (bottom)* culo *m.*
but·ter 1 *n* mantequilla *f.* **2** *vt* untar con mantequilla.
but·ter·cup botón *m* de oro.
but·ter·fly mariposa *f.*
but·tock nalga *f,* **buttocks** nalgas *fpl.*
but·ton 1 *n* botón *m.* **2** *vt* **to b. (up) one's jacket** abotonarse la chaqueta.
but·ton·hole ojal *m.*
buy 1 *n* **a good b.** una ganga. **2** *vt** comprar; **she bought that car from a neighbor** compró ese coche a un vecino.
buy·er comprador, -a *mf.*
buzz 1 *n (of bee)* zumbido *m; (of conversation)* rumor *m.* **2** *vi* zumbar.
▸ **buzz off** *vi fam* largarse.
by 1 *prep (indicating agent)* por; **composed by Bach** compuesto, -a por Bach; **a film by Almodóvar** una película de Almodóvar. ▪ *(via)* por; **he left by the back door** salió por la puerta trasera. ▪ *(manner)* en, con, por; **by car/train** en coche/tren; **by credit card** con tarjeta de crédito; **by chance** por casualidad; **by oneself** solo, -a; **you can obtain a ticket by filling in the coupon** puede conseguir una entrada rellenando el cupón. ▪ *(amount)* por; **little by little** poco a poco; **they are sold by the dozen** se venden por docenas; **to be paid by the hour** cobrar por horas; **he won by a foot** ganó por un pie. ▪ *(beside)* al lado de, junto a; **side by side** juntos. ▪ *(past)* **to walk by a building** pasar por delante de un edificio. ▪ *(time)* **by now** ya; **by then** para entonces; **we have to be there by nine** tenemos que estar allí para las nueve; **by the time we arrive** (para) cuando lleguemos. ▪ *(during)* de; **by day/night** de día/noche. ▪ *(according to)* según; **is that O.K. by you?** ¿te viene bien? **2** *adv* **to go by** *(past)* pasar; **she just walked by** pasó de largo; **by and by** con el tiempo; **by and large** en conjunto.
bye(-bye) ¡adiós!, ¡hasta luego!
by-e·lec·tion elección *f* parcial.
by·pass 1 *n (road)* carretera *f* de circunvalación. **2** *vt* evitar.
by·stand·er mirón, -ona *mf.*

C

cab taxi *m.*
cab·bage col *f.*
cab·in *(hut)* choza *f; (on ship)* camarote *m.*
cab·i·net *(furniture)* armario *m; (glass-fronted)* vitrina *f; (in government)* gabinete *m.*
cab·i·net meet·ing consejo *m* de ministros.
ca·ble cable *m.*
ca·ble car teleférico *m.*
ca·ble TV televisión *f* por cable.
cac·tus *(pl cacti)* cactus *m.*
ca·fé, caf·e·te·ria cafetería *f,* bar *m.*
caf·feine cafeína *f.*
cage jaula *f.*
cake pastel *m.*
cal·cu·late *vt* calcular.
cal·cu·la·tion cálculo *m.*
cal·cu·la·tor calculadora *f.*
cal·en·dar calendario *m.*
calf *(pl calves) (of cattle)* becerro, -a *mf,* ternero, -a *mf; (part of leg)* pantorrilla *f.*
call 1 *vt* llamar; *(meeting etc)* convocar; **what's he called?** ¿cómo se llama? **2** *vi* llamar; **to c. at sb's (house)** pasar por casa de algn. **3** *n* llamada *f; (visit)* visita *f; (phone)* **c.** llamada *f.*
▸ **call back** *vti (phone again)* llamar otra vez.
▸ **call in 1** *vt (doctor)* llamar. **2** *vi* entrar; **to call in on sb** ir a ver a algn.
▸ **call on** *vt* visitar; **to c. on sb for support** recurrir a algn en busca de apoyo.
▸ **call out 1** *vt (shout)* gritar; *(doctor)* hacer venir. **2** *vi* gritar.
▸ **call (up)** *vt* llamar (por teléfono).
call box cabina *f* telefónica.
calm 1 *adj (weather, sea)* en calma; *(relaxed)* tranquilo, -a; **keep c.!** ¡tranquilo, -a! **2** *n (of weather, sea)* calma *f.* **3** *vt* calmar.
▸ **calm down** *vi* calmarse.
calm·ly *adv* con calma, tranquilamente.
cal·o·rie caloría *f.*
cam·cord·er videocámara *f.*
came *pt* of **come**.
cam·el camello, -a *mf.*
cam·er·a cámara *f.*

camp 1 *n* campamento *m.* **2** *vi* **to go camping** ir de camping.
cam·paign campaña *f.*
camp bed cama *f* plegable.
camp·er *(person)* campista *mf; (vehicle)* caravana *f.*
camp·fire fogata *f.*
camp(·ing) site camping *m.*
cam·pus campus *m,* ciudad *f* universitaria.
can¹ *v aux (pt could)* poder; *(know how to)* saber; **I'll phone you as soon as I c.** te llamaré en cuanto pueda; **she can't do it** no puede hacerlo; **I cannot understand why** no entiendo por qué; **he could have come** podría haber venido; **c. you ski?** ¿sabes esquiar?; **she could have forgotten** puede (ser) que lo haya olvidado; **they can't be very poor** no deben ser muy pobres; **what c. it be?** ¿qué será?
can² *(tin)* lata *f.*
Ca·na·di·an *adj & n* canadiense *(mf).*
ca·nal canal *m.*
ca·nar·y canario *m.*
can·cel *vt (train, booking)* cancelar; *(contract)* anular; *(permission)* retirar.
can·cel·la·tion cancelación *f, (of contract)* anulación *f.*
can·cer cáncer *m.*
can·did *adj* franco, -a.
can·di·date candidato, -a *mf, (in state exam)* opositor, -a *mf.*
can·dle vela *f; (in church)* cirio *m.*
can·dle·stick palmatoria *f, (in church)* cirial *m.*
can·dy caramelo *m.*
cane 1 *n (walking stick)* bastón *m; (for punishment)* palmeta *f.* **2** *vt* castigar con la palmeta.
can·na·bis canabis *m.*
canned *adj* enlatado, -a; **c. foods** conservas *fpl.*
can·ni·bal *adj & n* caníbal *(mf).*
ca·noe canoa *f, (for sport)* piragua *f.*
ca·noe·ing piragüismo *m.*
can o·pen·er abrelatas *m.*
can·o·py *(awning)* toldo *m.*
can·teen *(restaurant)* comedor *m,* cantina *f.*
can·vas lona *f, (painting)* lienzo *m.*
can·yon cañón *m.*
cap gorro *m; (soldier's)* gorra *f; (of pen)* capuchón *m; (of bottle)* chapa *f.*
ca·pa·bil·i·ty habilidad *f.*
ca·pa·ble *adj (skillful)* hábil; *(able)* capaz **(of** de).
ca·pac·i·ty capacidad *f; (position)* puesto *m;* **in her c. as manageress** en calidad de gerente.
cape *(garment)* capa *f.*
cap·i·tal *(town)* capital *f, (money)* capital *m; (letter)* mayúscula *f.*
cap·size 1 *vt* hacer zozobrar. **2** *vi* zozobrar.
cap·sule cápsula *f.*
cap·tain capitán *m.*
cap·ture *vt* capturar; *(of troops) (town)* tomar.
car coche *m, Am* carro *m;* **by c.** en coche.
car·a·mel azúcar *m* quemado; *(sweet)* caramelo *m.*
car·a·van *(vehicle)* caravana *f.*
car·bon carbono *m;* **c. copy** copia *f* al papel carbón.
car·bu·re·tor carburador *m.*
card tarjeta *f, (of cardboard)* cartulina *f, (in file)* ficha *f.*
card·board cartón *m.*
car·di·gan rebeca *f.*
car·di·nal 1 *n* cardenal *m.* **2** *adj* **c. numbers** números *mpl* cardinales.
care 1 *vi (be concerned)* preocuparse **(about** por); **I don't c.** no me importa; **who cares?** ¿qué más da? **2** *n (attention, protection)* cuidado *m; (worry)* preocupación *f;* **to take c. of** cuidar; *(business)* ocuparse de; **take c.** *(be careful)* ten cuidado; *(as farewell)* ¡cuídate!; **to take c. not to do sth** guardarse de hacer algo.
▸ **care about** *vt (something)* preocuparse de; *(somebody)* tener cariño a.
▸ **care for** *vt (look after)* cuidar; **I don't c. for that sort of thing** no me hace gracia una cosa así; **would you c. for a coffee?** ¿te apetece un café?
ca·reer carrera *f.*
care·free *adj* despreocupado, -a.
care·ful *adj* cuidadoso, -a; *(cautious)* prudente; **to be c.** tener cuidado; **be c.!** ¡ojo!
care·ful·ly *adv (painstakingly)* cuidadosamente; *(cautiously)* con cuidado.
care·less *adj* descuidado, -a; *(about clothes)* desaliñado, -a; *(driving)* negligente.
car fer·ry transbordador *m* para coches.
car·ing *adj* humanitario, -a, afectuoso, -a.
car·na·tion clavel *m.*
car·ni·val carnaval *m.*
car·ol villancico *m.*
carp *(fish)* carpa *f.*
car·pen·ter carpintero, -a *mf.*
car·pen·try carpintería *f.*
car·pet alfombra *f, (fitted)* moqueta *f.*
car·pet·ing (wall to wall) c. moqueta *f.*
car·pet sweep·er barredora *f* para alfombras.
car·riage *(horse-drawn)* carruaje *m; (on train)* vagón *m,* coche *m.*
car·ri·er *(company)* transportista *mf; (of disease)* portador, -a *mf.*
car·rot zanahoria *f.*
car·ry 1 *vt* llevar; *(goods)* transportar; *(stock)* tener; *(responsibility, penalty)* conllevar; *(disease)* ser portador, -a de. **2** *vi (sound)* oírse.
▸ **carry away** *vt* llevarse; **to get carried away** entusiasmarse.
▸ **carry off** *vt (prize)* llevarse; **to c. it off** salir airoso, -a.
▸ **carry on 1** *vt* continuar; *(conversation)* mantener. **2** *vi* continuar; **c. on!** ¡adelante!
▸ **carry out** *vt (plan)* llevar a cabo; *(order)* cumplir; *(repairs)* hacer.
▸ **carry through** *vt (plan)* completar.
car·ry·on *(baggage)* bolsa *f* de viaje.
cart 1 *n (horse-drawn)* carro *m; (handcart)* carretilla *f.* **2** *vt* acarrear.
▸ **cart around** *vt fam* llevar y traer.
car·ton *(of cream etc)* paquete *m.*
car·toon *(strip)* tira *f* cómica; *(animated)* dibujos *mpl* animados.
car·tridge cartucho *m; (for pen)* recambio *m.*
carve *vt (wood)* tallar; *(stone, metal)* esculpir; *(meat)* trinchar.
car wash túnel *m* or tren *m* de lavado.
case¹ *(instance, medical)* caso *m; (legal)* causa *f,* **in any c.** en cualquier caso; **just in c.** por si acaso.
case² *(suitcase)* maleta *f; (small)* estuche *m; (soft)* funda *f.*
cash 1 *n* dinero *m* efectivo; **to pay c.** pagar al contado or en efectivo. **2** *vt (check)* cobrar.
cash·box caja *f.*
cash·ier cajero, -a *mf.*
cash price precio *m* al contado.
cash reg·is·ter caja *f* registradora.
ca·si·no casino *m.*

cas·se·role *(container)* cacerola *f*; *(food)* guisado *m*.

cas·sette casete *f*.

cas·sette play·er casete *m*.

cas·sette re·cord·er casete *m*.

cast 1 *vt** *(net, fishing line)* echar; *(light)* proyectar; *(glance)* lanzar; *(vote)* emitir; **to c. suspicion on sb** levantar sospechas sobre algn; *(play, film)* hacer el reparto de. **2** *n* **(plaster) c.** escayola *f*; *(of play)* reparto *m*.

cast·i·ron *adj* *(pan)* de hierro fundido; *(alibi)* a toda prueba.

cas·tle castillo *m*; *(in chess)* torre *f*.

cas·tor ruedecilla *f*.

ca·su·al *adj* informal; *(worker)* eventual; *(clothes)* (de) sport; *(unimportant)* casual.

ca·su·al·ty *(injured)* herido, -a *mf*; **casualties** víctimas *fpl*.

cat gato, -a *mf*.

cat·a·log catálogo *m*.

cat·a·pult tirachinas *m inv*.

ca·tas·tro·phe catástrofe *f*.

catch 1 *vt** *(thief, bus etc)* coger, *Am* agarrar; *(fish)* pescar; *(mouse etc)* atrapar; *(surprise)* sorprender; *(hear)* entender; **to c. fire** *(log)* prenderse; *(building)* incendiarse; **to c. one's breath** *(recover)* recuperar el aliento. **2** *vi** *(sleeve etc)* engancharse **(on** en); *(fire)* encenderse. **3** *n (of ball)* parada *f*; *(of fish)* presa *f*; *(on door)* pestillo *m*; *(drawback)* pega *f*.

▸ **catch on** *vi (become popular)* ganar popularidad; *(understand)* caer en la cuenta.

▸ **catch up** *vti* **to c. up (with) sb** *(reach)* alcanzar a algn; *(with news)* ponerse al corriente **(on** de); **to c. up with work** ponerse al día con el trabajo.

catch·ing *adj (disease)* contagioso, -a.

cat·e·go·ry categoría *f*.

▸ **cater for, cater to** *vt (need, taste)* atender a.

cat·er·pil·lar oruga *f*.

ca·the·dral catedral *f*.

Cath·o·lic *adj & n* católico, -a *(mf)*.

cau·li·flow·er coliflor *f*.

cause 1 *n (of event etc)* causa *f*; *(reason)* motivo *m*. **2** *vt* provocar; **to c. sb to do sth** hacer que algn haga algo.

cau·tion *(care)* cautela *f*; *(warning)* aviso *m*.

cau·tious *adj* cauteloso, -a.

cau·tious·ly *adv* con precaución.

cave cueva *f*.

▸ **cave in** *vi (roof etc)* derrumbarse.

cav·i·ty *(hole)* cavidad *f*.

CD *abbr of* **compact disc** CD *m*.

cease 1 *vt* **to c. doing** *or* **to do sth** dejar de hacer algo. **2** *vi* cesar.

cease-fire alto *m* el fuego.

ceil·ing techo *m*.

cel·e·brate 1 *vt* celebrar. **2** *vi* divertirse.

cel·e·bra·tion celebración *f*.

ce·leb·ri·ty celebridad *f*.

cel·er·y apio *m*.

cell *(in prison)* celda *f*; *(in organism)* célula *f*.

cel·lar sótano *m*; *(for wine)* bodega *f*.

cel·lo·phane celofán *m*.

ce·ment 1 *n* cemento *m*. **2** *vt (fix with cement)* unir con cemento.

ce·ment mix·er hormigonera *f*.

cem·e·ter·y cementerio *m*.

cen·sus censo *m*.

cent centavo *m*, céntimo *m*.

cen·ter 1 *n* centro *m*; **town c.** centro de la ciudad. **2** *vt (attention, interest)* centrar **(on** en).

cen·ti·grade *adj* centígrado, -a.

cen·ti·me·ter centímetro *m*.

cen·ti·pede ciempiés *m inv*.

cen·tral *adj* central.

Cen·tral A·mer·i·can *adj & n* centro-americano, -a *(mf)*.

cen·tral·ize *vt* centralizar.

cen·tu·ry siglo *m*.

ce·ram·ic *adj* de cerámica.

ce·re·al cereal *m*.

cer·e·mo·ny ceremonia *f*.

cer·tain 1 *adj (sure)* seguro, -a; *(true)* cierto, -a; **to make c. of sth** asegurarse de algo; **to a c. extent** hasta cierto punto. **2** *adv* **for c.** a ciencia cierta.

cer·tain·ly *adv* desde luego; **c. not** de ninguna manera.

cer·tain·ty certeza *f*; *(assurance)* seguridad *f*.

cer·tif·i·cate certificado *m*; *(from college)* diploma *m*.

cer·ti·fy *vt* certificar.

chain 1 *n* cadena *f*; *(of events)* serie *f*; **c. of mountains** cordillera *f*. **2** *vt* **to c. (up)** encadenar.

chair silla *f*; *(with arms)* sillón *m*; *(of meeting)* presidente *mf*.

chair lift telesilla *m*.

chair·man presidente *m*.

cha·let chalet *m*, chalé *m*.

chalk *(for writing)* tiza *f*.

chal·lenge 1 *vt* desafiar; *(authority etc)* poner a prueba; *(statement)* poner en duda; **to c. sb to do sth** retar a algn a que haga algo. **2** *n* desafío *m*.

chal·leng·ing *adj (idea)* desafiante; *(task)* que presenta un desafío.

cham·ber C. of Commerce Cámara *f* de Comercio.

cham·pagne *(French)* champán *m*; *(from Catalonia)* cava *m*.

cham·pi·on campeón, -ona *mf*.

cham·pi·on·ship campeonato *m*.

chance 1 *n (fortune)* azar *m*; *(opportunity)* oportunidad *f*; **by c.** por casualidad; **to take a c.** arriesgarse; **(the) chances are that ...** lo más probable es que .... **2** *vt* arriesgar.

chan·cel·lor *(head of state, in embassy)* canciller *m*.

chan·de·lier araña *f* (de luces).

change 1 *vt* cambiar; **to c. gear** cambiar de marcha; **to c. one's mind/the subject** cambiar de opinión/de tema; **to c. trains** hacer trasbordo; **to get changed** cambiarse de ropa. **2** *vi* cambiar(se); **I think he's changed** lo veo cambiado. **3** *n* cambio *m*; *(money after purchase)* vuelta *f*; **for a c.** para variar; **c. of scene** cambio de aires; **small c.** suelto *m*.

▸ **change over** *vi* **to c. over to sth** cambiar a algo, adoptar algo.

change·a·ble *adj (weather)* variable; *(person)* inconstante.

change·o·ver conversión *f*.

chang·ing room vestuario *m*.

chan·nel canal *m*; *(administrative)* vía *f*; **the English C.** el Canal de la Mancha.

chant 1 *n (of demonstrators)* eslogan *m*. **2** *vti (demonstrators)* corear.

cha·os caos *m*.

cha·ot·ic *adj* caótico, -a.

chap·el capilla *f*.

chapped *adj* agrietado, -a.

chap·ter capítulo *m*.

char *vt* carbonizar.

char·ac·ter carácter *m*; *(in play)* personaje *m*; *(person)* tipo *m*.

char·ac·ter·is·tic 1 *n* característica *f*. **2** *adj* característico, -a.

charge 1 *vt* cobrar; *(the enemy)* cargar contra; *(battery)* cargar; **to c. sb with a crime** acusar a algn de un crimen. **2** *vi (battery, troops)* cargar; **to c. about** andar a lo loco. **3** *n (cost)* precio *m*; *(in court)* acusación *f*; **bank charges** comisión *f*; **free of c.** gratis; **service c.** servicio *m*; **to be in c. of** estar a cargo de; **to take c. of** hacerse cargo de.

char·i·ty *(organization)* institución *f* benéfica.

charm 1 *n (quality)* encanto *m*; **lucky c.** amuleto *m*. **2** *vt* encantar.

charm·ing *adj* encantador, -a.

chart *(giving information)* tabla *f*; *(graph)* gráfico *m*; *(map)* carta *f* de navegación; *(of hit records)* **the charts** la lista de éxitos.

char·ter 1 *n (of institution)* estatutos *mpl*; *(of rights)* carta *f*; **c. flight** vuelo *m* chárter. **2** *vt (plane, boat)* fletar.

chase *vt* perseguir; *(hunt)* cazar.

▸ **chase after** *vt (someone)* correr detrás de; *(something)* andar tras.

▸ **chase away, chase off** *vt* ahuyentar.

chasm sima *f*, *fig* abismo *m*.

chas·sis chasis *m inv*.

chat 1 *n* charla *f*. **2** *vi* charlar.

chat·ter 1 *vi (person)* parlotear; *(teeth)* castañetear. **2** *n (of person)* parloteo *m*; *(of teeth)* castañeteo *m*.

chat·ter·box parlanchín, -ina *mf*.

chat·ty *adj* hablador, -a.

chauf·feur chófer *m*.

cheap 1 *adj* barato, -a; *(fare)* económico, -a; *(contemptible)* bajo, -a. **2** *adv* barato.

cheap·ly *adv* en plan económico.

cheat 1 *vt* engañar; **to c. sb out of sth** estafar algo a algn. **2** *vi (at games)* hacer trampa; *(on an exam etc)* copiar(se). **3** *n (trickster)* tramposo, -a *mf*.

check 1 *vt* verificar; *(facts)* comprobar; *(tickets)* controlar; *(tires, oil)* revisar; *(stop)* detener; *(in chess)* dar jaque a. **2** *vi* comprobar. **3** *n (of documents etc)* revisión *f*; *(of facts)* comprobación *f*; *(in chess)* jaque *m*; *(in restaurant etc)* cuenta *f*.

▸ **check in** *vi (at airport)* facturar; *(at hotel)* registrarse **(at** en).

▸ **check off** *vt (names on list etc)* tachar.

▸ **check on** *vt* verificar.

▸ **check out 1** *vi (of hotel)* dejar el hotel. **2** *vt (facts)* verificar.

▸ **check up** *vi* **to c. up on sth** comprobar algo.

check·book talonario *m* de cheques.

check·ers *(game)* damas *fpl*.

check in c. desk *(at airport)* mostrador *m* de facturación.

check·mate jaque mate *m*.

check·out *(counter)* caja *f*.

check·room guardarropa *f*; *(for luggage)* consigna *f*.

check·up *(medical)* chequeo *m*.

ched·dar queso *m* cheddar.

cheek mejilla *f*; *(nerve)* cara *f*; **what c.!** ¡vaya jeta!

cheek·y *adj* fresco, -a.

cheer 1 *vi* aclamar. **2** *vt (applaud)* aclamar. **3** *n* viva *m*; **cheers** aplausos *mpl*; **cheers!** *(before drinking)* ¡salud!

▸ **cheer up 1** *vi* animarse. **2** *vt* **to c. sb up** animar a algn.

cheer·ful *adj* alegre.

cheer·ing ovación *f*.

cheese queso *m*.

cheese·burg·er hamburguesa *f* de queso.

cheese·cake tarta *f* de queso.

chef chef *m*.

chem·i·cal 1 *n* sustancia *f* química. **2** *adj* químico, -a.

chem·ist farmacéutico, -a *mf*; *(scientist)* químico, -a *mf*.

chem·is·try química *f*.

cher·ry cereza *f*.

cher·ry bran·dy licor *m* de cerezas.

chess ajedrez *m*.

chess·board tablero *m* de ajedrez.

chest pecho *m*; *(for linen)* arca *f*; *(for valuables)* cofre *m*; **c. of drawers** cómoda *f*.

chest·nut *(nut)* castaña *f*.

chew *vt* masticar.

chew·ing gum chicle *m*.

chick pollito *m*.

chick·en *n* pollo *m*; *fam (coward)* gallina *m*.

▸ **chicken out** *vi* rajarse (por miedo).

chick·en·pox varicela *f*.

chick·pea garbanzo *m*.

chic·o·ry achicoria *f*.

chief 1 *n* jefe *m*. **2** *adj* principal.

chief·ly *adv (above all)* sobre todo; *(mainly)* principalmente.

chil·blain sabañón *m*.

child *(pl* **children)** niño, -a *mf*; *(son)* hijo *m*; *(daughter)* hija *f*.

child care *(for working parents)* servicio *m* de guardería.

child·hood infancia *f*, niñez *f*.

child·ish *adj* pueril.

Chi·le·an *adj & n* chileno, -a *(mf)*.

chill 1 *n (illness)* resfriado *m*; *(coldness)* fresco *m*. **2** *vt (meat)* refrigerar; *(wine)* enfriar.

chilled *adj (wine)* frío, -a.

chil·(l)i chile *m*.

chill·y *adj* frío, -a.

chime *vi* repicar, sonar.

chim·ney chimenea *f*.

chim·ney flue cañón *m*.

chim·pan·zee chimpancé *m*.

chin barbilla *f*.

chi·na loza *f*, bone *f*; **c.** porcelana *f*.

Chi·nese 1 *adj* chino, -a. **2** *n (person)* chino, -a *mf*; *(language)* chino *m*.

chip 1 *n (in cup)* mella *f*; *(microchip)* chip *m*; *(in gambling)* ficha *f*; **chips** patatas *fpl* fritas. **2** *vt (china, glass)* mellar.

chi·ro·po·dist pedicuro, -a *mf*.

chis·el cincel *m*.

chives *npl* cebollino *m sing*.

choc-ice *(ice cream)* helado *m* cubierto de chocolate.

chock-a-block, chock-full *adj* hasta los topes.

choc·o·late 1 *n* chocolate *m*; **chocolates** bombones *mpl*. **2** *adj* de chocolate.

choice elección *f*; **a wide c.** un gran surtido; **there's no c.** no hay más remedio.

choir coro *m*.

choke 1 *vt (person)* ahogar; *(obstruct)* obstruir. **2** *vi* ahogarse.

cho·les·ter·ol colesterol *m*.

choose* 1 *vt* elegir; *(decide on)* optar por. **2** *vi* elegir.

choos·(e)y *adj* exigente.
chop 1 *vt (wood)* cortar; *(tree)* talar; *(food)* cortar a pedacitos. 2 *n (of lamb, pork etc)* chuleta *f*.
▸**chop down** *vt (tree)* talar.
▸**chop off** *vt (branch, finger etc)* cortar.
▸**chop up** *vt* cortar en pedazos.
chop·per *n fam (helicopter)* helicóptero *m*.
chop·sticks *npl* palillos *mpl*.
chord *(musical)* acorde *m*.
chore tarea *f*.
cho·rus coro *m*; *(in song)* estribillo *m*.
chris·ten *vt* bautizar.
chris·ten·ing bautizo *m*.
Chris·tian *adj & n* cristiano, -a *(mf)*.
Chris·tian name nombre *m* de pila.
Christ·mas Navidad *f*; **Merry C.** feliz Navidad; **C. Day** (día *m* de) Navidad *f*; **C. Eve** Nochebuena *f*.
chrome cromo *m*.
chron·ic *adj* crónico, -a.
chry·san·the·mum crisantemo *m*.
chub·by *adj* rellenito, -a.
chuck *vt fam* tirar.
chum compañero, -a *mf*.
chunk pedazo *m*.
church iglesia *f*.
chute *(for refuse)* conducto *m*; *(slide)* tobogán *m*.
ci·der sidra *f*.
ci·gar puro *m*.
cig·a·rette cigarrillo *m*.
cig·a·rette butt colilla *f*.
cig·a·rette light·er mechero *m*.
cin·e·ma cine *m*.
cin·na·mon canela *f*.
cir·cle 1 *n* círculo *m*; *(of people)* corro *m*; **in business circles** en el mundo de los negocios. 2 *vt (move round)* dar la vuelta a. 3 *vi* dar vueltas.
cir·cuit circuito *m*.
cir·cu·lar *adj & n* circular *(f)*.
cir·cu·late 1 *vt (news)* hacer circular. 2 *vi* circular.
cir·cu·la·tion *(of blood)* circulación *f*; *(of newspaper)* tirada *f*.
cir·cum·fer·ence circunferencia *f*.
cir·cum·stance circunstancia *f*; **under no circumstances** en ningún caso.
cir·cus circo *m*.
cite *vt (quote)* citar.
cit·i·zen ciudadano, -a *mf*.
cit·y ciudad *f*.
cit·y cen·ter centro *m* urbano.
cit·y hall ayuntamiento *m*.
civ·ic *adj (authority, building)* municipal; *(duty, rights)* cívico, -a.
civ·il *adj* civil; *(polite)* educado, -a; **c. rights** derechos *mpl* civiles.
ci·vil·ian *adj & n* civil *(mf)*.
civ·i·li·za·tion civilización *f*.
civ·il ser·vant funcionario, -a *mf*.
civ·il ser·vice administración *f* pública.
claim 1 *vt (benefit, rights)* reclamar; *(assert)* afirmar. 2 *n (demand)* reclamación *f*; *(right)* derecho *m*; *(assertion)* pretensión *f*; **to put in a c.** pedir una indemnización.
clam almeja *f*.
clamp wheel c. cepo *m*.
clap *vi* aplaudir.
clap·ping aplauso(s) *m(pl)*.
clar·i·fy *vt* aclarar.
clar·i·net clarinete *m*.
clash 1 *vi (disagree)* estar en desacuerdo; *(colors)* desentonar; *(dates)* coincidir. 2 *n (sound)* sonido *m*; *(fight)* choque *m*; *(conflict)* conflicto *m*.
clasp 1 *n (on belt)* cierre *m*; *(on necklace)* broche *m*. 2 *vt (object)* agarrar.
class 1 *n* clase *f*; **second c. ticket** billete *m* de segunda (clase). 2 *vt* clasificar.
clas·sic 1 *adj* clásico, -a.
clas·si·fy *vt* clasificar.
class·mate compañero, -a *mf* de clase.
class·room aula *f*.
clause oración *f*.
claw *(of bird, lion)* garra *f*; *(of cat)* uña *f*; *(of crab)* pinza *f*.
clay arcilla *f*.
clean 1 *adj* limpio, -a; *(unmarked, pure)* sin defecto. 2 *adv* por completo; **it went c. through the middle** pasó justo por el medio. 3 *vt (room)* limpiar; **to c. one's teeth** lavarse los dientes.
clean·er limpiador, -a *mf*.
clean·ing limpieza *f*.
clean·ing wom·an señora *f* de la limpieza.
clean·ly *adv (to break, cut)* limpiamente.
cleans·ing c. lotion leche *f* limpiadora.
clear 1 *adj* claro, -a; *(road, day)* despejado, -a; *(obvious)* claro, -a; *(majority)* absoluto, -a; *(profit)* neto, -a; **to make sth c.** aclarar algo. 2 *adv* **stand c.!** ¡apártese!; **to stay c. of** evitar. 3 *vt (room)* vaciar; *(authorize)* autorizar; *(hurdle)* salvar; **to c. one's throat** aclararse la garganta; **to c. the table** quitar la mesa; **to c. sb of a charge** exculpar a algn de un delito. 4 *vi (sky)* despejarse.
▸**clear away** *vt* quitar.
▸**clear off** *vi fam* largarse; **c. off!** ¡largo!
▸**clear out** *vt (room)* limpiar a fondo; *(cupboard)* vaciar.
▸**clear up** 1 *vt (tidy)* recoger; *(arrange)* ordenar; *(mystery)* resolver. 2 *vi (weather)* despejarse.
clear·ance *(of area)* despeje *m*.
clear·ance sale liquidación *f* (de existencias).
clear-cut *adj* claro, -a.
clear·ing *(in wood)* claro *m*.
clear·ly *adv* claramente; *(at start of sentence)* evidentemente.
clear·way carretera *f* donde está prohibido parar.
clem·en·tine clementina *f*.
clench *vt (teeth, fist)* apretar.
cler·gy clero *m*.
cler·i·cal *adj (of an office)* de oficina.
clerk *(office worker)* oficinista *mf*; *(civil servant)* funcionario, -a *mf*; *(in shop)* dependiente, -a *mf*.
clev·er *adj (person)* inteligente; *(argument)* ingenioso, -a; **to be c. at sth** tener aptitud para algo.
click *(sound)* clic *m*.
cli·ent cliente *mf*.
cliff acantilado *m*.
cli·mate clima *m*.

cli·max *(peak)* punto *m* culminante.
climb 1 *vt (ladder)* subir por; *(mountain)* escalar; *(tree)* subir a. 2 *vi* subir; *(plants)* trepar; *fig (socially)* ascender. 3 *n* subida *f*, ascensión *f*.
▸**climb down** *vi* bajar.
climb·er alpinista *mf*, *Am* andinista *mf*.
cling* *vi (hang on)* agarrarse (**to** a); *(clothes)* ajustarse; **to c. together** unirse.
clin·ic *(in state hospital)* ambulatorio *m*; *(specialized)* clínica *f*.
clip¹ *vt (cut)* cortar; *(ticket)* picar.
clip² *n (for hair)* pasador *m*; *(for paper)* sujetapapeles *m inv*; *(brooch)* clip *m*.
▸**clip on** *vt (brooch)* prender (**to** a); *(documents)* sujetar (**to** a).
clip·pers *npl (for hair)* maquinilla *f* para rapar; *(for nails)* cortauñas *m inv*; *(for hedge)* tijeras *fpl* de podar.
clip·ping *(newspaper)* recorte *m*.
cloak *(garment)* capa *f*.
cloak·room guardarropa *m*; *(toilets)* servicios *mpl*.
clock reloj *m*; **to be open round the c.** estar abierto las 24 horas (del día).
clock·wise *adj & adv* en el sentido de las agujas del reloj.
close¹ 1 *adj (in space, time)* cercano, -a; *(contact)* directo, -a; **c. to** cerca de; *(relationship)* estrecho, -a; *(friend)* íntimo, -a; *(weather)* bochornoso, -a; **c. together** juntos. 2 *adv* cerca; **they live c. by** *or* **c. at hand** viven cerca.
close² 1 *vt* cerrar; *(bring to a close)* concluir; *(meeting)* levantar. 2 *vi (shut)* cerrar(se). 3 *n* fin *m*, final *m*.
▸**close down** *vti (business)* cerrar para siempre.
▸**close in on** *vi* **to c. in on sb** rodear a algn.
▸**close up** 1 *vt* cerrar del todo. 2 *vi* cerrarse; *(ranks)* apretarse.
closed *adj* cerrado, -a; **c.-circuit television** televisión *f* en circuito cerrado.
close·ly *adv (listen)* con atención; **c. contested/connected** muy reñido, -a/relacionado, -a; **to follow (events) c.** seguir de cerca (los acontecimientos).
clos·et armario *m*.
clos·ing time hora *f* de cierre.
clo·sure cierre *m*.
clot 1 *n (of blood)* coágulo *m*. 2 *vi* coagularse.
cloth paño *m*, *(rag)* trapo *m*; *(tablecloth)* mantel *m*.
clothes *npl* ropa *f sing*.
clothes hang·er percha *f*.
clothes-line tendedero *m*.
clothes peg pinza *f*.
clothes shop tienda *f* de ropa.
cloth·ing ropa *f*.
cloud *n* nube *f*.
▸**cloud over** *vi* nublarse.
cloud·y *adj (sky)* nublado, -a.
clove *(of garlic)* diente *f*.
clown payaso *m*.
club *(society)* club *m*; *(for golf)* palo *m*, *(in cards)* trébol *m*.
clue *(sign)* indicio *m*; *(to mystery)* pista *f*, *(in crossword)* clave *f*, *fam* **I haven't a c.** no tengo (ni) idea.
clum·sy *adj (person; awkward)* torpe; *(awkward)* tosco, -a.
clus·ter 1 *n* grupo *m*. 2 *vi* agruparse.
clutch 1 *vt* agarrar. 2 *n (in vehicle)* embrague *m*.
clut·ter *vt* **to c. (up)** llenar de cosas.
Co *abbr of* **Company** C., Cª, Cía.
coach 1 *n* autocar *m*; *(carriage)* carruaje *m*; *(of train)* coche *m*, vagón *m*. 2 *vt (student)* dar clases particulares a; *(team)* entrenar.
coal carbón *m*.
coal mine mina *f* de carbón.
coarse *adj (material)* basto, -a; *(language)* grosero, -a.
coast costa *f*.
coat 1 *n (overcoat)* abrigo *m*; *(short)* chaquetón *m*; *(of animal)* pelo *m*; *(of paint)* capa *f*. 2 *vt* cubrir (**with** de); *(with liquid)* bañar (**with** en).
coat hang·er percha *f*.
coat·ing capa *f*.
cob mazorca *f*.
cob·bled *adj* adoquinado, -a.
cob·web telaraña *f*.
co·caine cocaína *f*.
cock *(bird)* gallo *m*.
cock·le berberecho *m*.
cock·pit cabina *f* del piloto.
cock·roach cucaracha *f*.
cock·tail cóctel *m*.
co·coa cacao *m*.
co·co·nut coco *m*.
cod bacalao *m*.
code código *m*; *(symbol)* clave *f*; *(for telephone)* prefijo *m*.
cod-liv·er oil aceite *m* de hígado de bacalao.
co-ed 1 *adj* mixto, -a. 2 *n* colegio *m* mixto.
cof·fee café *m*.
cof·fee bar cafetería *f*.
cof·fee break pausa *f* para el café.
cof·fee·pot cafetera *f*.
cof·fee ta·ble mesita *f* de café.
cof·fin ataúd *m*.
co·gnac coñac *m*.
co·her·ent *adj* coherente.
coil 1 *vt* **to c. (up)** enrollar. 2 *n (loop)* vuelta *f*, *(of rope)* rollo *m*.
coin moneda *f*.
co·in·cide *vi* coincidir (**with** con).
co·in·ci·dence coincidencia *f*.
Coke® *abbr of* **Coca-Cola®** coca-cola *f*.
col·an·der colador *m*.
cold 1 *adj* frío, -a; **I'm c.** tengo frío; **it's c.** *(weather)* hace frío. 2 *n* frío *m*; *(illness)* resfriado *m*; **to catch a c.** resfriarse, acatarrarse; **to have a c.** estar resfriado, -a.
cold·ness frialdad *f*.
cole·slaw ensalada *f* de col.
col·lab·o·rate *vi* colaborar (**with** con).
col·lab·o·ra·tion colaboración *f*.
col·lapse 1 *vi (fall down)* derrumbarse; *(cave in)* hundirse. 2 *n (falling down)* derrumbamiento *m*; *(caving in)* hundimiento *m*.
col·lar *n (of garment)* cuello *m*; *(for dog)* collar *m*.
col·lar·bone clavícula *f*.
col·league colega *mf*.
col·lect 1 *vt (gather)* recoger; *(stamps etc)* coleccionar; *(taxes)* recaudar. 2 *vi (for charity)* hacer una colecta (**for** para). 3 *adv* **to call c.** llamar a cobro revertido.

col·lec·tion (of mail) recogida f; (of money) colecta f; (of stamps) colección f; (of taxes) recaudación f.
col·lec·tor (of stamps) coleccionista mf.
col·lege ≃ centro m de enseñanza superior, ≃ politécnico m; **to go to c.** seguir estudios superiores.
col·lide vi chocar.
col·li·sion choque m.
col·lo·qui·al adj coloquial.
co·logne (agua f de) colonia f.
Co·lom·bi·an adj & n colombiano, -a (mf).
co·lon (punctuation) dos puntos mpl.
colo·nel coronel m.
co·lo·ni·al adj colonial.
col·o·ny colonia f.
col·or 1 n color m; **c. film/television** película f/televisión f en color. **2** vt colorear.
col·ored adj (pencil) de color; (photograph) en color.
col·or·ful adj (with color) lleno, -a de color; (person) pintoresco, -a.
col·umn columna f.
co·ma coma m; **to go into a c.** entrar en coma.
comb 1 n peine m. **2** vt **to c. one's hair** peinarse.
com·bi·na·tion combinación f.
com·bine 1 vt combinar. **2** vi combinarse; (companies) asociarse.
come* vi venir; (arrive) llegar; (happen) suceder; **to c. apart/undone** desatarse/soltarse; **that's what comes of being too impatient** es lo que pasa por ser demasiado impaciente.
► **come about** vi ocurrir, suceder.
► **come across** vt (thing) encontrar por casualidad; **to c. across sb** tropezar con algn.
► **come along** vi (arrive) venir; (make progress) progresar; **c. along!** ¡venga!
► **come around 1** vt (corner) dar la vuelta a. **2** vi (visit) venir; (regain consciousness) volver en sí.
► **come away** vi (leave) salir; (part) desprenderse (**from** de).
► **come back** vi (return) volver.
► **come by 1** vt (acquire) adquirir. **2** vi (visit) **why don't you c. by?** ¿por qué no te pasas por casa?
► **come down** vi bajar; (rain) caer; **to c. down with the flu** pillar la gripe.
► **come forward** vi (advance) avanzar; (volunteer) ofrecerse.
► **come in** vi (enter) entrar; (arrive) (train) llegar; (tide) subir.
► **come into** vt (enter) entrar en; (inherit) heredar.
► **come off 1** vt (fall from) caerse de. **2** vi (button) caerse; (succeed) salir bien.
► **come on** vi (make progress) progresar; **c. on!** (hurry) ¡venga!
► **come out** vi salir (**of** de); (book) aparecer; (stain) quitarse; **to c. out (on strike)** declararse en huelga.
► **come over 1** vi venir. **2** vt **what's c. over you?** ¿qué te pasa?
► **come through** vt (cross) cruzar; (illness) recuperarse de; (accident) sobrevivir a.
► **come to 1** vi (regain consciousness) volver en sí. **2** vt (amount to) ascender a; (arrive at) llegar a.
► **come up** vi (rise) subir; (sun) salir; (approach) acercarse (**to** a); (difficulty, question) surgir.
► **come up against** vt (problems etc) encontrarse con.
► **come upon** vt = **come across**.
► **come up to** vt (equal) igualar.
► **come up with** vt (solution etc) encontrar.
come·back to make a c. reaparecer.
co·me·di·an cómico m.
com·e·dy comedia f.
com·fort 1 n comodidad f; (consolation) consuelo m. **2** vt consolar.
com·fort·a·ble adj cómodo, -a; (temperature) agradable.
com·fort·er edredón m.
com·ic 1 adj cómico, -a. **2** n tebeo m, comic m.
com·ic strip tira f cómica.
com·ing comings and goings idas y venidas fpl.
com·ma coma f.
com·mand 1 vt mandar. **2** n (order) orden f; (authority) mando m; (of language) dominio m.
com·mand·er comandante mf.
com·mem·o·rate vt conmemorar.
com·mence vti comenzar.
com·ment n comentario m.
► **comment on** vt (event etc) comentar.
com·men·tar·y comentario m.
com·men·ta·tor comentarista mf.
com·merce comercio m.
com·mer·cial adj comercial.
com·mis·sion comisión f.
com·mit vt (crime) cometer; **to c. suicide** suicidarse.
com·mit·ment compromiso m.
com·mit·tee comisión f, comité m.
com·mod·i·ty artículo m.
com·mon adj común; (ordinary) corriente.
com·mon·ly adv (generally) en general.
com·mon·place adj corriente.
com·mon sense sentido m común.
com·mo·tion alboroto m.
com·mu·nal adj (bathroom etc) comunitario, -a.
com·mu·ni·cate 1 vi comunicarse (**with** con). **2** vt comunicar.
com·mu·ni·ca·tion comunicación f.
com·mun·ion comunión f.
com·mu·ni·ty comunidad f; (people) colectividad f.
com·mu·ni·ty cen·ter centro m social.
com·mute vi viajar diariamente al lugar de trabajo.
com·mut·er persona f que viaja diariamente al lugar de trabajo.
com·mut·ing desplazarse diariamente al lugar de trabajo.
com·pact 1 adj compacto, -a; (style) conciso, -a. **2** n (for powder) polvera f.
com·pact disc disco m compacto.
com·pan·ion compañero, -a mf.
com·pa·ny compañía f; (business) empresa f; **to keep sb c.** hacer compañía a algn.
com·pa·ra·ble adj comparable (**to, with** con).
com·par·a·tive 1 adj comparativo, -a; (relative) relativo, -a. **2** n (in grammar) comparativo m.
com·pa·ra·tive·ly adv relativamente.
com·pare 1 vt comparar (**to, with** con); **(as) compared with** en comparación con. **2** vi compararse.
com·par·i·son comparación f.
com·part·ment (on train) departamento m.
com·pass brújula f; **(pair of) compasses** compás m.
com·pat·i·ble adj compatible.
com·pel vt (oblige) obligar; **to c. sb to do sth** obligar a algn a hacer algo.
com·pen·sate vti compensar; **to c. sb for sth** indemnizar a algn de algo.
com·pen·sa·tion (for loss) indemnización f.
com·pete vi competir.
com·pe·tent adj competente.

com·pe·ti·tion competencia f; (contest) concurso m.
com·pet·i·tive adj competitivo, -a.
com·pet·i·tor competidor, -a mf.
com·pile vt compilar.
com·plain vi quejarse (**of, about** de).
com·plaint queja f; (formal) reclamación f; (illness) enfermedad f.
com·ple·ment 1 n complemento m. **2** vt complementar.
com·plete 1 adj (entire) completo, -a; (absolute) total. **2** vt completar; (form) rellenar.
com·plete·ly adv completamente, por completo.
com·plex 1 adj complejo, -a. **2** n complejo m.
com·plex·ion tez f, fig aspecto m.
com·pli·cate vt complicar.
com·pli·cat·ed adj complicado, -a.
com·pli·ca·tion complicación f.
com·pli·ment cumplido m.
com·pli·men·ta·ry adj (praising) elogioso, -a; (free) gratuito, -a.
com·ply vi obedecer; **to c. with** (order) cumplir con.
com·pose vti componer; **to be composed of** componerse de; **to c. oneself** calmarse.
com·posed adj (calm) sereno, -a.
com·pos·er compositor, -a mf.
com·po·si·tion (essay) redacción f.
com·pound compuesto m.
com·pre·hen·sive adj completo, -a; (insurance) a todo riesgo; **c. school** escuela f secundaria.
com·prise vt (include) comprender; (consist of) constar de; (constitute) constituir.
com·pro·mise acuerdo m.
com·pul·sive adj compulsivo, -a.
com·pul·so·ry adj obligatorio, -a.
com·put·er ordenador m.
com·put·er·ized adj informatizado, -a.
com·put·er pro·gram·mer programador, -a mf de ordenadores.
com·put·er sci·ence informática f.
com·put·ing informática f.
con vt fam estafar.
con·ceal vt ocultar; (emotions) disimular.
con·cede vt conceder.
con·ceit·ed adj presuntuoso, -a.
con·ceiv·a·ble adj concebible.
con·ceive vti concebir.
con·cen·trate 1 vt concentrar. **2** vi **to c. on sth** concentrarse en algo.
con·cen·tra·tion concentración f.
con·cern 1 vt concernir; (worry) preocupar. **2** n (worry) preocupación f; (business) negocio m.
con·cerned adj (worried) preocupado, -a (**about** por).
con·cern·ing prep con respecto a.
con·cert concierto m.
con·ces·sion concesión f.
con·cise adj conciso, -a.
con·clude vti concluir.
con·clu·sion conclusión f.
con·crete 1 n hormigón m. **2** adj (made of concrete) de hormigón; (definite) concreto, -a.
con·demn vt condenar.
con·den·sa·tion condensación f.
con·di·tion condición f; **on c. that ...** a condición de que ...
con·di·tion·er acondicionador m.
con·dom preservativo m.
con·duct 1 n (behavior) conducta f. **2** vt (lead) guiar; (business, orchestra) dirigir.
con·duct·ed tour visita f guiada.
con·duc·tor (on bus) cobrador, -a mf; (on train) revisor, -a mf; (of orchestra) director, -a mf.
cone cono m; **ice-cream c.** cucurucho m.
con·fer 1 vt **to c. a title on sb** condecer un título a algn. **2** vi (discuss) deliberar.
con·fer·ence congreso m.
con·fess vti confesar; (to priest) confesarse.
con·fes·sion confesión f.
con·fet·ti confeti m.
con·fi·dence confianza f; **in c.** en confianza.
con·fi·dent adj seguro, -a.
con·fi·den·tial adj (secret) confidencial; (entrusted) de confianza.
con·fi·dent·ly adv con seguridad.
con·fine vt limitar.
con·firm vt confirmar.
con·fir·ma·tion confirmación f.
con·firmed adj empedernido, -a.
con·fis·cate vt confiscar.
con·flict 1 n conflicto m. **2** vi chocar (**with** con).
con·flict·ing adj contradictorio, -a.
con·form vi conformarse; **to c. to** or **with** (customs) amoldarse a; (rules) someterse a.
con·front vt hacer frente a.
con·fron·ta·tion confrontación f.
con·fuse vt (person) despistar; (thing) confundir (**with** con); **to get confused** confundirse.
con·fused adj (person) confundido, -a; (mind, ideas) confuso, -a.
con·fus·ing adj confuso, -a.
con·fu·sion confusión f.
con·gest·ed adj (street) repleto, -a de gente.
con·ges·tion congestión f.
con·grat·u·late vt felicitar.
con·grat·u·la·tions npl felicitaciones fpl; **c.!** ¡enhorabuena!
con·gre·gate vi congregarse.
con·gress congreso m.
con·gress·man diputado m, miembro m del Congreso.
con·gress·wom·an diputada f, miembro f del Congreso.
con·ju·gate vt conjugar.
con·ju·ga·tion conjugación f.
con·junc·tion conjunción f.
con·jur·er prestidigitador, -a mf.
con·jur·ing trick juego m de manos.
con man estafador m.
con·nect 1 vt unir; (wires) empalmar; (install) instalar; (electricity) conectar; (on phone) poner. **2** vi (train, flight) enlazar (**with** con).
con·nect·ed adj unido, -a; (events) relacionado, -a.
con·nec·tion conexión f; (installation) instalación f; (rail, flight) enlace m; (of ideas) relación f; (person) contacto m; **in c. with** (regarding) con respecto a.
con·quer vt (enemy, bad habit) vencer; (country) conquistar.
con·quest conquista f.

con·science conciencia f.
con·sci·en·tious adj concienzudo, -a.
con·scious adj (aware) consciente; (choice etc) deliberado, -a.
con·sen·sus consenso m.
con·sent 1 n consentimiento m. **2** vi consentir (**to** en).
con·se·quence consecuencia f.
con·se·quent·ly adv por consiguiente.
con·ser·va·tion conservación f.
con·ser·va·tive adj & n conservador, -a (mf).
con·ser·va·to·ry (greenhouse) invernadero m.
con·serve 1 vt conservar. **2** n conserva f.
con·sid·er vt (ponder on, regard) considerar; (keep in mind) tener en cuenta; **to c. doing sth** pensar hacer algo.
con·sid·er·a·ble adj considerable.
con·sid·er·ate adj considerado, -a.
con·sid·er·a·tion consideración f.
con·sid·er·ing prep teniendo en cuenta.
con·sign·ment envío m.
con·sist vi **to c. of** consistir en.
con·sis·ten·cy (of actions) coherencia f; (of mixture) consistencia f.
con·sis·tent adj (quality, results) constante; (behaviour) coherente.
con·so·la·tion consuelo m; **c. prize** premio m de consolación.
con·sole¹ vt consolar.
con·sole² consola f.
con·so·nant consonante f.
con·spic·u·ous adj (striking) llamativo, -a; (easily seen) visible.
con·spir·a·cy conjura f.
con·sta·ble policía m.
con·stant adj constante; (continuous) incesante; (loyal) fiel.
constant·ly adv constantemente.
con·sti·pat·ed adj estreñido, -a.
con·sti·tu·tion constitución f.
con·straint coacción f.
con·struct vt construir.
con·struc·tion construcción f.
con·struc·tive adj constructivo, -a.
con·sul cónsul mf.
con·su·late consulado m.
con·sult vti consultar (**about** sobre).
con·sul·tan·cy (firm) asesoría f, consulting m.
con·sult·ant (doctor) especialista mf; (in business) asesor, -a mf.
con·sul·ta·tion consulta f.
con·sume vt consumir.
con·sum·er consumidor, -a mf.
con·sump·tion consumo m.
con·tact 1 n contacto m. **2** vt ponerse en contacto con.
con·tact lens·es lentes fpl de contacto.
con·ta·gious adj contagioso, -a.
con·tain vt contener.
con·tain·er (box, package) recipiente m; (for shipping) contenedor m.
con·tem·po·rar·y adj & n contemporáneo, -a (mf).
con·tempt desprecio m.
▸ **con·tend with** vt (problem, person) enfrentarse a.
con·tent¹ contenido m; **table of contents** índice m de materias.
con·tent² adj contento, -a.
con·tent·ed adj satisfecho, -a.
con·test prueba f.
con·tes·tant concursante mf.
con·text contexto m.
con·ti·nent continente m; **(on) the C.** (en) Europa.
con·ti·nen·tal adj continental; (European) **C.** europeo, -a.
con·tin·u·al adj continuo, -a, constante.
con·tin·u·al·ly adv continuamente.
con·tin·ue vt continuar, seguir; **to c. to do sth** seguir or continuar haciendo algo.
con·tin·u·ous adj continuo, -a.
con·tin·u·ous·ly adv continuamente.
con·tra·cep·tion anticoncepción f.
con·tra·cep·tive adj & n anticonceptivo (m).
con·tract contrato m.
con·trac·tor contratista mf.
con·tra·dict vt contradecir.
con·tra·dic·tion contradicción f.
con·trar·y 1 n **on the c.** todo lo contrario. **2** adv **c. to** en contra de.
con·trast contraste m.
con·trast·ing adj opuesto, -a.
con·trib·ute 1 vt (money) contribuir; (ideas, information) aportar. **2** vi contribuir; (in discussion) participar; (to publication) colaborar (**to** en).
con·tri·bu·tion (of money) contribución f; (to publication) colaboración f.
con·trive vi **to c. to do sth** buscar la forma de hacer algo.
con·trived adj artificial.
con·trol 1 vt controlar; (person, animal) dominar; (vehicle) manejar; **to c. one's temper** controlarse. **2** n (power) control m; (authority) autoridad f; (in car, plane) (device) mando m; (on TV) botón m de control; **out of c.** fuera de control; **to be in c.** estar al mando; **to be under c.** (situation) estar bajo control; **to go out of c.** descontrolarse; **to lose c.** perder los estribos.
con·trol tow·er torre f de control.
con·va·lesce vi convalecer.
con·va·les·cence convalecencia f.
con·va·les·cent home clínica f de reposo.
con·ven·ience comodidad f.
con·ven·ience food comida f precocinada.
con·ven·ient adj (arrangement) conveniente; (time) oportuno, -a; (place) bien situado, -a.
con·vent convento m.
con·ver·sa·tion conversación f.
con·verse vi conversar.
con·ver·sion conversión f (**to** a; **into** en).
con·vert vt convertir (**into** en).
con·vert·i·ble 1 adj convertible. **2** n (car) descapotable m.
con·vey vt (carry) transportar; (sound) transmitir; (idea) comunicar.
con·vey·or belt cinta f transportadora.
con·vict vt declarar culpable a.
con·vic·tion (belief) creencia f, convicción f; (for crime) condena f.
con·vince vt convencer.
con·vinc·ing adj convincente.

con·voy convoy m.
cook 1 vt cocinar, guisar; (dinner) preparar. **2** vi (person) cocinar, guisar; (food) cocerse. **3** n cocinero, -a mf.
cook·book libro m de cocina.
cook·er cocina f.
cook·er·y cocina f.
cook·ie galleta f.
cook·ing cocina f.
cook·ing ap·ple manzana f ácida para cocinar.
cool 1 adj fresco, -a; (calm) tranquilo, -a; (reserved) frío, -a; **it's c.** (weather) hace fresquito. **2** n (coolness) fresco m; **to lose one's c.** perder la calma. **3** vt (air) refrescar; (drink) enfriar.
▸ **cool down, cool off** vi (something hot) enfriarse; fig calmarse; (feelings) enfriarse.
cool·er (for food) nevera f portátil.
cool·ness (calmness) calma f; (composure) aplomo m.
co·op·er·ate vi cooperar.
co·op·er·a·tion cooperación f.
coop up vt encerrar.
co·or·di·nate 1 vt coordinar. **2** n **coordinates** (clothes) coordinados mpl.
cope vi arreglárselas; **to c. with** (person, work) poder con; (problem) hacer frente a.
cop·per (metal) cobre m.
cop·y 1 n copia f; (of book) ejemplar m. **2** vti copiar.
▸ **copy down** vt (letter etc) pasar a limpio.
cord (string) cuerda f, (electrical) cordón m.
cor·dial (drink) licor m.
cor·don off vt acordonar.
cor·du·roy pana f.
core (of fruit) corazón m; fig centro m.
cork corcho m.
cork·screw sacacorchos m inv.
corn¹ (maize) maíz m; (grain) granos mpl; (seed) cereal m.
corn² (on foot) callo m.
corned beef carne f acecinada.
cor·ner 1 n (of street) esquina f; (bend in road) curva f; (of room) rincón m; (in soccer) **c. (kick)** córner m. **2** vt (enemy) arrinconar; (market) acaparar.
cor·net (for ice cream) cucurucho m.
corn·flakes npl copos mpl de maíz, cornflakes mpl.
corn·starch harina f de maíz.
corn·y adj gastado, -a.
cor·po·ral cabo m.
corps (pl **corps**) cuerpo m.
corpse cadáver m.
cor·rect 1 vt (mistake) corregir; (child) reprender. **2** adj correcto, -a; (behavior) formal.
cor·rec·tion corrección f.
cor·rect·ly adv correctamente.
cor·re·spond vi corresponder; (by letter) escribirse; **to c. to** equivaler a.
cor·re·spon·dence correspondencia f, **c. course** curso m por correspondencia.
cor·re·spond·ing adj (matching) correspondiente.
cor·ri·dor pasillo m.
cor·ru·gat·ed adj **c. iron** hierro m ondulado.
cor·rupt adj (person) corrupto, -a; (actions) deshonesto, -a.
cor·rup·tion corrupción f.
cos·met·ic cosmético m.
cos·mo·naut cosmonauta mf.
cost 1 n (price) precio m; coste m; **at all costs** a toda costa. **2** vti* costar, valer; **how much does it c.?** ¿cuánto cuesta?
Cos·ta Ri·can adj & n costarricense (mf).
cost·ly adj costoso, -a.
cos·tume traje m; **c. jewelery** bisutería f.
cot cuna f.
cot·tage casa f de campo.
cot·tage cheese requesón m.
cot·ton algodón m; (thread) hilo m.
cot·ton wool algodón m hidrófilo.
couch sofá m.
cou·chette litera f.
cough 1 vi toser. **2** n tos f.
▸ **cough up** vt fam **to c. up the money** soltar la pasta.
cough syr·up jarabe m para la tos.
could v aux of **can¹**.
coun·cil (body) consejo m; **town c.** consejo municipal.
coun·cil house ≃ vivienda f de protección oficial.
coun·cil·or concejal mf.
count¹ 1 vt contar. **2** vi contar; **that doesn't c.** eso no vale.
▸ **count in** vt incluir a, contar con.
▸ **count on** vt contar con.
▸ **count out** vt (banknotes) contar uno por uno.
count² (nobleman) conde m.
count·down cuenta f atrás.
coun·ter (in shop) mostrador m; (in bank) ventanilla f, (in board games) ficha f.
coun·ter- prefix contra-.
coun·ter·at·tack contraataque m.
coun·ter·clock·wise adj & adv en sentido inverso al de las agujas del reloj.
coun·ter·foil (of check) matriz f.
coun·ter·part homólogo, -a mf.
coun·try (state) país m; (rural area) campo m; **native c.** patria f.
coun·try·side (area) campo m; (scenery) paisaje m.
coun·ty condado m.
coup golpe m; **c. d'état** golpe de estado.
cou·ple (of people) pareja f, (of things) par m; **a married c.** un matrimonio; **a c. of times** un par de veces.
cou·pon cupón m.
cour·age valor m.
cou·ra·geous adj valiente.
cou·ri·er (messenger) mensajero, -a mf; (guide) guía mf turístico, -a.
course (of river) curso m; (of ship, plane) rumbo m; (series) ciclo m; (for golf) campo m; (of meal) plato m; (degree) carrera f; (in single subject) curso m; (short course) cursillo m; **in the c. of construction** en vías de construcción; **a c. of treatment** un tratamiento; **of c.** claro, por supuesto; **of c. not!** ¡claro que no!
court (of law) tribunal m; (royal) corte f; (for sport) pista f, cancha f.
cour·te·ous adj cortés.
cour·te·sy cortesía f, educación f.
court·room sala f de justicia.
court·yard patio m.
cous·in primo, -a mf.

cov·er 1 *vt* cubrir (**with** de); *(with lid)* tapar; *(hide)* disimular; *(protect)* abrigar; *(include)* abarcar. **2** *n* cubierta *f*; *(of chair etc)* funda *f*; *(of magazine)* portada *f*; *(in restaurant)* cubierto *m*; **full c.** *(in insurance)* cobertura *f* completa; **to take c.** refugiarse.
▸ **cover over** *vt (floor etc)* recubrir.
▸ **cover up 1** *vt* cubrir; *(crime)* encubrir. **2** *vi (person)* abrigarse; **to c. up for sb** encubrir a algn.
cov·er·age cobertura *f*.
cov·er·alls *npl* mono *m sing*.
cover charge *(in restaurant)* precio *m* del cubierto.
cov·er·ing 1 *n* cubierta *f*. **2** *adj (letter)* explicatorio, -a.
cow vaca *f*.
cow·ard cobarde *mf*.
cow·ard·ice cobardía *f*.
cow·ard·ly *adj* cobarde.
cow·boy vaquero *m*.
co·zy *adj (atmosphere)* acogedor, -a; *(bed)* calentito, -a.
crab cangrejo *m*.
crack 1 *vt (cup)* partir; *(nut)* cascar; *(whip)* hacer restallar; *(joke)* contar. **2** *vi (glass)* partirse; *(wall)* agrietarse; *fam* **to get cracking on sth** ponerse a hacer algo. **3** *n (in cup)* raja *f*, *(in wall, ground)* grieta *f*, *(of whip)* restallido *m*; *(of gun)* detonación *f*, *fam (drug)* crack *m*.
▸ **crack up** *vi (go insane)* desquiciarse; *(with laughter)* partirse de risa.
crack·er galleta *f* seca; *(firework)* petardo *m*.
crack·pot *fam* chiflado, -a *mf*.
cra·dle *(baby's)* cuna *f*.
craft *(occupation)* oficio *m*; *(art)* arte *m*; *(skill)* destreza *f*.
crafts·man artesano *m*.
craft·y *adj* astuto, -a.
cram 1 *vt* atiborrar; **crammed with** atestado, -a de. **2** *vi (for exam)* empollar.
cramp *(in leg etc)* calambre *m*.
cramped *adj* apretado, -a.
crane *(device)* grúa *f*.
crank *(handle)* manivela *f*, *fam (eccentric)* tipo *m* raro.
crash 1 *vt* **to c. one's car** tener un accidente con el coche. **2** *vi (car, plane)* estrellarse; *(collide)* chocar; **to c. into** estrellarse contra. **3** *n (noise)* estrépito *m*; *(collision)* choque *m*; *(of market)* quiebra *f*, **car/plane c.** accidente *m* de coche/avión.
crash course curso *m* intensivo.
crash hel·met casco *m* protector.
crash-land *vi* hacer un aterrizaje forzoso.
crate caja *f* (para embalaje).
crav·ing ansia *f*.
crawl 1 *vi (baby)* gatear; *(vehicle)* avanzar lentamente. **2** *n (swimming)* crol *m*.
cray·on cera *f*.
craze manía *f*, *(fashion)* moda *f*.
cra·zy *adj* loco, -a.
creak *vi (hinge)* chirriar.
cream *(of milk)* nata *f*, **c. colored** color crema.
cream cheese queso *m* crema.
cream·y *adj* cremoso, -a.
crease 1 *n (wrinkle)* arruga *f*, *(on trousers)* raya *f*. **2** *vt (clothes)* arrugar. **3** *vi* arrugarse.
cre·ate *vt* crear.
cre·a·tion creación *f*.
cre·a·tive *adj (person)* creativo, -a.
crea·ture *(animal)* criatura *f*.
crèche guardería *f*.
cred·i·ble *adj* creíble.
cred·it 1 *n (financial)* crédito *m*; *(merit)* honor *m*; **on c.** a crédito; **to be a c. to** hacer honor a. **2** *vt* **to c. sb's account** abonar en cuenta a algn.
cred·it card tarjeta *f* de crédito.
cred·it fa·cil·i·ties facilidades *fpl* de pago.
cred·it·wor·thy *adj* solvente.
creek cala *f*, riachuelo *m*.
creep* *vi (insect)* arrastrarse; *(cat)* deslizarse; *(person)* arrastrarse.
creep·y *adj fam* espeluznante.
cre·mate *vt* incinerar.
cre·ma·to·ri·um crematorio *m*.
crepe pa·per papel *m* crespón.
cress berro *m*.
crest *(of cock, wave)* cresta *f*, *(of hill)* cima *f*.
crew *(of plane, yacht)* tripulación *f*.
crib 1 *n (for baby)* cuna *f*. **2** *vt (copy)* copiar.
crick·et¹ *(insect)* grillo *m*.
crick·et² *(game)* cricket *m*.
crime delincuencia *f*, *(offence)* delito *m*.
crim·i·nal *adj & n* criminal *(mf)*.
crip·ple lisiado, -a *mf*.
cri·sis *(pl* **crises)** crisis *f inv*.
crisp *adj* crujiente; *(lettuce)* fresco, -a.
cri·te·ri·on *(pl* **criteria)** criterio *m*.
crit·ic crítico, -a *mf*.
crit·i·cal *adj* crítico, -a.
crit·i·cal·ly *adv* **c. ill** gravemente enfermo, -a.
crit·i·cism crítica *f*.
crit·i·cize *vt* criticar.
cro·chet ganchillo *m*.
crock·er·y loza *f*.
croc·o·dile cocodrilo *m*.
cro·cus crocus *m*.
crook *fam* caco *m*.
crook·ed *adj (stick, picture)* torcido, -a; *(path)* tortuoso, -a.
crop cultivo *m*; *(harvest)* cosecha *f*.
▸ **crop up** *vi* surgir.
cro·quet croquet *m*.
cross 1 *n* cruz *f*, *(of breeds)* cruce *m*; **c. section** sección *f* transversal. **2** *vt* cruzar. **3** *vi* cruzar; *(roads)* cruzarse. **4** *adj (angry)* enfadado, -a.
▸ **cross off, cross out** *vt* tachar.
▸ **cross over** *vi* cruzar.
cross-coun·try race cros *m*.
cross-eyed *adj* bizco, -a.
cross·ing **pedestrian c.** paso *m* de peatones; **sea c.** travesía *f*.
cross-ref·er·ence referencia *f* cruzada.
cross·roads cruce *m*; *fig* encrucijada *f*.
cross·walk paso *m* de peatones.
cross·word (puz·zle) crucigrama *m*.
crouch *vi* **to c. (down)** agacharse.
crow cuervo *m*.

crow·bar palanca *f*.
crowd 1 *n* muchedumbre *f*, *(gang)* pandilla *f*; **the c.** el vulgo; **there was such a c. there** había tantísima gente allí. **2** *vi* **to c. in/out** entrar/salir en tropel.
▸ **crowd round** *vt* apiñarse alrededor de.
crowd·ed *adj* lleno, -a, atestado, -a.
crown corona *f*.
cru·cial *adj* decisivo, -a.
crude *adj (manners, style)* grose- ro, -a.
cru·el *adj* cruel *(to* con).
cru·el·ty crueldad *f* *(to* hacia).
cru·et c. set vinagreras *fpl*.
cruise 1 *vi (ship)* hacer un crucero; *(car)* viajar a velocidad constante; *(plane)* viajar a velocidad de crucero. **2** *n (on ship)* crucero *m*.
crumb miga *f*.
crum·ble 1 *vt* desmigar. **2** *vi (wall)* desmoronarse; *(bread)* desmigajarse.
crum·bly *adj* que se desmigaja.
crum·my *adj fam* chungo, -a.
crum·ple *vt (clothes)* arrugar.
crunch 1 *vt (food)* mascar. **2** *n* crujido *m*.
crunch·y *adj* crujiente.
crush 1 *vt* aplastar; *(wrinkle)* arrugar; *(grind)* moler. **2** *n (of people)* gentío *m*.
crust corteza *f*.
crutch *(for walking)* muleta *f*.
cry 1 *vi* gritar; *(weep)* llorar. **2** *n* grito *m*; *(weep)* llanto *m*.
▸ **cry off** *vi* rajarse.
▸ **cry out** *vi* gritar; **to c. out for sth** pedir algo a gritos.
▸ **cry over** *vt* llorar por.
crys·tal cristal *m*.
cub *(young animal)* cachorro, -a *mf*; *(junior scout)* niño *m* explorador.
Cu·ban *adj & n* cubano, -a *(mf)*.
cube cubo *m*; *(of sugar)* terrón *m*.
cu·bic *adj* cúbico, -a.
cuck·oo cuco *m*.
cu·cum·ber pepino *m*.
cud·dle 1 *vt* abrazar. **2** *vi* abrazarse.
▸ **cuddle up to** *vt* acurrucarse contra.
cuddly toy muñeco *m* de peluche.
cue *(in play)* pie *m*; indicación *f*.
cuff *(of sleeve)* puño *m*; *(of trousers)* dobladillo *m*.
cuff-links *npl* gemelos *mpl*.
cul-de-sac callejón *m* sin salida.
cul·prit culpable *mf*.
cult culto *m*; **c. film** película *f* de culto.
cul·ti·vate *vt* cultivar.
cul·ti·vat·ed *adj (person)* culto, -a.
cul·tur·al *adj* cultural.
cul·ture cultura *f*.
cul·tured *adj (person)* culto, -a.
cum·ber·some *adj (bulky)* voluminoso, -a.
cun·ning 1 *adj* astuto, -a. **2** *n* astucia *f*.
cup taza *f*; *(trophy)* copa *f*.
cup·board armario *m*; *(on wall)* alacena *f*.
cur·a·ble *adj* curable.
curb bordillo *m*.
cure 1 *vt* curar. **2** *n (remedy)* cura *f*, remedio *m*.
cu·ri·os·i·ty curiosidad *f*.
cu·ri·ous *adj (inquisitive)* curioso, -a; *(odd)* extraño, -a.
curl 1 *vt (hair)* rizar. **2** *vi* rizarse. **3** *n (of hair)* rizo *m*.
▸ **curl up** *vi (cat etc)* enroscarse; *(person)* hacerse un ovillo.
curl·y *adj* rizado, -a.
cur·rant pasa *f* (de Corinto).
cur·ren·cy moneda *f*, **foreign c.** divisas *fpl*.
cur·rent *adj* actual; *(opinion)* general; *(year)* en curso.
cur·rent ac·count cuenta *f* corriente.
cur·rent af·fairs actualidad *f* *sing* (política).
cur·rent·ly *adv* actualmente.
cur·ric·u·lum *(pl* **curricula)** plan *m* de estudios; **c. vitae** *(resume)* currículum *m* (vitae).
cur·ry curry *m*.
curse *vi* blasfemar.
cur·sor cursor *m*.
cur·tain cortina *f*.
curt·s(e)y 1 *n* reverencia *f*. **2** *vi* hacer una reverencia *(to* a).
curve 1 *n* curva *f*. **2** *vi (road, river)* describir una curva.
cush·ion cojín *m*; *(large)* almohadón *m*.
cus·tard natillas *fpl*.
cus·to·dy custodia *f*; **to take into c.** detener.
cus·tom *(habit)* costumbre *f*.
cus·tom·ar·y *adj* habitual.
cus·tom·er cliente *mf*.
cus·toms *n sing or pl* aduana *f*.
cus·toms du·ty derechos *mpl* de aduana.
cus·toms of·fi·cer agente *mf* de aduana.
cut 1 *vt** cortar; *(stone)* tallar; *(reduce)* reducir; *(divide up)* dividir **(into** en). **2** *vi** cortar. **3** *n* corte *m*; *(in skin)* cortadura *f*, *(wound)* herida *f*, *(with knife)* cuchillada *f*, *(of meat)* clase *f* de carne; *(reduction)* reducción *f*.
▸ **cut away** *vt (remove)* cortar.
▸ **cut back** *vt (expenses)* reducir; *(production)* disminuir.
▸ **cut down** *vt (tree)* talar.
▸ **cut down on** *vt* reducir.
▸ **cut off** *vt (water etc)* cortar; *(place)* aislar; *(heir)* excluir.
▸ **cut out 1** *vt (from newspaper)* recortar; *(delete)* suprimir; *(person)* **to be c. out for sth** estar hecho, -a para algo; *fam* **c. it out!** ¡basta ya! **2** *vi (engine)* calarse.
▸ **cut up** *vt* cortar en pedazos.
cut·back reducción *f* **(in** de).
cute *adj* mono, -a, lindo, -a.
cut·ler·y cubiertos *mpl*.
cut·let chuleta *f*.
cut·ting 1 *n (from newspaper)* recorte *m*; *(plant)* esqueje *m*. **2** *adj (wind)* cortante; *(remark)* mordaz.
CV, cv *abbr of* **curriculum vitae** currículum *m* (vitae).
cy·cle 1 *n* ciclo *m*; *(bicycle)* bicicleta *f*; *(motorcycle)* moto *f*. **2** *vi* ir en bicicleta.
cy·cling ciclismo *m*.
cy·clist ciclista *mf*.

cyl·in·der cilindro *m*; *(for gas)* bombona *f*.
cym·bal platillo *m*.
cyn·i·cal *adj (sceptical)* descreído, -a, suspicaz; *(unscrupulous)* desaprensivo, -a, sin escrúpulos.
Czech 1 *adj* checo, -a. **2** *n (person)* checo, -a *mf*; *(language)* checo *m*.

D

dab *vt (apply)* aplicar; *(touch lightly)* tocar ligeramente.
dad, dad·dy *fam* papá *m*, papi *m*.
daf·fo·dil narciso *m*.
daft *adj (idea)* tonto, -a.
dai·ly 1 *adj* diario, -a. **2** *adv* diariamente. **3** *n (newspaper)* diario *m*.
dair·y lechería *f*; **d. farming** industria *f* lechera; **d. produce** productos *mpl* lácteos.
dai·sy margarita *f*.
dam *(barrier)* dique *m*; *(lake)* presa *f*.
dam·age 1 *n* daño *m*; *(to health, reputation)* perjuicio *m*. **2** *vt (harm)* dañar; *(spoil)* estropear.
dam·ag·ing *adj* perjudicial.
damn *fam* **1** *interj* d. (it)! ¡maldito, -a sea! **2** *n* **I don't give a d.** me importa un bledo. **3** *adj* maldito, -a. **4** *adv (very)* muy, sumamente.
damp 1 *adj* húmedo, -a; *(wet)* mojado, -a. **2** *n* humedad *f*.
damp·en *vt* humedecer.
damp·ness humedad *f*.
dance 1 *n* baile *m*; *(classical, tribal)* danza *f*. **2** *vti* bailar.
dance hall salón *m* de baile.
danc·er *(by profession)* bailarín, -ina *mf*; **she's a good d.** baila muy bien.
dan·de·li·on diente *m* de león.
dan·druff caspa *f*.
Dane danés, -esa *mf*.
dan·ger *(peril)* peligro *m*; *(risk)* riesgo *m*; *(of war etc)* amenaza *f*; **out of d.** fuera de peligro.
dan·ger·ous *adj* peligroso, -a; *(risky)* arriesgado, -a; *(harmful)* nocivo, -a; *(illness)* grave.
danger·ous·ly *adv* peligrosamente.
Dan·ish 1 *adj* danés, -esa. **2** *n (language)* danés *m*.
dare 1 *vi* atreverse, osar. **2** *vt (challenge)* desafiar; **to d. to do sth** atreverse a hacer algo.
dar·ing *adj* osado, -a.
dark 1 *adj (unlit, color)* oscuro, -a; *(hair, complexion)* moreno, -a; *(eyes, future)* negro, -a. **2** *n (darkness)* oscuridad *f*.
dark-haired *adj* moreno, -a.
dark·ness oscuridad *f*.
dark-skinned *adj* de piel oscura.
dar·ling *adj & n* querido, -a *(mf)*.
dart *(missile)* dardo *m*; **darts** *sing (game)* dardos *mpl*.
dart·board diana *f*.
dash 1 *n (hyphen)* guión *m*. **2** *vi (rush)* correr.
▶**dash off** *vi* salir corriendo.
dash·board salpicadero *m*.
da·ta *npl* datos *mpl*
da·ta·base base *m* de datos.
data proc·ess·ing *(act)* proceso *m* de datos; *(science)* informática *f*.
date¹ *n* fecha *f*; *(social event)* compromiso *m*; *(with girl, boy)* cita *f*; *(person dated)* ligue *m*; **what's the d. today?** ¿qué día es hoy?; **out of d.** *(ideas)* anticuado, -a; *(expression)* desusado, -a; *(invalid)* caducado, -a; **to be up to d.** estar al día.
▶**date back to, date from** *vt* datar de; *(origins etc)* remontarse a.
date² *(fruit)* dátil *m*.
dat·ed *(idea)* anticuado, -a; *(fashion)* pasado, -a de moda; *(expression)* desusado, -a.
daugh·ter hija *f*.
daugh·ter-in-law nuera *f*.
daw·dle *vi (walking)* andar despacio; *(waste time)* perder el tiempo.
dawn amanecer *m*.
day día *m*; **(on) the next** *or* **following d.** el *or* al día siguiente; **the d. after tomorrow** pasado mañana; **the d. before yesterday** anteayer.
day·break amanecer *m*.
day·light luz *f* del día.
day re·turn *(ticket)* billete *m* de ida y vuelta para el mismo día.
day·time día *m*.
dead 1 *adj* muerto, -a; **he was shot d.** le mataron a tiros. **2** *adv fam (tired, easy)* muy.
dead-end *(street)* callejón *m* sin salida.
dead·line *(date)* fecha *f* tope; *(time)* hora *f* tope.
dead·ly 1 *adj* mortal; *(weapon)* mortífero, -a; *(aim)* certero, -a. **2** *adv (extremely)* terriblemente, sumamente.
deaf 1 *adj* sordo, -a; **d. mute** sordomudo, -a *mf*. **2** *npl* **the d.** los sordos.
deaf·ness sordera *f*.
deal *(in business, politics)* trato *m*; *(amount)* cantidad *f*; *(at cards)* reparto *m*; **business d.** contrato *m*; **to do a d. with sb** *(transaction)* cerrar un trato con algn; *(agreement)* pactar algo con algn; **it's a d.!** ¡trato hecho!; **a good d. (of sth)** una gran parte (de algo); **a good d. slower** mucho más despacio.
▶**deal* in** *vt (goods)* comerciar en; *(drugs)* traficar con.
▶**deal* out** *vt* repartir.
▶**deal* with** *vt (firm, person)* tratar con; *(subject, problem)* abordar; *(in book etc)* tratar de.
deal·er *(in goods)* comerciante *mf*; *(in drugs)* traficante *mf*.
deal·ings *npl (relations)* trato *m* sing; *(in business)* negocios *mpl*.
dear 1 *adj (loved)* querido, -a; *(expensive)* caro, -a; *(in letter)* **D. Andrew** Querido Andrew; **D. Madam** Estimada señora; **D. Sir(s)** Muy señor(es) mío(s). **2** *n* querido, -a *mf*; **my d.** mi vida. **3** *interj* **oh d.!, d. me!** *(surprise)* ¡vaya por Dios!; *(disappointment)* ¡qué pena!
death muerte *f*.
death cer·tif·i·cate certificado *m* de defunción.
de·bate 1 *n* debate *m*. **2** *vti* discutir.
deb·it 1 *n* débito *m*. **2** *vt* **to d. sb's account** cargar una suma en la cuenta de algn.
debt deuda *f*.
debt·or deudor, -a *mf*.
de·but debut *m*; **to make one's d.** debutar.
dec·ade década *f*, decenio *m*.
de·caf·fein·at·ed *adj* descafeinado, -a.
de·cay *(of food, body)* descomposición *f*; *(of teeth)* caries *f inv*; *(of buildings)* desmoronamiento *m*.
de·ceive *vt (mislead)* engañar; *(lie to)* mentir.
De·cem·ber diciembre *m*.
de·cent *adj* decente; *(person)* honrado, -a; *(kind)* simpático, -a.

de·cep·tion engaño *m*.
de·cide 1 *vt* decidir; **to d. to do sth** decidir hacer algo. **2** *vi (reach decision)* decidirse.
▶**decide on** *vt (choose)* optar por.
dec·i·mal 1 *adj* decimal; **d. point** coma *f* (de fracción decimal). **2** *n* decimal *m*.
de·ci·sion decisión *f*.
de·ci·sive *adj (resolute)* decidido, -a; *(conclusive)* decisivo, -a.
deck *(of ship)* cubierta *f*.
deck-chair tumbona *f*.
de·clare *vt* declarar; *(winner, innocence)* proclamar.
de·cline *vi (decrease)* disminuir; *(amount)* bajar; *(business)* decaer; *(deteriorate)* deteriorarse; *(health)* empeorar.
dec·o·rate *vt (adorn)* decorar (**with** con); *(paint)* pintar; *(wallpaper)* empapelar.
dec·o·ra·tion *(decor)* decoración *f*.
dec·or·a·tive *adj* decorativo, -a.
dec·o·ra·tor decorador, -a *mf*; *(painter)* pintor, -a *mf*; *(paper-hanger)* empapelador, -a *mf*.
de·crease 1 *n* disminución *f*; *(in speed, size, price)* reducción *f*. **2** *vi* disminuir; *(price, temperature)* bajar; *(speed, size)* reducirse. **3** *vt* disminuir; *(price, temperature)* bajar.
de·cree 1 *n* decreto *m*; *(by court)* sentencia *f*. **2** *vt* decretar.
ded·i·cate *vt* consagrar, dedicar.
ded·i·cat·ed *adj* dedicado, -a, entregado, -a.
de·duct *vt* descontar (**from** de).
de·duc·tion *(conclusion)* conclusión *f*; *(subtraction)* descuento *m*.
deed *(act)* acto *m*; *(legal document)* escritura *f*.
deep *adj* profundo, -a; *(breath, sigh)* hondo, -a; *(voice)* bajo, -a; **it's ten meters d.** tiene diez metros de profundidad.
deep-freeze 1 *n* congelador *m*. **2** *vt* congelar.
deer *n inv* ciervo *m*.
de·fault *n* **by d.** por defaut, por omisión; **to win by d.** ganar por incomparecencia del adversario.
de·feat 1 *vt* derrotar. **2** *n (of army, team)* derrota *f*.
de·fect defecto *m*.
de·fec·tive *adj (faulty)* defectuoso, -a.
de·fend *vt* defender.
de·fen·dant acusado, -a *mf*.
de·fense defensa *f*.
de·fen·sive 1 *adj* defensivo, -a. **2** *n* **to be on the d.** estar a la defensiva.
de·fi·ant *adj (behavior)* desafiante; *(person)* insolente.
de·fi·cien·cy falta *f*, carencia *f*.
de·fi·cient *adj* deficiente; **to be d. in sth** carecer de algo.
def·i·cit déficit *m*.
de·fine *vt* definir; *(duties, powers)* delimitar.
def·i·nite *adj (clear)* claro, -a; *(progress)* notable; *(date, place)* determinado, -a.
def·i·nite·ly *adv* sin duda.
def·i·ni·tion definición *f*.
de·formed *adj* deforme.
de·frost *vt (freezer, food)* descongelar.
de·fy *vt* desafiar; *(law, order)* contravenir.
de·gen·er·ate *vi* degenerar (**into** en).
de·gree grado *m*; *(qualification)* título *m*; **to some d.** hasta cierto punto; **to have a d. in science** ser licenciado en ciencias.
de-icer anticongelante *m*.
de·ject·ed *adj* deprimido, -a.
de·lay 1 *vt (flight, train)* retrasar; *(person)* entretener; *(postpone)* aplazar. **2** *n* retraso *m*.
del·e·gate 1 *n* delegado, -a *mf*. **2** *vt* delegar (**to** en); **to d. sb to do sth** encargar a algn que haga algo.
del·e·ga·tion delegación *f*.
de·lete *vt* suprimir; *(cross out)* tachar.
de·lib·er·ate *adj (intentional)* deliberado, -a.
de·lib·er·ate·ly *adv (intentionally)* a propósito; *(unhurriedly)* pausadamente.
del·i·ca·cy *(food)* manjar *m* (exquisito).
del·i·cate *adj* delicado, -a; *(handwork)* fino, -a; *(instrument)* sensible; *(flavor)* fino, -a.
del·i·ca·tes·sen delicatessen *f*.
de·li·cious *adj* delicioso, -a.
de·light 1 *n (pleasure)* placer *m*; *(source of pleasure)* encanto *m*; **he took d. in it** le encantó. **2** *vt* encantar.
de·light·ed *adj* encantado, -a.
de·light·ful *adj (person)* encantador, -a; *(view)* muy agradable; *(meal, weather)* delicioso, -a.
de·lin·quent *adj & n* delincuente *(mf)*.
de·liv·er *vt (goods, letters)* repartir; *(parcel, manuscript etc)* entregar; *(speech, verdict)* pronunciar; *(baby)* dar a luz.
de·liv·er·y *(of goods)* reparto *m*; *(of package, manuscript etc)* entrega *f*; *(of baby)* parto *m*.
de·lude *vt* engañar; **don't d. yourself** no te hagas ilusiones.
de·lu·sion *(state, act)* engaño *m*; *(false belief)* ilusión *f* (vana); **delusions of grandeur** delirios *mpl* de grandeza.
de luxe *adj* de lujo *inv*.
de·mand 1 *n (request)* petición *f*; *(for pay rise, rights)* reclamación *f*; *(need)* necesidad *f*; *(claim)* exigencia *f*; *(economic)* demanda *f*; **to be in d.** ser solicitado, -a. **2** *vt* exigir; *(rights)* reclamar; **to d. that ...** insistir en que ... (+ *subjunctive*).
de·mand·ing *adj (hard to please)* exigente; *(job)* agotador, -a.
dem·er·a·ra (su·gar) azúcar *m* moreno.
dem·o *fam (demonstration)* manifestación *f*; **d. tape** maqueta *f*.
de·moc·ra·cy democracia *f*.
dem·o·crat·ic *adj* democrático, -a.
de·mol·ish *vt (building)* derribar.
dem·o·li·tion demolición *f*.
de·mon demonio *m*.
dem·on·strate 1 *vt* demostrar. **2** *vi (politically)* manifestarse.
dem·on·stra·tion *(proof)* demostración *f*; *(explanation)* explicación *f*; *(political)* manifestación *f*.
de·mon·stra·tive *adj* franco, -a.
dem·on·stra·tor manifestante *mf*.
de·mor·al·ize *vt* desmoralizar.
den *(of animal)* guarida *f*; *(study)* estudio *m*.
de·ni·al *(of charge)* desmentido *m*; *(of rights)* denegación *f*.
den·im dril *m*; **denims** tejanos *mpl*, vaqueros *mpl*.
de·nounce *vt* denunciar.
dent 1 *n* abolladura *f*. **2** *vt* abollar.
den·tal *adj* dental.
den·tist dentista *mf*.
den·tures *npl* dentadura *f* postiza.
de·ny *vt (refuse)* negar; *(rumor, report)* desmentir; *(charge)* rechazar; **to d. sb sth** negarle algo a algn.
de·o·dor·ant desodorante *m*.
de·part *vi* marcharse, irse; *(from subject)* desviarse (**from** de).

de·part·ment sección *f*, *(in university)* departamento *m*; *(in government)* ministerio *m*.
de·part·ment store grandes almacenes *mpl*.
de·par·ture partida *f*, *(of plane, train)* salida *f*.
de·pend 1 *vi (rely)* fiarse **(on, upon** de). **2** *v impers (be determined by)* depender **(on** de); **it depends on the weather** según el tiempo que haga; **that depends** según.
de·pend·a·ble *adj (person)* fiable.
de·pen·dent 1 *adj* dependiente; **to be d. on sth** depender de algo. **2** *n* **his/her d.** la persona a su cargo.
de·pict *vt (in painting)* representar; *(describe)* describir.
de·plor·a·ble *adj* lamentable.
de·plore *vt* deplorar.
de·pos·it 1 *n (in bank, on rented car)* depósito *m*; *(in river, test tube)* sedimento *m*; *(in wine)* poso *m*; *(on purchase)* señal *f*; *(on house)* entrada *f*. **2** *vt* depositar; *(into account)* ingresar.
de·pot almacén *m*; *(bus garage)* cochera *f* (de autobuses).
de·press *vt (discourage)* deprimir.
de·pressed *adj (person)* deprimido, -a; **to get d.** deprimirse.
de·pres·sion depresión *f*.
de·prive *vt* privar **(of** de).
de·prived *adj* necesitado, -a.
depth profundidad *f*, *(of emotion)* intensidad *f*.
dep·u·ty *(substitute)* suplente *mf*; **d. head** subdirector, -a *mf*.
de·rail·ment descarrilamiento *m*.
der·e·lict *adj* abandonado, -a.
de·rive *vt* sacar, obtener.
de·scend 1 *vi* descender; **to d. from** *(be related to)* descender de. **2** *vt (stairs)* bajar.
▸**descend upon** *vt (area)* invadir.
de·scen·dant descendiente *mf*.
de·scent descenso *m*.
de·scribe *vt* describir.
de·scrip·tion descripción *f*; *(type)* clase *f*.
des·ert¹ desierto *m*.
de·sert² *vt (place, family)* abandonar.
de·serve *vt (rest, punishment)* merecer; *(prize, praise)* ser digno, -a de.
de·sign 1 *n* diseño *m*; *(of building etc)* plano *m*; *(of room)* disposición *f*; *(pattern)* dibujo *m*. **2** *vt* diseñar.
des·ig·nate *vt* designar, nombrar.
de·sign·er diseñador, -a *mf*; **d. jeans** vaqueros *mpl* de marca.
de·sign·er clothes ropa *f* de marca.
de·sir·a·ble *adj* deseable; *(asset, offer)* atractivo, -a.
de·sire 1 *n* deseo *m*; **I haven't the slightest d. to go** no me apetece nada ir. **2** *vt* desear.
desk *(in school)* pupitre *m*; *(in office)* escritorio *m*; **(reception) d.** recepción *f*.
desk clerk recepcionista *mf*.
desk·top escritorio *m*; **d. publishing** autoedición *f*.
de·spair 1 *n* desesperación *f*. **2** *vi* desesperar(se) **(of** de).
des·patch *vt* = **dispatch**.
des·per·ate *adj (person, situation, action)* desesperado, -a; *(need)* apremiante; **to be d. for sth** necesitar algo con urgencia.
des·per·ate·ly *adv (need)* urgentemente; *(bad, busy)* terriblemente.
des·pi·ca·ble *adj* despreciable; *(behavior)* indigno, -a.
de·spise *vt* despreciar.
de·spite *prep* a pesar de.
des·sert postre *m*.
des·sert spoon cuchara *f* de postre.
des·ti·na·tion destino *m*.
des·ti·tute *adj* indigente.
de·stroy *vt* destruir; *(vehicle, old furniture)* destrozar.
de·struc·tion destrucción *f*.
de·struc·tive *adj (gale etc)* destructor, -a.
de·tach *vt (remove)* separar.
de·tach·a·ble *adj* separable **(from** de).
de·tached *adj (separated)* separado, -a.
de·tached house casa *f* independiente.
de·tail detalle *m*, pormenor *m*.
detailed *adj* detallado, -a.
de·tain *vt (police etc)* detener; *(delay)* retener.
de·tect *vt (error, movement)* advertir; *(difference)* notar; *(smell, sound)* percibir; *(discover)* descubrir.
de·tec·tive detective *mf*; **d. story** novela *f* policíaca.
de·tec·tor aparato *m* detector.
de·ten·tion *(of suspect etc)* detención *f*.
de·ter *vt (dissuade)* disuadir **(from** de); **to d. sb from doing sth** impedir a algn hacer algo.
de·ter·gent detergente *m*.
de·te·ri·o·rate *vi* deteriorarse.
de·te·ri·o·ra·tion empeoramiento *m*; *(of substance, friendship)* deterioro *m*.
de·ter·mi·na·tion *(resolution)* resolución *f*.
de·ter·mine *vt* determinar.
de·ter·mined *adj (person)* decidido, -a; *(effort)* enérgico, -a.
de·ter·rent fuerza *f* disuasoria.
de·tour desvío *m*.
dev·as·tat·ing *adj (news, results)* demoledor, -a.
de·vel·op 1 *vt* desarrollar; *(trade)* fomentar; *(plan)* elaborar; *(illness, habit)* contraer; *(interest)* mostrar; *(natural resources)* aprovechar; *(build on) (site)* urbanizar. **2** *vi (body, industry)* desarrollarse; *(system)* perfeccionarse; *(interest)* crecer.
▸**develop into** *vt* transformarse en.
de·vel·op·ment desarrollo *m*; *(of trade)* fomento *m*; *(of skill)* perfección *f*; *(of character)* formación *f*; *(advance)* avance *m*; *(exploitation)* explotación *f*; *(of land, site)* urbanización *f*; **there are no new developments** no hay ninguna novedad.
de·vi·ate *vi* desviarse **(from** de).
de·vice aparato *m*; *(mechanism)* mecanismo *m*.
dev·il diablo *m*, demonio *m*; *fam* **where the d. did you put it?** ¿dónde demonios lo pusiste?
de·vise *vt* idear.
de·vote *vt* dedicar.
de·vot·ed *adj* dedicado, -a **(to** a).
de·vo·tion devoción *f*; *(to cause)* dedicación *f*.
dew rocío *m*.
di·a·be·tes diabetes *f*.
di·a·bet·ic *adj & n* diabético, -a *(mf)*.
di·ag·nose *vt* diagnosticar.
di·ag·no·sis *(pl* **diagnoses)** diagnóstico *m*.
di·ag·o·nal *adj & n* diagonal *(f)*.
di·ag·o·nal·ly *adv* en diagonal, diagonalmente.
di·a·gram diagrama *m*; *(of process, system)* esquema *m*; *(of workings)* gráfico *m*.
di·al 1 *n (of clock)* esfera *f*; *(on machine)* botón *m* selector; *(on radio)* dial *m*; **d. tone** señal *f* para marcar. **2** *vti* marcar.

di·a·lect dialecto *m*.
di·a·log diálogo *m*.
di·am·e·ter diámetro *m*.
di·a·mond diamante *m*; *(shape)* rombo *m*.
di·a·per pañal *m*.
di·ar·rhe·a diarrea *f*.
di·a·ry diario *m*; *(for appointments)* agenda *f*.
dice 1 *n* dado *m*. **2** *vt (food)* cortar en cuadritos.
dic·tate 1 *vt (letter, order)* dictar. **2** *vi (order about)* dar órdenes.
dic·ta·tion dictado *m*.
dic·tion·ar·y diccionario *m*.
did *pt of* **do**.
die *vi* morir(se); **to be dying for sth/to do sth** morirse por algo/de ganas de hacer algo.
▸**die down** *vi (wind)* amainar; *(noise, excitement)* disminuir.
▸**die out** *vi* extinguirse.
die·sel *(oil)* gasoil *m*; **d. engine** motor *m* diesel.
di·et 1 *n (normal food)* dieta *f*; *(selected food)* régimen *m*. **2** *vi* estar a régimen.
dif·fer *vi (be unlike)* ser distinto, -a; *(disagree)* discrepar.
dif·fer·ence diferencia *f*; *(disagreement)* desacuerdo *m*; **it makes no d. (to me)** (me) da igual; **what d. does it make?** ¿qué más da?
dif·fer·ent *adj* distinto, -a.
dif·fer·ent·ly *adv* de otra manera.
dif·fi·cult *adj* difícil.
dif·fi·cul·ty dificultad *f*; *(problem)* problema *m*.
dig* 1 *vt (earth)* cavar; *(tunnel)* hacer; *(hole)* hacer. **2** *vi* cavar.
▸**dig out** *vt fig (find)* sacar; *(information)* descubrir.
▸**dig up** *vt (weeds)* arrancar; *(buried object)* desenterrar.
di·gest *vt (food)* digerir; *(facts)* asimilar.
di·ges·tion digestión *f*.
dig·ger escavadora *f*.
di·git *(number)* dígito *m*.
dig·i·tal *adj* digital.
dig·ni·ty dignidad *f*.
di·lap·i·dat·ed *adj* en mal estado.
di·lem·ma dilema *m*.
di·lute *vt* diluir; *(wine, milk)* aguar.
dim 1 *adj (light)* tenue; *(room)* oscuro, -a; *(outline)* borroso, -a; *(memory)* vago, -a; *fam (stupid)* torpe. **2** *vt (light)* bajar.
dime moneda *f* de diez centavos.
di·men·sion dimensión *f*.
di·min·ish *vti* disminuir.
din estrépito *m*.
dine *vi (formal use)* cenar.
din·er *(person)* comensal *mf*; *(restaurant)* restaurante *m* barato.
din·ghy bote *m*; **(rubber) d.** bote *m* neumático.
din·gy *adj (street, house)* oscuro, -a; *(dirty)* sucio, -a; *(colour)* desteñido, -a.
din·ing car vagón *m* restaurante.
din·ing room comedor *m*.
din·ner *(at midday)* comida *f*; *(in evening)* cena *f*.
din·ner jack·et smoking *m*.
din·ner par·ty cena *f*.
din·ner ser·vice vajilla *f*.
di·no·saur dinosaurio *m*.
dip 1 *n (bathe)* chapuzón *m*; *(of road)* pendiente *f*. **2** *vi (road)* bajar.
▸**dip into** *vt (savings)* echar mano de.
diph·thong diptongo *m*.
di·plo·ma diploma *m*.
dip·lo·mat diplomático, -a *mf*.
dip·lo·mat·ic *adj* diplomático, -a.
di·rect 1 *adj* directo, -a. **2** *adv* directamente. **3** *vt* dirigir; **can you d. me to a bank?** ¿me puede indicar dónde hay un banco?
di·rec·tion dirección *f*; **directions** *(to place)* señas *fpl*; **directions for use** modo *m* de empleo.
di·rect·ly 1 *adv (above etc)* justo; *(speak)* directamente; *(at once)* en seguida. **2** *conj* en cuanto.
di·rec·tor director, -a *mf*.
di·rec·to·ry *(for telephone)* guía *f* telefónica.
di·rec·to·ry as·sis·tance *(servicio m de)* información *f*.
dirt suciedad *f*.
dirt-cheap *adv & adj fam* tirado, -a.
dirt·y 1 *adj* sucio, -a; *(joke)* verde; *(mind)* pervertido, -a; **d. word** palabrota *f*; **to get d.** ensuciar algo. **2** *vt* ensuciar.
dis·a·bil·i·ty discapacidad *f*.
dis·a·bled 1 *adj* minusválido, -a. **2** *npl* **the d.** los minusválidos *mpl*.
dis·ad·van·tage desventaja *f*; *(obstacle)* inconveniente *m*.
dis·a·gree *vi (differ)* no estar de acuerdo **(with** con); *(quarrel)* reñir **(about** por); **garlic disagrees with me** el ajo no me sienta bien.
dis·a·gree·a·ble *adj* desagradable.
dis·a·gree·ment desacuerdo *m*; *(argument)* riña *f*.
dis·ap·pear *vi* desaparecer.
dis·ap·pear·ance desaparición *f*.
dis·ap·point *vt* decepcionar.
dis·ap·point·ing *adj* decepcionante.
dis·ap·point·ment decepción *f*.
dis·ap·prove *vi* **to d. of** desaprobar.
dis·arm 1 *vt* desarmar. **2** *vi* desarmarse.
dis·as·ter desastre *m*.
dis·as·trous *adj* desastroso, -a.
disc disco *m*.
dis·card *vt (old things)* deshacerse de; *(plan)* descartar.
dis·charge *vt (prisoner)* soltar; *(patient)* dar de alta; *(soldier)* licenciar; *(dismiss)* despedir.
dis·con·tin·ued *adj (article)* que no se fabrica más.
dis·ci·pline 1 *n* disciplina *f*. **2** *vt (child)* castigar; *(worker)* sancionar.
disc jock·ey disc-jockey *mf*, pinchadiscos *mf inv*.
dis·close *vt* revelar.
dis·co discoteca *f*.
dis·com·fort *(pain)* malestar *m*.
dis·con·nect *vt* desconectar **(from** de); *(gas, electricity)* cortar.
dis·con·tent·ed *adj* descontento, -a.
dis·co·theque discoteca *f*.
dis·count descuento *m*.
dis·cour·age *vt (dishearten)* desanimar; *(advances)* rechazar.
dis·cov·er *vt* descubrir; *(missing person, object)* encontrar.
dis·cov·er·y descubrimiento *m*.
dis·creet *adj* discreto, -a.
dis·crim·i·nate *vi* distinguir **(between** entre); **to d. against sth/sb** discriminar algo/a algn.

dis·crim·i·na·tion (*bias*) discriminación *f*.
dis·cuss *vt* discutir; (*in writing*) tratar de.
dis·cus·sion discusión *f*.
dis·ease enfermedad *f*.
dis·em·bark *vti* desembarcar.
dis·fig·ured *adj* desfigurado, -a.
dis·grace 1 *n* desgracia *f*. **2** *vt* deshonrar.
dis·grace·ful *adj* vergonzoso, -a.
dis·guise 1 *n* disfraz *m*; **in d.** disfrazado, -a. **2** *vt* (*person*) disfrazar (**as** de).
dis·gust 1 *n* repugnancia *f*, asco *m*. **2** *vt* (*revolt*) dar asco a.
dis·gust·ed *adj* disgustado, -a, indignado, -a.
dis·gust·ing *adj* repugnante; (*behavior, state of affairs*) intolerable.
dish (*for serving*) fuente *f*, (*course*) plato *m*; **to wash** *or* **do the dishes** fregar los platos.
▶**dish up** *vt* (*meal*) servir.
dish·cloth trapo *m* de fregar.
di·shev·eled *adj* (*hair*) despeinado, -a; (*appearance*) fraudulento, -a.
dis·hon·est *adj* (*person*) poco honrado, -a.
dis·hon·es·ty (*of person*) falta *f* de honradez.
dish·tow·el paño *m* de cocina.
dish·wash·er lavaplatos *m inv*.
dis·il·lu·sioned *adj* desilusionado, -a.
dis·in·cen·tive freno *m*.
dis·in·fect *vt* desinfectar.
dis·in·fec·tant desinfectante *m*.
disk disco *m*; (*for computer*) disquete *m*; **d. drive** unidad *f* de disquete, disquetera *f*.
dis·like 1 *n* antipatía *f* (**for, of** a, hacia). **2** *vt* tener antipatía hacia.
dis·lo·cate *vt* (*joint*) dislocar.
dis·mal *adj* (*prospect*) sombrío, -a; (*place, weather*) deprimente; (*person*) triste.
dis·man·tle *vt* desmontar.
dis·may 1 *n* consternación *f*. **2** *vt* consternar.
dis·miss *vt* (*employee*) despedir.
dis·miss·al (*of employee*) despido *m*.
dis·o·be·di·ence desobediencia *f*.
dis·o·be·di·ent *adj* desobediente.
dis·o·bey *vt* desobedecer; (*law*) violar.
dis·or·der (*untidiness*) desorden *m*; (*riot*) disturbio *m*; (*illness*) trastorno *m*.
dis·or·gan·ized *adj* desorganizado, -a.
dis·patch *vt* (*mail*) enviar; (*goods*) expedir.
dis·pel *vt* disipar.
dis·pens·er (*device*) máquina *f* expendedora; **cash d.** cajero *m* automático.
dis·perse 1 *vt* dispersar. **2** *vi* dispersarse.
dis·play 1 *n* (*exhibition*) exposición *f*, (*on computer screen*) visualización *f*. **2** *vt* mostrar; (*goods*) exponer; (*on computer screen*) visualizar; (*feelings*) manifestar.
dis·pleased *adj* contrariado, -a.
dis·pos·a·ble *adj* desechable.
dis·pos·al **at my d.** a mi disposición.
dis·pose *vi* **to d. of** (*trash*) tirar; (*unwanted object*) deshacerse de.
dis·pute 1 *n* (*disagreement*) discusión *f*, (*quarrel*) disputa *f*, **industrial d.** conflicto *m* laboral. **2** *vt* refutar.
dis·qual·i·fy *vt* (*team*) descalificar; (*make ineligible*) incapacitar.
dis·re·gard *vt* (*ignore*) ignorar.
dis·re·spect·ful *adj* irrespetuoso, -a.
dis·rupt (*meeting, traffic*) interrumpir; (*order*) trastornar; (*schedule etc*) desbaratar.
dis·rup·tion (*of meeting, traffic*) interrupción *f*, (*of schedule etc*) desbaratamiento *m*.
dis·sat·is·fac·tion descontento *m*.
dis·sat·is·fied *adj* descontento, -a.
dis·sent 1 *n* disconformidad *f*. **2** *vi* disentir.
dis·solve 1 *vt* disolver. **2** *vi* disolverse.
dis·suade *vt* disuadir (**from** de).
dis·tance distancia *f*, **in the d.** a lo lejos.
dis·tant *adj* (*place, time*) lejano, -a; (*look*) distraído, -a; (*aloof*) distante.
dis·taste aversión *f*.
dis·taste·ful *adj* desagradable.
dis·tinct *adj* (*different*) diferente; (*smell, change*) marcado, -a; (*idea, intention*) claro, -a; **as d. from** a diferencia de.
dis·tinc·tion (*difference*) diferencia *f*, (*excellence*) distinción *f*, (*in exam*) sobresaliente *m*.
dis·tinc·tive *adj* distintivo, -a.
dis·tinct·ly *adv* (*clearly*) claramente; (*definitely*) sensiblemente.
dis·tin·guish *vt* distinguir.
dis·tin·guished *adj* distinguido, -a.
dis·tort *vt* (*misrepresent*) deformar.
dis·tract *vt* distraer.
dis·trac·tion (*interruption*) distracción *f*, **to drive sb to d.** volver loco a algn.
dis·tress (*mental*) angustia *f*, (*physical*) dolor *m*.
dis·tress·ing *adj* penoso, -a.
dis·trib·ute *vt* distribuir.
dis·tri·bu·tion distribución *f*.
dis·trib·u·tor distribuidor, -a *mf*, (*in car engine*) delco *m*.
dis·trict (*of country*) región *f*, (*of town*) barrio *m*; **d. attorney** fiscal *mf*.
dis·trust *vt* desconfiar de.
dis·turb *vt* (*inconvenience*) molestar; (*silence*) romper; (*sleep*) interrumpir; (*worry*) perturbar; (*papers*) desordenar.
dis·tur·bance (*commotion*) disturbio *m*.
dis·turb·ing *adj* inquietante.
ditch zanja *f*, (*at roadside*) cuneta *f*, (*for irrigation*) acequia *f*.
dit·to ídem.
di·van diván *m*.
dive 1 *n* (*into water*) zambullida *f*, (*of diver*) buceo *m*; (*of plane*) picado *m*; (*in sport*) salto *m*. **2** *vi** zambullirse; (*diver*) bucear; (*plane*) bajar en picado; (*in sport*) saltar; **he dived for the phone** se precipitó hacia el teléfono.
div·er (*person*) buceador, -a *mf*, (*professional*) buzo *m*; (*from diving board*) saltador, -a *mf*.
di·ver·sion (*distraction*) distracción *f*.
di·vert *vt* desviar.
di·vide 1 *vt* dividir. **2** *vi* (*road, stream*) bifurcarse.
▶**divide off** *vt* separar.
▶**divide up** *vt* (*share out*) repartir.
div·i·dend dividendo *m*.
di·vine *adj* divino, -a.
div·ing submarinismo *m*; (*sport*) salto *m* de trampolín.
div·ing board trampolín *m*.
di·vi·sion división *f*, (*sharing*) reparto *m*; (*of organization*) sección *f*.
di·vorce 1 *n* divorcio *m*. **2** *vt* **she divorced him** se divorció de él.
di·vorced divorciado, -a; **to get d.** divorciarse.
diz·zi·ness vértigo *m*.

diz·zy *adj* (*person*) (*unwell*) mareado, -a.
DJ *abbr of* **disc jockey**.
do* 1 *v aux* (*in negatives and questions*) (*not translated in Spanish*) **do you drive?** ¿tienes carnet de conducir?; **don't you want to come?** ¿no quieres venir?; **he doesn't smoke** no fuma. ▪ (*emphatic*) (*not translated in Spanish*) **do come with us!** ¡ánimo, vente con nosotros!; **I do like your bag** me encanta tu bolso. ▪ (*substituting main verb*) (*not translated in Spanish*) **I don't believe him — neither do I** no le creo — yo tampoco; **I'll go if you do** si vas tú, voy yo; **I think it's dear, but he doesn't** a mí me parece caro pero a él no; **who went? — I did** ¿quién asistió? — yo. ▪ (*in question tags*) **he refused, didn't he?** dijo que no, ¿verdad?; **I don't like it, do you?** a mí no me gusta, ¿y a ti? **2** *vt* hacer; (*task*) realizar; (*duty*) cumplir con; (*distance*) recorrer; **what can I do for you?** ¿en qué puedo servirle?; **what do you do (for a living)?** ¿a qué te dedicas?; **he's done it!** ¡lo ha conseguido!; **we were doing eighty** íbamos a ochenta. **3** *vi* (*act*) hacer; **do as I tell you** haz lo que te digo; **how are you doing?** ¿qué tal?; **to do well** (*person*) tener éxito; (*business*) ir bien; **five dollars will do** con cinco dólares será suficiente; **that will do!** ¡basta ya!; **this cushion will do as a pillow** este cojín servirá de almohada.
▶**do away with** *vt* (*abolish*) abolir; (*discard*) deshacerse de.
▶**do for** *vt* (*destroy, ruin*) arruinar; **I'm done for if I don't finish this** estoy perdido, -a si no acabo esto.
▶**do in** *vt* **I'm done in** (*exhausted*) estoy hecho, -a polvo.
▶**do out** *vt* (*clean*) limpiar a fondo.
▶**do over** *vt* (*repeat*) repetir.
▶**do up** *vt* (*wrap*) envolver; (*belt etc*) abrochar; (*laces*) atar; (*dress up*) arreglar; (*redecorate*) renovar.
▶**do with** *vt* **I could do with a rest** (*need*) un descanso no me vendría nada mal; **to have** *or* **be to do with** (*concern*) tener que ver con.
▶**do without** *vt* pasar sin, prescindir de.
dock 1 *n* **the docks** el muelle. **2** *vi* (*ship*) atracar.
dock·er estibador *m*.
dock·yard astillero *m*.
doc·tor médico, -a *mf*, (*academic*) doctor, -a *mf*.
doc·tor·ate doctorado *m*.
doc·trine doctrina *f*.
doc·u·ment documento *m*.
doc·u·men·ta·ry *adj & n* documental (*m*).
dodge *vt* (*blow*) esquivar; (*pursuer*) despistar; (*tax*) evadir.
dodg·em coche *m* de choque.
does 3rd person sing pres of **do**.
dog perro, -a *mf*.
dog·gy bag (*in restaurant*) bolsita *f* para llevarse los restos de la comida.
dog·house perrera *f*, *fam* **to be in the d.** estar en desgracia.
do·ing **it was none of my d.** yo no tuve nada que ver.
do-it-your·self bricolaje *m*.
doll (*toy*) muñeca *f*.
dol·lar dólar *m*.
doll·house casa *f* de muñecas.
dol·phin delfín *m*.
do·main (*sphere*) campo *m*, esfera *f*, (*territory*) dominio *m*; **d. name** nombre *m* de dominio.
dome cúpula *f*.
do·mes·tic *adj* (*appliance, pet*) doméstico, -a; (*flight, news*) nacional; (*trade, policy*) interior.
dom·i·nant *adj* dominante.
dom·i·nate *vti* dominar.
Do·min·i·can *adj & n* dominicano, -a (*mf*).
dom·i·no (*pl* **dominoes**) (*piece*) ficha *f* de dominó; **dominoes** (*game*) dominó *m sing*.
do·nate *vt* donar.
do·na·tion donativo *m*.
done 1 *pp of* **do**. **2** *adj* (*finished*) terminado, -a; (*meat*) hecho, -a; (*vegetables*) cocido, -a.
don·key burro, -a *mf*.
do·nor donante *mf*.
door puerta *f*.
door·bell timbre *m* (de la puerta).
door·knob pomo *m*.
door knock·er picaporte *m*.
door·man portero *m*.
door·mat felpudo *m*.
door·step peldaño *m*.
door·way entrada *f*.
dope 1 *n fam* (*drug*) chocolate *m*. **2** *adj* tonto, -a.
dor·mi·to·ry (*in school*) dormitorio *m*; (*in university*) colegio *m* mayor.
dos·age (*amount*) dosis *f inv*.
dose dosis *f inv*.
dot punto *m*.
dot·ted line línea *f* de puntos.
dou·ble 1 *adj* doble. **2** *adv* doble; **folded d.** doblado, -a por la mitad; **it's d. the price** cuesta dos veces más. **3** *n* **to earn d.** ganar el doble.
▶**double back** *vi* **to d. back on one's tracks** volver sobre sus pasos.
▶**double up** *vi* (*bend*) doblarse.
dou·ble bed cama *f* de matrimonio.
dou·ble-breast·ed *adj* cruzado, -a.
dou·ble-cross *vt* engañar, traicionar.
dou·ble glaz·ing doble acristalamiento *m*.
doubt 1 *n* duda *f*, **no d.** sin duda; **to be in d. about sth** dudar algo. **2** *vt* dudar.
doubt·ful *adj* **I'm a bit d. about it** no me convence del todo; **it's d. whether ...** no se sabe seguro si ...
doubt·less *adv* sin duda, seguramente.
dough (*for bread*) masa *f*, (*for pastries*) pasta *f*, *fam* (*money*) pasta *f*.
dough·nut rosquilla *f*, dónut® *m*.
dove paloma *f*.
down 1 *adv* (*to or at lower level*) abajo; (*to floor*) al suelo; (*to ground*) a tierra; **to go d.** (*price, person*) bajar; **d. there** allí abajo; **to be d. with a cold** estar resfriado, -a; **to feel d.** estar deprimido, -a. **2** *prep* (*along*) por; **to go d. the road** bajar la calle.
down-and-out *adj* vagabundo, -a *mf*.
down·fall (*of régime*) caída *f*, (*of person*) perdición *f*.
down·hill *adv* **to go d.** ir cuesta abajo.
down pay·ment entrada *f*, fianza *f*.
down·pour chaparrón *m*.
down·right 1 *adj* (*liar, rogue*) declarado, -a; (*lie*) manifiesto, -a. **2** *adv* (*totally*) completamente.
down·stairs 1 *adv* abajo; (*to first floor*) a la planta baja; **to go d.** bajar la escalera. **2** *adj* (*on first floor*) de la planta baja.
down-to-earth *adj* realista.
down·town *adv* en el centro (de la ciudad).
down·ward(s) *adv* hacia abajo.
doze 1 *vi* dormitar. **2** *n* cabezada *f*, **to have a d.** echar una cabezada.
▶**doze off** *vi* quedarse dormido, -a.

doz·en docena *f*; **half a d./a d. eggs** media docena/una docena de huevos.

Dr *abbr of* **Doctor** Doctor, -a *mf*; Dr., Dra.

drab *adj* (*dreary*) gris; (*color*) pardo, -a.

draft (*of cold air*) corriente *f* (de aire); **d. (beer)** cerveza *f* de barril.

draft·y *adj* **this room is very d.** en esta habitación hay mucha corriente.

drag 1 *vt* (*pull*) arrastrar. **2** *vi* (*trail*) arrastrarse; (*person*) rezagarse.

▸**drag along** *vt* arrastrar.

▸**drag on** *vi* (*war, strike*) hacerse interminable.

▸**drag out** *vt* (*speech etc*) alargar.

drag·on dragón *m*.

drain 1 *n* (*for water*) desagüe *m*; (*grating*) sumidero *m*. **2** *vt* (*marsh etc*) avenar; (*reservoir*) desecar. **3** *vi* **to d. (away)** (*liquid*) irse.

drain·ing board escurridero *m*.

drain·pipe tubo *m* de desagüe.

dra·ma (*play*) obra *f* de teatro; (*subject*) teatro *m*; (*tense situation*) drama *m*.

dra·mat·ic *adj* (*change*) impresionante; (*moment*) emocionante; (*of the theater*) dramático, -a.

dra·mat·i·cal·ly *adv* (*to change*) de forma espectacular.

drapes *npl* cortinas *fpl*.

dras·tic *adj* (*severe*) drástico, -a; (*change*) radical.

dras·ti·cal·ly *adv* radicalmente.

draw 1 *vt** (*picture*) dibujar; (*line*) trazar; (*curtains*) (*open*) descorrer; (*close*) correr; (*attract*) atraer; (*attention*) llamar. **2** *vi** (*sketch*) dibujar; **they drew two all** empataron a dos. **3** *n* (*score*) empate *m*.

▸**draw in** *vi* (*days*) acortarse.

▸**draw near (to)** *vt* acercarse (a).

▸**draw on** *vt* (*savings*) recurrir a; (*experience*) aprovecharse de.

▸**draw out** *vt* (*withdraw*) sacar.

▸**draw up** *vt* (*contract*) preparar; (*plan*) esbozar.

draw·back inconveniente *m*.

draw·er cajón *m*.

draw·ing dibujo *m*.

draw·ing pin chincheta *f*.

draw·ing room sala *f* de estar.

dread 1 *vt* temer. **2** *n* temor *m*.

dread·ful *adj* (*shocking*) espantoso, -a; (*awful*) fatal.

dread·ful·ly *adv* (*horribly*) terriblemente; (*very*) muy.

dream 1 *n* sueño *m*; (*marvel*) maravilla *f*. **2** *vti** soñar (**of, about** con).

▸**dream up** *vt* (*excuse*) inventarse; (*plan*) idear.

drea·ry *adj* (*gloomy*) triste; (*boring*) aburrido, -a.

drench *vt* empapar.

dress 1 *n* vestido *m*; (*clothing*) ropa *f*. **2** *vt* (*person*) vestir; (*wound*) vendar; (*salad*) aliñar; **he was dressed in a gray suit** llevaba (puesto) un traje gris. **3** *vi* vestirse.

▸**dress up** *vi* (*in disguise*) disfrazarse (**as** de); (*in best clothes*) vestirse elegante.

dress·er (*in bedroom*) tocador *m*.

dress·ing (*bandage*) vendaje *m*; (*salad*) **d.** aderezo *m*, aliño *m*; **d. room** (*in theater*) camerino *m*; **d. table** tocador *m*.

dress·mak·er modista *mf*.

drew *pt of* **draw**.

drib·ble 1 *vi* (*baby*) babear; (*liquid*) gotear. **2** *vt* (*ball*) regatear.

dried *adj* (*fruit*) seco, -a; (*milk*) en polvo.

drier = **dryer**.

drift *vi* (*boat*) ir a la deriva; (*person*) ir sin rumbo, vagar; **they drifted away** se marcharon poco a poco.

drill 1 *n* (*handtool*) taladro *m*; **dentist's d.** fresa *f*; **pneumatic d.** martillo *m* neumático. **2** *vt* (*wood etc*) taladrar.

drink 1 *vti** beber; **to have sth to d.** tomarse algo; **to d. to sth/sb** brindar por algo/algn. **2** *n* bebida *f*; (*alcoholic*) copa *f*.

▸**drink up 1** *vt* beberse todo. **2** *vi* **d. up!** ¡bébelo todo!

drink·a·ble *adj* potable; (*not unpleasant*) agradable.

drink·ing wa·ter agua *f* potable.

drip 1 *n* goteo *m*; *fam* (*person*) necio, -a *mf*. **2** *vi* gotear; **he was dripping with sweat** el sudor le caía a gotas.

drip-dry *adj* que no necesita planchado.

drive 1 *vt** (*vehicle*) conducir, *Am* manejar; (*person*) llevar; (*stake*) hincar; (*nail*) clavar; (*compel*) forzar; **to d. sb mad** volver loco, -a a algn. **2** *vi** (*in car*) conducir, *Am* manejar. **3** *n* camino *m* de entrada; (*energy*) energía *f*; **to go for a d.** dar una vuelta en coche; **left-hand d.** conducción *f* por la izquierda.

▸**drive along** *vti* (*in car*) conducir.

▸**drive back 1** *vt* (*enemy*) rechazar; (*passenger*) llevar de vuelta a. **2** *vi* volver en coche.

▸**drive in** *vt* (*nail*) clavar.

▸**drive off** *vi* salir (en coche).

▸**drive on** *vi* (*after stopping*) continuar.

▸**drive out** *vt* expulsar.

▸**drive up** *vi* llegar en coche.

driv·el tonterías *fpl*.

driv·er (*of car, bus*) conductor, -a *mf*; (*of train*) maquinista *mf*; (*of lorry*) camionero, -a *mf*.

driv·er's li·cense carnet *m* de conducir.

drive·way *n* camino *m* de entrada.

driv·ing les·son clase *f* de conducir.

driv·ing school autoescuela *f*.

driv·ing test examen *m* de conducir.

driz·zle 1 *n* llovizna *f*. **2** *vi* lloviznar.

droop *vi* (*flower*) marchitarse.

drop 1 *n* (*liquid*) gota *f*; (*descent*) desnivel *m*; (*in price*) bajada *f*; (*in temperature*) descenso *m*. **2** *vt* (*let fall*) dejar caer; (*lower*) bajar; (*reduce*) disminuir; (*abandon*) (*subject, charge etc*) abandonar. **3** *vi* (*object*) caerse; (*voice, price, temperature*) bajar; (*speed*) disminuir.

▸**drop behind** *vi* quedarse atrás.

▸**drop in, drop round** *vi* (*visit*) pasarse (**at** por).

▸**drop off 1** *vi* (*fall asleep*) quedarse dormido, -a. **2** *vt* (*deliver*) dejar en casa (de algn).

▸**drop out** *vi* (*of college*) dejar los estudios; (*of society*) marginarse; (*of competition*) retirarse.

drought sequía *f*.

drown 1 *vt* ahogar; (*place*) inundar. **2** *vi* ahogarse; **he drowned** murió ahogado.

drows·y *adj* soñoliento, -a; **to feel d.** tener sueño.

drug 1 *n* (*medicine*) medicamento *m*; (*narcotic*) droga *f*; **to be on drugs** drogarse. **2** *vt* (*person*) drogar; (*food, drink*) adulterar con drogas.

drug ad·dict drogadicto, -a *mf*.

drug·store establecimiento *m* donde se compran medicamentos, periódicos etc.

drum tambor *m*; (*container*) bidón *m*; **to play the drums** tocar la batería.

drum·mer (*in band*) tambor *mf*; (*in pop group*) batería *mf*.

drunk 1 *adj* borracho, -a; **to get d.** emborracharse. **2** *n* borracho, -a *mf*.

drunk·ard borracho, -a *mf*.

drunk·en *adj* (*driver*) borracho, -a; **d. driving** conducir en estado de embriaguez.

dry 1 *adj* seco, -a. **2** *vt* secar. **3** *vi* **to d. (off)** secarse.

▸**dry up 1** *vt* secar. **2** *vi* secarse.

dry-clean *vt* lavar en seco.

dry-clean·er (*shop*) tintorería *f*.

dry·er secadora *f*.

du·al *adj* doble, dual.

dub *vt* (*subtitle*) doblar (**into** a).

du·bi·ous *adj* (*morals etc*) dudoso, -a; (*doubting*) indeciso, -a.

duch·ess duquesa *f*.

duck¹ pato, -a *mf*; (*as food*) pato *m*.

duck² *vi* (*bow down*) agacharse. **2** *vt* (*evade*) esquivar.

due 1 *adj* (*expected*) esperado, -a; (*money*) pagadero, -a; **the train is d. (to arrive) at ten** el tren debe llegar a las diez; **in d. course** a su debido tiempo; **to be d. to** deberse a. **2** *adv* (*north etc*) derecho hacia.

du·el duelo *m*.

duf·fel coat trenca *f*.

duke duque *m*.

dull *adj* (*boring*) pesado, -a; (*place*) sin interés; (*light*) apagado, -a; (*weather*) gris; (*sound, ache*) sordo, -a.

du·ly *adv* (*properly*) debidamente; (*as expected*) como era de esperar.

dumb *adj* mudo, -a; (*stupid*) tonto, -a.

dump 1 *n* (*tip*) vertedero *m*; *fam* (*place*) lugar *m* de mala muerte; (*town*) poblacho *m*; (*dwelling*) tugurio *m*. **2** *vt* (*garbage*) verter.

dump truck volquete *m*.

dun·ga·rees *npl* mono *m sing*.

du·plex casa *f* adosada; **d. apartment** dúplex *m inv*.

du·pli·cate duplicado *m*; **in d.** por duplicado.

du·ra·ble *adj* duradero, -a.

du·ra·tion duración *f*.

dur·ing *prep* durante.

dusk crepúsculo *m*; **at d.** al anochecer.

dust 1 *n* polvo *m*. **2** *vt* (*furniture*) quitar el polvo a.

dust·er (*for housework*) trapo *m* (del polvo).

dust·y *adj* polvoriento, -a.

Dutch 1 *adj* holandés, -esa. **2** *n* (*language*) holandés *m*; **the D.** los holandeses *mpl*.

Dutch·man holandés *m*.

Dutch·wom·an holandesa *f*.

du·ty deber *m*; (*task*) función *f*; (*tax*) impuesto *m*; **to be on d.** estar de servicio; (*doctor, soldier*) estar de guardia; **d. chemist** farmacia *f* de guardia; **customs d.** derechos *mpl* de aduana.

du·ty-free *adj* libre de impuestos.

du·vet edredón *m*.

DVD *abbr of* **digital versatile disk, digital video disk** DVD *m*; **D. player** reproductor *m* or lector *m* de DVD.

dwarf (*pl* **dwarves**) enano, -a *mf*.

dye 1 *n* tinte *m*. **2** *vt* teñir; **to d. one's hair black** teñirse el pelo de negro.

dy·nam·ic *adj* dinámico, -a.

dy·na·mite dinamita *f*.

dy·na·mo dínamo *f*.

dys·lex·ic *adj* disléxico, -a.

E

each 1 *adj* cada; **e. day/month** todos los días/meses. **2** *pron* cada uno, -a; **we bought one e.** nos compramos uno cada uno; **e. other** el uno al otro; **they hate e. other** se odian.

ea·ger *adj* (*anxious*) impaciente (**to** por); (*keen*) deseoso, -a.

ea·ger·ly *adv* (*anxiously*) con impaciencia; (*keenly*) con ilusión.

ea·ger·ness impaciencia *f* (**to do** por hacer); (*keenness*) afán *m*.

ea·gle águila *f*.

ear oreja *f*; (*inner ear*) oído *m*; (*of corn*) espiga *f*.

ear·ache dolor *m* de oídos.

ear·ly 1 *adj* (*before usual time*) temprano, -a; **to have an e. night** acostarse pronto; **you're e.!** ¡qué pronto has venido! ▪ (*at first stage, period*) **in her e. forties** a los cuarenta y pocos; **in e. July** a principios de julio. ▪ (*in the near future*) **an e. reply** una respuesta pronta. **2** *adv* (*before the expected time*) temprano; **to leave e.** irse pronto; **e. on** al principio; **earlier on** antes; **five minutes e.** con cinco minutos de adelanto; **as e. as possible** tan pronto como sea posible; **to book e.** reservar con tiempo; **at the earliest** cuanto antes.

earn *vt* ganarse; (*money*) ganar; **to earn one's living** ganarse la vida.

ear·nest 1 *adj* serio, -a, formal. **2** *n* **in e.** de veras, en serio.

earn·ings *npl* ingresos *mpl*.

ear·phones *npl* auriculares *mpl*, cascos *mpl*.

ear·plug tapón *m* para los oídos.

ear·ring pendiente *m*.

earth *n* tierra *f*; (*electric*) toma *f* de tierra; **to be down to e.** ser práctico, -a; *fam* **where/why on e. ...?** ¿pero dónde/por qué demonios ...?

earth·quake terremoto *m*.

ease 1 *n* (*lack of difficulty*) facilidad *f*; (*affluence*) comodidad *f*; (*freedom from discomfort*) tranquilidad *f*; **at e.** relajado, -a. **2** *vt* (*pain*) aliviar; (*move gently*) deslizar con cuidado.

▸**ease off, ease up** *vi* (*decrease*) disminuir; (*slow down*) ir más despacio.

ea·sel caballete *m*.

eas·i·ly *adv* fácilmente; **e. the best** con mucho el mejor.

east 1 *n* este *m*. **2** *adj* del este, oriental. **3** *adv* al este.

east·bound *adj* (con) dirección este.

Eas·ter Semana Santa *f*; **E. Sunday** Domingo *m* de Resurrección.

east·ern *adj* oriental, del este.

east·ward(s) *adv* hacia el este.

eas·y 1 *adj* fácil; (*comfortable*) cómodo, -a; *fam* **I'm e.!** me da lo mismo; **e. chair** butacón *m*. **2** *adv* **go e. on the wine** no te pases con el vino; **to take things e.** tomarse las cosas con calma; **take it e.!** ¡tranquilo!

eas·y-go·ing *adj* (*calm*) tranqui- lo, -a; (*lax*) despreocupado, -a; (*undemanding*) poco exigente.

eat* *vt* comer.

▸**eat away** *vt* desgastar; (*metal*) corroer.

▸**eat out** *vi* comer fuera.

▸**eat up** *vt* (*meal*) terminar; (*petrol*) consumir; (*miles*) tragar.

eau de Co·logne colonia *f*.

ec·cen·tric *adj & n* excéntrico, -a (*mf*).

ech·o 1 *n* (*pl* **echoes**) eco *m*. **2** *vt* (*repeat*) repetir. **3** *vi* resonar.

ec·o·nom·ic *adj* económico, -a; (*profitable*) rentable.

ec·o·nom·i·cal *adj* económico, -a.

e·con·o·mize *vi* economizar (**on** en).

e·con·o·my *(national)* economía *f*, *(saving)* ahorro *m*; **e. class** (clase *f*) turista *f*.
edge 1 *n* borde *m*; *(of knife)* filo *m*; *(of water)* orilla *f*, **on the e. of town** en las afueras de la ciudad; **to have the e. on sb** llevar ventaja a algn; **to be on e.** tener los nervios de punta. **2** *vi* **to e. closer** acercarse lentamente; **to e. forward** avanzar poco a poco.
ed·i·ble *adj* comestible.
ed·it *vt* editar; *(proofs)* corregir; *(newspaper)* ser redactor, -a de; *(film, TV program)* montar; *(cut)* cortar.
▸**edit out** *vt* suprimir.
e·di·tion edición *f*.
ed·i·tor *(of book)* editor, -a *mf*, *(of newspaper)* redactor, -a *mf*, *(of film, TV program)* montador, -a *mf*.
ed·i·to·ri·al 1 *adj* **e. staff** redacción *f*. **2** *n* editorial *m*.
ed·u·cate *vt* educar.
ed·u·cat·ed *adj* culto, -a.
ed·u·ca·tion *(schooling)* enseñanza *f*, *(training)* formación *f*, *(studies)* estudios *mpl*; *(culture)* cultura *f*.
ed·u·ca·tion·al *adj* educativo, -a.
eel anguila *f*.
ef·fect efecto *m*; *(impression)* impresión *f*, **in e.** efectivamente; **to come into e.** entrar en vigor; **to have an e. on** afectar a; **to no e.** sin resultado alguno; **effects** *(possessions)* efectos *mpl*.
ef·fec·tive *adj (successful)* eficaz; *(impressive)* impresionante.
ef·fec·tive·ly *adv (successfully)* eficazmente; *(in fact)* en efecto.
ef·fi·cien·cy *(of person)* eficacia *f*, *(of machine)* rendimiento *m*.
ef·fi·cient *adj* eficaz; *(person)* eficiente; *(machine)* de buen rendimiento.
ef·fi·cient·ly *adv* eficazmente; **to work e.** tener buen rendimiento.
ef·fort esfuerzo *m*; *(attempt)* intento *m*; **to make an e.** hacer un esfuerzo.
eg *abbr* p. ej.
egg 1 *n* huevo *m*. **2** *vt* **to e. sb on (to do sth)** empujar a algn (a hacer algo).
egg cup huevera *f*.
egg·plant berenjena *f*.
egg tim·er reloj *m* de arena.
egg white clara *f* de huevo.
e·go ego *m*; *fam* amor propio; *fam* **e. trip** autobombo *m*.
E·gyp·tian *adj & n* egipcio, -a *(mf)*.
ei·der·down edredón *m*.
eight *adj & n* ocho *(m) inv*.
eight·een *adj & n* dieciocho *(m) inv*.
eighth *adj & n* octavo, -a *(mf)*.
eight·y *adj & n* ochenta *(m) inv*.
ei·ther 1 *pron (affirmative)* cualquiera; *(negative)* ninguno, ninguna, ni el uno ni el otro, ni la una ni la otra; **e. of them** cualquiera de los dos; **I don't want e. of them** no quiero ninguno de los dos. **2** *adj (both)* cada, los dos, las dos; **on e. side** en ambos lados. **3** *conj* o; **e. … or …** o … o …; **e. Friday or Saturday** o (bien) el viernes o el sábado. **4** *adv (after negative)* tampoco; **I don't want to do it e.** yo tampoco quiero hacerlo.
e·lab·o·rate 1 *vt (devise)* elaborar; *(explain)* explicar detalladamente. **2** *vi* explicarse; **to e. on sth** explicar algo con más detalles. **3** *adj (complicated)* complicado, -a; *(detailed)* detallado, -a; *(style)* esmerado, -a.
e·las·tic 1 *adj* elástico, -a; *fig* flexible; **e. band** goma elástica. **2** *n* elástico *m*.
el·bow 1 *n* codo *m*. **2** *vt* **to e. sb** dar un codazo a algn.
eld·er *adj* mayor.
eld·er·ly 1 *adj* anciano, -a. **2** *npl* **the e.** los ancianos.
eld·est 1 *adj* mayor. **2** *n* el/la mayor.
e·lect *vt* elegir.
e·lec·tion 1 *n* elección *f*, **general e.** elecciones *fpl* generales. **2** *adj* electoral.
e·lec·tor·ate electorado *m*.
e·lec·tric *adj* eléctrico, -a; *fig* electrizante.
e·lec·tri·cal *adj* eléctrico, -a.
e·lec·tric blan·ket manta *f* eléctrica.
e·lec·tric chair silla *f* eléctrica.
e·lec·tri·cian electricista *mf*.
e·lec·tric·i·ty electricidad *f*, **e. bill** recibo *m* de la luz.
e·lec·tric shock electrochoque *m*.
e·lec·tro·cute *vt* electrocutar.
e·lec·tron·ic *adj* electrónico, -a.
e·lec·tron·ics *(science)* electrónica *f*, *(of machine)* componentes *mpl* electrónicos.
el·e·gance elegancia *f*.
el·e·gant *adj* elegante.
el·e·gant·ly *adv* con elegancia.
el·e·ment elemento *m*; *(electrical)* resistencia *f*.
el·e·men·ta·ry *adj (not developed)* rudimentario, -a; *(easy)* fácil; **e. school** escuela *f* primaria.
el·e·phant elefante *m*.
el·e·va·tor ascensor *m*.
e·lev·en *adj & n* once *(m) inv*.
e·lev·enth *adj & n* undécimo, -a *(mf)*.
el·i·gi·ble *adj* apto, -a; **he isn't e. to vote** no tiene derecho al voto.
e·lim·i·nate *vt* eliminar.
e·lite elite *f*.
else *adv* **anything e.?** ¿algo más?; **everything e.** todo lo demás; **no-one e.** nadie más; **someone e.** otro, -a; **something e.** otra cosa; **somewhere e.** en otra parte; **what e.?** ¿qué mas?; **where e.?** ¿en qué otro sitio?; **or e.** si no.
else·where *adv* en otra parte.
e·lude *vt (avoid)* esquivar; **his name eludes me** no consigo acordarme de su nombre.
em·bark *vi* embarcar(se); **to e. upon sth** emprender algo.
em·bar·rass *vt* avergonzar.
em·bar·rass·ing *adj* embarazoso, -a; *(situation)* violento, -a.
em·bar·rass·ment vergüenza *f*.
em·bas·sy embajada *f*.
em·blem emblema *m*.
em·brace 1 *vt* abrazar; *(include)* abarcar. **2** *vi* abrazarse. **3** *n* abrazo *m*.
em·broi·der *vt* bordar; *(story, truth)* adornar.
em·broi·der·y bordado *m*.
em·bry·o embrión *m*.
em·er·ald esmeralda *f*.
e·merge *vi* salir; *(problem)* surgir; **it emerged that …** resultó que ….
e·mer·gen·cy emergencia *f*, *(medical)* urgencia *f*, **in an e.** en caso de emergencia; **e. exit** salida *f* de emergencia; **e. landing** aterrizaje *m* forzoso; **state of e.** estado *m* de excepción.
em·i·grate *vi* emigrar.
e·mo·tion emoción *f*.
e·mo·tion·al *adj* emocional; *(moving)* conmovedor, -a.
em·per·or emperador *m*.
em·pha·sis énfasis *m*; **to place e. on sth** hacer hincapié en algo.
em·pha·size *vt* subrayar.
em·pire imperio *m*.
em·ploy *vt* emplear; *(time)* ocupar.
em·ploy·ee empleado, -a *mf*.
em·ploy·er empresario, -a *mf*.
em·ploy·ment empleo *m*.
em·ploy·ment a·gen·cy agencia *f* de colocaciones.
emp·ty 1 *adj* vacío, -a; **e. promises** promesas *fpl* vanas. **2** *vt* vaciar. **3** *vi* vaciarse. **4** *npl* **empties** envases *mpl*.
emp·ty-hand·ed *adv* con las manos vacías.
e·mul·sion e. (paint) pintura *f* mate.
en·a·ble *vt* **to e. sb to do sth** permitir a algn hacer algo.
e·nam·el esmalte *m*.
en·chant·ing *adj* encantador, -a.
en·close *vt (surround)* rodear; *(fence in)* cercar; *(in envelope)* adjuntar; **please find enclosed** le enviamos adjunto.
en·clo·sure *(fenced area)* cercado *m*; *(in envelope)* documento *m* adjunto.
en·coun·ter 1 *n* encuentro *m*. **2** *vt* encontrarse con; *(problems)* tropezar con.
en·cour·age *vt (urge)* animar; *(help to develop)* fomentar.
en·cour·age·ment estímulo *m*.
en·cy·clo·pe·dia enciclopedia *f*.
end 1 *n (of stick)* punta *f*, *(of street)* final *m*; *(conclusion)* fin *m*, final *m*; *(aim)* objetivo *m*; **in the e.** al final; **for hours on e.** hora tras hora; **to put an e. to** acabar con; **it makes my hair stand on e.** me pone el pelo de punta. **2** *vt* acabar, terminar. **3** *vi* acabarse, terminarse.
▸**end up** *vi* terminar; **to e. up doing sth** terminar por hacer algo.
en·dan·ger *vt* poner en peligro.
end·ing final *m*.
en·dive escarola *f*.
end·less *adj* interminable.
en·dorse *vt (check etc)* endosar; *(approve)* aprobar; *(support)* apoyar.
en·dorse·ment *(on check etc)* endoso *m*; *(approval)* aprobación *f*.
en·dur·ance resistencia *f*.
en·dure *vt (bear)* aguantar. **2** *vi* perdurar.
en·e·my *adj & n* enemigo, -a *(mf)*.
en·er·get·ic *adj* enérgico, -a.
en·er·gy 1 *n* energía *f*. **2** *adj* energético, -a.
en·force *vt (law)* hacer cumplir.
en·gaged *adj* prometido, -a; *(busy)* ocupado, -a; **to get e.** prometerse; **it's e.** *(phone)* está comunicando.
en·gage·ment *(to marry)* noviazgo *m*; *(appointment)* cita *f*.
en·gage·ment ring anillo *m* de compromiso.
en·gine motor *m*; *(of train)* locomotora *f*.
en·gine driv·er maquinista *mf*.
en·gi·neer ingeniero, -a *mf*, *(on train)* maquinista *mf*.
en·gi·neer·ing ingeniería *f*.
Eng·lish 1 *adj* inglés, -esa. **2** *n (language)* inglés *m*; **the E.** los ingleses *mpl*.
Eng·lish·man inglés *m*.
Eng·lish-speak·ing *adj* de habla inglesa.
Eng·lish·wom·an inglesa *f*.
en·grave *vt* grabar.
en·grav·ing grabado *m*.
en·joy *vt* disfrutar; **to e. oneself** pasarlo bien; **he enjoys swimming** le gusta nadar.
en·joy·able *adj* agradable.
en·joy·ment disfrute *m*.
en·large *vt* ampliar.
en·light·en *vt* iluminar.
en·list 1 *vt (recruit)* reclutar; **to e. sb's help** conseguir ayuda de algn. **2** *vi (in the army)* alistarse.
e·nor·mous *adj* enorme.
e·nor·mous·ly *adv* enormemente; **I enjoyed myself e.** lo pasé genial.
e·nough 1 *adj* bastante, suficiente; **e. books** bastantes libros; **have we got e. gas?** ¿tenemos suficiente gasolina? **2** *adv* bastante; **sure e.** en efecto. **3** *n* lo suficiente; **e. to live on** lo suficiente para vivir; **it isn't e.** no basta; **I've had e.!** ¡estoy harto!
en·quire = **inquire**.
en·quir·y = **inquiry**.
en·roll 1 *vt* matricular. **2** *vi* matricularse.
en·roll·ment matrícula *f*.
en·sure *vt* asegurar.
en·tail *vt* suponer.
en·ter 1 *vt (go into)* entrar en; *(data into computer)* introducir; *(join)* ingresar en; **to e. one's name for a course** matricularse en un curso. **2** *vi* entrar.
▸**enter into** *vt (agreement)* firmar; *(negotiations)* iniciar.
en·ter·prise empresa *f*, **free e.** libre empresa.
en·ter·pris·ing *adj* emprendedor, -a.
en·ter·tain 1 *vt (amuse)* divertir; *(consider)* considerar. **2** *vi (have guests)* tener invitados.
en·ter·tain·er artista *mf*.
en·ter·tain·ing *adj* divertido, -a.
en·ter·tain·ment diversión *f*, *(show)* espectáculo *m*.
en·thu·si·asm entusiasmo *m*.
en·thu·si·ast entusiasta *mf*.
en·thu·si·as·tic *adj* entusiasta; *(praise)* caluroso, -a; **to be e. about sth** entusiasmarse por algo.
en·thu·si·as·ti·cal·ly *adv* con entusiasmo.
en·tire *adj* todo, -a; **the e. family** toda la familia.
en·tire·ly *adv (completely)* totalmente; *(solely)* exclusivamente.
en·ti·tle *vt (permit)* dar derecho a; **to be entitled to** tener derecho a.
en·trance entrada *f*, *(admission)* ingreso *m*; **e. examination** examen *m* de ingreso.
en·trant *(in competition)* participante *mf*.
en·try *(entrance)* entrada *f*; **no e.** dirección prohibida.
en·try form hoja *f* de inscripción.
en·ve·lope sobre *m*.
en·vi·ous *adj* envidioso, -a; **to feel e.** tener envidia.
en·vi·ron·ment entorno *m*; *(natural)* medio ambiente *m*.
en·vi·ron·men·tal *adj* medio ambiental.
envisage, en·vi·sion *vt (imagine)* imaginarse; *(foresee)* prever.
en·vy 1 *n* envidia *f*. **2** *vt* envidiar.
ep·i·dem·ic 1 *n* epidemia *f*. **2** *adj* epidémico, -a.
ep·i·sode episodio *m*.
e·qual 1 *adj* igual; **to be e. to the occasion** estar a la altura de las circunstancias. **2** *n* igual *mf*; **to treat sb as an e.** tratar a algn de igual a igual. **3** *vt* equivaler a.
e·qual·i·ty igualdad *f*.
e·qual·ize *vi (in sport)* empatar.
e·qual·ly *adv* igualmente; **e. pretty** igual de bonito; **to share sth e.** dividir algo en partes iguales.
e·qua·tion ecuación *f*.
e·qua·tor ecuador *m*.
e·quip *vt (supply)* equipar; *(person)* proveer.

e·quip·ment *(materials)* equipo *m.*
e·quiv·a·lent *adj & n* equivalente *(m).*
e·ra era *f.*
e·rase *vt* borrar.
e·ras·er goma *f* de borrar.
e·rect 1 *adj (upright)* erguido, -a. **2** *vt (monument)* erigir.
e·ro·sion *(of land)* erosión *f.*
er·rand recado *m.*
er·rat·ic *adj (performance, behavior)* irregular; *(weather)* muy variable; *(person)* caprichoso, -a.
er·ror error *m.*
e·rupt *vi (volcano)* entrar en erupción; *(violence)* estallar.
e·rup·tion erupción *f.*
es·ca·la·tor escalera *f* mecánica.
es·cape 1 *n* fuga *f,* *(of gas)* escape *m;* **e. route** vía *f* de escape. **2** *vi* escaparse. **3** *vt (avoid)* evitar; **the name escapes me** se me escapa el nombre.
es·cort 1 *n (bodyguard etc)* escolta *f.* **2** *vt (protect)* escoltar.
Es·ki·mo *adj & n* esquimal *(mf).*
es·pe·cial·ly *adv* especialmente.
es·pres·so café *m* exprés.
es·say *(at school)* redacción *f.*
es·sen·tial *adj* esencial.
es·sen·tial·ly *adv* esencialmente.
es·tab·lish *vt (found)* establecer; *(business)* montar; **to e. the truth** demostrar la verdad.
es·tab·lished *adj (person)* establecido, -a; *(fact)* conocido, -a.
es·tab·lish·ment establecimiento *m;* **the E.** el sistema.
es·tate *(land)* finca *f,* *(property)* bienes *mpl;* *(inheritance)* herencia *f,* **(housing) e.** urbanización *f.*
es·ti·mate 1 *n (calculation)* cálculo *m;* *(likely cost of work)* presupuesto *m.* **2** *vt* calcular.
etch·ing aguafuerte *m.*
e·ter·nal *adj* eterno, -a, incesante.
ethics ética *f.*
et·i·quette etiqueta *f.*
EU *abbr of* **European Union** UE.
Euro- *prefix* Euro-.
Eu·ro·pe·an *adj & n* europeo, -a *(mf).*
e·vac·u·ate *vt* evacuar.
e·vade *vt* evadir.
e·val·u·ate *vt* evaluar.
e·vap·o·rate 1 *vi* evaporarse. **2** *vt* evaporar.
eve víspera *f;* **on the e. of** en vísperas de.
e·ven 1 *adj (smooth)* liso, -a; *(regular)* uniforme; *(equally balanced)* igual; *(number)* par; *(in football game etc)* **to be e.** ir empatados, -as; **to get e. with sb** desquitarse con algn. **2** *adv* aun; **e. now** incluso ahora; **e. the children knew** hasta los niños lo sabían; **e. as** mientras; **e. if** incluso si; **e. though** aunque. ▪ *(with negative)* si siquiera; **she can't e. write her name** ni siquiera sabe escribir su nombre. ▪ *(before comparative)* aun, todavía; **e. worse** aun peor.
eve·ning *(early)* tarde *f,* *(late)* noche *f,* **in the e.** por la tarde/noche; **tomorrow e.** mañana por la tarde/noche.
eve·ning class clase *f* nocturna.
e·ven·ly *adv (uniformly)* de modo uniforme; *(fairly)* equitativamente.
e·vent *(happening)* suceso *m;* *(in sport)* prueba *f,* **at all events** en todo caso; **in the e. of fire** en caso de incendio.
e·ven·tu·al *adj (ultimate)* final; *(resulting)* consiguiente.
e·ven·tu·al·ly *adv* finalmente.
ev·er *adv (always)* siempre; **for e.** para siempre; **stronger than e.** más fuerte que nunca; **have you e. been there?** ¿has estado allí alguna vez?; **how e. did you manage it?** ¿cómo diablos lo conseguiste?; *fam* **so ...** muy ...; **thank you e. so much** muchísimas gracias.
eve·ry *adj (each)* cada; *(all)* todos, -as; **e. now and then** de vez en cuando; **e. day** todos los días; **e. other day** cada dos días; **e. one of you** todos, -as vosotros, -as; **e. citizen** todo ciudadano.
eve·ry·bod·y *pron* todo el mundo, todos, -as; **e. who ...** todos los que ...
eve·ry·day *adj* de todos los días; **an e. occurrence** un suceso cotidiano.
eve·ry·one *pron* **= everybody.**
eve·ry·place *adv* en todos sitios.
eve·ry·thing *pron* todo; **he eats e.** come de todo; **e. I have** todo lo que tengo.
eve·ry·where *adv* por *or* en todas partes; **e. I go** por todas partes adonde voy.
ev·i·dence *n (proof)* evidencia *f,* *(in court case)* testimonio *m;* *(sign)* indicio *m;* **to give e.** prestar declaración.
ev·i·dent *adj* evidente.
ev·i·dent·ly *adv* evidentemente.
e·vil 1 *adj (wicked)* malvado, -a; *(harmful)* nocivo, -a. **2** *n* mal *m.*
e·voke *vt* evocar.
ewe oveja *f.*
ex her e. su marido; **his e.** su ex mujer.
ex- *prefix* ex-; **ex-minister** ex ministro *m.*
ex·act *adj* exacto, -a; **this e. spot** ese mismo lugar.
ex·act·ly *adv* exactamente; **e.!** ¡exacto!
ex·ag·ger·ate *vti* exagerar.
ex·ag·ger·a·tion exageración *f.*
ex·am examen *m.*
ex·am·i·na·tion examen *m;* *(medical)* reconocimiento *m;* **to sit an e.** hacer un examen.
ex·am·ine *vt* examinar; *(customs)* registrar; *(medically)* reconocer a.
ex·am·in·er examinador, -a *mf.*
ex·am·ple ejemplo *m;* **for e.** por ejemplo.
ex·ceed *vt* exceder.
ex·ceed·ing·ly *adv* extremadamente.
ex·cel *vi* sobresalir.
ex·cel·lent *adj* excelente.
ex·cept *prep* excepto; **e. for the little ones** excepto los pequeños; **e. that ...** salvo que ...
ex·cep·tion excepción *f,* **with the e. of** a excepción de; **to take e. to sth** ofenderse por algo.
ex·cep·tion·al *adj* excepcional.
ex·cep·tion·al·ly *adv* excepcionalmente.
ex·cerpt extracto *m.*
ex·cess 1 *n* exceso *m.* **2** *adj* excedente; **e. baggage** exceso *m* de equipaje; **e. fare** suplemento *m.*
ex·ces·sive *adj* excesivo, -a.
ex·ces·sive·ly *adv* excesivamente, en exceso.
ex·change 1 *n* cambio *m;* **(telephone) e.** central *f* telefónica; **in e. for** a cambio de. **2** *vt* intercambiar; **to e. blows** golpearse.
ex·change rate tipo *m* de cambio.
ex·cite *vt (enthuse)* entusiasmar; *(arouse)* provocar; **to get excited** entusiasmarse.
ex·cit·ed *adj* ilusionado, -a; emocionado, -a.

ex·cite·ment *(emotion)* emoción *f.*
ex·cit·ing *adj* emocionante.
ex·claim *vi* exclamar.
ex·cla·ma·tion exclamación *f.*
ex·cla·ma·tion point signo *m* de admiración.
ex·clude *vt* excluir; *(from club)* no admitir.
ex·clu·sive 1 *adj* exclusivo, -a; *(select)* selecto, -a. **2** *n (in newspaper)* exclusiva *f.*
ex·clu·sive·ly *adv* exclusivamente.
ex·cur·sion excursión *f.*
ex·cuse 1 *vt* disculpar; *(exempt)* dispensar; *(justify)* justificar; **e. me!** con permiso. **2** *n* excusa *f,* **to make excuses** dar excusas.
ex·e·cute *vt (order)* cumplir; *(task)* realizar; *(person)* ejecutar.
ex·e·cu·tion *(of order)* cumplimiento *m;* *(of task)* realización *f,* *(of person)* ejecución *f.*
ex·ec·u·tive *adj & n* ejecutivo, -a *(mf).*
ex·empt 1 *vt* eximir **(from** de). **2** *adj* exento, -a; **e. from tax** libre de impuesto.
ex·emp·tion exención *f.*
ex·er·cise 1 *n* ejercicio *m;* **e. book** cuaderno *m.* **2** *vt (rights, duties)* ejercer; *(dog)* sacar de paseo. **3** *vi* hacer ejercicio.
ex·er·cise book cuaderno *m.*
ex·ert *vt (influence)* ejercer; **to e. oneself** esforzarse.
ex·er·tion esfuerzo *m.*
ex·haust 1 *vt* agotar. **2** *n (gas)* gases *mpl* de combustión; **e. pipe** tubo *m* de escape.
ex·haust·ed *adj* agotado, -a.
ex·haust·ing *adj* agotador, -a.
ex·hib·it 1 *n* objeto *m* expuesto. **2** *vt* exponer; *(manifest)* mostrar.
ex·hi·bi·tion exposición *f.*
ex·hib·i·tor expositor, -a *mf.*
ex·ile 1 *n (banishment)* exilio *m;* *(person)* exiliado, -a *mf.* **2** *vt* exiliar.
ex·ist *vi* existir; *(stay alive)* subsistir.
ex·is·tence existencia *f.*
ex·ist·ing *adj* actual.
ex·it salida *f.*
ex·or·bi·tant *adj* exorbitante.
ex·pand 1 *vt* ampliar. **2** *vi (grow)* ampliarse; *(metal)* dilatarse.
▸ **expand on** *vt* ampliar.
ex·panse extensión *f.*
ex·pan·sion *(in size)* expansión *f,* *(of gas, metal)* dilatación *f.*
ex·pan·sion slot ranura *f* de expansión.
ex·pect 1 *vt (anticipate)* esperar; *(suppose)* suponer; **to e. sth from sb/sth** esperar algo de algn/algo; **to e. to do sth** contar con hacer algo; **she's expecting a baby** está esperando un niño. **2** *vi* **to be expecting** estar embarazada.
ex·pec·ta·tion esperanza *f,* **contrary to e.** contrariamente a lo que se esperaba.
ex·pe·di·tion expedición *f.*
ex·pel *vt* expulsar.
ex·pen·di·ture desembolso *m.*
ex·pense gasto *m;* **to spare no e.** no escatimar gastos; *fig* **at the e. of** a costa de.
ex·pen·sive *adj* caro, -a.
ex·pe·ri·ence 1 *n* experiencia *f.* **2** *vt (sensation)* experimentar; *(difficulty, loss)* sufrir.
ex·pe·ri·enced *adj* experimentado, -a.
ex·per·i·ment 1 *n* experimento *m.* **2** *vi* experimentar **(on, with** con).
ex·pert *adj & n* experto, -a *(mf).*
ex·per·tise pericia *f.*
ex·pi·ra·tion vencimiento *m.*
ex·pi·ra·tion date fecha *f* de caducidad.
ex·pire *vi (come to an end)* terminar; *(policy, contract)* vencer; *(ticket)* caducar.
ex·pired *adj (ticket)* caducado, -a.
ex·plain *vt* explicar; *(clarify)* aclarar; **to e. oneself** justificarse.
▸ **explain away** *vt* justificar.
ex·pla·na·tion explicación *f,* *(clarification)* aclaración *f.*
ex·plic·it *adj* explícito, -a.
ex·plode 1 *vt* hacer explotar. **2** *vi (bomb)* explotar; **to e. with anger** montar en cólera.
ex·ploit 1 *n* hazaña *f.* **2** *vt* explotar.
ex·plo·ra·tion exploración *f.*
ex·plore *vt* explorar.
ex·plor·er explorador, -a *mf.*
ex·plo·sion explosión *f.*
ex·plo·sive 1 *adj* explosivo, -a. **2** *n* explosivo *m.*
ex·port 1 *vt* exportar. **2** *n* exportación *f.*
ex·pose *vt (uncover)* exponer; *(secret)* revelar; *(plot)* descubrir.
ex·press 1 *adj (explicit)* expreso, -a; *(letter)* urgente. **2** *n (train)* expreso *m.* **3** *vt* expresar.
ex·pres·sion expresión *f.*
ex·press·way autopista *f.*
ex·tend 1 *vt (enlarge)* ampliar; *(lengthen)* alargar; *(prolong)* prolongar; *(increase)* aumentar. **2** *vi (stretch)* extenderse; *(last)* prolongarse.
ex·ten·sion extensión *f,* *(of time)* prórroga *f,* *(of building)* anexo *m.*
ex·ten·sive *adj* extenso, -a.
ex·ten·sive·ly *adv* extensamente; *(frequently)* con frecuencia.
ex·tent *(area)* extensión *f,* **to some e.** hasta cierto punto; **to a large e.** en gran parte; **to such an e.** hasta tal punto.
ex·te·ri·or *adj & n* exterior *(m).*
ex·ter·nal *adj* externo, -a.
ex·tin·guish·er extintor *m.*
ex·tra 1 *adj* extra; *(spare)* de sobra. **2** *adv* extra; **e. fine** extra fino. **3** *n (additional charge)* suplemento *m;* *(in film)* extra *mf.*
ex·tract 1 *n* extracto *m.* **2** *vt (tooth, information)* extraer.
ex·tra·cur·ric·u·lar *adj* extracurricular.
ex·traor·di·nar·y *adj* extraordinario, -a; *(strange)* raro, -a.
ex·trav·a·gant *adj (wasteful)* derrochador, -a; *(excessive)* exagerado, -a.
ex·treme 1 *adj* extremo, -a; **an e. case** un caso excepcional. **2** *n* extremo *m;* **in the e.** en sumo grado.
ex·treme·ly *adv* extremadamente; **I'm e. sorry** lo siento de veras.
eye *n* ojo *m;* **I couldn't believe my eyes** no podía creerlo; **not to take one's eyes off sb/sth** no quitar la vista de encima a algn/algo; **to catch sb's e.** llamar la atención de algn; **to turn a blind e.** hacer la vista gorda **(to** a); **with an e. to** con miras a; **to keep an e. on sb/sth** vigilar a algn/algo.
eye·brow ceja *f.*
eye·glasses *npl* gafas *fpl.*
eye·lash pestaña *f.*
eye·lid párpado *m.*
eye·lin·er lápiz *m* de ojos.
eye·shad·ow sombra *f* de ojos.
eye·sight vista *f.*

F

fab·ric *(cloth)* tejido *m.*
fab·u·lous *adj* fabuloso, -a.
face 1 *n* cara *f*; *(surface)* superficie *f*; **f. to f.** cara a cara; **she slammed the door in my f.** me dio con la puerta en las narices; **in the f. of danger** ante el peligro; **to pull faces** hacer muecas; **f. down/up** boca abajo/ arriba; **to save f.** salvar las apariencias. **2** *vt (look onto)* dar a; *(be opposite)* estar enfrente de; *(problem)* hacer frente a; **to f. up to** hacer cara a; *(tolerate)* aguantar. **3** *vi* **to f. on to** dar a; **to f. towards** mirar hacia.
fa·cil·i·tate *vt* facilitar.
fa·cil·i·ty *(ease)* facilidad *f*; **facilities** *(means)* facilidades *fpl*; *(rooms, equipment)* instalaciones *fpl.*
fact hecho *m*; *(reality)* realidad *f*; **as a matter of f.** de hecho; **in f.** en realidad.
fac·tor factor *m.*
fac·to·ry fábrica *f.*
fac·tu·al *adj* **a f. error** un error de hecho.
fade *vi (colour)* desteñirse; *(flower)* marchitarse; *(light)* apagarse.
▸**fade away, fade out** *vi* desvanecerse.
▸**fade in** *vt* hacer aparecer gradualmente.
fail 1 *n (at school)* suspenso *m*; **without f.** sin falta. **2** *vt (exam)* suspender; **to f. to do sth** *(be unable)* no poder hacer algo; *(neglect)* dejar de hacer algo. **3** *vi (show, film)* fracasar; *(brakes)* fallar; *(at school)* suspender; *(health)* deteriorarse.
failed *adj (attempt, poet)* fracasado, -a.
fail·ing 1 *n (shortcoming)* defecto *m*; *(weakness)* punto *m* débil. **2** *prep* a falta de.
fail·ure fracaso *m*; *(at school)* suspenso *m*; *(person)* fracasado, -a *mf*; *(breakdown)* avería *f*; **power f.** apagón *m*; **heart f.** paro *m* cardíaco; **her f. to answer** el hecho de que no contestara.
faint 1 *adj (sound)* débil; *(color)* pálido, -a; *(outline)* borroso, -a; *(recollection)* vago, -a; *(giddy)* mareado, -a; **I haven't the faintest idea** no tengo la más mínima idea. **2** *n* desmayo *m.* **3** *vi* desmayarse.
faintly *adv (with little strength)* débilmente; *(unclearly)* vagamente.
fair¹ 1 *adj (impartial)* imparcial; *(just)* justo, -a; *(hair)* rubio, -a; *(weather)* bueno, -a; **it's not f.** no hay derecho; **f. enough!** ¡vale!; **a f. number** un buen número. **2** *adv* **to play f.** jugar limpio.
fair² feria *f*; **trade f.** feria *f* de muestras.
fair-haired *adj* rubio, -a.
fairly *adv (justly)* justamente; *(moderately)* bastante.
fair play juego *m* limpio.
fair-sized *adj* bastante grande.
fair·y hada *f*; **f. tale** cuento *m* de hadas.
faith fe *f*; *(trust)* confianza *f.*
faith·ful *adj* fiel.
faith·ful·ly *adv* **yours f.** *(in letter)* le saluda atentamente.
fake 1 *adj* falso, -a. **2** *n (object)* falsificación *f*; *(person)* impostor, -a *mf.* **3** *vt (forge)* falsificar; *(feign)* fingir.
fall 1 *n* caída *f*; *(decrease)* baja *f*; otoño *m*; **falls** *(waterfall)* cascada *f*; **Niagara Falls** las cataratas del Niágara. **2** *vi** caer, caerse; *(temperature, prices)* bajar; **night was falling** anochecía; **to f. asleep** dormirse; **to f. ill** caer enfermo, -a; **to f. in love** enamorarse.
▸**fall apart** *vi (of machine)* deshacerse.
▸**fall back on** *vt (as last resort)* recurrir a.
▸**fall behind** *vi (in race)* quedarse atrás; **to f. behind with one's work** retrasarse en el trabajo.
▸**fall down** *vi (picture etc)* caerse; *(building)* derrumbarse.
▸**fall for** *vt (person)* enamorarse de; *(trick)* dejarse engañar por.
▸**fall in** *vi (roof)* desplomarse.
▸**fall off** *vi (drop off)* caer; *(part)* desprenderse; *(diminish)* disminuir.
▸**fall out** *vi (hair)* caerse; *(quarrel)* pelearse.
▸**fall over** *vi* caerse.
▸**fall through** *vi (plan)* fracasar.
false *adj* falso, -a; **f. teeth** dentadura *f* postiza; **f. alarm** falsa alarma *f.*
fame fama *f.*
fa·mil·iar *adj (common)* conocido, -a; **his face is f.** su cara me suena; **to be on f. terms with sb** *(know well)* tener confianza con algn.
fa·mil·iar·i·ty familiaridad *f* (**with** con); *(intimacy)* confianza *f.*
fa·mil·iar·ize *vt (make acquainted)* familiarizar (**with** con); **to become familiarized with sth** familiarizarse con algo.
fam·i·ly familia *f*; **f. doctor** médico *m* de cabecera; **f. planning** planificación *f* familiar; **f. tree** árbol *m* genealógico.
fa·mous *adj* famoso, -a (**for** por).
fan *(held in hand)* abanico *m*; *(electric)* ventilador *m*; *(person)* aficionado, -a *mf*, *(of pop star etc)* fan *mf*; **football f.** hincha *mf.*
fan·cy 1 *adj* de fantasía; **f. goods** artículos *mpl* de fantasía. **2** *n (whim)* capricho *m*; **to take a f. to sth** encapricharse con algo; **what takes your f.?** ¿qué se le antoja? **3** *vt (imagine)* imaginarse; *(like, want)* apetecer; *fam* **f. that!** ¡fíjate!; **do you f. a drink?** ¿te apetece una copa?
fan heat·er estufa *f* de aire.
fan·tas·tic *adj* fantástico, -a.
fan·ta·sy fantasía *f.*
far 1 *adj (distant)* lejano, -a; **at the f. end** en el otro extremo. **2** *adv (distant)* lejos; **f. off** a lo lejos; **farther back** más atrás; **how f. is it to Chicago?** ¿cuánto hay de aquí a Chicago?; **as f. as I can** en lo que puedo; **as f. as I know** que yo sepa; **as f. as possible** en lo posible; **f. from complaining, he seemed pleased** lejos de quejarse, parecía contento; **in so f. as ...** en la medida en que ...; **to go too f.** pasarse de la raya; **f. into the night** hasta muy entrada la noche; **so f.** *(in time)* hasta ahora; **by f.** con mucho; **f. cleverer** mucho más listo, -a; **f. too much** demasiado.
far·a·way *adj* lejano, -a.
farce farsa *f.*
fare *(ticket price)* tarifa *f*, precio *m* del billete; *(for boat)* pasaje *m*; *(passenger)* pasajero, -a *mf.*
fare·well 1 *interj (old use)* ¡adiós! **2** *n* despedida *f.*
far-fetched *adj* rebuscado, -a.
farm 1 *n* granja *f*, *Am* hacienda *f.* **2** *vt* cultivar.
▸**farm out** *vt* encargar fuera.
farm·er granjero, -a *mf*, *Am* hacendado, -a *mf.*
farm·house granja *f*, *Am* hacienda *f.*
farm·ing 1 *n (agriculture)* agricultura *f*, *(of land)* cultivo *m.* **2** *adj* agrícola.
farm·yard corral *m.*
far-off *adj* lejano, -a.
far-reach·ing *adj* de gran alcance.
far·ther *adv* más lejos.
far·thest 1 *adj* más lejano, -a. **2** *adv* más lejos.
fas·ci·nate *vt* fascinar.
fas·ci·nat·ing *adj* fascinante.
fas·ci·na·tion fascinación *f.*
fash·ion *(manner)* manera *f*, *(latest style)* moda *f*; **to go/be out of f.** pasar/no estar de moda; **f. parade** desfile *m* de modelos.
fash·ion show pase *m* de modelos.
fast 1 *adj (quick)* rápido, -a; *(clock)* adelantado, -a. **2** *adv* rápidamente, deprisa; **how f.?** ¿qué velocidad?; **f. asleep** profundamente dormido, -a.
fas·ten *vt (attach)* sujetar; *(fix)* fijar; *(belt)* abrochar; *(bag)* asegurar; *(shoelaces)* atar.
fas·ten·er cierre *m.*
fat 1 *adj* gordo, -a; *(thick)* grueso, -a; *(meat)* poco magro, -a. **2** *n* grasa *f*; **cooking f.** manteca *f* de cerdo.
fa·tal *adj (accident, illness)* mortal; *(ill-fated)* funesto, -a.
fa·tal·ly *adv* **f. wounded** mortalmente herido, -a.
fate destino *m.*
fa·ther padre *m*; **my f. and mother** mis padres.
Fa·ther Christ·mas Papá *m* Noel.
fa·ther-in-law suegro *m.*
fa·tigue fatiga *f.*
fat·ten·ing *adj* que engorda.
fat·ty 1 *adj (food)* graso, -a. **2** *n fam (person)* gordinflón, -ona *mf.*
fau·cet grifo *m.*
fault *(defect)* defecto *m*; *(in merchandise)* desperfecto *m*; *(blame)* culpa *f*; **to find f. with** poner reparos a; **to be at f.** tener la culpa.
fault·y *adj* defectuoso, -a.
fa·vor 1 *n* favor *m*; **in f. of** a favor de; **to ask sb a f.** pedirle un favor a algn. **2** *vt (treat favorably)* favorecer; *(approve)* estar a favor de.
fa·vor·a·ble *adj* favorable.
fa·vor·ite *adj & n* favorito, -a *(mf).*
fax 1 *n* fax *m.* **2** *vt (document)* mandar por fax; **to f. sb** mandar un fax a algn.
fear 1 *n* miedo *m*; **for f. of** por temor a. **2** *vt* temer; **I f. it's too late** me temo que ya es tarde.
fear·ful *adj (person)* temeroso, -a; *(frightening)* espantoso, -a.
fear·less *adj* intrépido, -a.
feast banquete *m.*
feat hazaña *f.*
feath·er pluma *f*; **f. duster** plumero *m.*
fea·ture 1 *n (of face)* facción *f*, *(characteristic)* característica *f*; **f. film** largometraje *m.* **2** *vi* figurar.
Feb·ru·ar·y febrero *m.*
fed·er·al *adj* federal.
fed up *adj fam* harto, -a (**with** de).
fee *(of lawyer, doctor)* honorarios *mpl.*
fee·ble *adj* débil.
feed* 1 *vt (give food to)* dar de comer a; **to f. a baby** *(breastfeed)* amamantar a un bebé; *(with bottle)* dar el biberón a un bebé. **2** *vi* comer; *(cows, sheep)* pacer.
feed·back feedback *m*; *fig* reacción *f.*
feel 1 *vi** *(have emotion, sensation)* sentirse; *(have opinion)* opinar; **how do you f.?** ¿qué tal te encuentras?; **I f. bad about it** me da pena; **to f. happy** sentirse feliz; **to f. cold/sleepy** tener frío/sueño; **I feel that ...** me parece que ...; **it feels like summer** parece verano; **I f. sure that ...** estoy seguro, -a de que ...; **I f. like an ice cream** me apetece un helado; **to f. like doing sth** tener ganas de hacer algo. **2** *vt** *(touch)* tocar; *(sense)* sentir; *(the cold)* notar; **she feels like a failure** se siente inútil. **3** *n (touch, sensation)* tacto *m.*
▸**feel for** *vt (have sympathy for)* compadecer.
▸**feel up to** *vt* tener ánimos para.
feel·ing *(emotion)* sentimiento *m*; *(physical)* sensación *f*, *(opinion)* opinión *f*; **I had the f. that ...** *(impression)* tuve la impresión de que ...; **to express one's feelings** expresar sus opiniones.
feet *npl see* **foot.**
fell *pt of* **fall.**
fel·low 1 *n* tipo *m*, tío *m.* **2 f. citizen** conciudadano, -a *mf*, **f. countryman/countrywoman** compatriota *mf.*
fel·o·ny crimen *m*, delito *m* mayor.
felt¹ *pt & pp of* **feel.**
felt² fieltro *m.*
felt-tip(ped) pen rotulador *m.*
fe·male 1 *adj* femenino, -a; *(animal)* hembra. **2** *n (animal)* hembra *f*, *(woman)* mujer *f*; *(girl)* chica *f.*
fem·i·nine *adj* femenino, -a.
fence 1 *n* cerca *f.* **2** *vi (in sport)* practicar la esgrima.
▸**fence in** *vt* meter en un cercado.
fenc·ing *(sport)* esgrima *f.*
fend *vi* **to f. for oneself** valerse por sí mismo.
▸**fend off** *vt (blow)* parar; *(attack)* rechazar.
fend·er *(on car)* parachoques *m inv.*
fern helecho *m.*
fe·ro·cious *adj* feroz.
fer·ry 1 *n (small)* barca *f* de pasaje; *(large, for cars)* ferry *m.* **2** *vt* transportar.
fer·tile *adj* fértil.
fer·til·iz·er abono *m.*
fes·ti·val festival *m.*
fes·tive *adj* festivo, -a; **the f. season** las fiestas de Navidad.
fes·tiv·i·ty **the festivities** las fiestas.
fetch *vt (go for)* ir a buscar; *(bring)* traer.
fete fiesta *f.*
feud 1 *n* enemistad *f* duradera. **2** *vi* pelear.
fe·ver fiebre *f.*
fe·ver·ish *adj* febril.
few 1 *adj (not many)* pocos, -as; **as f. as** solamente; **a f.** unos, -as, algunos, -as; **in the next f. days** dentro de unos días; **she has fewer books than I thought** tiene menos libros de lo que pensaba; **quite a f.** un buen número. **2** *pron (not many)* pocos, -as; **there are too f.** no hay suficientes; **a f.** *(some)* algunos, -as; **who has the fewest?** ¿quién tiene menos?
fi·an·cé prometido *m.*
fi·an·cée prometida *f.*
fi·ber fibra *f.*
fic·tion ficción *f.*
fid·dle *fam n (musical instrument)* violín *m.*
▸**fiddle about** *vi* juguetear (**with** con).
fidg·et *vi* moverse; **stop fidgeting!** ¡estáte quieto!; **to f. with sth** jugar con algo.
field 1 *n* campo *m*; *(oil field, coal field etc)* yacimiento *m.* **2** *vt (in sport) (ball)* parar y devolver; *(team)* presentar.
field trip viaje *m* de estudios.
field·work trabajo *m* de campo.
fierce *adj (animal)* feroz; *(argument)* acalorado, -a; *(heat, competition)* intenso, -a.
fif·teen *adj & n* quince *(m) inv.*
fif·teenth *adj & n* decimoquinto, -a *(mf).*
fifth *adj & n* quinto, -a *(mf).*
fif·ti·eth *adj & n* quincuagésimo, -a *(mf).*
fif·ty 1 *adj* cincuenta *inv*; **a f.-f. chance** una probabilidad del cincuenta por ciento; **to go f.-f.** ir a medias. **2** *n* cincuenta *m inv.*
fig *(fruit)* higo *m.*

fight 1 *vt** combatir; *(bull)* lidiar. **2** *vi** pelear(se); *(quarrel)* reñir; *fig (struggle)* luchar (**for/against** por/contra). **3** *n* pelea *f*; *(boxing)* combate *m*; *(quarrel)* riña *f*; *fig (struggle)* lucha *f*.
▸**fight back 1** *vt (tears)* contener. **2** *vi (recover ground)* resistir.
▸**fight off** *vt (attack)* rechazar.
▸**fight out** *vt* arreglar discutiendo *or* peleando.
fight·er *(person)* combatiente *mf*; *(boxing)* púgil *m*; *fig* luchador, -a *mf*; **f. (plane)** (avión *m* de) caza *m*.
fig·ure¹ 1 *n (numeral)* cifra *f*; *(form, outline)* forma *f*; *(shape, statue, character)* figura *f*; **she has a good f.** tiene buen tipo; **f. of speech** figura retórica. **2** *vt fam* imaginarse. **3** *vi (appear)* figurar; *fam* **that figures** eso tiene sentido.
fig·ure² *vt (guess)* imaginar.
▸**figure on** *vt* **to f. on doing sth** esperar hacer algo.
▸**figure out** *vt* comprender; **I can't f. it out** no me lo explico.
file 1 *n (tool)* lima *f*; *(folder)* carpeta *f*; *(archive)* archivo *m*; *(of computer)* fichero *m*; *(line)* fila *f*; **on f.** archivado, -a; **in single f.** en fila india. **2** *vt (smooth)* limar; *(put away)* archivar. **3** *vi* **to f. past** desfilar.
▸**file away** *vt (put away)* archivar; *(in card catalog)* clasificar.
▸**file down** *vt* limar.
▸**file in/out** *vi* entrar/salir en fila.
fil·ing clasificación *f*.
fil·ing cab·i·net archivador *m*; *(for cards)* fichero *m*.
fill 1 *vt (space, time)* llenar (**with** de); *(post, requirements)* cubrir. **2** *vi* llenarse (**with** de).
▸**fill in 1** *vt (space, form)* rellenar; *(time)* pasar; *(inform) fam* poner al corriente (**on** de). **2** *vi* **to f. in for sb** sustituir a algn.
▸**fill out** *vt (form)* rellenar.
▸**fill up 1** *vt* llenar hasta arriba; **f. her up!** ¡llénelo! **2** *vi* llenarse.
fil·let filete *m*; **f. steak** filete *m*.
fill·ing 1 *adj* que llena mucho. **2** *n (stuffing)* relleno *m*; *(in tooth)* empaste *m*.
fill·ing sta·tion gasolinera *f*.
film 1 *n* película *f*. **2** *vt* filmar. **3** *vi* rodar.
film star estrella *f* de cine.
fil·ter 1 *n* filtro *m*; **f. lane** carril *m* de acceso. **2** *vt* filtrar. **3** *vi (traffic)* **to f. to the right** girar a la derecha.
filth *(dirt)* porquería *f*, *fig* porquerías *fpl*.
filth·y *adj (dirty)* asqueroso, -a; *(obscene)* obsceno, -a.
fin *(of fish)* aleta *f*.
fi·nal 1 *adj* último, -a; *(definitive)* definitivo, -a. **2** *n (sport)* final *f*.
fi·nal·ize *vt* ultimar; *(date)* fijar.
fi·nal·ly *adv* finalmente.
fi·nance 1 *n* finanzas *fpl*; **finances** fondos *mpl*. **2** *vt* financiar.
fi·nan·cial *adj* financiero, -a.
find 1 *vt** *(locate, think)* encontrar; *(discover)* descubrir; **it has been found that ...** se ha comprobado que ...; **I found it impossible to get away** me resultó imposible irme. **2** *n* hallazgo *m*.
▸**find out 1** *vt (inquire)* averiguar; *(discover)* descubrir. **2** *vi* **to f. out about sth** informarse sobre algo; *(discover)* enterarse de algo.
fine¹ 1 *n (sum of money)* multa *f*. **2** *vt* multar.
fine² 1 *adj (delicate etc)* fino, -a; *(excellent)* excelente; *(weather)* bueno, -a; **it was f.** hacía buen tiempo. **2** *adv* muy bien. **3** *interj* ¡vale!
fin·ger dedo *m* (de la mano); **to keep one's fingers crossed** esperar que todo salga bien.
fin·ger·nail uña *f*.
fin·ger·print huella *f* dactilar.
fin·ger·tip punta *f* or yema *f* del dedo.
fin·ish 1 *n* fin *m*; *(of race)* llegada *f*. **2** *vt (complete)* acabar, terminar; *(use up)* agotar; **to f. doing sth** terminar de hacer algo. **3** *vi* acabar, terminar.
▸**finish off** *vt (complete)* terminar completamente; *(kill)* rematar.
▸**finish up 1** *vt* acabar; **to f. up doing sth** acabar haciendo algo. **2** *vi* **to f. up in jail** ir a parar a la cárcel.
fin·ished *adj (product)* acabado, -a; *fam (exhausted)* rendido, -a.
Finn finlandés, -esa *mf*.
Finn·ish 1 *adj* finlandés, -esa. **2** *n (language)* finlandés *m*.
fir abeto *m*.
fire 1 *n* fuego *m*; *(accident etc)* incendio *m*; *(heater)* estufa *f*; *(gunfire)* fuego *m*; **to open f.** abrir fuego. **2** *vt (gun)* disparar (**at** a); *(dismiss)* despedir. **3** *vi (shoot)* disparar (**at** sobre).
fire a·larm alarma *f* de incendios.
fire bri·gade (cuerpo *m* de) bomberos *mpl*.
fire·crack·er petardo *m*.
fire ex·it salida *f* de emergencia.
fire ex·tin·guish·er extintor *m*.
fire·man bombero *m*.
fire·place chimenea *f*; *(hearth)* hogar *m*.
fire·wood leña *f*.
fire·works *npl* fuegos *mpl* artificiales.
firm 1 *adj* firme. **2** *n* empresa *f*.
first 1 *adj* primero, -a; *(before masculine singular noun)* primer; **for the f. time** por primera vez; **in the f. place** en primer lugar. **2** *adv (before anything else)* primero; **f. and foremost** ante todo; **at f.** al principio. **3** *n* **the f.** el primero, la primera; **the f. of April** el uno *or* el primero de abril; **from the (very) f.** desde el principio.
first aid primeros auxilios.
first-class 1 *adj* de primera clase. **2** *adv* **to travel f.** viajar en primera.
first·ly *adv* en primer lugar.
fish 1 *n (pl* **fish**) pez *m*; *(as food)* pescado *m*. **2** *vi* pescar.
fish·er·man pescador *m*.
fish·ing pesca *f*; **to go f.** ir de pesca.
fish·ing rod caña *f* de pescar.
fish shop pescadería *f*.
fish stick palito *m* de pescado.
fist puño *m*.
fit¹ 1 *vt (clothes)* ir bien a; *(slot)* encajar; *(install)* colocar; **that suit doesn't f. you** ese traje no te queda bien; **a car fitted with a radio** un coche provisto de radio; **she doesn't f. the description** no responde a la descripción. **2** *vi (be of right size)* caber; *(be suitable)* encajar; *(facts etc)* cuadrar. **3** *adj (suitable)* apto, -a (**for** para); *(healthy)* en (plena) forma; **are you f. to drive?** ¿estás en condiciones de conducir?; **to keep f.** mantenerse en forma. **4** *n* **to be a good f.** encajar bien.
fit² *(attack)* ataque *m*; *fig* arrebato *m*; **by fits and starts** a trompicones.
▸**fit in 1** *vi (tally)* cuadrar (**with** con); **he didn't f. in with his colleagues** no encajó con sus compañeros de trabajo. **2** *vt (find time for)* encontrar un hueco para.
▸**fit on** *vt* **to f. sth on(to) sth** colocar *or* encajar algo en algo.
▸**fit out** *vt* equipar.
fit·ness *(health)* (buen) estado *m* físico.
fit·ted *adj* empotrado, -a; **f. carpet** moqueta *f*.
fit·ting *adj* apropiado, -a.
fit·ting room probador *m*.
fit·tings *npl* accesorios *mpl*; **light f.** apliques *mpl* eléctricos.
five *adj & n* cinco *(m) inv*; **f. hundred** quinientos, -as.
fix 1 *n* **to be in a f.** estar en un apuro. **2** *vt (fasten)* fijar; *(date, price)* fijar; *(repair)* arreglar; *(food, drink)* preparar; **he'll f. it with the boss** *(arrange)* se las arreglará con el jefe.
▸**fix on** *vt (lid etc)* encajar.
▸**fix up** *vt (arrange)* arreglar; **to f. sb up with sth** proveer a algn de algo.
fix·ture *(in sport)* encuentro *m*; **fixtures** *(in building)* accesorios *mpl*.
fizzy *adj (water)* con gas.
flag 1 *n* bandera *f*; *(on ship)* pabellón *m*. **2** *vi (interest)* decaer; *(conversation)* languidecer.
flake 1 *n (of snow)* copo *m*; *(of skin, soap)* escama *f*. **2** *vi (paint)* desconcharse.
flame llama *f*; **to go up in flames** incendiarse.
flam·ma·ble *adj* inflamable.
flan tarta *f* rellena; **fruit f.** tarta *f* de fruta.
flan·nel *(material)* franela *f*.
flap 1 *vt (wings, arms)* batir. **2** *vi (wings)* aletear; *(flag)* ondear. **3** *n (of envelope, pocket)* solapa *f*; **to get into a f.** ponerse nervioso, -a.
flare 1 *n (distress signal)* bengala *f*. **2** *vi (fire)* llamear; *(trouble)* estallar.
flash 1 *n (of light)* destello *m*; *(of lightning)* relámpago *m*; *(for camera)* flash *m*. **2** *vt (torch)* dirigir; **he flashed his card** enseñó rápidamente su carnet. **3** *vi (sudden light)* destellar; *(shine)* brillar; **a car flashed past** un coche pasó como un rayo.
flash·light linterna *f*.
flask frasco *m*; **(thermos) f.** termo *m*.
flat 1 *adj (surface)* llano, -a; *(beer)* sin gas; *(battery)* descargado, -a; *(tire)* desinflado, -a; *(dull)* soso, -a; *(in music)* **B f.** si *m* bemol. **2** *adv* **to fall f. on one's face** caerse de bruces; **to go f. out** ir a todo gas. **3** *n (flat tire)* pinchazo *m*.
flat·ly *adv* rotundamente.
flat·ten *vt (make level)* allanar; *(crush)* aplastar.
flat·ter *vt* halagar; *(clothes, portrait)* favorecer.
fla·vor 1 *n* sabor *m*. **2** *vt (food)* sazonar (**with** con).
fla·vor·ing condimento *m*; **artificial f.** aroma *m* artificial.
flaw *(failing)* defecto *m*; *(fault)* desperfecto *m*.
flea pulga *f*.
flea mar·ket rastro *m*.
flee* 1 *vt* huir. **2** *vi* huir (**from** de).
fleet flota *f*.
Flem·ish 1 *adj* flamenco, -a. **2** *n (language)* flamenco *m*.
flesh carne *f*; *(of fruit)* pulpa *f*; **in the f.** en persona.
flex *vt (muscles)* flexionar.
flex·i·ble *adj* flexible.
flick 1 *n (of finger)* capirotazo *m*. **2** *vt (finger)* dar un capirotazo a.
▸**flick off** *vt (piece of fluff)* quitar con un dedo.
▸**flick through** *vt* hojear.
flick·er *vi (eyes)* parpadear; *(flame)* vacilar.
flies *npl (on trousers)* bragueta *f*.
flight vuelo *m*; *(escape)* huida *f*; *(of stairs)* tramo *m*; **to take f.** darse a la fuga.
flight at·ten·dant azafata *f*.
flim·sy *adj (cloth)* ligero, -a; *(structure)* poco sólido, -a; *(excuse)* poco convincente.
fling* *vt* arrojar.
flint *(in lighter)* piedra *f* de mechero.
flip 1 *n (flick)* capirotazo *m*. **2** *vt (toss)* tirar (al aire); **to f. a coin** echar a cara o cruz.
▸**flip through** *vt (book)* hojear.
flip-flop *(footwear)* chancleta *f*.
float 1 *n* flotador *m*; *(in procession)* carroza *f*. **2** *vi* flotar.
flock 1 *n* rebaño *m*; *(of birds)* bandada *f*. **2** *vi* acudir en masa.
flood 1 *n* inundación *f*; *(of river)* riada *f*. **2** *vt* inundar. **3** *vi (river)* desbordarse.
flood·light foco *m*.
floor *(of room)* suelo *m*; *(storey)* piso *m*; **first f.** planta *f* baja.
floor·board tabla *f* (del suelo).
flop 1 *n (failure)* fracaso *m*. **2** *vi* fracasar.
flop·py *adj* flojo, -a.
flop·py disk disquete *m*, disco *m* flexible.
flo·rist florista *mf*; **f.'s** floristería *f*.
floun·der *inv (fish)* platija *f*.
flour harina *f*.
flour·ish 1 *n (gesture)* ademán *m* (teatral). **2** *vt (brandish)* agitar. **3** *vi (thrive)* florecer; *(plant)* crecer.
flow 1 *n* flujo *m*; *(of traffic)* circulación *f*; *(of people, goods)* movimiento *m*. **2** *vi (blood, river)* fluir; *(traffic)* circular.
flow chart organigrama *m*.
flow·er 1 *n* flor *f*. **2** *vi* florecer.
flow·er bed arriate *m*.
flow·er shop floristería *f*.
flu gripe *f*.
flu·ent *adj (eloquent)* fluido, -a; **he speaks f. German** habla el alemán con soltura.
flu·ent·ly *adv (to speak)* con soltura.
fluff *(down)* pelusa *f*.
flu·id líquido *m*.
flunk *vt fam* catear.
flu·o·res·cent *adj* fluorescente.
flush 1 *adj* **f. with** *(level)* a ras de. **2** *n (blush)* rubor *m*. **3** *vt* **to f. the lavatory** tirar de la cadena. **4** *vi (blush)* ruborizarse.
flute flauta *f*.
flut·ter *vi (leaves, birds)* revolotear; *(flag)* ondear.
fly¹* 1 *vt (plane)* pilotar. **2** *vi (bird, plane)* volar; *(go by plane)* ir en avión; *(flag)* ondear.
▸**fly over** *vt (country etc)* sobrevolar.
fly² *(insect)* mosca *f*; **f. spray** spray *m* matamoscas.
fly³ *(on trousers)* bragueta *f*.
fly·ing 1 *adj (soaring)* volante; *(rapid)* rápido, -a. **2** *n (action)* vuelo *m*; *(aviation)* aviación *f*.
fly·ing sau·cer platillo *m* volante.
fly-o·ver paso *m* elevado.
foam espuma *f*; **f. rubber** goma *f* espuma.
fo·cus 1 *vt* centrar (**on** en). **2** *vi* **to f. on sth** enfocar algo; *fig* centrarse en algo. **3** *n* foco *m*.
fog niebla *f*; *(at sea)* bruma *f*.
fog·gy *adj* **it is f.** hay niebla.
foil 1 *n* **aluminum f.** papel *m* de aluminio. **2** *vt (plot)* frustrar.
fold 1 *n (crease)* pliegue *m*. **2** *vt* doblar; **to f. one's arms** cruzar los brazos. **3** *vi* **to f. (up)** *(chair etc)* plegarse.
▸**fold away** *vt* plegar.
fold·er carpeta *f*.
fold·ing *adj (chair etc)* plegable.
folk *npl (people)* gente *f*.
folk mu·sic música *f* folk.
fol·low 1 *vt* seguir; *(understand)* comprender. **2** *vi (come after)* seguir; *(result)* resultar; *(understand)* entender; **that doesn't f.** eso no es lógico.
▸**follow around** *vt* **to f. sb around** seguir a algn por todas partes.

▶**follow on** *vi (come after)* venir detrás.
▶**follow up** *vt (idea)* llevar a cabo; *(clue)* investigar.
follower seguidor, -a *mf.*
fol·low·ing 1 *adj* siguiente. **2** *n* seguidores *mpl.*
fond *adj* **to be f. of sb** tenerle mucho cariño a algn; **to be f. of doing sth** ser aficionado, -a a hacer algo.
font *(of characters)* fuente *f.*
food comida *f.*
food poi·son·ing intoxicación *f* alimenticia.
fool 1 *n* tonto, -a *mf;* **to play the f.** hacer el tonto. **2** *vt (deceive)* engañar. **3** *vi (joke)* bromear.
▶**fool around** *vi* hacer el tonto.
fool·ish *adj (silly)* tonto, -a; *(unwise)* estúpido, -a.
fool·ish·ly *adv* estúpidamente.
foot 1 *n (pl feet)* pie *m; (of animal)* pata *f;* **on f.** a pie; **to put one's f. in it** meter la pata. **2** *vt* **to f. the bill** *(pay)* pagar la cuenta.
foot·ball fútbol americano *m; (ball)* balón *m.*
foot·bridge puente *m* para peatones.
foot·path sendero *m.*
foot·print pisada *f.*
foot·step paso *m.*
for *prep (purpose)* para; **what's this f.?** ¿para qué sirve esto?; **f. sale** en venta. ▪ *(because of, on behalf of)* por; **famous f. its cuisine** famoso, -a por su cocina; **will you do it f. me?** ¿lo harás por mí? ▪ *(instead of)* por; **can you go f. me?** ¿puede ir por mí? ▪ *(during)* por, durante; **I was ill f. a month** estuve enfermo durante un mes; **I've been here f. three months** hace tres meses que estoy aquí. ▪ *(distance)* por; **I walked f. ten kilometers** caminé diez kilómetros. ▪ *(at a point in time)* para; **I can do it f. next Monday** puedo hacerlo para el lunes que viene; **f. the last time** por última vez. ▪ *(in exchange for)* por; **I got the car f. five hundred dollars** conseguí el coche por quinientos dólares. ▪ *(in favor of)* a favor de; **are you f. or against?** ¿estás a favor o en contra? ▪ *(towards)* hacia, por; **affection f. sb** cariño hacia algn. ▪ **it's time f. you to go** es hora de que os marchéis.
for·bid* *vt* prohibir; **to f. sb to do sth** prohibirle a algn hacer algo.
force 1 *n* fuerza *f;* **to come into f.** entrar en vigor; **the (armed) forces** las fuerzas armadas. **2** *vt* forzar; **to f. sb to do sth** forzar a algn a hacer algo.
fore·cast 1 *n* pronóstico *m,* previsión *f.* **2** *vt** pronosticar.
fore·head frente *f.*
for·eign *adj* extranjero, -a; *(trade, policy)* exterior.
for·eign·er extranjero, -a *mf.*
fore·man capataz *m.*
fore·most *adj* principal; **first and f.** ante todo.
fore·run·ner precursor, -a *mf.*
fore·see* *vt* prever.
for·est bosque *m.*
for·ev·er *adv (constantly)* siempre; *(for good)* para siempre.
forge *vt (counterfeit)* falsificar; *(metal)* forjar.
▶**forge ahead** *vi* hacer grandes progresos.
for·ger·y falsificación *f.*
for·get* **1** *vt* olvidar; **I forgot to close the window** se me olvidó cerrar la ventana. **2** *vi* olvidarse.
▶**forget about** *vt* olvidar.
for·get·ful *adj* olvidadizo, -a.
for·give* *vt* perdonar; **to f. sb for sth** pendonarle algo a algn.
fork 1 *n (cutlery)* tenedor *m; (farming)* horca *f; (in road)* bifurcación *f.* **2** *vi (roads)* bifurcarse.
▶**fork out** *vt fam (money)* soltar.
form 1 *n* forma *f; (type)* clase *f; (document)* formulario *m; (at school)* clase *f;* **on/on top/off f.** en/en plena/en baja forma. **2** *vt* formar. **3** *vi* formarse.
for·mal *adj (official)* oficial; *(party, dress)* de etiqueta; *(person)* formalista.
for·mal·i·ty formalidad *f.*
for·mal·ly *adv* oficialmente.
for·mat 1 *n* formato *m.* **2** *vt (computer disk)* formatear.
for·ma·tion formación *f.*
for·mer *adj (time)* anterior; *(one-time)* antiguo, -a; *(first)* aquél/aquélla; **the f. champion** el ex-campeón.
for·mer·ly *adv* antes, antiguamente.
for·mu·la fórmula *f.*
for·mu·late *vt* formular.
fort fortaleza *f.*
forth *adv fml* **and so f.** y así sucesivamente; **to go back and f.** ir de acá para allá.
forth·com·ing *adj (event)* próximo, -a; *(communicative)* comunicativo, -a; **no money was f.** no hubo oferta de dinero.
for·ti·eth *adj & n* cuadragésimo, -a *(mf).*
fort·night quincena *f.*
for·tress fortaleza *f.*
for·tu·nate *adj* afortunado, -a; **it was f. that he came** fue una suerte que viniera.
for·tu·nate·ly *adv* afortunadamente.
for·tune *(luck, fate)* suerte *f; (money)* fortuna *f.*
for·ty *adj & n* cuarenta *(m) inv.*
fo·rum foro *m.*
for·ward 1 *adv (also forwards) (direction and movement)* hacia adelante; **from this day f.** de ahora en adelante. **2** *adj (person)* fresco, -a. **3** *n (in sport)* delantero, -a *mf.* **4** *vt (send on)* remitir; *(goods)* expedir.
fos·sil fósil *m.*
fos·ter *adj* **f. child** niño(a) *mf* en régimen de acogida; **f. home** hogar *m* de acogida; **f. parents** padres *mpl* de acogida.
foul 1 *adj (smell)* fétido, -a; *(taste)* asqueroso, -a; *(language)* grosero, -a. **2** *n (in football etc)* falta *f.*
found¹ *pt & pp of* **find**.
found² *vt (establish)* fundar.
found·er fundador, -a *mf.*
foun·tain fuente *f.*
foun·tain pen pluma estilográfica *f.*
four *adj & n* cuatro *(m) inv;* **on all fours** a gatas.
four·teen *adj & n* catorce *(m) inv.*
fourth *adj & n* cuarto, -a *(mf).*
fowl aves *fpl* de corral.
fox zorro, -a *mf.*
foy·er vestíbulo *m.*
frac·tion fracción *f.*
frac·ture 1 *n* fractura *f.* **2** *vt* fracturar.
frag·ile *adj* frágil.
frag·ment fragmento *m.*
fra·grance fragancia *f.*
frail *adj* frágil.
frame 1 *n (of window, door, picture)* marco *m; (of machine)* armazón *m;* **f. of mind** estado *m* de ánimo. **2** *vt (picture)* enmarcar; *(question)* formular; *(innocent person)* incriminar.

frame·work **within the f. of ...** dentro del marco de ....
franc franco *m.*
fran·chise *(right to vote)* derecho *m* al voto; *(right to sell product)* concesión *f,* licencia *f.*
frank *adj* franco, -a.
frank·ly *adv* francamente.
frank·ness franqueza *f.*
fran·tic *adj (anxious)* desesperado, -a; *(hectic)* frenético, -a.
fran·ti·cal·ly *adv* desesperadamente.
fraud fraude *m; (person)* impostor, -a *mf.*
fray *vi (cloth)* deshilacharse.
freck·le peca *f.*
freck·led *adj* pecoso, -a.
free 1 *adj* libre; **f. (of charge)** gratuito, -a; *(generous)* generoso, -a. **2** *adv* **(for) f.** gratis. **3** *vt (liberate)* poner en libertad.
free·dom libertad *f.*
free·way autopista *f.*
freeze* **1** *vt* congelar. **2** *vi (liquid)* helarse; *(food)* congelarse.
▶**freeze up, freeze over** *vi* helarse; *(windshield)* cubrirse de hielo.
freez·er congelador *m.*
freez·ing *adj* glacial; **above/below f. point** sobre/bajo cero.
freight *(transport)* transporte *m; (goods, price)* flete *m;* **f. train** tren *m* de mercancías.
French 1 *adj* francés, -esa. **2** *n (language)* francés *m, pl* **the F.** los franceses.
French fries *npl* patatas *fpl* fritas.
French·man francés *m.*
French·wom·an francesa *f.*
fre·quent *adj* frecuente.
fre·quent·ly *adv* frecuentemente.
fresh *adj* fresco, -a; *(new)* nuevo, -a; **in the f. air** al aire libre.
fresh·en up *vi* asearse.
fret *vi* preocuparse **(about** por).
Fri·day viernes *m.*
fridge nevera *f,* frigorífico *m.*
fried *adj* frito, -a.
friend amigo, -a *mf;* **a f. of mine** un, -a amigo, -a mío, -a.
friend·ly *adj (person)* simpático, -a; *(atmosphere)* acogedor, -a.
friend·ship amistad *f.*
fright *(fear)* miedo *m; (shock)* susto *m;* **to get a f.** pegarse un susto.
fright·en *vt* asustar.
▶**frighten away, frighten off** *vt* ahuyentar.
fright·ened *adj* asustado, -a; **to be f. of sb** tenerle miedo a algn.
fright·en·ing *adj* espantoso, -a.
frill *(dress)* volante *m.*
fringe *(edge)* borde *m, fig* **on the f. of society** al margen de la sociedad.
frog rana *f.*
from *prep (time)* desde, a partir de; **f. the eighth to the seventeenth** desde el ocho hasta el diecisiete; **f. time to time** de vez en cuando. ▪ *(price, number)* desde, de; **dresses f. ten dollars** vestidos desde diez dólares. ▪ *(origin)* de; **he's f. Malaga** es de Málaga; **the train f. Bilbao** el tren procedente de Bilbao. ▪ *(distance)* de; **the town is four miles f. the coast** el pueblo está a cuatro millas de la costa. ▪ *(remove, subtract)* a; **he took the book f. the child** le quitó el libro al niño. ▪ *(according to)* según, por; **f. what the author said** según lo que dijo el autor. ▪ *(position)* desde, de; **f. here** desde aquí.
front 1 *n* parte *f* delantera; *(of building)* fachada *f; (military, political, of weather)* frente *m;* **in f. (of)** delante (de). **2** *adj* delantero, -a.
front door puerta *f* principal.
fron·tier frontera *f.*
frost *n (covering)* escarcha *f, (freezing)* helada *f.*
frost·bite congelación *f.*
frost·y *adj fig* glacial; **it will be a f. night tonight** esta noche habrá helada.
froth espuma *f.*
frown *vi* fruncir el ceño.
▶**frown upon** *vt* desaprobar.
fro·zen *adj (liquid, feet etc)* helado, -a; *(food)* congelado, -a.
fruit fruta *f,* **fruits** *(rewards)* frutos *mpl.*
fruit sal·ad macedonia *f* de frutas.
frus·trate *vt* frustrar.
frus·trat·ed *adj* frustrado, -a.
frus·trat·ing *adj* frustrante.
frus·tra·tion frustración *f.*
fry *vt* freír.
fry·ing pan sartén *f.*
fu·el combustible *m; (for engines)* carburante *m.*
fu·gi·tive fugitivo, -a *mf.*
ful·fill *vt (task, ambition)* realizar; *(promise)* cumplir; *(wishes)* satisfacer.
ful·fill·ing *adj* que llena.
full 1 *adj* lleno, -a **(of** de); *(complete)* completo, -a; **I'm f. (up)** no puedo más. **2** *n* **in f.** en su totalidad.
full board pensión *f* completa.
full-scale *adj (model)* de tamaño natural.
full stop punto *m.*
full-time *adj* de jornada completa. **2** *adv* **to work f.** trabajar a jornada completa.
ful·ly *adv* completamente.
fumes *npl* humo *m.*
fun *(amusement)* diversión *f;* **in** *or* **for f.** en broma; **to have f.** pasarlo bien; **to make f. of sb** reírse de algn.
func·tion 1 *n* función *f; (ceremony)* acto *m; (party)* recepción *f.* **2** *vi* funcionar.
func·tion·al *adj* funcional.
fund 1 *n* fondo *m;* **funds** fondos *mpl.* **2** *vt (finance)* financiar.
fu·ner·al funeral *m;* **f. home** funeraria *f.*
fun·nel *(for liquids)* embudo *m; (of ship)* chimenea *f.*
fun·ny *adj (peculiar)* raro, -a; *(amusing)* divertido, -a; *(ill)* mal; **I found it very f.** me hizo mucha gracia.
fur *(of living animal)* pelo *m; (of dead animal)* piel *f.*
fu·ri·ous *adj (angry)* furioso, -a.
fur·nace horno *m.*
fur·nish *vt (house)* amueblar.
fur·ni·ture muebles *mpl;* **a piece of f.** un mueble.
fur·ther 1 *adj (new)* nuevo, -a; *(additional)* otro, -a. **2** *adv* más lejos; *(more)* más; **f. back** más atrás.
fur·ther ed·u·ca·tion estudios *mpl* superiores.
fur·ther·more *adv* además.
fur·thest *adj* más lejano, -a.
fu·ry furia *f.*
fuse 1 *n* fusible *m; (of bomb)* mecha *f.* **2** *vi* **the lights fused** se fundieron los plomos.

fuss 1 n (commotion) jaleo m; **to kick up a f.** armar un escándalo; **to make a f. of** (pay attention to) mimar a. **2** vi preocuparse (**about** por).

▶ **fuss over** vt consentir a.

fuss·y adj (nitpicking) quisquilloso, -a; (thorough) exigente.

fu·ture 1 n futuro m; **in the near f.** en un futuro próximo. **2** adj futuro, -a.

fuzz·y adj (hair) muy rizado, -a; (blurred) borroso, -a.

G

gadg·et aparato m.

Gael·ic 1 adj gaélico, -a. **2** n (language) gaélico m.

gag 1 n mordaza f; (joke) chiste m. **2** vt amordazar.

gai·e·ty regocijo m.

gai·ly adv alegremente.

gain 1 n ganancia f; (increase) aumento m. **2** vt (obtain) ganar; (increase) aumentar; **to g. weight** aumentar de peso.

▶ **gain on** vt ganar terreno a.

ga·la gala f.

ga·lax·y galaxia f.

gale vendaval m.

gal·lant adj (chivalrous) galante.

gal·ler·y galería f.

gal·li·vant vi fam callejear.

gal·lon galón m.

gal·lop 1 n galope m. **2** vi galopar.

gam·ble 1 n (risk) riesgo m; (bet) apuesta f. **2** vi (bet) jugar; (take a risk) arriesgarse.

▶ **gamble away** vt (lose) perder en el juego.

gam·bler jugador, -a mf.

gam·bling juego m.

game juego m; (match) partido m; (of bridge) partida f.

gang (of criminals) banda f; (of youths) pandilla f.

▶ **gang up** vi confabularse (**on** contra).

gang·ster gángster m.

gang·way pasarela f.

gap hueco m; (blank space) blanco m; (in time) intervalo m; (gulf) diferencia f; (deficiency) laguna f.

gape vi (person) mirar boquiabierto, -a.

ga·rage garaje m; (for repairs) taller m mecánico; (gas station) gasolinera f.

gar·bage basura f; **g. can** cubo m de la basura.

gar·ban·zo g. (bean) garbanzo m.

gar·den jardín m.

gar·den·er jardinero, -a mf.

gar·den·ing jardinería f.

gar·gle vi hacer gárgaras.

gar·land guirnalda f.

gar·lic ajo m.

gar·ment prenda f.

gas 1 n gas m; gasolina f; **g. cooker** cocina f de gas; **g. fire** estufa f de gas. **2** vt (asphyxiate) asfixiar con gas.

gash 1 n herida f profunda. **2** vt **he gashed his forehead** se hizo una herida en la frente.

gas·o·line gasolina f.

gasp 1 n (cry) grito m sordo; (breath) bocanada f. **2** vi (in surprise) quedar boquiabierto, -a; (breathe) jadear.

gas sta·tion gasolinera f.

gas·sy adj gaseoso, -a.

gas tank depósito m de gasolina.

gas·works fábrica f de gas.

gate puerta f; (at stadium) entrada f.

gate·crash vti colarse.

gath·er vt (collect) juntar; (pick up) recoger; (bring together) reunir; (understand) suponer; **to g. speed** ir ganando velocidad; **I g. that ...** tengo entendido que .... **2** vi (come together) reunirse.

▶ **gather around** vi agruparse.

gath·er·ing reunión f.

gaud·y adj chillón, -ona.

gauge 1 n (of railway) ancho m de vía; (calibrator) indicador m. **2** vt (judge) juzgar.

gaunt adj (lean) demacrado, -a; (desolate) lúgubre.

gauze gasa f.

gave pt of **give**.

gay adj (homosexual) gay; (happy) alegre.

gaze 1 n mirada f fija. **2** vi mirar fijamente.

▶ **gaze at** vt mirar fijamente.

GB abbr of **Great Britain**.

gear 1 n (equipment) equipo m; (belongings) bártulos mpl; (clothing) ropa f; (in car etc) marcha f. **2** vt adaptar (**to** a).

gear·box caja f de cambios.

geese npl see **goose**.

gel gel m; (for hair) gomina f.

gem piedra f preciosa.

gen·der género m.

gen·er·al 1 adj general; **in g.** en general; **the g. public** el público. **2** n (in army) general m.

gen·er·al·ly adv generalmente.

gen·er·a·tion generación f.

gen·er·a·tion gap abismo m or conflicto m generacional.

gen·er·a·tor generador m.

gen·er·os·i·ty generosidad f.

gen·er·ous adj generoso, -a; (plentiful) copioso, -a.

gen·er·ous·ly adv generosamente.

gen·ius (person) genio m; (gift) don m.

gen·tle adj dulce; (breeze) suave.

gen·tle·man caballero m.

gen·tle·ness (mildness) ternura f; (kindness) amabilidad f.

gent·ly con cuidado.

gents npl servicio m de caballeros.

gen·u·ine adj auténtico, -a; (sincere) sincero, -a.

gen·u·ine·ly adv auténticamente.

ge·o·graph·i(·)c(al) adj geográfico, -a.

ge·og·ra·phy geografía f.

ge·o·met·ri(·)c(al) adj geométrico, -a.

ge·om·e·try geometría f.

germ microbio m.

Ger·man 1 adj alemán, -ana; **G. measles** rubeola f. **2** n alemán, -ana mf; (language) alemán m.

Ger·man shep·herd (dog) pastor m alemán.

ges·ture gesto m.

get* 1 vt (obtain) obtener, conseguir; (earn) ganar; (fetch) (something) traer; (somebody) ir a por; (receive) recibir; (bus, train, thief etc) coger, Am agarrar; (understand) entender; (on phone) **g. me Mr Brown** póngame con el Sr. Brown; **can I g. you something to eat?** ¿te traigo algo de comer?; **g. him to call me** dile que me llame; **to g. one's hair cut** cortarse el pelo; **to g. sb to do sth** (ask) persuadir a algn de que haga algo. **2** vi (become) ponerse; **to g. late** hacerse tarde; **to g. dressed** vestirse; **to g. married** casarse; **to g. to** (come to) llegar a; **to g. to know sb** llegar a conocer a algn.

▶ **get across** vt (idea etc) hacer comprender.

▶ **get along** vi (manage) arreglárselas; (two people) llevarse bien.

▶ **get around 1** vi (person) salir; (news) difundirse. **2** vt (problem) salvar; (difficulty) vencer.

▶ **get around to** vi **if I g. around to it** si tengo tiempo; **I'll g. around to it later** encontraré tiempo para hacerlo más tarde.

▶ **get at** vt (reach) alcanzar; (criticize) criticar.

▶ **get away** vi escaparse.

▶ **get back 1** vi (return) volver; **g. back!** (move backwards) ¡atrás! **2** vt (recover) recuperar.

▶ **get by** vi (manage) arreglárselas; **she can g. by in French** sabe defenderse en francés.

▶ **get down 1** vt (depress) deprimir. **2** vi (descend) bajar.

▶ **get in 1** vi (arrive) llegar; (politician) ser elegido, -a. **2** vt (buy) comprar; (collect) recoger.

▶ **get into** vt (house, car) entrar en; fig **to g. into bad habits** adquirir malas costumbres; **to g. into trouble** meterse en un lío.

▶ **get off 1** vt (bus etc) bajarse de; (remove) quitarse. **2** vi bajarse; (escape) escaparse; **to g. off lightly** salir bien librado, -a.

▶ **get on 1** vt (board) subir a. **2** vi (board) subirse; (make progress) hacer progresos; **how are you getting on?** ¿cómo te van las cosas?; **to g. on well (with sb)** llevarse bien (con algn); (continue) **to g. on with sth** seguir con algo.

▶ **get on to** vt (find) (person) localizar; (find out) descubrir; (continue) pasar a.

▶ **get out 1** vt (object) sacar. **2** vi (of room etc) salir (**of** de); (of train) bajar (**of** de); (news) difundirse; (secret) hacerse público.

▶ **get over** vt (illness) recuperarse de; (difficulty) vencer; (convey) hacer comprender.

▶ **get through 1** vi (message) llegar; (on phone) **to g. through to sb** conseguir comunicar con algn. **2** vt (consume) consumir; **to g. through a lot of work** trabajar mucho.

▶ **get together** vi (people) reunirse.

▶ **get up 1** vi (rise) levantarse. **2** vt (wake up) despertar.

▶ **get up to** vt hacer; **to g. up to mischief** hacer de las suyas.

get-to-geth·er reunión f.

ghast·ly adj espantoso, -a.

gher·kin pepinillo m.

ghet·to gueto m.

ghost fantasma m.

gi·ant adj & n gigante (m).

gid·dy adj mareado, -a; **it makes me g.** me da vértigo; **to feel g.** sentirse mareado, -a.

gift regalo m; (talent) don m.

gift·ed adj dotado, -a.

gig fam (concert) actuación f.

gi·gan·tic adj gigantesco, -a.

gig·gle vi reírse tontamente.

gim·mick truco m; (in advertising) reclamo m.

gin ginebra f; **g. and tonic** gin tonic m.

gin·ger 1 adj (hair) pelirrojo, -a. **2** n jengibre m.

gi·raffe jirafa f.

girl chica f; (child) niña f; (daughter) hija f.

girl·friend novia f; (female friend) amiga f.

give* vt dar; **to g. sb sth as a present** regalar algo a algn.

▶ **give away** vt (present) regalar; (disclose) revelar.

▶ **give back** vt devolver.

▶ **give in 1** vi (admit defeat) darse por vencido, -a; (surrender) rendirse. **2** vt (hand in) entregar.

▶ **give off** vt (smell etc) despedir.

▶ **give out** vt repartir.

▶ **give up** vt (idea) abandonar; **to g. up smoking** dejar de fumar; **to g. oneself up** entregarse.

giv·en 1 adj (particular) dado, -a. **2** conj (considering) dado, -a.

glad adj contento, -a; **to be g.** alegrarse.

glad·ly adv con mucho gusto.

glam·or·ous adj atractivo, -a.

glam·our atractivo m; (charm) encanto m.

glance 1 n vistazo m. **2** vi echar un vistazo (**at** a).

gland glándula f.

glare 1 n (look) mirada f feroz. **2** vi (look) lanzar una mirada furiosa (**at** a).

glar·ing adj (light) deslumbrante; (obvious) evidente.

glass (material) vidrio m; (drinking vessel) vaso m; **pane of g.** cristal m; **wine g.** copa f (para vino); **glasses** (spectacles) gafas fpl.

glee gozo m.

glide vi (plane) planear.

glid·ing vuelo m sin motor.

glim·mer fig (trace) destello m.

glimpse 1 n atisbo m. **2** vt atisbar.

glit·ter·ing adj reluciente.

globe globo m.

gloom (obscurity) penumbra f; (melancholy) melancolía f.

gloom·y adj (dismal) deprimente; (despondent) pesimista; (sad) triste.

glo·ri·fied adj fam con pretensiones; **a g. boarding house** una pensión con pretensiones.

glo·ri·ous adj (momentous) glorioso, -a; (splendid) espléndido, -a.

glo·ry gloria f; (splendor) esplendor m.

gloss (sheen) brillo m; **g. (paint)** esmalte m.

gloss·y adj lustroso, -a; **g. magazine** revista f de lujo.

glove guante m; **g. compartment** guantera f.

glow 1 n brillo m. **2** vi brillar.

glue 1 n pegamento m. **2** vt pegar (**to** a).

glum adj alicaído, -a.

glut·ton glotón, -ona mf.

gnat mosquito m.

gnaw vti (chew) roer.

go* 1 vi ir; (depart) irse, marcharse; (bus) salir; (disappear) desaparecer; (function) funcionar; (become) quedarse, volverse; (fit) caber; (time) pasar; **how's it going?** ¿qué tal (te van las cosas)?; **to get** or **be going** marcharse; **to be going to** (in the future) ir a; (on the point of) estar a punto de; **there are only two weeks to go** sólo quedan dos semanas; **to let sth go** soltar algo. **2** n (try) intento m; (turn) turno m; **to have a go at sth** probar suerte con algo; **it's your go** te toca a ti; **to have a go at sb** criticar a algn.

▶**go about 1** *vt (task)* emprender; **how do you go about it?** ¿cómo hay que hacerlo? **2** *vi (rumor)* correr.
▶**go after** *vt (pursue)* andar tras.
▶**go against** *vt (oppose)* ir en contra de; *(be unfavorable to)* ser desfavorable a.
▶**go ahead** *vi (proceed)* proceder; **we'll go on ahead** iremos adelante.
▶**go along** *vt (street)* ir por.
▶**go along with** *vt (agree)* estar de acuerdo con; *(accompany)* acompañar.
▶**go around** *vi (revolve)* dar vueltas; **to go around to sb's house** pasar por casa de algn.
▶**go away** *vi* marcharse.
▶**go back** *vi (return)* volver.
▶**go back on** *vt* **to go back on one's word** faltar a su palabra.
▶**go back to** *vt* volver a; *(date from)* datar de.
▶**go by** *vi* pasar; **as time goes by** con el tiempo.
▶**go down** *vi (descend)* bajar; *(sun)* ponerse; *(ship)* hundirse; *(diminish)* disminuir; *(temperature)* bajar.
▶**go down with** *vt (disease)* coger.
▶**go for** *vt (fetch)* ir por; *(attack)* atacar, lanzarse sobre; **the same goes for you** lo mismo te digo a ti *or* vale para ti
▶**go in** *vi* entrar.
▶**go in for** *vt (exam)* presentarse a.
▶**go into** *vt (enter)* entrar en; *(matter)* investigar.
▶**go off** *vi (leave)* irse, marcharse; *(bomb)* explotar; *(gun)* dispararse; *(alarm)* sonar; *(food)* pasarse.
▶**go on** *vi (continue)* seguir, continuar; *(happen)* pasar; *(light)* encenderse; **to go on talking** seguir hablando.
▶**go out** *vi (leave)* salir; *(fire, light)* apagarse.
▶**go over** *vt (cross)* atravesar; *(revise)* repasar.
▶**go over to** *vt (switch to)* pasar a; **to go over to the enemy** pasarse al enemigo.
▶**go through** *vt (endure)* sufrir; *(examine)* examinar; *(search)* registrar; *(spend)* gastar.
▶**go under** *vi (ship)* hundirse; *(business)* fracasar.
▶**go up** *vi* subir.
▶**go with** *vt (accompany)* ir con; *(colors)* hacer juego con.
▶**go without** *vt* pasarse sin.
go·a·head **to give sb the g.** dar luz verde a algn.
goal gol *m*; *(aim, objective)* meta *f*.
goal·keep·er portero, -a *mf*.
goat *(male)* macho cabrío *m*; *(female)* cabra *f*.
god dios *m*.
god·daugh·ter ahijada *f*.
god·fa·ther padrino *m*.
god·moth·er madrina *f*.
god·send **to be a g.** venir como agua de mayo.
god·son ahijado *m*.
gog·gles *npl (for diving)* gafas *fpl* de bucear; *(protective)* gafas *fpl* protectoras.
go·ing *adj (price)* corriente.
go·ings-on *npl* tejemanejes *mpl*.
gold 1 *n* oro *m*. **2** *adj* de oro; *(color)* dorado, -a.
gold·en *adj* de oro; *(color)* dorado, -a.
gold·fish pez *m* de colores.
gold-plat·ed *adj* chapado, -a en oro.
golf golf *m*.
golf·er golfista *mf*.
gone *pp* of **go**.
good 1 *adj (before noun)* buen, -a; *(after noun)* bueno, -a; *(kind)* amable; *(generous)* generoso, -a; *(morally correct)* correcto, -a; **g. afternoon, g. evening** buenas tardes; **g. morning** buenos días; **g. night** buenas noches; **to have a g. time** pasarlo bien; **be g.!** ¡pórtate bien!; **he's g. at languages** tiene facilidad para los idiomas; **he's in a g. mood** está de buen humor. **2** *n* bien *m*; **for your own g.** por tu propio bien; **it's no g. waiting** no sirve de nada esperar. **3** *adv* **she's gone for g.** se ha ido para siempre. **4** *interj* **g.!** ¡muy bien!
good·bye *interj* ¡adiós!
good-look·ing *adj* guapo, -a.
good·ness bondad *f*; **my g.!** ¡Dios mío!
goods *npl (possessions)* bienes *mpl*; *(commercial)* mercancías *fpl*.
good will buena voluntad *f*.
goose *(pl* **geese)** ganso *m*, oca *f*.
goose·ber·ry grosella *f* espinosa.
goose·flesh, goose·pim·ples *npl* carne *f* de gallina.
gorge desfiladero *m*.
gor·geous *adj* magnífico, -a; *(person)* atractivo, -a.
go·ril·la gorila *m*.
gos·pel **the G.** el Evangelio
gos·sip *(rumor)* cotilleo *m*; *(person)* chismoso, -a *mf*.
got *pt & pp* of **get**.
got·ten *pp* of **get**.
gour·met gourmet *mf*.
gov·ern *vt* gobernar; *(determine)* determinar.
gov·ern·ment gobierno *m*.
gov·er·nor *(ruler)* gobernador, -a *mf*; *(of school)* administrador, -a *mf*.
gown *(dress)* vestido *m* largo; *(of lawyer, professor)* toga *f*.
GP *abbr* of **general practitioner** médico *m* de cabecera.
grab *vt* agarrar; **to g. hold of sb** agarrarse a algn.
grace gracia *f*, *(elegance)* elegancia *f*.
grace·ful *adj* elegante; *(movement)* garboso, -a.
grade 1 *n (rank)* categoría *f*, *(in army)* rango *m*; *(mark)* nota *f*, *(class)* clase *f*. **2** *vt* clasificar.
grad·u·al *adj* gradual.
grad·u·al·ly *adv* poco a poco.
grad·u·ate 1 *n* licenciado, -a *mf*. **2** *vi (from university)* licenciarse **(in** en).
grad·u·a·tion cer·e·mo·ny ceremonia *f* de entrega de los títulos.
graf·fi·ti *npl* grafiti *mpl*.
graft 1 *n* injerto *m*. **2** *vt* injertar **(on to** en).
grain *(cereals)* cereales *mpl*; *(particle)* grano *m*.
gram gramo *m*.
gram·mar gramática *f*.
gram·mar school ≃ instituto *m* de Bachillerato.
gram·mat·i·cal *adj* gramatical.
grand *adj (splendid)* grandioso, -a; *(impressive)* impresionante.
grand·child nieto, -a *mf*.
grand·dad *fam* abuelo *m*.
grand·daugh·ter nieta *f*.
grand·fa·ther abuelo *m*.
grand·ma *fam* abuelita *f*.
grand·moth·er abuela *f*.
grand·par·ents *npl* abuelos *mpl*.
grand·son nieto *m*.

gran·ny *fam* abuelita *f*.
grant 1 *vt (give)* conceder; *(accept)* admitir; **to take for granted** dar por sentado. **2** *n (for study)* beca *f*, *(subsidy)* subvención *f*.
grape uva *f*, **g. juice** mosto *m*.
grape·fruit pomelo *m*.
graph gráfica *f*.
graph·ic *adj* gráfico, -a; **g. arts** artes *fpl* gráficas.
graph·ics *(computer)* g. gráficas *fpl*.
grasp 1 *vt* agarrar; *(understand)* comprender. **2** *n (grip)* agarrón *m*; *(understanding)* comprensión *f*.
grass hierba *f*, *(lawn)* césped *m*.
grass·hop·per saltamontes *m* inv.
grate 1 *vt (food)* rallar. **2** *vi* chirriar. **3** *n (fireplace)* rejilla *f*.
grate·ful *adj* agradecido, -a; **to be g. for** agradecer.
grat·er rallador *m*.
grat·i·fy·ing *adj* grato, -a.
grat·i·tude agradecimiento *m*.
grave¹ tumba *f*.
grave² *adj (situation)* grave.
grav·el gravilla *f*.
grave·yard cementerio *m*.
grav·i·ty gravedad *f*.
gra·vy salsa *f*.
gray *adj (color)* gris; *(hair)* cano, -a; *(sky)* nublado, -a.
graze 1 *vt (scratch)* rasguñar; *(brush against)* rozar. **2** *vi (cattle)* pacer. **3** *n* rasguño *m*.
grease 1 *n* grasa *f*. **2** *vt* engrasar.
grease·proof pa·per papel *m* apergaminado.
greas·y *adj (hair, food)* graso, -a.
great *adj* grande; *(before sing noun)* gran; *fam (excellent)* estupendo, -a; **a g. many** muchos, -as; **to have a g. time** pasarlo en grande.
great-grand·fa·ther bisabuelo *m*.
great-grand·moth·er bisabuela *f*.
great·ly *adv (with adjective)* muy; *(with verb)* mucho.
greed, gree·di·ness *(for food)* gula *f*, *(for money)* codicia *f*.
greed·y *adj (for food)* glotón, -ona; *(for money)* codicioso, -a **(for** de).
Greek 1 *adj* griego, -a. **2** *n (person)* griego, -a *mf*, *(language)* griego *m*.
green 1 *n (color)* verde *m*; *(for golf)* campo *m*; **greens** verduras *fpl*. **2** *adj* verde.
green·house invernadero *m*; **g. effect** efecto *m* invernadero.
greet *vt* saludar.
greet·ing saludo *m*.
gre·nade granada *f*.
grey *adj* = **gray**.
grey·hound galgo *m*.
grid *(on map)* cuadrícula *f*, *(of electricity etc)* red *f* nacional.
grief pena *f*, dolor *m*.
grieve *vi* **to g. for sb** llorar la muerte de algn.
grill 1 *vt (food)* asar a la parrilla. **2** *n* parrilla *f*, *(dish)* parrillada *f*.
grim *adj (landscape)* lúgubre; *(manner)* severo, -a; *(unpleasant)* desagradable.
grime mugre *f*.
grim·y *adj* mugriento, -a.
grin 1 *vi* sonreír abiertamente. **2** *n* sonrisa abierta.
grind* **1** *vt* moler; **to g. one's teeth** hacer rechinar los dientes.
grip 1 *n (hold)* agarrón *m*; *(handle)* asidero *m*. **2** *vt* agarrar; **to be gripped by fear** ser presa del miedo.
grip·ping *adj (film, story)* apasionante.
groan 1 *n* gemido *m*. **2** *vi* gemir.
gro·cer tendero, -a *mf*.
gro·cer·y *(shop)* tienda *f* de ultramarinos; **g. store** supermercado *m*.
groin ingle *f*.
groom *(bridegroom)* novio *m*.
groove *(furrow etc)* ranura *f*, *(of record)* surco *m*.
grope *vi* **to g. for sth** buscar algo a tientas.
▶**grope about** *vi* andar a tientas; *(looking for sth)* buscar a tientas.
gross *adj* grosero, -a; *(not net)* bruto, -a.
gross·ly *adv* enormemente.
gross na·tion·al prod·uct producto *m* nacional bruto.
ground¹ suelo *m*; *(terrain)* terreno *m*; **grounds** *(gardens)* jardines *mpl*; *(reason)* motivo *m* sing.
ground² *adj (coffee)* molido, -a; *(meat)* picado, -a.
ground·work trabajo *m* preparatorio.
group grupo *m*.
grow* **1** *vt (cultivate)* cultivar; **to g. a beard** dejarse (crecer) la barba. **2** *vi* crecer; *(increase)* aumentar; *(become)* volverse.
▶**grow into** *vt* convertirse en.
▶**grow out of** *vt (phase etc)* superar; **he's grown out of his shirt** se le ha quedado pequeña la camisa.
▶**grow up** *vi* crecer.
growl 1 *vi* gruñir. **2** *n* gruñido *m*.
grown *adj* crecido, -a.
grown-up *adj & n* adulto, -a *(mf)*; **the grown-ups** los mayores.
growth crecimiento *m*; *(increase)* aumento *m*; *(development)* desarrollo *m*; *(diseased part)* bulto *m*.
grub *fam (food)* comida *f*.
grub·by *adj* sucio, -a.
grudge 1 *n* rencor *m*; **to bear sb a g.** guardar rencor a algn. **2** *vt* **he grudges me my success** me envidia el éxito.
gru·el·ing *adj* penoso, -a.
grue·some *adj* espantoso, -a.
grum·ble *vi* refunfuñar.
grump·y *adj* gruñón, -ona.
grunt 1 *vi* gruñir. **2** *n* gruñido *m*.
guar·an·tee 1 *n* garantía *f*. **2** *vt* garantizar; *(assure)* asegurar.
guard 1 *vt (protect)* proteger; *(keep watch over)* vigilar; *(control)* guardar. **2** *n (sentry)* guardia *mf*, *(on train)* jefe *m* de tren; **to be on one's g.** estar en guardia; **to stand g.** montar la guardia.
guard·i·an guardián, -ana *mf*, *(of minor)* tutor, -a *mf*.
Gua·te·ma·lan *adj & n* guatemalteco, -a *(mf)*.
guess 1 *vti* adivinar; *fam* suponer. **2** *n* conjetura *f*, *(estimate)* cálculo *m*; **to have** *or* **make a g.** intentar adivinar.
guess·work conjetura *f*.
guest invitado, -a *mf*, *(in hotel)* cliente, -a *mf*, huésped, -a *mf*.
guest·house casa *f* de huéspedes.
guid·ance orientación *f*.
guide 1 *vt* guiar. **2** *n (person)* guía *mf*, *(guidebook)* guía *f*.
guide·line pauta *f*.
guild gremio *m*.

guilt culpabilidad *f.*
guilt·y *adj* culpable (**of** de).
guinea pig conejillo *m* de Indias.
gui·tar guitarra *f.*
gui·tar·ist guitarrista *mf.*
gulf golfo *m; fig* abismo *m.*
gull gaviota *f.*
gulp trago *m.*
gum¹ **1** *n* goma *f.* **2** *vt* pegar con goma.
gum² *(around teeth)* encía *f.*
gun *(handgun)* pistola *f; (rifle)* fusil *m; (cannon)* cañón *m.*
▶ **gun down** *vt* matar a tiros.
gun·fire tiros *mpl.*
gun·man pistolero *m.*
gun·point at g. a punta de pistola.
gun·pow·der pólvora *f.*
gun·shot tiro *m.*
gush *vi* brotar.
gust *(of wind)* ráfaga *f.*
gut 1 *n (inside body)* intestino *m; guts (entrails)* tripas *fpl; fam (courage)* agallas *fpl.* **2** *vt (fish)* destripar; *(destroy)* destruir por dentro.
gut·ter *(in street)* cuneta *f; (on roof)* canalón *m.*
guy *fam* tipo *m,* tío *m.*
gym *(gymnasium)* gimnasio *m; (gymnastics)* gimnasia *f.*
gy·ne·col·o·gist ginecólogo, -a *mf.*

H

hab·it costumbre *f;* **to be in the h. of doing sth** soler hacer algo; **to get into the h. of doing sth** acostumbrarse a hacer algo.
hab·i·tat hábitat *m.*
hack 1 *n (cut)* corte *m; (with an ax)* hachazo *m.* **2** *vt (with knife, ax)* cortar.
had *pt & pp of* **have.**
had·dock abadejo *m.*
hag bruja *f.*
hag·gle *vi* regatear.
hail 1 *n* granizo *m;* **a h. of bullets** una lluvia de balas. **2** *vi* granizar.
hail·stone granizo *m.*
hair pelo *m; (on arm, leg)* vello *m;* **to have long h.** tener el pelo largo.
hair·brush cepillo *m* (para el pelo).
hair·cut corte *m* de pelo; **to have a h.** cortarse el pelo.
hair·do *fam* peinado *m.*
hair·dress·er peluquero, -a *mf;* **h.'s (shop)** peluquería *f.*
hair·dry·er, hair·dri·er secador *m* (de pelo).
hair·grip horquilla *f.*
hair·pin bend curva *f* muy cerrada.
hair·rais·ing *adj* espeluznante.
hair·spray laca *f* (para el pelo).
hair·style peinado *m.*
hair·y *adj (with hair)* peludo, -a; *fam (frightening)* espeluznante.
half 1 *n (pl halves)* mitad *f; (period in match)* tiempo *m;* **he's four and a h.** tiene cuatro años y medio; **to cut in h.** cortar por la mitad. **2** *adj* medio, -a; **h. a dozen/an hour** media docena/hora; **h. fare** media tarifa *f.* **3** *adv* a medias; **h. asleep** medio dormido, -a; **h. past one** la una y media.
half board media pensión *f.*
half·heart·ed *adj* poco entusiasta.
half-hour media hora *f.*
half term *(holiday)* vacación *f* a mitad de trimestre.
half-time descanso *m.*
half·way *adv* a medio camino.
hal·i·but mero *m.*
hall *(lobby)* vestíbulo *m; (building)* sala *f;* **h. of residence** colegio *m* mayor.
Hal·low·e('·)en víspera *f* de Todos los Santos.
hall·stand percha *f.*
hall·way vestíbulo *m.*
halt alto *m;* **to call a h. to sth** poner fin a algo.
halve *vt* reducir a la mitad.
ham jamón *m.*
ham·burg·er hamburguesa *f.*
ham·mer 1 *n* martillo *m.* **2** *vt (nail)* clavar; *fig* **to h. home** insistir sobre. **3** *vi* dar golpes.
ham·mer·ing *fam (defeat)* paliza *f.*
ham·mock hamaca *f.*
ham·per¹ cesta *f.*
ham·per² *vt* dificultar.
ham·ster hámster *m.*
hand 1 *n* mano *f; (worker)* trabajador, -a *mf; (of clock)* aguja *f;* **by h.** a mano; **(close) at h.** a mano; **on the one/other h.** por una/otra parte; **to get out of h.** descontrolarse; **to be on h.** estar a mano; **to have a h. in** intervenir en; **to give sb a h.** echarle una mano a algn; **to give sb a big h.** *(applause)* dedicar a algn una gran ovación. **2** *vt (give)* dar.
▶ **hand back** *vt* devolver.
▶ **hand in** *vt (homework)* entregar.
▶ **hand out** *vt* repartir.
▶ **hand over** *vt* entregar.
hand·bag bolso *m.*
hand·book manual *m.*
hand·brake freno *m* de mano.
hand·cuff 1 *vt* esposar. **2** *npl* **handcuffs** esposas *fpl.*
hand·ful puñado *m.*
hand gre·nade granada *f* de mano.
hand·i·cap 1 *n (physical)* minusvalía *f; (in sport)* hándicap *m.* **2** *vt* impedir.
hand·i·capped *adj (physically)* minusválido, -a; *(mentally)* retrasado, -a; *fig* desfavorecido, -a.
hand·ker·chief pañuelo *m.*
han·dle 1 *n (of knife)* mango *m; (of cup)* asa *f; (of door)* pomo *m; (of drawer)* tirador *m.* **2** *vt* manejar; *(problem)* encargarse de; *(people)* tratar; **'h. with care'** 'frágil'.
han·dle·bars *npl* manillar *m.*
hand lug·gage equipaje *m* de mano.
hand·made *adj* hecho, -a a mano.
hand·out *(leaflet)* folleto *m; (charity)* limosna *f.*
hand·rail pasamanos *m inv.*

hand·shake apretón *m* de manos.
hand·some *adj (person)* guapo, -a; *(substantial)* considerable.
hand·writ·ing letra *f.*
hand·y *adj (useful)* útil; *(nearby)* a mano; *(dexterous)* diestro, -a.
hand·y·man manitas *m inv.*
hang* **1** *vt* colgar; *(head)* bajar. **2** *vi* colgar *(from* de*); (in air)* flotar; *(criminal)* ser ahorcado, -a; **to h. oneself** ahorcarse.
▶ **hang around 1** *vi fam* no hacer nada; *(wait)* esperar. **2** *vt (bar etc)* frecuentar.
▶ **hang on** *vi* agarrarse; *(wait)* esperar; **to h. on to sth** *(keep)* guardar.
▶ **hang out 1** *vt (washing)* tender. **2** *vi* **his tongue was hanging out** le colgaba la lengua.
▶ **hang up** *vt (picture, telephone)* colgar.
han·gar hangar *m.*
hang·er percha *f.*
hang-glid·er alta *f* delta.
hang·o·ver resaca *f.*
hang-up *fam (complex)* complejo *m.*
hap·pen *vi* suceder, ocurrir; **if you h. to see my friend** si por casualidad ves a mi amigo.
hap·pen·ing acontecimiento *m.*
hap·pi·ly *adv (with pleasure)* felizmente; *(fortunately)* afortunadamente.
hap·pi·ness felicidad *f.*
hap·py *adj* feliz; **h. birthday!** ¡feliz cumpleaños!
ha·rass *vt* acosar.
ha·rass·ment hostigamiento *m,* acoso *m.*
har·bor 1 *n* puerto *m.* **2** *vt (criminal)* encubrir; *(doubts)* abrigar.
hard 1 *adj* duro, -a; *(solid)* sólido, -a; *(difficult)* difícil; *(harsh)* severo, -a; *(strict)* estricto, -a; **h. of hearing** duro, -a de oído; **to be h. up** estar sin blanca; **to take a h. line** tomar medidas severas; **h. drugs** droga *f* dura; **a h. worker** un trabajador concienzudo; **h. luck!** ¡mala suerte!; **h. evidence** pruebas definitivas; **h. currency** divisa *f* fuerte. **2** *adv (forcibly)* fuerte; *(with application)* mucho.
hard·ball béisbol *m.*
hard-boiled *adj* duro, -a.
hard-core *adj* irreductible.
hard disk disco *m* duro.
hard·en 1 *vt* endurecer. **2** *vi* endurecerse.
hard·ly *adv* apenas; **h. anyone/ever** casi nadie/nunca; **he had h. begun when ...** apenas había comenzado cuando ....
hard·ness dureza *f; (difficulty)* dificultad *f.*
hard·ship privación *f.*
hard·ware *(goods)* ferretería *f; (computer equipment)* hardware *m;* **h. store** ferretería *f.*
hard-wear·ing *adj* duradero, -a.
hard-work·ing *adj* muy trabajador, -a.
hare liebre *f.*
harm 1 *n* daño *m.* **2** *vt* hacer daño a.
harm·ful *adj* perjudicial (**to** para).
harm·less *adj* inofensivo, -a.
har·mon·i·ca armónica *f.*
har·mo·ni·ous *adj* armonioso, -a.
har·mo·ny armonía *f.*
har·ness 1 *n (for horse)* arreos *mpl.* **2** *vt (horse)* enjaezar.
harp arpa *f.*
▶ **harp on** *vi fam* hablar sin parar; **to h. on about sth** hablar sin parar sobre algo.
harsh *adj* severo, -a; *(voice)* áspero, -a; *(sound)* discordante.
harsh·ly *adv* duramente.
harsh·ness dureza *f; (discordancy)* discordancia *f.*
har·vest 1 *n* cosecha *f; (of grapes)* vendimia *f.* **2** *vt* cosechar, recoger.
has *3rd person sing pres of* **have.**
has·sle *fam* **1** *n (nuisance)* rollo *m; (problem)* lío *m; (wrangle)* bronca *f.* **2** *vt* fastidiar.
haste prisa *f.*
has·ten *vi* apresurarse.
has·ti·ly *adv (quickly)* de prisa.
hast·y *adj* apresurado, -a; *(rash)* precipitado, -a.
hat sombrero *m.*
hatch¹ escotilla *f;* **serving h.** ventanilla *f.*
hatch² **1** *vt (egg)* empollar. **2** *vi (bird)* salir del huevo.
hatch·back coche *m* de 3/5 puertas.
hate 1 *n* odio *m.* **2** *vt* odiar.
hate·ful *adj* odioso, -a.
ha·tred odio *m.*
haul 1 *n (journey)* trayecto *m.* **2** *vt* tirar; *(drag)* arrastrar.
haunt 1 *n* guarida *f.* **2** *vt (of ghost)* aparecerse en; *fig* atormentar; *(frequent)* frecuentar.
haunt·ed *adj* embrujado, -a.
have* **1** *vt* tener; *(party, meeting)* hacer; **h. you got a car?** ¿tienes coche?; **to h. a cigarette** fumarse un cigarrillo; **h. breakfast/lunch/tea/dinner** desayunar/comer/merendar/cenar; **what will you h.?** ¿qué quieres tomar?; **can I h. your pen for a moment?** *(borrow)* ¿me dejas tu bolígrafo un momento? ▪ **to h. to** *(obligation)* tener que, deber; **I h. to go now** tengo que irme ya. ▪ *(make happen)* hacer; **I'll h. someone come around** haré que venga alguien. **2** *v aux (compound)* haber; **yes I h.!** ¡que sí!; **you haven't seen my book, h. you?** no has visto mi libro, ¿verdad?; **he's been to France, hasn't he?** ha estado en Francia, ¿verdad?
▶ **have on** *vt (wear)* vestir; *fam* **to h. sb** tomarle el pelo a algn.
▶ **have out** *vt* **to h. it out with sb** ajustar cuentas con algn.
▶ **have over** *vt (invite)* recibir.
hav·oc to play h. with hacer estragos en.
hawk halcón *m.*
hay heno *m.*
hay fe·ver fiebre *f* del heno.
hay·stack almiar *m.*
haz·ard 1 *n* peligro *m,* riesgo *m.* **2** *vt* arriesgar; **to h. a guess** intentar adivinar.
haze *(mist)* neblina *f.*
ha·zel·nut avellana *f.*
haz·y *adj* nebuloso, -a.
he *pers pron* él; **he who** el que.
head 1 *n* cabeza *f; (mind)* mente *f; (of company)* director, -a *mf; (of coin)* cara *f;* **to be h. over heels in love** estar locamente enamorado, -a; **to keep one's h.** mantener la calma; **to lose one's h.** perder la cabeza; **heads or tails** cara o cruz. **2** *adj* principal; **h. office** sede *f.* **3** *vt (list etc)* encabezar.
▶ **head for** *vt* dirigirse hacia.
head·ache dolor *m* de cabeza; *fig* quebradero *m* de cabeza.
head·band cinta *f* para la cabeza
head·ing título *m; (of letter)* membrete *m.*
head·light faro *m.*
head·line titular *m.*
head·mas·ter director *m.*
head·mis·tress directora *f.*
head·phones *npl* auriculares *mpl.*

head·quar·ters *npl* oficina *f* central; *(military)* cuartel *m* general.
head teach·er director, -a *mf.*
head·wait·er jefe *m* de comedor.
head·way **to make h.** avanzar.
heal **1** *vi* cicatrizar. **2** *vt* curar.
health salud *f*; *fig* prosperidad *f*; **to be in good/bad h.** estar bien/mal de salud; **h. foods** alimentos *mpl* naturales; **h. service** ≃ Insalud *m.*
health·y *adj* sano, -a; *(good for health)* saludable.
heap **1** *n* montón *m.* **2** *vt* amontonar; *(praises)* colmar de; **to h. praises on sb** colmar a algn de elogios.
hear* *vt* oír; *(listen to)* escuchar; *(find out)* enterarse de; *(evidence)* oír; **I won't h. of it!** ¡ni hablar!; **to h. from sb** tener noticias de algn.
hear·ing oído *m*; *(legal)* audiencia *f.*
hear·ing aid audífono *m.*
hearse coche *m* fúnebre.
heart corazón *m*; **hearts** corazones; **at h.** en el fondo; **to lose h.** desanimarse.
heart at·tack infarto *m* (de miocardio).
heart·beat latido *m* del corazón.
heart-break·ing *adj* desgarrador, -a.
heart·en·ing *adj* alentador, -a.
heart·y *adj (person)* francote; *(meal)* abundante; **to have a h. appetite** ser de buen comer.
heat **1** *n* calor *m*; *(in sport)* eliminatoria *f.* **2** *vt* calentar.
▸**heat up** *vi (warm up)* calentarse.
heat·er calentador *m.*
heath *(land)* brezal *m.*
heath·er brezo *m.*
heat·ing calefacción *f.*
heat·wave ola *f* de calor.
heave *vt (lift)* levantar; *(haul)* tirar; *(push)* empujar; *(throw)* arrojar.
heav·en cielo *m*; **for heaven's sake!** ¡por Dios!
heav·i·ly *adv* **it rained h.** llovió mucho; **to sleep h.** dormir profundamente.
heav·y **1** *adj* pesado, -a; *(rain, meal)* fuerte; *(traffic)* denso, -a; *(loss)* grande; **is it h.?** ¿pesa mucho?; **a h. drinker/smoker** un, -a bebedor, -a/fumador, -a empedernido, -a.
heav·y·weight peso *m* pesado.
He·brew **1** *adj* hebreo, -a; **2** *n (person)* hebre, -a *mf*; *(language)* hebreo *m.*
hec·tic *adj* agitado, -a.
hedge **1** *n* seto *m.* **2** *vt* **to h. one's bets** cubrirse.
hedge·hog erizo *m.*
heel talón *m*; *(of shoe)* tacón *m.*
heft·y *adj (person)* fornido, -a; *(package)* pesado, -a.
height altura *f*; *(of person)* estatura *f*; **what h. are you?** ¿cuánto mides?
heir heredero *m.*
heir·ess heredera *f.*
held *pt & pp of* **hold**.
hel·i·cop·ter helicóptero *m.*
hell infierno *m*; *fam* **what the h. are you doing?** ¿qué diablos estás haciendo?; *fam* **go to h.!** ¡vete a hacer puñetas!; *fam* **a h. of a party** una fiesta estupenda; *fam* **she's had a h. of a day** ha tenido un día fatal; *fam* **h.!** ¡demonios!
hel·lo *interj* ¡hola!; *(on phone)* ¡diga!; *(showing surprise)* ¡hala!
helm timón *m.*
hel·met casco *m.*
help **1** *n* ayuda *f*; **h.!** ¡socorro!; **(daily) h.** asistenta *f.* **2** *vt* ayudar; **can I h. you?** *(in shop)* ¿qué desea?; **h. yourself!** *(to food etc)* ¡sírvete!; **I couldn't h. laughing** no pude evitar reirme; **I can't h. it** no lo puedo remediar.
▸**help out** *vt* **to h. sb out** echarle una mano a algn.
help·er ayudante, -a *mf.*
help·ful *adj (person)* amable; *(thing)* útil.
help·ing ración *f.*
help·less *adj (defenseless)* desamparado, -a; *(powerless)* impotente.
hem dobladillo *m.*
▸**hem in** *vt* cercar, rodear.
hem·i·sphere hemisferio *m.*
hem·or·rhage hemorragia *f.*
hen gallina *f.*
hep·a·ti·tis hepatitis *f.*
her **1** *poss adj (one thing)* su; *(more than one)* sus; *(to distinguish male from female)* de ella; **are they h. books or his?** ¿los libros son de ella o de él? **2** *object pron (direct object)* la; **I saw h. recently** la vi hace poco. ▪ *(indirect object)* le; *(with other third person pronouns)* se; **he gave h. money** le dio dinero; **they handed it to h.** se lo entregaron. ▪ *(after prep)* ella; **for h.** para ella. ▪ *(emphatic)* ella; **look, it's h.!** ¡mira, es ella!
herb hierba *f*; **herb tea** infusión *f.*
herd *(of cattle)* manada *f*; *(of goats)* rebaño *m.*
here **1** *adv* aquí; **h.!** ¡presente!; **h. you are!** ¡toma! **2** *interj* **look h., you can't do that!** ¡oiga, no puede hacer eso!
he·red·i·tar·y *adj* hereditario, -a.
her·mit ermitaño, -a *mf.*
he·ro (*pl* **heroes**) héroe *m*; *(in novel)* protagonista *m.*
he·ro·ic *adj* heroico, -a.
her·o·in heroína *f.*
her·o·ine heroína *f*; *(in novel)* protagonista *f.*
her·ring arenque *m.*
hers *poss pron (attribute) (one thing)* suyo, -a; *(more than one)* suyos, -as; *(to distinguish male from female)* de ella; **they are h. not his** son de ella, no de él. ▪ *(one thing)* el suyo, la suya; *(more than one)* los suyos, las suyas.
her·self *pers pron (reflexive)* se; **she dressed h.** se vistió. ▪ *(alone)* ella misma; **she was by h.** estaba sola. ▪ *(emphatic)* **she told me so h.** eso me dijo ella misma.
hes·i·tant *adj* vacilante.
hes·i·tate *vi* vacilar.
hes·i·ta·tion indecisión *f.*
het up *adj* nervioso, -a.
hey *interj* ¡oye!; ¡oiga!
hi *interj* ¡hola!
hic·cup hipo *m*; *(minor problem)* problemilla *m*; **to have hiccups** tener hipo.
hide[1]* **1** *vt (conceal)* esconder; *(obscure)* ocultar. **2** *vi* esconderse, ocultarse.
hide[2] *(skin)* piel *f.*
hide-and-seek escondite *m.*
hid·e·ous *adj (horrific)* horroroso, -a; *(extremely ugly)* espantoso, -a.
hide·ous·ly *adv* horrorosamente.
hide-out escondrijo *m.*
hid·ing **a good h.** una buena paliza.
hid·ing place escondite *m.*
hi·er·ar·chy jerarquía *f.*
hi-fi hifi *m.*
high **1** *adj* alto, -a; *(price)* elevado, -a; *(drugged)* colcado, -a; **how h. is that wall?** ¿qué altura tiene esa pared?; **it's three feet h.** tiene tres pies de alto; **h. wind** viento *m* fuerte; **to have a h. opinion of sb** tener muy buena opinión de algn. **2** *adv* alto; **to fly h.** volar a gran altura.
high-class *adj* de alta categoría.
high den·si·ty *adj* de alta densidad.
high·er *adj* superior; **h. education** enseñanza *f* superior.
high·lands *npl* tierras *fpl* altas.
high·light **1** *n (in hair)* reflejo *m*; *(of event)* atracción *f* principal. **2** *vt* hacer resaltar; *(with highlighter)* subrayar con marcador.
high·light·er marcador *m.*
high·ly *adv (very)* sumamente; **to speak h. of sb** hablar muy bien de algn.
high-pitched *adj* estridente.
high-pro·file *adj (person)* prominente, destacado(a); *(campaign)* de gran alcance.
high-rise *adj* **h. building** rascacielos *m inv.*
high school instituto *m* de enseñanza media.
high-speed *adj* **h. train** tren *m* de alta velocidad.
high street calle *f* mayor.
high-tech *adj* de alta tecnología.
high·way autopista *f.*
hi·jack **1** *vt* secuestrar. **2** *n* secuestro *m.*
hi·jack·er secuestrador, -a *mf*, *(of planes)* pirata *mf* del aire.
hi·jack·ing secuestro *m.*
hike **1** *n (walk)* excursión *f.* **2** *vi* ir de excursión.
hik·er excursionista *mf.*
hi·lar·i·ous *adj* graciosísimo, -a.
hill colina *f*; *(slope)* cuesta *f.*
hill·side ladera *f.*
hill·y *adj* accidentado, -a.
him *object pron (direct object)* lo, le; **hit h.!** ¡pégale!; **she loves h.** lo quiere. ▪ *(indirect object)* le; *(with other third person pronouns)* se; **give h. the money** dale el dinero; **give it to h.** dáselo. ▪ *(after prep)* él; **it's not like h. to say that** no es propio de él decir eso. ▪ *(emphatic)* él; **it's h.** es él.
him·self *pers pron (reflexive)* se; **he hurt h.** se hizo daño. ▪ *(alone)* por sí mismo; **by h.** solo. ▪ *(emphatic)* él mismo; **he told me so h.** me lo dijo él mismo.
hin·der *vt* dificultar.
Hin·du *adj & n* hindú *(mf).*
hinge bisagra *f.*
▸**hinge on** *vt* depender de.
hint **1** *n* indirecta *f*; *(clue)* pista *f*; *(advice)* consejo *m.* **2** *vi* lanzar indirectas. **3** *vt (imply)* insinuar.
▸**hint at** *vt* aludir a.
hip cadera *f.*
hip·po·pot·a·mus hipopótamo *m.*
hire *vt (rent)* alquilar; *(employ)* contratar.
his **1** *poss adj (one thing)* su; *(more than one)* sus; *(to distinguish male from female)* de él; **he washed h. face** se lavó la cara; **is it h. dog or hers?** ¿el perro es de él o de ella? **2** *poss pron (attribute) (one thing)* suyo, -a; *(more than one)* suyos, -as; *(to distinguish male from female)* de él. ▪ *(one thing)* el suyo, la suya; *(more than one)* los suyos, las suyas.
His·pan·ic **1** *adj* hispánico, -a. **2** *n* hispano, -a *mf.*
hiss **1** *n* siseo *m*; *(in theater)* silbido *m.* **2** *vti* silbar.
his·tor·ic *adj* histórico, -a.
his·tor·i·cal *adj* histórico, -a.
his·to·ry historia *f.*
hit **1** *n (blow)* golpe *m*; *(success)* éxito *m.* **2** *vt** *(strike)* pegar; *(affect)* afectar; **he was h. in the leg** le dieron en la pierna; **the car h. the kerb** el coche chocó contra el bordillo.
▸**hit back** *vi (reply to criticism)* replicar.
▸**hit out** *vi* **to h. out at sb** atacar a algn.
▸**hit (up)on** *vt* dar con; **we h. on the idea of ...** se nos ocurrió la idea de ....
hit-and-run driv·er conductor *m* que atropella a algn y no para.
hitch **1** *n* dificultad *f.* **2** *vi (hitchhike)* hacer autostop.
hitch·hike *vi* hacer autostop.
hitch·hik·er autostopista *mf.*
hitch·hik·ing autostop *m.*
HIV *abbr of* **human immunodeficiency virus** virus *m* de inmunodeficiencia humano, VIH *m*; **to be HIV positive/negative** ser/no ser seropositivo, -a.
hive colmena *f.*
hoard **1** *n (provisions)* reservas *fpl*; *(money etc)* tesoro *m.* **2** *vt (objects)* acumular; *(money)* atesorar.
hoard·ing *(billboard)* valla *f* publicitaria.
hoarse *adj* ronco, -a; **to be h.** tener la voz ronca.
hoax *(joke)* broma *f* pesada; *(trick)* engaño *m.*
hob·by pasatiempo *m.*
ho·bo vagabundo, -a *mf.*
hock·ey hockey *m.*
hold **1** *vt** *(keep in hand)* tener (en la mano); *(grip)* agarrar; *(opinion)* sostener; *(contain)* dar cabida a; *(meeting)* celebrar; *(reserve) (ticket)* guardar; *(at police station etc)* detener; *(office)* ocupar; **to h. sb's hand** cogerle la mano a algn; **the jug holds a liter** en la jarra cabe un litro; **to h. one's breath** contener la respiración; **to h. sb hostage** retener a algn como rehén; **to h. the line** no colgar. **2** *vi** *(rope)* aguantar; *(offer)* ser válido, -a. **3** *n (in ship)* bodega *f*; *(control)* control *m*; **to get h. of** *(grip)* coger; *(get in touch with)* localizar.
▸**hold back** *vt (crowd)* contener; *(feelings)* reprimir; *(truth)* ocultar; *(suspect)* retener; *(store)* guardar.
▸**hold down** *vt (control)* dominar; *(job)* desempeñar.
▸**hold on** *vi (keep a firm grasp)* agarrarse bien; *(wait)* esperar; **h. on!** *(on phone)* ¡no cuelgue!
▸**hold on to** *vt (to stop oneself from falling)* agarrarse a; *(to stop something from falling)* agarrar; *(keep)* guardar.
▸**hold out** **1** *vt (hand)* tender. **2** *vi (last) (things)* durar; *(person)* resistir.
▸**hold up** *vt (support)* apuntalar; *(rob) (train)* asaltar; *(bank)* atracar; *(delay)* retrasar; **we were held up for half an hour** sufrimos media hora de retraso.
hold·er *(receptacle)* recipiente *m*; *(owner)* poseedor, -a *mf*, *(bearer)* portador, -a *mf*, *(of passport)* titular *mf.*
hold·up *(robbery)* atraco *m*; *(delay)* retraso *m*; *(in traffic)* atasco *m.*
hole agujero *m*; *(large, in golf)* hoyo *m.*
hol·i·day *(one day)* (día *m* de) fiesta *f*; *(several days)* vacaciones *fpl.*
hol·low **1** *adj* hueco, -a; *(cheeks, eyes)* hundido, -a. **2** *n* hueco *m.*
hol·ly acebo *m.*
ho·ly *adj* sagrado, -a; *(blessed)* bendito, -a.
Ho·ly Ghost Espíritu *m* Santo.
home **1** *n* casa *f*, hogar *m*; *(institution)* asilo *m*; *(country)* patria *f*; **at h.** en casa; **make yourself at h.!** ¡estás en tu casa!; **old people's h.** asilo *m* de ancianos; **to play at h.** jugar en casa. **2** *adj (domestic)* del hogar; *(political)* interior; *(native)* natal; **h. affairs** asuntos *mpl* interiores. **3** *adv* en casa; **to go h.** irse a casa; **to leave h.** irse de casa.
home com·put·er ordenador *m* doméstico.
home help asistenta *f.*
home·land patria *f*; *(birthplace)* tierra *f* natal.
home·less **1** *adj* sin hogar. **2** *npl* **the h.** los sin hogar.

home·made *adj* casero, -a.
home·sick *adj* to be h. tener morriña.
home·town ciudad *f* natal.
home·work deberes *mpl*.
ho·mo·sex·u·al *adj & n* homosexual *(mf)*.
Hon·du·ran *adj & n* hondureño, -a *(mf)*.
hon·est *adj* honrado, -a; *(sincere)* sincero, -a; *(fair)* justo, -a.
hon·est·ly *adv* honradamente; **h.?** ¿de verdad?
hon·es·ty honradez *f*.
hon·ey miel *f, fam (endearment)* cariño *m*.
hon·ey·moon luna *f* de miel.
honk *vi (person in car)* tocar la bocina.
hon·or 1 *n* honor *m*. **2** *vt (respect)* honrar; *(obligation)* cumplir.
hon·or·a·ble *adj (person)* honrado, -a; *(actions)* honroso, -a.
hood *(of garment)* capucha *f, (of car)* capota *f; (bonnet)* capó *m*.
hoof *(pl* hoofs *or* hooves) *(of horse)* casco *m; (of cow, sheep)* pezuña *f*.
hook gancho *m; (for fishing)* anzuelo *m;* **to take the phone off the h.** descolgar el teléfono.
▸**hook up** *vti* conectar (**with** con).
hooked *adj (nose)* aguileño, -a; *(addicted)* enganchado, -a (**on** a); **to get h.** engancharse.
hook·y to play h. hacer novillos.
hoo·li·gan gamberro, -a *mf*.
hoop aro *m*.
hoot 1 *n (owl)* grito *m;* **hoots of laughter** carcajadas *fpl*. **2** *vi (owl)* ulular; *(train)* silbar; *(siren)* pitar.
Hoo·ver® **1** *n* aspiradora *f*. **2** *vt* to h. pasar la aspiradora a.
hop 1 *vi* saltar; **to h. on one leg** andar a la pata coja. **2** *n (small jump)* brinco *m*.
hope 1 *n* esperanza *f, (false)* ilusión *f;* **to have little h. of doing sth** tener pocas posibilidades de hacer algo. **2** *vti* esperar; **I h. so/not** espero que sí/no.
▸**hope for** *vt* esperar.
hope·ful *adj (confident)* optimista; *(promising)* prometedor, -a.
hope·ful·ly *adv* **h. she won't come** esperemos que no venga.
hope·less *adj* desesperado, -a; **to be h. at sports** ser negado, -a para los deportes.
hope·less·ly *adv* desesperadamente; **h. lost** completamente perdido, -a.
hops *npl* lúpulo *m*.
hop·scotch to play h. jugar al tejo.
ho·ri·zon horizonte *m*.
hor·i·zon·tal *adj* horizontal.
horn cuerno *m; (on car)* bocina *f*.
hor·ri·ble *adj* horrible.
hor·ri·bly *adv* horriblemente.
hor·rif·ic *adj* horrendo, -a.
hor·ri·fy *vt* horrorizar.
hor·ror horror *m;* **a little h.** un diablillo.
hor·ror film película *f* de terror.
horse caballo *m*.
horse·back on h. a caballo.
horse·pow·er caballo *m* (de vapor).
horse race carrera *f* de caballos.
horse·shoe herradura *f*.
hose *(pipe)* manguera *f*.
hose·pipe manguera *f*.
hos·pi·ta·ble *adj* hospitalario, -a.
hos·pi·tal hospital *m*.
hos·pi·tal·i·ty hospitalidad *f*.
hos·pi·tal·ize *vt* hospitalizar.
host 1 *n (at home)* anfitrión *m; (on TV)* presentador *m*. **2** *vt (TV show etc)* presentar.
hos·tage rehén *m;* **to take sb h.** tomar a algn como rehén.
hos·tel hostal *m*.
host·ess *(at home etc)* anfitriona *f, (on TV)* presentadora *f*.
hos·tile *adj* hostil.
hos·til·i·ty hostilidad *f*.
hot *adj* caliente; *(weather)* caluroso, -a; *(spicy)* picante; *(temper)* fuerte; **it's very h.** hace mucho calor; **to feel h.** tener calor; **it's not so h.** *(not very good)* no es nada del otro mundo.
hot·cake crepe *f*, panqueque *m, Esp* tortita *f*.
hot dog perrito *m* caliente.
ho·tel hotel *m*.
hot-wa·ter bot·tle bolsa *f* de agua caliente.
hound 1 *n* perro *m* de caza. **2** *vt* acosar.
hour hora *f*, **60 miles an h.** 60 millas por hora; **by the h.** por horas.
hour·ly 1 *adj* cada hora. **2** *adv* por horas.
house 1 *n* casa *f; (in theater)* sala *f;* **at my h.** en mi casa. **2** *vt* alojar; *(store)* guardar.
house·hold hogar *m;* **h. products** productos *mpl* domésticos.
house·keep·ing administración *f* doméstica.
house-warm·ing par·ty fiesta *f* que se da al estrenar casa.
house·wife ama *f* de casa.
house·work trabajo *m* doméstico.
hous·ing vivienda *f*.
hous·ing es·tate urbanización *f*.
hov·el casucha *f*.
hov·er *vi (bird)* cernerse; *(helicopter)* permanecer inmóvil (en el aire).
hov·er·craft aerodeslizador *m*.
how *adv* ¿cómo?; **h. are you?** ¿cómo estás?; **h. do you do?** mucho gusto; **h. funny!** ¡qué divertido!; **h. about ...?** ¿y si ...?; **h. about a stroll?** ¿qué te parece un paseo?; **h. old is she?** ¿cuántos años tiene?; **h. tall are you?** ¿cuánto mides?; **¿h. many?** ¿cuántos, -as?; **h. much?** ¿cuánto, -a?
how·e·ver *adv* no obstante, sin embargo; **h. difficult it may be** por difícil que sea; **h. much** por mucho que (+ *subjunctive*).
howl 1 *n* aullido *m*. **2** *vi* aullar.
HQ *abbr of* **headquarters**.
hub·cap tapacubos *m inv*.
hud·dle 1 *n* grupo *m*. **2** *vi* to h. (**up** *or* **together**) acurrucarse.
hug 1 *vt* abrazar. **2** *n* abrazo *m*.
huge *adj* enorme.
hull casco *m*.
hum 1 *vt (tune)* tararear. **2** *vi (bees, engine)* zumbar. **3** *n (of bees)* zumbido *m*.
hu·man 1 *adj* humano, -a. **h. race** raza *f* humana. **2** *n* ser *m* humano.
hu·man be·ing ser *m* humano.
hu·man·i·ty humanidad *f;* **the humanities** las humanidades.
hum·ble *adj* humilde.
hu·mid *adj* húmedo, -a.
hu·mid·i·ty humedad *f*.
hu·mil·i·ate *vt* humillar.
hu·mil·i·a·tion humillación *f*.
hu·mor humor *m*.

hu·mor·ous *adj (person, story)* gracioso, -a; *(writer)* humorístico, -a.
hump *(on back)* joroba *f, (small hill)* montículo *m*.
hunch *(idea)* corazonada *f*.
hun·dred 1 *n* cien *m*, ciento *m; (rough number)* centenar *m;* **a h. and twenty-five** ciento veinticinco; **five h.** quinientos, -as. **2** *adj* cien; **a h. people** cien personas; **a h. per cent** cien por cien; **two h. chairs** doscientas sillas.
hun·dredth *adj & n* centésimo, -a *(mf)*.
Hun·gar·i·an *adj & n* húngaro, -a *(mf)*.
hun·ger hambre *m;* **h. strike** huelga *m* de hambre.
hun·gry *adj* to be h. tener hambre.
hunt 1 *vt* cazar. **2** *vi (for game)* cazar; *(search)* buscar. **3** *n* caza *f, (search)* búsqueda *f*.
▸**hunt down** *vt* perseguir.
hunt·er cazador, -a *mf*.
hunt·ing caza *f, (expedition)* cacería *f*.
hur·dle *(in sport)* valla *f, fig* obstáculo *m*.
hurl *vt* lanzar.
hur·rah, hur·ray *interj* ¡hurra!; **h. for John!** ¡viva John!
hur·ri·cane huracán *m*.
hur·ry 1 *vi* darse prisa. **2** *vt* meter prisa a. **3** *n* to be in a h. tener prisa.
▸**hurry up** *vi (go faster)* darse prisa.
hurt 1 *vt** hacer daño a; *(wound)* herir; *(mentally)* ofender. **2** *vi** doler; **my arm hurts** me duele el brazo. **3** *adj (physically)* herido, -a; *(mentally)* dolido, -a.
hus·band marido *m*, esposo *m*.
hush 1 *n* silencio *m*. **2** *interj* ¡silencio!
hus·tle 1 *vt (jostle)* empujar; *(hurry along)* meter prisa a. **2** *n* h. and bustle ajetreo *m*.
hut cabaña *f, (shed)* cobertizo *m*.
hy·dro·gen hidrógeno *m*.
hy·giene higiene *f*.
hy·gien·ic *adj* higiénico, -a.
hymn himno *m;* **h. book** cantoral *m*.
hy·per·mar·ket hipermercado *m*.
hy·phen guión *m*.
hy·phen·at·ed *adj (word)* (escrito, -a) con guión.
hyp·no·tize *vt* hipnotizar.
hyp·oc·ri·sy hipocresía *f*.
hyp·o·crite hipócrita *mf*.
hy·poth·e·sis *(pl* hypotheses) hipótesis *f*.
hys·ter·i·cal *adj* histérico, -a.
hys·ter·i·cal·ly *adv (to cry)* histéricamente.

I

I *pers pron* yo.
ice hielo *m*.
ice·berg iceberg *m*.
ice-cold *adj* helado, -a.
ice cream helado *m*.
ice cube cubito *m* de hielo.
ice-skat·ing patinaje *m* sobre hielo.
i·ci·cle carámbano *m*.
ic·ing alcorza *f*.
ic·ing sug·ar azúcar *m* glas.
i·con icono *m*.
ic·y *adj (road etc)* helado, -a; *(smile)* glacial.
ID ID card documento *m* nacional de identidad, DNI *m*.
i·de·a idea *f*.
i·de·al *adj & n* ideal *(m)*.
i·de·al·ly *adv (if possible)* de ser posible.
i·den·ti·cal *adj* idéntico, -a.
i·den·ti·fi·ca·tion identificación *f, (papers)* documentación *f*.
i·den·ti·fy 1 *vt* identificar. **2** *vi* identificarse (**with** con).
i·den·ti·ty identidad *f*.
id·i·om modismo *m*.
id·i·ot idiota *mf*.
id·i·ot·ic *adj* idiota.
i·dle *adj* holgazán, -ana; *(not working) (person)* desempleado, -a.
i·dol ídolo *m*.
i·dol·ize *vt* idolatrar.
i.e. *abbr* a saber.
if *conj* si; **if I were rich** si fuera rico, -a; **if I were you** yo en tu lugar.
ig·loo iglú *m*.
ig·no·rance ignorancia *f*.
ig·no·rant *adj* ignorante (**of** de).
ig·nore *vt (warning, remark)* no hacer caso de; *(behavior, fact)* pasar por alto.
ill 1 *adj* enfermo, -a; *(bad)* malo, -a. **2** *n* mal *m*.
il·le·gal *adj* ilegal.
il·leg·i·ble *adj* ilegible.
il·lit·er·ate *adj* analfabeto, -a.
ill·ness enfermedad *f*.
il·lu·sion ilusión *f*.
il·lus·trate *vt* ilustrar.
il·lus·tra·tion ilustración *f*.
im·age imagen *f*.
i·mag·i·nar·y *adj* imaginario, -a.
i·mag·i·na·tion imaginación *f*.
i·mag·ine *vt* imaginarse; *(think)* suponer.
im·be·cile *fam* imbécil *mf*.
im·i·tate *vt* imitar.
im·i·ta·tion 1 *n* imitación *f*. **2** *adj* de imitación.
im·mac·u·late *adj* impecable.
im·ma·ture *adj* inmaduro, -a.
im·me·di·ate *adj* inmediato, -a.
im·me·di·ate·ly 1 *adv* inmediatamente. **2** *conj (as soon as)* en cuanto.
im·mense *adj* inmenso, -a.
im·mense·ly *adv* sumamente.
im·mi·grant *adj & n* inmigrante *(mf)*.
im·mi·gra·tion inmigración *f*.
im·mi·nent *adj* inminente.

im·mor·tal *adj* inmortal.
im·mune *adj* inmune.
im·mu·nize *vt* inmunizar (**against** contra).
im·pact impacto *m*; *(crash)* choque *m*.
im·pa·tience impaciencia *f*.
im·pa·tient *adj* impaciente.
im·pa·tient·ly *adv* con impaciencia.
im·per·a·tive *(form of verb)* imperativo *m*.
im·per·son·ate *vt* hacerse pasar por; *(famous people)* imitar.
im·per·son·a·tor *(on TV etc)* imitador, -a *mf*.
im·per·ti·nent *adj* impertinente.
im·pe·tus ímpetu *m*; *fig* impulso *m*.
im·ple·ment 1 *n (tool)* herramienta *f*. **2** *vt (decision, plan)* llevar a cabo.
im·pli·ca·tion implicación *f*; *(consequence)* consecuencia *f*.
im·plic·it *adj (implied)* implícito, -a; *(trust)* absoluto, -a; *(faith)* incondicional.
im·ply *vt (hint)* dar a entender.
im·po·lite *adj* maleducado, -a.
im·port 1 *n* importación *f*. **2** *vt* importar.
im·por·tance importancia *f*; **of little i.** de poca importancia.
im·por·tant *adj* importante; **it's not i.** no importa.
im·port·er importador, -a *mf*.
im·pose 1 *vt* imponer (**on, upon** a). **2** *vi* **to i. on** or **upon** *(take advantage of)* abusar de.
im·pos·ing *adj* imponente.
im·po·si·tion would it be an i. if …? ¿le molestaría si …?
im·pos·si·bil·i·ty imposibilidad *f*.
im·pos·si·ble *adj* imposible.
im·pos·tor impostor, -a *mf*.
im·prac·ti·cal *adj* poco práctico, -a.
im·press *vt* impresionar.
im·pres·sion impresión *f*; **to be under the i. that …** tener la impresión de que …
im·pres·sive *adj* impresionante.
im·pris·on *vt* encarcelar.
im·prob·a·ble *adj* improbable.
im·prop·er *adj (indecent)* indecente.
im·prove 1 *vt* mejorar. **2** *vi* mejorarse.
▸**improve on** *vt* superar.
im·prove·ment mejora *f*.
im·pro·vise *vti* improvisar.
im·pu·dent *adj* insolente.
im·pulse impulso *m*.
im·pul·sive *adj* irreflexivo, -a.
im·pul·sive·ly *adv* de forma impulsiva.
im·pu·ri·ty impureza *f*.
in 1 *prep (place)* en; **in prison** en la cárcel; **in the distance** a lo lejos; **she arrived in New York** llegó a Nueva York. ▪ *(time) (during)* en, durante; **in May/1945** en mayo/1945; **in spring** en primavera; **in the daytime** durante el día; **in the morning** por la mañana. ▪ *(time) (within)* dentro de. ▪ *(time) (after)* al cabo de. ▪ *(manner)* en, de; **in a loud/quiet voice** en voz alta/baja; **in French** en francés; **dressed in blue** vestido, -a de azul; **in uniform** de uniforme. ▪ *(ratio, numbers)* de; **one in six** uno de cada seis; **two meters in length** dos metros de largo. ▪ *(after superlative)* de; **the smallest car in the world** el coche más pequeño del mundo. **2** *adv* **to be in** *(at home)* estar (en casa); *(in fashion)* estar de moda; **the bus is in** el autobús ha llegado.
in·a·bil·i·ty incapacidad *f*.
in·ac·ces·si·ble *adj* inaccesible.
in·ac·cu·ra·cy *(error)* inexactitud *f*.
in·ac·cu·rate *adj* incorrecto, -a.
in·ad·e·qua·cy *(lack)* insuficiencia *f*; *(inability)* incompetencia *f*.
in·ad·e·quate *adj (lacking)* insuficiente; *(unsuitable)* inadecuado, -a.
in·ap·pro·pri·ate *adj (behavior)* poco apropiado, -a.
in·au·gu·rate *vt (building)* inaugurar.
in·au·gu·ra·tion *(of building)* inauguración *f*.
Inc, inc *abbr of* **Incorporated** ≃ S.A.
in·ca·pa·ble *adj* incapaz (**of doing sth** de hacer algo).
in·cense 1 *vt* enfurecer. **2** *n* incienso *m*.
in·cen·tive incentivo *m*.
inch pulgada *f (approx 2.54 cm)*.
in·ci·dent incidente *m*.
in·ci·den·tal·ly *adv* por cierto, a propósito.
in·cite *vt* incitar; **to i. sb to do sth** incitar a algn a hacer algo.
in·cite·ment incitación *f*.
in·cli·na·tion deseo *m*; **my i. is to stay** yo prefiero quedarme.
in·cline 1 *vt* **she's incined to be aggressive** tiende a ser agresiva. **2** *vi (slope)* inclinarse.
in·clude *vt* incluir (**in** en); *(in price)* comprender (**in** en).
in·clud·ing *prep* incluso, inclusive.
in·clu·sive *adj* inclusivo, -a; **the rent is i. of bills** el alquiler incluye las facturas.
in·come ingresos *mpl*; *(from investment)* réditos *mpl*.
in·come tax impuesto *m* sobre la renta.
in·com·pat·i·ble *adj* incompatible (**with** con).
in·com·pe·tent *adj* incompetente.
in·com·plete *adj* incompleto, -a.
in·con·ceiv·a·ble *adj* inconcebible.
in·con·sid·er·ate *adj* desconsiderado, -a.
in·con·sis·ten·cy inconsecuencia *f*.
in·con·sis·tent *adj* inconsecuente; **your evidence is i. with the facts** su testimonio no concuerda con los hechos.
in·con·spic·u·ous *adj* que pasa desapercibido, -a.
in·con·ven·ience 1 *n* molestia *f*; *(disadvantage)* inconvenientes *mpl*; **the i. of living out here** los inconvenientes de vivir aquí. **2** *vt* molestar.
in·con·ven·ient *adj* molesto, -a; *(time)* inoportuno, -a.
in·cor·po·rate *vt (include)* incluir; *(contain)* contener.
in·cor·rect *adj* incorrecto, -a.
in·crease 1 *n* aumento *m*; *(in number)* incremento; *(in price etc)* subida *f*. **2** *vt* aumentar; *(price etc)* subir. **3** *vi* aumentar.
in·creas·ing *adj* creciente.
in·creas·ing·ly *adv* cada vez más.
in·cred·i·ble *adj* increíble.
in·cred·i·bly *adv* increíblemente.
in·cu·ba·tor incubadora *f*.
in·cur *vt (blame)* incurrir en; *(debt)* contraer; *(loss)* sufrir.
in·cur·a·ble *adj* incurable.
in·de·cent *adj* indecente.
in·de·ci·sive *adj* indeciso, -a.
in·deed *adv (in fact)* efectivamente; **it's very hard i.** es verdaderamente difícil; **thank you very much i.** muchísimas gracias.

in·def·i·nite *adj* indefinido, -a.
in·def·i·nite·ly *adv* indefinidamente.
in·de·pend·ence independencia *f*.
in·de·pend·ent *adj* independiente; **to become i.** independizarse.
in·de·pend·ent·ly *adv* independientemente.
in·dex 1 *n (in book)* índice *m*; *(in library)* catálogo *m*. **2** *vt* catalogar.
in·dex card ficha *f*.
in·dex fin·ger dedo *m* índice.
in·dex-linked *adj* sujeto, -a al aumento de la inflación.
In·di·an *adj & n (of America)* indio, -a *(mf)*; *(of India)* hindú *(mf)*.
in·di·cate 1 *vt* indicar. **2** *vi (driving)* poner el intermitente.
in·di·ca·tion indicio *m*.
in·di·ca·tor indicador *m*; *(on car)* intermitente *m*.
in·dif·fer·ence indiferencia *f*.
in·dif·fer·ent *adj (uninterested)* indiferente; *(mediocre)* regular.
in·di·ges·tion indigestión *f*; **to have i.** tener un empacho.
in·dig·nant *adj* indignado, -a; **to get i. about sth** indignarse por algo.
in·di·rect *adj* indirecto, -a.
indi·rect·ly *adv* indirectamente.
in·dis·creet *adj* indiscreto, -a.
in·dis·crim·i·nate *adj* indiscriminado, -a.
in·dis·crim·i·nate·ly *adv (at random)* indistintamente, sin criterio.
in·dis·tin·guish·a·ble *adj* indistinguible.
in·di·vid·u·al 1 *adj (separate)* individual; *(for one)* particular; *(characteristic)* particular. **2** *n (person)* individuo *m*.
in·di·vid·u·al·ly *adv* individualmente.
in·door *adj (plant)* interior; **i. pool** piscina cubierta.
in·doors *adv (inside)* dentro (de casa).
in·duce *vt (persuade)* inducir; *(cause)* producir.
in·dulge 1 *vt (child)* consentir; *(person)* complacer; *(whim)* ceder a, satisfacer; **to i. oneself** darse gusto. **2** *vi* darse el gusto (**in** de).
in·dul·gent *adj* indulgente.
in·dus·tri·al *adj* industrial; *(accident)* laboral; **i. dispute** conflicto *m* laboral; **i. estate** polígono *m* industrial.
in·dus·try industria *f*.
in·ed·i·ble *adj* incomible.
in·ef·fec·tive *adj* ineficaz.
in·ef·fi·cien·cy ineficacia *f*; *(of person)* incompetencia *f*.
in·ef·fi·cient *adj* ineficaz; *(person)* inepto, -a.
in·ept *adj (person)* inepto, -a; *(remark)* estúpido, -a.
in·e·qual·i·ty desigualdad *f*.
in·ev·i·ta·ble *adj* inevitable.
in·ev·i·ta·bly *adv* inevitablemente.
in·ex·cus·a·ble *adj* inexcusable.
in·ex·pen·sive *adj* económico, -a.
in·ex·pe·ri·enced *adj* inexperto, -a.
in·ex·pli·ca·ble *adj* inexplicable.
in·fal·li·ble *adj* infalible.
in·fa·mous *adj* infame.
in·fan·cy infancia *f*.
in·fant niño, -a *mf*.
in·fan·try infantería *f*.
in·fat·u·at·ed *adj* encaprichado, -a (**with** con).
in·fat·u·a·tion encaprichamiento *m*.
in·fect *vt* infectar.
in·fec·tion infección *f*.
in·fec·tious *adj (disease)* infeccioso, -a; *fig* contagioso, -a.
in·fer *vt* inferir (**from** de).
in·fe·ri·or *adj* inferior (**to** a).
in·fe·ri·or·i·ty inferioridad *f*.
in·fest *vt* infestar (**with** de).
in·fi·nite *adj* infinito, -a.
in·fi·nite·ly *adv* infinitamente.
in·fin·i·tive infinitivo *m*.
in·fin·i·ty infinidad *f*.
in·firm *adj (ailing)* enfermizo, -a; *(weak)* débil.
in·flamed *adj* inflamado, -a; **to become i.** inflamarse.
in·flam·ma·tion inflamación *f*.
in·flate *vt* inflar.
in·fla·tion inflación *f*.
in·flex·i·ble *adj* inflexible.
in·flict *vt (damage)* causar (**on** a); *(defeat)* infligir (**on** a).
in·flu·ence 1 *n* influencia *f*; **to be under the i. (of drink)** llevar unas copas de más; *(formally)* estar en estado de embriaguez. **2** *vt* influir en.
in·flu·en·tial *adj* influyente.
in·flu·en·za gripe *f*.
in·flux afluencia *f*.
in·fo *fam* información *f*.
in·form *vt* informar (**of, about** de, sobre).
in·for·mal *adj (occasion, behavior)* informal; *(language, treatment)* familiar; *(unofficial)* no oficial.
in·for·mal·ly *adv (to speak, behave)* de manera informal.
in·for·ma·tion información *f*; **a piece of i.** un dato.
information technology informática *f*.
in·form·a·tive *adj* informativo, -a.
in·fu·ri·ate *vt* poner furioso, -a.
in·fu·ri·at·ing *adj* exasperante.
in·gen·ious *adj* ingenioso, -a.
in·grat·i·tude ingratitud *f*.
in·gre·di·ent ingrediente *m*.
in·hab·it *vt* vivir en, ocupar.
in·hab·i·tant habitante *mf*.
in·hale *vt (gas)* inhalar; *(air)* aspirar.
in·her·it *vt* heredar (**from** de).
in·her·i·tance herencia *f*.
in·hib·it *vt (freedom)* limitar; *(person)* cohibir; **to be inhibited** *(person)* sentirse cohibido, -a.
in·hi·bi·tion cohibición *f*.
in·hos·pi·ta·ble *adj* inhospitalario, -a.
in·hu·man *adj* inhumano, -a.
in·i·tial 1 *adj* inicial. **2** *n* **initials** *(of name)* iniciales *fpl*; *(of abbreviation)* siglas *fpl*.
in·i·tial·ly *adv* al principio.
in·i·ti·ate *vt (reform)* promover; *(lawsuit)* entablar.
in·ject *vt (drug etc)* inyectar.
in·jec·tion inyección *f*.

in·jure *vt* herir; **to i. oneself** hacerse daño.
in·jured 1 *adj* herido, -a. **2** *npl* **the i.** los heridos.
in·ju·ry herida *f*.
in·jus·tice injusticia *f*.
ink tinta *f*.
ink-jet print·er impresora *f* de chorro de tinta.
in·kling *(idea)* idea *f* vaga, indicio *m*.
in·land 1 *adj* (del) interior. **2** *adv (travel)* tierra adentro.
in-laws *npl* familia *f* política.
in·mate *(of prison)* preso, -a *mf*.
inn *(with lodging)* posada *f*.
in·ner *adj* interior; **i. city** casco *m* urbano.
in·ning *(in baseball)* turno *m* para batear, *Am* inning *m*.
in·no·cence inocencia *f*.
in·no·cent *adj & n* inocente *(mf)*.
in·oc·u·late *vt* inocular.
in·oc·u·la·tion inoculación *f*.
in·put *(of data)* input *m*, entrada *f*.
in·quire 1 *vt* preguntar. **2** *vi* preguntar **(about** por); *(find out)* informarse **(about** de).
▶**inquire into** *vt* investigar.
in·quir·y pregunta *f*, *(investigation)* investigación *f*; **'inquiries'** 'información'.
in·quis·i·tive *adj* curioso, -a; *(questioning)* preguntón, -ona.
in·sane *adj* loco, -a.
in·san·i·ty locura *f*.
in·scrip·tion *(on stone, coin)* inscripción *f*, *(in book, on photo)* dedicatoria *f*.
in·sect insecto *m*; **i. bite** picadura *f*.
in·sec·ti·cide insecticida *m*.
in·se·cure *adj* inseguro, -a.
in·sen·si·tive *adj* insensible.
in·sen·si·tiv·i·ty insensibilidad *f*.
in·sert *vt* introducir.
in·side 1 *n* interior *m*; **on the i.** por dentro; **to turn sth i. out** volver algo al revés. **2** *adj* interior; **i. lane** carril *m* interior. **3** *adv (be)* dentro, adentro; *(run etc)* (hacia) adentro. **4** *prep (place)* dentro de.
in·sid·er *(of firm)* empleado, -a *mf* de la empresa.
in·sight *(quality)* perspicacia *f*.
in·sig·nif·i·cant *adj* insignificante.
in·sin·cere *adj* poco sincero, -a.
in·sist 1 *vi* insistir **(on** en). **2** *vt* **to i. that** ... insistir en que ....
in·sis·tence insistencia *f*.
in·sis·tent *adj* insistente.
in·so·lence insolencia *f*.
in·so·lent *adj* insolente.
in·som·ni·a insomnio *m*.
in·spect *vt* inspeccionar.
in·spec·tion inspección *f*.
in·spec·tor inspector, -a *mf*; *(on bus, train)* revisor, -a *mf*.
in·spi·ra·tion inspiración *f*.
in·spire *vt* inspirar; **to i. respect in sb** infundir respeto a algn.
in·stall *vt* instalar.
in·stall·ment *(of payment)* plazo *m*; *(of novel, program)* entrega *f*.
in·stance caso *m*; **for i.** por ejemplo.
in·stant 1 *n (moment)* instante *m*. **2** *adj* inmediato, -a; *(coffee, meal)* instantáneo, -a.
in·stant·ly *adv* inmediatamente.
in·stant re·play repetición *f*.
in·stead 1 *adv* en cambio. **2** *prep* **i. of** en vez de.
in·stinct instinto *m*.
in·stinc·tive *adj* instintivo, -a.
in·stinc·tive·ly *adv* instintivamente.
in·sti·tu·tion institución *f*.
in·struct *vt* instruir; *(order)* mandar.
in·struc·tion instructions instrucciones *fpl*; **'instructions for use'** 'modo de empleo'.
in·struc·tive *adj* instructivo, -a.
in·struc·tor instructor, -a *mf*; *(of driving)* profesor, -a *mf*.
in·stru·ment instrumento *m*.
in·stru·men·tal *adj (music)* instrumental; **to be i. in sth** contribuir decisivamente a algo.
in·suf·fi·cient *adj* insuficiente.
in·su·late *vt* aislar **(against, from** de).
in·su·la·tion aislamiento *m*.
in·sult 1 *n* insulto *m*. **2** *vt* insultar.
in·sur·ance seguro *m*; **i. company** compañía *f* de seguros.
in·sure *vt* asegurar **(against** contra).
in·tact *adj* intacto, -a.
in·take *(of food)* consumo *m*; *(of students, recruits)* número *m* de admitidos.
in·te·grate 1 *vt* integrar. **2** *vi* integrarse.
in·teg·ri·ty integridad *f*, honradez *f*.
in·tel·lect intelecto *m*.
in·tel·lec·tu·al *adj & n* intelectual *(mf)*.
in·tel·li·gence inteligencia *f*.
in·tel·li·gent *adj* inteligente.
in·tel·li·gi·ble *adj* inteligible.
in·tend *vt (mean)* tener la intención de.
in·tense *adj* intenso, -a.
in·tense·ly *adv (extremely)* sumamente.
in·ten·si·fy *vt* intensificar.
in·ten·si·ty intensidad *f*.
in·ten·sive *adj* intensivo, -a; **i. care unit** unidad *f* de vigilancia intensiva.
in·tent *adj* **to be i. on doing sth** estar resuelto, -a a hacer algo.
in·ten·tion intención *f*.
in·ten·tion·al *adj* deliberado, -a.
in·ten·tion·al·ly *adv* a propósito.
in·ter·act *vi (people)* interrelacionarse.
in·ter·ac·tive *adj* interactivo, -a.
in·ter·cept *vt* interceptar.
in·ter·change *(on motorway)* cruce *m*.
in·ter·change·a·ble *adj* intercambiable.
in·ter·com *(at entrance)* portero *m* automático.
in·ter·con·nect·ed *adj (facts etc)* interrelacionado, -a.
in·ter·course *(sexual)* relaciones *fpl* sexuales.
in·ter·est 1 *n* interés *m*; **i. rate** tipo *m* de interés. **2** *vt* interesar; **to be interested in** interesarse en; **I'm not interested** no me interesa.
in·ter·est·ing *adj* interesante.
in·ter·fere *vi (meddle)* entrometerse **(in** en).
in·ter·fer·ence *(meddling)* intromisión *f*, *(on radio etc)* interferencia *f*.

in·ter·im *n fml* **in the i.** en el ínterin. **2** *adj* interino, -a, provisional.
in·te·ri·or 1 *adj* interior. **2** *n* interior *m*.
in·ter·me·di·ar·y intermediario, -a *mf*.
in·ter·me·di·ate *adj* intermedio, -a.
in·ter·mis·sion *(at cinema, in theater)* intermedio *m*; *(in music)* interludio *m*.
in·tern *(doctor)* interno, -a *mf*.
in·ter·nal *adj* interior; *(dispute, injury)* interno, -a.
In·ter·nal Rev·e·nue Ser·vice Hacienda *f*.
in·ter·na·tion·al *adj* internacional.
in·ter·pret *vt* interpretar.
in·ter·pret·er intérprete *mf*.
in·ter·ro·gate *vt* interrogar.
in·ter·ro·ga·tion interrogatorio *m*.
in·ter·rupt *vti* interrumpir.
in·ter·rup·tion interrupción *f*.
in·ter·sect 1 *vt* cruzar. **2** *vi* cruzarse.
in·ter·sec·tion *(crossroads)* cruce *m*.
in·ter·state 1 *n* autopista *f* interestatal. **2** *adj* entre estados.
in·ter·val *(of time, space)* intervalo *m*.
in·ter·vene *vi (person)* intervenir **(in** en); *(event)* sobrevenir.
in·ter·ven·tion intervención *f*.
in·ter·view 1 *n* entrevista *f*. **2** *vt* entrevistar.
in·ter·view·er entrevistador, -a *mf*.
in·ti·mate *adj* íntimo, -a.
in·tim·i·date *vt* intimidar.
in·to *prep (motion)* en, a; **to get i. a car** subir a un coche; **to go i. a house** entrar a una casa; **to change dollars i. pesos** cambiar dólares en *or* por pesos; **to translate sth i. French** traducir algo al francés; *fam* **to be i. sth** ser aficionado, -a a algo.
in·tol·er·a·ble *adj* intolerable.
in·tox·i·cate *vt* embriagar.
in·tox·i·cat·ed *adj* borracho, -a.
in·tran·si·tive *adj* intransitivo, -a.
in·tro·duce *vt (person, program)* presentar **(to** a); *(bring in)* introducir **(into, to** en).
in·tro·duc·tion *(of person, program)* presentación *f*, *(in book, bringing in)* introducción *f*.
in·trude *vi* entrometerse **(into, on** en); *(disturb)* molestar.
in·trud·er intruso, -a *mf*.
in·tru·sion intrusión *f*.
in·tu·i·tion intuición *f*.
in·un·date *vt* inundar **(with** de); **I was inundated with offers** me llovieron las ofertas.
in·vade *vt* invadir.
in·vad·er invasor, -a *mf*.
in·va·lid¹ *(disabled person)* minusválido, -a *mf*, *(sick person)* enfermo, -a *mf*.
in·val·id² *adj* nulo, -a.
in·val·u·a·ble *adj* inestimable.
in·var·i·a·bly *adv (always)* invariablemente.
in·va·sion invasión *f*.
in·vent *vt* inventar.
in·ven·tion invento *m*.
in·ven·tor inventor, -a *mf*.
in·ven·to·ry inventario *m*.
in·vert·ed *adj* **(in) i. commas** (entre) comillas *fpl*.
in·vest *vt* invertir **(in** en).
in·ves·ti·gate *vt (crime, subject)* investigar; *(cause, possibility)* estudiar.
in·ves·ti·ga·tion *(of crime)* investigación *f*, *(of cause)* examen *m*.
in·ves·ti·ga·tor investigador, -a *mf*.
in·ves·tor inversor, -a *mf*.
in·vig·or·at·ing *adj* vigorizante.
in·vis·i·ble *adj* invisible.
in·vi·ta·tion invitación *f*.
in·vite *vt* invitar **(to** a); *(comments etc)* solicitar; *(criticism)* provocar.
in·vit·ing *adj (attractive)* atractivo, -a; *(food)* apetitoso, -a.
in·voice 1 *n* factura *f*. **2** *vt* facturar.
in·voke *vt fml* invocar.
in·volve *vt (entail)* suponer; *(concern)* implicar **(in** en); **to be involved in an accident** sufrir un accidente.
in·volved *adj (complicated)* complicado, -a; *(romantically)* enredado, -a.
in·volve·ment *(participation)* participación *f*, *(in crime)* implicación *f*; **emotional i.** relación *f* sentimental.
in·ward 1 *adj* interior. **2** *adv* = **inwards**.
in·wards *adv* hacia dentro.
IQ *abbr of* **intelligence quotient** coeficiente *m* intelectual, CI *m*.
IRA *abbr of* **individual retirement account** cuenta *f* de retiro *or* jubilación individual.
I·ra·ni·an *adj & n* iraní *(mf)*.
I·ra·qi *adj & n* iraquí *(mf)*.
i·ris *(of eye)* iris *m inv*; *(plant)* lirio *m*.
I·rish 1 *adj* irlandés, -esa. **2** *npl* **the I.** los irlandeses.
I·rish·man irlandés *m*.
I·rish·wom·an irlandesa *f*.
i·ron 1 *n* hierro *m*; *(for clothes)* plancha *f*; **the i. and steel industry** la industria siderúrgica. **2** *vt (clothes)* planchar.
i·ron·i(·)c(al) *adj* irónico, -a.
i·ron·ing **to do the i.** planchar.
i·ron·ing board tabla *f* de planchar.
i·ro·ny ironía *f*.
ir·ra·tion·al *adj* irracional.
ir·reg·u·lar *adj* irregular.
ir·rel·e·vance irrelevancia *f*.
ir·rel·e·vant *adj* no pertinente.
ir·re·sist·i·ble *adj* irresistible.
ir·re·spec·tive *adj* **i. of** sin tener en cuenta.
ir·ri·gate *vt* regar.
ir·ri·ta·ble *adj* irritable.
ir·ri·tate *vt (annoy)* irritar, fastidiar.
ir·ri·tat·ing *adj* irritante.
ir·ri·ta·tion *(annoyance)* fastidio *m*; *(bad mood)* mal humor *m*.
is 3rd person sing pres of **be**.
Is·lam·ic *adj* islámico, -a.
is·land isla *f*.
i·so·late *vt* aislar **(from** de).
i·so·lat·ed *adj* aislado, -a.
i·so·la·tion aislamiento *m*.
is·sue 1 *n (matter)* cuestión *f*, *(of journal etc)* ejemplar *m*. **2** *vt (book)* publicar; *(currency etc)* emitir; *(passport)* expedir; *(supplies)* repartir; *(order, instructions)* dar.
it *pers pron (subject)* él, ella *(often omitted)*; **it's here** está aquí. • *(direct object)* lo, la; **I don't**

believe it no me lo creo. ▪ *(indirect object)* le; **give it a kick** dale una patada. ▪ *(after prep)* él, ella, ello; **we'll talk about it later** ya hablaremos de ello. ▪ *(impersonal)* **it's late** es tarde; **it's me** soy yo; **it's raining** está lloviendo; **who is it?** ¿quién es?
I·tal·ian 1 *adj* italiano, -a. **2** *n (person)* italiano, -a *mf*; *(language)* italiano *m.*
i·tal·ic *adj* **in italics** en cursiva.
itch 1 *n* picor *m.* **2** *vi (skin)* picar.
itch·y *adj* que pica.
i·tem *(in list)* artículo *m*; *(in collection)* pieza *f*; *(on agenda)* asunto *m*; **i. of clothing** prenda *f* de vestir; **news i.** noticia *f.*
its *poss adj (one thing)* su; *(more than one)* sus.
it·self *pers pron* ▪ *(reflexive)* se; **the cat scratched i.** el gato se rascó. ▪ *(emphatic)* él *or* ella mismo, -a.
i·vo·ry marfil *m.*
i·vy hiedra *f.*

J

jab 1 *n* pinchazo *m*; *(poke)* golpe *m* seco. **2** *vt* pinchar.
jack *(for car)* gato *m*; *(cards)* sota *f.*
jack·et chaqueta *f*; *(of suit)* americana *f*; **j. potatoes** patatas *fpl* al horno.
ja·cuz·zi jacuzzi *m.*
jag·ged *adj* dentado, -a.
jail 1 *n* cárcel *f.* **2** *vt* encarcelar.
jam¹ mermelada *f.*
jam² 1 *n (blockage)* atasco *m.* **2** *vt (cram)* meter a la fuerza; *(block)* atascar. **3** *vi (door)* atrancarse; *(brakes)* agarrotarse.
▸**jam into** *vt (crowd)* apretarse en; **to j. sth into sth** meter algo a la fuerza en algo.
jam jar pote *m* de mermelada.
jam-packed *adj fam (with people)* atestado, -a; *(with things)* atiborrado, -a.
jan·i·tor portero *m*, conserje *m.*
Jan·u·ar·y enero *m.*
Jap·a·nese 1 *adj* japonés, -esa. **2** *n (person)* japonés, -esa *mf*; *(language)* japonés *m.*
jar *(glass)* tarro *m*; *(earthenware)* tinaja *f.*
jaun·dice ictericia *f.*
jave·lin jabalina *f.*
jaw mandíbula *f.*
jay·walk·ing imprudencia *f* peatonal.
jazz jazz *m.*
jea·lous *adj* celoso, -a; *(envious)* envidioso, -a; **to be j. of** tener celos de.
jeal·ous·y celos *mpl*; *(envy)* envidia *f.*
jeans *npl* vaqueros *npl*, tejanos *mpl.*
jeep jeep *m.*
jeer 1 *n (boo)* abucheo *m.* **2** *vi (boo)* abuchear; *(mock)* burlarse.
jeer·ing *adj* burlón, -ona.
Jell-O®, jel·lo gelatina *f.*
jel·ly gelatina *f.*
jeop·ard·ize *vt* poner en peligro; *(agreement etc)* comprometer.
jerk 1 *n (jolt)* sacudida *f*, *fam (idiot)* imbécil *mf.* **2** *vt (shake)* sacudir.
jer·sey jersey *m.*
jet reactor *m*; **j. engine** reactor *m.*
jet lag desfase *m* horario.
Jew judío, -a *mf.*
jew·el joya *f*, *(in watch)* rubí *m.*
jew·el·er joyero, -a *mf.*
jew·el·ry joyas *fpl*, alhajas *fpl.*
Jew·ish *adj* judío, -a.
jig·saw *(puzzle)* rompecabezas *m inv.*
jin·gle *vi* tintinear.
jit·ters *npl* **to get the j.** ponerse nervioso, -a.
job trabajo *m*; *(task)* tarea *f*; *(occupation)* (puesto *m* de) trabajo *m*; **we had a j. to ...** nos costó (trabajo) ...; **it's a good j. that ...** menos mal que ...
job cen·ter oficina *f* de empleo.
job·less *adj* parado, -a.
jock·ey jinete *m.*
jog 1 *n* trote *m.* **2** *vt* empujar; *(memory)* refrescar. **3** *vi (run)* hacer footing.
john *fam* meódromo *m.*
join 1 *vt* juntar; *(road)* empalmar con; *(river)* desembocar en; *(meet)* reunirse con; *(group)* unirse a; *(institution)* entrar en; *(army)* alistarse a; *(party)* afiliarse a; *(club)* hacerse socio, -a de. **2** *vi* unirse; *(roads)* empalmar; *(rivers)* confluir; *(become a member)* afiliarse; *(club)* hacerse socio, -a. **3** *n* juntura *f.*
▸**join in 1** *vi* participar. **2** *vt* participar en.
joint 1 *n* articulación *f*; *(of meat)* corte *m* de carne para asar; *(once roasted)* asado *m*; *(drugs)* porro *m.* **2** *adj* colectivo, -a; **j. (bank) account** cuenta *f* conjunta.
joint·ly *adv* conjuntamente, en común.
joke 1 *n* chiste *m*; *(prank)* broma *f.* **2** *vi* estar de broma.
jok·er bromista *mf*; *(in cards)* comodín *m.*
jol·ly *adj* alegre.
jolt 1 *n* sacudida *f.* **2** *vi* moverse a sacudidas. **3** *vt* sacudir.
jos·tle 1 *vt* dar empujones a. **2** *vi* dar empujones.
▸**jot down** *vt* apuntar.
jour·nal·ist periodista *mf.*
jour·ney viaje *m*; *(distance)* trayecto *m.*
joy alegría *f.*
joy·ful *adj* alegre.
joy·stick palanca *f* de mando; *(of video game)* joystick *m.*
judge 1 *n* juez *mf*, jueza *f.* **2** *vt* juzgar; *(estimate)* considerar; *(assess)* valorar. **3** *vi* juzgar.
judg(e)·ment sentencia *f*; *(opinion)* opinión *f.*
ju·di·cial *adj* judicial.
ju·do judo *m.*
jug jarra *f*; **milk j.** jarra de leche.
jug·gle *vi* hacer juegos malabares (**with** con).
jug·gler malabarista *mf.*
juice jugo *m*; *(of citrus fruits)* zumo *m.*
juic·y *adj* jugoso, -a.
Ju·ly julio *m.*
jum·ble 1 *n* revoltijo *m.* **2** *vt* revolver.
jum·bo *adj* gigante.
jum·bo jet jumbo *m.*

jump 1 *n* salto *m*; *(sudden increase)* subida repentina *f.* **2** *vi* saltar; *(start)* sobresaltarse; *(increase)* aumentar de golpe. **3** *vt* saltar; **to j. the line** colarse.
▸**jump in, jump on 1** *vt (train etc)* subirse a. **2** *vi* subir.
jump rope comba *f.*
jump·y *adj fam* nervioso, -a.
junc·tion *(of roads)* cruce *m.*
June junio *m.*
jun·gle jungla *f.*
jun·ior 1 *adj (lower in rank)* subalterno, -a; *(younger)* menor; **j. team** equipo juvenil. **2** *n (of lower rank)* subalterno, -a *mf*; *(younger person)* menor *mf.*
jun·ior high school = instituto *m* de enseñanza secundaria.
junk trastos *mpl.*
junk shop tienda *f* de segunda mano.
ju·ry jurado *m.*
just 1 *adj (fair)* justo, -a. **2** *adv (at this very moment)* ahora mismo, en este momento; *(only)* solamente; *(barely)* por poco; *(exactly)* exactamente; **he had j. arrived** acababa de llegar; **he was j. leaving when Rosa arrived** estaba a punto de salir cuando llegó Rosa; **j. as I came in** justo cuando entré; **I only j. caught the bus** cogí el autobús por los pelos; **j. about** casi; **j. as fast as** tan rápido como.
jus·tice justicia *f.*
jus·ti·fi·ca·tion justificación *f.*
jus·ti·fy *vt* justificar.
▸**jut out** *vi* sobresalir.

K

kan·ga·roo canguro *m.*
ka·ra·te kárate *m.*
ke·bab pincho moruno *m.*
keen *adj (eager)* entusiasta; *(intense)* profundo, -a; *(mind, senses)* agudo, -a.
keep 1 *n* **to earn one's k.** ganarse el pan. **2** *vt** mantener; *(letters, memories, silence, secret)* guardar; *(retain possession of)* quedarse con; *(hold back)* entretener; *(in prison)* detener; *(promise)* cumplir; *(diary, accounts)* llevar; **to k. sb waiting** hacer esperar a algn; **to k. doing sth** seguir haciendo algo; **she keeps forgetting her keys** siempre se olvida las llaves; **to k. going** seguir adelante. **3** *vi* (food)* conservarse.
▸**keep away 1** *vt* mantener a distancia. **2** *vi* mantenerse a distancia.
▸**keep back 1** *vt (information)* callar; *(money etc)* retener. **2** *vi (crowd)* mantenerse atrás.
▸**keep down** *vt* **to k. prices down** mantener los precios bajos.
▸**keep off** *vt* **k. off the grass** prohibido pisar la hierba.
▸**keep on 1** *vt (clothes etc)* no quitarse; *(continue to employ)* mantener a; **it keeps on breaking** siempre se está rompiendo. **2** *vi* **the rain kept on** la lluvia siguió/continuó; **he just kept on** *(talking, complaining)* siguió machacando; **k. straight on** sigue todo derecho.
▸**keep out 1** *vt* no dejar pasar. **2** *vi* no entrar; **k. out** *(sign)* prohibida la entrada
▸**keep to** *vt (subject)* limitarse a; **to k. to one's room** quedarse en el cuarto; **k. to the point!** ¡cíñete a la cuestión!; **to k. to the left** circular por la izquierda.
▸**keep up 1** *vt* mantener. **2** *vi (in race etc)* no rezagarse.
▸**keep up with** *vt* **to k. up with the times** estar al día.
ken·nel caseta *f* para perros.
Ken·yan *adj & n* keniano, -a *(mf).*
kept *pt & pp of* **keep.**
ker·o·sene queroseno *m.*
ketch·up ketchup *m.*
ket·tle hervidor *m.*
key 1 *n (for lock)* llave *f*; *(of piano, typewriter)* tecla *f.* **2** *adj* clave.
key·board teclado *m.*
key ring llavero *m.*
kick 1 *n (from person)* puntapié *m.* **2** *vi (animal)* cocear; *(person)* dar patadas. **3** *vt* dar un puntapié a.
▸**kick down, kick in** *vt (door etc)* derribar a patadas.
▸**kick off** *vi fam* empezar; *(of footballer)* sacar.
▸**kick out** *vt* echar a patadas.
kick-off saque *m* inicial.
kid¹ *fam (child)* niño, -a *mf*; **the kids** los críos.
kid² 1 *vt* tomar el pelo a. **2** *vi* tomar el pelo.
kid·nap *vt* secuestrar.
kid·nap·per secuestrador, -a *mf.*
kid·ney riñón *m.*
kill *vt* matar.
kill·er asesino, -a *mf.*
kill·ing *(of person)* asesinato *m*; *(of animal)* matanza *f.*
ki·lo kilo *m.*
kil·o·gram kilogramo *m.*
kil·o·me·ter kilómetro *m.*
kin familiares *mpl*; parientes *mpl.*
kind¹ *n* clase *f*; **what k. of?** ¿qué tipo de? **2** *adv fam* **k. of** en cierta manera.
kind² *adj* amable.
kin·der·gar·ten jardín *m* de infancia.
kind·ly 1 *adj (kindlier, kindliest)* amable, bondadoso, -a. **2** *adv fml (please)* por favor; **to look k. on** aprobar.
kind·ness amabilidad *f.*
king rey *m.*
king·dom reino *m.*
ki·osk quiosco *m.*
kiss 1 *n* beso *m.* **2** *vt* besar. **3** *vi* besarse.
kit *(gear)* equipo *m*; *(clothing)* ropa *f*; *(toy model)* maqueta *f.*
kitch·en cocina *f.*
kite *(toy)* cometa *f.*
kit·ten gatito, -a *mf.*
klutz *fam (stupid person)* bobo, -a *mf*, *Esp* chorra *mf*; *(clumsy person)* torpe *mf*, *Esp* patoso, -a *mf.*
knack **to get the k. of doing sth** cogerle el truquillo a algo.
knee rodilla *f.*
kneel* *vi* **to k. (down)** arrodillarse.
knew *pt of* **know.**
knick·ers *npl* bragas *fpl.*
knife *(pl* **knives)** cuchillo *m.*
knight caballero *m*; *(in chess)* caballo *m.*
knit 1 *vt* tejer; *(join)* juntar. **2** *vi* hacer punto; *(bone)* soldarse.

knit·ting punto *m*.
knit·ting nee·dle aguja *f* de hacer punto.
knob *(of stick)* puño *m*; *(of drawer)* tirador *m*; *(button)* botón *m*.
knock 1 *n* golpe *m*; **there was a k. at the door** llamaron a la puerta. **2** *vt* golpear. **3** *vi* chocar (**against, into** contra); *(at door)* llamar (**at** a).
▶**knock down** *vt (demolish)* derribar; *(car)* atropellar.
▶**knock off** *vt* tirar.
▪**knock out** *vt (make unconscious)* dejar sin conocimiento; *(in boxing)* derrotar por K.O.
▶**knock over** *vt* volcar; *(car)* atropellar.
knock·er *(on door)* aldaba *f*.
knot 1 *n* nudo *m*. **2** *vt* anudar.
know* 1 *vt* saber; *(be acquainted with)* conocer; **she knows how to ski** sabe esquiar; **we got to k. each other at the party** nos conocimos en la fiesta. **2** *vi* saber; **to let sb k.** avisar a algn.
know-how conocimiento *m* práctico.
know-it-all *fam* sabihondo, -a *mf*, sabelotodo *mf*.
knowl·edge conocimiento *m*; *(learning)* conocimientos *mpl*.
known *adj* conocido, -a.
knuck·le nudillo *m*.
Ko·ran Corán *m*.
Ko·re·an *adj & n* coreano, -a *(mf)*.

L

lab *fam* laboratorio *m*.
la·bel 1 *n* etiqueta *f*. **2** *vt* poner etiqueta a.
la·bor 1 *n (work)* trabajo *m*; *(workforce)* mano *f* de obra; **to be in l.** estar de parto. **2** *adj (market etc)* laboral; **L. day** día *m* de los trabajadores. **3** *vi (work)* trabajar (duro).
lab·o·ra·to·ry laboratorio *m*.
la·bor·er peón *m*; **farm l.** peón *m* agrícola.
la·bor un·ion sindicato *m*.
lace *n (fabric)* encaje *m*; **laces** cordones *mpl*; **to do up one's laces** atarse los cordones.
lack 1 *n* falta *f*. **2** *vt* carecer de. **3** *vi* carecer (**in** de).
lad chaval *m*.
lad·der escalera *f* (de mano).
la·dle cucharón *m*.
la·dy señora *f*; **'Ladies'** *(restroom)* 'Señoras'.
la·dy·bug mariquita *f*.
la·ger cerveza *f* (rubia).
lake lago *m*.
lamb cordero *m*; *(meat)* carne *f* de cordero.
lame *adj* cojo, -a.
lamp lámpara *f*.
lamp·post farola *f*.
lamp·shade pantalla *f*.
land 1 *n* tierra *f*; *(country)* país *m*; *(property)* tierras *fpl*; **piece of l.** terreno *m*; **by l.** por tierra. **2** *vt (plane)* hacer aterrizar. **3** *vi (plane)* aterrizar; *(passengers)* desembarcar.
land·ing *(of staircase)* rellano *m*; *(of plane)* aterrizaje *m*.
land·la·dy *(of apartment)* propietaria *f*, casera *f*; *(of boarding house)* patrona *f*; *(of pub)* dueña *f*.
land·lord *(of apartment)* propietario *m*, casero *m*; *(of pub)* dueño *m*.
land·own·er terrateniente *mf*.
land·scape paisaje *m*.
land·slide desprendimiento *m* de tierras.
lane *(in country)* camino *m*; *(in town)* callejón *m*; *(of highway)* carril *m*.
lan·guage idioma *m*, lengua *f*.
lan·guage lab·o·ra·to·ry laboratorio *m* de idiomas.
lan·tern farol *m*.
lap¹ *(knees)* rodillas *fpl*.
lap² *(circuit)* vuelta *f*.
la·pel solapa *f*.
lap·top laptop (computer) *Esp* ordenador *m* or *Am* computadora *f* portátil.
lar·ce·ny hurto *m*.
lar·der despensa *f*.
large *adj* grande; *(amount)* importante; **by and l.** por lo general.
large·ly *adv (mainly)* en gran parte; *(chiefly)* principalmente.
large-scale *adj (project, problem etc)* de gran envergadura; *(map)* a gran escala.
lark *(bird)* alondra *f*.
la·ser láser *m*; **l. printer** impresora *f* láser.
last 1 *adj (final, most recent)* último, -a; *(past)* pasado, -a; *(previous)* anterior; **l. but one** penúltimo, -a; **l. month** el mes pasado; **l. night** anoche. **2** *adv (on final occasion)* por última vez; *(at the end)* en último lugar; *(in race etc)* último; **at (long) l.** por fin. **3** *n* el último, la última. **4** *vi (time)* durar; *(hold out)* aguantar.
last·ly *adv* por último.
latch pestillo *m*.
late 1 *adj (not on time)* tardío, -a; *(hour)* avanzado, -a; *(far on in time)* tarde; **to be five minutes l.** llegar con cinco minutos de retraso; **in the l. afternoon** a última hora de la tarde. **2** *adv* tarde; **l. at night** a altas horas de la noche.
late·com·er rezagado, -a *mf*.
late·ly *adv* últimamente.
Lat·in 1 *adj* latino, -a; **L. America** América *f* Latina, Latinoamérica *f*; **L. American** latinoamericano, -a *(mf)*. **2** *n* latino, -a *mf*; *(language)* latín *m*.
lat·ter 1 *n (last)* último, -a; *(second of two)* segundo, -a. **2** *pron* éste, -a.
laugh 1 *n* risa *f*. **2** *vi* reír, reírse.
▶**laugh about** *vt* **to l. about sb/sth** reírse de algn/algo.
▶**laugh at** *vt* **to l. at sb/sth** reírse de algn/algo.
laugh·ter risa *f*.
launch 1 *n (vessel)* lancha *f*; *(of product)* lanzamiento *m*. **2** *vt (rocket, new product)* lanzar; *(ship)* botar; *(film, play)* estrenar.
Laun·dro·mat® lavandería *f* automática.
laun·dry *(place)* lavandería *f*; *(dirty clothes)* ropa *f* sucia; **to do the l.** lavar la ropa.
lav·a·to·ry retrete *m*; *(room)* baño *m*; **public l.** servicios *mpl*.
law ley *f*; *(as subject)* derecho *m*.
law court tribunal *m* de justicia.
lawn césped *m*.
lawn·mow·er cortacésped *m*.
law·suit pleito *m*.
law·yer abogado, -a *mf*.

lay* *vt (place)* poner; *(cable, trap)* tender; *(foundations)* echar; *(table, eggs)* poner; *(set down)* asentar.
▶**lay down** *vt (put down)* poner.
▶**lay off** *vt (dismiss)* despedir.
▶**lay on** *vt (provide)* proveer de; *(food)* preparar.
▶**lay out** *vt (open out)* extender; *(arrange)* disponer; *(ideas)* exponer; *(spend)* gastar.
lay·a·bout vago, -a *mf*.
lay·er capa *f*.
lay·man lego, -a *mf*.
lay·out *(arrangement)* disposición *f*; *(presentation)* presentación *f*.
la·zy *adj* vago, -a.
lead¹ *(metal)* plomo *m*; *(in pencil)* mina *f*.
lead² 1 *n (front position)* delantera *f*; *(advantage)* ventaja *f*; *(leash)* correa *f*; *(electric cable)* cable *m*; **to be in the l.** ir en cabeza; **to take the l.** *(in race)* tomar la delantera; *(score)* adelantarse. **2** *vt* (conduct)* conducir; *(be the leader of)* dirigir; *(life)* llevar; **to l. sb to think sth** hacer a algn pensar algo. **3** *vi* (road)* llevar (**to** a); *(in race)* llevar la delantera.
▶**lead away** *vt* llevar.
▶**lead on** *vt (deceive)* engañar, timar.
▶**lead to** *vt (result in)* dar lugar a.
lead·er jefe, -a *mf*; *(political)* líder *mf*.
lead·ing *adj (main)* principal.
leaf *(pl* **leaves**) hoja *f*.
leaf·let folleto *m*.
leak 1 *n (of gas, liquid)* escape *m*; *(of information)* filtración *f*. **2** *vi (gas, liquid)* escaparse. **3** *vt (information)* filtrar.
lean* 1 *vi* inclinarse; *(thing)* estar inclinado; **to l. on/against** apoyarse en/contra. **2** *vt* apoyar (**on** en).
▶**lean forward** *vi* inclinarse hacia delante.
▶**lean over** *vi* inclinarse.
leap 1 *n (jump)* salto *m*. **2** *vi** saltar.
leap year año *m* bisiesto.
learn* 1 *vt* aprender; *(find out about)* enterarse de; **to l. (how) to ski** aprender a esquiar. **2** *vi* aprender; **to l. about** or **of** *(find out)* enterarse de.
learn·er *(beginner)* principiante *mf*.
learn·ing *(knowledge)* conocimientos *mpl*; *(erudition)* saber *m*.
lease 1 *n* contrato *m* de arrendamiento. **2** *vt* arrendar.
leash correa *f*.
least 1 *adj* menor. **2** *adv* menos. **3** *n* lo menos; **at l.** por lo menos.
leath·er 1 *n (fine)* piel *f*; *(heavy)* cuero *m*. **2** *adj* de piel.
leave¹* 1 *vt* dejar; *(go away from)* abandonar; *(go out of)* salir de; **I have two cookies left** me quedan dos galletas. **2** *vi (go away)* irse, marcharse; *(go out)* salir; **the train leaves in five minutes** el tren sale dentro de cinco minutos.
▶**leave behind** *vt* dejar atrás.
▶**leave on** *vt (clothes)* dejar puesto, -a; *(lights, radio)* dejar encendido, -a.
▶**leave out** *vt (omit)* omitir.
leave² *(time off)* vacaciones *fpl*.
lec·ture 1 *n* conferencia *f*; *(at university)* clase *f*; **to give a l.** dar una conferencia (**on** sobre). **2** *vi (at university)* dar clases.
lec·tur·er conferenciante *mf*; *(at university)* profesor, -a *mf*.
leek puerro *m*.
left¹ 1 *adj* izquierdo, -a. **2** *adv* a la izquierda. **3** *n* izquierda *f*; **on the l.** a mano izquierda.
left² *pt & pp* de **leave¹**.
left-hand *adj* **on the l. side** a mano izquierda.
left-hand·ed *adj* zurdo, -a.
left·o·vers *npl* sobras *fpl*.
leg pierna *f*; *(of animal, table)* pata *f*.
le·gal *adj* legal; *(permitted by law)* lícito, -a; *(relating to the law)* jurídico, -a.
le·gal hol·i·day fiesta *f* nacional.
le·gal·ly *adv* legalmente.
leg·end leyenda *f*.
leg·i·ble *adj* legible.
leg·is·la·tion legislación *f*.
leg·is·la·tive *adj* legislativo, -a.
leg·is·la·ture asamblea *f* legislativa.
le·git·i·mate *adj* legítimo, -a.
lei·sure ocio *m*; *(free time)* tiempo *m* libre; **l. activities** pasatiempos *mpl*.
lem·on limón *m*; **l. juice** zumo *m* de limón; **l. tea** té *m* con limón.
lem·on·ade gaseosa *f*.
lend* *vt* prestar.
lend·er entidad *f* de crédito.
length largo *m*; *(duration)* duración *f*; *(section of string etc)* trozo *m*.
length·en 1 *vt* alargar; *(lifetime)* prolongar. **2** *vi* alargarse; *(lifetime)* prolongarse.
length·y *adj (lengthier, lengthiest)* largo, -a; *(meeting, discussion)* prolongado, -a.
le·nient *adj* indulgente.
lens *(of spectacles)* lente *f*; *(of camera)* objetivo *m*.
len·til lenteja *f*.
leop·ard leopardo *m*.
le·o·tard mallas *fpl*.
less menos; **l. and l.** cada vez menos; **a year l. two days** un año menos dos días.
les·son clase *f*; *(in book)* lección *f*.
let* 1 *vt* dejar; *(rent out)* alquilar; **to l. sb do sth** dejar a algn hacer algo; **to l. go of sth** soltar algo; **to l. sb know** avisar a algn. **2** *v aux* **l. him wait** que espere; **l.'s go!** ¡vamos!, ¡vámonos!
▶**let down** *vt (lower)* bajar; *(fail)* defraudar.
▶**let in** *vt (admit)* dejar entrar.
▶**let off** *vt (bomb)* hacer explotar; *(fireworks)* hacer estallar; **to l. sb off** *(pardon)* perdonar.
▶**let on** *vi fam* **don't l. on** *(reveal information)* no se lo digas.
▶**let out** *vt (release)* soltar; *(news)* divulgar; *(secret)* revelar; *(cry)* soltar.
▶**let up** *vi (cease)* cesar.
let·down decepción *f*.
let·ter *(of alphabet)* letra *f*; *(written message)* carta *f*.
let·ter·box buzón *m*.
let·tuce lechuga *f*.
lev·el 1 *adj (flat)* llano, -a; *(even)* nivelado, -a; **to be l. with** estar a nivel de. **2** *n* nivel *m*; **to be on a l. with** estar al mismo nivel que.
lev·el crossing paso *m* a nivel.
lev·er palanca *f*.
li·a·ble *adj* **the river is l. to freeze** el río tiene tendencia a helarse.
li·ar mentiroso, -a *mf*.
li·bel 1 *n* libelo *m*. **2** *vt* difamar, calumniar.
lib·er·al 1 *adj* liberal; *(abundant)* abundante; **L. Party** Partido *m* Liberal. **2** *n* **L.** liberal *mf*.
lib·er·ty libertad *f*; **to be at l. to say sth** ser libre de decir algo.
li·brar·i·an bibliotecario, -a *mf*.
li·brar·y biblioteca *f*.
Lib·y·an *adj & n* libio, -a *(mf)*.

lice *npl see* **louse**.
li·cense *(permit)* permiso *m*; **l. plate** *(of car)* placa *f* de la) matrícula *f*.
lick *vt* lamer.
lic·o·rice regaliz *m*.
lid *(cover)* tapa *f*; *(of eye)* párpado *m*.
lie¹ 1 *vi* mentir. **2** *n* mentira *f*.
lie²* *vi (act)* acostarse; *(state)* estar acostado, -a.
▸ **lie around** *vi (person)* estar tumbado, -a; *(things)* estar tirado, -a.
▸ **lie down** *vi* acostarse.
life *(pl* **lives)** vida *f*; **to come to l.** cobrar vida.
life belt cinturón *m* salvavidas.
life·boat *(on ship)* bote *m* salvavidas; *(on shore)* lancha *f* de socorro.
life·guard socorrista *mf*.
life in·sur·ance seguro *m* de vida.
life jack·et chaleco *m* salvavidas.
life·style estilo *m* de vida.
life·time vida *f*; **in his l.** durante su vida.
lift 1 *vt* levantar; *(head etc)* alzar; *(pick up)* coger. **2** *n* **to give sb a l.** llevar a algn en coche.
▸ **lift out** *vt (take out)* sacar.
▸ **lift up** *vt* levantar.
light¹ 1 *n* luz *f*; *(lamp)* lámpara *f*; *(headlight)* faro *m*; **to set l. to sth** prender fuego a algo; **have you got a l.?** ¿tiene fuego? **2** *vt* (illuminate)* iluminar; *(ignite)* encender. **3** *adj* claro, -a; *(hair)* rubio, -a.
▸ **light up 1** *vt* iluminar. **2** *vi* iluminarse; *(light cigarette)* encender un cigarrillo.
light² 1 *adj* ligero, -a; *(rain)* fino, -a. **2** *adv* **to travel l.** ir ligero, -a de equipaje.
light bulb bombilla *f*.
light·er (cigarette) l. mechero *m*.
light·house faro *m*.
light·ing *(act)* iluminación *f*.
light·ning *(flash)* relámpago *m*; *(which hits the earth)* rayo *m*.
like¹ 1 *prep (similar to)* parecido, -a a; *(the same as)* igual que; **l. that** así; **what's he l.?** ¿cómo es?; **to feel l.** tener ganas de. **2** *adj* parecido, -a; *(equal)* igual.
like² 1 *vt* **do you l. chocolate?** ¿te gusta el chocolate?; **he likes dancing** le gusta bailar; **I would l. a coffee** quisiera un café; **would you l. to go now?** ¿quieres que nos vayamos ya? **2** *vi* querer; **as you l.** como quieras.
like·a·ble *adj* simpático, -a.
like·li·hood probabilidad *f*.
like·ly 1 *adj* probable; **he's l. to cause trouble** es probable que cause problemas. **2** *adv* probablemente; **not l.!** ¡ni hablar!
like·wise *adv (also)* asimismo.
lik·ing *(for thing)* afición *f*; *(for person)* simpatía *f*; *(for friend)* cariño *m*.
lil·y lirio *m*.
limb miembro *m*.
lime *(fruit)* lima *f*; *(tree)* limero *m*.
lim·it 1 *n* límite *m*; *(maximum)* máximo *m*; *(minimum)* mínimo *m*. **2** *vt (restrict)* limitar **(to** a).
lim·ou·sine limusina *f*.
limp 1 *vi* cojear. **2** *n* cojera *f*.
line¹ línea *f*; *(straight)* raya *f*; *(of writing)* renglón *m*; *(of poetry)* verso *m*; *(row)* fila *f*; *(of trees)* hilera *f*; *(of people waiting)* cola *f*; *(rope)* cuerda *f*; *(telephone)* línea *f*; *(of railway)* vía *f*.
line² *vt (clothes)* forrar.
▸ **line up 1** *vt (arrange in rows)* poner en fila; **he has something lined up for this evening** tiene algo organizado para esta noche. **2** *vi (people)* ponerse en fila; *(in line)* hacer cola.
lin·en *(sheets etc)* ropa *f* blanca.
lin·er transatlántico *m*.
line-up *(of team)* alineación *f*; *(of band)* formación *f*; *(of police suspects)* rueda *f* de reconocimiento *or* identificación.
lin·ger *vi* tardar; *(dawdle)* rezagarse; *(smell, doubt)* persistir; *fig (memory)* perdurar.
lin·guis·tics lingüística *f*.
lin·ing forro *m*.
link 1 *n (of chain)* eslabón *m*; *(connection)* conexión *f*. **2** *vt* unir.
▸ **link up** *vi* unirse; *(meet)* encontrarse.
lino linóleo *m*.
lint brush cepillo *m* de la ropa.
li·on león *m*.
lip labio *m*.
lip·stick lápiz *m* de labios.
li·queur licor *m*.
liq·uid *adj & n* líquido, -a *(m)*.
liq·ui·date *vt* liquidar.
liq·uor bebidas *fpl* alcohólicas.
list 1 *n* lista *f*; *(catalog)* catálogo *m*. **2** *vt (make a list of)* hacer una lista de; *(put on a list)* poner en una lista.
lis·ten *vi* escuchar; **to l. to sth/sb** escuchar algo/a algn.
▸ **listen out** *vi* estar atento, -a **(for** a).
lis·ten·er oyente *mf*.
li·ter litro *m*.
lit·er·al·ly *adv* literalmente.
lit·er·ar·y *adj* literario, -a.
lit·er·a·ture literatura *f*; *(documentation)* folleto *m* informativo.
lit·i·ga·tion litigio *m*.
lit·ter *(trash)* basura *f*; *(papers)* papeles *mpl*; *(offspring)* camada *f*.
lit·ter bin papelera *f*.
lit·tle *adj* pequeño, -a; **a l. dog** un perrito; **a l. house** una casita. **2** *pron* poco *m*; **save me a l.** guárdame un poco; **a l. cheese** un poco de queso. **3** *adv* poco; **l. by l.** poco a poco; **as l. as possible** lo menos posible; **l. milk/money** poca leche/poco dinero.
live¹ *vti* vivir; **to l. an interesting life** llevar una vida interesante.
live² *adj (TV etc)* en directo; *(wire)* con corriente.
▸ **live off, live on** *vt (food, money)* vivir de.
▸ **live on** *vi (memory)* persistir.
▸ **live through** *vt* sobrevivir a, vivir.
▸ **live together** *vi* vivir juntos.
▸ **live up to** *vt (promises)* cumplir con; **to l. up to expectations** estar a la altura de lo que se esperaba.
▸ **live with** *vt* vivir con.
live·ly *adj (person)* vivo, -a; *(place)* animado, -a.
liv·er hígado *m*.
liv·ing 1 *adj* vivo, -a. **2** *n* vida *f*; **to earn** *or* **make one's l.** ganarse la vida.
liv·ing room sala *f* de estar.
liz·ard *(large)* lagarto *m*; *(small)* lagartija *f*.
load 1 *n (cargo)* carga *f*; *(weight)* peso *m*; *fam* **loads of** montones de; *fam* **that's a l. of garbage!** ¡no son más que tonterías! **2** *vt* cargar.
▸ **load up** *vti* cargar.
loaf *(pl* **loaves)** pan *m*.

loan 1 *n (to individual)* préstamo *m*; *(to company etc)* empréstito *m*; **on l.** prestado, -a. **2** *vt* prestar.
lob·by *(hall)* vestíbulo *m*.
lob·ster langosta *f*.
lo·cal *adj* local; *(person)* del pueblo.
lo·cal ar·e·a net·work red *f* local.
lo·cal·i·ty localidad *f*.
lo·cal·ly *adv* en *or* de la localidad.
lo·cate *vt (situate)* ubicar; *(find)* localizar.
lo·ca·tion ubicación *f*.
lock¹ 1 *n (on door etc)* cerradura *f*; *(bolt)* cerrojo *m*; *(padlock)* candado *m*; *(on canal)* esclusa *f*. **2** *vt* cerrar con llave *or* cerrojo *or* candado.
lock² *(of hair)* mechón *m*.
▸ **lock in** *vt (person)* encerrar a.
▸ **lock out** *vt (person)* cerrar la puerta a.
▸ **lock up** *vt (house)* cerrar; *(in jail)* meter en la cárcel.
lock·er armario *m* ropero.
lock·et medallón *m*.
lodge 1 *n (gamekeeper's)* casa *f* del guarda; *(porter's)* portería *f*; *(hunter's)* refugio *m*. **2** *vt (accommodate)* alojar; *(complaint)* presentar. **3** *vi (live)* alojarse; *(get stuck)* meterse **(in** en).
lodg·er huésped, -a *mf*.
lodg·ing alojamiento *m*; **l. house** casa *f* de huéspedes.
loft desván *m*.
log *(wood)* tronco *m*; *(for fire)* leño *m*.
log·ic lógica *f*.
log·i·cal *adj* lógico, -a.
lol·li·pop chupachup® *m*.
lone *adj (solitary)* solitario, -a; *(single)* solo, -a.
lone·li·ness soledad *f*.
lone·ly *adj (person)* solo, -a; *(place)* solitario, -a.
long¹ 1 *adj (size)* largo, -a; *(time)* mucho, -a; **it's three meters l.** tiene tres metros de largo; **it's a l. way** está lejos; **at l. last** por fin; **how l. is the film?** ¿cuánto tiempo dura la película? **2** *adv* mucho tiempo; **as l. as the exhibition lasts** mientras dure la exposición; **as l. as** *or* **so l. as you don't mind** con tal de que no te importe; **before l.** dentro de poco; **how l. have you been here?** ¿cuánto tiempo llevas aquí?
long-dis·tance *adj* de larga distancia; **l. call** conferencia *f* interurbana.
long-term *adj* largo plazo.
look 1 *n (glance)* mirada *f*; *(appearance)* aspecto *m*; **to take a l. at** echar un vistazo a. **2** *vi* mirar; *(seem)* parecer; **he looks well** tiene buena cara; **she looks like her father** se parece a su padre.
▸ **look after** *vt* ocuparse de, cuidar de.
▸ **look around 1** *vi* mirar alrededor; *(turn head)* volver la cabeza. **2** *vt (house, shop)* ver.
▸ **look at** *vt* mirar.
▸ **look back** *vi* mirar hacia atrás; **to l. back on sth** *(remember)* recordar algo.
▸ **look for** *vt* buscar.
▸ **look forward to** *vt* esperar con ilusión; **I l. forward to hearing from you** *(in letter)* espero noticias suyas.
▸ **look into** *vt* investigar.
▸ **look onto** *vt* dar a.
▸ **look out** *vi* **the bedroom looks out onto the garden** el dormitorio da al jardín; **l. out!** ¡cuidado!, ¡ojo!
▸ **look over** *vt (examine)* revisar; *(place)* inspeccionar.
▸ **look up 1** *vi (glance upwards)* alzar la vista. **2** *vt (look for)* buscar.
lookout *(person)* centinela *mf*; *(place)* mirador *m*; **to be on the l. for** estar al acecho de.
loom¹ telar *m*.
loom² *vi (of mountain)* alzarse; *(threaten)* amenazar.
loop lazo *m*.
loop·hole *fig* escapatoria *f*.
loose 1 *adj (not secure)* flojo, -a; *(papers, hair, clothes)* suelto, -a; *(baggy)* holgado, -a; *(not packaged)* a granel; **to set sb l.** soltar a algn; **l. change** suelto *m*. **2** *n* **to be on the l.** *(prisoner)* andar suelto.
loos·en *vt* aflojar; *(belt)* desabrochar.
lord señor *m*.
lose* *vti* perder; **to l. to sb** perder contra algn.
los·er perdedor, -a *mf*.
loss pérdida *f*.
lost *adj* perdido, -a; **to get l.** perderse; **get l.!** *fam* ¡vete a la porra!
lost and found oficina *f* de objetos perdidos.
lot a l. of *(much)* mucho, -a; *(many)* muchos, -as; **he feels a l. better** se encuentra mucho mejor; **lots of** montones de; **what a l. of bottles!** ¡qué cantidad de botellas!
lo·tion loción *f*.
lot·ter·y lotería *f*.
loud 1 *adj (voice)* alto, -a; *(noise)* fuerte; *(protests, party)* ruidoso, -a. **2** *adv* **to read/think out l.** leer/pensar en voz alta.
loud·ly *adv (to speak etc)* en voz alta.
loud·speak·er altavoz *m*.
lous·y *adj fam* fatal; **a l. trick** una cochinada.
love 1 *n* amor *m*; **to be in l. with sb** estar enamorado, -a de algn; **to make l.** hacer el amor. **2** *vt (person)* querer; *(sport etc)* ser muy aficionado, -a a; **he loves cooking** le encanta cocinar.
love·ly *adj (charming)* encantador, -a; *(beautiful)* precioso, -a; *(delicious)* riquísimo, -a.
lov·er *(enthusiast)* aficionado, -a *mf*.
lov·ing *adj* cariñoso, -a.
low 1 *adj* bajo, -a; *(poor)* pobre; *(reprehensible)* malo, -a; **to feel l.** sentirse deprimido, -a. **2** *adv* bajo.
low·er 1 *adj* inferior. **2** *vt* bajar; *(reduce)* reducir; *(price)* rebajar.
low-fat *adj (milk)* desnatado, -a; *(food)* light *inv*.
loy·al *adj* leal.
loy·al·ty lealtad *f*, fidelidad *f*.
loz·enge pastilla *f*.
LP LP *m*, elepé *m*.
luck suerte *f*; **bad l.!** ¡mala suerte!; **good l.!** ¡(buena) suerte!
luck·i·ly *adv* afortunadamente.
luck·y *adj (person)* afortunado, -a; *(charm)* de la suerte; **that was l.** ha sido una suerte.
lu·di·crous *adj* ridículo, -a.
lug·gage equipaje *m*.
luke·warm *adj (water etc)* tibio, -a.
lull·a·by nana *f*.
lum·ber maderos *mpl*.
lum·ber·yard almacén *m* maderero, maderería *f*, *RP* barraca *f* maderera.
lu·mi·nous *adj* luminoso, -a.
lump *(of coal etc)* trozo *m*; *(of sugar, earth)* terrón *m*; *(swelling)* bulto *m*.
lump sum suma *f* global.

M

lu·na·tic *adj & n* loco, -a *(mf)*.
lunch comida *f*, almuerzo *m*; **l. hour** hora *f* de comer.
lung pulmón *m*.
lux·u·ri·ous *adj* lujoso, -a.
lux·u·ry lujo *m*.

mac(c)aroni macarrones *mpl*.
ma·chine máquina *f*.
ma·chin·er·y *(machines)* maquinaria *f*; *(workings of machine)* mecanismo *m*.
mack·er·el *inv* caballa *f*.
mad *adj* loco, -a; **to be m. about sth/sb** estar loco, -a por algo/algn; **to be m. at sb** estar enfadado, -a con algn.
Mad·am señora *f*.
made *pt & pp of* **make**.
mad·man loco *m*.
mad·ness locura *f*.
mag·a·zine *(periodical)* revista *f*.
mag·got gusano *m*.
mag·ic 1 *n* magia *f*. **2** *adj* mágico, -a; **m. wand** varita *f* mágica.
mag·i·cal *adj* mágico, -a.
ma·gi·cian *(wizard)* mago, -a *mf*; *(conjuror)* prestidigitador, -a *mf*.
mag·is·trate juez, -a *mf* de paz.
mag·net imán *m*.
mag·nif·i·cent *adj* magnífico, -a.
mag·ni·fy·ing glass lupa *f*.
ma·hog·a·ny caoba *f*.
maid criada *f*.
mail 1 *n* correo *m*. **2** *vt (post)* echar (al buzón).
mail·box buzón *m*.
mail·man cartero *m*.
main *adj (problem, door etc)* principal; *(square, mast, sail)* mayor; *(office)* central; **the m. thing is to keep calm** lo esencial es mantener la calma; **m. road** carretera *f* principal. **2** *n (pipe, wire)* conducto *m* principal; **the mains** *(water or gas system)* la conducción; *(electrical)* la red (eléctrica).
main·land continente *m*.
main·ly *adv* principalmente; *(for the most part)* en su mayoría.
main·tain *vt (road, machine)* conservar en buen estado; **to m. that** sostener que.
main·te·nance *(of vehicle, road)* mantenimiento *m*; *(divorce allowance)* pensión *f*.
maî·tre d' jefe *m* de sala.
maize maíz *m*.
maj·es·ty majestad *f*.
ma·jor 1 *adj* principal; *(contribution, operation)* importante. **2** *n (officer)* comandante *m*.
ma·jor·ette majorette *f*.
ma·jor·i·ty mayoría *f*.
make 1 *vt** hacer; *(manufacture)* fabricar; *(clothes, curtains)* confeccionar; *(meal)* preparar; *(decision)* tomar; *(earn)* ganar; **to be made of** ser de; **to m. sb do sth** obligar a algn a hacer algo; **to m. do with sth** arreglárselas con algo; **I don't know what to m. of it** no sé qué pensar de eso; **we've made it!** *(succeeded)* ¡lo hemos conseguido! **2** *n (brand)* marca *f*.
▸**make out 1** *vt (list, receipt)* hacer; *(check)* extender; *(perceive)* distinguir; *(understand)* entender; *(claim)* pretender. **2** *vi* **how did you m. out?** ¿qué tal te fue?
▸**make up 1** *vt (list)* hacer; *(assemble)* montar; *(invent)* inventar; *(apply cosmetics to)* maquillar; *(one's face)* maquillarse; *(loss)* compensar. **2** *vi* **to m. up (with sb)** hacer las paces (con algn).
▸**make up for** *vt (loss, damage)* compensar por; *(lost time, mistake)* recuperar.
mak·er fabricante *mf*.
make-up *(cosmetics)* maquillaje *m*.
ma·lar·i·a malaria *f*.
male 1 *adj (animal, plant)* macho; *(person)* varón; *(sex)* masculino. **2** *n (person)* varón *m*; *(animal, plant)* macho *m*.
mal·ice *(wickedness)* malicia *f*.
ma·li·cious *adj (wicked)* malévolo, -a.
mall *(shopping)* centro *m* comercial.
mam·mal mamífero *m*.
man *(pl men)* hombre *m*; **old m.** viejo *m*; **young m.** joven *m*; *(humanity)* el hombre; *(human being)* ser *m* humano.
man·age 1 *vt (company, household)* llevar; *(money, affairs, person)* manejar; *(achieve)* conseguir; **to m. to do sth** lograr hacer algo. **2** *vi (cope physically)* poder; *(financially)* arreglárselas.
man·age·ment dirección *f*.
man·ag·er *(of company, bank)* director, -a *mf*; *(of department)* jefe, -a *mf*.
man·ag·ing di·rec·tor director, -a *mf* gerente.
man·da·rin *(fruit)* mandarina *f*.
mane *(of horse)* crin *f*; *(of lion)* melena *f*.
ma·neu·ver 1 *n* maniobra *f*. **2** *vt* maniobrar; *(person)* manejar. **3** *vi* maniobrar.
ma·ni·ac maníaco, -a *mf*, *fam* loco, -a *mf*.
man·kind la humanidad.
man·made *adj (lake)* artificial; *(fibers, fabric)* sintético, -a.
man·ner *(way, method)* manera *f*, modo *m*; *(way of behaving)* forma *f* de ser; **(good) manners** buenos modales *mpl*; **bad manners** falta *f sing* de educación.
man·pow·er mano *f* de obra.
man·tel·piece *(shelf)* repisa *f* de chimenea; *(fireplace)* chimenea *f*.
man·u·al *adj & n* manual *(m)*.
man·u·fac·ture 1 *vt* fabricar. **2** *n* fabricación *f*.
man·u·fac·tur·er fabricante *mf*.
ma·nure estiércol *m*.
man·y 1 *adj* muchos, -as; **a great m.** muchísimos, -as; **as m. ... as ...** tantos, -as ... como ...; **how m. days?** ¿cuántos días?; **not m. books** pocos libros; **so m. flowers!** ¡cuántas flores!; **too m.** demasiados, -as. **2** *pron* muchos, -as.
map *(of country)* mapa *m*; *(of town, bus)* plano *m*.
mar·a·thon maratón *m or f*.
mar·ble *(stone)* mármol *m*; *(glass ball)* canica *f*.
March marzo *m*.
march 1 *n* marcha *f*. **2** *vi* marchar.
mare yegua *f*.
mar·ga·rine margarina *f*.
mar·gin margen *m*.
ma·rine 1 *adj* marino, -a. **2** *n* soldado *m* de infantería de marina; **the M. Corps** la infantería de marina.

mark 1 *n (trace)* huella *f*; *(stain)* mancha *f*; *(symbol)* signo *m*; *(sign, token)* señal *f*; *(in exam etc)* nota *f*. **2** *vt (make mark on)* marcar; *(stain)* manchar; *(exam)* corregir.
▸**mark out** *vt (area)* delimitar.
mark·er *(pen)* rotulador *m*.
mar·ket mercado *m*.
mar·ket·ing marketing *m*.
mar·ma·lade mermelada *f* (de cítricos).
mar·riage *(state)* matrimonio *m*; *(wedding)* boda *f*.
mar·ried *adj* casado, -a.
mar·row *(bone)* **m.** médula *f*; *(vegetable)* calabacín *m*.
mar·ry *vt* casarse con; *(priest)* casar; **to get married** casarse.
marsh pantano *m*; **salt m.** marisma *f*.
mar·shal 1 *n (in army)* mariscal *m*; *(sheriff)* policía *mf*; *(police or fire chief)* jefe, -a *mf*. **2** *vt (troops)* formar; *(facts etc)* ordenar.
Mar·tian *n & adj* marciano, -a *(mf)*.
mar·vel·ous *adj* maravilloso, -a.
mar·zi·pan mazapán *m*.
mas·car·a rímel *m*.
mas·cot mascota *f*.
mas·cu·line *adj* masculino, -a.
mash *vt* **to m. (up)** machacar; **mashed potatoes** puré *m* de patatas.
mask máscara *f*.
mass¹ *(in church)* misa *f*; **to say m.** decir misa.
mass² **1** *n* masa *f*; *(large quantity)* montón *m*; *(of people)* multitud *f*. **2** *adj* masivo, -a.
mas·sa·cre 1 *n* masacre *f*. **2** *vt* masacrar.
mas·sage 1 *n* masaje *m*. **2** *vt* dar masaje a.
mas·seur masajista *m*.
mas·seuse masajista *f*.
mas·sive *adj* enorme.
mast mástil *m*; *(radio etc)* torre *f*.
mas·ter 1 *n (of dog, servant)* amo *m*; *(of household)* señor *m*; *(teacher)* profesor *m*; **m.'s degree** ≃ máster *m*. **2** *vt (person, situation)* dominar; *(subject, skill)* llegar a dominar.
mas·ter·piece obra *f* maestra.
mat *(rug)* alfombrilla *f*; *(doormat)* felpudo *m*; *(rush mat)* estera *f*.
match¹ cerilla *f*.
match² **1** *n (sport)* partido *m*. **2** *vt (be in harmony with)* armonizar con; *(colors, clothes)* hacer juego con; **they are well matched** *(teams)* van iguales; *(couple)* hacen buena pareja. **3** *vi (harmonize)* hacer juego.
▸**match up to** *vt* estar a la altura de.
match·box caja *f* de cerillas.
match·ing *adj* a juego.
match·stick cerilla *f*.
ma·te·ri·al *(substance)* materia *f*; *(cloth)* tejido *m*; **materials** *(ingredients, equipment)* materiales *mpl*.
ma·ter·nal *adj* maternal; *(uncle etc)* materno, -a.
ma·ter·ni·ty maternidad *f*.
ma·ter·ni·ty hos·pi·tal maternidad *f*.
math matemáticas *fpl*.
math·e·mat·i·cal *adj* matemático, -a.
math·e·mat·ics matemáticas *fpl*.
mat·i·née *(cinema)* sesión *f* de tarde; *(theater)* función *f* de tarde.
mat·ter 1 *n (affair, question)* asunto *m*; *(problem)* problema *m*; *(substance)* materia *f*; **what's the m.?** ¿qué pasa? **2** *vi* importar; **it doesn't m.** no importa, da igual.
mat·tress colchón *m*.
ma·ture *adj* maduro, -a.
max·i·mum 1 *n* máximo *m*. **2** *adj* máximo, -a.
May mayo *m*.
may *v aux (pt* might*) (possibility, probability)* poder, ser posible; **he m.** *or* **might come** puede que venga; **you m.** *or* **might as well stay** más vale que te quedes. ▪ *(permission)* poder; **m. I?** ¿me permite?; **you m. smoke** pueden fumar. ▪ *(wish)* ojalá (+ *subjunctive*); **m. you always be happy!** ¡ojalá seas siempre feliz!
may·be *adv* quizá(s), tal vez.
may·on·naise mayonesa *f*.
may·or *(man)* alcalde *m*; *(woman)* alcaldesa *f*.
maze laberinto *m*.
MBA *abbr of* **Master of Business Administration** MBA *m*, máster *m* en administración de empresas
me *pron (as object)* me; **he gave it to me** me lo dio; **listen to me** escúchame; **she knows me** me conoce. ▪ *(after prep)* mí; **it's for me** es para mí; **with me** conmigo. ▪ *(emphatic)* yo; **it's me** soy yo; **what about me?** y yo, ¿qué?
mead·ow prado *m*.
meal *(food)* comida *f*.
mean¹* *vt (signify)* querer decir; *(intend)* pensar; *(wish)* querer; **what do you m. by that?** ¿qué quieres decir con eso?; **I m. it** (te) lo digo en serio; **she was meant to arrive on the 7th** tenía que *or* debía llegar el día 7; **they m. well** tienen buenas intenciones; **I didn't m. to do it** lo hice sin querer.
mean² *adj (miserly)* tacaño, -a; *(unkind)* malo, -a; *(bad-tempered)* malhumorado, -a.
mean·ing sentido *m*.
mean·ing·ful *adj* significativo, -a.
mean·ing·less *adj* sin sentido.
mean·ness *(miserliness)* tacañería *f*; *(nastiness)* maldad *f*.
means *sing or pl (method)* medio *m*; *(resources, wealth)* recursos *mpl* (económicos); **by m. of** por medio de, mediante; **by all m.!** ¡por supuesto!; **by no m.** de ninguna manera.
mean·time **in the m.** mientras tanto.
mean·while *adv* mientras tanto.
mea·sles sarampión *m*.
meas·ure 1 *n* medida *f*; *(ruler)* regla *f*. **2** *vt (object, area)* medir.
▸**measure up** *vi* **to m. up to sth** estar a la altura de algo.
meas·ure·ment medida *f*.
meat carne *f*.
me·chan·ic mecánico, -a *mf*.
me·chan·i·cal *adj* mecánico, -a.
mech·a·nism mecanismo *m*.
med·al medalla *f*.
med·al·ist medalla *mf*; **to be a gold m.** ser medalla de oro.
me·di·a *npl* medios *mpl* de comunicación.
med·i·cal *adj (treatment)* médico, -a; *(book)* de medicina.
med·i·ca·tion medicación *f*.
med·i·cine *(science)* medicina *f*; *(drug etc)* medicamento *m*.
med·i·cine cab·i·net botiquín *m*.
me·di·e·val *adj* medieval.
Med·i·ter·ra·ne·an 1 *adj* mediterráneo, -a. **2** *n* **the M.** el Mediterráneo.
me·di·um *adj* mediano, -a.
me·di·um-sized *adj* de tamaño mediano.

meet* 1 *vt (by chance)* encontrar; *(by arrangement)* reunirse con; *(pass in street etc)* toparse con; *(get to know)* conocer; *(await arrival of)* esperar; *(collect)* ir a buscar; **pleased to m. you!** ¡mucho gusto! 2 *vi (by chance)* encontrarse; *(by arrangement)* reunirse; *(formal meeting)* entrevistarse; *(get to know each other)* conocerse.
▸ **meet with** *vt (difficulty)* tropezar con; *(loss)* sufrir; *(success)* tener; *(person)* reunirse con.
meet·ing *(prearranged)* cita *f*; *(formal)* entrevista *f*; *(of committee etc)* reunión *f*; *(of assembly)* sesión *f*.
mel·o·dy melodía *f*.
mel·on melón *m*.
melt 1 *vt (metal)* fundir. 2 *vi (snow)* derretirse; *(metal)* fundirse.
mem·ber miembro *mf*; *(of a society)* socio, -a *mf*; *(of party, union)* afiliado, -a *mf*.
mem·o *(official)* memorándum *m*; *(personal)* apunte *m*.
mem·o·ra·ble *adj* memorable.
me·mo·ri·al 1 *adj (plaque etc)* conmemorativo, -a. 2 *n* monumento conmemorativo.
mem·o·ry memoria *f*; *(recollection)* recuerdo *m*.
men *npl see* **man**.
mend *vt* reparar; *(clothes)* remendar; *(socks etc)* zurcir.
men·tal *adj* mental; **m. home, m. hospital** hospital *m* psiquiátrico; **m. illness** enfermedad *f* mental.
men·tal·ly *adv* **to be m. handicapped** ser un, -a disminuido, -a psíquico, -a.
men·tion 1 *n* mención *f*. 2 *vt* mencionar; **don't m. it!** ¡de nada!
men·u *(à la carte)* carta *f*; *(fixed meal)* menú *m*; **today's m.** menú del día; *(computer)* menú *m*.
mer·cy misericordia *f*; **at the m. of** a la merced de.
mere *adj* mero, -a.
mere·ly *adv* simplemente.
merge *vi* unirse; *(roads)* converger; *(companies)* fusionarse.
merg·er *(of companies)* fusión *f*.
mer·it 1 *n (of person)* mérito *m*; *(of plan etc)* ventaja *f*. 2 *vt* merecer.
mer·ry *adj* alegre; *(tipsy)* achispado, -a; **M. Christmas!** ¡Felices Navidades!
mer·ry-go-round tiovivo *m*.
mesh malla *f*.
mess *(confusion)* confusión *f*; *(disorder)* desorden *m*; *(mix-up)* lío *m*; *(dirt)* suciedad *f*.
▸ **mess about, mess around** 1 *vt* fastidiar. 2 *vi (act the fool)* hacer el tonto.
▸ **mess around with** *vt (fiddle with)* manosear.
▸ **mess up** *vt (make untidy)* desordenar; *(dirty)* ensuciar; *(spoil)* estropear.
mes·sage recado *m*.
mes·sen·ger mensajero, -a *mf*.
mess·y *adj (untidy)* desordenado, -a; *(dirty)* sucio, -a.
met·al 1 *n* metal *m*. 2 *adj* metálico, -a.
met·a·phor metáfora *f*.
me·ter¹ contador *m*.
me·ter² metro *m*.
meth·od método *m*.
me·thod·i·cal *adj* metódico, -a.
met·ric *adj* métrico, -a.
mew maullido *m*.
Mex·i·can *adj & n* mejicano, -a *(mf)*, mexicano, -a *(mf)*.
mice *npl see* **mouse**.
mi·cro·chip microchip *m*.
mi·cro·phone micrófono *m*.
mi·cro·scope microscopio *m*.
mi·cro·wave (ov·en) *(horno m)* microondas *m inv*.
mid *adj* **(in) m. afternoon** a media tarde; **(in) m. April** a mediados de abril.
mid-air *adj (collision, explosion)* en el aire.
mid·day mediodía *m*.
mid·dle 1 *adj* de en medio; **the M. Ages** la Edad Media. 2 *n* medio *m*; *(waist)* cintura *f*; **in the m.** of en medio de; **in the m. of winter** en pleno invierno.
mid·dle-aged *adj* de mediana edad.
mid·dle-class *adj* de clase media.
mid·night medianoche *f*.
midst **in the m. of** en medio de.
mid·way *adv* a medio camino.
mid·wife comadrona *f*.
might *v aux see* **may**.
might·y 1 *adj* **(mightier, mightiest)** *(strong)* fuerte; *(powerful)* poderoso, -a; *(great)* enorme. 2 *adv fam* cantidad de, muy.
mild *adj (person, character)* apacible; *(climate)* templado, -a; *(punishment)* leve; *(tobacco, taste)* suave.
mile milla *f*, *fam* **miles better** muchísimo mejor.
mile·age kilometraje *m*.
mil·i·tar·y *adj* militar.
milk leche *f*.
milk choc·o·late chocolate *m* con leche.
milk·man lechero *m*.
milk shake batido *m*.
mill *(grinder)* molino *m*; *(for coffee)* molinillo *m*; *(factory)* fábrica *f*.
mil·li·me·ter milímetro *m*.
mil·lion millón *m*.
mil·lion·aire millonario, -a *mf*.
mime *vt* imitar.
mim·ic *vt* imitar.
mince(-meat) carne *f* picada.
mincer picadora *f* de carne.
mind 1 *n (intellect)* mente *f*, *(brain)* cabeza *f*; **what kind of car do you have in m.?** ¿en qué clase de coche estás pensando?; **to be in two minds** estar indeciso, -a; **to my m.** a mi parecer. 2 *vt (child)* cuidar; *(house)* vigilar; *(be careful of)* tener cuidado con; *(object to)* tener inconveniente en; **m. the step!** ¡ojo con el escalón!; **I wouldn't m. a cup of coffee** me vendría bien un café; **never m.** no importa. 3 *vi (object)* **do you m. if I open the window?** ¿le importa que abra la ventana?
mine¹ *poss pron* (el) mío, (la) mía, (los) míos, (las) mías; **a friend of m.** un amigo mío; **these gloves are m.** estos guantes son míos; **which is m.?** ¿cuál es el mío?
mine² *(for coal etc)* mina *f*.
min·er minero, -a *mf*.
min·er·al *adj* mineral.
min·er·al wa·ter agua *f* mineral.
min·i- *prefix* mini-.
min·i·a·ture 1 *n* miniatura *f*. 2 *adj* (en) miniatura.
min·i·mum *adj* mínimo, -a.
min·ing 1 *n* minería *f*, explotación *f* de minas. 2 *adj* minero, -a.
min·is·ter ministro, -a *mf*; *(of church)* pastor, -a *mf*.
min·is·try *(political)* ministerio *m*; *(in church)* sacerdocio *m*.
mi·nor *adj (lesser)* menor; *(unimportant)* sin importancia.
mi·nor·i·ty minoría *f*.
mint *(herb)* menta *f*, *(sweet)* pastilla *f* de menta.

mi·nus *prep* **5 m. 3** 5 menos 3; **m. 10 degrees** 10 grados bajo cero.
min·ute¹ minuto *m*; **just a m.** (espera) un momento.
mi·nute² *adj (tiny)* diminuto, -a.
mir·a·cle milagro *m*.
mi·rac·u·lous *adj* milagroso, -a.
mir·ror espejo *m*; **rear-view m.** retrovisor *m*.
mis·be·have *vi* portarse mal.
mis·cel·la·ne·ous *adj* variado, -a.
mis·chief *(naughtiness)* travesura *f*, *(evil)* malicia *f*; **to get up to m.** hacer travesuras.
mis·chie·vous *adj (naughty)* travieso, -a; *(playful)* juguetón, -ona; *(wicked)* malicioso, -a.
mis·de·mean·or delito *m* menor.
mi·ser avaro, -a *mf*.
mis·er·a·ble *adj (sad)* triste; *(wretched)* miserable.
mi·ser·ly *adj* tacaño, -a.
mis·er·y *(sadness)* tristeza *f*, *(wretchedness)* desgracia *f*, *(suffering)* sufrimiento *m*; *(poverty)* miseria *f*.
mis·for·tune desgracia *f*.
mis·hap contratiempo *m*.
mis·lay* *vt* extraviar.
mis·lead* *vt* despistar; *(deliberately)* engañar.
mis·lead·ing *adj (erroneous)* erróneo, -a; *(deliberately)* engañoso, -a.
miss¹ señorita *f*.
miss² 1 *vt (train etc)* perder; *(opportunity)* dejar pasar; *(regret absence of)* echar de menos; **you have missed the point** no has captado la idea. 2 *vi (throw etc)* fallar; *(shot)* errar; **is anything missing?** ¿falta algo?
▸ **miss out** 1 *vt (omit)* saltarse. 2 *vi* **don't worry, you're not missing out** no te preocupes, no te pierdes nada.
▸ **miss out on** *vt* perderse.
mis·sile misil *m*; *(object thrown)* proyectil *m*.
miss·ing *adj (lost)* perdido, -a; *(disappeared)* desaparecido, -a; *(absent)* ausente; **m. person** desaparecido, -a *mf*; **three cups are m.** faltan tres tazas.
mis·sion misión *f*.
mist *(fog)* niebla *f*, *(thin)* neblina *f*, *(at sea)* bruma *f*.
mis·take 1 *n* error *m*; **by m.** por equivocación; *(unintentionally)* sin querer; **to make a m.** cometer un error. 2 *vt (meaning)* malentender; **to m. Jack for Bill** confundir a Jack con Bill.
mis·tak·en *adj* erróneo, -a; **you are m.** estás equivocado, -a.
mis·tak·en·ly *adv* por error.
mis·treat maltratar.
mis·tress *(of house)* ama *f*, *(primary school)* maestra *f*, *(secondary school)* profesora *f*, *(lover)* amante *f*.
mis·trust 1 *n* recelo *m*. 2 *vt* desconfiar de.
mist·y *adj (day)* de niebla; *(window etc)* empañado, -a.
mis·un·der·stand* *vti* malentender.
mis·un·der·stand·ing malentendido *m*; *(disagreement)* desavenencia *f*.
mit·ten manopla *f*.
mix 1 *vt* mezclar. 2 *vi (blend)* mezclarse **(with** con).
▸ **mix up** *vt (ingredients)* mezclar bien; *(confuse)* confundir **(with** con); *(papers)* revolver.
mixed *adj (assorted)* surtido, -a; *(varied)* variado, -a; *(school)* mixto, -a.
mix·er *(for food)* batidora *f*.
mix·ture mezcla *f*.
mix-up confusión *f*.
moan 1 *n* gemido *m*. 2 *vi (groan)* gemir; *(complain)* quejarse **(about** de).
mob 1 *n* multitud *f*. 2 *vt* acosar.
mo·bile *adj* móvil.
mo·bile phone teléfono *m* móvil.
mod·el 1 *n* modelo *mf*, *(scale)* **m.** maqueta *f*. 2 *adj (railway)* en miniatura.
mo·dem módem *m*.
mod·er·ate *adj* moderado, -a; *(reasonable)* razonable; *(average)* regular; *(ability)* mediocre.
mod·er·a·tion moderación *f*.
mod·ern *adj* moderno, -a; **m. languages** lenguas *fpl* modernas.
mod·ern·ize *vt* modernizar.
mod·est *adj* modesto, -a; *(chaste)* púdico, -a; *(price)* módico, -a; *(success)* discreto, -a.
mod·es·ty *(humility)* modestia *f*, *(chastity)* pudor *m*.
mod·i·fi·ca·tion modificación *f*.
mod·i·fy *vt* modificar.
moist *adj* húmedo, -a.
mois·ture humedad *f*.
mold¹ *(fungus)* moho *m*.
mold² 1 *n (shape)* molde *m*. 2 *vt* moldear; *(clay)* modelar.
mold·y *adj* mohoso, -a; **to go m.** enmohecerse.
mole¹ *(beauty spot)* lunar *m*.
mole² *(animal)* topo *m*.
mom *fam* mamá *f*.
mo·ment momento *m*.
Mon·day lunes *m*.
mon·ey dinero *m*.
mon·ey or·der giro *m* postal.
mon·i·tor *(of computer)* monitor *m*.
monk monje *m*.
mon·key mono *m*.
mo·nop·o·lize *vt (attention etc)* acaparar.
mo·not·o·nous *adj* monótono -a.
mo·not·o·ny monotonía *f*.
mon·ster monstruo *m*.
month mes *m*.
month·ly 1 *adj* mensual. 2 *adv* mensualmente.
mon·u·ment monumento *m*.
moo *vi* mugir.
mood humor *m*; **to be in a good/bad m.** estar de buen/mal humor; **to be in the m. for (do-ing) sth** estar de humor para (hacer) algo.
mood·y *adj (changeable)* de humor variable; *(bad-tempered)* malhumorado, -a.
moon luna *f*.
moon·light luz *f* de la luna.
moor *(heath)* páramo *m*.
moose *inv* alce *m*.
mop *(for floor)* fregona *f*.
▸ **mop up** *vt (liquids)* limpiar.
mo·ped ciclomotor *m*.
mor·al 1 *adj* moral. 2 *n* moraleja *f*, **morals** moral *f sing*, moralidad *f sing*.
mo·rale moral *f*.
more 1 *adj* más; **and what is m.** y lo que es más; **is there any m. tea?** ¿queda más té?; **I've no m. money** no me queda más dinero. 2 *pron* más; **how many m.?** ¿cuántos más?; **I need some m.** necesito más; **many/much m.** muchos, -as/mucho más; **m. than a hundred** más de cien. 3 *adv* más; **I won't do it any m.** no lo volveré a hacer; **m. and m. difficult** cada vez más difícil; más

or less más o menos; **she doesn't live here any m.** ya no vive aquí.

more·o·ver *adv* además.

morn·ing mañana *f*, *(before dawn)* madrugada *f*; **in the m.** por la mañana; **on Monday mornings** los lunes por la mañana; **tomorrow m.** mañana por la mañana.

Mo·roc·can *adj & n* marroquí *(mf)*.

mor·tal *adj & n* mortal *(mf)*.

mort·gage hipoteca *f*.

mort·gage com·pa·ny sociedad *f* hipotecaria.

Mos·lem *adj & n* musulmán, -ana *(mf)*.

mosque mezquita *f*.

mos·qui·to *(pl mosquitoes)* mosquito *m*.

moss musgo *m*.

most 1 *adj (greatest in quantity etc)* más; *(the majority of)* la mayor parte de; **this house suffered (the) m. damage** esta casa fue la más afectada; **who made (the) m. mistakes?** ¿quién cometió más errores?; **m. of the time** la mayor parte del tiempo; **m. people** la mayoría de la gente. **2** *pron (greatest part)* la mayor parte; *(greatest number)* lo máximo; *(the majority of people)* la mayoría; **at the (very) m.** como máximo. **3** *adv* más; **the m. intelligent student** el estudiante más inteligente; **what I like m.** lo que más me gusta; **m. of all** sobre todo.

most·ly *adv (chiefly)* en su mayor parte; *(generally)* generalmente; *(usually)* normalmente.

mo·tel motel *m*.

moth mariposa *f* nocturna; **clothes m.** polilla *f*.

moth·er madre *f*; **M.'s Day** Día *m* de la Madre.

moth·er-in-law suegra *f*.

mo·tion 1 *n (movement)* movimiento *m*; *(gesture)* ademán *m*. **2** *vi* **to m. (to) sb to do sth** hacer señas a algn para que haga algo.

mo·ti·vat·ed *adj* motivado, -a.

mo·tive *(reason)* motivo *m*.

mo·tor *(engine)* motor *m*.

mo·tor·boat *(lancha)* motora *f*.

mo·tor·cy·cle motocicleta *f*.

mo·tor·cy·clist motociclista *mf*.

mo·tor·ist automovilista *mf*.

mount 1 *n (horse)* montura *f*, *(for photograph)* marco *m*. **2** *vt (horse)* subirse *or* montar a; *(photograph)* enmarcar. **3** *vi (go up)* subir; *(get on horse, bike)* montar.

▸ **mount up** *vi (increase)* subir; *(accumulate)* acumularse.

moun·tain montaña *f*; **m. bike** bicicleta *f* de montaña.

moun·tain·eer alpinista *mf*, *Am* andinista *mf*.

moun·tain·eer·ing alpinismo *m*, *Am* andinismo *m*.

moun·tain·ous *adj* montañoso, -a.

mourn *vti* **to m. (for) sb** llorar la muerte de algn.

mourn·ing luto *m*; **in m.** de luto.

mouse *(pl mice)* ratón *m*.

mousse *(dessert)* mousse *f*.

mouth *(pl mouths)* boca *f*, *(of river)* desembocadura *f*.

mouth·wash enjuague *m* bucal.

move 1 *n (movement)* movimiento *m*; *(in game)* jugada *f*, *(turn)* turno *m*; *(course of action)* medida *f*, *(to new home)* mudanza *f*. **2** *vt* mover; *(transfer)* trasladar; *(affect emotionally)* conmover; **to m. house** mudarse (de casa); **to m. job** cambiar de trabajo. **3** *vi (change position)* moverse; *(change house)* mudarse (de casa); *(change post)* trasladarse; *(leave)* marcharse; *(in game)* hacer una jugada.

▸ **move about, move around 1** *vt* cambiar de sitio. **2** *vi (be restless)* ir y venir.

▸ **move along 1** *vt (move forward)* hacer avanzar. **2** *vi (move forward)* avanzar.

▸ **move away** *vi (move aside)* apartarse; *(change house)* mudarse (de casa).

▸ **move back 1** *vt (to original place)* volver a. **2** *vi (withdraw)* retirarse; *(to original place)* volver.

▸ **move forward** *vti* avanzar.

▸ **move in** *vi (into new home)* instalarse.

▸ **move on** *vi (go forward)* avanzar; *(time)* transcurrir.

▸ **move out** *vi (leave house)* mudarse.

▸ **move over** *vi* correrse hacia un lado.

▸ **move up** *vi (go up)* subir; *(move along)* correrse hacia un lado, hacer sitio.

move·ment movimiento *m*; *(gesture)* ademán *m*; *(trend)* corriente *f*; *(of goods, capital)* circulación *f*.

mov·ie película *f*.

mov·ing *adj (that moves)* móvil; *(car etc)* en marcha; *(touching)* conmovedor, -a.

mow* *vt (lawn)* cortar.

mow·er cortacésped *m or f*.

Mr *abbr of* mister señor *m*, Sr.

Mrs *abbr* señora *f*, Sra.

MS *abbr of* Master of Science Licenciado, -a *mf* en Ciencias.

much 1 *adj* mucho, -a; **as m. … as** tanto, a … como; **how m. chocolate?** ¿cuánto chocolate?; **so m.** tanto, -a. **2** *adv* mucho; **as m. as** tanto como; **as m. as possible** todo lo posible; **how m.?** ¿cuánto?; **how m. is it?** ¿cuánto es?; **m. better** mucho mejor; **m. more** mucho más; **too m.** demasiado. **3** *pron* mucho; **I thought as m.** lo suponía; **m. of the town was destroyed** gran parte de la ciudad quedó destruida.

Ms *abbr* señora *f*, Sra.

mud barro *m*.

mud·dle 1 *n* desorden *m*; *(mix-up)* embrollo *m*; **to get into a m.** hacerse un lío. **2** *vt* **to m. (up)** confundir.

mud·dy *adj* fangoso, -a; *(hands)* cubierto, -a de barro; *(liquid)* turbio, -a.

mug¹ *(large cup)* tazón *m*; *(beer)* jarra *f*.

mug² *vt (assault)* asaltar.

mug·ger asaltante *mf*.

mule mulo, -a *mf*.

mul·ti·ple 1 *adj* múltiple. **2** *n* múltiplo *m*.

mul·ti·pli·ca·tion multiplicación *f*.

mul·ti·ply *vt* multiplicar **(by** por).

mum·ble 1 *vt* decir entre dientes. **2** *vi* hablar entre dientes.

mum·my *fam* mami *f*.

mumps paperas *fpl*.

mu·nic·i·pal *adj* municipal.

mur·der 1 *n* asesinato *m*. **2** *vt* asesinar.

mur·der·er asesino *m*.

mur·mur 1 *vti* murmurar. **2** *n* murmullo *m*.

mus·cle músculo *m*.

mus·cu·lar *adj (person)* musculoso, -a.

mu·se·um museo *m*.

mush·room seta *f*, *(food)* champiñón *m*.

mu·sic música *f*.

mu·si·cal 1 *adj* musical; **to be m.** estar dotado, -a para la música. **2** *n* musical *m*.

mu·si·cian músico, -a *mf*.

Mus·lim *adj & n* musulmán, -ana *(mf)*.

mus·sel mejillón *m*.

must *v aux (obligation)* deber, tener que; **you m. arrive on time** tienes que *or* debes llegar a la hora. ▪ *(probability)* deber (de); **he m. be ill** debe (de) estar enfermo.

mus·tache bigote *m*.

mus·tard mostaza *f*.

must·y *adj* que huele a cerrado *or* a humedad.

mute 1 *adj* mudo, -a. **2** *n (person)* mudo, -a *mf*; *(for musical instrument)* sordina *f*.

mut·ter *vti* murmurar.

mut·ton *(carne f* de) cordero *m*.

mu·tu·al *adj* mutuo, -a; *(shared)* común.

muz·zle *(for animal)* bozal *m*.

my *poss* mi; **I washed my hair** me lavé el pelo; **my cousins** mis primos; **my father** mi padre; **one of my friends** un amigo mío.

my·self *pers pron (emphatic)* yo mismo, -a; **my husband and m.** mi marido y yo. ▪ *(reflexive)* me; **I hurt m.** me hice daño. ▪ *(after prep)* mí (mismo, -a).

mys·te·ri·ous *adj* misterioso, -a.

mys·ter·y misterio *m*.

myth mito *m*.

N

nail 1 *n (of finger, toe)* uña *f*, *(metal)* clavo *m*. **2** *vt* clavar.

▸ **nail down** *vt* clavar.

nail·file lima *f* de uñas.

nail pol·ish, nail var·nish esmalte *m or* laca *f* de uñas.

na·ïve *adj* ingenuo, -a.

naked *adj* desnudo, -a.

name 1 *n* nombre *m*; *(surname)* apellido *m*; *(reputation)* reputación *f*; **what's your n.?** ¿cómo te llamas? **2** *vt* llamar; *(appoint)* nombrar.

name·ly *adv* a saber.

nan·ny niñera *f*.

nap *(sleep)* siesta *f*; **to have a n.** echar la *or* una siesta.

nap·kin (table) *n.* servilleta *f*.

nap·py pañal *m*.

nar·ra·tive 1 *n (genre)* narrativa *f*, *(story)* narración *f*. **2** *adj* narrativo, -a.

nar·row 1 *adj (passage, road etc)* estrecho, -a. **2** *vi* estrecharse.

▸ **narrow down** *vt* reducir.

narrow·ly *adv (closely)* de cerca; *(by a small margin)* por poco.

nasti·ly *adv (to behave)* antipáticamente.

nas·ty *adj (unpleasant)* desagradable; *(unfriendly)* antipático, -a; *(malicious)* mal intencionado, -a.

na·tion nación *f*.

na·tion·al *adj* nacional.

na·tion·al·i·ty nacionalidad *f*.

na·tive 1 *adj (place)* natal; **n. language** lengua *f* materna. **2** *n* nativo, -a *mf*.

nat·u·ral *adj* natural; *(normal)* normal; *(born)* nato, -a.

nat·u·ral·ly *adv (of course)* naturalmente; *(by nature)* por naturaleza; *(in a relaxed manner)* con naturalidad.

na·ture naturaleza *f*; **n. study** historia *f* natural.

naugh·ty *adj (child)* travieso, -a.

nau·seous *adj* **to feel n.** tener ganas de vomitar.

na·val *adj* naval; **n. officer** oficial *mf* de marina.

na·vel ombligo *m*.

nav·i·gate 1 *vt (river)* navegar por; *(ship)* gobernar. **2** *vi* navegar.

nav·i·ga·tion navegación *f*.

na·vy marina *f*; **n. blue** azul *m* marino.

near 1 *adj (space)* cercano, -a; *(time)* próximo, -a; **in the n. future** en un futuro próximo; **it was a n. thing** poco faltó. **2** *adv (space)* cerca; **that's n. enough** ya vale. **3** *prep* cerca de; **n. the end of the film** hacia el final de la película.

near·by 1 *adj* cercano, -a. **2** *adv* cerca.

near·ly *adv* casi; **very n.** casi, casi; **we haven't n. enough** no alcanza ni con mucho.

neat *adj (room, habits etc)* ordenado, -a; *(appearance)* pulcro, -a.

neat·ly *adv (carefully)* cuidadosamente; *(cleverly)* hábilmente.

nec·es·sar·i·ly *adv* necesariamente.

nec·es·sar·y *adj* necesario, -a; **to do what is n.** hacer lo que haga falta; **if n.** si es preciso.

ne·ces·si·ty necesidad *f*; *(article)* requisito *m* indispensable.

neck cuello *m*; *(of animal)* pescuezo *m*.

neck·lace collar *m*.

nec·tar·ine nectarina *f*.

need 1 *n* necesidad *f*; *(poverty)* indigencia *f*; **if n. be** si fuera necesario; **there's no n. for you to do that** no hace falta que hagas eso. **2** *vt* necesitar; *(require)* requerir; **I n. to see him** tengo que verle. **3** *v aux* tener que, deber; **n. he go?** ¿tiene que ir?; **you needn't wait** no hace falta que esperes.

nee·dle aguja *f*.

need·less·ly *adv* innecesariamente.

nee·dle·work *(sewing)* costura *f*, *(embroidery)* bordado *m*.

neg·a·tive 1 *adj* negativo, -a. **2** *n (in grammar)* negación *f*, *(photo)* negativo *m*.

ne·glect *vt (not look after)* descuidar; **to n. to do sth** *(omit to do)* no hacer algo.

ne·glect·ed *adj (appearance)* desarreglado, -a; *(garden)* descuidado, -a; **to feel n.** sentirse desatendido, -a.

neg·li·gence negligencia *f*.

neg·li·gent *adj* negligente.

ne·go·ti·ate *vti* negociar.

ne·go·ti·a·tion negociación *f*.

neigh *vi* relinchar.

neigh·bor vecino, -a *mf*.

neigh·bor·hood *(district)* vecindad *f*, barrio *m*; *(people)* vecindario *m*.

neigh·bor·ing *adj* vecino, -a.

nei·ther 1 *adj & pron* ninguno de los dos, ninguna de las dos. **2** *adv & conj* ni; **n. … nor** ni … ni; **it's n. here nor there** no viene al caso; **she was not there and n. was her sister** ella no estaba, ni su hermana tampoco.

ne·on neón *m*; **n. light** luz *f* de neón.

neph·ew sobrino *m*.

nerve nervio *m*; *(courage)* valor *m*; *(cheek)* descaro *m*; **to get on sb's nerves** poner los nervios de punta a algn.

nerv·ous *adj (apprehensive)* nervioso, -a; *(afraid)* miedoso, -a; *(timid)* tímido, -a; **to be n.** tener miedo.

nest nido *m*.

net¹ red *f*.

net² *adj* neto, -a.

net·ting *(wire)* alambrada *f*.

net·tle ortiga *f.*
net·work red *f.*
neu·tral 1 *adj* neutro, -a. **2** *n (gear)* punto *m* muerto.
nev·er *adv* nunca, jamás; **he n. complains** no se queja nunca; **n. again** nunca (ja)más.
nev·er-end·ing *adj* interminable.
nev·er·the·less *adv* sin embargo, no obstante.
new *adj* nuevo, -a.
new·born *adj* recién nacido, -a.
new·com·er recién llegado, -a *mf; (to job etc)* nuevo, -a *mf.*
new·ly *adv* recién.
news noticias *fpl;* **a piece of n.** una noticia.
news bul·le·tin boletín *m* informativo.
news·flash noticia *f* de última hora.
news·let·ter hoja *f* informativa.
news·pa·per periódico *m.*
next 1 *adj (in position)* de al lado; *(in time)* próximo, -a; *(in order)* siguiente, próximo, -a; **the n. day** el día siguiente; **n. Friday** el viernes que viene. **2** *adv* después; *(next time)* la próxima vez; **what shall we do n.?** ¿qué hacemos ahora? **3** *prep* **n. to** al lado de.
next-door *adj* de al lado; **our n. neighbor** el vecino *or* la vecina de al lado.
nib plumilla *f.*
nib·ble *vti* mordisquear.
nice *adj (person)* simpático, -a; *(thing)* agradable; *(nice-looking) Esp* bonito, -a, *Am* lindo, -a; **n. and cool** fresquito, -a; **to smell/taste n.** oler/saber bien.
nice·ly *adv* muy bien.
nick·el moneda *f* de cinco centavos.
nick·el-and-dime store = tienda de productos muy baratos.
nick·name apodo *m.*
niece sobrina *f.*
night noche *f;* **at twelve o'clock at n.** a las doce de la noche; **last n.** anoche; **to have a n. out** salir por la noche.
night·club sala *f* de fiestas; *(disco)* discoteca *f.*
night·gown camisón *m.*
night·in·gale ruiseñor *m.*
night·mare pesadilla *f.*
night·stand mesita *f* or mesilla *f* de noche, *RP* mesa *f* de luz, *Méx* buró *m.*
night·time noche *f;* **at n.** por la noche.
night watch·man vigilante *m* nocturno.
nil nada *f; (in sport)* cero *m.*
nine *adj & n* nueve *(m) inv;* **n. hundred** novecientos, -as.
nine·teen *adj & n* diecinueve *(m) inv.*
nine·ty *adj & n* noventa *(m) inv.*
ninth *adj & n* noveno, -a *(mf).*
nip *vt (pinch)* pellizcar; *(bite)* morder.
nip·ple *(female)* pezón *m; (male)* tetilla *f.*
ni·tro·gen nitrógeno *m.*
no 1 *adv* no; **no longer** ya no; **no less than** no menos de. **2** *adj* ninguno, -a; **she has no children** no tiene hijos; **I have no idea** no tengo (ni) idea; **no sensible person** ninguna persona razonable; **'no parking'** 'prohibido aparcar'; **¡no way!** ¡ni hablar!
no·ble *adj* noble.
no·bod·y *pron* nadie; **there was n. there** no había nadie; **n. else** nadie más.
nod 1 *n (in agreement)* señal *m* de asentimiento. **2** *vi (in agreement)* asentir con la cabeza. **3** *vt* **to n. one's head** inclinar la cabeza.
▸ **nod off** *vi* dormirse.
noise ruido *m;* **to make a n.** hacer ruido.
nois·i·ly *adv* ruidosamente.
nois·y *adj* ruidoso, -a.
nom·i·nate *vt (appoint)* nombrar.
nom·i·na·tion *(proposal)* propuesta *f; (appointment)* nombramiento *m.*
non- *prefix* no.
none *pron* ninguno, -a; **n. at all** nada en absoluto.
none·the·less *adv* no obstante, sin embargo.
non·ex·ist·ent *adj* inexistente.
non·fic·tion obras *fpl* de no ficción.
non·sense tonterías *fpl;* **that's n.** eso es absurdo.
non·smok·er no fumador, -a *mf.*
non·stick *adj* antiadherente.
non·stop 1 *adj* continuo, -a; *(train)* directo, -a. **2** *adv* sin parar.
noo·dles *npl* fideos *mpl,* tallarines *mpl.*
noon mediodía *m;* **at n.** a mediodía.
nor *conj* ni, ni … tampoco; **neither … n.** ni … ni; **neither you n.** I ni tú ni yo; **n. do I** (ni) yo tampoco.
norm norma *f.*
nor·mal *adj* normal.
nor·mal·ly *adv* normalmente.
north 1 *n* norte *m.* **2** *adv* hacia el norte. **3** *adj* del norte; **n. wind** viento del norte.
north·bound *adj* (con) dirección norte.
north·east nor(d)este *m.*
north·ern *adj* del norte.
north·ern·er norteño, -a *mf.*
north·ward *adj & adv* hacia el norte.
north·west noroeste *m.*
Nor·we·gian 1 *adj* noruego, -a. **2** *n (person)* noruego, -a *mf; (language)* noruego *m.*
nose nariz *f;* **her n. is bleeding** le está sangrando la nariz.
nose·bleed hemorragia *f* nasal.
nos·tril orificio *m* nasal.
nos·y *adj* entrometido, -a.
not *adv* no; **he's n. in today** hoy no está; **n. at all** en absoluto; **thank you — n. at all** gracias — no hay de qué; **n. one (of them) said thank you** nadie me dio las gracias.
no·ta·ble *adj* notable.
no·ta·bly *adv* notablemente.
note 1 *n (in music, written)* nota *f; (money)* billete *m* (de banco); **to take n. of** *(notice)* prestar atención a; **to take notes** *(at lecture)* tomar apuntes. **2** *vt (write down)* anotar; *(notice)* darse cuenta de.
note·book cuaderno *m.*
note·pad bloc *m* de notas.
note·pa·per papel *m* de carta.
noth·ing 1 *n* nada; **I saw n.** no vi nada; **for n.** *(free)* gratis; **it's n. to do with you** no tiene nada que ver contigo; **n. else** nada más; **n. much** poca cosa. **2** *adv* **she looks n. like her sister** no se parece en nada a su hermana.
no·tice 1 *n (warning)* aviso *m; (attention)* atención *f; (in newspaper etc)* anuncio *m; (sign)* aviso *m;* **he gave a month's n.** presentó la dimisión con un mes de antelación; **at short n.** con poca antelación; **until further n.** hasta nuevo aviso; **to take n. of sth** prestar atención a algo. **2** *vt* darse cuenta de.
no·tice·a·ble *adj* obvio, -a, evidente.

no·ti·fi·ca·tion aviso *m.*
no·ti·fy *vt* avisar.
no·tion idea *f.*
no·to·ri·ous *adj pej* tristemente célebre.
nought cero *m.*
noun sustantivo *m.*
nour·ish·ing *adj* nutritivo, -a.
nov·el¹ novela *f.*
nov·el² *adj* original.
nov·el·ist novelista *mf.*
No·vem·ber noviembre *m.*
now 1 *adv* ahora; *(at present, these days)* actualmente; **just n., right n.** ahora mismo; **from n. on** de ahora en adelante; **n. and then, n. and again** de vez en cuando; **n. (then)** ahora bien; **n., n.!** ¡de eso nada! **2** *conj* **n. (that)** ahora que.
now·a·days *adv* hoy (en) día.
no·where *adv* en ninguna parte; **it's n. near ready** no está preparado, ni mucho menos.
noz·zle boquilla *f.*
nu·clear *adj* nuclear.
nude *adj* desnudo, -a; **in the n.** al desnudo.
nudge 1 *vt* dar un codazo a. **2** *n* codazo *m.*
nui·sance pesadez *f, (person)* pesado, -a *mf;* **what a n.!** ¡qué lata!
numb *adj (without feeling)* entumecido, -a.
num·ber 1 *n* número *m;* **have you got my (phone) n.?** ¿tienes mi (número de) teléfono?; **a n. of people** varias personas. **2** *vt (put a number on)* numerar.
nu·mer·al número *m.*
nu·mer·ous *adj* numeroso, -a.
nun monja *f.*
nurse 1 *n* enfermera *f, (male)* enfermero *m.* **2** *vt (look after)* cuidar.
nurs·er·y guardería *f, (in house)* cuarto *m* de los niños; *(garden center)* vivero *m.*
nurs·er·y rhyme canción *f* infantil.
nurs·er·y school jardín *m* de infancia.
nurs·ing n. home clínica *f.*
nut *(fruit)* fruto *m* seco; *(for bolt)* tuerca *f.*
nut·crack·er cascanueces *m inv.*
nut·shell in a n. en pocas palabras.
ny·lon 1 *n* nailon *m;* **nylons** medias *fpl* de nailon. **2** *adj* de nailon.

O

oak roble *m.*
oar remo *m.*
oats avena *f.*
o·be·di·ence obediencia *f.*
o·be·di·ent *adj* obediente.
o·bey *vt* obedecer; *(law)* cumplir.
ob·ject¹ *(thing)* objeto *m; (aim, purpose)* objetivo *m; (in grammar)* complemento *m.*
ob·ject² *vi* oponerse (to a); **do you o. to my smoking?** ¿le molesta que fume?
ob·jec·tion objeción *f.*
ob·jec·tive objetivo *m.*
ob·li·ga·tion obligación *f.*
o·blige *vt (compel)* obligar; *(do a favor for)* hacer un favor a; **I'm obliged to do it** me veo obligado, -a a hacerlo.
o·blig·ing *adj* solícito, -a.
o·blique *adj* oblicuo, -a, inclinado, -a.
ob·scene *adj* obsceno, -a.
ob·scure 1 *adj* oscuro, -a; *(author, poet)* desconocido, -a. **2** *vt (truth)* ocultar.
ob·ser·vant *adj* observador, -a.
ob·ser·va·tion observación *f, (surveillance)* vigilancia *f.*
ob·serve *vt* observar; *(on surveillance)* vigilar; *(remark)* advertir.
ob·ses·sion obsesión *f.*
ob·sta·cle obstáculo *m.*
ob·sti·nate *adj (person)* obstina-do, -a.
ob·struct *vt* obstruir; *(pipe etc)* atascar; *(view)* tapar; *(hinder)* estorbar; *(progress)* dificultar.
ob·tain *vt* obtener.
ob·vi·ous *adj* obvio, -a, evidente.
ob·vi·ous·ly *adv* evidentemente; **o.!** ¡claro!
oc·ca·sion ocasión *f, (event)* acontecimiento *m.*
oc·ca·sion·al *adj* eventual.
oc·ca·sion·al·ly *adv* de vez en cuando.
oc·cu·pant ocupante *mf, (tenant)* inquilino, -a *mf.*
oc·cu·pa·tion *(job, profession)* profesión *f, (task)* trabajo *m.*
oc·cu·py *vt (live in)* habitar en; **to o. one's time in doing sth** dedicar su tiempo a hacer algo; **to keep oneself occupied** mantenerse ocupado, -a.
oc·cur *vi (event)* suceder; *(change)* producirse; *(be found)* encontrarse; **it occurred to me that** … se me ocurrió que …
oc·cur·rence acontecimiento *m.*
o·cean océano *m.*
o'clock *adv* **(it's) one o'c.** (es) la una; **(it's) two o'c.** (son) las dos.
Oc·to·ber octubre *m.*
oc·to·pus pulpo *m.*
odd 1 *adj (strange)* raro, -a; *(occasional)* esporádico, -a; *(extra)* adicional; *(not even)* impar; *(unpaired)* desparejado, -a; **the o. customer** algún que otro cliente; **o. job** trabajillo *m;* **to be the o. man out** estar de más; **an o. sock** un calcetín suelto. **2** *adv* y pico; **twenty o. people** veinte y pico *or* veintitantas personas.
odd·ly *adv* extrañamente.
odds *npl (chances)* probabilidades *fpl; (in betting)* puntos *mpl* de ventaja; **the o. are that …** lo más probable es que … *(+ subjunctive);* **at o. with sb** reñido, -a con algn; **o. and ends** *(small things)* cositas *fpl.*
o·dor olor *m; (fragrance)* perfume *m.*
of *prep* de; **a friend of mine** un amigo mío; **there are four of us** somos cuatro; **two of them** dos de ellos; **that's very kind of you** es usted muy amable.
off 1 *prep* de; **she fell o. her horse** se cayó del caballo; **a house o. the road** una casa apartada de la carretera; **I'm o. to New York** me voy a Nueva York. **2** *adv (absent)* fuera; **I have a day o.** tengo un día libre; **to be o. sick** estar de baja por enfermedad. ▪ **his arrival is three days o.** faltan tres días para su llegada; **six miles o.** a seis millas. ▪ **I'm o. to New York** me voy a Nueva York; **she ran o.** se fue corriendo. ▪ **ten percent o.** un descuento del diez por ciento. ▪ **with his shoes o.** descalzo. ▪ **on and o.** de vez en cuando. **3** *adj* **to be o.** *(meat, fish)* estar pasado, -a; *(milk)* estar agrio, -a; *(gas etc)* estar apagado, -a; *(water)* estar cortado, -a; *(cancelled)* estar can-

celado, -a; **on the o. chance** por si acaso; **the o. season** la temporada baja; **you're better o. like that** así estás mejor.
of·fend *vt* ofender.
of·fend·er *(criminal)* delincuente *mf*.
of·fense *(in law)* delito *m*; **to take o. at sth** ofenderse por algo.
of·fen·sive 1 *n (military)* ofensiva *f*. **2** *adj (insulting)* ofensivo, -a; *(repulsive)* repugnante.
of·fer 1 *vt* ofrecer; *(propose)* proponer; *(provide)* proporcionar; **to o. to do a job** ofrecerse para hacer un trabajo. **2** *n* oferta *f*; *(proposal)* propuesta *f*; **on o.** de oferta.
of·fer·ing ofrecimiento *m*; *(in religious ceremony)* ofrenda *f*.
off·hand 1 *adj (abrupt)* brusco, -a. **2** *adv* de improviso.
of·fice *(room)* despacho *m*; *(building)* oficina *f*; *(position)* cargo *m*.
of·fi·cer oficial *mf*; **(police) o.** agente *mf* de policía.
of·fi·cial 1 *adj* oficial. **2** *n* funcionario, -a *mf*.
of·fi·cial·ly *adv* oficialmente.
off-line *adj (computer, user)* desconectado, -a.
off·spring *inv (child)* vástago *m*; *(children)* progenitura *f*.
of·ten *adv* a menudo; **every so o.** de vez en cuando.
oh *interj* ¡oh!
oil 1 *n* aceite *m*; *(crude)* petróleo *m*. **2** *vt* engrasar.
oil·can aceitera *f*.
oil change cambio *m* de aceite.
oint·ment pomada *f*.
OK, o·kay 1 *interj* ¡vale! **2** *adj* bien; **is it OK if ...?** ¿está bien si ...?
old *adj* viejo, -a; *(previous)* antiguo, -a; **an o. man** un anciano; **o. age** vejez *f*; **how o. are you?** ¿cuántos años tienes?; **she's five years o.** tiene cinco años.
old-fash·ioned *adj (outdated)* a la antigua; *(unfashionable)* anticua- do, -a.
ol·ive *(tree)* olivo *m*; *(fruit)* aceituna *f*, oliva *f*.
O·lym·pic *adj* olímpico, -a; **O. Games** Juegos *mpl* Olímpicos.
om·e·let tortilla *f*; **Spanish o.** tortilla española *or* de patatas.
o·mis·sion omisión *f*.
o·mit *vt* omitir; *(accidentally)* pasar por alto; *(forget)* olvidarse (**to** de).
on 1 *prep (position)* sobre, encima de, en; **it's on the table** está encima de *or* sobre la mesa; **on page four** en la página cuatro; **a town on the coast** un pueblo en la costa; **on the right** a la derecha; **on the way** en el camino. ▪ *(time)* **on April 3rd** el tres de abril; **on a sunny day** un día de sol; **on Monday** el lunes; **on the following day** al día siguiente; **on his arrival** a su llegada; **on time** a tiempo. ▪ *(means)* **on the radio** en la radio; **to play sth on the piano** tocar algo al piano; **on TV** en la tele; **on the phone** al teléfono; **on foot** a pie; **on the train/plane** en tren/avión. ▪ *(about)* sobre; **a lecture on numismatics** una conferencia sobre numismática. **2** *adj* **to be on** *(TV, radio, light)* estar encendido, -a; *(engine)* estar en marcha; *(tablecloth)* estar puesto; **she had a coat on** llevaba un abrigo puesto; **that film was on last week** pusieron esa película la semana pasada. **3** *adv* **have you anything on tonight?** ¿tienes algún plan para esta noche?; **he talks on and on** habla sin parar; **to work on** seguir trabajando.
once 1 *adv (one time)* una vez; *(formerly)* en otro tiempo; **o. a week** una vez por semana; **o. in a while** de vez en cuando; **o. more** una vez más; **at o.** en seguida; **don't speak all at o.** no habléis todos a la vez. **2** *conj* una vez que.
one 1 *adj* un, una; **he'll come back o. day** un día volverá. **2** *dem pron* **any o.** cualquiera; **that o.** ése, ésa; *(distant)* aquél, aquélla; **the blue ones** los azules, las azules; **the o. on the table** el *or* la que está encima de la mesa; **the ones that, the ones who** los *or* las que; **this o.** éste, ésta. **3** *indef pron* uno, -a *mf*; **give me o.** dame uno; **o. by o.** uno tras otro; **o. never knows** nunca se sabe; **to cut o.'s finger** cortarse el dedo; **o. another** el uno al otro; **they love o. another** se quieren. **4** *n (digit)* uno *m*; **a hundred and o.** ciento uno.
one·self *pron* uno, -a mismo, -a *mf*; *(reflexive)* sí mismo, -a *mf*; **to talk to o.** hablar para sí; **by o.** solo, -a.
one-way *adj (ticket)* de ida; *(street)* de dirección única.
on·ion cebolla *f*.
on-line *adj (computer, user)* conectado, -a.
on·look·er espectador, -a *mf*.
on·ly 1 *adv* solamente, sólo; **he has o. just left** acaba de marcharse hace un momento; **o. yesterday** ayer mismo. **2** *adj* único, -a. **3** *conj* pero.
on·to *prep see* **on**.
on·ward(s) *adv* en adelante; **from this time o.** de ahora en adelante.
o·paque *adj* opaco, -a.
o·pen 1 *adj* abierto, -a; **wide o.** abierto de par en par; **in the o. air** al aire libre; **o. ticket** billete *m* abierto. **2** *vt* abrir; *(exhibition etc)* inaugurar; *(negotiations, conversation)* entablar. **3** *vi* abrirse. **4** *n* **in the o.** al aire libre; *fig* **to bring into the o.** hacer público.
▸**open out 1** *vt* desplegar. **2** *vi (flowers)* abrirse; *(view)* extenderse.
▸**open up 1** *vt (market etc)* abrir; *(possibilities)* crear. **2** *vi* abrirse.
o·pen·ing *(act)* apertura *f*; *(beginning)* comienzo *m*; *(aperture)* abertura *f*; *(gap)* brecha *f*; *(in market)* oportunidad *f*.
o·pen·ly *adv* abiertamente.
o·pen-mind·ed *adj* sin prejuicios.
o·pen·ness *(frankness)* franqueza *f*.
op·er·a ópera *f*.
op·er·ate 1 *vi (function)* funcionar; *(act)* actuar; *(surgeon)* operar. **2** *vt (switch on)* accionar; *(control)* manejar; *(business)* dirigir.
op·er·at·ing sys·tem sistema *m* operativo.
op·er·a·tion *(of machine)* funcionamiento *m*; *(surgical)* operación *f*.
op·er·a·tor *(of machine)* operario, -a *mf*; *(telephone)* operador, -a *mf*.
o·pin·ion opinión *f*; **in my o.** en mi opinión.
op·po·nent adversario, -a *mf*.
op·por·tu·ni·ty oportunidad *f*; *(prospect)* perspectiva *f*.
op·pose *vt* oponerse a.
op·posed *adj* opuesto, -a; **to be o. to sth** estar en contra de algo.
op·pos·ing *adj* adversario, -a.
op·po·site 1 *adj (facing)* de enfrente; *(page)* contiguo, -a; *(contrary)* contrario, -a; **in the o. direction** en dirección contraria. **2** *n* lo contrario *m*; **quite the o.!** ¡al contrario! **3** *prep* enfrente de. **4** *adv* enfrente.
op·po·si·tion oposición *f*, **in o.** to en contra de.
opt *vi* **to o. for** optar por; **to o. to do sth** optar por hacer algo.
op·ti·cal *adj* óptico, -a.
op·ti·cian óptico, -a *mf*.
op·ti·mist optimista *mf*.
op·ti·mis·tic *adj* optimista.
op·tion opción *f*; **I have no o.** no tengo más remedio.
op·tion·al *adj* optativo, -a.
or *conj* o; *(before a word beginning with a stressed* o *or* ho*)* u; *(with negative)* ni; **he can't read or write** no sabe leer ni escribir.
o·ral 1 *adj* oral. **2** *n* examen *m* oral.
or·ange 1 *n* naranja *f*. **2** *adj* de color naranja.
or·ange juice zumo *m* de naranja.
or·bit órbita *f*.
or·chard huerto *m*.
or·ches·tra orquesta *f*.
or·deal mala experiencia *f*.
or·der 1 *n (sequence, command)* orden *m*; *(commission)* pedido *m*; **to put in o.** ordenar; **is your passport in o.?** ¿tienes el pasaporte en regla?; **'out of o.'** 'averiado'; **to be on o.** estar pedido; **in o. that** para que *(+ subjunctive)*, a fin de que *(+ subjunctive)*; **in o. to** para *(+ infinitive)*, a fin de *(+ infinitive)*. **2** *vt (command)* ordenar; *(goods)* encargar; **to o. sb to do sth** mandar a algn hacer algo; **to o. a dish** pedir un plato.
or·di·nance *(decree)* ordenanza *f*, decreto *m*.
or·di·nar·y 1 *adj* normal; *(average)* corriente. **2** *n* **out of the o.** fuera de lo común.
ore mineral *m*.
or·gan órgano *m*.
or·gan·ic *adj* orgánico, -a.
or·gan·i·za·tion organización *f*.
or·gan·ize *vt* organizar.
or·gan·iz·er organizador, -a *mf*.
O·ri·en·tal *adj & n* oriental *(mf)*.
or·i·gin origen *m*.
o·rig·i·nal 1 *adj* original; *(first)* primero, -a; *(novel)* original. **2** *n* original *m*.
o·rig·i·nal·i·ty originalidad *f*.
o·rig·i·nal·ly *adv (at first)* en un principio.
o·rig·i·nate 1 *vt* originar. **2** *vi* **to o. from** *or* **in** tener su origen en.
or·na·ment adorno *m*.
or·phan huérfano, -a *mf*.
or·phan·age orfanato *m*.
or·tho·dox *adj* ortodoxo, -a.
os·trich avestruz *f*.
oth·er 1 *adj* otro, -a; **the o. one** el otro, la otra. **2** *pron* otro, -a *mf*; **many others** otros muchos; **the others** los otros, los demás; **we see each o. quite often** nos vemos con bastante frecuencia.
oth·er·wise *adv (if not)* si no; *(differently)* de otra manera; *(in other respects)* por lo demás.
ought *v aux* deber; **I thought I o. to tell you** creí que debía decírtelo; **she o. to do it** debería hacerlo; **you o. to see the exhibition** deberías ver la exposición. ▪ *(expectation)* **he o. to pass the exam** seguramente aprobará el examen; **that o. to do** con eso bastará.
ounce onza *f*.
our *poss adj* nuestro, -a.
ours *poss pron* (el) nuestro, (la) nuestra, (los) nuestros, (las) nuestras; **a friend of o.** un amigo nuestro.
our·selves *pers pron pl (reflexive)* nos; *(emphatic)* nosotros mismos, nosotras mismas; **by o.** a solas.
out 1 *adv (outside, away)* fuera; **o. there** ahí fuera; **to go o.** salir. **2** *prep* **o. of** *(place)* fuera de; *(cause, motive)* por; *(made from)* de; *(short of, without)* sin; **move o. of the way!** ¡quítate de en medio!; **he jumped o. the window** saltó por la ventana; **o. of danger** fuera de peligro; **forty o. of fifty** cuarenta de cada cincuenta. **3** *adj* **to be o.** *(unfashionable)* estar pasado, -a de moda; *(not lit)* estar apagado, -a; *(eliminated from game)* quedar eliminado, -a; **the sun is o.** ha salido el sol; **she's o.** *(not in)* ha salido.
out·break *(of war)* comienzo *m*; *(of disease)* brote *m*; *(of violence)* ola *f*.
out·burst *(of anger)* arrebato *m*.
out·come resultado *m*.
out·dat·ed *adj* anticuado, -a.
out·do* *vt* exceder; **to o. sb** superar a algn.
out·door *adj* al aire libre; *(clothes)* de calle.
out·doors *adv* al aire libre.
out·er *adj* exterior.
out·er space espacio *m* sideral.
out·fit *(kit, equipment)* equipo *m*; *(set of clothes)* conjunto *m*.
out·grow* *vt* **he's outgrowing all his clothes** toda la ropa se le está quedando pequeña; **he'll o. it** se le pasará con la edad.
out·ing excursión *f*.
out·law 1 *n* proscrito, -a *mf*. **2** *vt* prohibir.
out·let *(for goods)* mercado *m*.
out·line *(draft)* bosquejo *m*; *(outer line)* contorno *m*; *(silhouette)* perfil *m*; *(sketch)* boceto *m*.
out·look *(point of view)* punto *m* de vista; *(prospect)* perspectiva *f*.
out·num·ber *vt* exceder en número.
out-of-doors *adv* al aire libre.
out·put producción *f*; *(of machine)* rendimiento *m*.
out·rage 1 *n* ultraje *m*; **it's an o.!** ¡es un escándalo! **2** *vt* **to be outraged by sth** indignarse por algo.
out·ra·geous *adj (behavior)* escandaloso, -a; *(clothes)* extravagante.
out·right *adv (completely)* por completo; *(directly)* directamente.
out·set comienzo *m*, principio *m*.
out·side 1 *prep* fuera de; *(beyond)* más allá de; *(other than)* aparte de. **2** *adj (exterior)* exterior, externo, -a. **3** *adv* (a)fuera. **4** *n* exterior *m*; **on the o.** por fuera.
out·sid·er *(stranger)* extraño, -a *mf*; *(in election)* candidato, -a *mf* con pocas posibilidades de ganar.
out·skirts *npl* afueras *fpl*.
out·stand·ing *adj (exceptional)* destacado, -a; *(unpaid, unresolved)* pendiente.
out·ward *adj (appearance)* externo, -a; **the o. journey** el viaje de ida.
out·ward(s) *adv* hacia (a)fuera.
o·val 1 *adj* ovalado, -a. **2** *n* óvalo *m*.
ov·en horno *m*.
o·ver 1 *prep (above)* encima de; *(across)* al otro lado de; *(during)* durante; *(more than)* más de; **the bridge o. the river** el puente que cruza el río; **all o. Spain** por toda España; **it's all o. the carpet** está por toda la alfombra; **o. the phone** por teléfono; **men o. twenty-five** hombres mayores de veinticinco años. **2** *adv (more)* más; *(again)* otra vez; *(in excess)* de más; **o. there** allá; **all o.** por todas partes; **o. and o. (again)** una y otra vez; **there are still some o.** todavía quedan algunos. **3** *adj (finished)* acabado, -a; **it's (all) o.** se acabó; **the danger is o.** ha pasado el peligro.
o·ver·all 1 *adj* total. **2** *adv (on the whole)* en conjunto. **3** *n* guardapolvo *m*; **overalls** mono *m* sing.
o·ver·board *adv* por la borda.
o·ver·charge *vt (charge too much)* cobrar de más.
o·ver·coat abrigo *m*.
o·ver·come* *vt (conquer)* vencer; *(overwhelm)* abrumar; *(surmount)* superar.
o·ver·do* *vt (carry too far)* exagerar; *(in cooking)* cocer *or* asar demasiado.
o·ver·draft crédito *m* al descubierto.
o·ver·due *adj (rent, train etc)* atrasado, -a.
o·ver·eat *vi* comer en exceso.
o·ver·ex·cit·ed *adj* sobreexcitado, -a.
o·ver·flow *vi (river)* desbordarse; *(cup etc)* derramarse.
o·ver·head *adj* (por) encima de la cabeza.
o·ver·hear *vt* oír por casualidad.
o·ver·heat *vi* recalentarse.
o·ver·joyed *adj* rebosante de alegría.
o·ver·lap *vi* superponerse.
ov·er·leaf *adv* al dorso.
o·ver·load *vt* sobrecargar.

o·ver·look *vt (fail to notice)* pasar por alto; *(ignore)* no hacer caso de; *(have a view of)* tener vista a.

o·ver·night 1 *adv* por la noche; **we stayed there o.** pasamos la noche allí. **2** *adj (journey)* de noche.

o·ver·pass *(bridge)* paso *m* elevado.

o·ver·rat·ed *adj* sobrestimado, -a.

o·ver·seas 1 *adv* en ultramar; **to live o.** vivir en el extranjero. **2** *adj* de ultramar; *(visitor)* extranjero, -a; *(trade)* exterior.

o·ver·sight descuido *m*.

o·ver·sleep *vi* quedarse dormido, -a.

o·ver·spend *vi* gastar demasiado.

o·ver·take* *vt* adelantar.

o·ver·time horas *fpl* extra.

o·ver·turn *vti* volcar.

o·ver·weight *adj* **to be o.** ser gordo, -a.

o·ver·whelm *vt (defeat)* aplastar; *(overpower)* abrumar.

o·ver·whelm·ing *adj (defeat)* aplastante; *(desire)* irresistible.

o·ver·work *vi* trabajar demasiado.

owe *vt* deber.

ow·ing *adj* o. to debido a.

owl búho *m*.

own 1 *adj* propio, -a; **it's his o. fault** es culpa suya. **2** *pron* **my o., your o., his o.** *etc* lo mío, lo tuyo, lo suyo *etc*; **to get one's o. back** tomarse la revancha; **on one's o.** *(without help)* uno, -a mismo, -a; *(alone)* solo, -a. **3** *vt* poseer.

▸**own up** *vi* to o. up (to) confesar.

own·er propietario, -a *mf*.

ox·y·gen oxígeno *m*.

oys·ter ostra *f*.

o·zone ozono *m*; **o. layer** capa *f* de ozono.

P

pace *(step)* paso *m*; *(speed)* ritmo *m*.

Pa·cif·ic the P. (Ocean) el (océano) Pacífico.

pac·i·fi·er *(of baby)* chupete *m*.

pack 1 *n* paquete *m*; *(rucksack)* mochila *f*; *(of cards)* baraja *f*; *(of hounds)* jauría *f*. **2** *vt (goods)* embalar; *(in suitcase)* poner; *(fill)* atestar; *(press down) (snow)* apretar; **to p. one's bags** hacer las maletas; *fig* marcharse. **3** *vi (baggage)* hacer las maletas.

▸**pack away** *vt (tidy away)* guardar.

▸**pack up** *fam* **1** *vt (give up)* dejar. **2** *vi (stop working)* terminar; *(machine etc)* estropearse.

pack·age *(parcel, software)* paquete *m*.

pack·age tour viaje *m* todo incluido.

pack·ag·ing embalaje *m*.

packed *adj (place)* atestado, -a.

packed lunch almuerzo *m* (para tomar fuera).

pack·et paquete *m*.

pack·ing embalaje *m*.

pact pacto *m*.

pad 1 *n* almohadilla *f*; *(of paper)* bloc *m*. **2** *vt (chair)* rellenar.

pad·ded *adj (cell)* acolchado, -a.

pad·dle¹ *(oar)* pala *f*.

pad·dle² *vi* chapotear.

pad·lock candado *m*.

page¹ página *f*.

page² *(at club etc)* botones *m inv*.

pain dolor *m*; *(grief)* sufrimiento *m*; **to take pains over sth** esmerarse en algo.

pain·ful *adj* doloroso, -a.

pain·kill·er analgésico *m*.

paint 1 *n* pintura *f*. **2** *vt* pintar; **to p. sth white** pintar algo de blanco.

paint·brush pincel *m*; *(for walls)* brocha *f*.

paint·er pintor, -a *mf*.

paint·ing cuadro *m*; *(activity)* pintura *f*.

paint strip·per quitapinturas *m inv*.

pair *(of gloves, shoes)* par *m*; *(of people, cards)* pareja *f*.

pa·ja·mas *npl* pijama *m*.

Pak·i·stan·i *adj & n* paquistaní *(mf)*.

pal *fam* amigo, -a *mf*.

pal·ace palacio *m*.

pal·ate paladar *m*.

pale *adj (skin)* pálido, -a; *(color)* claro, -a.

Pal·es·tin·i·an *adj & n* palestino, -a *(mf)*.

pal·ette paleta *f*.

palm *(of hand)* palma *f*; *(tree)* palmera *f*; **p. leaf** palma *f*.

pam·phlet folleto *m*.

pan *(saucepan)* cazuela *f*.

pan·cake crepe *f*.

pane cristal *m*, vidrio *m*.

pan·el *(of wall)* panel *m*; *(of instruments)* tablero *m*; *(jury)* jurado *m*.

pan·ic 1 *n* pánico *m*; **to get into a p.** ponerse histérico, -a. **2** *vi* **he panicked** le entró pánico.

pant *vi* jadear.

pant·ies *npl* bragas *fpl*.

pan·to·mime *(play)* función *f* musical navideña.

pan·try despensa *f*.

pants *npl (underpants) (ladies')* bragas *fpl*; *(men's)* calzoncillos *mpl*; *(trousers)* pantalón *m*.

pant·y·hose panties *mpl*.

pa·per papel *m*; *(newspaper)* periódico *m*; *(exam)* examen *m*; *(essay)* trabajo *m* (escrito).

pa·per·back libro *m* en rústica.

pa·per·clip clip *m*.

pa·per knife cortapapeles *m inv*.

pap·er·work papeleo *m*.

par *(parity)* igualdad *f*; *(in golf)* par *m*.

par·a·chute paracaídas *m inv*.

pa·rade desfile *m*.

par·a·dise paraíso *m*.

par·af·fin parafina *f*.

par·a·graph párrafo *m*.

Par·a·guay·an *adj & n* paraguayo, -a *(mf)*.

par·a·le·gal ayudante *mf* de un abogado, *RP* procurador, -a *mf*

par·al·lel *adj* paralelo, -a (**to, with** a).

par·a·lyze *vt* paralizar.

par·a·site parásito *m*.

par·a·sol sombrilla *f*.

par·cel paquete *m*.

par·don 1 *n* perdón *m*; **I beg your p.** (Vd.) perdone; **(I beg your) p.?** ¿cómo (dice)? **2** *vt* perdonar; **p. me!** ¡Vd. perdone!

par·ents *npl* padres *mpl*.

par·ish parroquia *f*.

park 1 *n* parque *m*. **2** *vt (car)* estacionar, *Esp* aparcar.

park·ing aparcamiento *m*; **'no p.'** 'prohibido aparcar'.

park·ing light luz *f* de estacionamiento.

park·ing lot aparcamiento *m*.

park·ing me·ter parquímetro *m*.

park·ing space aparcamiento *m*.

park·ing tick·et multa *f* de aparcamiento.

par·lia·ment parlamento *m*.

par·rot loro *m*.

pars·ley perejil *m*.

pars·nip chirivía *f*.

part 1 *n* parte *f*; *(piece)* trozo *m*; *(of machine, engine)* pieza *f*; *(in play etc)* papel *m*; **for the most p.** en la mayor parte; **to take p. in sth** participar en algo; **in these parts** por estos lugares. **2** *(partly)* en parte. **3** *vi* separarse; *(say goodbye)* despedirse.

▸**part with** *vt* separarse de.

par·tial *adj* parcial; **to be p. to sth** ser aficionado, -a a algo.

par·tic·i·pant participante *mf*.

par·tic·i·pate *vi* participar (**in** en).

par·tic·i·pa·tion participación *f*.

par·ti·ci·ple participio *m*.

par·ti·cle board madera *f* aglomerada.

par·tic·u·lar 1 *adj (special)* particular; *(fussy)* exigente; **in this p. case** en este caso concreto. **2** *npl* **particulars** pormenores *mpl*; **to take down sb's particulars** tomar nota de los datos personales de algn.

par·tic·u·lar·ly *adv* particularmente.

part·ing *(in hair)* raya *f*.

par·ti·tion *(wall)* tabique *m*.

part·ly *adv* en parte.

part·ner compañero, -a *mf*; *(in dancing, tennis)* pareja *f*; *(in business)* socio, -a *mf*.

part·ner·ship *(in business)* sociedad *f*.

par·tridge perdiz *f*.

part-time 1 *adj (work etc)* de media jornada. **2** *adv* a tiempo parcial.

par·ty *(celebration)* fiesta *f*; *(group)* grupo *m*; *(political)* partido *m*.

pass 1 *n (of mountain)* desfiladero *m*; *(permit)* permiso *m*; *(in football etc)* pase *m*. **2** *vt* pasar; *(overtake)* adelantar; *(exam, law)* aprobar. **3** *vi* pasar; *(car)* adelantar; *(people)* cruzarse; *(in football etc)* hacer un pase; *(in exam)* aprobar; **we passed on the stairs** nos cruzamos en la escalera.

▸**pass away** *vi* pasar a mejor vida.

▸**pass by 1** *vt* pasar de largo. **2** *vi* pasar cerca; **if you're ever passing by** si alguna vez pasas por aquí.

▸**pass off 1** *vt* **to p. oneself off as sth** hacerse pasar por algo. **2** *vi (happen)* transcurrir.

▸**pass on** *vt (hand on)* transmitir. **2** *vi (die)* pasar a mejor vida.

▸**pass out** *vi (faint)* desmayarse.

▸**pass over** *vt (disregard)* pasar por alto.

▸**pass through** *vi* estar de paso.

▸**pass up** *vt (opportunity)* renunciar a; *(offer)* rechazar.

pass·a·ble *adj (road)* transitable; *(acceptable)* pasable.

pas·sage *(hallway)* pasillo *m*; *(in music, text)* pasaje *m*.

pas·sage·way *(interior)* pasillo *m*; *(exterior)* pasaje *m*.

pas·sen·ger pasajero, -a *mf*.

pas·ser-by transeúnte *mf*.

pass·ing 1 *n (of time)* transcurso *m*; **in p.** de pasada. **2** *adj* que pasa; **p. grade** *(in exam)* aprobado *m*.

pas·sion pasión *f*.

pas·sion·ate *adj* apasionado, -a.

pas·sive *adj* pasivo, -a.

pass·port pasaporte *m*.

pass·word contraseña *f*.

past 1 *n* pasado *m*; **in the p.** antiguamente. **2** *adj* pasado, -a; *(former)* anterior; **in the p. weeks** en las últimas semanas. **3** *adv* por delante; **to run p.** pasar corriendo. **4** *prep (beyond)* más allá de; *(more than)* más de; **it's five p. ten** son las diez y cinco.

pas·ta pasta *f*.

paste 1 *n* pasta *f*; *(glue)* engrudo *m*. **2** *vt (stick)* pegar.

pas·teur·ized *adj* pasteurizado, -a.

pas·time pasatiempo *m*.

pas·try *(dough)* pasta *f*; *(cake)* pastel *m*.

pas·ture pasto *m*.

pat *vt* acariciar.

patch *(of material)* parche *m*; *(of color)* mancha *f*; **to go through a bad p.** pasar por una mala racha.

▸**patch up** *vt (garment)* poner un parche en; **to p. up a quarrel** hacer las paces (**with** con).

pat·ent 1 *n (for product)* patente *f*. **2** *adj (obvious)* patente, evidente. **3** *vt (product)* patentar.

path sendero *m*; *(route)* camino *m*.

pa·thet·ic *adj* patético, -a; *(hopeless)* malísimo, -a.

path·way sendero *m*.

pa·tience paciencia *f*; **to lose one's p. with sb** perder la paciencia con algn.

pa·tient 1 *adj* paciente. **2** *n* paciente *mf*.

pa·tient·ly *adv* con paciencia.

pat·i·o patio *m*.

pa·tri·ot·ic *adj (person)* patriota; *(speech, act)* patriótico, -a.

pa·trol 1 *n* patrulla *f*. **2** *vt* patrullar por.

pa·tron *(of charity)* patrocinador, -a *mf*; *(of arts)* mecenas *m inv*; *(customer)* cliente, -a *mf* habitual; **p. saint** *(santo, -a mf)* patrón, -ona *mf*.

pat·tern *(in sewing)* patrón *m*; *(design)* dibujo *m*.

pause 1 *n* pausa *f*; *(in conversation)* silencio *m*. **2** *vi* hacer una pausa.

pave *vt* pavimentar; *(with stones)* empedrar; **to p. the way for sb/sth** preparar el terreno para algn/algo.

paved *adj* pavimentado, -a.

pave·ment acera *f*; *(road surface)* calzada *f*.

pa·vil·ion pabellón *m*.

pav·ing stone losa *f*.

paw *(foot)* pata *f*; *(of cat)* garra *f*.

pawn *(in chess)* peón *m*.

pay 1 *n (wages)* paga *f*. **2** *vt** pagar; *(attention)* prestar; *(visit)* hacer; *(be profitable for)* compen-

sar; **to be** *or* **get paid** cobrar; **to p. sb a compliment** halagar a algn. **3** *vi** pagar; *(be profitable)* ser rentable; **to p. for sth** pagar (por) algo.
▸ **pay back** *vt* reembolsar.
▸ **pay in** *vt (money)* ingresar.
▸ **pay off** *vt (debt)* liquidar.
▸ **pay out** *vt (spend)* gastar (**on** en).
▸ **pay up 1** *vt (bill)* liquidar, saldar. **2** *vi* pagar.
pay·a·ble *adj* pagadero, -a.
pay·check sueldo *m*.
pay·ment pago *m*.
pay·phone teléfono *m* público.
pay slip nómina *f*.
pea guisante *m*.
peace paz *f*; *(calm)* tranquilidad *f*; **at** *or* **in p.** en paz; **p. and quiet** tranquilidad.
peace·ful *adj (non-violent)* pacífico, -a; *(calm)* tranquilo, -a.
peach melocotón *m*.
pea·cock pavo *m* real.
peak *(of mountain)* pico *m*; *(summit)* cima *f*; **p. hours** horas *fpl* punta.
peaky *adj fam (ill)* pálido, -a.
pea·nut cacahuete *m*.
pear pera *f*.
pearl perla *f*.
peb·ble guijarro *m*; *(small)* china *f*.
pe·can *(nut)* pacana *f*.
peck *vt (bird)* picotear.
peck·ish *adj* **to feel p.** empezar a tener hambre.
pe·cu·liar *adj (odd)* extraño, -a; *(particular)* característico, -a.
pe·cu·li·ar·i·ty *(characteristic)* característica *f*.
ped·al 1 *n* pedal *m*. **2** *vi* pedalear.
pe·des·tri·an peatón, -ona *mf*.
pe·des·tri·an cross·ing paso *m* de peatones.
peek 1 *n* ojeada *f*. **2** *vi* **to p. at sth** mirar algo a hurtadillas.
peel 1 *n* piel *f*; *(of orange, lemon)* cáscara *f*. **2** *vt (fruit)* pelar. **3** *vi (paint)* desconcharse; *(skin)* pelarse.
▸ **peel off** *vt (skin of fruit)* pelar; *(clothes)* quitarse.
peel·er potato p. pelapatatas *m inv*.
peep 1 *n (glance)* ojeada *f*; *(furtive look)* mirada *f* furtiva. **2** *vi* **to p. at sth** echar una ojeada a algo.
peer *vi* mirar detenidamente.
peg clavija *f*; *(for coat, hat)* colgador *m*.
pen¹ pluma *f*.
pen² *(for animals)* corral *m*.
pen·al·ty *(punishment)* pena *f*; *(in sport)* castigo *m*; *(in soccer)* penalti *m*.
pen·cil lápiz *m*.
pen·cil case estuche *m* de lápices.
pen·cil sharp·en·er sacapuntas *m inv*.
pen·du·lum péndulo *m*.
pen·e·trate *vt (break through, grasp)* penetrar; *(forest, territory)* adentrarse en.
pen·guin pingüino *m*.
pen·i·cil·lin penicilina *f*.
pen·in·su·la península *f*.
pen·knife navaja *f*.
pen·ni·less *adj* sin dinero.
pen·ny *(pl* **pennies***)* centavo *m*.
pen pal amigo, -a *mf* por carta.
pen·sion pensión *f*; **retirement p.** jubilación *f*.
pen·sion·er jubilado, -a *mf*.
peo·ple *npl* gente *f sing*; *(individuals)* personas *fpl*; *(nation)* pueblo *m sing*; **old p.'s home** asilo *m* de ancianos; **p. say that ...** se dice que ....
pep·per *(spice)* pimienta *f*; *(fruit)* pimiento *m*.
pep·per·mint hierbabuena *f*; *(sweet)* pastilla *f* de menta.
per *prep* por; **5 times p. week** 5 veces a la semana; **p. day/annum** al *or* por día/año; **p. capita** *or* **person** per cápita.
per·ceive *vt* percibir.
percent *adv* por ciento.
per·cent·age porcentaje *m*.
perch 1 *n (for bird)* percha *f*. **2** *vi (bird)* posarse (**on** en).
per·co·la·tor cafetera *f* de filtro.
per·fect 1 *adj* perfecto, -a; **p. tense** tiempo *m* perfecto. **2** *vt* perfeccionar.
per·fec·tion perfección *f*.
per·fect·ly *adv* perfectamente; *(absolutely)* completamente.
per·form 1 *vt (task)* realizar; *(piece of music)* interpretar; *(play)* representar. **2** *vi (machine)* funcionar; *(musician)* tocar; *(actor)* actuar.
per·form·ance *(of task)* realización *f*; *(of piece of music)* interpretación *f*; *(of play)* representación *f*; *(in sport)* actuación *f*; *(of machine etc)* rendimiento *m*.
per·form·er *(singer)* intérprete *mf*; *(actor)* actor *m*, actriz *f*.
per·fume perfume *m*.
per·haps *adv* tal vez, quizá(s).
per·il *(danger)* peligro *m*.
pe·ri·od período *m*; *(stage)* etapa *f*; *(at school)* clase *f*; *(full stop)* punto *m*; *(menstruation)* regla *f*.
pe·ri·od·i·cal 1 *n* revista *f*. **2** *adj* periódico, -a.
pe·riph·er·al periférico *m*.
perk extra *m*.
▸ **perk up** *vi* animarse.
perm 1 *n* permanente *f*. **2** *vt* **to have one's hair permed** hacerse la permanente.
per·ma·nent *adj* permanente; *(address, job)* fijo, -a.
per·ma·nent·ly *adv* permanentemente.
per·mis·sion permiso *m*.
per·mit 1 *n* permiso *m*. **2** *vt* **to p. sb to do sth** permitir a algn hacer algo.
per·pen·dic·u·lar *adj* perpendicular.
per·se·cute *vt* perseguir.
per·se·cu·tion persecución *f*.
per·se·ver·ance perseverancia *f*.
per·se·vere *vi* perseverar.
per·sist *vi* empeñarse (**in** en).
per·sist·ent *adj (person)* perseverante; *(continual)* constante.
per·son persona *f*; **in p.** en persona.
per·son·al *adj (private)* personal; *(friend)* íntimo, -a; *(pej comment etc)* indiscreto, -a; **he will make a p. appearance** estará aquí en persona.
per·son·al·i·ty personalidad *f*.
per·son·al·ly *adv (for my part)* personalmente; *(in person)* en persona.
per·son·nel personal *m*.
per·suade *vt* persuadir; **to p. sb to do sth** persuadir a algn para que haga algo.

per·sua·sion persuasión *f*.
per·ti·nent *adj (relevant)* pertinente; **p. to** relacionado, -a con, a propósito de.
Pe·ru·vi·an *adj & n* peruano, -a *(mf)*.
pes·si·mist pesimista *mf*.
pes·si·mis·tic *adj* pesimista.
pest *(animal, insect)* plaga *f*; *fam (person)* pelma *mf*; *(thing)* lata *f*.
pes·ter *vt* molestar.
pet 1 *n* animal *m* doméstico. **2** *adj (favorite)* preferido, -a.
pet·al pétalo *m*.
pe·ti·tion petición *f*.
pe·tro·le·um petróleo *m*.
pet·ti·coat enaguas *fpl*.
pet·ty *adj (trivial)* insignificante; *(small-minded)* mezquino, -a.
pet·ty cash dinero *m* para gastos pequeños.
phar·ma·cist farmacéutico, -a *mf*.
phar·ma·cy farmacia *f*.
phase 1 *n* fase *f*. **2** *vt* **to p. sth in/out** introducir/retirar algo progresivamente.
PhD Doctor, -a *mf* en Filosofía.
pheas·ant faisán *m*.
phe·nom·e·nal *adj* fenomenal.
phe·nom·e·non *(pl* **phenomena***)* fenómeno *m*.
phi·los·o·pher filósofo, -a *mf*.
phil·o·soph·i·cal *adj* filosófico, -a.
phi·los·o·phy filosofía *f*.
phlegm flema *f*.
phone 1 *n* teléfono *m*. **2** *vt* llamar por teléfono a.
phone book guía *f* telefónica.
phone booth cabina *f* telefónica.
phone call llamada *f* (telefónica).
phone card tarjeta *f* telefónica.
phone numb·er número *m* de teléfono.
pho·net·ic *adj* fonético, -a.
pho·to foto *f*.
pho·to·cop·i·er fotocopiadora *f*.
pho·to·cop·y 1 *n* fotocopia *f*. **2** *vt* fotocopiar.
pho·to·graph 1 *n* fotografía *f*. **2** *vt* fotografiar.
pho·tog·ra·pher fotógrafo, -a *mf*.
pho·tog·ra·phy fotografía *f*.
phrase frase *f*.
phrase·book libro *m* de frases.
phys·i·cal *adj* físico, -a.
phys·i·cal·ly *adv* físicamente; **p. handicapped** minusválido, -a.
phy·si·cian médico, -a *mf*.
phys·ics física *f*.
pi·an·ist pianista *mf*.
pi·an·o piano *m*.
pick 1 *n (tool)* pico *m*; **take your p.** *(choice)* elige el que quieras. **2** *vt (choose)* escoger; *(team)* seleccionar; *(flowers, fruit)* coger; *(lock)* forzar; **to p. one's nose** hurgarse la nariz.
▸ **pick at** *vt* **she picked at her food** picoteó la comida con desgana.
▸ **pick on** *vt (persecute)* meterse con.
▸ **pick out** *vt (choose)* elegir; *(identify)* identificar.
▸ **pick up 1** *vt (object on floor)* recoger; *(telephone)* descolgar; *(collect)* recoger; *(shopping, person)* buscar; *(acquire)* conseguir; *(learn)* aprender; **to p. up speed** ganar velocidad. **2** *vi (improve)* mejorarse.
pick·ax piqueta *f*.
pick·le *vt (food)* conservar en adobo *or* escabeche; **pickled onions** cebollas *fpl* en vinagre.
pick·pock·et carterista *mf*.
pic·nic comida *f* de campo, picnic *m*.
pic·ture 1 *n (painting)* cuadro *m*; *(drawing)* dibujo *m*; *(portrait)* retrato *m*; *(photo)* foto *f*; *(on TV)* imagen *f*; *(at cinema)* película *f*. **2** *vt (imagine)* imaginarse.
pic·ture frame marco *m*.
pic·tur·esque *adj* pintoresco, -a.
pie *(fruit) (big)* tarta *f*, *(small)* pastel *m*; *(meat etc)* empanada *f*; *(pasty)* empanadilla *f*.
piece pedazo *m*; *(of paper)* trozo *m*; *(part)* pieza *f*; *(coin)* moneda *f*; **a p. of news** una noticia; **to break sth into pieces** hacer algo pedazos.
pier embarcadero *m*, muelle *m*.
pierce *vt* perforar.
pierc·ing *adj (sound etc)* penetrante.
pig cerdo *m*.
pi·geon paloma *f*.
pi·geon·hole casilla *f*.
pig·gy·back **to give sb a p.** llevar a algn a cuestas.
pig·tail trenza *f*.
pile 1 *n* montón *m*. **2** *vt* amontonar.
▸ **pile up 1** *vt (things)* amontonar; *(riches, debts)* acumular. **2** *vi* amontonarse.
piles *sing (illness)* hemorroides *fpl*.
pile·up choque *m* en cadena.
pill píldora *f*; **to be on the p.** estar tomando la píldora (anticonceptiva).
pil·lar pilar *m*, columna *f*.
pil·lar box buzón *m*.
pil·low almohada *f*.
pil·low·case funda *f* de almohada.
pi·lot piloto *m*.
pim·ple espinilla *f*.
pin 1 *n* alfiler *m*. **2** *vt (onto board)* clavar con chinchetas.
▸ **pin up** *vt* clavar con chinchetas.
pin·a·fore *(apron)* delantal *m*.
pin·ball flipper *m*.
pin·cers *npl (tool)* tenazas *fpl*.
pinch 1 *n (nip)* pellizco *m*; **a p. of salt** una pizca de sal. **2** *vt* pellizcar; *fam (steal)* birlar.
pin·cush·ion acerico *m*.
pine *(tree)* pino *m*.
pine·ap·ple piña *f*.
pink *adj* rosa *inv*.
pink·ie dedo *m* meñique.
pint pinta *f (0,47 litro)*; **a p. of beer** una cerveza.
pi·o·neer 1 *n (settler)* pionero, -a *mf*; *(forerunner)* precursor, -a *mf*. **2** *vt* ser pionero, -a en.
pip *(seed)* pepita *f*.
pipe tubería *f*; *(for smoking)* pipa *f*.
pi·rate pirata *m*.
pi·rat·ed *adj (book, record, CD)* pirateado, -a.
pis·ta·chi·o pistacho *m*.
pis·tol pistola *f*.
pit hoyo *m*; *(large)* hoya *f*; *(coal mine)* mina *f* de carbón; *(of fruit)* hueso *m*.

pitch 1 vt (throw) lanzar; (tent) armar. **2** n (for sport) campo m; (throw) lanzamiento m.
pitch-black, pitch-dark adj negro, -a como boca de lobo.
pitch·er (container) cántaro m, jarro m.
pit·y 1 n (compassion) compasión f, (shame) lástima f; **what a p.!** ¡qué pena! **2** vt compadecerse de.
piz·za pizza f.
plac·ard pancarta f.
place 1 n sitio m, lugar m; (seat) sitio m; (on bus) asiento m; (position on scale) posición f; (house) casa f, (building) lugar m; **to take p.** tener lugar; **to take sb's p.** sustituir a algn; **in the first p.** en primer lugar; **we're going to his p.** vamos a su casa. **2** vt poner, colocar; (face, person) recordar.
place·mat tapete m individual.
place·ment (for trainee, student) colocación f en prácticas.
place set·ting cubierto m.
plague peste f.
plain adj (clear) claro, -a; (simple) sencillo, -a; (unattractive) poco atractivo, -a; **the p. truth** la verdad lisa y llana. **2** n (land) llanura f.
plain·ly adv claramente; (simply) sencillamente; **to speak p.** hablar con franqueza.
plait 1 n trenza f. **2** vt trenzar.
plan 1 n plan m. **2** vt (for future) planear; (economy) planificar; (intend) pensar; **to p. on doing sth** tener la intención de hacer algo.
▸**plan for** vt (disaster) prevenirse contra.
plane¹ avión m.
plane² (tool) cepillo m.
plane³ p. (tree) plátano m.
plan·et planeta m.
plank tabla f.
plant¹ 1 n planta f. **2** vt (flowers) plantar; (bomb) colocar.
plant² (factory) planta f (industrial).
plas·ter yeso m; (for broken limb) escayola f.
plas·ter cast (for broken arm) escayola f.
plas·tic 1 n plástico m. **2** adj (cup, bag) de plástico.
plas·tic sur·ger·y cirugía f plástica.
plate plato m; (sheet) placa f.
plat·form plataforma f, (at meeting) tribuna f, (at station) andén m.
plau·si·ble adj plausible.
play 1 vt (game) jugar a; (team) jugar contra; (instrument, tune) tocar; (part) hacer (el papel) de; **to p. a record** poner un disco; fig **to p. a part in sth** participar en algo. **2** vi jugar (**with** con). **3** n obra f de teatro.
▸**play back** vt (tape) volver a poner.
▸**play down** vt quitar importancia a.
play·er jugador, -a mf, (in play) (man) actor m; (woman) actriz f.
play·ground (in school) patio m de recreo; (recreation ground) parque m infantil.
play·group jardín m de infancia.
play·ing card carta f.
play·ing field campo m de deportes.
play·time recreo m.
plea (request) petición f, súplica f; (in court) alegato m.
plead 1 vt **to p. sb's cause** defender la causa de algn; **to p. ignorance** (give as excuse) alegar ignorancia. **2** vi (beg) rogar, suplicar; **to p. with sb to do sth** suplicar a algn que haga algo; (in court) **to p. guilty/not guilty** declararse culpable/inocente.
pleas·ant adj agradable.
pleas·ant·ly adv agradablemente.
please 1 adv por favor; '**p. do not smoke**' 'se ruega no fumar'. **2** vt (give pleasure to) complacer. **3** vi **do as you p.** haz lo que quieras.
pleased adj (happy) contento, -a; (satisfied) satisfecho, -a; **p. to meet you!** ¡encantado, -a!
pleas·ing adj (pleasant) agradable.
pleas·ure placer m; **with p.** con mucho gusto.
pleat pliegue m.
pleat·ed adj plisado, -a.
pledge 1 n promesa f. **2** vt prometer.
plen·ti·ful adj abundante.
plen·ty p. of potatoes muchas patatas; **p. of time** tiempo de sobra.
pli·ers npl alicates mpl, tenazas fpl.
plot¹ 1 n (conspiracy) complot m; (story) argumento m. **2** vi conspirar.
plot² (ground) terreno m; (for building) solar m.
plow 1 n arado m. **2** vt arar.
pluck vt (flowers) coger; (chicken) desplumar.
plug 1 n (in bath etc) tapón m; (electric) enchufe m; **2/3 pin p.** clavija bipolar/tripolar. **2** vt (hole) tapar.
▸**plug in 1** vt enchufar. **2** vi enchufarse.
plum (fruit) ciruela f.
plumb·er fontanero, -a mf.
plumb·ing (system) fontanería f.
plump adj (person) rechoncho, -a; (baby) rellenito, -a.
plunge 1 vt (immerse) sumergir; (thrust) arrojar. **2** vi (dive) zambullirse; (fall) caer.
plu·ral adj & n plural (m); **in the p.** en plural.
plus prep más; **three p. four makes seven** tres más cuatro hacen siete.
p.m. (from midday to early evening) de la tarde; (at night) de la noche.
pneu·mat·ic adj neumático, -a.
pneu·mat·ic drill martillo m neumático.
poach vt (egg) escalfar.
PO Box apartado m (de Correos).
pock·et bolsillo m.
pock·et·book bolso m.
pock·et·ful a p. of un bolsillo de.
pock·et mon·ey dinero m de bolsillo.
po·em poema m.
po·et poeta mf.
po·et·ic adj poético, -a.
po·et·ry poesía f.
point 1 n (sharp end) punta f, (place) punto m; (score) tanto m; (moment) **at that p.** en aquel momento; **to be on the p. of doing sth** estar a punto de hacer algo; **there's no p. in going** no merece la pena ir; **six p. three** seis coma tres; **up to a p.** hasta cierto punto; **power p.** toma f de corriente; **points** (on railway) agujas fpl. **2** vt (way etc) indicar; **to p. a gun at sb** apuntar a algn con una pistola. **3** vi **to p. at sth/sb** (with finger) señalar algo/a algn con el dedo.
▸**point out** vt indicar; (mention) hacer resaltar.
point·ed adj (sharp) puntiagudo, -a.
point·less adj sin sentido.
poi·son 1 n veneno m. **2** vt envenenar.
poi·son·ous adj (plant, snake) venenoso, -a; (gas) tóxico, -a.
poke vt (fire) atizar; (with finger) dar con la punta del dedo a; (with stick) dar con la punta del bastón a; **to p. one's head out** asomar la cabeza.
▸**poke about, poke around** vi fisgonear or hurgar en.

pok·er (for fire) atizador m.
po·lar adj polar.
po·lar bear oso m polar.
Pole polaco, -a mf.
pole¹ palo m.
pole² (north, south) polo m.
po·lice npl policía f sing.
po·lice car coche m patrulla.
po·lice·man policía m.
po·lice sta·tion comisaría f.
po·lice·wom·an (mujer f) policía f.
pol·i·cy política f, (insurance) póliza f (de seguros).
po·li·o poliomielitis f.
Po·lish 1 adj polaco, -a. **2** n (language) polaco m.
pol·ish 1 vt pulir; (furniture) encerar; (shoes) limpiar. **2** n (for furniture) cera f, (for shoes) betún m; (for nails) esmalte m.
▸**polish off** vt (food) zamparse.
▸**polish up** vt fig perfeccionar.
po·lite adj educado, -a.
po·lite·ly adv educadamente.
po·lite·ness educación f.
po·lit·i·cal adj político, -a.
pol·i·ti·cian político, -a mf.
pol·i·tics política f.
poll votación f, (survey) encuesta f; **to go to the polls** acudir a las urnas.
pol·len polen m.
poll·ing sta·tion colegio m electoral.
pol·lute vt contaminar.
pol·lu·tion contaminación f.
po·lo p. neck sweater jersey m de cuello vuelto.
pol·y·es·ter poliéster m.
pol·y·tech·nic politécnico m.
pol·y·thene polietileno m.
pom·e·gran·ate granada f.
pond estanque m.
po·ny poney m.
po·ny·tail cola f de caballo.
poo·dle caniche m.
pool (of water, oil etc) charco m; **swimming p.** piscina f.
pooped adj fam hecho, -a polvo.
poor 1 adj pobre; (quality) malo, -a. **2** npl **the p.** los pobres.
poor·ly 1 adv (badly) mal. **2** adj (ill) enfermo, -a.
pop 1 vt (burst) hacer reventar. **2** vi (burst) reventar; fam **I'm just popping over to Ian's** voy un momento a casa de Ian. **3** n (drink) gaseosa f, fam (father) papá m; (music) música f pop.
▸**pop in** vi fam entrar un momento.
pop·corn palomitas fpl.
Pope the P. el Papa.
pop·py amapola f.
Pop·si·cle® polo m.
pop sing·er cantante mf pop.
pop·u·lar adj popular; (fashionable) de moda.
pop·u·lar·i·ty popularidad f.
pop·u·lat·ed adj thinly p. poco poblado.
pop·u·la·tion población f.
porch (of house) porche m; (veranda) terraza f.
pork carne f de cerdo.
por·ridge gachas fpl de avena.
port (harbor, of computer) puerto m.
por·ta·ble adj & n portátil (m).
por·ter (in hotel etc) portero, -a mf.
port·fo·li·o (for papers, of artist, politician) cartera f.
port·hole portilla f.
por·tion (part, piece) parte f, (of food) ración f.
por·trait retrato m.
Por·tu·guese 1 adj portugués, -esa. **2** n (person) portugués, -esa mf, (language) portugués m.
pose 1 vt (problem) plantear; (threat) representar. **2** vi (for painting) posar; **to p. as** hacerse pasar por.
posh adj elegante; (person) presumido, -a; (accent) de clase alta.
po·si·tion posición f, (location) situación f, (rank) rango m; **to be in a p. to do sth** estar en condiciones de hacer algo.
pos·i·tive adj positivo, -a; (sign) favorable; (sure) seguro, -a.
pos·i·tive·ly adv (constructively) positivamente; (to answer) afirmativamente; (for emphasis) verdaderamente, realmente.
pos·sess vt poseer.
pos·ses·sions npl bienes mpl.
pos·ses·sive adj posesivo, -a.
pos·si·bil·i·ty posibilidad f.
pos·si·ble adj posible; **as much as p.** todo lo posible; **as often as p.** cuanto más mejor; **as soon as p.** cuanto antes.
pos·si·bly adv posiblemente; (perhaps) quizás; **I can't p. come** no puedo venir de ninguna manera.
post¹ (wooden) poste m.
post² (job) puesto m.
▸**post up** vt (notice) fijar.
post·age franqueo m.
post·age stamp sello m (de correos).
post·al adj postal.
post·al or·der giro m postal.
post·card (tarjeta f) postal f.
post·er póster m; (advertising) cartel m.
post·grad·u·ate posgraduado, -a mf.
post·man cartero m.
post·mark matasellos m inv.
post of·fice oficina f de correos; **where is the p.?** ¿dónde está correos?
post·pone vt aplazar.
post·pone·ment aplazamiento m.
pot (for cooking) olla f, (for flowers) maceta f.
po·ta·to (pl potatoes) patata f, Am papa f.
po·tent adj potente.
po·ten·tial 1 adj potencial. **2** n potencial m.
pot·ter alfarero, -a mf.
pot·ter·y (craft, place) alfarería f, (objects) cerámica f.
pot·ty orinal m.
pouch bolsa f pequeña; (of animal) bolsa f abdominal.

poul·try *(live)* aves *fpl* de corral; *(food)* pollos *mpl.*
pounce *vi* to p. on abalanzarse encima de.
pound¹ *(weight)* libra *f.*
pound² *(for dogs)* perrera *f; (for cars)* depósito *m* de coches.
pour 1 *vt* verter; **to p. sb a drink** servirle una copa a algn. **2** *vi* **it's pouring with rain** está lloviendo a cántaros.
▸**pour away** *vt (liquid)* vaciar.
▸**pour in** *vi (water)* entrar a raudales; *(applications)* llegar sin parar.
▸**pour out 1** *vt* verter. **2** *vi (liquid, people)* salir a raudales.
pov·er·ty pobreza *f.*
pow·der 1 *n* polvo *m.* **2** *vt* **to p. one's nose** empolvarse la cara.
pow·dered *adj (milk)* en polvo.
pow·er fuerza *f; (energy)* energía *f; (ability, authority)* poder *m; (nation)* potencia *f;* **to be in p.** estar en el poder.
pow·er·ful *adj (influential)* poderoso, -a; *(engine, machine)* potente.
pow·er point enchufe *m.*
pow·er sta·tion central *f* eléctrica.
prac·ti·cal *adj* práctico, -a.
prac·ti·cal joke broma *f* pesada.
prac·ti·cal·ly *(almost)* casi.
prac·tice 1 *n (exercise)* práctica *f; (in sport)* entrenamiento *m; (rehearsal)* ensayo *m; (habit)* costumbre *f; (way of doing sth)* práctica *f;* **to be out of p.** no estar en forma; **in p.** en la práctica. **2** *vt* practicar; *(principle)* poner en práctica; *(profession)* ejercer. **3** *vi* practicar; *(in sport)* entrenar; *(rehearse)* ensayar; *(doctor)* practicar; *(lawyer)* ejercer.
praise 1 *n* alabanza *f.* **2** *vt* alabar.
prank travesura *f; (joke)* broma *f.*
prawn gamba *f.*
pray *vi* rezar.
prayer oración *f.*
preach *vi* predicar.
pre·cau·tion precaución *f.*
pre·cede *vt* preceder.
prec·e·dent precedente *m.*
pre·ced·ing *adj* precedente.
pre·cinct *(administrative, police division)* distrito *m.*
pre·cious *adj* precioso, -a.
pre·cise *adj* preciso, -a; *(meticulous)* meticuloso, -a.
pre·co·cious *adj* precoz.
pred·a·tor depredador *m.*
pre·de·ces·sor antecesor, -a *mf.*
pre·dic·a·ment apuro *m,* aprieto *m.*
pre·dict *vt* predecir.
pre·dict·a·ble *adj* previsible.
pre·dic·tion pronóstico *m.*
pref·ace prefacio *m.*
pre·fer *vt* preferir; **I p. coffee to tea** prefiero el café al té.
pref·er·a·ble *adj* preferible (**to** a).
pref·er·a·bly *adv* preferentemente.
pref·er·ence preferencia *f.*
pre·fix prefijo *m.*
preg·nan·cy embarazo *m.*
preg·nant *adj* embarazada.
pre·his·tor·i(·)c(al) *adj* prehistórico, -a.
prej·u·dice *(bias)* prejuicio *m.*
pre·lim·i·nar·y *adj* preliminar.
pre·ma·ture *adj* prematuro, -a.
prem·is·es *npl* local *m;* **on the p.** en el local.
pre·mi·um prima *f.*
prep·a·ra·tion preparación *f; (plan)* preparativo *m.*
pre·pare 1 *vt* preparar; **to p. to do sth** prepararse para hacer algo. **2** *vi* prepararse (**for** para).
pre·pared *adj (ready)* preparado, -a; **to be p. to do sth** *(willing)* estar dispuesto, -a a hacer algo.
prep·o·si·tion preposición *f.*
pre·school *adj* preescolar.
pre·scribe *vt (medicine)* recetar.
pre·scrip·tion *(medical)* receta *f.*
pres·ence presencia *f; (attendance)* asistencia *f.*
pres·ent¹ 1 *adj (in attendance)* presente; *(current)* actual; **p. tense** (tiempo *m*) presente *m.* **2** *n (time)* presente *m;* **at p.** actualmente.
pre·sent² 1 *vt (opportunity)* ofrecer; *(problems)* plantear; *(prize)* entregar; *(introduce) (person, program)* presentar; **to p. sb with sth** obsequiar a algn con algo. **2** *n (gift)* regalo *m.*
pres·en·ta·tion presentación *f;* **p. ceremony** ceremonia *f* de entrega.
pre·sent·er animador, -a *mf.*
pres·ent·ly *adv (soon)* dentro de poco; *(now)* ahora.
pres·er·va·tion conservación *f.*
pre·ser·va·tive conservante *m.*
pre·serve 1 *vt (keep)* mantener. **2** *n* conserva *f.*
pre·side *vi* presidir; **to p. over** *or* **at sth** presidir algo.
pres·i·den·cy presidencia *f.*
pres·i·dent presidente, -a *mf.*
pres·i·den·tial *adj* presidencial.
press 1 *vt* apretar; *(button)* pulsar; *(iron)* planchar; *(urge)* presionar; **to p. sb to do sth** presionar a algn para que haga algo. **2** *vi (push)* apretar; **to p. (down) on sth** hacer presión sobre algo. **3** *n (newspapers)* prensa *f.*
▸**press on** *vi* seguir adelante.
press con·fer·ence rueda *f* de prensa.
pres·sure presión *f;* **to bring p. (to bear) on sb** ejercer presión sobre algn.
pres·sure cook·er olla *f* a presión.
pres·sure gauge manómetro *m.*
pre·sume *vt* suponer.
pre·tend *vti* fingir.
pre·text pretexto *m;* **on the p. of** so pretexto de.
pret·ty 1 *adj (thing)* bonito, -a; *(person)* guapo, -a. **2** *adv* bastante; **p. much the same** más o menos lo mismo.
pre·vail *vi* predominar; **to p. upon** *or* **on sb to do sth** *(persuade)* persuadir *or* convencer a algn para que haga algo.
pre·vent *vt* impedir; *(accident)* evitar; **to p. sb from doing sth** impedir a algn hacer algo.
pre·ven·tion prevención *f.*
pre·vi·ous *adj* anterior.
pre·vi·ous·ly *adv* previamente.
prey presa *f, fig* víctima *f.*
price precio *m.*
price list lista *f* de precios.
pric·ey *adj fam* carillo(a).

prick *vt* picar; **to p. one's finger** pincharse el dedo.
prick·ly *adj* espinoso, -a; *(touchy)* enojadizo, -a.
pride 1 *n* orgullo *m; (arrogance)* soberbia *f;* **to take p. in sth** enorgullecerse de algo. **2** *vt* **to p. oneself on** enorgullecerse de.
priest sacerdote *m,* cura *m.*
pri·mar·i·ly *adv* ante todo.
pri·mar·y 1 *adj* principal; **p. education/school** enseñanza *f*/escuela *f* primaria. **2** *n (election)* (elección *f*) primaria *f.*
Prime Min·is·ter primer, -a ministro, -a *mf.*
prime num·ber número *m* primo.
prim·i·tive *adj* primitivo, -a.
prim·rose primavera *f.*
prince príncipe *m;* **P. Charming** Príncipe Azul.
prin·cess princesa *f.*
prin·ci·pal 1 *adj* principal. **2** *n (of college etc)* director, -a *mf.*
prin·ci·ple principio *m;* **on p.** por principio.
print 1 *vt (publish)* publicar; *(write)* escribir con letra de imprenta. **2** *n* letra *f; (of hand, foot)* huella *f; (of photo)* copia *f;* **out of p.** agotado, -a.
▸**print out** *vt* imprimir.
print·ed *adj* impreso(a); **printed matter** impresos *mpl.*
print·er *(person)* impresor, -a *mf; (machine)* impresora *f.*
print·ing *(industry)* imprenta *f; (process)* impresión *f.*
print-out impresión *f.*
pri·or *adj* anterior; **without p. warning** sin previo aviso.
pri·or·i·ty prioridad *f.*
pris·on prisión *f.*
pris·on·er preso, -a *mf;* **to hold sb p.** detener a algn.
pri·va·cy intimidad *f.*
pri·vate 1 *adj* privado, -a; *(individual)* particular; *(personal)* personal; *(letter)* confidencial. **2** *n (soldier)* soldado *m* raso.
pri·vate·ly *adv* en privado; *(personally)* personalmente.
prize premio *m.*
prize-giv·ing distribución *f* de premios.
prize-win·ner premiado, -a *mf.*
pro¹ pro *m;* **the pros and cons** los pros y los contras.
pro² *abbr of* **professional** *fam* profesional *mf.*
pro³ *prefix (in favour of)* pro-.
prob·a·ble *adj* probable.
prob·a·bly *adv* probablemente.
probe 1 *n (medical instrument, spacecraft)* sonda *f; (investigation)* sondeo *m.* **2** *vt (with medical instrument)* sondar; *(investigate)* investigar.
▸**probe into** *vt* investigar.
prob·lem problema *m.*
prob·lem·at·i(·)c(al) *adj* problemático, -a.
pro·ceed *vi* proceder, seguir; **to p. to do sth** ponerse a hacer algo.
pro·ceeds *npl* ganancias *fpl.*
proc·ess 1 *n* proceso *m;* **in the p. of** en vías de. **2** *vt* procesar.
proc·essed cheese queso *m* fundido.
pro·ces·sion desfile *m; (religious)* procesión *f.*
proc·es·sor procesador *m.*
pro·duce 1 *vt* producir; *(manufacture)* fabricar; *(give birth to)* dar a luz a; *(show)* enseñar; *(bring out)* sacar. **2** *n* productos *mpl.*
pro·duc·er productor, -a *mf; (manufacturer)* fabricante *mf.*
pro·duc·tion producción *f; (manufacture)* fabricación *f;* **p. line** cadena *f* de montaje.
pro·duc·tive *adj* productivo, -a.
pro·duc·tiv·i·ty productividad *f.*
pro·fes·sion profesión *f.*
pro·fes·sion·al 1 *adj* profesional; *(polished)* de gran calidad. **2** *n* profesional *mf.*
pro·fes·sor catedrático, -a *mf.*
prof·it 1 *n* beneficio *m;* **to make a p. on** sacar beneficios de. **2** *vi* **to p. from** aprovecharse de.
prof·it·a·ble *adj* rentable; *(worthwhile)* provechoso, -a.
pro·found *adj* profundo, -a.
pro·gram 1 *n* programa *m; (plan)* plan *m.* **2** *vti* programar.
pro·gram·ming programación *f.*
prog·ress 1 *n* progreso *m;* **to make p.** hacer progresos; **in p.** en curso. **2** *vi* avanzar; *(develop)* desarrollarse; *(medically)* mejorar.
pro·gres·sive *adj (increasing)* progresivo, -a; *(in politics)* progresista.
pro·hib·it *vt* prohibir; **to p. sb from doing sth** prohibir a algn hacer algo.
proj·ect proyecto *m; (at school)* trabajo *m.*
pro·jec·tor proyector *m.*
pro·long *vt* prolongar.
prom·e·nade *(at seaside)* paseo *m* marítimo.
prom·i·nent *adj (important)* importante; *(famous)* eminente.
prom·ise 1 *n* promesa *f;* **to show p.** ser prometedor, -a. **2** *vti* prometer.
prom·is·ing *adj* prometedor, -a.
pro·mote *vt* ascender; *(product)* promocionar.
pro·mo·tion *(in rank)* ascenso *m; (of product)* promoción *f.*
prompt *adj (quick)* rápido, -a; *(punctual)* puntual. **2** *adv* **at 2 o'clock p.** a las 2 en punto.
prone *adj* **to be p. to do sth** ser propenso, -a a hacer algo.
pro·noun pronombre *m.*
pro·nounce *vt* pronunciar.
pro·nun·ci·a·tion pronunciación *f.*
proof prueba *f.*
prop¹ 1 *n (physical support)* puntal *m; (psychological support)* sostén *m.* **2** *vt (lean)* apoyar.
▸**prop up** *vt* apoyar.
prop² *(in theatre)* fam accesorio *m.*
prop·a·gan·da propaganda *f.*
pro·pel·ler hélice *f.*
prop·er *adj* adecuado, -a; *(real)* auténtico, -a; **p. noun** nombre propio.
prop·er·ly *(suitably, correctly, decently)* correctamente.
prop·er·ty *(possession)* propiedad *f;* **personal p.** bienes *mpl.*
pro·por·tion proporción *f; (part, quantity)* parte *f.*
pro·por·tion·al *adj* proporcional (**to** a).
pro·pos·al propuesta *f;* **p. of marriage** propuesta de matrimonio.
pro·pose 1 *vt* proponer; *(suggest)* sugerir. **2** *vi (ask to marry)* declararse.
prop·o·si·tion propuesta *f.*
props *npl (in theater)* accesorios *mpl.*
prose prosa *f; (translation)* traducción *f* inversa.
pros·e·cute *vt* procesar.
pros·e·cu·tion *(action)* proceso *m,* juicio *m;* **the p.** *(in court)* la acusación.
pros·pect *(outlook)* perspectiva *f; (hope)* esperanza *f.*
pros·per·i·ty prosperidad *f.*
pros·per·ous *adj* próspero, -a.
pro·tect *vt* **to p. sb from sth** proteger a algn de algo.

pro·tec·tion protección f.
pro·tec·tive adj protector, -a.
pro·test 1 n protesta f. **2** vi protestar.
Prot·es·tant adj & n protestante (mf).
pro·test·er manifestante mf.
proud adj orgulloso, -a; (arrogant) soberbio, -a.
proud·ly adv con orgullo; (arrogantly) con soberbia.
prove vt demostrar; **it proved to be disastrous** resultó desastroso, -a.
prov·erb refrán m, proverbio m.
pro·vide vt proporcionar; (supplies) suministrar.
pro·vid·ed conj p. (that) con tal de que.
prov·ince provincia f.
pro·vin·cial adj provincial; pej provinciano, -a.
pro·vi·sion·al adj provisional.
pro·voke vt provocar.
prowl vi merodear; **to p. about** or **around** rondar.
prowl·er merodeador m.
prune[1] ciruela f pasa.
prune[2] vt (roses etc) podar.
psy·chi·at·ric adj psiquiátrico, -a.
psy·chi·a·trist psiquiatra mf.
psy·cho·log·i·cal adj psicológico, -a.
psy·chol·o·gist psicólogo, -a mf.
psy·chol·o·gy psicología f.
pub bar m.
pub·lic 1 adj público, -a; **p. holiday** fiesta f nacional. **2** n **the p.** el público; **in p.** en público.
pub·li·ca·tion publicación f.
pub·lic·i·ty publicidad f.
pub·lic·ly adv públicamente.
pub·lish vt publicar, editar.
pub·lish·er editor, -a mf.
pub·lish·ing (business) industria f editorial.
pud·ding pudín m; (dessert) postre m.
pud·dle charco m.
puff 1 n (of smoke) bocanada f. **2** vi (person) jadear; **to p. on one's pipe** chupar la pipa.
pull 1 n **to give sth a p.** (tug) dar un tirón a algo. **2** vt (tug) dar un tirón a; (drag) tirar de; **to p. a muscle** sufrir un tirón en un músculo; **to p. the trigger** apretar el gatillo; **to p. sth to pieces** hacer pedazos algo.
▸ **pull apart** vt desmontar.
▸ **pull down** vt (building) derribar.
▸ **pull in 1** vt (crowds) atraer. **2** vi **to p. in(to the station)** llegar a la estación.
▸ **pull out 1** vt (withdraw) retirar. **2** vi (car) **to p. out to overtake** salirse para adelantar.
▸ **pull over** vi hacerse a un lado.
▸ **pull through** vi reponerse.
▸ **pull up 1** vt (uproot) desarraigar; (draw close) acercar. **2** vi (stop) pararse.
pull·o·ver jersey m.
pulse (in body) pulso m.
pump 1 n bomba f. **2** vt bombear.
▸ **pump up** vt (tire) inflar.
pump·kin calabaza f.
punch[1] **1** n (for making holes) perforadora f. **2** vt (ticket) picar.
punch[2] **1** n (blow) puñetazo m. **2** vt (with fist) dar un puñetazo a.
punc·tu·al adj puntual.
punc·tu·a·tion puntuación f.
punc·ture 1 n pinchazo m. **2** vt (tire) pinchar.
pun·ish vt castigar.
pun·ish·ment castigo m.
pu·pil[1] (at school) alumno, -a mf.
pu·pil[2] (in eye) pupila f.
pup·pet títere m.
pup·py cachorro, -a mf (de perro).
pur·chase 1 n compra f. **2** vt comprar.
pur·chas·er comprador, -a mf.
pur·chas·ing pow·er poder m adquisitivo.
pure adj puro, -a.
pure·ly adv simplemente.
pur·ple adj morado, -a.
pur·pose propósito m; **on p.** a propósito.
pur·pose·ly adv adrede.
purse (bag) bolso m.
pur·sue vt (criminal) perseguir; (person) seguir.
pur·suit (of criminal) persecución f; (of animal) caza f; (of pleasure) búsqueda f; (pastime) pasatiempo m.
push 1 n empujón m; **to give sb a p.** dar un empujón a algn. **2** vt empujar; (button) pulsar; **to p. one's finger into a hole** meter el dedo en un agujero. **3** vi empujar.
▸ **push aside** vt (object) apartar.
▸ **push in** vi colarse.
▸ **push off** vi fam **p. off!** ¡lárgate!
▸ **push on** vi (continue) seguir adelante.
▸ **push through** vt (crowd) abrirse paso entre; (law) hacer aceptar (a la fuerza).
pushed adj **to be p. for time/money** estar justo, -a de tiempo/dinero.
push·y adj (pushier, pushiest) fam agresivo, -a.
puss, puss·y minino m.
put[*] vt poner; (place) colocar; (insert) meter; (express) expresar; (invest) (money) invertir; **to p. a stop to sth** poner término a algo; **to p. a question to sb** hacer una pregunta a algn.
▸ **put across** vt (idea etc) comunicar.
▸ **put aside** vt (money) ahorrar; (time) reservar.
▸ **put away** vt (tidy up) recoger; (save money) ahorrar.
▸ **put back** vt (postpone) aplazar.
▸ **put by** vt (money) ahorrar.
▸ **put down** vt (set down) dejar; (criticize) criticar; (write down) apuntar.
▸ **put forward** vt (theory) exponer; (proposal) hacer.
▸ **put in** vt (install) instalar; (complaint, request) presentar; (time) pasar.
▸ **put off** vt (postpone) aplazar; (switch off) (radio, light) apagar; **to p. sb off (doing) sth** (dissuade) disuadir a algn de (hacer) algo.
▸ **put on** vt (clothes) poner(se); (switch on) (radio) poner; (light) encender; **to p. on weight** engordar.
▸ **put out** vt (switch off, extinguish) apagar; (place outside) sacar; (extend) (arm) extender; (hand) tender; (annoy) molestar; (inconvenience) incordiar.
▸ **put through** vt (on telephone) **p. me through to Pat, please** póngame con Pat, por favor.
▸ **put together** vt (assemble) montar.
▸ **put up** vt (raise) levantar; (picture) colocar; (curtains) colgar; (tent) armar; (prices) subir; (accommodate) alojar; **to p. up a fight** ofrecer resistencia.
▸ **put up with** vt aguantar.

put·ty masilla f.
puz·zle 1 n rompecabezas m inv; (mystery) misterio m. **2** vt dejar perplejo, -a.
puz·zling adj extraño, -a.
py·lon torre f (de conducción eléctrica).
pyr·a·mid pirámide f.

Q

qual·i·fi·ca·tion (diploma etc) título m.
qual·i·fied adj capacitado, -a; **q. teacher** profesor m titulado.
qual·i·fy vi (in competition) quedar clasificado, -a; **to q. as** (doctor etc) sacar el título de.
qual·i·ty (excellence) calidad f; (attribute) cualidad f.
quan·ti·ty cantidad f.
quar·rel 1 n (argument) riña f, pelea f. **2** vi (argue) reñir.
quar·rel·ing disputas fpl.
quar·ry cantera f.
quart cuarto m de galón (0,94 litros).
quar·ter cuarto m; (coin) cuarto m (de dólar); (district) barrio m; **it's a q. to three, it's a q. of three** son las tres menos cuarto.
quar·ter·back quarterback m, Méx mariscal m de campo
quartz cuarzo m; **q. watch** reloj m de cuarzo.
queen reina f.
queer adj (strange) extraño, -a.
quench vt apagar.
que·ry (question) pregunta f.
ques·tion 1 n pregunta f; (problem, issue) asunto m; **to ask sb a q.** hacer una pregunta a algn; **out of the q.** imposible; **that's out of the q.** ¡ni hablar! **2** vt (interrogate) interrogar; (query) poner en duda.
ques·tion·a·ble adj (doubtful) dudoso, -a; (debatable) discutible.
ques·tion mark signo m de interrogación.
ques·tion·naire cuestionario m.
quib·ble vi poner pegas (**with** a).
quiche quiche f.
quick adj (fast) rápido, -a; **be q.!** ¡date prisa!
quick·ly adv deprisa.
qui·et adj (silent) silencioso, -a; (calm, not crowded) tranquilo, -a.
qui·et·ly adv (silently) silenciosamente; (calmly) tranquilamente; **he spoke q.** habló en voz baja.
quit[*] **1** vt (leave) dejar; **q. making that noise!** ¡deja de hacer ese ruido! **2** vi (go) irse; (resign) dimitir.
quite adv (entirely) totalmente; (rather) bastante; **q. a few** bastantes; **q. often** con bastante frecuencia; **q. (so)!** ¡exacto!
quiz q. show concurso m.
quo·ta (proportional share) cuota f, parte f; (prescribed amount, number) cupo m.
quo·ta·tion cita f; (commercial) cotización f.
quo·ta·tion marks npl comillas fpl.
quote 1 vt (cite) citar; **to q. a price** dar un presupuesto. **2** n cita f; (commercial) presupuesto m.

R

rab·bi rabino m.
rab·bit conejo, -a mf.
ra·bies rabia f.
race[1] **1** n (in sport) carrera f. **2** vt (car, horse) hacer correr; **I'll r. you!** ¡te echo una carrera! **3** vi (go quickly) correr.
race[2] (people) raza f.
race·horse caballo m de carreras.
ra·cial adj racial.
rac·ing carreras fpl.
rac·ing bike (motorbike) moto f de carreras; (bicycle) bicicleta f de carreras.
rac·ing car coche m de carreras.
rac·ing driv·er piloto mf de carreras.
rac·ism racismo m.
ra·cist adj & n racista (mf).
rack (shelf) estante m; (for clothes) percha f; **luggage r.** portaequipajes m inv; **roof r.** baca f.
rack·et[1] (din) jaleo m.
rack·et[2] (for tennis etc) raqueta f.
ra·dar radar m.
ra·di·a·tion radiación f.
ra·di·a·tor radiador m.
rad·i·cal adj radical.
ra·di·o radio f; **on the r.** en or por la radio; **r. station** emisora f (de radio).
ra·di·o·ac·tive adj radiactivo, -a.
rad·ish rábano m.
ra·di·us radio m.
raf·fle rifa f.
raft balsa f.
rag (torn piece) harapo m; (for cleaning) trapo m; **rags** (clothes) trapos mpl.
rage 1 n (fury) cólera f. **2** vi (person) estar furioso, -a.
rag·ged adj (clothes) hecho, -a jirones; (person) harapiento, -a.
raid 1 n (by police) redada f; (robbery etc) atraco m. **2** vt (police) hacer una redada (en); (rob) asaltar.
rail barra f; (railing) barandilla f; (on railroad) carril m; **by r.** (send sth) por ferrocarril; (travel) en tren.
rail·ings npl verja f sing.
rail·road ferrocarril m.
rail·road sta·tion estación f de ferrocarril.
rail·road track vía f férrea.
rail·way line vía f férrea.
rain 1 n lluvia f; **in the r.** bajo la lluvia. **2** vi llover; **it's raining** llueve.
rain·bow arco m iris.
rain·coat impermeable m.
rain·y adj lluvioso, -a.

raise 1 *n* aumento *m* (de sueldo). **2** *vt* levantar; *(voice)* subir; *(increase)* aumentar; *(money, help)* reunir; *(issue, question)* plantear; *(crops, children)* criar.

rai·sin pasa *f.*

rake 1 *n (garden tool)* rastrillo *m.* **2** *vt (leaves)* rastrillar.

ral·ly *(political)* mitin *m.*

▸**rally around** *vi (help out)* echar una mano.

ram 1 *n (sheep)* carnero *m.* **2** *vt (drive into place)* hincar; *(crash into)* chocar con.

ram·ble *(walk)* caminata *f.*

ramp rampa *f.*

ran *pt of* **run**.

ranch rancho *m.*

ran·dom 1 *n* **at r.** al azar. **2** *adj* fortuito, -a; **r. selection** selección *f* hecha al azar.

range 1 *n (of mountains)* cordillera *f*; *(of products)* gama *f*; *(of missile)* alcance *m*; *(stove)* cocina *f* de carbón. **2** *vi (extend)* extenderse (**to** hasta); **prices r. from five to twenty dollars** los precios oscilan entre cinco y veinte dólares.

rank *(position in army)* graduación *f*; *(in society)* rango *m*; **(taxi) r.** parada *f* de taxis.

ran·som rescate *m.*

rape 1 *n* violación *f.* **2** *vt* violar.

rap·id *adj* rápido, -a.

rap·id·ly *adv* rápidamente.

rap·ist violador, -a *mf.*

rare *adj* poco común; *(steak)* poco hecho, -a.

rare·ly *adv* raras veces.

ras·cal granuja *mf.*

rash[1] *(on skin)* sarpullido *m.*

rash[2] *adj (reckless)* impetuoso, -a; *(words, actions)* precipitado, -a.

rash·ly *adv* a la ligera.

rasp·ber·ry frambuesa *f.*

rat rata *f.*

rate 1 *n* tasa *f*; **at any r.** *(anyway)* en cualquier caso; *(of interest, exchange)* tipo *m*; **at the r. of** *(speed)* a la velocidad de; *(quantity)* a razón de. **2** *vt (estimate)* estimar; *(evaluate)* tasar; *(consider)* considerar.

rath·er *adv (quite)* más bien, bastante; *(more accurately)* mejor dicho; **r. than** *(instead of)* en vez de; *(more than)* más que; **she would r. stay here** prefiere quedarse aquí.

rat·ing *(score)* valoración *f.*

ra·tio razón *f.*

ra·tion 1 *n (allowance)* ración *f*; **rations** víveres *mpl.* **2** *vt* racionar.

ra·tion·al *adj* racional.

ra·tion·ing racionamiento *m.*

rat·tle 1 *n (toy)* sonajero *m*; *(instrument)* carraca *f.* **2** *vt (keys etc)* hacer sonar. **3** *vi* sonar; *(metal)* repiquetear; *(glass)* tintinear; *(window, shelves)* vibrar.

rav·en·ous *adj* **I'm r.** tengo un hambre que no veo.

raw *adj (uncooked)* crudo, -a; **r. material** materia *f* prima; **r. flesh** carne *f* viva.

ray rayo *m.*

ra·zor *(for shaving)* maquinilla *f* de afeitar.

ra·zor blade hoja *f* de afeitar.

reach 1 *vt (arrive at)* llegar a; *(contact)* localizar. **2** *vi* alcanzar. **3** *n (range)* alcance *m*; **out of r.** fuera del alcance; **within r.** al alcance.

▸**reach out** *vi (with hand)* extender la mano.

re·act *vi* reaccionar.

re·ac·tion reacción *f.*

re·ac·tor reactor *m.*

read* *vt* leer; *(decipher)* descifrar.

▸**read about** *vt* leer.

▸**read out** *vt* leer en voz alta.

▸**read up on** *vt* estudiar.

read·er lector, -a *mf*; *(book)* libro *m* de lectura.

read·i·ly *adv (easily)* fácilmente; *(willingly)* de buena gana.

read·ing lectura *f*; *fig* interpretación *f.*

read·y *adj (prepared)* listo, -a; *(willing)* dispuesto, -a; **r. to** *(about to)* a punto de; **r. cash** dinero *m* en efectivo.

read·y-cooked *adj* precocinado, -a.

read·y-made *adj* confeccionado, -a; *(food)* preparado, -a.

re·al *adj* verdadero, -a; *(genuine)* auténtico, -a.

re·al es·tate bienes *mpl* inmuebles.

re·al es·tate a·gent agente *mf* inmobiliario, -a.

re·al·is·tic *adj* realista.

re·al·i·ty realidad *f.*

re·al·ize *vt (become aware of)* darse cuenta de; **don't you r. that ...?** ¿no te das cuenta de que ...?

re·al·ly *adv (truly)* verdaderamente; **r.?** ¿de veras?

re·al·tor agente *mf* inmobiliario, -a.

rear[1] **1** *n (back part)* parte *f* de atrás. **2** *adj* trasero, -a; **r. entrance** puerta *f* de atrás.

rear[2] **1** *vt (breed, raise)* criar. **2** *vi* **to r. up** *(horse)* encabritarse.

re·ar·range *vt (furniture)* colocar de otra manera; *(set new date)* fijar otra fecha para.

rea·son 1 *n* motivo *m*; **for no r.** sin razón. **2** *vi (argue, work out)* razonar.

rea·son·a·ble *adj (fair)* razonable; *(sensible)* sensato, -a.

rea·son·a·bly *adv (fairly, quite)* bastante.

rea·son·ing razonamiento *m.*

re·as·sure *vt (comfort)* tranquilizar; *(restore confidence in)* dar confianza a.

re·as·sur·ing *adj* consolador, -a.

re·bel 1 *adj & n* rebelde *(mf).* **2** *vi* rebelarse (**against** contra).

re·bel·lion rebelión *f.*

re·bound 1 *n (of ball)* rebote *m.* **2** *vi (ball)* rebotar.

re·build *vt* reconstruir.

re·call *vt (remember)* recordar.

re·ceipt *(paper)* recibo *m*; **receipts** *(takings)* recaudación *f sing.*

re·ceive *vt* recibir.

re·ceiv·er *(of phone)* auricular *m*; *(radio)* receptor *m.*

re·cent *adj* reciente; **in r. years** en los últimos años.

re·cent·ly *adv* recientemente.

re·cep·tion *(party, of TV pictures etc)* recepción *f*; *(welcome)* acogida *f*; **r. (desk)** recepción *f.*

re·cep·tion·ist recepcionista *mf.*

re·charge *vt (battery)* recargar.

rec·i·pe receta *f.*

re·cip·i·ent receptor, -a *mf*; *(of letter)* destinatario, -a *mf.*

re·cite *vti* recitar.

reck·less *adj (unwise)* imprudente.

reck·on *vt (calculate)* calcular; *fam (think)* creer.

▸**reckon on** *vt* contar con.

▸**reckon with** *vt (take into account)* contar con.

re·claim *vt (recover)* recuperar; *(demand back)* reclamar; *(marshland etc)* convertir.

rec·og·nize *vt* reconocer.

rec·ol·lect *vt* recordar.

rec·ol·lec·tion recuerdo *m.*

rec·om·mend *vt* recomendar.

rec·om·men·da·tion recomendación *f.*

re·cord 1 *n (of music etc)* disco *m*; *(in sport etc)* récord *m*; *(document)* documento *m*; *(case history)* historial *m* médico; **public records** archivos *mpl.* **2** *vt (relate)* hacer constar; *(note down)* apuntar; *(music, voice)* grabar.

re·cord·ed *adj* grabado, -a.

re·cord·er *(musical instrument)* flauta *f*; **(tape) r.** magnetófono *m*; **(video) r.** vídeo *m.*

re·cord·ing grabación *f.*

re·cord play·er tocadiscos *m inv.*

re·cov·er 1 *vt (items, time)* recuperar; *(consciousness)* recobrar. **2** *vi (from illness etc)* reponerse; *(economy)* recuperarse.

rec·re·a·tion *(entertainment)* diversión *f*; *(school playtime)* recreo *m.*

re·cruit recluta *m.*

rec·tan·gle rectángulo *m.*

rec·tan·gu·lar *adj* rectangular.

re·cy·cle *vt* reciclar.

red 1 *adj* rojo, -a; **r. light** semáforo *m* en rojo; **r. wine** vino *m* tinto; **to go r.** ponerse colorado, -a; **to have r. hair** ser pelirrojo, -a. **2** *n (color)* rojo *m*; **to be in the r.** estar en números rojos.

red-hand·ed *adj* **to catch sb r.** coger a algn con las manos en la masa.

red·head pelirrojo, -a *mf.*

red-hot *adj* al rojo vivo.

re·di·rect *vt (forward)* remitir a la nueva dirección.

re·do* *vt (exercise, house)* rehacer.

re·duce *vt* reducir.

re·duc·tion *(decrease)* reducción *f*; *(cut in price)* descuento *m.*

re·dun·dan·cy despido *m.*

re·dun·dant *adj* **to be made r.** perder el empleo; **to make sb r.** despedir a algn.

reed *(plant)* caña *f.*

reef arrecife *m.*

reel *(spool)* bobina *f*, carrete *m.*

re·fec·to·ry refectorio *m.*

re·fer 1 *vt* **to r. a matter to a tribunal** remitir un asunto a un tribunal. **2** *vi (allude)* referirse (**to** a).

ref·e·ree 1 *n* árbitro, -a *mf.* **2** *vt* arbitrar.

ref·er·ence referencia *f*; *(character report)* informe *m*; **with r. to** referente a, con referencia a.

ref·er·en·dum referéndum *m.*

re·fill 1 *n (replacement)* recambio *m*; *(another drink)* otra copa *f.* **2** *vt* rellenar.

re·flect 1 *vt (light, attitude)* reflejar; **to be reflected** reflejarse. **2** *vi (think)* reflexionar.

re·flec·tion *(indication, mirror image)* reflejo *m.*

re·flex reflejo *m.*

re·form 1 *n* reforma *f.* **2** *vt* reformar.

re·frain *vi* abstenerse (**from** de).

re·fresh *vt* refrescar.

re·fresh·er course cursillo *m* de reciclaje.

re·fresh·ing *adj* refrescante.

re·fresh·ment refresco *m.*

re·frig·er·a·tor nevera *f.*

ref·uge refugio *m*; **to take r.** refugiarse.

ref·u·gee refugiado, -a *mf.*

re·fund 1 *n* reembolso *m.* **2** *vt* reembolsar.

re·fus·al negativa *f.*

re·fuse 1 *vt (reject)* rechazar; **to r. sb sth** negar algo a algn; **to r. to do sth** negarse a hacer algo. **2** *vi* negarse.

re·gain *vt* recuperar.

re·gard 1 *n (concern)* consideración *f*, **with r. to, as regards** (con) respecto a; **give him my regards** dale recuerdos de mi parte. **2** *vt (consider)* considerar.

re·gard·ing *prep* (con) respecto a.

re·gard·less 1 *prep* **r. of** a pesar de; **r. of the outcome** pase lo que pase. **2** *adv* a toda costa.

reg·i·ment regimiento *m.*

re·gion región *f*, zona *f*; **in the r. of** aproximadamente.

re·gion·al *adj* regional.

reg·is·ter 1 *n* registro *m.* **2** *vt (record)* registrar; *(letter)* certificar. **3** *vi (enter one's name)* inscribirse; *(at university)* matricularse.

reg·is·tra·tion inscripción *f*; *(at university)* matrícula *f.*

re·gret 1 *n (remorse)* remordimiento *m*; *(sadness)* pesar *m.* **2** *vt* arrepentirse de, lamentar.

reg·u·lar 1 *adj* regular; *(usual)* normal; *(frequent)* frecuente.

reg·u·lar·ly *adv* con regularidad.

reg·u·late *vt* regular.

reg·u·la·tion 1 *n (control)* regulación *f*; *(rule)* regla *f.* **2** *adj* reglamentario, -a.

re·hears·al ensayo *m.*

re·hearse *vti* ensayar.

reign 1 *n* reinado *m.* **2** *vi* reinar.

rein·deer reno *m.*

re·in·force *vt (strengthen)* reforzar.

re·in·force·ments *npl* refuerzos *mpl.*

reins *(for horse)* riendas *fpl.*

re·in·state *vt (to job)* reincorporar.

re·ject *vt* rechazar.

re·jec·tion rechazo *m.*

re·joice *vi* regocijarse (**at, over** de).

re·late 1 *vt (connect)* relacionar; *(tell)* contar. **2** *vi* relacionarse (**to** con).

re·lat·ed *adj (linked)* relacionado, -a (**to** con); **to be r. to sb** ser pariente de algn.

re·la·tion *(link)* relación *f*; *(family)* pariente, -a *mf*; **in** *or* **with r. to** (con) respecto a.

re·la·tion·ship *(link)* relación *f*; *(between people)* relaciones *fpl.*

rel·a·tive 1 *n* pariente, -a *mf.* **2** *adj* relativo, -a.

rel·a·tive·ly *adv* relativamente.

re·lax 1 *vi* relajarse; **r.!** ¡cálmate! **2** *vt (calm)* relajar; *(loosen)* aflojar.

re·lax·a·tion *(rest)* relajación *f.*

re·laxed *adj* relajado, -a.

re·lease 1 *n (setting free)* liberación *f*; *(of product)* puesta *f* en venta; *(of film)* estreno *m*; *(press release)* comunicado *m.* **2** *vt (set free)* poner en libertad; *(let go)* soltar; *(product, record)* poner a la venta; *(film)* estrenar.

rel·e·vance pertinencia *f.*

rel·e·vant *adj* pertinente (**to** a); **it is not r.** no viene al caso.

re·li·a·bil·i·ty *(of person)* formalidad *f*; *(of thing)* fiabilidad *f.*

re·li·a·ble *adj (person)* de fiar; *(thing)* fiable.

re·lief alivio *m*; *(aid)* auxilio *m*; *(in art, geography)* relieve *m.*

re·lieve *vt* aliviar; *(substitute)* relevar.

re·li·gion religión *f.*

re·li·gious *adj* religioso, -a.

rel·ish *(seasoning)* condimento *m.*

re·load *vt (gun, camera)* recargar.

re·luc·tance desgana *f.*

re·luc·tant *adj* reacio, -a; **to be r. to do sth** estar poco dispuesto, -a a hacer algo.
re·luc·tant·ly *adv* de mala gana.
▸**re·ly on** *vt (count on)* contar con; *(be dependent on)* depender de.
re·main *vi (stay)* permanecer, quedarse; *(be left)* quedar.
re·main·ing *adj* restante.
re·mark 1 *n* comentario *m*. **2** *vt* comentar.
re·mark·a·ble *adj (extraordinary)* extraordinario, -a.
re·mark·a·bly *adv* extraordinariamente.
re·me·di·al *adj* **r. classes** clases *fpl* para niños atrasados en los estudios.
rem·e·dy 1 *n* remedio *m*. **2** *vt* remediar.
re·mem·ber 1 *vt (recall)* acordarse de. **2** *vi* acordarse.
re·mind *vt* recordar; **r. me to do it** recuérdame que lo haga.
re·mind·er *n* aviso *m*.
re·morse *n* remordimiento *m*.
re·mote *adj (far away)* remoto, -a; *(isolated)* aislado, -a.
re·mote con·trol *n* mando *m* a distancia.
re·mov·al *(moving house)* mudanza *f*, *(getting rid of)* eliminación *f*; **r. man** hombre *m* de la mudanza; **r. van** camión *m* de mudanzas.
re·move *vt* quitar.
re·new *vt (contract etc)* renovar; *(talks etc)* reanudar.
rent 1 *n (of building, car, TV)* alquiler *m*. **2** *vt* alquilar.
▸**rent out** *vt* alquilar.
rent·al *(of house etc)* alquiler *m*.
rent·al car coche *m* de alquiler.
re·or·gan·ize *vt* reorganizar.
re·pair 1 *n* reparación *f*, **in good/bad r.** en buen/mal estado. **2** *vt* arreglar; *(car)* reparar; *(clothes)* remendar.
re·pair·man técnico *m*.
re·pay *vt* devolver; *(debt)* liquidar.
re·pay·ment pago *m*.
re·peat 1 *vt* repetir. **2** *n (repetition)* repetición *f*, *(on TV)* reposición *f*.
re·peat·ed *adj* repetido, -a.
re·peat·ed·ly *adv* repetidas veces.
re·pel *vt (fight off)* repeler.
rep·e·ti·tion repetición *f*.
re·pet·i·tive *adj* repetitivo, -a.
re·place *vt (put back)* volver a poner en su sitio; *(substitute)* sustituir.
re·place·ment *(person)* sustituto, -a *mf*, *(part)* pieza *f* de recambio.
re·play repetición *f*.
rep·li·ca réplica *f*.
re·ply 1 *n* respuesta *f*. **2** *vi* responder.
re·port 1 *n* informe *m*; *(piece of news)* noticia *f*; *(in newspaper, on TV etc)* reportaje *m*; *(rumor)* rumor *m*; **school r.** informe *m* escolar. **2** *vt (tell police, authorities about)* denunciar; *(journalist)* hacer un reportaje sobre; **it is reported that ...** se dice que ... **3** *vi (committee etc)* hacer un informe; *(journalist)* hacer un reportaje; *(to work etc)* presentarse.
re·port·ed *adj* **r. speech** estilo *m* indirecto.
re·port·ed·ly *adv* según se dice.
re·port·er periodista *mf*.
rep·re·sent *vt* representar.
rep·re·sen·ta·tive representante *mf*.
re·pro·duce 1 *vt* reproducir. **2** *vi* reproducirse.
re·pro·duc·tion reproducción *f*.
rep·tile reptil *m*.
re·pub·lic república *f*.
re·pub·li·can *adj & n* republicano, -a *(mf)*; **R. Party** Partido *m* Republicano.
rep·u·ta·ble *adj (company etc)* acreditado, -a; *(person, products)* de toda confianza.
rep·u·ta·tion reputación *f*.
re·quest 1 *n* petición *f*. **2** *vt* pedir.
re·quire *vt (need)* necesitar; *(demand)* exigir.
re·quired *adj* necesario, -a.
res·cue 1 *n* rescate *m*. **2** *vt* rescatar.
re·search 1 *n* investigación *f*. **2** *vti* investigar.
re·search·er investigador, -a *mf*.
re·sem·blance semejanza *f*.
re·sem·ble *vt* parecerse a.
re·sent *vt* ofenderse por.
re·sent·ment resentimiento *m*.
res·er·va·tion reserva *f*.
re·serve 1 *n* reserva *f*, *(in sport)* suplente *mf*; **to keep sth in r.** guardar algo de reserva. **2** *vt* reservar.
re·served *adj* reservado, -a.
res·er·voir embalse *m*, pantano *m*.
res·i·dence *(home)* residencia *f*, *(address)* domicilio *m*.
res·i·dent *adj & n* residente *(mf)*.
res·i·den·tial *adj* residencial.
re·sign 1 *vt* to **r. oneself to sth** resignarse a algo. **2** *vi* dimitir.
res·ig·na·tion *(from a job)* dimisión *f*.
re·sist *vt (not yield)* resistir; *(oppose)* oponerse a; **I couldn't r. telling her** no pude resistir a la tentación de decírselo.
re·sis·tance resistencia *f*.
re·sit *vt (exam)* volver a presentarse a.
re·sort *(recourse)* recurso *m*; *(place)* lugar *m* de vacaciones; **as a last r.** como último recurso; **tourist r.** centro *m* turístico.
▸**resort to** *vt* recurrir a.
re·source recurso *m*.
re·spect 1 *n (reference)* respeto *m*; **in that r.** a ese respecto; **with r. to** con referencia a. **2** *vt* respetar.
re·spect·a·ble *adj* respetable; *(clothes)* decente.
re·spec·tive *adj* respectivo, -a.
re·spond *vi* responder a.
re·sponse *(reply)* respuesta *f*, *(reaction)* reacción *f*.
re·spon·si·bil·i·ty responsabilidad *f*.
re·spon·si·ble *adj* responsable *(for* de).
rest¹ 1 *n (break)* descanso *m*, *(peace)* tranquilidad *f*. **2** *vt (lean)* apoyar. **3** *vi* descansar.
rest² the **r.** *(remainder)* el resto *m*; **the r. of the day** el resto del día; **the r. of the girls** las demás chicas.
res·tau·rant restaurante *m*.
rest·ful *adj* relajante.
rest·less *adj* inquieto, -a.
re·store *vt (give back)* devolver; *(repair)* restaurar.
re·strain *vt* contener; **to r. one's anger** reprimir la cólera; **to r. oneself** contenerse.
re·straint *(restriction)* restricción *f*, *(moderation)* moderación *f*.
re·strict *vt* restringir.
re·strict·ed *adj* restringido, -a; **r. area** zona *f* restringida.

re·stric·tion restricción *f*.
rest·room aseos *mpl*.
re·sult resultado *m*; **as a r. of** como consecuencia de.
re·sume 1 *vt (journey, work, conversation)* reanudar; *(control)* reasumir. **2** *vi* recomenzar.
ré·su·mé resumen *m*.
re·tail 1 *n* **r. price** precio *m* de venta al público. **2** *vt* vender al por menor. **3** *adv* al por menor.
re·tail·er detallista *mf*.
re·tain *vt* conservar.
re·tire *vi (stop working)* jubilarse; *(withdraw)* retirarse; **to r. for the night** irse a la cama.
re·tired *adj* jubilado, -a.
re·tire·ment jubilación *f*.
re·treat 1 *n (of troops)* retirada *f*, *(shelter)* refugio *m*. **2** *vi* retirarse *(from* de).
re·trieve *vt (recover)* recuperar; *(of dog)* cobrar.
re·turn 1 *n (coming or going back)* regreso *m*, *(giving back)* devolución *f*, *(profit)* beneficio *m*; **r. ticket** billete *m* de ida y vuelta. **2** *vt (give back)* devolver. **3** *vi (come or go back)* regresar.
re·turn·a·ble *adj (bottle)* retornable.
re·veal *vt (make known)* revelar; *(show)* dejar ver.
rev·e·la·tion revelación *f*.
re·venge venganza *f*; **to take r. on sb for sth** vengarse de algo en algn.
re·verse 1 *adj* inverso, -a. **2** *n* quite the **r.** todo lo contrario; **r. (gear)** marcha *f* atrás. **3** *vt* to **r. the charges** poner una conferencia a cobro revertido. **4** *vi (in car)* dar marcha atrás; **to r. in/out** entrar/salir marcha atrás.
re·vert *vi* volver *(to* a).
re·view 1 *n (in press)* crítica *f*. **2** *vt (book etc)* hacer una crítica de.
re·vise *vt (look over)* revisar; *(at school)* repasar.
re·vi·sion revisión *f*, *(at school)* repaso *m*.
re·viv·al *(of interest, custom, country)* resurgimiento *m*, *(of play)* reposición *f*.
re·vive *vt (unconscious person)* reanimar.
re·volt rebelión *f*.
re·volt·ing *adj* repugnante.
rev·o·lu·tion revolución *f*.
rev·o·lu·tion·ar·y *adj & n* revolucionario, -a *(mf)*.
re·volve *vi* girar; *fig* to **r. around** girar en torno a.
re·volv·er revólver *m*.
re·volv·ing *adj* giratorio, -a; **r. door** puerta *f* giratoria.
re·ward 1 *n* recompensa *f*. **2** *vt* recompensar.
re·wind* 1 *vt (tape)* rebobinar. **2** *vi* rebobinarse.
rhet·o·ric retórica *f*.
rheu·ma·tism reúma *m*.
rhi·noc·er·os rinoceronte *m*.
rhu·barb ruibarbo *m*.
rhyme 1 *n* rima *f*, *(poem)* poema *m*. **2** *vi* rimar.
rhythm ritmo *m*.
rib costilla *f*.
rib·bon cinta *f*, *(in hair etc)* lazo *m*.
rice arroz *m*.
rich 1 *adj* rico, -a. **2** *npl* the **r.** los ricos.
rich·es *npl* riquezas *fpl*.
rid *vt* to get **r. of sth** deshacerse de algo.
rid·dle *(puzzle)* adivinanza *f*, *(mystery)* enigma *m*.
ride 1 *n* paseo *m*; **a short bus r.** un corto trayecto en autobús; **horse r.** paseo a caballo. **2** *vt** *(bicycle, horse)* montar en; **can you r. a bike?** ¿sabes montar en bici? **3** *vi* (on horse)* montar a caballo; *(travel) (on bus, train etc)* viajar.
rid·er *(of horse) (man)* jinete *m*, *(woman)* amazona *f*, *(of bicycle)* ciclista *mf*, *(of motorbike)* motociclista *mf*.
ridge *(of mountain)* cresta *f*.
ri·dic·u·lous *adj* ridículo, -a.
rid·ing equitación *f*.
ri·fle rifle *m*.
rig (oil) r. *(onshore)* torre *f* de perforación; *(offshore)* plataforma *f* petrolífera.
right 1 *adj (not left)* derecho, -a; *(correct)* correcto, -a; *(suitable)* adecuado, -a; *(proper)* apropiado, -a; *(exact) (time)* exacto, -a; **all r.** de acuerdo; **r.?** ¿vale?; **that's r.** eso es; **isn't that r.?** ¿no es verdad?; **the r. word** la palabra justa; **to be r.** tener razón; **the r. time** *(appropriate time)* el momento oportuno; **r. angle** ángulo *m* recto. **2** *n (right side)* derecha *f*, *(right hand)* mano *f* derecha; *(in politics)* the **R.** la derecha; *(lawful claim)* derecho *m*; **r. and wrong** el bien y el mal. **3** *adv (correctly)* bien; *(to the right)* a la derecha; **r. away** en seguida; **to turn r.** girar a la derecha; **go r. on** sigue recto; **r. at the top** en todo lo alto; **r. in the middle** justo en medio; **r. to the end** hasta el final.
right-hand *adj* derecho, -a.
right-hand·ed *adj (person)* que usa la mano derecha, diestro, -a.
right·ly *adv* debidamente; **and r. so** y con razón.
right-wing *adj* de derechas, derechista.
rig·id *adj* rígido, -a.
rim *(edge)* borde *m*.
rind *(of fruit, cheese)* corteza *f*.
ring¹ 1 *n (of doorbell, alarm clock)* timbre *m*, *(of phone)* llamada *f*. **2** *vt* (bell)* tocar; *(on phone)* llamar por teléfono. **3** *vi* (bell, phone etc)* sonar.
ring² 1 *n* sortija *f*, *(wedding ring)* anillo *m*; *(metal hoop)* aro *m*; *(circle)* círculo *m*; *(group of people)* corro *m*; *(in boxing)* cuadrilátero *m*; *(for bullfights)* ruedo *m*. **2** *vt (surround)* rodear.
▸**ring out** *vi (bell etc)* resonar.
ring·lead·er cabecilla *m*.
rinse *vt* aclarar; *(dishes)* enjuagar.
▸**rinse out** *vt* enjuagar.
ri·ot 1 *n (disturbance)* disturbio *m*; **r. police** policía *f* antidisturbios. **2** *vi* amotinarse.
rip 1 *n (tear)* rasgón *m*. **2** *vt* rasgar. **3** *vi* rasgarse.
▸**rip off** *vt fam* to **r. sb off** timar a algn.
▸**rip up** *vt* hacer pedacitos.
ripe *adj* maduro, -a.
rip·en *vti* madurar.
rip-off *fam* timo *m*.
rise 1 *n (of slope, hill)* cuesta *f*, *(in prices, temperature)* subida *f*, *(of wages)* aumento *m*; **to give r. to** ocasionar. **2** *vi* (prices, temperature)* subir; *(wages)* aumentar; *(from bed)* levantarse; *(stand up)* levantarse; *(city, building)* erguirse.
ris·ing 1 *adj (sun)* naciente; *(tide)* creciente; *(prices)* en aumento. **2** *n (rebellion)* levantamiento *m*.
risk 1 *n* riesgo *m*; **at r.** en peligro; **to take risks** arriesgarse. **2** *vt* arriesgar; **I'll r. it** correré el riesgo.
risk·y *adj* arriesgado, -a.
rit·u·al *adj & n* ritual *(m)*.
ri·val 1 *adj & n* rival *(mf)*. **2** *vt* rivalizar con.
riv·er río *m*.
road carretera *f*, *(street)* calle *f*, *(way)* camino *m*; **r. accident** accidente *m* de tráfico; **r. safety** seguridad *f* vial.
road·side borde *m* de la carretera.

road·way calzada f.
road·works npl obras fpl.
roam 1 vt vagar por. **2** vi vagar.
roar 1 n (of lion) rugido m; (of bull, sea, wind) bramido m. **2** vi (lion, crowd) rugir; (bull, sea, wind) bramar.
roast 1 adj (meat) asado, -a; **r. beef** rosbif m. **2** n asado m. **3** vt (meat) asar; (coffee, nuts) tostar. **4** vi asarse.
rob vt robar; (bank) atracar.
rob·ber ladrón, -a mf; **bank r.** atracador, -a mf.
rob·ber·y robo m.
robe (ceremonial) toga f, bata f.
rob·in petirrojo m.
ro·bot robot m.
rock 1 n roca f, (stone) piedra f, (music) música f rock. **2** vt (chair) mecer; (baby) acunar; (shake) sacudir. **3** vi (move back and forth) mecerse; (shake) vibrar.
rock·et 1 n cohete m. **2** vi (prices) dispararse.
rock·ing chair mecedora f.
rod (of metal) barra f, (stick) vara f, **fishing r.** caña f de pescar.
rogue granuja m.
role, rôle papel m; **to play a r.** desempeñar un papel.
roll 1 n rollo m; **(bread) r.** bollo m; (of drum) redoble m. **2** vt hacer rodar. **3** vi (ball) rodar; (animal) revolcarse.
▶**roll by** vi (years) pasar.
▶**roll down** vt (blinds) bajar; (sleeves) bajarse; (hill) bajar rodando.
▶**roll over** vi dar una vuelta.
▶**roll up** vt (paper etc) enrollar; (blinds) subir; **to r. up one's sleeves** (ar)remangarse.
roll·er rodillo m, **rollers** (for hair) rulos mpl.
roll·er skate patín m de ruedas.
roll·ing pin rodillo m (de cocina).
roll·ing stock material m rodante.
Ro·man adj & n romano, -a (mf).
Ro·man Cath·o·lic adj & n católico, -a (mf) (romano, -a).
ro·mance (love affair) aventura f amorosa.
ro·man·tic adj & n romántico, -a (mf).
roof tejado m; (of car) techo m.
roof rack baca f.
room habitación f, (space) espacio m; **single r.** habitación individual; **make r. for me** hazme sitio.
room·mate compañero, -a mf de habitación.
room·y adj amplio, -a.
root raíz f, **to take r.** echar raíces.
▶**root for** vt **to r. for a team** animar a un equipo.
▶**root out, root up** vt arrancar de raíz.
rope (small) cuerda f, (big) soga f.
▶**rope off** vt acordonar.
rose rosa f, **r. bush** rosal m.
rot vi pudrirse.
ro·ta·tion rotación f.
rot·ten adj (decayed) podrido, -a; fam (very bad) malísimo, -a; (health) enfermo, -a; **I feel r.** me encuentro fatal.
rough adj (surface, skin) áspero, -a; (terrain) accidentado, -a; (road) desigual; (sea) agitado, -a; (rude) grosero, -a; (violent) violento, -a; (approximate) aproximado, -a; (plan etc) preliminar; **r. draft** borrador m; **r. sketch** esbozo m.
rough·ly adv (crudely) toscamente; (not gently) bruscamente; (approximately) aproximadamente.
round 1 adj redondo, -a. **2** n (of drinks) ronda f, (at golf) partido m; (at cards) partida f, (in boxing) round m; (in a competition) eliminatoria f, **rounds** (doctor's) visita f sing. **3** adv **all year r.** durante todo el año; **to invite sb r.** invitar a algn a casa. **4** prep (place etc) alrededor de; **r. here** por aquí; **r. the corner** a la vuelta de la esquina.
▶**round up** vt (cattle) acorralar; (people) reunir.
round·a·bout 1 n (merry-go-round) tiovivo m; (on road) glorieta f. **2** adj indirecto, -a.
round trip viaje m de ida y vuelta.
route ruta f, (of bus) línea f.
rou·tine rutina f.
row¹ fila f, **three times in a r.** tres veces seguidas.
row² vi (in a boat) remar.
row³ 1 n (quarrel) bronca f, (noise) jaleo m. **2** vi pelearse.
row·boat bote m de remos.
row house casa f adosada.
roy·al 1 adj real. **2** npl **the Royals** los miembros de la Familia Real.
roy·al·ty (royal person(s)) miembro(s) m(pl) de la Familia Real; **royalties** derechos mpl de autor.
rub 1 vt frotar; (hard) restregar; (massage) friccionar. **2** vi rozar (**against** contra).
▶**rub down** vt frotar; (horse) almohazar; (surface) raspar.
▶**rub in** vt (cream etc) frotar con.
▶**rub off** vt (erase) borrar.
▶**rub out** vt borrar.
rub·ber (substance) caucho m; (eraser) goma f (de borrar).
rub·ble escombros mpl.
ru·by rubí m.
ruck·sack mochila f.
rud·der timón m.
rude adj (impolite) maleducado, -a; (foul-mouthed) grosero, -a.
rude·ness (impoliteness) falta f de educación; (offensiveness) grosería f.
rug alfombra f.
rug·by rugby m.
ru·in 1 n ruina f, **in ruins** en ruinas. **2** vt arruinar; (spoil) estropear.
rule 1 n regla f, (of monarch) reinado m; **as a r.** por regla general. **2** vti (govern) gobernar; (monarch) reinar.
▶**rule out** vt descartar.
rul·er (monarch) soberano, -a mf; (for measuring) regla f.
rul·ing 1 adj (in charge) dirigente; **the r. party** el partido en el poder. **2** n (of judge) fallo m.
rum ron m.
Ru·ma·ni·an 1 adj rumano, -a. **2** n (person) rumano, -a mf; (language) rumano m.
rum·mage sale mercadillo m de caridad.
ru·mor 1 n rumor m. **2** vt **it is rumored that** se rumorea que.
run 1 n (act of running, in stocking) carrera f, (trip) vuelta f, **on the r.** fugado, -a; **to go for a r.** hacer footing; (in car) dar un paseo; **in the long r.** a largo plazo; **ski r.** pista f de esquí. **2** vt* correr; (business) llevar; (company) dirigir; (organize) organizar; **to r. errands** hacer recados; **to r. a program** pasar un programa. **3** vi* (person, river) correr; (color) desteñirse; (operate) funcionar; (film, play) estar en cartel; **your nose is running** tienes catarro; **trains r. every two hours** hay trenes cada dos horas; **we're running low on milk** nos queda poca leche.
▶**run across** vt (meet) tropezar con.
▶**run away** vi fugarse.
▶**run down** vt (stairs) bajar corriendo; (knock down) atropellar.
▶**run in** vi entrar corriendo.
▶**run into** vt (room etc) entrar corriendo en; (people, problems) tropezar con; (crash into) chocar contra.
▶**run off** vi escaparse.
▶**run out** vi (exit) salir corriendo; (finish) agotarse; (contract) vencer; **to r. out of** quedarse sin.
▶**run over** vt (knock down) atropellar.
run·a·way adj (vehicle) incontrolado, -a; (inflation) galopante; (success) clamoroso, -a.
rung (of ladder) peldaño m.
run·ner-up subcampeón, -ona mf.
run·ning 1 n atletismo m; (management) dirección f. **2** adj **r. water** agua f corriente; **three weeks r.** tres semanas seguidas.
run·ny adj (nose) que moquea.
run·way pista f (de aterrizaje y despegue).
rush 1 n (hurry) prisa f, (hustle and bustle) ajetreo m; **there's no r.** no corre prisa. **2** vt (do hastily) hacer de prisa; **to r. sb to hospital** llevar a algn urgentemente al hospital. **3** vi (go quickly) precipitarse.
▶**rush around** vi correr de un lado a otro.
▶**rush off** vi irse corriendo.
rush hour hora f punta.
Rus·sian 1 adj ruso, -a. **2** n (person) ruso, -a mf; (language) ruso m.
rust 1 n herrumbre f. **2** vi oxidarse.
rust·y adj oxidado, -a.
RV abbr of **recreational vehicle** autocaravana f.
rye centeno m; **r. bread** pan m de centeno.

S

sack 1 n (bag) saco m. **2** vt (employee) despedir a.
sa·cred adj sagrado, -a.
sac·ri·fice 1 n sacrificio m. **2** vt sacrificar.
sad adj triste.
sad·den vt entristecer.
sad·dle n (for horse) silla f (de montar).
sad·ly adv tristemente.
sad·ness tristeza f.
safe 1 adj (unharmed) ileso, -a; (out of danger) a salvo; (not dangerous) inocuo, -a; (secure, sure) seguro, -a; **s. and sound** sano, -a y salvo, -a. **2** n (for money etc) caja f fuerte.
safe·guard 1 n (protection) salvaguarda f, (guarantee) garantía f. **2** vt proteger, salvaguardar.
safe·ly adv con toda seguridad; **to arrive s.** llegar sin accidentes.
safe·ty seguridad f.
safe·ty belt cinturón m de seguridad.
safe·ty pin imperdible m.
sag vi (roof) hundirse.
said 1 pt & pp of **say 2** adj dicho, -a.
sail 1 n (canvas) vela f, (trip) paseo m en barco; **to set s.** zarpar. **2** vt (ship) gobernar. **3** vi ir en barco; (set sail) zarpar.
sail·board tabla f de windsurf.
sail·boat barco m de vela.
sail·ing navegación f, (yachting) vela f.
sail·or marinero m.
saint n santo, -a mf; (before all masculine names except those beginning **Do** or **To**) San; (before feminine names) Santa.
sake n **for the s. of** por (el bien de); **for your own s.** por tu propio bien.
sal·ad ensalada f.
sal·ad bowl ensaladera f.
sal·ad dress·ing aliño m.
sal·a·ry salario m.
sale venta f, (at low prices) rebajas fpl; **for** or **on s.** en venta.
sale price adj (article) a precio rebajado.
sales·clerk dependiente, -a mf.
sales·man vendedor m; (in shop) dependiente m; (commercial representative) representante m.
sales tax impuesto m de venta.
sales·wom·an vendedora f, (in shop) dependienta f, (commercial representative) representante f.
sa·li·va saliva f.
salm·on salmón m.
sa·lon salón m.
salt 1 n sal f, **bath salts** sales de baño. **2** vt (add salt to) echar sal a.
salt cel·lar salero m.
salt·y adj salado, -a.
sal·va·tion salvación f, **S. Army** Ejército m de Salvación.
same 1 adj mismo, -a; **at the s. time** al mismo tiempo; **the two cars are the s.** los dos coches son iguales. **2** pron el mismo, la misma, lo mismo; **all the s., just the s.** aun así; **it's all the s. to me** (a mí) me da igual.
sam·ple 1 n muestra f. **2** vt (wines) catar; (dish) probar.
sand arena f.
san·dal sandalia f.
sand cas·tle castillo m de arena.
sand·pa·per papel m de lija.
sand·wich (roll) bocadillo m; (sliced bread) sandwich m.
sand·y adj (earth, beach) arenoso, -a; (hair) rubio, -a, rojizo, -a.
san·i·tar·y s. napkin compresa f.
San·ta Claus Papá Noel m.
sar·dine sardina f.
sat pt & pp of **sit**.
satch·el cartera f (de colegial).
sat·el·lite satélite m; **s. dish** antena f parabólica.
sat·in satén m.
sat·is·fac·tion satisfacción f.
sat·is·fac·to·ry adj satisfactorio, -a.
sat·is·fy vt satisfacer; (fulfill) cumplir con.
sat·is·fy·ing adj satisfactorio, -a.
sat·u·rate vt saturar (**with** de).
Sat·ur·day sábado m.
sauce salsa f.
sauce·pan cacerola f, (large) olla f.

sau·cer platillo *m*.
Sau·di A·ra·bi·an *adj & n* saudita *(mf)*, saudí *(m)*.
sau·na sauna *f*.
sau·sage *(frankfurter)* salchicha *f*, *(cured)* salchichón *m*; *(spicy)* chorizo *m*.
save 1 *vt (rescue)* rescatar; *(put by, computer file)* guardar; *(money)* ahorrar; *(food)* almacenar; **it saved him a lot of trouble** le evitó muchos problemas. **2** *n (in soccer)* parada *f*.
sav·ings *npl* ahorros *mpl*.
sav·ings ac·count cuenta *f* de ahorros.
sav·ings bank caja *f* de ahorros.
saw¹ *n (tool)* sierra *f*. **2** *vti* * serrar.
▸ **saw off** *vt* serrar.
saw² *pt of* **see**.
sax·o·phone saxofón *m*.
say* *vt* decir; **it is said that ...** se dice que ...; **that is to s.** es decir; **what does the sign s.?** ¿qué pone en el letrero?; **shall we s. Friday then?** ¿quedamos el viernes, pues?
say·ing refrán *m*.
scab *(on cut)* costra *f*.
scaf·fold·ing andamio *m*.
scald *vt* escaldar.
scale¹ *(of fish, on skin)* escama *f*, *(in boiler)* incrustaciones *fpl*.
scale² escala *f*, *(extent)* alcance *m*.
scales *npl (pair of)* **s.** *(shop, kitchen)* balanza *f sing*; *(bathroom)* báscula *f sing*.
scan 1 *vt (text, graphics)* escanear; *(scrutinize)* escrutar; *(glance at)* ojear. **2** *n (by ultrasound)* exploración *f* ultrasónica; *(in gynaecology etc)* ecografía *f*.
scan·dal escándalo *m*; *(gossip)* chismes *mpl*.
Scan·di·na·vi·an *adj & n* escandinavo, -a *(mf)*.
scan·ner escáner *m*.
scar cicatriz *f*.
scarce *adj* escaso, -a.
scarce·ly *adv* apenas.
scar·ci·ty escasez *f*.
scare *vt* asustar.
▸ **scare away, scare off** *vt* ahuyentar.
scare·crow espantapájaros *m inv*.
scarf *(pl* **scarves** *or* **scarfs*) *(long, woolen)* bufanda *f*, *(square)* pañuelo *m*.
scar·let *adj* **s. fever** escarlatina *f*.
scar·y *adj* espantoso, -a; *(film)* de terror.
scat·ter 1 *vt (papers etc)* esparcir; *(disperse)* dispersar. **2** *vi* dispersarse.
sce·nar·i·o *(of film)* guión *m*; *(situation)* situación *f* hipotética.
scene *(in theater etc)* escena *f*, *(place)* lugar *m*; **to make a s.** *(fuss)* montar un espectáculo.
scen·er·y *(landscape)* paisaje *m*; *(in theater)* decorado *m*.
scent *(smell)* olor *m*; *(perfume)* perfume *m*.
sched·ule 1 *n (plan, agenda)* programa *m*; *(timetable)* horario *m*; **on s.** a la hora (prevista); **to be behind s.** llevar retraso. **2** *vt (plan)* programar.
sched·uled *adj* previsto, -a; **s. flight** vuelo *m* regular.
scheme *(plan)* plan *m*; *(project)* proyecto *m*; *(trick)* ardid *m*.
schmuck *fam* lelo, -a *mf*.
schol·ar *(learned person)* erudito, -a *mf*; *(pupil)* alumno, -a *mf*.
schol·ar·ship *(grant)* beca *f*.
school *(primary)* escuela *f*, *(secondary)* colegio *m*; *(university)* universidad *f*, **s. year** año *m* escolar.
school·boy alumno *m*.
school·girl alumna *f*.
school·mate compañero, -a *mf* de clase.
school·teach·er profesor, -a *mf*, *(primary school)* maestro, -a *mf*.
sci·ence ciencia *f*, *(school subject)* ciencias *fpl*.
sci·ence fic·tion ciencia-ficción *f*.
sci·en·tif·ic *adj* científico, -a.
scis·sors *npl* tijeras *fpl*.
scold *vt* regañar, reñir.
scone bollo *m*.
scoop *(in press)* exclusiva *f*.
scoot·er *(child's)* patinete *m*; *(adult's)* Vespa® *f*.
scope *(range)* alcance *m*; *(freedom)* libertad *f*.
scorch *vt (burn)* quemar; *(singe)* chamuscar.
score 1 *n (in sport)* tanteo *m*; *(cards, golf)* puntuación *f*, *(result)* resultado *m*; *(twenty)* veintena *f*, *(music)* partitura *f*. **2** *vt (goal)* marcar; *(points)* conseguir. **3** *vi (in sport)* marcar un tanto; *(soccer)* marcar un gol; *(keep the score)* llevar el marcador.
scorn desprecio *m*.
Scot escocés, -esa *mf*.
Scotch 1 *adj* **S. tape**® cinta *f* adhesiva, celo® *m*. **2** *n (whiskey)* whisky *m* escocés.
Scots *adj* escocés, -esa.
Scots·man escocés *m*.
Scots·wom·an escocesa *f*.
scoun·drel canalla *m*.
scout boy s. boy *m* scout; **(talent) s.** cazatalentos *m inv*.
scram·ble 1 *vi* trepar; **to s. up a tree** trepar a un árbol. **2** *vt* **scrambled eggs** huevos *mpl* revueltos. **3** *n (climb)* subida *f*, *fig* **it's going to be a s.** *(rush)* va a ser muy apresurado.
scrap¹ 1 *n (small piece)* pedazo *m*; **scraps** *(of food)* sobras *fpl*. **2** *vt (discard)* desechar; *(idea)* descartar.
scrap² 1 *n (fight)* pelea *f*. **2** *vi* pelearse **(with con)**.
scrap·book álbum *m* de recortes.
scrape 1 *vt (paint, wood)* raspar; *(graze)* arañarse. **2** *vi (rub)* rozar. **3** *n (trouble)* lío *m*.
▸ **scrape through** *vti (exam)* aprobar por los pelos.
scrap met·al chatarra *f*.
scrap pa·per papel *m* de borrador.
scratch 1 *n (on skin, paintwork)* arañazo *m*; **to be up to s.** dar la talla; **to start from s.** partir de cero. **2** *vt (with nail, claw)* arañar; *(paintwork)* rayar; *(to relieve itching)* rascarse.
scream 1 *n* chillido *m*. **2** *vt (insults etc)* gritar. **3** *vi* **to s. at sb** chillar a algn.
screen *(movable partition)* biombo *m*; *(cinema, TV, computer)* pantalla *f*.
screw 1 *n* tornillo *m*. **2** *vt* atornillar; **to s. sth down** *or* **in** *or* **on** fijar algo con tornillos.
screw·driv·er destornillador *m*.
scrib·ble *vt (message etc)* garabatear.
script *(of film)* guión *m*; *(in exam)* examen *m*.
scrub *vt* frotar.
scrub brush estregadera *f*.
scrum *(in rugby)* melée *f*, **s. half** medio *m* melée.
scu·ba div·ing submarinismo *m*.
sculp·ture escultura *f*.
scum *(on liquid)* espuma *f*, *fig* escoria *f*.
sea mar *m or f*, **by the s.** a orillas del mar; **out at s.** en alta mar; **to go by s.** ir en barco.
sea·food mariscos *mpl*.
sea·front paseo *m* marítimo.
sea·gull gaviota *f*.

seal¹ *(animal)* foca *f*.
seal² 1 *n (official stamp)* sello *m*; *(airtight closure)* cierre *m* hermético. **2** *vt (with official stamp)* sellar; *(with wax)* lacrar; *(close)* cerrar.
▸ **seal off** *vt (area)* acordonar.
seam *(in cloth)* costura *f*.
search 1 *vt (files etc)* buscar en; *(building, suitcase)* registrar; *(person)* cachear. **2** *vi* buscar; **to s. through** registrar. **3** *n* búsqueda *f*, *(of person)* cacheo *m*; **in s. of** en busca de.
sea·shell concha *f* marina.
sea·shore *(beach)* playa *f*.
sea·sick *adj* **to get s.** marearse.
sea·sick·ness mareo *m*.
sea·side playa *f*.
sea·son¹ *(of year)* estación *f*, *(for sport etc)* temporada *f*, **high/low s.** temporada *f* alta/baja.
sea·son² *(food)* sazonar.
sea·son·al *adj* estacional.
sea·son·ing condimento *m*.
sea·son tick·et abono *m*.
seat 1 *n* asiento *m*; *(place)* plaza *f*, *(in cinema, theater)* localidad *f*, *(in government)* escaño *m*; **to take a s.** sentarse. **2** *vt (guests etc)* sentar; *(accommodate)* tener cabida para.
seat·ing asientos *mpl*.
sea·weed alga *f* (marina).
sec·ond¹ 1 *adj* segundo, -a; **every s. day** cada dos días. **2** *n (in series)* segundo, -a *mf*; *(gear)* segunda *f*, **the s. of October** el dos de octubre. **3** *adv* **to come s.** terminar en segundo lugar.
sec·ond² *(time)* segundo *m*.
sec·ond·ar·y *adj* secundario, -a.
sec·ond-class 1 *adj* de segunda clase. **2** *adv* **to travel s.** viajar en segunda.
sec·ond·hand *adj & adv* de segunda mano.
sec·ond·ly *adv* en segundo lugar.
se·cret *adj* secreto, -a; **in s.** en secreto.
sec·re·tar·y secretario, -a *mf*.
se·cret·ly *adv* en secreto.
sec·tion sección *f*.
sec·u·lar *adj (music, art)* profano, -a.
se·cure 1 *adj* seguro, -a; *(window, door)* bien cerrado, -a; *(ladder etc)* firme. **2** *vt (fix)* sujetar; *(window, door)* cerrar bien; *(obtain)* obtener.
se·cure·ly *adv (firmly)* firmemente.
se·cu·ri·ty seguridad *f*, *(financial guarantee)* fianza *f*.
se·dan *(automobile)* turismo *m*.
se·da·tion sedación *f*.
sed·a·tive *adj & n* sedante *(m)*.
see* *vti* ver; **let's s.** a ver; **s. you (later)/soon!** ¡hasta luego/pronto!; **to s. sb home** acompañar a algn a casa.
▸ **see about** *vt (deal with)* ocuparse de.
▸ **see off** *vt (say goodbye to)* despedirse de.
▸ **see out** *vt (show out)* acompañar hasta la puerta.
▸ **see through** *vt fam* **to s. through sb** verle el plumero a algn; **to s. sth through** *(carry out)* llevar algo a cabo.
▸ **see to** *vt (deal with)* ocuparse de.
seed semilla *f*, *(of fruit)* pepita *f*.
see·ing *conj* **s. that** dado que.
seek* **1** *vt (look for)* buscar; *(ask for)* solicitar. **2** *vi* buscar; **to s. to do sth** procurar hacer algo.
seem *vi* parecer; **I s. to remember his name was Colin** creo recordar que su nombre era Colin; **it seems to me that** me parece que; **so it seems** eso parece.
seem·ing·ly *adv* aparentemente, según parece.
see·saw balancín *m*.
seg·ment segmento *m*; *(of orange)* gajo *m*.
seize *vt (grab)* agarrar; **to s. an opportunity** aprovechar una ocasión; **to s. power** hacerse con el poder.
sel·dom *adv* rara vez, raramente.
se·lect *vt (thing)* escoger; *(team)* seleccionar.
se·lec·tion *(people or things chosen)* selección *f*, *(range)* surtido *m*.
se·lec·tive *adj* selectivo, -a.
self-as·sur·ance confianza *f* en uno mismo.
self-as·sured *adj* seguro, -a de uno mismo, -a.
self-con·fi·dence confianza *f* en uno mismo, -a.
self-con·fi·dent *adj* seguro, -a de uno mismo, -a.
self-con·scious *adj* cohibido, -a.
self-con·trol autocontrol *m*.
self-de·fense *f* autodefensa *f*.
self-em·ployed *adj (worker)* autónomo, -a.
self-ev·i·dent *adj* evidente, patente.
self·ish *adj* egoísta.
self-re·spect amor *m* propio.
self-righ·teous *adj* santurrón, -ona.
self-serv·ice 1 *n (in shop etc)* autoservicio *m*. **2** *adj* de autoservicio.
sell* **1** *vt* vender. **2** *vi* venderse.
▸ **sell out** *vt* **we're sold out of sugar** se nos ha agotado el azúcar; **sold out** *(sign at theater)* agotadas las localidades.
sell·er vendedor, -a *mf*.
se·mes·ter semestre *m*.
semi- *prefix* semi-.
sem·i·cir·cle semicírculo *m*.
sem·i·co·lon punto y coma *m*.
sem·i·con·duc·tor semiconductor *m*.
sem·i·de·tached casa *f* adosada.
sem·i·fi·nal semifinal *f*.
sem·i·nar seminario *m*.
sem·o·li·na sémola *f*.
sen·ate senado *m*.
sen·a·tor senador, -a *mf*.
send* **1** *vt* enviar; *(cause to become)* volver. **2** *vi* **to s. for sb** mandar llamar a algn.
▸ **send away 1** *vt (dismiss)* despedir. **2** *vi* **s. away for sth** escribir pidiendo algo.
▸ **send back** *vt (goods etc)* devolver.
▸ **send in** *vt (application etc)* mandar; *(troops)* enviar.
▸ **send off** *vt (letter etc)* enviar; *(player)* expulsar.
▸ **send on** *vt (luggage) (ahead)* facturar.
▸ **send out** *vt (person)* echar; *(invitations)* enviar.
▸ **send up** *vt* hacer subir; *(make fun of)* burlarse de.
send·er remitente *mf*.
sen·ior 1 *adj (in age)* mayor; *(in rank)* superior; *(with longer service)* más antiguo, -a; **William Armstrong S.** William Armstrong padre. **2** *n (at school)* estudiante *mf* del último curso; **she's three years my s.** *(in age)* me lleva tres años.
sen·sa·tion sensación *f*.
sen·sa·tion·al *adj (marvelous)* sensacional.

sense 1 *n (faculty)* sentido *m*; *(of word)* significado *m*; *(meaning)* sentido *m*; **s. of direction/humor** sentido *m* de la orientación/del humor; **common s.** sentido *m* común; **it doesn't make s.** no tiene sentido; **to come to one's senses** recobrar el juicio. **2** *vt* sentir.
sense·less *adj (absurd)* absurdo, -a.
sen·si·ble *adj (wise)* sensato, -a; *(choice)* acertado, -a; *(clothes, shoes)* práctico, -a.
sen·si·tive *adj* sensible; *(touchy)* susceptible; *(skin)* delicado, -a.
sen·si·tiv·i·ty sensibilidad *f*; *(touchiness)* susceptibilidad *f*.
sen·tence 1 *n* frase *f*; *(legal)* sentencia *f*; **life s.** cadena *f* perpetua. **2** *vt (judge)* condenar.
sen·ti·ment *(sentimentality)* sensiblería *f*; *(feeling)* sentimiento *m*; *(opinion)* opinión *f*.
sep·a·rate 1 *vt* separar (**from** de). **2** *vi* separarse. **3** *adj* separado, -a; *(different)* distinto, -a.
sep·a·rate·ly *adv* por separado.
sep·a·ra·tion separación *f*.
Sep·tem·ber se(p)tiembre *m*.
se·quence *(order)* orden *m*; *(series)* sucesión *f*.
ser·geant sargento *m*; *(of police)* cabo *m*.
se·ri·al *(on TV etc)* serial *m*; *(soap opera)* telenovela *f*.
se·ries *inv* serie *f*.
se·ri·ous *adj* serio, -a; *(causing concern)* grave; **I am s.** hablo en serio.
se·ri·ous·ly *adv (in earnest)* en serio; *(dangerously, severely)* gravemente.
ser·vant *(domestic)* criado, -a *mf*.
serve *vt* servir; *(customer)* atender; **it serves him right** bien merecido lo tiene.
▸**serve out, serve up** *vt* servir.
serv·er *(for computers)* servidor *m*.
serv·ice 1 *n* servicio *m*; *(maintenance)* mantenimiento *m*; **s. (charge) included** servicio incluido. **2** *vt (car, machine)* revisar.
serv·ice ar·e·a área *f* de servicio.
serv·ice sta·tion estación *f* de servicio.
ses·sion sesión *f*.
set[1] **1** *vt* (put, place)* poner, colocar; *(time, price)* fijar; *(record)* establecer; *(mechanism etc)* ajustar; **to s. one's watch** poner el reloj en hora; **to s. the table** poner la mesa; **to s. sb free** poner en libertad a algn. **2** *vi* (sun, moon)* ponerse; *(jelly, jam)* cuajar; **to s. to** *(begin)* ponerse a. **3** *n (stage) (for film)* plató *m*; *(in theater)* escenario *m*; *(scenery)* decorado *m*; **shampoo and s.** lavado y marcado *m*. **4** *adj (task, idea)* fijo, -a; *(date, time)* señalado, -a; *(ready)* listo, -a; **s. phrase** frase *f* hecha; **to be s. on doing sth** estar empeñado, -a en hacer algo.
▸**set about** *vt (begin)* empezar.
▸**set aside** *vt (time, money)* reservar.
▸**set back** *vt (delay)* retrasar.
▸**set down** *vt (luggage etc)* dejar (en el suelo).
▸**set off 1** *vi (depart)* salir. **2** *vt (bomb)* hacer estallar; *(burglar alarm)* hacer sonar.
▸**set out 1** *vi (depart)* salir; **to s. out for ...** partir hacia ...; **to s. out to do sth** proponerse hacer algo. **2** *vt (arrange)* disponer; *(present)* presentar.
▸**set up 1** *vt (tent, stall)* montar; *(business etc)* establecer. **2** *vi* establecerse.
set[2] *(series)* serie *f*; *(of golf clubs, keys etc)* juego *m*; *(of tools)* estuche *m*; *(of people)* grupo *m*; *(in math)* conjunto *m*; *(tennis)* set *m*; **TV s.** televisor *m*; **chess s.** juego *m* de ajedrez.
set·back revés *m*, contratiempo *m*.
set·tee sofá *m*.
set·ting *(background)* marco *m*.
set·tle 1 *vt (decide on)* acordar; *(date, price)* fijar; *(debt)* pagar; *(account)* saldar. **2** *vi (bird, insect)* posarse; *(put down roots)* afincarse; **to s. into an armchair** acomodarse en un sillón.
▸**settle down** *vi (put down roots)* instalarse; *(marry)* casarse; *(child)* calmarse; *(situation)* normalizarse.
▸**settle with** *vt (pay debt to)* ajustar cuentas con.
set·tle·ment *(agreement)* acuerdo *m*; *(colony)* asentamiento *m*.
set·tler colono, -a *mf*.
sev·en *adj & n* siete *(m) inv*.
sev·en·teen *adj & n* diecisiete *(m) inv*.
sev·enth *adj & n* séptimo, -a *(mf)*.
sev·en·ti·eth *adj & n* septuagésimo, -a *(mf)*.
sev·en·ty *adj & n* setenta *(m) inv*; **in the seventies** en los (años) setenta.
sev·er·al 1 *adj* varios, -as. **2** *pron* algunos, -as.
se·vere *adj* severo, -a; *(climate, blow)* duro, -a; *(illness, loss)* grave.
se·ver·i·ty severidad *f*.
sew* *vti* coser.
▸**sew on** *vt* coser.
▸**sew up** *vt (mend)* remendar.
sew·er alcantarilla *f*.
sew·ing costura *f*.
sew·ing ma·chine máquina *f* de coser.
sex sexo *m*; **s. education** educación *f* sexual; **to have s. with sb** tener relaciones sexuales con algn.
sex·u·al *adj* sexual.
sex·y *adj* sexy.
sh! *interj* ¡chitón!, ¡chh!
shab·by *adj (garment)* raído, -a; *(unkempt)* desaseado, -a.
shade *(shadow)* sombra *f*; *(lampshade)* pantalla *f*; *(of color)* matiz *m*; **in the s.** a la sombra.
shad·ow sombra *f*.
shad·y *adj (place)* a la sombra.
shaft *(of tool)* mango *m*; *(of mine)* pozo *m*; *(of elevator)* hueco *m*; *(beam of light)* rayo *m*.
shake* 1 *vt* sacudir; *(bottle)* agitar; **the news shook him** la noticia le conmocionó; **to s. hands with sb** estrechar la mano a algn; **to s. one's head** negar con la cabeza. **2** *vi (person, building)* temblar.
shall *v aux (used to form future tense) (first person only)* **I s.** (*or* **I'll**) **buy it** lo compraré; **I s. not** (*or* **I shan't**) **say anything** no diré nada. ▪ *(used to form questions) (usually first person)* **s. I close the door?** ¿cierro la puerta?; **s. we go?** ¿nos vamos?
shal·low *adj* poco profundo, -a.
shame vergüenza *f*; *(pity)* pena *f*; **what a s.!** ¡qué lástima!
shame·ful *adj* vergonzoso, -a.
sham·poo 1 *n* champú *m*. **2** *vt (one's hair)* lavarse.
shape forma *f*; **to take s.** tomar forma; **in good/bad s.** *(condition)* en buen/mal estado; **to be in good s.** *(health)* estar en forma.
share 1 *n (portion)* parte *f*; *(financial)* acción *f*. **2** *vt (divide)* dividir; *(have in common)* compartir.
▸**share in** *vt* participar en.
▸**share out** *vt* repartir.
share·hold·er accionista *mf*.
shark *(fish)* tiburón *m*.
sharp 1 *adj (razor, pencil, knife)* afilado, -a; *(needle)* puntiagudo, -a; *(bend)* cerrado, -a; *(pain, cry)* agudo, -a. **2** *adv* **at 2 o'clock s.** a las dos en punto.
sharp·en *vt (knife)* afilar; *(pencil)* sacar punta a.
sharp·en·er sacapuntas *m*.
sharp·ly *adv (abruptly)* bruscamente.
shat·ter 1 *vt* hacer añicos. **2** *vi* hacerse añicos.
shave 1 *n* afeitado *m*; **to have a s.** afeitarse. **2** *vt (person)* afeitar. **3** *vi* afeitarse.
shav·er (electric) s. máquina *f* de afeitar.
shav·ing brush brocha *f* de afeitar.
shav·ing cream crema *f* de afeitar.
shawl chal *m*.
she *pers pron* ella.
shed[1] *(in garden)* cobertizo *m*; *(workmen's storage)* barraca *f*.
shed[2] *vt (blood, tears)* derramar.
sheep *inv* oveja *f*.
sheep·skin piel *f* de carnero.
sheer *adj (utter)* total, puro, -a; *(cliff)* escarpado, -a; *(drop)* vertical; *(stockings)* fino, -a.
sheet *(on bed)* sábana *f*; *(of paper)* hoja *f*; *(of tin, glass, plastic)* lámina *f*; *(of ice)* capa *f*.
shelf (*pl* **shelves**) *(on bookcase)* estante *m*; **shelves** estantería *f*.
shell 1 *n (of egg, nut)* cáscara *f*; *(of tortoise etc)* caparazón *m*; *(of snail etc)* concha *f*; *(from gun)* obús *m*. **2** *vt (peas)* desvainar; *(with guns)* bombardear.
shell·fish *inv* marisco *m*; mariscos *mpl*.
shel·ter 1 *n (protection)* abrigo *m*; **to take s.** refugiarse (**from** de); **bus s.** marquesina *f*. **2** *vt* proteger. **3** *vi* refugiarse.
shelv·ing estanterías *fpl*.
shep·herd pastor *m*.
sher·iff sheriff *m*.
sher·ry jerez *m*.
shield *n* escudo *m*; *(of policeman)* placa *f*. **2** *vt* proteger (**from** de).
shift 1 *n (change)* cambio *m*; *(period of work, group of workers)* turno *m*; **(gear) s.** cambio *m* de velocidades. **2** *vt (change)* cambiar; *(move)* cambiar de sitio. **3** *vi (move)* mover; *(change place)* cambiar de sitio.
shin espinilla *f*.
shine 1 *vi** brillar. **2** *vt (lamp)** dirigir; (*pt & pp* **shined**) *(polish)* sacar brillo a; *(shoes)* limpiar. **3** *n* brillo *m*.
shin·y *adj* brillante.
ship barco *m*.
ship·ping barcos *mpl*.
ship·wreck 1 *n* naufragio *m*. **2** *vt* **to be shipwrecked** naufragar.
ship·yard astillero *m*.
shirt camisa *f*.
shiv·er 1 *vi (with cold)* tiritar; *(with fear)* temblar. **2** *n* escalofrío *m*.
shock 1 *n (jolt)* choque *m*; *(scare)* susto *m*; *(in medical sense)* shock *m*. **2** *vt (scandalize)* escandalizar.
shock ab·sorb·er amortiguador *m*.
shock·ing *adj (causing horror)* espantoso, -a; *(disgraceful)* escandaloso, -a.
shoe zapato *m*; **shoes** calzado *m sing*.
shoe·lace cordón *m* (de zapatos).
shoe pol·ish betún *m*.
shoot 1 *n (on plant)* brote *m*; *(of vine)* sarmiento *m*. **2** *vt* (fire on)* pegar un tiro a; *(wound)* herir (de bala); *(kill)* matar; *(execute)* fusilar; *(film)* rodar, filmar; *(with still camera)* fotografiar. **3** *vi* (with gun)* disparar (**at sb** sobre, a algn).
▸**shoot down** *vt (aircraft)* derribar.
▸**shoot off** *vi (leave quickly)* salir a escape.
▸**shoot up** *vi (prices)* dispararse.
shoot·ing 1 *n (shots)* tiros *mpl*; *(murder)* asesinato *m*; *(hunting)* caza *f*; *(of film)* rodaje *m*. **2** *adj (pain)* punzante.
shoot·ing star estrella *f* fugaz.
shop 1 *n* tienda *f*; *(large store)* almacén *m*. **2** *vi* hacer compras; **to go shopping** ir de compras.
shop as·sis·tant dependiente, -a *mf*.
shop·keep·er tendero, -a *mf*.
shop·ping *(purchases)* compras *fpl*.
shop·ping bag bolsa *f* de la compra.
shop·ping bas·ket cesta *f* de la compra.
shop·ping cen·ter centro *m* comercial.
shop win·dow escaparate *m*.
shore *(of sea, lake)* orilla *f*; *(coast)* costa *f*.
short 1 *adj* corto, -a; *(not tall)* bajo, -a; **in a s. while** dentro de un rato; **in the s. term** a corto plazo; **'Bob' is s. for 'Robert'** 'Bob' es el diminutivo de 'Robert'; **to be s. of food** andar escaso, -a de comida. **2** *adv* **to cut s.** *(vacation)* interrumpir; *(meeting)* suspender; **we're running s. of coffee** se nos está acabando el café.
short·age escasez *f*.
short·cut atajo *m*.
short·en *vt (skirt, visit)* acortar.
short·hand typ·ist taquimecanógrafo, -a *mf*.
short·ly *adv (soon)* dentro de poco; **s. after** poco después.
shorts *npl* **a pair of s.** un pantalón corto; *(underpants)* unos calzoncillos.
short·sight·ed *adj (person)* miope.
short-term *adj* a corto plazo.
shot[1] *(act, sound)* disparo *m*; *(sport)* tiro *m* (a puerta); *(photography)* foto *f*; *(in film)* toma *f*.
shot[2] *pt & pp of* **shoot**.
shot·gun escopeta *f*.
should *v aux (duty)* deber; **all employees s. wear helmets** todos los empleados deben llevar casco; **he s. have been an architect** debería haber sido arquitecto. ▪ *(probability)* deber de; **he s. have finished by now** ya debe de haber acabado. ▪ *(conditional use)* **if anything strange s. happen** si pasara algo raro; **I s. like to ask a question** quisiera hacer una pregunta.
shoul·der hombro *m*; *(beside road)* arcén *m*.
shoul·der bag bolso *m* (de bandolera).
shout 1 *n* grito *m*. **2** *vti* gritar; **to s. at sb** gritar a algn.
shout·ing gritos *mpl*.
shove 1 *n* empujón *m*. **2** *vt* empujar. **3** *vi* empujar; *(jostle)* dar empellones.
shov·el 1 *n* pala *f*. **2** *vt* mover con pala.
show 1 *vt* (ticket etc)* mostrar; *(painting etc)* exponer; *(film)* poner; *(latest plans etc)* presentar; *(teach)* enseñar; *(temperature, way etc)* indicar; **to s. sb to the door** acompañar a algn hasta la puerta. **2** *vi* (be visible)* notarse; **what's showing?** *(at cinema)* ¿qué ponen? **3** *n (entertainment)* espectáculo *m*; **on s.** expuesto, -a; **boat s.** salón *m* náutico; **motor s.** salón *m* del automóvil.
▸**show off 1** *vt (flaunt)* hacer alarde de. **2** *vi* farolear.
▸**show up 1** *vt (embarrass)* dejar en evidencia. **2** *vi (arrive)* aparecer.
show·er *(rain)* chaparrón *m*; *(bath)* ducha *f*; **to have a s.** ducharse.
show·ing *(cinema performance)* sesión *f*.
show-off farolero, -a *mf*.
shrimp camarón *m*.
shrink* 1 *vt* encoger. **2** *vi* encoger(se).
shrub arbusto *m*.
shrug *vt* **to s. one's shoulders** encogerse de hombros.
shud·der *vi (person)* estremecerse.
shuf·fle *vt (cards)* barajar.
shut 1 *vt** cerrar. **2** *vi** cerrarse. **3** *adj* cerrado, -a.
▸**shut down 1** *vt (factory)* cerrar. **2** *vi (factory)* cerrar.
▸**shut off** *vti (gas, water etc)* cortar.
▸**shut out** *vt (lock out)* dejar fuera a.

▸**shut up 1** vt (close) cerrar; (imprison) encerrar. **2** vi (keep quiet) callarse.
shut·ter (on window) postigo m.
shut·tle (plane) puente m aéreo; **(space)** s. transbordador m espacial.
shy adj (timid) tímido, -a; (reserved) reservado, -a.
shy·ness timidez f.
sick adj (ill) enfermo, -a; fam (fed up) harto, -a; **s. leave** baja f por enfermedad; **to feel s.** (about to vomit) tener ganas de devolver; **to be s.** devolver.
sick·ness (illness) enfermedad f; (nausea) náuseas fpl.
side n lado m; (of coin etc) cara f; (of hill) ladera f; (edge) borde m; (of lake, river) orilla f; (team) equipo m; (in politics) partido m; **by the s. of** junto a; **by my s.** a mi lado; **s. by s.** juntos; **she's on our s.** está de nuestro lado; **to take sides with sb** ponerse de parte de algn.
side·board aparador m.
side·burns npl patillas fpl.
side·light piloto m.
side·walk acera f.
side·ways adv de lado.
sid·ing (on railroad) apartadero m, vía f muerta.
siege sitio m, cerco m; **to lay s. to** sitiar.
sieve colador m; (coarse) criba f.
sift vt tamizar.
sigh 1 vi suspirar. **2** n suspiro m.
sight 1 n (faculty) vista f; (spectacle) espectáculo m; **at first s.** a primera vista; **to catch s. of** divisar; **to lose s. of sth/sb** perder algo/a algn de vista; **within s.** a la vista.
sight·see·ing to go s. hacer turismo.
sign 1 n (signal) señal f; (trace) rastro m; (notice) anuncio m; (board) letrero m. **2** vti (letter etc) firmar.
▸**sign on** vi (worker) firmar un contrato; (unemployed person) apuntarse al paro.
▸**sign up** vi (soldier) alistarse; (worker) firmar un contrato.
sig·nal 1 n señal f. **2** vt (direction etc) indicar.
sig·na·ture firma f.
sig·nif·i·cant adj (important) importante.
sig·nif·i·cant·ly adv (markedly) sensiblemente.
sig·ni·fy vt (mean) significar; (show, make known) indicar.
sign·post poste m indicador.
si·lence 1 n silencio m. **2** vt acallar.
si·lent adj silencioso, -a; (film) mudo, -a; **to remain s.** guardar silencio.
si·lent·ly adv silenciosamente.
silk seda f.
sill (of window) alféizar m.
sil·ly adj (stupid) tonto, -a; (ridiculous) ridículo, -a.
sil·ver 1 n (metal) plata f; (tableware) vajilla f de plata. **2** adj de plata; **s. paper** papel m de plata.
sil·ver-plat·ed adj plateado, -a.
sil·ver·ware vajilla f de plata.
sim·i·lar adj semejante (**to** a); **to be s.** parecerse.
sim·i·lar·i·ty semejanza f.
sim·ple adj sencillo, -a.
sim·pli·fy vt simplificar.
sim·ply adv (only) simplemente; (just, merely) meramente.
si·mul·ta·ne·ous adj simultáneo, -a.
si·mul·ta·ne·ous·ly adv simultáneamente.
sin pecado m.
since 1 adv (ever) **s.** desde entonces. **2** prep desde; **she has been living here s. 1975** vive aquí desde 1975. **3** conj (time) desde que; **how long is it s. you last saw him?** ¿cuánto tiempo hace (desde) que lo viste por última vez? ▪ (because, as) ya que.
sin·cere adj sincero, -a.
sin·cere·ly adv sinceramente; **Yours s.** (in letter) (le saluda) atentamente.
sin·cer·i·ty sinceridad f.
sing* vti cantar.
sing·er cantante mf.
sin·gle 1 adj solo, -a; (unmarried) soltero, -a; **s. bed/room** cama f/habitación f individual. **2** n (record) single m.
▸**single out** vt (choose) escoger.
sin·gle-mind·ed adj resuelto, -a.
sin·gu·lar 1 adj (noun form etc) singular. **2** n singular m.
sin·gu·lar·ly adv excepcionalmente.
sin·is·ter adj siniestro, -a.
sink¹ (in kitchen) fregadero m.
sink²* vi (ship) hundirse.
▸**sink in** vi (penetrate) penetrar; fig causar impresión.
sip vt beber a sorbos.
sir señor m; (title) sir.
si·ren sirena f.
sis·ter hermana f.
sis·ter-in-law cuñada f.
sit* 1 vt (child etc) sentar (**in, on** en); (exam) presentarse a. **2** vi (action) sentarse; (be seated) estar senta- do, -a.
▸**sit around** vi holgazanear.
▸**sit down** vi sentarse.
▸**sit up** vi incorporarse.
site (area) lugar m; **building s.** solar m; (under construction) obra f.
sit·ting room sala f de estar.
sit·u·at·ed adj **to be s.** estar situado, -a.
sit·u·a·tion situación f.
six adj & n seis (m) inv.
six·teen adj & n dieciséis (m) inv.
sixth 1 adj sexto, -a. **2** n (in series) sexto, -a mf; (fraction) sexto m.
six·ti·eth adj & n sexagésimo, -a (mf).
six·ty adj & n sesenta (m) inv.
size tamaño m; (of garment) talla f; (of shoes) número m; (of person) estatura f.
skate 1 n patín m. **2** vi patinar.
skate·board monopatín m.
skat·er patinador, -a mf.
skat·ing patinaje m.
skat·ing rink pista f de patinaje.
skel·e·ton esqueleto m.
sketch n (preliminary drawing) bosquejo m; (on TV etc) sketch m. **2** vt (preliminary drawing) bosquejar.
skew·er pincho m, broqueta f.
ski 1 n esquí m. **2** vi esquiar; **to go skiing** ir a esquiar.
skid 1 n patinazo m. **2** vi patinar.
ski·er esquiador, -a mf.
ski·ing esquí m.
skilled adj (dextrous) hábil, diestro, -a; (expert) experto, -a; (worker) cualificado, -a.

skill·ful adj hábil.
ski lift telesquí m; (with seats) telesilla f.
skill (ability) habilidad f; (technique) técnica f.
skilled adj (worker) cualificado, -a.
skim milk leche f desnatada.
skin piel f; (of face) cutis m; (complexion) tez f; (of fruit) piel f.
skin-div·ing submarinismo m.
skin·ny adj flaco, -a.
skip¹ 1 vi (jump) saltar, brincar; (with rope) saltar a la comba. **2** vt (omit) saltarse.
skip² (container) contenedor m.
skirt falda f.
skull calavera f; (cranium) cráneo m.
sky cielo m; **s. blue** azul m celeste.
sky·scrap·er rascacielos m inv.
slack adj (not taut) flojo, -a; **business is s.** hay poco negocio.
slack·en vt (rope) aflojar; (speed) reducir.
slacks npl pantalones mpl.
slam 1 n (of door) portazo m. **2** vt (bang) cerrar de golpe; **to s. the door** dar un portazo. **3** vi cerrarse de golpe.
slang jerga f popular.
slant 1 n inclinación f. **2** vi inclinarse.
slap 1 n palmada f; (in face) bofetada f. **2** vt pegar con la mano; (hit in face) dar una bofetada a; **to s. sb on the back** dar a algn una palmada en la espalda.
slate pizarra f.
slaugh·ter 1 n (of animals) matanza f; (of people) carnicería f. **2** vt (animals) matar; (people) masacrar.
slave esclavo, -a mf.
slav·er·y esclavitud f.
sleep 1 n sueño m. **2** vi* dormir; **to go to s.** dormirse.
▸**sleep in** vi (oversleep) quedarse dormido, -a.
sleep·er (on train) (coach) coche-cama m; (berth) litera f.
sleep·ing bag saco m de dormir.
sleep·ing car coche-cama m.
sleep·ing pill somnífero m.
sleep·y adj **to be** or **feel s.** tener sueño.
sleet 1 n aguanieve f. **2** vi **it's sleeting** cae aguanieve.
sleeve (of garment) manga f; (of record) funda f.
sleigh trineo m.
slen·der adj (thin) delgado, -a; fig (hope, chance) remoto, -a.
slept pt & pp of **sleep**.
slice 1 n (of bread) rebanada f; (of cake) trozo m; (of meat) loncha f. **2** vt (food) cortar en rodajas.
slide 1 n (in playground) tobogán m; (photographic) diapositiva f; **s. projector** proyector m de diapositivas. **2** vt* deslizar; (furniture) correr. **3** vi* deslizarse; (slip) resbalar.
slid·ing adj (door, window) corredizo, -a.
slight adj (small) pequeño, -a; (trivial) leve; **not in the slightest** en absoluto.
slight·ly adv (a little) ligeramente.
slim 1 adj (person) delgado, -a; (slender) esbelto, -a. **2** vi adelgazar.
slim·y adj (slimier, slimiest) (muddy) lodoso, -a; (snail) baboso, -a; fig (person) zalamero, -a.
sling 1 n (for arm) cabestrillo m. **2** vt* (throw) tirar.
slip 1 n (mistake) error m; (moral) desliz m; (under skirt) combinación f; (of paper) papelito m. **2** vi (slide) resbalar. **3** vt **to s. sth into sth** meter algo en algo; **to s. sth to sb** dar algo a algn con disimulo.
▸**slip away** vi (person) escabullirse.
▸**slip off** vt (clothes) quitarse rápidamente.
▸**slip on** vt (clothes) ponerse rápidamente.
▸**slip out** vi (leave) salir.
▸**slip up** vi (make a mistake) equivocarse.
slip·per zapatilla f.
slip·per·y adj resbaladizo, -a.
slit (opening) hendidura f; (cut) raja f.
slo·gan (e)slogan m, lema m.
slope 1 n (incline) cuesta f; (of mountain) ladera f; (of roof) vertiente f. **2** vi inclinarse.
slop·ing adj inclinado, -a.
slot (for coin) ranura f; (opening) rendija f.
slot ma·chine (for gambling) (máquina f) tragaperras f inv; (vending machine) distribuidor m automático.
slow 1 adj lento, -a; (clock) atrasado, -a; (stupid) torpe; **in s. motion** a cámara lenta; **to be s. to do sth** tardar en hacer algo. **2** adv despacio.
▸**slow down, slow up** vi ir más despacio; (in car) reducir la velocidad.
slow·ly adv despacio.
slug (animal) babosa f.
slump 1 n (drop in sales etc) bajón m; (economic depression) crisis f económica. **2** vi (sales etc) caer de repente; (prices) desplomarse; (the economy) hundirse.
slums barrios bajos mpl.
sly adj (cunning) astuto, -a.
smack 1 n (slap) bofetada f. **2** vt (slap) dar una bofetada a; (hit) golpear.
small adj pequeño, -a; (in height) bajo, -a; **s. change** cambio m.
small·pox viruela f.
smart adj (elegant) elegante; (clever) listo, -a.
smash 1 vt (break) romper; (shatter) hacer pedazos. **2** vi (break) romperse; (shatter) hacerse pedazos.
▸**smash into** vt (vehicle) estrellarse contra.
smash·ing adj fam estupendo, -a.
smell 1 n (sense) olfato m; (odor) olor m. **2** vt* oler. **3** vi* oler (**of** a); (stink) apestar; **it smells good/like lavender** huele bien/a lavanda.
smell·y adj (smellier, smelliest) fam maloliente, apestoso, -a.
smile 1 n sonrisa f. **2** vi sonreír.
smock (blouse) blusón m.
smoke 1 n humo m. **2** vi fumar; (chimney etc) echar humo. **3** vt (tobacco) fumar; **to s. a pipe** fumar en pipa.
smok·er (person) fumador, -a mf; (compartment) vagón m de fumadores.
smooth adj (surface) liso, -a; (skin) suave; (beer, wine) suave; (flight) tranquilo, -a.
▸**smooth out** vt (creases) alisar.
▸**smooth over** vt **to s. things over** limar asperezas.
smooth·ly adv sobre ruedas.
smug·gle vt pasar de contrabando.
smug·gler contrabandista mf.
smug·gling contrabando m.
snack bocado m.
snack bar cafetería f.
snail caracol m.
snake (big) serpiente f; (small) culebra f.
snap 1 n (photo) (foto f) instantánea f. **2** vt (branch etc) partir (en dos). **3** vi (break) romperse.
▸**snap off** vt (branch etc) arrancar.

snap·shot (foto f) instantánea f.

snatch 1 vt (grab) arrebatar. **2** vi **to s. at** intentar agarrar.

sneak·ers npl zapatillas fpl de deporte.

sneer vi **to s. at** hacer un gesto de desprecio a.

sneeze 1 n estornudo m. **2** vi estornudar.

sniff vt (flower etc) oler.

snip vt cortar a tijeretazos.

snook·er billar m ruso.

snore 1 n ronquido m. **2** vi roncar.

snor·ing ronquidos mpl.

snow 1 n nieve f. **2** vi nevar; **it's snowing** está nevando.

snow·ball bola f de nieve.

snow·drift ventisquero m.

snow·flake copo m de nieve.

snow·man hombre m de nieve.

snow·plow quitanieves m inv.

snow·storm nevada f.

so 1 adv (to such an extent) tanto; **he was so tired that …** estaba tan cansado que …; **so long!** ¡hasta luego! ▪ (degree) tanto; **we loved her so (much)** la queríamos tanto; **so many books** tantos libros. ▪ (thus, in this way) así; **and so on, and so forth** y así sucesivamente; **if so en** este caso; **I think/hope so** creo/espero que sí. ▪ (also) **I'm going to Spain — so am I** voy a España — yo también. **2** conj (expresses result) así que; **so you like England, do you?** así que te gusta Inglaterra, ¿no? ▪ (expresses purpose) para que; **I'll put the key here so (that) every-one can see it** pongo la llave aquí para que todos la vean.

soak 1 vt (washing, food) remojar. **2** vi (washing, food) estar en remojo.

▸**soak up** vt absorber.

soaked through adj (person) empapado, -a.

soak·ing adj (object) empapado, -a; (person) calado, -a hasta los huesos.

soap jabón m.

soap flakes jabón m en escamas.

soap pow·der jabón m en polvo.

soap·y adj jabonoso, -a.

sob 1 n sollozo m. **2** vi sollozar.

so·ber adj (not drunk, moderate) sobrio, -a.

soc·cer fútbol m.

soc·cer play·er futbolista mf.

so·cial adj social; **s. climber** arribista mf, **s. security** seguridad f social; **s. welfare** seguro m social; **s. work** asistencia f social; **s. worker** asistente, -a mf social.

so·cial·ist adj & n socialista (mf).

so·ci·e·ty sociedad f.

sock calcetín m.

sock·et (for electricity) enchufe m.

so·da s. water soda f, (fizzy drink) gaseosa f.

so·fa sofá m; **s. bed** sofá m cama.

soft adj (not hard) blando, -a; (skin, color, hair, light, music) suave; (drink) no alcohólico, -a; **s. drinks** refrescos mpl.

soft·ball = juego parecido al béisbol jugado en un campo más pequeño y con una pelota más blanda.

soft·en 1 vt (leather, heart) ablandar; (skin) suavizar. **2** vi (leather, heart) ablandarse; (skin) suavizarse.

soft·ly adv (gently) suavemente; (quietly) silenciosamente.

soft·ware software m; **s. package** paquete m.

soil (earth) tierra f.

so·lar adj solar.

sol·dier soldado m.

sole¹ (of foot) planta f, (of shoe, sock) suela f.

sole² (fish) lenguado m.

sole·ly adv (only) únicamente; (entirely) exclusivamente.

sol·emn adj solemne.

so·lic·i·tor abogado, -a mf.

sol·id 1 adj (not liquid) sólido, -a; (firm) firme; (not hollow, pure) (metal) macizo, -a; (reliable) formal. **2** n sólido m.

sol·i·dar·i·ty solidaridad f.

so·lo solo m.

so·lu·tion solución f.

solve vt resolver.

sol·vent adj & n solvente (m).

some 1 adj (with plural nouns) unos, -as, algunos, -as; (several) varios, -as; (a few) unos, -as cuantos, -as; **there were s. roses** había unas rosas. ▪ (with singular nouns) algún, alguna; (a little) un poco de; **there's s. wine left** queda un poco de vino. ▪ (certain) cierto, -a; **to s. extent** hasta cierto punto. ▪ (unspecified) algún, alguna; **s. day** algún día; **s. other time** otro día. ▪ (quite a lot of) bastante; **it's s. distance away** queda bastante lejos. **2** pron algunos, -as, unos, -as. ▪ (a few) unos, -as cuantos, -as. ▪ (a little) un poco.

some·bod·y pron alguien; **s. else** otro, -a.

some·how adv (in some way) de alguna forma; (for some reason) por alguna razón.

some·one pron = **somebody**.

some·place adv = **somewhere**.

som·er·sault (by acrobat etc) voltereta f.

some·thing pron & n algo; **is s. the matter?** ¿le pasa algo?; **s. else** otra cosa; **s. of the kind** algo por el estilo.

some·time adv algún día.

some·times adv a veces.

some·what adv un tanto.

some·where adv (in some place) en alguna parte; (to some place) a alguna parte.

son hijo m.

song canción f, (of bird) canto m.

son-in-law yerno m.

soon adv (within a short time) dentro de poco; (quickly) rápidamente; (early) pronto; **s. after-wards** poco después; **as s. as** en cuanto; **as s. as possible** cuanto antes; **I would just as s. stay at home** prefiero quedarme en casa; **I would (just) as s. read as watch TV** tanto me da leer como ver la tele.

soot hollín m.

soothe vt (calm) tranquilizar; (pain) aliviar.

so·phis·ti·cat·ed adj sofisticado, -a.

sore 1 adj (aching) dolorido, -a; (painful) doloroso, -a; fam (angry) enfadado, -a; **to have a s. throat** tener dolor de garganta. **2** n llaga f.

sor·row pena f.

sor·ry 1 adj **I feel very s. for her** me da mucha pena; **to be s. (about sth)** sentir (algo); **I'm s. I'm late** siento llegar tarde. **2** interj (apology) ¡perdón!; (for repetition) ¿cómo?

sort 1 n (kind) clase f, tipo m; (brand) marca f, **it's a s. of teapot** es una especie de tetera. **2** vt (classify) clasificar.

▸**sort out** vt (classify) clasificar; (put in order) ordenar; (problem) solucionar.

soul alma f.

sound¹ n sonido m; (noise) ruido m; **I don't like the s. of it** no me gusta nada la idea. **2** vt (bell, trumpet) tocar. **3** vi (trumpet, bell, alarm) sonar; (give an impression) parecer; **it sounds inter-esting** parece interesante.

sound² 1 adj (healthy) sano, -a; (in good condition) en buen estado; (safe, dependable) seguro, -a. **2** adv **to be s. asleep** estar profundamente dormido, -a.

sound·proof adj insonorizado, -a.

soup sopa f, (thin, clear) caldo m.

sour adj (fruit, wine) agrio, -a; (milk) cortado, -a.

source fuente f.

south 1 n sur m; **in the s. of England** en el sur de Inglaterra. **2** adj del sur. **3** adv (location) al sur; (direction) hacia el sur.

south·bound adj (con) dirección sur.

south·east n & adj sudeste (m).

south·ern adj del sur.

south·ern·er sureño, -a mf.

south·ward adj & adv hacia el sur.

south·west n & adj suroeste (m).

sou·ve·nir recuerdo m.

sov·er·eign·ty soberanía f.

sow* vt sembrar.

space 1 n espacio m; (room) sitio m. **2** vt (also **s. out**) espaciar.

space age era f espacial.

space·ship nave f espacial.

space shut·tle transbordador m espacial.

spa·cious adj espacioso, -a.

spade¹ (for digging) pala f.

spade² (in cards) (international pack) pica f, (Spanish pack) espada f.

spa·ghet·ti espaguetis mpl.

span vt (river etc) extenderse sobre, atravesar; (period of time etc) abarcar.

Span·iard español, -a mf.

Span·ish 1 adj español, -a. **2** n (language) español m, castellano m; **the S.** los españoles.

spank vt zurrar.

spank·ing cachete m.

spare 1 vt (do without) prescindir de; **can you s. me 10?** ¿me puedes dejar 10?; **I can't s. the time** no tengo tiempo; **there's none to s.** no sobra nada; **s. me the details** ahórrate los detal-les. **2** adj (left over) sobrante; (surplus) de sobra; **a s. moment** un momento libre; **s. part** (pieza f de) recambio m; **s. room** cuarto m de los invitados; **s. wheel** rueda f de recambio. **3** n (for car etc) (pieza f de) recambio m.

spark chispa f.

spar·kle vi (diamond, glass) destellar; (eyes) brillar.

spar·kling adj **s. wine** vino m espumoso.

spark·plug bujía f.

spar·row gorrión m.

speak* **1** vt (utter) decir; (language) hablar. **2** vi hablar; **to s. to sb** hablar con algn; **speaking!** ¡al habla!; **who's speaking, please?** ¿de parte de quién?

▸**speak up** vi hablar más fuerte.

speak·er (in dialog) interlocutor, -a mf, (lecturer) conferenciante mf, (of language) hablante mf, (loudspeaker) altavoz m; **(public) s.** orador, -a mf.

spear lanza f.

spe·cial adj especial.

spe·cial·ist especialista mf.

spe·ci·al·i·ty especialidad f.

spe·cial·ize vi especializarse (in en).

spe·cial·ly adv (specifically) especialmente; (on purpose) a propósito.

spe·ci·al·ty especialidad f.

spe·cies inv especie f.

spe·cif·ic adj específico, -a; (precise) preciso, -a; **to be s.** concretar.

spec·i·fi·ca·tion specifications datos mpl específicos.

spec·i·men (sample) muestra f, (example) ejemplar m.

spec·ta·cle (display) espectáculo m; **spectacles** (glasses) gafas fpl, Am lentes mpl, Am anteo-jos mpl.

spec·tac·u·lar adj espectacular.

spec·ta·tor espectador, -a mf.

spec·trum espectro m.

spec·u·late vi especular.

spec·u·la·tion especulación f.

speech (faculty) habla f, (address) discurso m; **to give a s.** pronunciar un discurso.

speed 1 n velocidad f, (rapidity) rapidez f. **2** vi* (exceed speed limit) conducir con exceso de velocidad.

▸**speed up 1** vt acelerar. **2** vi (person) darse prisa.

speed·boat lancha f rápida.

speed lim·it velocidad f máxima.

speed·om·e·ter velocímetro m.

spell¹* vt (write) escribir; (letter by letter) deletrear; **how is that spelled?** ¿cómo se escribe eso?

spell² (magical) hechizo m.

spell³ (period) período m; (short period) rato m; **cold s.** ola f de frío.

spell·ing ortografía f.

spend* vt (money) gastar (**on** en); (time) pasar.

sphere esfera f.

spice 1 n especia f. **2** vt (food) sazonar.

spic·y adj sazonado, -a; (hot) picante.

spi·der araña f; **s.'s web** telaraña f.

spike (sharp point) punta f.

spill* **1** vt (liquid) derramar. **2** vi (liquid) derramarse.

▸**spill over** vi desbordarse.

spin* vt (wheel etc) hacer girar; (washing) centrifugar.

spin·ach espinacas fpl.

spine (of back) columna f vertebral.

spi·ral espiral f.

spire aguja f.

spir·its npl (alcoholic drinks) licores mpl.

spir·i·tu·al adj espiritual.

spit¹* vti escupir.

spit² (for cooking) asador m.

spite in s. of a pesar de; **in s. of the fact that** a pesar de que.

spite·ful adj (remark) malévolo, -a.

splash 1 vt (spray) salpicar. **2** vi **to s. (about)** (in water) chapotear.

splen·did adj espléndido, -a.

splin·ter (wood) astilla f.

split 1 n (crack) grieta f, (tear) desgarrón m. **2** vt* (crack) hender; (cut) partir; (tear) rajar; (divide) dividir.

▸**split up 1** vt (break up) partir; (divide up) dividir; (share out) repartir. **2** vi (couple) separarse.

spoil* vt (ruin) estropear; (child) mimar.

spoke¹ pt of **speak**.

spoke² (of wheel) radio m.

spo·ken *pp of* **speak**.
spokes·man portavoz *mf*.
sponge 1 *n* esponja *f*. **2** *vt (wash)* lavar con esponja.
▶**sponge down** *vt* lavar con esponja.
sponge cake bizcocho *m*.
spon·sor 1 *vt* patrocinar. **2** *n* patrocinador, -a *mf*.
spon·ta·ne·ous *adj* espontáneo, -a.
spool bobina *f*.
spoon cuchara *f*; *(small)* cucharita *f*.
spoon·ful cucharada *f*.
sport deporte *m*.
sports·man deportista *m*.
sports·wom·an deportista *m*.
spot 1 *n (dot)* punto *m*; *(on fabric)* lunar *m*; *(stain)* mancha *f*; *(pimple)* grano *m*; *(place)* sitio *m*; **to decide sth on the s.** decidir algo en el acto. **2** *vt (notice)* notar; *(see)* ver.
spot·less *adj (very clean)* impecable.
spot·light foco *m*.
spot·ted *adj (speckled)* moteado, -a.
spouse cónyuge *mf*.
spout *(of jug)* pico *m*; *(of teapot)* pitorro *m*.
sprain 1 *n* esguince *m*. **2** *vt* **to s. one's ankle** torcerse el tobillo.
spray 1 *n (aerosol)* spray *m*. **2** *vt (insecticide, perfume)* pulverizar.
spray can aerosol *m*.
spread 1 *n (for bread)* pasta *f*, **cheese s.** queso *m* para untar. **2** *vt* *(unfold)* desplegar; *(lay out)* extender; *(butter etc)* untar; *(news)* difundir; *(rumor)* hacer correr; *(panic)* sembrar. **3** *vi* *(stretch out)* extenderse; *(news)* difundirse; *(rumor)* correr; *(disease, fire)* propagarse.
spread·sheet hoja *f* de cálculo.
spring¹ *(season)* primavera *f*.
spring² **1** *n (of water)* fuente *f*; *(of watch etc)* resorte *m*. **2** *vi* *(jump)* saltar.
spring·board trampolín *m*.
spring on·ion cebolleta *f*.
spring·time primavera *f*.
sprin·kle *vt (with water)* rociar (**with** de); *(with sugar)* espolvorear (**with** de).
sprin·kler *(for water)* aspersor *m*.
sprout (Brussels) sprouts coles *fpl* de Bruselas.
spur espuela *f*.
spurt *vi (liquid)* chorrear.
spy 1 *n* espía *mf*. **2** *vi* espiar (**on** a).
spy·ing espionaje *m*.
square 1 *n* cuadrado *m*; *(in town)* plaza *f*. **2** *adj* cuadrado, -a; **a s. meal** una buena comida.
squash¹ *vt (crush)* aplastar.
squash² *(sport)* squash *m*.
squat *vi (crouch)* agacharse.
squeak *vi (hinge, wheel)* chirriar; *(shoes)* crujir.
squeal 1 *n* chillido *m*. **2** *vi (animal, person)* chillar.
squeeze 1 *vt* apretar; *(lemon etc)* exprimir; *(sponge)* estrujar. **2** *vi* **to s. in** apretujarse. **3** *n (pressure)* estrujón *m*; *(of hand)* apretón *m*; *(hug)* abrazo *m*; *(crush)* apiñamiento *m*.
▶**squeeze up** *vi (on bench etc)* correrse.
squint 1 *n* bizquera *f*; **to have a s.** ser bizco, -a. **2** *vi* ser bizco, -a; **to s. at sth** *(with eyes half-closed)* mirar algo con los ojos entrecerrados.
squir·rel ardilla *f*.
squirt 1 *vt* lanzar a chorro. **2** *vi* **to s. out** salir a chorros.
St. *abbr of* **Saint** San, Sto., Sta; *abbr of* **Street** c/.
stab *vt* apuñalar.
sta·bil·i·ty estabilidad *f*.
sta·ble¹ *adj* estable.
sta·ble² *(for horses)* cuadra *f*.
stack 1 *n (pile)* montón *m*; *fam* **stacks of ...** un montón de ... **2** *vt (pile up)* amontonar.
sta·di·um estadio *m*.
staff *(personnel)* personal *m*; *(of army)* estado *m* mayor.
staff·room sala *f* de profesores.
stag venado *m*.
stage 1 *n (platform)* plataforma *f*; *(in theater)* escenario *m*; *(of development, journey)* etapa *f*; **in stages** por etapas. **2** *vt (play)* poner en escena.
stag·ger *vi* tambalearse. **2** *vt (hours, work)* escalonar.
stain 1 *n* mancha *f*. **2** *vt* manchar.
stained glass win·dow vidriera *f* de colores.
stain·less *adj (steel)* inoxidable.
stair peldaño *m*; **stairs** escalera *f sing*.
stair·case escalera *f*.
stake *(stick)* estaca *f*.
stale *adj (food)* pasado, -a; *(bread)* duro, -a.
stalk *(of plant)* tallo *m*; *(of fruit)* rabo *m*.
stall 1 *n (in market)* puesto *m*; *(in theater)* **stalls** platea *f sing*. **2** *vi (of engine)* calarse.
stam·mer 1 *n* tartamudeo *m*. **2** *vi* tartamudear.
stamp 1 *n (postage stamp)* sello *m*, *Am* estampilla *f*; *(with foot)* patada *f*. **2** *vt (with postage stamp)* poner el sello a; **self-addressed stamped envelope** sobre *m* franqueado; **to s. one's feet** patear.
▶**stamp out** *vt (racism etc)* acabar con.
stamp col·lect·ing filatelia *f*.
stance postura *f*.
stand 1 *n (of lamp, sculpture)* pie *m*; *(market stall)* puesto *m*; *(at exhibition)* stand *m*; *(in stadium)* tribuna *f*; **newspaper s.** quiosco *m* de prensa. **2** *vt* *(place)* poner, colocar; *(tolerate)* aguantar. **3** *vi* *(be upright)* estar de pie; *(get up)* levantarse; *(be situated)* encontrarse; *(remain unchanged)* permanecer.
▶**stand around** *vi* estar sin hacer nada; *(wait)* esperar.
▶**stand aside** *vi* apartarse.
▶**stand back** *vi (allow sb to pass)* abrir paso.
▶**stand by 1** *vi (do nothing)* quedarse sin hacer nada; *(be ready)* estar listo, -a. **2** *vt (person)* apoyar.
▶**stand down** *vi fig* retirarse.
▶**stand for** *vt (mean)* significar; *(tolerate)* aguantar.
▶**stand in** *vi* sustituir (**for** -).
▶**stand out** *vi (mountain etc, fig person)* destacar(se).
▶**stand up** *vi (get up)* ponerse de pie; *fig* **to s. up for sb** defender a algn; *fig* **to s. up to sb** hacer frente a algn.
stan·dard 1 *n (level)* nivel *m*; *(criterion)* criterio *m*; *(norm)* estándar *m inv*; **s. of living** nivel de vida. **2** *adj* normal.
stand·by *adj* **s. ticket** billete *m* sin reserva.
stand·ing *adj (not sitting)* de pie.
stand·point punto *m* de vista.
stand·still **at a s.** *(car, traffic)* parado, -a; *(industry)* paralizado, -a; **to come to a s.** *(car, traffic)* pararse; *(industry)* paralizarse.
stank *pt of* **stink**.

sta·ple 1 *n (fastener)* grapa *f*. **2** *vt* grapar.
sta·pler grapadora *f*.
star 1 *n* estrella *f*. **2** *vt (film)* tener como protagonista. **3** *vi (in film)* protagonizar.
stare 1 *n* mirada *f* fija. **2** *vi* mirar fijamente; **to s. at sb** mirar fijamente a algn.
start 1 *n (beginning)* principio *m*; *(of race)* salida *f*; *(advantage)* ventaja *f*. **2** *vt (begin)* empezar, comenzar; **to s. doing sth** empezar a hacer algo. **3** *vi (begin)* empezar, comenzar; *(engine)* arrancar; *(take fright)* asustarse; **starting from Monday** a partir del lunes.
▶**start off** *vi (leave)* salir.
▶**start on** *vt* empezar.
▶**start up 1** *vt (engine)* arrancar. **2** *vi (car)* arrancar.
start·er *(in car)* motor *m* de arranque; *(food)* entrada *f*.
star·tle *vt* asustar.
star·va·tion hambre *m*.
starve *vi* pasar hambre; **to s. to death** morirse de hambre.
starv·ing *adj* **I'm s.!** estoy muerto, -a de hambre.
state 1 *n* estado *m*; **The States** (los) Estados Unidos. **2** *vt* declarar.
state·ment declaración *f*; *(financial)* estado *m* de cuenta; **monthly s.** balance *m* mensual.
states·man estadista *m*.
stat·ic *adj* estático, -a.
sta·tion estación *f*.
sta·tion·ar·y *adj (not moving)* inmóvil.
sta·tion·er·y *(paper)* papel *m* de escribir; *(pens, ink etc)* artículos *mpl* de escritorio.
sta·tion·mas·ter jefe *m* de estación.
sta·tion wag·on camioneta *f*.
sta·tis·tic estadística *f*.
stat·ue estatua *f*.
stay 1 *n* estancia *f*. **2** *vi (remain)* quedarse; *(reside temporarily)* alojarse; **she's staying with us for a few days** ha venido a pasar unos días con nosotros.
▶**stay away** *vi (not attend)* no asistir; **s. away from her** no te acerques a ella.
▶**stay in** *vi* quedarse en casa.
▶**stay out** *vi* **to s. out all night** no volver a casa en toda la noche.
▶**stay out of** *vt (not interfere in)* no meterse en.
▶**stay up** *vi (not go to bed)* no acostarse; *(fence etc)* mantenerse en pie.
stead·i·ly *adv (improve)* constantemente; *(walk)* con paso seguro; *(gaze)* fijamente; *(rain, work)* sin parar.
stead·y *adj* firme; *(prices)* estable; *(demand, speed)* constante.
steak bistec *m*.
steal* *vti* robar.
steam 1 *n* vapor *m*. **2** *vt (food)* cocer al vapor.
▶**steam up** *vi (window etc)* empañarse.
steam·roll·er apisonadora *f*.
steel acero *m*; **s. industry** industria *f* siderúrgica.
steep *adj (hill etc)* empinado, -a; *(price, increase)* excesivo, -a.
stee·ple aguja *f*.
steer *vt* dirigir; *(car)* conducir; *(ship)* gobernar.
steer·ing wheel volante *m*.
stem *(of plant)* tallo *m*; *(of glass)* pie *m*.
ste·nog·ra·pher taquígrafo *m*.
step 1 *n* paso *m*; *(measure)* medida *f*; *(stair)* peldaño *m*; **s. by s.** poco a poco; **steps** *(outdoor)* escalinata *f sing*; *(indoor)* escalera *f sing*. **2** *vi* dar un paso.
▶**step aside** *vi* apartarse.
▶**step back** *vi* retroceder.
▶**step down** *vi* renunciar; *(resign)* dimitir.
▶**step forward** *vi (volunteer)* ofrecerse.
▶**step in** *vi* intervenir.
▶**step into/out of** *vt (car etc)* entrar en/salir de.
▶**step up** *vt* aumentar.
step·broth·er hermanastro *m*.
step·daugh·ter hijastra *f*.
step·fa·ther padrastro *m*.
step·lad·der escalera *f* de tijera.
step·moth·er madrastra *f*.
step·sis·ter hermanastra *f*.
step·son hijastro *m*.
ster·e·o 1 *n* estéreo *m*. **2** *adj* estereo(fónico, -a).
ster·il·ize *vt* esterilizar.
ster·ling *n* libras *fpl* esterlinas
stew estofado *m*, cocido *m*.
stew·ard *(on plane)* auxiliar *m* de vuelo.
stew·ard·ess *(on plane)* azafata *f*.
stick¹ palo *m*; *(walking stick)* bastón *m*.
stick² **1** *vt* meter; *(with glue etc)* pegar; **he stuck his head out of the window** asomó la cabeza por la ventana. **2** *vi (become attached)* pegarse; *(window, drawer)* atrancarse.
▶**stick down** *vt (stamp)* pegar.
▶**stick on** *vt (stamp)* pegar.
▶**stick out 1** *vi (project)* sobresalir; *(be noticeable)* resaltar. **2** *vt (tongue)* sacar.
▶**stick to** *vt (principles)* atenerse a.
▶**stick up** *vt (poster)* fijar.
▶**stick up for** *vt* defender.
stick·er *(label)* etiqueta *f* adhesiva; *(with slogan)* pegatina *f*.
stick·ing plas·ter tirita *f*, curita *f*.
stick·y *adj* pegajoso, -a; *(label)* engomado, -a.
stiff *adj* rígido, -a; *(joint)* entumecido, -a; **to have a s. neck** tener tortícolis.
sti·fle 1 *vt* sofocar. **2** *vi* sofocarse.
sti·fling *adj* sofocante.
still 1 *adv (up to this time)* todavía, aún; *(nonetheless)* no obstante; *(however)* sin embargo; *(with comparative) (even)* aún; **s. colder** aún más frío. **2** *adj (calm)* tranquilo, -a; *(motionless)* inmóvil.
stim·u·late *vt* estimular.
sting 1 *n* picadura *f*. **2** *vt* picar.
stink* *vi* apestar (**of** a).
▶**stink out** *vt (room)* apestar.
stir *vt (liquid)* remover.
▶**stir up** *vt (memories, curiosity)* despertar.
stir·rup estribo *m*.
stitch puntada *f*; *(in knitting)* punto *m*; *(for surgery etc)* punto *m* (de sutura).
stock 1 *n (goods)* existencias *fpl*; *(selection)* surtido *m*; *(broth)* caldo *m*; **out of s.** agotado, -a; **to have sth in s.** tener existencias de algo; **stocks and shares** acciones *fpl*. **2** *vt (have in stock)* tener existencias de.
▶**stock up** *vi* abastecerse (**on, with** de).
Stock Ex·change Bolsa *f* (de valores).
stock·ing media *f*; **a pair of stockings** unas medias.
Stock Mar·ket Bolsa *f*.
stock·pile *vt* almacenar; *(accumulate)* acumular.

stock·y *adj* (**stockier, stockiest**) *(squat)* rechoncho, -a; *(heavily built)* fornido, -a.
sto·len *pp of* **steal**.
stom·ach estómago *m*; **s. upset** trastorno *m* gástrico.
stone piedra *f*.
stool taburete *m*.
stop 1 *n* parada *f*, *(break)* pausa *f*; **to come to a s.** pararse; **to put a s. to sth** poner fin a algo. **2** *vt* parar; *(gas, water supply)* cortar; *(prevent)* evitar; **to s. sb from doing sth** impedir a algn hacer algo; **to s. doing sth** dejar de hacer algo. **3** *vi* *(person, moving vehicle)* pararse; *(cease)* terminar; *(stay)* pararse.
▶ **stop by** *vi* pasarse; **I'll s. by at the office** me pasaré por la oficina.
▶ **stop off** *vi* pararse un rato.
▶ **stop up** *vt* *(hole)* tapar.
stop-off parada *f*, *(flying)* escala *f*.
stop·o·ver parada *f*.
stop·watch cronómetro *m*.
store 1 *n* *(stock)* provisión *f*, *(warehouse)* almacén *m*; *(shop)* tienda *f*; **department s.** gran almacén *m*. **2** *vt* *(furniture, computer data)* almacenar; *(keep)* guardar; **to s. (up)** acumular.
store·room despensa *f*.
stork cigüeña *f*.
storm tormenta *f*, *(with wind)* vendaval *m*.
storm·y *adj* *(weather)* tormentoso, -a.
sto·ry¹ *(tale)* historia *f*, *(account)* relato *m*; *(article)* artículo *m*; *(plot)* trama *f*; **tall s.** cuento *m* chino.
sto·ry² piso *m*.
stove *(for heating)* estufa *f*, *(cooker)* cocina *f*, *(oven)* horno *m*.
straight 1 *adj* *(not bent)* recto, -a; *(hair)* liso, -a; *(honest)* honrado, -a; *(answer)* sincero, -a; *(drink)* solo, -a. **2** *adv* *(in a straight line)* en línea recta; *(directly)* directamente; *(frankly)* francamente; **keep s. ahead** sigue todo recto; **s. away** en seguida.
straight·en *vt* *(sth bent)* enderezar, poner derecho, -a; *(tie, picture)* poner bien; *(hair)* alisar.
▶ **straighten out** *vt* *(problem)* resolver.
straight·for·ward *adj* *(easy)* sencillo, -a.
strain 1 *vt* *(eyes, voice)* forzar; *(heart)* cansar; *(liquid)* filtrar; *(vegetables, tea)* colar. **2** *n* tensión *f*, *(effort)* esfuerzo *m*; *(exhaustion)* agotamiento *m*.
strain·er colador *m*.
strand *(of thread)* hebra *f*, *(of hair)* pelo *m*.
strand·ed *adj* **to leave stranded** dejar plantado, -a.
strange *adj* *(unknown)* desconocido, -a; *(unfamiliar)* nuevo, -a; *(odd)* extraño, -a.
strang·er *(unknown person)* desconocido, -a *mf*, *(outsider)* forastero, -a *mf*.
stran·gle *vt* estrangular.
strap *(on bag)* correa *f*, *(on dress)* tirante *m*.
straw paja *f*, *(for drinking)* pajita *f*.
straw·ber·ry fresa *f*, *(large)* fresón *m*.
streak *(line)* raya *f*, *(in hair)* reflejo *m*; **s. of lightning** rayo *m*.
stream *(brook)* arroyo *m*; *(current)* corriente *f*, *(flow)* flujo *m*.
street calle *f*; **the man in the s.** el hombre de la calle.
street·car tranvía *m*.
street lamp farol *m*.
street map, street plan (plano *m*) callejero *m*.
strength fuerza *f*, *(of rope etc)* resistencia *f*, *(of emotion, color)* intensidad *f*.
strength·en *vt* reforzar; *(intensify)* intensificar.
stress 1 *n* estrés *m*; *(emphasis)* hincapié *m*; *(on word)* acento *m*. **2** *vt* *(emphasize)* subrayar; *(word)* acentuar.
stress·ful *adj* estresante.
stretch *vt* *(elastic)* estirar; *(arm, hand)* alargar. **2** *vi* estirarse. **3** *n* *(of land)* extensión *f*, *(of time)* intervalo *m*.
▶ **stretch out 1** *vt* *(arm, hand)* alargar; *(legs)* estirar. **2** *vi* *(countryside, years etc)* extenderse.
stretch·er camilla *f*.
strict *adj* estricto, -a.
strict·ly *adv* *(categorically)* terminantemente; *(precisely)* estrictamente; **s. speaking** en sentido estricto.
strict·ness severidad *f*.
stride *n* zancada *f*. **2** *vi** **to s. (along)** andar a zancadas.
strike 1 *vt** *(hit)* golpear; *(collide with)* chocar contra; *(match)* encender; *(impress)* impresionar; **the clock struck three** el reloj dio las tres; **it strikes me …** me parece … **2** *vi** *(workers)* declararse en huelga. **3** *n* *(by workers)* huelga *f*, **on s.** en huelga; **to go (out) on s.** declararse en huelga; **to call a s.** convocar una huelga.
▶ **strike out** *vi* **to s. out at sb** arremeter contra algn.
▶ **strike up** *vt* *(friendship)* trabar; *(conversation)* entablar; *(tune)* empezar a tocar.
strik·er *(worker)* huelguista *mf*.
strik·ing *adj* *(eye-catching)* llamativo, -a; *(impressive)* impresionante.
string *(cord, of guitar)* cuerda *f*.
strip¹ *vi* *(undress)* desnudarse.
strip² tira *f*, *(of metal)* cinta *f*, lámina *f*.
▶ **strip off** *vi* *(undress)* desnudarse.
stripe raya *f*.
striped *adj* a rayas.
strive* *vi* **to s. to do sth** esforzarse por hacer algo.
stroke 1 *n* *(blow)* golpe *m*; *(in swimming)* brazada *f*, *(illness)* apoplejía *f*; **a s. of luck** un golpe de suerte. **2** *vt* acariciar.
stroll *vi* dar un paseo; **he strolled across the square** cruzó la plaza a paso lento. **2** *n* paseo *m*.
stroll·er *(for baby)* cochecito *m*.
strong *adj* fuerte; *(durable)* sólido, -a.
struc·ture estructura *f*, *(building)* edificio *m*.
strug·gle 1 *vi* luchar. **2** *n* lucha *f*, *(physical fight)* pelea *f*.
stub *(of cigarette)* colilla *f*, *(of check)* matriz *f*.
stub·born *adj* testarudo, -a.
stub·born·ness testarudez *f*.
stuck 1 *pt & pp of* **stick²**. **2** *adj* *(caught, jammed)* atrancado, -a; **I'm s.** *(unable to carry on)* no puedo seguir.
stud *(on clothing)* tachón *m*.
stu·dent estudiante *mf*.
stu·di·o *(TV etc)* estudio *m*; *(artist's)* taller *m*; **s. apartment** estudio *m*.
stud·y 1 *vti* estudiar; **to s. to be a doctor** estudiar para médico. **2** *n* estudio *m*.
stuff 1 *vt* *(container)* llenar (**with** de); *(in cooking)* rellenar (**with** con *or* de); *(cram)* atiborrar (**with** de). **2** *n* *(material)* material *m*; *(things)* cosas *fpl*, trastos *mpl*.
stuffed up *adj* *(nose)* tapado, -a.
stuff·ing relleno *m*.
stuff·y *adj* *(room)* mal ventilado, -a; *(atmosphere)* cargado, -a.
stum·ble *vi* tropezar; *fig* **to s. across** *or* **on** tropezar *or* dar con.
stump *(of tree)* tocón *m*.
stun *vt* aturdir; *(news etc)* sorprender.
stunned *adj* *(amazed)* estupefacto, -a.
stun·ning *adj* *(blow)* duro, -a; *(news)* sorprendente; *fam* *(woman, outfit)* fenomenal.
stu·pid *adj* estúpido, -a.

stu·pid·i·ty estupidez *f*.
stur·dy *adj* robusto, -a.
stut·ter 1 *vi* tartamudear. **2** *n* tartamudeo *m*.
sty *(pen)* pocilga *f*.
style estilo *m*; *(of dress)* modelo *m*; *(fashion)* moda *f*.
styl·ish *adj* con estilo.
sub·ject 1 *n* *(citizen)* súbdito *m*; *(topic)* tema *m*; *(at school)* asignatura *f*, *(of sentence)* sujeto *m*. **2** *vt* someter.
sub·junc·tive subjuntivo *m*.
sub·ma·rine 1 *n* submarino *m*. **2** *adj* submarino, -a.
sub·scribe *vi* suscribirse (**to** a).
sub·scrib·er abonado, -a *mf*.
sub·scrip·tion *(to magazine)* suscripción *f*, abono *m*.
sub·side *vi* *(land)* hundirse; *(floodwater)* bajar.
sub·si·dy subvención *f*.
sub·stance sustancia *f*.
sub·stan·tial *adj* *(sum, loss)* importante; *(meal)* abundante.
sub·sti·tute 1 *vt* sustituir. **2** *n* *(person)* suplente *mf*, *(thing)* sucedáneo *m*.
sub·sti·tu·tion sustitución *f*.
sub·ti·tle subtítulo *m*.
sub·tle *adj* sutil.
sub·tract *vt* restar.
sub·trac·tion resta *f*.
sub·urb barrio *m* periférico; **the suburbs** las afueras.
sub·ur·ban *adj* suburbano, -a.
sub·way *(underground railway)* metro *m*.
suc·ceed *vi* *(person)* tener éxito; **to s. in doing sth** conseguir hacer algo.
suc·cess éxito *m*.
suc·cess·ful *adj* de éxito; *(business)* próspero, -a; **to be s. in doing sth** lograr hacer algo.
suc·ces·sion sucesión *f*, serie *f*, **in s.** sucesivamente.
suc·ces·sive *adj* sucesivo, -a, consecutivo, -a.
suc·ces·sor sucesor, -a *mf*.
such 1 *adj* *(of that sort)* tal, semejante; **artists s. as Monet** artistas como Monet. ▪ *(so much, so great)* tanto, -a; **he's always in s. a hurry** siempre anda con tanta prisa; **s. a lot of books** tantos libros. **2** *adv* *(so very)* tan; **it's s. a long time** hace tanto tiempo; **she's s. a clever woman** es una mujer tan inteligente.
suck 1 *vt* *(liquid)* sorber, chupar; *(at breast)* mamar. **2** *vi* *(baby)* mamar.
▶ **suck up** *vt* *(with straw)* aspirar.
sud·den *adj* *(hurried)* repentino, -a; *(unexpected)* imprevisto, -a; **all of a s.** de repente.
sud·den·ly *adv* de repente.
suds *npl* espuma *f* de jabón.
sue 1 *vt* demandar. **2** *vi* presentar una demanda.
suede ante *m*, *(for gloves)* cabritilla *f*.
suf·fer *vti* sufrir; **to s. from** sufrir de.
suf·fer·er *(from disease)* enfermo, -a *mf*.
suf·fer·ing *(affliction)* sufrimiento *m*; *(pain, torment)* dolor *m*.
suf·fi·cient *adj* suficiente, bastante.
suf·fi·cient·ly *adv* suficientemente, bastante.
suf·fix sufijo *m*.
suf·fo·cate 1 *vt* asfixiar. **2** *vi* asfixiarse.
sug·ar 1 *n* azúcar *m or f*. **2** *vt* azucarar.
sug·ar bowl azucarero *m*.
sug·gest *vt* *(propose)* sugerir; *(advise)* aconsejar; *(indicate, imply)* indicar.
sug·ges·tion *(proposal)* sugerencia *f*.
su·i·cide suicidio *m*.
suit 1 *n* traje *m* de chaqueta; *(in cards)* palo *m*. **2** *vt* *(be convenient for)* convenir a; *(be right, appropriate for)* ir bien a; **red really suits you** el rojo te favorece mucho; **s. yourself!** ¡como quieras!
suit·a·ble *adj* *(convenient)* conveniente; *(appropriate)* adecuado, -a; **the most s. woman for the job** la mujer más indicada para el puesto.
suit·case maleta *f*.
suite *(of furniture)* tresillo *m*; *(of hotel rooms, music)* suite *f*.
sulk *vi* enfurruñarse.
sul·tan·a *(raisin)* pasa *f* (de Esmirna).
sum *(arithmetic problem, amount)* suma *f*, *(total amount)* total *m*; *(of money)* importe *m*.
▶ **sum up** *vt* resumir.
sum·ma·rize *vt* resumir.
sum·ma·ry resumen *m*.
sum·mer 1 *n* verano *m*. **2** *adj* *(vacation etc)* de verano; *(resort)* de veraneo.
sum·mer·time verano *m*.
sum·mon *vt* *(meeting, person)* convocar; *(aid)* pedir.
▶ **summon up** *vt* *(resources)* reunir; **to s. up one's courage** armarse de valor.
sum·mons 1 *n* *(call)* llamada *f*, llamamiento *m*; *(to court)* citación *f* judicial. **2** *vt* *(to court)* citar.
sun sol *m*.
sun·bathe *vi* tomar el sol.
sun·burn quemadura *f* de sol.
sun·burnt *adj* *(burnt)* quemado, -a por el sol; *(tanned)* bronceado, -a.
sun·dae helado *m* de fruta y nueces.
Sun·day domingo *m*.
sun·glass·es *npl* gafas *fpl* de sol.
sun·lamp lámpara *f* solar.
sun·light (luz *f* del) sol *m*.
sun·ny *adj* *(day)* de sol; **it is s.** hace sol.
sun·rise salida *f* del sol.
sun·roof *(on car)* techo *m* corredizo.
sun·set puesta *f* del sol.
sun·shade sombrilla *f*.
sun·shine (luz *f* del) sol *m*.
sun·stroke insolación *f*.
sun·tan bronceado *m*; **s. oil** (aceite *m*) bronceador *m*; **s. lotion** leche *f* bronceadora.
sun·tanned *adj* bronceado, -a.
su·per *adj fam* fenomenal.
su·perb *adj* espléndido, -a.
su·per·fi·cial *adj* superficial.
su·per·in·ten·dent *(of apartment building)* portero, -a *mf*.
su·pe·ri·or *adj* superior.
su·pe·ri·or·i·ty superioridad *f*.
su·per·mar·ket supermercado *m*.
su·per·sti·tion superstición *f*.
su·per·sti·tious *adj* supersticioso, -a.
su·per·vise *vt* supervisar; *(watch over)* vigilar.
su·per·vi·sor supervisor, -a *mf*.

sup·per cena *f*; **to have s.** cenar.
sup·ple *adj* flexible.
sup·ple·ment 1 *n* suplemento *m*. **2** *vt* complementar.
sup·ply 1 *n* (*provision*) suministro *m*; (*delivery*) provisión *f*; **supplies** (*food*) víveres *mpl*. **2** *vt* (*provide*) suministrar; (*with provisions*) aprovisionar; (*information*) facilitar.
sup·port 1 *n* soporte *m*; (*moral*) apoyo *m*. **2** *vt* (*weight etc*) sostener; (*back*) apoyar; (*team*) ser (hincha) de; (*family*) mantener.
sup·port·er (*political*) partidario, -a *mf*; (*in sport*) hincha *mf*.
sup·por·tive *adj* he was supportive (of) apoyó mucho (a), fue muy comprensivo (con).
sup·pose *vt* suponer; (*presume*) creer; **I s. not/so** supongo que no/sí; **you're not supposed to smoke in here** no está permitido fumar aquí dentro; **you're supposed to be in bed** deberías estar acostado ya.
sup·press *vt* suprimir; (*feelings, laugh etc*) contener; (*news, truth*) callar; (*revolt*) sofocar.
sure *adj* seguro, -a; **I'm s. (that) …** estoy seguro, -a de que …; **make s. that it's ready** asegúrate de que esté listo.
sure·ly *adv* (*without a doubt*) seguramente; **s. not!** ¡no puede ser!
sur·face superficie *f*; **s. area** área *f* de la superficie; **by s. mail** por vía terrestre *or* marítima.
surf·board tabla *f* de surf.
surf·ing surf *m*, surfing *m*.
surge 1 *n* (*growth*) alza *f*; (*of sea, sympathy*) oleada *f*; *fig* (*of anger, energy*) arranque *m*. **2** *vi* **to s. forward** (*people*) avanzar en tropel.
sur·geon cirujano, -a *mf*.
sur·ger·y (*operation*) cirugía *f*; **s. hours** horas *fpl* de consulta.
sur·gi·cal *adj* quirúrgico, -a; **s. spirit** alcohol *m* de 90°.
sur·name apellido *m*.
sur·plus 1 *n* (*of goods*) excedente *m*; (*of budget*) superávit *m*. **2** *adj* excedente.
sur·prise 1 *n* sorpresa *f*; **to take sb by s.** coger desprevenido, -a a algn. **2** *adj* (*visit*) inesperado, -a; **s. attack** ataque *m* sorpresa. **3** *vt* sorprender.
sur·prised *adj* sorprendido, -a; **I should not be s. if it rained** no me extrañaría que lloviera.
sur·pris·ing *adj* sorprendente.
sur·pris·ing·ly *adv* de modo sorprendente.
sur·ren·der *vi* (*give in*) rendirse.
sur·round *vt* rodear.
sur·round·ing *adj* circundante.
sur·round·ings *npl* alrededores *mpl*.
sur·veil·lance vigilancia *f*.
sur·vey (*of trends etc*) encuesta *f*.
sur·vey·or agrimensor, -a *mf*.
sur·vive 1 *vi* sobrevivir. **2** *vt* sobrevivir a.
sur·vi·vor superviviente *mf*.
sus·pect 1 *n* sospechoso, -a *mf*. **2** *vt* (*person*) sospechar (**of** de); (*think likely*) imaginar.
sus·pend *vt* suspender; (*pupil*) expulsar por un tiempo.
sus·pend·ers *npl* tirantes *mpl*.
sus·pense suspense *m*.
sus·pen·sion suspensión *f*.
sus·pi·cion sospecha *f*; (*mistrust*) recelo *m*; (*doubt*) duda *f*; (*trace*) pizca *f*.
sus·pi·cious *adj* (*arousing suspicion*) sospechoso, -a; (*distrustful*) receloso, -a; **to be s. of sb** desconfiar de algn.
swal·low¹ *vt* (*drink, food*) tragar.
swal·low² (*bird*) golondrina *f*.
▸**swallow down** *vt* tragarse.
swamp ciénaga *f*.
swan cisne *m*.
swap 1 *n* intercambio *m*. **2** *vt* cambiar.
swarm enjambre *m*.
sway *vi* (*swing*) balancearse; (*totter*) tambalearse.
swear* 1 *vt* (*vow*) jurar. **2** *vi* (*curse*) decir palabrotas.
swear·word palabrota *f*.
sweat 1 *n* sudor *m*. **2** *vi* sudar.
sweat·er suéter *m*.
sweat·shirt sudadera *f*.
Swede (*person*) sueco, -a *mf*.
Swed·ish 1 *adj* sueco, -a. **2** *n* (*language*) sueco *m*.
sweep* *vti* barrer.
▸**sweep aside** *vt* apartar bruscamente; (*objections*) rechazar.
▸**sweep away** *vt* (*dust*) barrer; (*storm*) arrastrar.
▸**sweep out** *vt* (*room*) barrer.
▸**sweep up** *vi* barrer.
sweet 1 *adj* dulce; (*sugary*) azucarado, -a; (*pleasant*) agradable; (*person, animal*) encantador, -a. **2** *n* (*candy*) caramelo *m*; (*chocolate*) bombón *m*; (*dessert*) postre *m*.
sweet·corn maíz *m* dulce.
sweet·en *vt* (*tea etc*) azucarar.
sweet·ly *adv* dulcemente.
sweet shop confitería *f*.
swell 1 *n* (*of sea*) marejada *f*, oleaje *m*. **2** *adj fam* fenomenal. **3** *vi** (*part of body*) hincharse; (*river*) subir.
▸**swell up** *vi* hincharse.
swell·ing hinchazón *f*.
swerve *vi* (*car*) dar un viraje brusco.
swift 1 *adj* rápido, -a, veloz. **2** *n* (*bird*) vencejo *m* (común).
swim 1 *vi** nadar; **to go swimming** ir a nadar. **2** *vt** (*the Mississippi*) pasar a nado. **3** *n* baño *m*; **to go for a s.** ir a darse un baño.
swim·mer nadador, -a *mf*.
swim·ming natación *f*.
swim·ming pool piscina *f*.
swim·ming trunks bañador *m*.
swim·suit bañador *m*.
swing 1 *n* (*for playing*) columpio *m*. **2** *vi** (*move back and forth*) balancearse; (*arms, legs*) menearse; (*on swing*) columpiarse. **3** *vt** (*arms, legs*) menear.
Swiss 1 *adj* suizo, -a. **2** *n inv* (*person*) suizo, -a *mf*; **the S.** *pl* los suizos.
switch 1 *n* (*for light etc*) interruptor *m*. **2** *vt* (*jobs, direction*) cambiar de.
▸**switch off** *vt* apagar.
▸**switch on** *vt* encender.
▸**switch over** *vi* cambiar (**to** a).
swol·len *adj* (*ankle, face*) hinchado, -a.
swop *vt* = **swap**.
sword espada *f*.
syl·la·ble sílaba *f*.
syl·la·bus programa *m* de estudios.
sym·bol símbolo *m*.
sym·bol·ic *adj* simbólico, -a.
sym·me·try simetría *f*.
sym·pa·thet·ic *adj* (*showing pity*) compasivo, -a; (*understanding*) comprensivo, -a; (*kind*) amable.

sym·pa·thize *vi* (*show pity*) compadecerse (**with** de); (*understand*) comprender.
sym·pa·thy (*pity*) compasión *f*; (*condolences*) pésame *m*; (*understanding*) comprensión *f*; **to express one's s.** dar el pésame.
sym·pho·ny sinfonía *f*.
symp·tom síntoma *m*.
syn·a·gogue sinagoga *f*.
syn·o·nym sinónimo *m*.
sy·ringe jeringuilla *f*.
syr·up jarabe *m*, almíbar *m*.
sys·tem sistema *m*.

T

ta *interj fam* gracias.
tab (*flap*) lengüeta *f*.
ta·ble mesa *f*; **to lay** *or* **set the t.** poner la mesa.
ta·ble·cloth mantel *m*.
ta·ble·mat salvamanteles *m inv*.
ta·ble·spoon cuchara *f* de servir.
ta·ble·spoon·ful cucharada *f*.
tab·let (*pill*) pastilla *f*.
tack (*small nail*) tachuela *f*.
tack·le *vt* (*task*) emprender; (*problem*) abordar; (*grapple with*) agarrar; (*in sport*) placar; (*in soccer*) entrar a.
tack·y *adj fam* (*shoddy*) cutre.
tact tacto *m*.
tact·ful *adj* diplomático, -a.
tac·tic táctica *f*; **tactics** táctica *f sing*.
taf·fy caramelo *m* duro.
tag (*label*) etiqueta *f*.
tail cola *f*.
tai·lor sastre *m*.
take* *vt* tomar; (*bus etc*) coger; (*accept*) aceptar; (*win*) ganar; (*prize*) llevarse; (*eat, drink*) tomar; (*accompany*) llevar; (*endure*) aguantar; (*consider*) considerar; (*require*) requerir; **she's taking (a degree in) law** estudia derecho; **to t. an exam (in …)** examinarse (de …); **it takes an hour to get there** se tarda una hora en ir hasta allí; **it takes courage** se necesita valor.
▸**take after** *vt* parecerse a.
▸**take along** *vt* llevar (consigo).
▸**take apart** *vt* (*machine*) desmontar.
▸**take away** *vt* (*carry off*) llevarse; (*in math*) restar (**from** de); **to t. sth away from sb** quitarle algo a algn.
▸**take back** *vt* (*give back*) devolver; (*receive back*) recuperar; (*withdraw*) retirar.
▸**take down** *vt* (*lower*) bajar; (*write*) apuntar.
▸**take in** *vt* (*include*) abarcar; (*understand*) entender; (*deceive*) engañar.
▸**take off 1** *vt* quitar; (*lead or carry away*) llevarse; (*deduct*) descontar; **he took off his jacket** se quitó la chaqueta. **2** *vi* (*plane*) despegar.
▸**take on** *vt* (*undertake*) encargarse de; (*acquire*) tomar; (*employ*) contratar.
▸**take out** *vt* sacar; **he's taking me out to dinner** me ha invitado a cenar fuera; (*insurance*) sacarse; (*stain, tooth*) quitar.
▸**take over 1** *vt* (*office, post*) tomar posesión de. **2** *vi* **to t. over from sb** relevar a algn.
▸**take up** *vt* (*occupy*) ocupar; **I've taken up the guitar** he empezado a tocar la guitarra.
take·off (*of plane*) despegue *m*.
take·o·ver (*of company*) absorción *f*.
tak·ings *npl* (*of shop, business*) recaudación *f sing*.
takeout 1 *n* (*food*) comida *f* para llevar; (*restaurant*) restaurante *m* de comida para llevar. **2** *adj* (*food*) para llevar.
tale cuento *m*; **to tell tales** contar chismes.
tal·ent talento *m*.
tal·ent·ed *adj* dotado, -a.
talk 1 *vi* hablar; (*chat*) charlar; (*gossip*) chismorrear. **2** *vt* hablar; **to t. nonsense** decir tonterías. **3** *n* (*conversation*) conversación *f*; (*words*) palabras *fpl*; (*gossip*) chismes *mpl*; (*lecture*) charla *f*; **there's t. of …** se habla de …
▸**talk into** *vt* **to t. sb into sth** convencer a algn para que haga algo.
▸**talk out of** *vt* **to t. sb out of sth** disuadir a algn de que haga algo.
▸**talk over** *vt* discutir.
talk·a·tive *adj* hablador, -a.
tall *adj* alto, -a; **a tree ten meters t.** un árbol de diez metros (de alto); **how t. are you?** ¿cuánto mides?
tam·bou·rine pandereta *f*.
tame 1 *adj* (*animal*) domado, -a; (*by nature*) manso, -a. **2** *vt* domar.
tam·pon tampón *m*.
tan 1 *n* (*of skin*) bronceado *m*. **2** *vt* (*skin*) broncear. **3** *vi* ponerse moreno, -a.
tan·ger·ine clementina *f*.
tan·gled *adj* enredado, -a.
tank (*container*) depósito *m*; (*with gun*) tanque *m*.
tank·er (*ship*) tanque *m*; (*for oil*) petrolero *m*.
tap¹ *vt* (*knock*) golpear suavemente; (*with hand*) dar una palmadita a. **2** *vi* **to t. at the door** llamar suavemente a la puerta. **3** *n* golpecito *m*.
tap² (*for water*) grifo *m*.
tape 1 *n* cinta *f*; **sticky t.** cinta *f* adhesiva. **2** *vt* pegar (con cinta adhesiva); (*record*) grabar (en cinta).
tape meas·ure cinta *f* métrica.
tape re·cord·er magnetófono *m*, casete *m*.
tar alquitrán *m*.
tar·get (*object aimed at*) blanco *m*; (*purpose*) meta *f*.
tar·iff tarifa *f*, arancel *m*.
tar·pau·lin lona *f*.
tart (*to eat*) tarta *f*.
tar·tan tartán *m*.
task tarea *f*.
taste 1 *n* (*sense*) gusto *m*; (*flavor*) sabor *m*; (*liking*) afición *f*; **it has a burnt t.** sabe a quemado; **in bad t.** de mal gusto; **to have (good) t.** tener (buen) gusto. **2** *vt* (*sample*) probar. **3** *vi* **to t. of sth** saber a algo.
tast·y *adj* sabroso, -a.
tat·tered *adj* hecho, -a jirones.
tat·too 1 *vt* tatuar. **2** *n* (*mark*) tatuaje *m*.
tax 1 *n* impuesto *m*; **t. free** exento, -a de impuestos; **t. collector** recaudador, -a *mf* (de impuestos). **2** *vt* gravar; (*patience etc*) poner a prueba.

tax·a·ble *adj* imponible.
tax·i taxi *m*.
tax·i driv·er taxista *mf*.
tax·i rank parada *f* de taxis.
tax·pay·er contribuyente *mf*.
tea té *m*; *(meal)* merienda *f*.
tea·bag bolsita *f* de té.
tea break descanso *m*.
teach* 1 *vt* enseñar; *(subject)* dar clases de; **to t. sb (how) to do sth** enseñar a algn a hacer algo. **2** *vi* ser profesor, -a.
teach·er profesor, -a *mf*.
teach·ing enseñanza *f*.
tea·cup taza *f* de té.
team equipo *m*.
▸**team up** *vi* **to t. up with sb** juntarse con algn.
tea·pot tetera *f*.
tear[1] lágrima *f*; **to be in tears** estar llorando.
tear[2] **1** *vt** rasgar; **to t. sth out of sb's hands** arrancarle algo de las manos a algn. **2** *vi** *(cloth)* rasgarse. **3** *n* desgarrón *m*.
▸**tear off** *vt* arrancar.
▸**tear out** *vt* arrancar.
▸**tear up** *vt* hacer pedazos.
tease *vt* tomar el pelo a.
tea ser·vice *or* **set** juego *m* de té.
tea·spoon cucharilla *f*.
tea·spoon·ful cucharadita *f*.
teat *(of bottle)* tetina *f*.
tea·time hora *f* del té.
tea tow·el paño *m* (de cocina).
tech·ni·cal *adj* técnico, -a.
tech·ni·cian técnico, -a *mf*.
tech·nique técnica *f*.
tech·no·log·i·cal *adj* tecnológico, -a.
tech·nol·o·gy tecnología *f*.
ted·dy bear oso *m* de felpa.
teen·age *adj* adolescente.
teen·ag·er adolescente *mf*.
tee-shirt camiseta *f*.
teeth *npl see* **tooth**.
tee·to·tal·ler abstemio, -a *mf*.
tel·e·com·mu·ni·ca·tions *npl* telecomunicaciones *fpl*.
tel·e·gram telegrama *m*.
tel·e·phone 1 *n* teléfono *m*; **to speak to sb on the t.** hablar por teléfono con algn. **2** *vt* telefonear a, llamar por teléfono a.
tel·e·phone booth cabina *f* (telefónica).
tel·e·phone call llamada *f* telefónica.
tel·e·phone di·rec·to·ry guía *f* telefónica.
tel·e·phone num·ber número *m* de teléfono.
tel·e·scope telescopio *m*.
tel·e·vise *vt* televisar.
tel·e·vi·sion televisión *f*; **t. (set)** televisor *m*; **on t.** en la televisión.
tell* 1 *vt* decir; *(relate)* contar; *(inform)* comunicar; *(order)* mandar; *(distinguish)* distinguir; **to t. sb about sth** contarle algo a algn; **to t. sb to do sth** decir a algn que haga algo. **2** *vi* **who can t.?** *(know)* ¿quién sabe?
▸**tell off** *vt* reñir.
tell·er *(cashier)* cajero, -a *mf*.
tell·tale chivato, -a *mf*.
tem·per *(mood)* humor *m*; **to keep one's t.** no perder la calma; **to lose one's t.** perder los estribos.
tem·per·a·ture temperatura *f*; **to have a t.** tener fiebre.
tem·ple *(building)* templo *m*.
tem·po·rar·i·ly *adj* temporalmente, *Am* temporariamente.
tem·po·rar·y *adj* provisional; *(setback, improvement)* momentáneo, -a; *(teacher)* sustituto, -a.
tempt *vt* tentar; **to t. sb to do sth** incitar a algn a hacer algo.
temp·ta·tion tentación *f*.
tempt·ing *adj* tentador, -a.
ten *adj & n* diez *(m) inv*.
ten·an·cy *(of house)* alquiler *m*; *(of land)* arrendamiento *m*.
ten·ant *(of house)* inquilino, -a *mf*.
tend *vi (be inclined)* tender, tener tendencia (**to** a).
ten·den·cy tendencia *f*.
ten·der *adj (affectionate)* cariñoso, -a; *(meat)* tierno, -a.
ten·nis tenis *m*.
ten·nis court pista *f* de tenis.
tense[1] *adj* tenso, -a.
tense[2] *(of verb)* tiempo *m*.
ten·sion tensión *f*.
tent tienda *f* de campaña.
tenth *adj & n* décimo, -a *(mf)*.
term *(period)* período *m*; *(of study)* trimestre *m*; *(word)* término *m*; **terms** *(conditions)* condiciones *fpl*; **to be on good/bad terms with sb** tener buenas/malas relaciones con algn.
ter·mi·nal 1 terminal *f*; *(for computer)* terminal *m*. **2** *adj (patient, illness)* terminal.
ter·mi·nate 1 *vt* terminar; **to t. a pregnancy** abortar. **2** *vi* terminarse.
ter·race *(of houses)* hilera *f* de casas; *(patio)* terraza *f*.
ter·raced hous·es casas *fpl* (de estilo uniforme) en hilera.
ter·ri·ble *adj* terrible; **I feel t.** me encuentro fatal.
ter·ri·bly *adv* terriblemente.
ter·ri·fic *adj* fenomenal.
ter·ri·fy *vt* aterrorizar.
ter·ri·fy·ing *adj* aterrador, -a.
ter·ri·to·ry territorio *m*.
ter·ror terror *m*.
ter·ror·ist *adj & n* terrorista *(mf)*.
ter·ror·ize *vt* aterrorizar.
test 1 *vt* probar; *(analyze)* analizar. **2** *n (of product)* prueba *f*; *(in school)* examen *m*; *(of blood)* análisis *m*.
tes·ta·ment testamento *m*; **Old/New T.** Antiguo/Nuevo Testamento.
tes·ti·mo·ny testimonio *m*, declaración *f*.
test tube probeta *f*.
text 1 *n* texto *m*; **t. (message)** mensaje *m* de texto. **2** *vt (send text message to)* enviar un mensaje de texto a.
text·book libro *m* de texto.
tex·tile 1 *n* tejido *m*. **2** *adj* textil.
tex·ture textura *f*.
Thai *adj & n* tailandés, -esa *(mf)*.
than *conj* que; *(with numbers)* de; **he's older t. me** es mayor que yo; **more interesting t. we thought** más interesante de lo que creíamos; **more t. once** más de una vez; **more t. ten people** más de diez personas.
thank *vt* agradecer; **t. you** gracias.
thank·ful *adj* agradecido, -a.
thanks *npl* gracias *fpl*; **no, t.** no, gracias; **t. to** gracias a.
thanks·giv·ing T. Day Día *m* de Acción de Gracias.
that 1 *dem adj (pl* **those**) *(masculine)* ese; *(feminine)* esa; *(further away) (masculine)* aquel; *(feminine)* aquella; **at t. time** en aquella época; **t. book** ese/aquel libro; **t. one** ése/aquél. **2** *dem pron (pl* **those**) ése *m*, ésa *f*; *(further away)* aquél *m*, aquélla *f*, *(indefinite)* eso; *(remote)* aquello; **after t.** después de eso; **like t.** así; **don't talk like t.** no hables así; **t.'s right** eso es; **t.'s where I live** allí vivo yo; **what's t.?** ¿qué es eso?; **who's t.?** ¿quién es?; **all those I saw** todos los que vi; **there are those who say that ...** hay quien dice que .... **3** *rel pron* que; **all t. you said** todo lo que dijiste; **the letter t. I sent you** la carta que te envié; **the car t. they came in** el coche en el que vinieron; **the moment t. you arrived** el momento en que llegaste. **4** *conj* que; **come here so t. I can see you** ven aquí para que te vea; **he said (t.) he would come** dijo que vendría. **5** *adv* así de, tan; **that much** tanto, -a; **cut off t. much** córteme un trozo así de grande; **t. old** tan viejo; **we haven't got t. much money** no tenemos tanto dinero.
thaw 1 *vt (snow)* derretir; *(food, freezer)* descongelar. **2** *vi* descongelarse; *(snow)* derretirse. **3** *n* deshielo *m*.
the *def art* el, la; *pl* los, las; **at** *or* **to t.** al, a la; *pl* a los, a las; **of** *or* **from t.** del, de la; *pl* de los, de las; **the voice of the people** la voz del pueblo; **George t. Sixth** Jorge Sexto.
the·a·ter teatro *m*.
theft robo *m*.
their *poss adj* su; *(pl)* sus.
theirs *poss pron* (el) suyo, (la) suya; *(pl)* (los) suyos, (las) suyas.
them *pers pron pl (direct object)* los, las; *(indirect object)* les; **I know t.** los *or* las conozco; **I shall tell t. so** se lo diré (a ellos *or* ellas); **it's t.!** ¡son ellos!; **speak to t.** hábleles. ▪ *(with preposition)* ellos, ellas; **walk in front of t.** camine delante de ellos; **with t.** con ellos.
them·selves *pers pron pl (as subject)* ellos mismos, ellas mismas; *(as direct or indirect object)* se; *(after a preposition)* sí mismos, sí mismas; **they did it by t.** lo hicieron ellos solos.
then 1 *adv (at that time, in that case)* entonces; *(next, afterwards)* luego; **since t.** desde entonces; **till t.** hasta entonces; **go t.** pues vete. **2** *conj* entonces.
the·o·ry teoría *f*.
there *adv (indicating place)* allí, allá; *(nearer speaker)* ahí; **is Peter t.?** ¿está Peter?; **that man t.** aquel hombre; **t. is, t. are** hay; **t. were six of us** éramos seis.
there·fore *adv* por lo tanto.
ther·mom·e·ter termómetro *m*.
Ther·mos® **T. (flask)** termo *m*.
these 1 *dem adj pl* estos, -as. **2** *dem pron pl* éstos, -as; *see* **this**.
the·sis tesis *f inv*.
they *pron* ellos, ellas; **t. are dancing** están bailando; **t. alone** ellos solos. ▪ *(indefinite)* **t. say that ...** se dice que ....
thick *adj (book, slice, material)* grueso, -a; *(wood, vegetation)* espeso, -a; **a wall two meters t.** un muro de dos metros de espesor.
thick·en 1 *vt* espesar. **2** *vi* espesarse.
thick·ness *(of wall etc)* espesor *m*; *(of wire, lips)* grueso *m*; *(of liquid, forest)* espesura *f*.
thief *(pl* **thieves**) ladrón, -ona *mf*.
thigh muslo *m*.
thim·ble dedal *m*.
thin 1 *adj* delgado, -a; *(hair, vegetation)* ralo, -a; *(liquid)* claro, -a; **a t. slice** una loncha fina. **2** *vt* **to t. (down)** *(paint)* diluir.
thing cosa *f*; **my things** *(clothing)* mi ropa *f sing*; *(possessions)* mis cosas.
think* 1 *vt* pensar, creer; **I t. so/not** creo que sí/no; **I thought as much** ya me lo imaginaba. **2** *vi* pensar **(of, about** en); **what do you t.?** ¿a ti qué te parece?
▸**think over** *vt* reflexionar; **we'll have to t. it over** lo tendremos que pensar.
▸**think up** *vt* idear.
thin·ly *adv* ligeramente.
third 1 *adj* tercero, -a; *(before masculine singular noun)* tercer; **(on) the t. of March** el tres de marzo. **2** *n (in series)* tercero, -a *mf*; *(fraction)* tercera parte *f*.
third·ly *adv* en tercer lugar.
thirst sed *f*.
thirst·y *adj* **to be t.** tener sed.
thir·teen *adj & n* trece *(m)*.
thir·ty *adj & n* treinta *(m)*.
this 1 *dem adj (pl* **these**) *(masculine)* este; *(feminine)* esta; **t. book/these books** este libro/estos libros; **t. one** éste, ésta. **2** *(pl* **these**) *dem pron (indefinite)* esto; **t. is different** esto es distinto; **it was like t.** fue así; **t. is where we met** fue aquí donde nos conocimos; **it should have come before t.** debería haber llegado ya; *(introduction)* **t. is Mr Álvarez** le presento al Sr. Álvarez; *(on the phone)* **t. is Julia (speaking)** soy Julia. ▪ *(specific person or thing)* éste *m*, ésta *f*; **I prefer these to those** me gustan más éstos que aquéllos. **3** *adv* **he got t. far** llegó hasta aquí; **t. small/big** así de pequeño/grande.
thorn espina *f*.
thor·ough *adj (careful)* minucioso, -a; *(work)* concienzudo, -a; *(knowledge)* profundo, -a; **to carry out a t. inquiry into a matter** investigar a fondo un asunto.
thor·ough·ly *adv (carefully)* a fondo; *(wholly)* completamente.
those 1 *dem adj* esos, -as; *(remote)* aquellos, -as. **2** *dem pron* ésos, -as; *(remote)* aquéllos, -as; *(with rel)* los, las; *see* **that 1 & 2**.
though 1 *conj* aunque; **as t.** como si; **it looks as t. he's gone** parece que se ha ido. **2** *adv* sin embargo.
thought 1 *pt & pp of* **think**. **2** *(act of thinking)* pensamiento *m*; *(reflection)* reflexión *f*.
thought·ful *adj (considerate)* atento, -a.
thought·less *adj (person)* desconsiderado, -a; *(action)* irreflexivo, -a.
thou·sand *adj & n* mil *(m) inv*; **thousands of people** miles de personas.
thread 1 *n* hilo *m*. **2** *vt (needle)* enhebrar.
threat amenaza *f*.
threat·en *vt* amenazar; **to t. to do sth** amenazar con hacer algo.
threat·en·ing *adj* amenazador, -a.
three *adj & n* tres *(m) inv*.
thresh·old umbral *m*.
threw *pt of* **throw**.
thrill *(excitement)* emoción *f*.
thrilled *adj* emocionado, -a; **I'm t. about the trip** estoy muy ilusionado, -a con el viaje.
thrill·er *(book)* novela *f* de suspense; *(film)* película *f* de suspense.
thrill·ing *adj* emocionante.
thrive* *vi (person)* rebosar de salud; *(business)* prosperar; **he thrives on it** le viene de maravilla.
thriv·ing *adj* próspero, -a.
throat garganta *f*.
throne trono *m*.
through 1 *prep (place)* a través de, por; **to look t. the window** mirar por la ventana. ▪ *(time)* a lo largo de; **all t. his life** durante toda su vida. ▪ *(by means of)* por, mediante. ▪ *(because of)* a *or* por causa de; **t. ignorance** por ignorancia. **2** *adj* **a t. train** un tren directo. **3** *adv (from one*

side to the other) de un lado a otro; **to let sb t.** dejar pasar a algn; **to get t. to sb** comunicar con algn; **I'm t. with him** he terminado con él.

through·out 1 *prep* por todo, -a; **t. the year** durante todo el año. **2** *adv (place)* en todas partes; *(time)* todo el tiempo.

throw* *vt* tirar; *(to the ground)* derribar; *(party)* dar.

▶ **throw away** *vt (trash, money)* tirar; *(money)* malgastar; *(opportunity)* perder.

▶ **throw out** *vt (trash)* tirar; *(person)* echar.

▶ **throw up** *vti* devolver.

thrust* 1 *vt* empujar con fuerza; **he t. a letter into my hand** me puso una carta violentamente en la mano. **2** *n (push)* empujón *m*; *(of aircraft)* empuje *m*.

thud ruido *m* sordo.

thug *(lout)* gamberro *m*; *(criminal)* criminal *m*.

thumb pulgar *m*.

thumb·tack chincheta *f*.

thun·der 1 *n* trueno *m*. **2** *vi* tronar.

thun·der·storm tormenta *f*.

Thurs·day jueves *m*.

thus *adv* así, de esta manera; **and t. ...** así que ....

tick¹ 1 *n (sound)* tic-tac *m*; *(mark)* marca *f* de visto bueno. **2** *vi* hacer tic-tac. **3** *vt* marcar.

▶ **tick off** *vt (mark)* marcar.

▶ **tick over** *vi (engine)* funcionar al ralentí.

tick² *(insect)* garrapata *f*.

tick·et *(for bus etc)* billete *m*; *(for theater)* entrada *f*; *(for lottery)* décimo *m*; *(receipt)* recibo *m*.

tick·et col·lec·tor revisor, -a *mf*.

tick·et of·fice taquilla *f*.

tick·le *vt* hacer cosquillas a.

tick·lish *adj* **to be t.** *(person)* tener cosquillas.

tic-tac-toe tres en raya *m*.

tide marea *f*.

ti·di·ly *adv (to put away)* ordenadamente.

ti·dy 1 *adj (room, habits)* ordenado, -a; *(appearance)* arreglado, -a. **2** *vt* arreglar. **3** *vi* **to t. (up)** ordenar las cosas.

tie 1 *vt (shoelaces etc)* atar; **to t. a knot** hacer un nudo. **2** *n (around neck)* corbata *f*; *(match)* partido *m*; *(draw)* empate *m*.

▶ **tie up** *vt (parcel, dog)* atar.

ti·ger tigre *m*.

tight 1 *adj* apretado, -a; *(clothing)* ajustado, -a; *(seal)* hermético, -a; **my shoes are too t.** me aprietan los zapatos. **2** *adv* estrechamente; *(seal)* herméticamente; **hold t.** agárrate fuerte; **shut t.** bien cerrado, -a.

tight·en 1 *vt (screw)* apretar, *(rope)* tensar; *fig* **to t. (up) restrictions** intensificar las restricciones. **2** *vi* apretarse; *(cable)* tensarse.

tights *npl (thin)* panties *mpl*; *(thick)* leotardos *mpl*.

tile 1 *n (of roof)* teja *f*; *(glazed)* azulejo *m*; *(for floor)* baldosa *f*. **2** *vt (roof)* tejar; *(wall)* alicatar; *(floor)* embaldosar.

till¹ *(for cash)* caja *f*.

till² 1 *prep* hasta; **from morning t. night** de la mañana a la noche; **t. then** hasta entonces. **2** *conj* hasta que.

tilt 1 *vi* **to t. over** volcarse; **to t. (up)** inclinarse. **2** *vt* inclinar.

tim·ber madera *f* (de construcción).

time 1 *n* tiempo *m*; *(era)* época *f*; *(point in time)* momento *m*; *(time of day)* hora *f*; *(occasion)* vez *f*; **all the t.** todo el tiempo; **for some t. (past)** desde hace algún tiempo; **I haven't seen him for a long t.** hace mucho (tiempo) que no lo veo; **in a short t.** en poco tiempo; **in t.** a tiempo; **in three weeks' t.** dentro de tres semanas; **(at) any t. (you like)** cuando quiera; **at that t.** (en aquel) entonces; **at the same t.** al mismo tiempo; **at times** a veces; **from t. to t.** de vez en cuando; **he may turn up at any t.** puede llegar en cualquier momento; **on t.** puntualmente; **what's the t.?** ¿qué hora es?; **t. of the year** época *f* del año; **to have a good/bad t.** pasarlo bien/mal; **four at a t.** cuatro a la vez; **next t.** la próxima vez; **three times four** tres (multiplicado) por cuatro; **four times as big** cuatro veces más grande. **2** *vt (speech)* calcular la duración de; *(race)* cronometrar; *(choose the time of)* escoger el momento oportuno para.

tim·er *(device)* temporizador *m*.

time·ta·ble horario *m*.

tim·id *adj* tímido, -a.

tim·ing *(timeliness)* oportunidad *f*; *(coordination)* coordinación *f*; *(in race)* cronometraje *m*.

tin *(metal)* estaño *m*; *(container)* lata *f*.

tin·foil papel *m* de estaño.

tinned *adj* enlatado, -a; **t. food** conservas *fpl*.

tin-o·pen·er abrelatas *m inv*.

ti·ny *adj* diminuto, -a.

tip¹ *(end)* punta *f*; *(of cigarette)* colilla *f*.

tip² 1 *n (gratuity)* propina *f*; *(advice)* consejo *m*. **2** *vt* dar una propina a.

tip³ 1 *vt* inclinar. **2** *vi* **to t. (up)** ladearse; *(cart)* bascular.

▶ **tip over 1** *vt* volcar. **2** *vi* volcarse.

tipped cig·a·rette cigarrillo *m* con filtro.

tip·toe on t. de puntillas.

tire¹ *(of vehicle)* neumático *m*.

tire² 1 *vt* cansar. **2** *vi* cansarse.

▶ **tire out** *vt* agotar.

tired *adj* cansado, -a; **t. out** rendido, -a; **to be t.** estar cansado, -a; **to be t. of sth** estar harto, -a de algo.

tired·ness cansancio *m*.

tir·ing *adj* agotador, -a.

tis·sue *(handkerchief)* Kleenex® *m*.

ti·tle título *m*.

to 1 *prep (with place)* a; *(towards)* hacia; **he went to France/Japan** fue a Francia/al Japón; **I'm going to Mary's** voy a casa de Mary; **it is thirty miles to New York** Nueva York está a treinta millas; **the train to Madrid** el tren de Madrid; **to the east** hacia el este; **to the right** a la derecha. ▪ *(time)* **ten (minutes) to six** las seis menos diez. ▪ *(with indirect object)* a; **he gave it to his cousin** se lo dio a su primo. ▪ *(towards)* **he was very kind to me** se portó muy bien conmigo. ▪ *(with infinitive)* **to buy/to come** comprar/venir; *(in order to)* para; *(with verbs of motion)* a; **he did it to help me** lo hizo para ayudarme; **he stopped to talk** se detuvo a hablar; **difficult to do** difícil de hacer; **ready to listen** dispuesto, -a a escuchar; **the first to complain** el primero en quejarse; **this is the time to do it** éste es el momento de hacerlo; **to have a great deal to do** tener mucho que hacer.

toad sapo *m*.

toad·stool hongo *m* (venenoso).

toast 1 *n* **slice of t.** tostada *f*. **2** *vt* tostar.

toast·er tostador *m* (de pan).

to·bac·co tabaco *m*.

to·bac·co·nist t.'s (shop) estanco *m*.

to·bog·gan tobogán *m*.

to·day *adv* hoy.

tod·dler niño, -a *mf* pequeño, -a.

toe dedo *m* del pie.

toe·nail uña *f* del dedo del pie.

tof·fee caramelo *m*.

to·geth·er *adv* junto, -a, juntos, -as; **all t.** todos juntos; **t. with** junto con.

toi·let wáter *m*; *(public)* servicios *mpl*.

toi·let pa·per *or* **tissue** papel *m* higiénico.

toi·let·ries *npl* artículos *mpl* de aseo.

toi·let roll rollo *m* de papel higiénico.

toi·let wa·ter *(perfume)* agua *f* de colonia.

to·ken *(for telephone)* ficha *f*; **book t.** vale *m* para comprar libros.

told *pt & pp of* **tell**.

tol·er·ance tolerancia *f*.

tol·er·ant *adj* tolerante.

tol·er·ate *vt* tolerar.

toll *(for road)* peaje *m*.

toll-free num·ber teléfono *m* gratuito.

to·ma·to *(pl* **tomatoes***)* tomate *m*.

tomb tumba *f*.

to·mor·row *adv* mañana; **the day after t.** pasado mañana; **t. night** mañana por la noche.

ton tonelada *f*; *fam* **tons of** montones de.

tone tono *m*.

tongs *npl (for sugar, hair)* tenacillas *fpl*; **(fire) t.** tenazas *fpl*.

tongue lengua *f*.

ton·ic *(drink)* tónica *f*.

to·night *adv* esta noche.

tonne = **ton**.

ton·sil amígdala *f*.

ton·sil·li·tis amigdalitis *f*.

too *adv (also)* también; *(excessively)* demasiado; **t. much/many** demasiado, -a, demasiados, -as; **ten dollars t. much** diez dólares de más; **t. much money** demasiado dinero; **t. old** demasiado viejo.

took *pt of* **take**.

tool *(utensil)* herramienta *f*.

tooth *(pl* **teeth***)* diente *m*.

tooth·ache dolor *m* de muelas.

tooth·brush cepillo *m* de dientes.

tooth·paste pasta *f* dentífrica.

tooth·pick mondadientes *m inv*.

top¹ 1 *n (upper part)* parte *f* de arriba; *(of hill)* cumbre *f*; *(of tree)* copa *f*; *(surface)* superficie *f*; *(of list etc)* cabeza *f*; *(of bottle etc)* tapón *m*; *(best)* lo mejor; **on t. of** encima de. **2** *adj (part)* superior, de arriba; *(best)* mejor; **the t. floor** el último piso.

▶ **top up** *vt* llenar hasta el tope.

top² *(toy)* peonza *f*.

top·ic tema *m*.

torch *(burning)* antorcha *f*.

tor·ment *vt* atormentar.

tor·na·do tornado *m*.

tor·toise tortuga *f* de tierra.

tor·toise-shell 1 *adj* de carey. **2** *n* carey *m*.

tor·ture 1 *vt* torturar; *(cause anguish)* atormentar. **2** *n* tortura *f*; *(anguish)* tormento *m*.

toss 1 *vt (ball)* tirar; *(throw about)* sacudir; **to t. a coin** echar a caro o cruz. **2** *vi* **to t. about** agitarse; *(in sport)* **to t. (up)** sortear.

to·tal total *m*; *(in check)* importe *m*.

to·tal·ly *adv* totalmente.

touch 1 *vt* tocar; *(lightly)* rozar; *(emotionally)* conmover. **2** *vi* tocarse; *(lightly)* rozarse. **3** *n* toque *m*; *(light contact)* roce *m*; *(sense of touch)* tacto *m*; **in t. with sb** en contacto con algn.

▶ **touch down** *vi (plane)* aterrizar.

touch·down *(of plane)* aterrizaje *m*; *(in football)* ensayo *m*.

touch·y *adj (person)* susceptible.

tough *adj (material, competitor etc)* fuerte; *(test, criminal, meat)* duro, -a; *(punishment)* severo, -a; *(problem)* difícil.

tour 1 *n (journey)* viaje *m*; *(of palace etc)* visita *f*; *(of city)* recorrido *m* turístico; *(of theatrical company, team)* gira *f*; **on t.** de gira. **2** *vt (country)* viajar por; *(building)* visitar. **3** *vi* estar de viaje.

tour·ism turismo *m*.

tour·ist turista *mf*; **t. class** clase *f* turista.

tour·ist of·fice oficina *f* de información turística.

tour·na·ment torneo *m*.

tow *vt* remolcar.

to·wards *prep* hacia; **our duty t. others** nuestro deber para con los demás.

tow·el toalla *f*.

tow·er torre *f*.

tow·er block torre *f*.

town ciudad *f*; *(small)* pueblo *m*; **to go into t.** ir al centro.

town coun·cil ayuntamiento *m*.

town hall ayuntamiento *m*.

town·house casa *f* de la ciudad.

town·ship municipio *m*.

tow truck grúa *f*.

tox·ic *adj* tóxico, -a.

toy juguete *m*.

toy·shop juguetería *f*.

trace 1 *n (sign)* indicio *m*, vestigio *m*. **2** *vt (drawing)* calcar; *(locate)* seguir la pista de.

trac·ing pa·per papel *m* de calco.

track *(mark)* huellas *fpl*; *(pathway)* camino *m*; *(for running)* pista *f*; *(of railroad)* vía *f*; *(on record)* canción *f*; **to be on the right t.** ir por buen camino; **to be on the wrong t.** haberse equivocado.

track·suit chandal *m*.

trac·tor tractor *m*.

trade 1 *n (job)* oficio *m*; *(sector)* industria *f*; *(commerce)* comercio *m*. **2** *vi* comerciar (**in** en). **3** *vt* **to t. sth for sth** trocar algo por algo.

trade·mark marca *f* (de fábrica); **registered t.** marca registrada.

trad·er comerciante *mf*.

trade un·ion sindicato *m*.

trad·ing comercio *m*.

tra·di·tion tradición *f*.

tra·di·tion·al *adj* tradicional.

traf·fic *n* tráfico *m*.

traf·fic jam atasco *m*.

traf·fic lights *npl* semáforo *m sing*.

traf·fic sign señal *f* de tráfico.

trag·e·dy tragedia *f*.

trag·ic *adj* trágico, -a.

trail 1 *vt* **to t. sth (along)** *(drag)* arrastrar algo. **2** *vi (drag)* arrastrarse; **to t. (along)** *(linger)* rezagarse. **3** *n* senda *f*; *(bigger)* pista *f*; *(of smoke)* estela *f*.

trail·er *(behind vehicle)* remolque *m*; *(caravan)* caravana *f*.

train¹ *n* tren *m*; **to go by t.** ir en tren.

train² **1** *vt (in sport)* entrenar; *(animal)* amaestrar; *(teach)* formar. **2** *vi* entrenarse; *(be taught)* prepararse.

trained *adj (skilled)* cualificado, -a.

train·ee aprendiz, -a *mf.*

train·er *(in sport)* entrenador, -a *mf; (of dogs)* amaestrador, -a *mf; (of lions)* domador, -a *mf.*

train·ing entrenamiento *m; (instruction)* formación *f.*

trai·tor traidor, -a *mf.*

tram tranvía *m.*

tramp *(person)* vagabundo, -a *mf.*

tran·quil·iz·er tranquilizante *m.*

trans·fer **1** *vt* trasladar; *(funds)* transferir; **a transferred charge call** una conferencia a cobro revertido. **2** *n* traslado *m; (of funds)* transferencia *f; (picture, design)* calcomanía *f.*

trans·fu·sion transfusión *f* (de sangre).

tran·sis·tor transistor *m.*

tran·sit in t. de tránsito.

tran·si·tive *adj* transitivo, -a.

trans·late *vt* traducir.

trans·la·tion traducción *f.*

trans·la·tor traductor, -a *mf.*

trans·mis·sion transmisión *f.*

trans·mit *vt* transmitir.

trans·par·ent *adj* transparente.

trans·plant trasplante *m.*

trans·port **1** *vt* transportar. **2** *n* transporte *m.*

trap **1** *n* trampa *f.* **2** *vt (animal, fugitive)* atrapar; **to t. sb into doing sth** lograr con ardides que algn haga algo.

trap door trampilla *f.*

trash *(inferior goods)* bazofia *f; (household waste)* basura *f, fam (worthless thing)* birria *f, fam (nonsense)* tonterías *fpl.*

trash can cubo *m* de la basura.

trash dump vertedero *m.*

trash·y *adj fam (book, film)* sin valor.

trav·el **1** *vi* viajar; *(vehicle, electric current)* ir; **to t. through** recorrer. **2** *vt* recorrer. **3** *n* viajes *mpl;* **t. agency** agencia *f* de viajes; **t. sickness** mareo *m.*

trav·el·er viajero, -a *mf;* **t.'s check** cheque *m* de viaje.

trav·el·ing **1** *adj (salesman)* ambulante. **2** *n* los viajes *mpl;* **I'm fond of t.** me gusta viajar.

tray *(for food)* bandeja *f.*

treach·er·ous *adj (dangerous)* peligroso, -a.

tread* *vi* pisar.

▶ **tread on** *vt* pisar.

treas·ure tesoro *m.*

treas·ur·er tesorero, -a *mf.*

treat **1** *n (present)* regalo *m.* **2** *vt* tratar; *(regard)* considerar; **he treated them to dinner** les invitó a cenar.

treat·ment *(of person)* trato *m; (of subject, patient)* tratamiento *m.*

treb·le **1** *vt* triplicar. **2** *vi* triplicarse.

tree árbol *m.*

trem·ble *vi* temblar.

tre·men·dous *adj (huge)* enorme; *(success)* arrollador, -a; *(shock etc)* tremendo, -a; *fam (marvellous)* estupendo, -a.

trench *(ditch)* zanja *f, (for troops)* trinchera *f.*

trend·y *adj (* **trendier, trendiest** *) fam (person)* moderno, -a; *(clothes)* a la última.

tri·al *(in court)* juicio *m.*

tri·an·gle triángulo *m.*

tri·an·gu·lar *adj* triangular.

tribe tribu *f.*

trib·ute *(mark of respect)* homenaje *m;* **to pay t. to** rendir homenaje a.

trick **1** *n (ruse)* ardid *m; (dishonest)* engaño *m; (practical joke)* broma *f, (of magic, knack)* truco *m;* **to play a t. on sb** gastarle una broma a algn. **2** *vt* engañar.

trick·le **1** *vi (water)* gotear. **2** *n* hilo *m.*

trick·y *adj (situation)* delicado, -a; *(problem)* difícil.

tri·cy·cle triciclo *m.*

trig·ger *(of gun)* gatillo *m.*

trim *vt (cut)* recortar; *(expenses)* disminuir.

trip **1** *n (journey)* viaje *m; (excursion)* excursión *f.* **2** *vi* **to t. (up)** *(stumble)* tropezar **(over** con).

tri·ple **1** *vt* triplicar. **2** *vi* triplicarse.

tri·umph **1** *n* triunfo *m.* **2** *vi* triunfar.

triv·i·al *adj* trivial.

trol·ley carro *m.*

trom·bone trombón *m.*

troop·er *(soldier)* soldado *m* de caballería; *(policeman)* policía *mf.*

troops tropas *fpl.*

tro·phy trofeo *m.*

trop·i·cal *adj* tropical.

trot **1** *vi* trotar. **2** *n* trote *m.*

trou·ble **1** *n (misfortune)* desgracia *f, (problems)* problemas *mpl; (effort)* esfuerzo *m;* **to be in t.** estar en un apuro; **it's not worth the t.** no merece la pena; **to take the t. to do sth** molestarse en hacer algo; **to have liver t.** tener problemas de hígado. **2** *vt (distress)* afligir; *(worry)* preocupar; *(bother)* molestar.

trou·sers *npl* pantalón *m sing.*

trout trucha *f.*

tru·ant **to play t.** hacer novillos.

truck camión *m.*

true *adj* verdadero, -a; *(faithful)* fiel; **to come t.** cumplirse; **it's not t.** no es verdad; **it's t. that ...** es verdad que ....

trump *(in card game)* triunfo *m.*

trum·pet trompeta *f.*

trunk *(of tree, body)* tronco *m; (of elephant)* trompa *f, (case)* baúl *m; (of car)* maletero *m.*

trunks *npl (swimming)* **t.** bañador *m sing.*

trust **1** *n* confianza *f.* **2** *vt (rely upon)* fiarse de; **to t. sb with sth** confiar algo a algn.

truth verdad *f.*

try **1** *vt (attempt)* intentar; *(test)* probar. **2** *vi* intentar; **to t. to do sth** tratar de *or* intentar hacer algo. **3** *n (attempt)* tentativa *f, (in rugby)* ensayo *m.*

▶ **try on** *vt (dress)* probarse.

try out *vt* probar.

try·ing *adj (person)* molesto, -a, pesado, -a.

T-shirt camiseta *f.*

tub *(container)* tina *f, (bath)* bañera *f.*

tube tubo *m; (in body)* conducto *m.*

tuck *vt* **to t. in the bedclothes** remeter la ropa de la cama; **to t. sb in** arropar a algn; **to t. one's shirt into one's trousers** meterse la camisa por dentro (de los pantalones).

Tues·day martes *m.*

tuft *(of hair)* mechón *m; (of wool etc)* copo *m.*

tug **1** *vt (pull at)* tirar de; *(haul along)* arrastrar; *(boat)* remolcar. **2** *n (boat)* remolcador *m.*

tug·boat remolcador *m.*

tu·i·tion instrucción *f;* **private t.** clases *fpl* particulares; **t. fees** tasas *fpl.*

tu·lip tulipán *m.*

tum·ble **1** *vi (person)* caerse. **2** *n* caída *f.*

tum·ble dry·er secadora *f.*

tum·bler *(glass)* vaso *m.*

tum·my *fam* estómago *m; (belly)* barriga *f.*

tu·mor tumor *m.*

tu·na atún *m.*

tune **1** *n (melody)* melodía *f; in/out of* **t.** afinado/desafinado; **to sing out of t.** desafinar. **2** *vt (instrument)* afinar; *(engine)* poner a punto.

▶ **tune in to** *vt (on radio etc)* sintonizar.

tun·ing *(of instrument)* afinación *f.*

Tu·ni·sian *adj & n* tunecino, -a *(mf).*

tun·nel túnel *m.*

tur·ban turbante *m.*

tur·key pavo *m.*

Turk turco, -a *mf.*

Turk·ish **1** *adj* turco, -a. **2** *n (language)* turco *m.*

turn **1** *vt (revolve)* girar; *(page, head, gaze)* volver; *(change)* transformar **(into** en); **he's turned forty** ha cumplido los cuarenta. **2** *vi (revolve)* girar; *(change direction)* torcer; *(turn round)* volverse; *(become)* volverse; **to t. to sb** *(for help)* acudir a algn. **3** *n (of wheel)* vuelta *f, (in road)* curva *f, (in game, line)* turno *m; it's your* **t.** te toca a ti; **to take turns (at doing sth)** turnarse (para hacer algo).

▶ **turn around** *vi (of person)* volverse.

▶ **turn away** **1** *vt (person)* rechazar. **2** *vi* volver la cabeza; *(move away)* alejarse.

▶ **turn back** **1** *vt (person)* hacer retroceder. **2** *vi* volverse.

▶ **turn down** *vt (gas, radio etc)* bajar; *(reject)* rechazar.

▶ **turn into** **1** *vt* convertir en. **2** *vi* convertirse en.

▶ **turn off** *vt (light, TV, radio, engine)* apagar; *(water, gas)* cortar; *(faucet)* cerrar.

▶ **turn on** *vt (light, TV, radio, engine)* encender; *(water, gas)* abrir la llave de; *(faucet)* abrir.

▶ **turn out** **1** *vt (extinguish)* apagar. **2** *vi* **it turns out that ...** resulta que ...; **things have turned out well** las cosas han salido bien.

▶ **turn over** **1** *vt (turn upside down)* poner al revés; *(page)* dar la vuelta a. **2** *vi* volverse.

▶ **turn round** **1** *vt* volver. **2** *vi (rotate)* girar.

▶ **turn up** **1** *vt (collar)* levantar; *(TV, volume)* subir; *(light)* aumentar la intensidad de. **2** *vi (arrive)* presentarse.

turn·ing *(in road)* salida *f.*

tur·nip nabo *m.*

turn·pike autopista *f* de peaje.

turn·up *(of trousers)* vuelta *f.*

tur·tle tortuga *f.*

tur·tle·neck a **t. sweater** un jersey de cuello alto.

tusk colmillo *m.*

tu·tor *(at university)* tutor, -a *mf;* **private t.** profesor, -a *mf* particular.

TV TV.

tweez·ers *npl* pinzas *fpl.*

twelfth *adj & n* duodécimo, -a *(mf).*

twelve *adj & n* doce *(m) inv;* **t. o'clock** las doce.

twen·ti·eth *adj & n* vigésimo, -a *(mf).*

twen·ty *adj & n* veinte *(m) inv.*

twice *adv* dos veces; **he's t. as old as I am** tiene el doble de años que yo; **t. as big** el doble de grande.

twig ramita *f.*

twi·light crepúsculo *m.*

twin *n* mellizo, -a *mf;* **identical twins** gemelos *mpl* (idénticos); **t. beds** camas *fpl* gemelas.

twine bramante *m.*

twirl **1** *vt* girar rápidamente. **2** *vi (spin)* girar rápidamente; *(dancer)* piruetear.

twist **1** *vt* torcer; **to t. one's ankle** torcerse el tobillo. **2** *n (movement)* torsión *f, (in road)* vuelta *f.*

▶ **twist off** *(lid)* desenroscar.

two *adj & n* dos *(m) inv.*

two-way *adj (street)* de dos direcciones.

type **1** *n (kind)* tipo *m; (print)* caracteres *mpl.* **2** *vti* escribir a máquina.

type·writ·er máquina *f* de escribir.

type·writ·ten *adj* escrito, -a a máquina.

typ·i·cal *adj* típico, -a.

typ·ing mecanografía *f.*

typ·ist mecanógrafo, -a *mf.*

U

UFO *abbr of* **unidentified flying object** OVNI *m.*

ug·li·ness fealdad *f.*

ug·ly *adj* feo, -a; *(situation)* desagradable.

ul·cer *(sore)* llaga *f, (internal)* úlcera *f.*

ul·ti·mate *adj (final)* último, -a; *(aim)* final; *(basic)* esencial.

um·brel·la paraguas *m inv.*

um·pire árbitro *m.*

ump·teen *adj fam* muchísimos, -as, la tira de.

un·a·ble *adj* **to be u. to do sth** no poder hacer algo.

un·ac·cept·a·ble *adj* inaceptable.

un·ac·cus·tomed *adj* **he's u. to this climate** no está acostumbrado a este clima.

u·nan·i·mous *adj* unánime.

u·nan·i·mous·ly *adv* unánimemente.

un·at·trac·tive *adj (idea, appearance)* poco atractivo, -a.

un·a·vail·a·ble *adj* no disponible; **Mr Smith is u. today** Mr Smith no le puede atender hoy.

un·a·void·a·ble *adj* inevitable; *(accident)* imprevisible.

un·a·void·a·bly *adv* inevitablemente.

un·a·ware **1** *adj* **to be u. of sth** ignorar algo. **2** *adv (without knowing)* inconscientemente; **it caught me u.** me cogió desprevenido.

un·bear·a·ble *adj* insoportable.

un·be·liev·a·ble *adj* increíble.

un·break·a·ble *adj* irrompible.

un·but·ton *vt* desabrochar.

un·cer·tain *adj (not certain)* incierto, -a; *(doubtful)* dudoso, -a; *(hesitant)* indeciso, -a.

un·cer·tain·ty incertidumbre *f.*

un·changed *adj* igual.

un·cle tío *m.*

un·clear *adj* poco claro, -a.
un·com·fort·a·ble *adj* incómodo, -a.
un·com·mon *adj (rare)* poco común.
un·con·nect·ed *adj* no relacionado, -a.
un·con·scious *adj* inconsciente (**of** de).
un·con·sti·tu·tion·al *adj* inconstitucional, anticonstitucional.
un·con·vinc·ing *adj* poco convincente.
un·co·op·er·a·tive *adj* poco cooperativo, -a.
un·cork *vt (bottle)* descorchar.
un·cov·er *vt* destapar; *(discover)* descubrir.
un·dam·aged *adj (article etc)* sin desperfectos.
un·de·cid·ed *adj (person)* indeciso, -a.
un·de·ni·a·ble *adj* innegable.
un·der 1 *prep* debajo de; *(less than)* menos de; **u. the circumstances** dadas las circunstancias; **u. there** allí debajo. **2** *adv* debajo.
un·der- *prefix (below)* sub-, infra-; *(insufficiently)* insuficientemente.
un·der·charge *vt* cobrar menos de lo debido.
un·der·clothes *npl* ropa *f sing* interior.
un·der·done *adj* poco hecho, -a.
un·der·es·ti·mate *vt* subestimar.
un·der·go* *vt* experimentar; *(change)* sufrir; *(test etc)* pasar por.
un·der·grad·u·ate estudiante *mf* universitario, -a.
un·der·ground *adj* subterráneo, -a.
un·der·line *vt* subrayar.
un·der·mine *vt* socavar, minar.
un·der·neath 1 *prep* debajo de. **2** *adv* debajo. **3** *n* parte *f* inferior.
un·der·pants *npl* calzoncillos *mpl*.
un·der·pass paso *n* subterráneo.
un·der·shirt camiseta *f*.
un·der·stand* *vti* entender.
un·der·stand·a·ble *adj* comprensible.
un·der·stand·ing 1 *n (intellectual grasp)* comprensión *f*; *(agreement)* acuerdo *m*. **2** *adj* comprensivo, -a.
un·der·stood 1 *pt & pp of* **understand**. **2** *adj (agreed on)* convenido, -a.
un·der·take* *vt (responsibility)* asumir; *(task, job)* encargarse de; *(promise)* comprometerse a.
un·der·tak·er empresario, -a *mf* de pompas fúnebres; **undertaker's** funeraria *f*.
un·der·tak·ing *(task)* empresa *f*.
un·der·wa·ter 1 *adj* submarino, -a. **2** *adv* bajo el agua.
un·der·wear *inv* ropa *f* interior.
un·do* *vt* deshacer; *(button)* desabrochar.
un·done *adj (knot etc)* deshecho, -a; **to come u.** *(shoelace)* desatarse; *(button, blouse)* desabrocharse; *(necklace etc)* soltarse.
un·doubt·ed·ly *adv* indudablemente.
un·dress 1 *vt* desnudar. **2** *vi* desnudarse.
un·eas·y *adj (worried)* preocupado, -a; *(disturbing)* inquietante; *(uncomfortable)* incómodo, -a.
un·em·ployed 1 *adj* **to be u.** estar en paro. **2** *npl* **the u.** los parados.
un·em·ploy·ment paro *m*.
un·e·ven *adj (not level)* desigual; *(bumpy)* accidentado, -a; *(variable)* irregular.
un·e·vent·ful *adj* sin acontecimientos.
un·ex·pect·ed *adj (unhoped for)* inesperado, -a; *(event)* imprevisto, -a.
un·ex·pect·ed·ly *adv* inesperadamente.
un·fair *adj* injusto, -a.
un·fair·ly *adv* injustamente.
un·fair·ness injusticia *f*.
un·faith·ful *adj (friend)* desleal; *(husband, wife)* infiel.
un·fa·mil·iar *adj (unknown)* desconocido, -a; **to be u. with sth** no conocer bien algo.
un·fash·ion·a·ble *adj* pasado, -a de moda; *(ideas etc)* poco popular.
un·fas·ten *vt (knot)* desatar; *(clothing, belt)* desabrochar.
un·fa·vor·a·ble desfavorable.
un·fin·ished *adj* inacabado, -a.
un·fit *adj (food, building)* inadecuado, -a; *(person)* no apto, -a (**for** para); *(incompetent)* incompetente; *(physically)* incapacitado, -a; **to be u.** no estar en forma.
un·fold *vt (sheet)* desdoblar; *(newspaper)* abrir.
un·for·get·ta·ble *adj* inolvidable.
un·for·giv·a·ble *adj* imperdonable.
un·for·tu·nate *adj (person, event)* desgraciado, -a; **how u.!** ¡qué mala suerte!
un·for·tu·nate·ly *adv* desgraciadamente.
un·friend·ly *adj* antipático, -a.
un·fur·nished *adj* sin amueblar.
un·grate·ful *adj (unthankful)* desagradecido, -a.
un·hap·pi·ness tristeza *f*.
un·hap·py *adj* triste.
un·harmed *adj* ileso, -a, indemne.
un·health·y *adj (ill)* enfermizo, -a; *(unwholesome)* malsano, -a.
un·help·ful *adj (advice)* inútil; *(person)* poco servicial.
un·hook *vt (from hook)* descolgar; *(clothing)* desabrochar.
un·hurt *adj* ileso, -a.
un·hy·gi·en·ic *adj* antihigiénico, -a.
u·ni·form *adj & n* uniforme *(m)*.
un·im·por·tant *adj* poco importante.
un·in·hab·it·ed *adj* despoblado, -a.
un·in·jured *adj* ileso, -a.
un·in·ten·tion·al *adj* involunta-rio, -a.
un·in·ter·est·ing *adj* poco interesante.
un·ion 1 *n* unión *f*, *(organization)* sindicato *m*. **2** *adj* sindical.
u·nique *adj* único, -a.
u·nit unidad *f*, *(piece of furniture)* módulo *m*; *(team)* equipo *m*; **kitchen u.** mueble *m* de cocina.
u·nite 1 *vt* unir. **2** *vi* unirse.
u·ni·ver·sal *adj* universal.
u·ni·verse universo *m*.
u·ni·ver·si·ty 1 *n* universidad *f*. **2** *adj* universitario, -a.
un·just *adj* injusto, -a.
un·kind *adj (not nice)* poco amable; *(cruel)* despiadado, -a.
un·know·ing·ly inconscientemente, inadvertidamente.
un·known *adj* desconocido, -a.
un·lead·ed *adj (gasoline)* sin plomo.
un·less *conj* a menos que (+ *subjunctive*), a no ser que (+ *subjunctive*).
un·like *prep* a diferencia de.
un·like·ly *adj (improbable)* poco probable.
un·lim·it·ed *adj* ilimitado, -a.
un·load *vti* descargar.
un·lock *vt* abrir (con llave).
un·luck·y *adj (unfortunate)* desgraciado, -a; **to be u.** *(person)* tener mala suerte; *(thing)* traer mala suerte.
un·made *adj (bed)* deshecho, -a.
un·mar·ried *adj* soltero, -a.
un·nec·es·sar·y *adj* innecesario, -a.
un·no·ticed *adj* desapercibido, -a; **to let sth pass u.** pasar algo por alto.
un·oc·cu·pied *adj (house)* desocupado, -a; *(seat)* libre.
un·pack 1 *vt (boxes)* desembalar; *(suitcase)* deshacer. **2** *vi* deshacer la(s) maleta(s).
un·paid *adj (bill, debt)* impagado, -a; *(work)* no retribuido, -a.
un·pleas·ant *adj (not nice)* desagradable; *(unfriendly)* antipático, -a (**to** con).
un·plug *vt* desenchufar.
un·pop·u·lar *adj* impopular; **to make oneself u.** ganarse la antipatía de algn.
un·pre·dict·a·ble *adj* imprevisible.
un·pre·pared *adj (speech etc)* improvisado, -a; *(person)* desprevenido, -a.
un·rea·son·a·ble *adj* poco razonable; *(demands)* desmedido, -a.
un·rec·og·niz·a·ble *adj* irreconocible.
un·re·lat·ed *adj (not connected)* no relacionado, -a.
un·re·li·a·ble *adj (person)* de poca confianza; *(information)* que no es de fiar; *(machine)* poco fiable.
un·rest *(social etc)* malestar *m*.
un·roll *vt* desenrollar.
un·safe *adj (activity, journey)* peligroso, -a; *(building, car, machine)* inseguro, -a; **to feel u.** sentirse expuesto, -a.
un·sat·is·fac·to·ry *adj* insatisfactorio, -a.
un·screw *vt* destornillar.
un·skilled *adj (worker)* no cualificado, -a.
un·sta·ble *adj* inestable.
un·stead·i·ly *adv (to walk)* con paso inseguro.
un·stead·y *adj (not firm)* inestable; *(table, chair)* cojo, -a; *(hand, voice)* tembloroso, -a.
un·suc·cess·ful *adj (person, negotiation)* fracasado, -a; *(attempt, effort)* vano, -a; *(candidate)* derrotado, -a; **to be u. at sth** no tener éxito con algo.
un·suc·cess·ful·ly *adv* sin éxito.
un·suit·a·ble *adj (person)* no apto, -a; *(thing)* inadecuado, -a.
un·suit·ed *adj (person)* no apto, -a; *(thing)* impropio, -a (**to** para).
un·sure *adj* poco seguro, -a; **to be u. of sth** no estar seguro, -a de algo.
un·tan·gle *vt* desenmarañar.
un·ti·dy *adj (room, person)* desordenado, -a; *(hair)* despeinado, -a; *(appearance)* desaseado, -a.
un·tie *vt* desatar.
un·til 1 *conj* hasta que; **u. she gets back** hasta que vuelva. **2** *prep* hasta; **u. now** hasta ahora; **not u. Monday** hasta el lunes no.
un·true *adj (false)* falso, -a.
un·used *adj (car)* sin usar; *(stamp)* sin matar.
un·u·su·al *adj (rare)* poco común; *(exceptional)* excepcional.
un·u·su·al·ly *adv* excepcionalmente.
un·veil *vt* descubrir.
un·want·ed *adj* no deseado, -a.
un·well *adj* **to be u.** estar malo, -a.
un·will·ing *adj* **to be u. to do sth** no estar dispuesto, -a a hacer algo.
un·will·ing·ly *adv* de mala gana.
un·wor·thy *adj* indigno, -a.
un·wrap *vt (gift)* desenvolver; *(package)* deshacer.
un·zip *vt* bajar la cremallera de.
up 1 *prep (movement)* **to climb up the mountain** escalar la montaña; **to walk up the street** ir calle arriba. ▪ *(position)* en lo alto de; **further up the street** más adelante (en la misma calle). **2** *adv (upwards)* arriba; **further up** hacia arriba; **from ten dollars up** de diez dólares para arriba; **right up (to the top)** hasta arriba (del todo); **to go** *or* **come up** subir; **to walk up and down** ir de un lado a otro. ▪ *(towards)* hacia; **to come** *or* **go up to sb** acercarse a algn. ▪ *(increased)* **bread is up** el pan ha subido. ▪ *(wrong)* **what's up (with you)?** ¿qué pasa (contigo)?; **something must be up** debe pasar algo. ▪ **up to** *(as far as, until)* hasta; **I can spend up to five dollars** puedo gastar un máximo de cinco dólares; **up to here** hasta aquí; **up to now** hasta ahora. ▪ **to be up to** *(depend on)* depender de; *(be capable of)* estar a la altura de; **he's up to something** está tramando algo. **3** *adj (out of bed)* levantado, -a; *(finished)* terminado, -a; **time's up** (ya) es la hora. **4** *vt (increase)* aumentar. **5** *n* **ups and downs** altibajos *mpl*.
up·date *vt* actualizar, poner al día.
up·grade 1 *vt (promote)* ascender; *(improve)* mejorar la calidad de; *(software, hardware)* actualizar. **2** *n (of software, hardware)* actualización *f*.
up·hill *adv* cuesta arriba.
up·hold* *vt* sostener.
up·on *prep* sobre.
up·per *adj* superior.
up·right 1 *adj (vertical)* vertical; *(honest)* honrado, -a. **2** *adv* derecho.
up·roar tumulto *m*.
up·scale *adj (newspaper, program)* dirigido, -a a un público selecto.
up·set 1 *vt* (shock)* trastornar; *(worry)* preocupar; *(displease)* disgustar; *(spoil)* desbaratar; *(make ill)* sentar mal a. **2** *adj (shocked)* alterado, -a; *(displeased)* disgustado, -a; **to have an u. stomach** sentirse mal del estómago.
up·side-down al revés.
up·stairs 1 *adv* arriba. **2** *n* piso *m* de arriba.
up-to-date *adj (current)* al día; *(modern)* moderno, -a; **to be u. with sth** estar al tanto de algo.
up·town zona *f* residencial.
up·ward(s) *adv* hacia arriba; **from ten (years) u.** a partir de los diez años; *fam* **u. of** algo más de.
urge *vt (incite)* incitar; *(press)* instar; *(plead)* exhortar; *(advocate)* preconizar; **to u. that sth should be done** insistir en que se haga algo.
ur·gen·cy urgencia *f*.
ur·gent *adj* urgente; *(need, tone)* apremiante.
ur·gent·ly *adv* urgentemente.
u·rine orina *f*.
U·ru·guay·an *adj & n* uruguayo, -a *(mf)*.
us *pers pron (as object)* nos; *(after prep, 'to be')* nosotros, -as; **she wouldn't believe it was us** no creía que fuéramos nosotros; **let's forget it** olvidémoslo.
us·age *(habit, custom)* costumbre *f*, *(linguistic)* uso *m*.
use 1 *vt* utilizar; *(consume)* consumir; **what is it used for?** ¿para qué sirve? **2** *n* uso *m*; **'not in u.'** 'no funciona'; **to be of u.** servir; **to make (good) u. of sth** aprovechar algo; **it's no u.** es inútil; **it's no u. crying** no sirve de nada llorar.
▸**use up** *vt* acabar; *(food)* consumir; *(gas)* agotar; *(money)* gastar.
used¹ *adj (second-hand)* usado, -a.
used² 1 *v aux* **where did you u. to live?** ¿dónde vivías (antes)?; **I u. to play the piano** solía tocar el piano; **I u. not to like it** antes no me gustaba. **2** *adj* **to be u. to sth** estar acostumbrado, -a a algo.
use·ful *adj* útil; *(practical)* práctico, -a; **to come in u.** venir bien.
use·ful·ness utilidad *f*.

use·less *adj* inútil.
us·er usuario, -a *mf.*
us·er-friend·ly *adj* de fácil manejo.
u·su·al *adj* corriente; **as u.** como siempre.
u·su·al·ly *adv* normalmente.
u·ten·sil utensilio *m*; **kitchen utensils** batería *f sing* de cocina.
u·til·i·ty (public) u. empresa *f* de servicio público.
ut·ter¹ *vt (words)* pronunciar; *(cry, threat)* lanzar.
ut·ter² *adj* total.
ut·ter·ly *adv* completamente.
U-turn cambio *m* de sentido.

V

va·can·cy *(job)* vacante *f*; *(room)* habitación *f* libre.
va·cant *adj (empty)* vacío, -a; *(room, seat)* libre.
va·ca·tion vacaciones *fpl*; **on v.** de vacaciones.
va·ca·tion·er summer v. veraneante *mf.*
vac·ci·nate *vt* vacunar.
vac·ci·na·tion vacuna *f.*
vac·cine vacuna *f.*
vac·uum 1 *vt* limpiar con aspiradora. **2** *n* vacío *m.*
vacuum clean·er aspiradora *f.*
vague *adj (imprecise)* vago, -a; *(indistinct)* borroso, -a.
vague·ly *adv* vagamente.
vain *adj* **in v.** en vano.
val·id *adj* válido, -a.
val·ley valle *m.*
val·u·a·ble 1 *adj* valioso, -a. **2** *npl* **valuables** objetos *mpl* de valor.
val·ue valor *m*; **to get good v. for money** sacarle jugo al dinero.
valve *(of machine, heart)* válvula *f.*
van furgoneta *f.*
van·dal gamberro, -a *mf.*
van·dal·ize *vt* destrozar.
va·nil·la vainilla *f.*
van·ish *vi* desaparecer.
var·i·a·ble *adj & n* variable *(f).*
var·i·ant variante *f.*
var·ied *adj* variado, -a.
va·ri·e·ty *(diversity)* variedad *f*; *(assortment)* surtido *m*; **for a v. of reasons** por razones diversas.
va·ri·e·ty show espectáculo *m* de variedades.
var·i·ous *adj* diversos, -as.
var·nish 1 *n* barniz *m.* **2** *vt* barnizar.
var·y *vti* variar.
vase florero *m.*
Vas·e·line® vaselina *f.*
vast *adj* vasto, -a.
VAT *abbr of* **value added tax** IVA *m.*
VCR *abbr of* **video cassette recorder** (grabador *m* de) vídeo *m.*
veal ternera *f.*
veg·e·ta·ble verdura *f.*
veg·e·tar·i·an *adj & n* vegetariano, -a *(mf).*
veg·e·ta·tion vegetación *f.*
ve·hi·cle vehículo *m.*
veil velo *m.*
vein vena *f.*
vel·vet terciopelo *m.*
vend·ing ma·chine máquina *f* expendedora.
ven·dor vendedor, -a *mf.*
Ve·ne·tian blind persiana *f* graduable.
Ven·e·zue·lan *adj & n* venezolano, -a *(mf).*
ven·ti·la·tion ventilación *f.*
ven·ture 1 *vt* arriesgar, aventurar; **he didn't v. to ask** no se atrevió a preguntarlo. **2** *vi* arriesgarse; **to v. out of doors** atreverse a salir. **3** *n* empresa *f* arriesgada, aventura *f.*
ven·ue *(meeting place)* lugar *m* de reunión; *(for concert etc)* local *m.*
verb verbo *m.*
ver·bal *adj* verbal.
ver·dict veredicto *m*; *(opinion)* opinión *f.*
verge *(of road)* arcén *m.*
verse *(stanza)* estrofa *f*; *(poetry)* versos *mpl*; *(of song)* copla *f.*
ver·sion versión *f.*
ver·sus *prep* contra.
ver·ti·cal *adj* vertical.
ver·y *adv* muy; **v. much** muchísimo; **at the v. latest** como máximo; **the v. first/last** el primero/último de todos; **at this v. moment** en este mismo momento.
vest *(undershirt)* camiseta *f*, chaleco *m.*
vet veterinario, -a *mf.*
vet·er·an veterano, -a *mf*, **(war) v.** ex combatiente *mf.*
vi·a *prep* por.
vi·brate *vi* vibrar *(with* de*).*
vi·bra·tion vibración *f.*
vic·ar párroco *m.*
vice¹ vicio *m.*
vice² *(tool)* torno *m* de banco.
vi·cious *adj (violent)* violento, -a; *(malicious)* malintencionado, -a; *(cruel)* cruel.
vic·tim víctima *f.*
vic·to·ry victoria *f.*
vid·e·o vídeo *m*; **v. (cassette)** videocasete *m*; **v. (cassette recorder)** vídeo *m.*
vid·e·o cam·er·a videocámara *f.*
vid·e·o game videojuego *m.*
vid·e·o·tape cinta *f* de vídeo.
view *(sight)* vista *f*, *(opinion)* opinión *f*; **to come into v.** aparecer; **in v. of the fact that …** dado que ….
view·er *(of TV)* televidente *mf.*
view·find·er visor *m.*
view·point punto *m* de vista.
vil·la *(country house)* casa *f* de campo.

vil·lage *(small)* aldea *f*, *(larger)* pueblo *m.*
vil·lag·er aldeano, -a *mf.*
vil·lain villano, -a *mf*, *(in movie, play)* malo, -a *mf.*
vin·e·gar vinagre *m.*
vine·yard viñedo *m.*
vi·o·lence violencia *f.*
vi·o·lent *adj* violento, -a.
vi·o·lent·ly *adv* violentamente.
vi·o·lin violín *m.*
VIP *abbr of* **very important person** *fam* vip *mf.*
vir·gin *n* virgen *f.*
vir·tu·al *adj* virtual; **v. reality** realidad *f* virtual.
vir·tu·al·ly *adv (almost)* prácticamente.
vir·tue virtud *f*, **by v. of** en virtud de.
vi·rus virus *m inv.*
vi·sa visado *m*, *Am* visa *f.*
vis·i·ble *adj* visible.
vis·it 1 *vt* visitar. **2** *n* visita *f*, **to pay sb a v.** hacerle una visita a algn.
vis·it·ing hours *npl* horas *fpl* de visita.
vis·i·tor *(guest)* invitado, -a *mf*; *(tourist)* turista *mf.*
vi·tal *adj (essential)* fundamental.
vi·tal·ly *adv* **it's v. important** es de vital importancia.
vi·ta·min vitamina *f.*
viv·id *adj (color)* vivo, -a; *(description)* gráfico, -a.
vo·cab·u·lar·y vocabulario *m.*
vo·ca·tion·al *adj* profesional
vod·ka vodka *m or f.*
voice voz *f*, **at the top of one's v.** a voz en grito.
vol·ca·no *(pl* volcanoes*)* volcán *m.*
volt·age voltaje *m.*
vol·ume volumen *m.*
vol·un·tar·y *adj* voluntario, -a.
vol·un·teer 1 *n* voluntario, -a *mf.* **2** *vi* ofrecerse *(for* para*).*
vom·it *vti* vomitar.
vote 1 *n* voto *m*; *(voting)* votación *f.* **2** *vti* votar.
vot·er votante *mf.*
vouch·er vale *m.*
vow·el vocal *f.*
voy·age viaje *m*; *(crossing)* travesía *f.*
vul·gar *adj (coarse)* ordinario, -a; *(in poor taste)* de mal gusto.

W

wad *(of paper)* taco *m*; *(of cotton wool)* bolita *f*, *(of money)* fajo *m.*
wad·dle *vi* andar como los patos.
wade *vi* caminar por el agua.
wad·ing pool piscina *f* para niños.
wa·fer barquillo *m.*
wag 1 *vt* menear. **2** *vi (tail)* menearse.
wage earn·er asalariado, -a *mf.*
wages *npl* salario *m sing.*
wag·on camión *m*; *(of train)* vagón *m.*
waist cintura *f.*
wait 1 *n* espera *f*, *(delay)* demora *f.* **2** *vi* esperar; **to keep sb waiting** hacer esperar a algn.
▸ **wait behind** *vi* quedarse.
▸ **wait up** *vi* **to w. up for sb** esperar a algn levantado, -a.
wait·er camarero *m.*
wait·ing 'no w.' 'prohibido aparcar'.
wait·ing room sala *f* de espera.
wait·ress camarera *f.*
wait·staff camareros *mpl.*
wake* 1 *vt* **to w. sb (up)** despertar a algn. **2** *vi* **to w. (up)** despertar(se).
walk 1 *n (long)* caminata *m*; *(short)* paseo *m*; **it's an hour's w.** está a una hora de camino; **to go for a w.** dar un paseo. **2** *vt (dog)* pasear. **3** *vi* andar; *(to a specific place)* ir andando.
▸ **walk away** *vi* alejarse.
▸ **walk in** *vi* entrar.
▸ **walk off** *vi* marcharse; **to walk off with sth** *(steal, win easily)* llevarse algo.
▸ **walk out** *vi* salir.
walk·er paseante *mf*, *(in sport)* marchador, -a *mf.*
walk·ing *(hiking)* excursionismo *m.*
walk·ing stick bastón *m.*
Walk·man® *(pl* Walkmans*)* Walkman® *m.*
wall *(exterior)* muro *m*; *(interior)* pared *f.*
wal·let cartera *f.*
wall·pa·per 1 *n* papel *m* pintado. **2** *vt* empapelar.
wal·nut nuez *f.*
wal·rus morsa *f.*
wan·der 1 *vt* **to w. the streets** vagar por las calles. **2** *vi (aimlessly)* vagar; *(stray)* desviarse; *(mind)* divagar; **his glance wandered round the room** recorrió el cuarto con la mirada.
▸ **wander about** *vi* deambular.
want *vt* querer; *(desire)* desear; *(need)* necesitar; **to w. to do sth** querer hacer algo; **you're wanted on the phone** te llaman al teléfono.
war guerra *f*, **to be at w.** estar en guerra *(with* con*).*
ward *(of hospital)* sala *f.*
war·den *(of residence)* guardián, -ana *mf*; **game w.** guarda *m* de coto.
ward·robe armario *m* *(ropero).*
ware·house almacén *m.*
warm 1 *adj* caliente; *(water)* tibio, -a; **a w. day** un día de calor; **I am w.** tengo calor; **it is (very) w. today** hoy hace (mucho) calor. **2** *vt* calentar.
▸ **warm up 1** *vt* calentar; *(soup)* (re)calentar. **2** *vi* calentarse; *(food)* (re)calentarse; *(person)* entrar en calor.
warmth calor *m.*
warn *vt* advertir *(about* sobre; **against** contra*)*; **he warned me not to go** me advirtió que no fuera; **to w. sb that …** advertir a algn que …
warn·ing *(of danger)* advertencia *f*, *(notice)* aviso *m.*
warn·ing light piloto *m.*
war·rant 1 *n (legal order)* orden *f* judicial. **2** *vt (justify)* justificar; *(guarantee)* garantizar.
war·ran·ty *(for goods)* garantía *f.*

war·ri·or guerrero, -a *mf.*
war·ship buque *m* de guerra.
wart verruga *f.*
war·time tiempos *mpl* de guerra.
war·y *adj* (**warier, wariest**) cauteloso, -a; **to be w. of doing sth** dudar en hacer algo; **to be w. of sb/sth** recelar de algn/algo.
was *pt of* **be**.
wash 1 *n* **to have a w.** lavarse. **2** *vt* lavar; *(dishes)* fregar; **to w. one's hair** lavarse el pelo. **3** *vi (have a wash)* lavarse.
▸**wash away** *vt (of sea)* llevarse; *(traces)* borrar.
▸**wash off** *vi* quitarse lavando.
▸**wash out 1** *vt (stain)* quitar lavando. **2** *vi* quitarse lavando.
▸**wash up** *vi* lavarse rápidamente.
wash·a·ble *adj* lavable.
wash·ba·sin lavabo *m.*
wash·cloth manopla *f.*
wash·ing *(action)* lavado *m*; *(of clothes)* colada *f*; **(dirty) w.** ropa *f* sucia; **to do the w.** hacer la colada.
wash·ing ma·chine lavadora *f.*
wash·room servicios *mpl.*
wasp avispa *f.*
waste 1 *n (unnecessary use)* desperdicio *m*; *(of resources, effort, money)* derroche *m*; *(of time)* pérdida *f*; *(trash)* basura *f*; **radioactive w.** desechos *mpl* radiactivos. **2** *vt (squander)* desperdiciar; *(resources)* derrochar; *(time, chance)* perder.
waste·bin cubo *m* de la basura.
waste ground *(in town)* descampado *m.*
waste·pa·per papeles *mpl* usados.
waste·pa·per bas·ket papelera *f.*
watch 1 *n* reloj *m.* **2** *vt (observe)* observar; *(keep an eye on)* vigilar; *(be careful of)* tener cuidado con. **3** *vi (look)* mirar.
▸**watch out** *vi* **w. out!** ¡cuidado!
▸**watch out for** *vt* tener cuidado con; *(wait for)* esperar.
watch·strap correa *f* (de reloj).
wa·ter 1 *n* agua *f.* **2** *vt (plants)* regar.
▸**water down** *vt (drink)* aguar.
wa·ter·col·or acuarela *f.*
wa·ter·cress berro *m.*
wa·ter·fall cascada *f*; *(very big)* catarata *f.*
wa·ter·ing can regadera *f.*
wa·ter·mel·on sandía *f.*
wa·ter·proof *adj (material)* impermeable; *(watch)* sumergible.
wa·ter-ski·ing esquí *m* acuático.
wa·ter·tight *adj* hermético, -a.
wave 1 *n (at sea)* ola *f*; *(in hair, radio)* onda *f.* **2** *vt* agitar; *(brandish)* blandir. **3** *vi* agitar el brazo; **she waved (to me)** *(greeting)* me saludó con la mano; *(goodbye)* se despidió (de mí) con la mano.
wave·length longitud *f* de onda.
wav·y *adj* ondulado, -a.
wax 1 *n* cera *m.* **2** *vt* encerar.
way *n (route, road)* camino *m*; *(distance)* distancia *f*; *(means, manner)* manera *f*; **on the w.** en el camino; **on the w. here** de camino para aquí; **which is the w. to the station?** ¿por dónde se va a la estación?; **w. in** entrada *f*; **w. out** salida *f*; **on the w. back** en el viaje de regreso; **on the w. up/down** en la subida/bajada; **(get) out of the w.!** ¡quítate de en medio!; **you're in the w.** estás estorbando; **come this w.** venga por aquí; **which w. did he go?** ¿por dónde se fue?; **that w.** por allá; **a long w. off** lejos; **do it this w.** hazlo así; **which w. did you do it?** ¿cómo lo hiciste?; **no w.!** ¡ni hablar!
we *pers pron* nosotros, -as.
weak *adj* débil; *(team, piece of work, tea)* flojo, -a.
weak·en 1 *vt* debilitar; *(argument)* quitar fuerza a. **2** *vi* debilitarse; *(concede ground)* ceder.
weak·ness debilidad *f*; *(character flaw)* punto *m* flaco.
wealth riqueza *f.*
wealth·y *adj* rico, -a.
weap·on arma *f.*
wear 1 *vt* (clothes)* llevar (puesto, -a); *(shoes)* calzar; **he wears glasses** lleva gafas; **he was wearing a jacket** llevaba chaqueta. **2** *n (deterioration)* desgaste *m*; **normal w. and tear** desgaste *m* natural.
▸**wear off** *vi (effect, pain)* pasar.
▸**wear out 1** *vt* gastar; *fig (exhaust)* agotar. **2** *vi* gastarse.
wea·ry *adj (tired)* cansado, -a.
wea·sel comadreja *f.*
weath·er tiempo *m*; **the w. is fine** hace buen tiempo; **to feel under the w.** no encontrarse bien.
weath·er fore·cast parte *m* meteorológico.
weave* *vt* tejer; *(intertwine)* entretejer.
web *(of spider)* telaraña *f.*
wed·ding boda *f.*
wed·ding ring alianza *f.*
wedge 1 *n* cuña *f*; *(for table leg)* calce *m.* **2** *vt* calzar.
Wednes·day miércoles *m.*
wee *adj esp Scot* pequeñito, -a.
weed mala hierba *f.*
week semana *f*; **a w. (ago) today/yesterday** hoy hace/ayer hizo una semana; **a w. today** de aquí a ocho días.
week·day día *m* laborable.
week·end fin *m* de semana; **at** *or* **on the w.** el fin de semana.
week·ly 1 *adj* semanal. **2** *adv* semanalmente. **3** *n (magazine)* semanario *m.*
weep* *vi* llorar.
weigh *vti* pesar.
weight peso *m*; **to lose w.** adelgazar; **to put on w.** engordar.
weird *adj* raro, -a.
wel·come 1 *adj (person)* bienvenido, -a; *(news)* grato, -a; *(change)* oportuno, -a; **to make sb w.** acoger a algn calurosamente; **you're w.!** ¡no hay de qué! **2** *n (greeting)* bienvenida *f.* **3** *vt* acoger; *(more formally)* darle la bienvenida a; *(news)* acoger con agrado; *(decision)* aplaudir.
weld *vt* soldar.
wel·fare *(social security)* seguridad *f* social.
well[1] *(for water)* pozo *m.*
well[2] **1** *adj (healthy)* bien; **he's w.** está bien (de salud); **to get w.** reponerse; **all is w.** todo va bien. **2** *adv (properly)* bien; **w. done!** ¡muy bien!; **as w.** también; **as w. as** así como; **children as w. as adults** tanto niños como adultos. **3** *interj (surprise)* ¡vaya!; **w., as I was saying** pues (bien), como iba diciendo.
well-be·haved *adj (child)* formal; *(dog)* manso.
well-be·ing bienestar *m.*
well-in·formed *adj* bien informado, -a.
wel·ling·tons *npl* botas *fpl* de goma.
well-known *adj* (bien) conocido, -a.
well-man·nered *adj* educado, -a.
well-off *adj* acomodado, -a.
well-to-do *adj* acomodado, -a.
Welsh 1 *adj* galés, -esa. **2** *n (language)* galés *m*; **the W.** *pl* los galeses.
Welsh·man galés *m.*
Welsh·wom·an galesa *f.*
went *pt of* **go**.
were *pt of* **be**.
west 1 *n* oeste *m*; **in** *or* **to the w.** al oeste. **2** *adj* occidental. **3** *adv* al oeste.
west·bound *adj* (con) dirección oeste.
west·ern 1 *adj* del oeste, occidental. **2** *n (film)* western *m.*
west·ward *adj* hacia el oeste.
west·wards *adv* hacia el oeste.
wet 1 *adj* mojado, -a; *(slightly)* húmedo, -a; *(rainy)* lluvioso, -a; **'w. paint'** 'recién pintado'. **2** *vt** mojar.
whale ballena *f.*
wharf (*pl* **wharves**) muelle *m.*
what 1 *adj (in questions)* qué; **ask her w. color she likes** pregúntale qué color le gusta. **2** *pron (in questions)* qué; **w. are you talking about?** ¿de qué estás hablando?; **he asked me w. I thought** me preguntó lo que pensaba; **I didn't know w. to say** no sabía qué decir; **w. about your father?** ¿y tu padre (qué)?; **w. about going tomorrow?** ¿qué te parece si vamos mañana?; **w. did you do that for?** ¿por qué hiciste eso?; **w. (did you say)?** ¿cómo?; **w. is it?** *(definition)* ¿qué es?; **what's the matter?** ¿qué pasa?; **w.'s it called?** ¿cómo se llama?; **w.'s this for?** ¿para qué sirve esto? **3** *interj* **w. a goal!** ¡qué golazo!
what·ev·er 1 *adj* **w. day you want** cualquier día que quieras; **of w. color** no importa de qué color; **nothing w.** nada en absoluto; **with no interest w.** sin interés alguno. **2** *pron (anything, all that)* (todo) lo que; **do w. you like** haz lo que quieras; **don't tell him w. you do** no se te ocurra decírselo; **w. (else) you find** cualquier (otra) cosa que encuentres.
wheat trigo *m.*
wheel 1 *n* rueda *f.* **2** *vt (bicycle)* empujar.
wheel·bar·row carretilla *f.*
wheel·chair silla *f* de ruedas.
when 1 *adv* cuando; *(in questions)* cuándo; **w. did he arrive?** ¿cuándo llegó?; **tell me w. to go** dime cuándo he de irme; **the days w. I work** los días en que trabajo. **2** *conj* cuando; **I'll tell you w. she comes** te lo diré cuando llegue.
when·ev·er *conj (when)* cuando; *(every time)* siempre que.
where *adv (in questions)* dónde; *(direction)* adónde; *(at, in which)* donde; *(direction)* adonde; **w. are you going?** ¿adónde vas?; **w. do you come from?** ¿de dónde es usted?; **tell me w. you went** dime adónde fuiste.
where·a·bouts 1 *adv* **w. do you live?** ¿por dónde vives? **2** *n* paradero *m.*
where·as *conj (but, while)* mientras que.
where·by *adv* por el *or* la *or* lo cual.
wher·ev·er *conj* dondequiera que; **I'll find him w. he is** le encontraré dondequiera que esté; **sit w. you like** siéntate donde quieras.
wheth·er *conj (if)* si; **I don't know w. it is true** no sé si es verdad; **I doubt w. he'll win** dudo que gane.
which 1 *adj* qué; **w. color do you prefer?** ¿qué color prefieres?; **w. one?** ¿cuál?; **w. way?** ¿por dónde?; **tell me w. dress you like** dime qué vestido te gusta. **2** *pron (in questions)* cuál, cuáles; **w. of you did it?** ¿quién de vosotros lo hizo? ▪ *(relative)* que; *(after preposition)* que, el/la que, los/las que; **here are the books (w.) I have read** aquí están los libros que he leído; **the accident (w.) I told you about** el accidente de que te hablé; **the car in w. he was traveling** el coche en (el) que viajaba; **this is the one (w.) I like** éste es el que me gusta; **I played three sets, all of w. I lost** jugué tres sets, todos los cuales perdí. ▪ *(referring to a clause)* lo cual; **he won, w. made me very happy** ganó, lo cual me alegró mucho.
which·ev·er 1 *adj* el/la que, cualquiera que; **I'll take w. books you don't want** tomaré los libros que no quieras; **w. system you choose** cualquiera que sea el sistema que elijas. **2** *pron* el que, la que.
while 1 *conj (time)* mientras; *(although)* aunque; *(whereas)* mientras que; **he fell asleep w. driving** se durmió mientras conducía. **2** *n (length of time)* rato *m*; **in a little w.** dentro de poco.
whim capricho *m.*
whine *vi (child)* lloriquear; *(complain)* quejarse.
whip 1 *n (for punishment)* látigo *m.* **2** *vt (as punishment)* azotar; *(cream etc)* batir.
▸**whip out** *vt* sacar rápidamente.
whirl *vi* **to w. (round)** girar con rapidez; *(leaves etc)* arremolinarse.
whisk 1 *n (for cream)* batidor *m*; *(electric)* batidora *f.* **2** *vt (cream etc)* batir.
whisk·ers *(of cat)* bigotes *mpl.*
whis·key whisky *m.*
whis·per 1 *n* susurro *m.* **2** *vt* decir en voz baja. **3** *vi* susurrar.
whis·tle 1 *n (instrument)* pito *m*; *(sound)* silbido *m.* **2** *vt (tune)* silbar. **3** *vi (person, kettle, wind)* silbar; *(train)* pitar.
white 1 *adj* blanco, -a; **to go w.** *(face)* palidecer; *(hair)* encanecer; **w. coffee** café *m* con leche. **2** *n (color, of eye)* blanco *m*; *(of egg)* clara *f.*
white·wash *vt (wall)* blanquear.
whiz(z) *vi (sound)* silbar; **to w. past** pasar volando.
who *pron (in questions) sing* quién; *pl* quiénes; **w. are they?** ¿quiénes son?; **w. is it?** ¿quién es?; **I don't know w. did it** no sé quién lo hizo. ▪ *rel (defining)* que; *(nondefining)* quien, quienes, el/la cual, los/las cuales; **those w. don't know** los que no saben; **Elena's mother, w. is very rich ...** la madre de Elena, la cual es muy rica ...
who·ev·er *pron* quienquiera que; **give it to w. you like** dáselo a quien quieras; **w. you are** quienquiera que seas.
whole 1 *adj (entire)* entero, -a; *(in one piece)* intacto, -a; **a w. week** una semana entera; **he took the w. lot** se los llevó todos. **2** *n* **the w. of New York** todo Nueva York; **on the w.** en general.
whole·meal *adj* integral.
whole·sale *adv* al por mayor.
whole·sal·er mayorista *mf.*
whol·ly *adv* enteramente, completamente.
whom *pron (question)* a quién. ▪ *(after preposition)* **of** *or* **from w.?** ¿de quién? ▪ *rel* a quien, a quienes; **those w. I have seen** aquéllos a quienes he visto. ▪ *rel (after preposition)* quien, quienes, el/la cual, los/las cuales; **my brothers, both of w. are miners** mis hermanos, que son mineros los dos.
whoop·ing cough tos *f* ferina.
whose 1 *pron* de quién, de quiénes; **w. are these gloves?** ¿de quién son estos guantes? ▪ *rel* cuyo(s)/cuya(s); **the man w. children we saw** el hombre a cuyos hijos vimos. **2** *adj* **w. car/house is this?** ¿de quién es este coche/esta casa?
why *adv* por qué; *(for what purpose)* para qué; **w. did you do that?** ¿por qué hiciste eso?; **w. not go to bed?** ¿por qué no te acuestas?; **I don't know w. he did it** no sé por qué lo hizo; **there's no reason w. you shouldn't go** no hay motivo para que no vayas.
wick mecha *f.*
wick·ed *adj* malvado, -a; *(awful)* malísimo, -a.
wick·er 1 *n* mimbre *f.* **2** *adj* de mimbre.
wide 1 *adj (road, trousers)* ancho, -a; *(area, knowledge, support, range)* amplio, -a; **it is ten**

meters w. tiene diez metros de ancho. **2** *adv* **w. awake** totalmente despierto, -a; **w. open** abierto, -a de par en par.
wide·ly *adv (to travel etc)* extensamente.
wid·en 1 *vt* ensanchar; *(interests)* ampliar. **2** *vi* ensancharse.
wide·spread *adj (unrest, belief)* general; *(damage)* extenso, -a.
wid·ow viuda *f.*
wid·ow·er viudo *m.*
width anchura *f.*
wife (*pl* **wives**) esposa *f.*
wig peluca *f.*
wild *adj (animal, tribe)* salvaje; *(plant)* silvestre; *(temperament, behavior)* alocado, -a; *(appearance)* desordenado, -a; *(passions etc)* desenfrenado, -a.
wil·der·ness desierto *m.*
wild·life fauna *f.*
wild·ly *adv (rush round etc)* como un, -a loco, -a; *(hit out)* a tontas y a locas.
will[1] 1 *n* voluntad *f*; *(testament)* testamento *m*; **good/ill w.** buena/mala voluntad; **of my own free w.** por mi propia voluntad; **to make one's w.** hacer testamento. **2** *vt* **fate willed that ...** el destino quiso que ...
will[2] *v aux* **they w. come** vendrán; **w. he be there? — yes, he w.** ¿estará allí? — sí (, estará); **you w.** *or* **you'll tell him, won't you?** se lo dirás, ¿verdad?; **you w. be here at eleven!** ¡debes estar aquí a las once!; **be quiet, w. you! — no, I won't!** ¿quiere callarse? — no quiero; **will you have a drink? — yes, I w.** ¿quiere tomar algo? — sí, por favor.
will·ing *adj (obliging)* complaciente; **to be w. to do sth** estar dispuesto, -a a hacer algo.
will·ing·ly *adv* de buena gana.
will·ing·ness buena voluntad *f.*
wil·low w. (tree) sauce *m.*
win 1 *n* victoria *f.* **2** *vt** ganar; *(prize)* llevarse; *(victory)* conseguir. **3** *vi** ganar.
wind[1] viento *m*; *(in stomach)* gases *mpl.*
wind[2]* 1 *vt (onto a reel)* enrollar; *(clock)* dar cuerda a. **2** *vi (road, river)* serpentear.
▸**wind back** *vt (film, tape)* rebobinar.
▸**wind on** *vt (film, tape)* avanzar.
wind·mill molino *m* (de viento).
win·dow ventana *f*, *(of vehicle, of ticket office etc)* ventanilla *f*, **(shop) w.** escaparate *m.*
win·dow box jardinera *f.*
win·dow clean·er limpiacristales *mf inv.*
win·dow-pane cristal *m.*
win·dow·sill alféizar *m.*
wind·shield parabrisas *m inv*; **w. wiper** limpiaparabrisas *m inv.*
wind·surf·ing windsurfing *m.*
wind·y *adj* **it is very w. today** hoy hace mucho viento.
wine vino *m*; **w. list** lista *f* de vinos.
wine·glass copa *f* (para vino).
wing ala *f.*
wink 1 *n* guiño *m.* **2** *vi (person)* guiñar el ojo.
win·ner ganador, -a *mf.*
win·ning *adj (person, team)* ganador, -a; *(number)* premiado, -a.
win·nings *npl* ganancias *fpl.*
win·ter 1 *n* invierno *m.* **2** *adj* de invierno.
wipe *vt* limpiar; **to w. one's feet/nose** limpiarse los pies/la nariz.
▸**wipe away** *vt (tear)* enjugar.
▸**wipe off** *vt* quitar frotando.
▸**wipe out** *vt (erase)* borrar.
▸**wipe up** *vi* secar los platos.
wip·er *(in vehicle)* limpiaparabrisas *m.*
wire alambre *m*; *(electric)* cable *m.*
wire mesh/net·ting tela *f* metálica.
wir·ing *(of house)* instalación *f* eléctrica.
wis·dom *(good sense) (of person)* cordura *f*, *(of action)* sensatez *f*, *(learning)* sabiduría *f.*
wise *adj* sabio, -a; **a w. man** un sabio; **it would be w. to keep quiet** sería prudente callarse.
wish 1 *n (desire)* deseo *m* (**for** de); **give your mother my best wishes** salude a su madre de mi parte; **with best wishes, Peter** *(at end of letter)* saludos de Peter. **2** *vt (want)* desear; **I w. I could stay longer** me gustaría poder quedarme más tiempo; **I w. you had told me!** ¡ojalá me lo hubieras dicho!; **to w. for sth** desear algo.
wit *(humour)* ingenio *m*; *(person)* ingenioso, -a *mf*, **wits** *(intelligence)* inteligencia *f*, *fig* **to be at one's wits' end** estar para volverse loco, -a.
witch bruja *f.*
with *prep* con; **the man w. the glasses** el hombre de las gafas; **w. no hat** sin sombrero; **he went w. me/you** fue conmigo/contigo; **he's w. Ford** trabaja para Ford; **to fill a vase w. water** llenar un jarrón de agua; **it is made w. butter** está hecho con mantequilla.
with·draw* 1 *vt* retirar; *(statement)* retractarse de; **to w. money from the bank** sacar dinero del banco. **2** *vi* retirarse; *(drop out)* renunciar.
with·draw·al retirada *f.*
with·er *vi* marchitarse.
with·hold* *vt (money)* retener; *(decision)* aplazar; *(consent)* negar; *(information)* ocultar.
with·in *prep (inside)* dentro de; **w. five kilometers of the town** a menos de cinco kilómetros de la ciudad; **w. the hour** dentro de una hora; **w. the next five years** durante los cinco próximos años.
with·out *prep* sin; **w. a coat** sin abrigo; **he did it w. my knowing** lo hizo sin que lo supiera yo.
wit·ness 1 *n (person)* testigo *mf.* **2** *vt (see)* presenciar.
wob·bly *adj* poco firme; *(table, chair)* cojo, -a.
wolf (*pl* **wolves**) lobo *m.*
wom·an (*pl* **women**) mujer *f*, **old w.** vieja *f.*
won·der 1 *n* **no w. he hasn't come** con razón no ha venido. **2** *vt (ask oneself)* preguntarse; **I w. why** ¿por qué será? **3** *vi* **it makes you w.** te da qué pensar.
won·der·ful *adj* maravilloso, -a.
won't = **will not**.
wood *(forest)* bosque *m*; *(material)* madera *f*, *(for fire)* leña *f.*
wood·en *adj* de madera.
wood·work *(craft)* carpintería *f.*
wool lana *f.*
wool·en 1 *adj* de lana. **2** *npl* **woolens** géneros *mpl* de lana.
word palabra *f*, **in other words ...** es decir ...; **I'd like a w. with you** quiero hablar contigo un momento; **words** *(of song)* letra *f.*
word·ing expresión *f*, **I changed the w. slightly** cambié algunas palabras.
word proc·ess·ing procesamiento *m* de textos.
word proc·es·sor procesador *m* de textos.
wore *pt of* **wear**.
work 1 *n* trabajo *m*; **his w. in the field of physics** su labor en el campo de la física; **out of w.** parado, -a; **a piece of w.** un trabajo; **a w. of art** una obra de arte; **works** *(factory)* fábrica *f.* **2** *vt (drive)* hacer trabajar; *(machine)* manejar; *(mechanism)* accionar. **3** *vi* trabajar (**on, at** en); *(machine)* funcionar; *(drug)* surtir efecto; *(system)* funcionar.
▸**work out 1** *vt (plan)* idear; *(problem)* solucionar; *(solution)* encontrar; *(amount)* calcular. **2** *vi (train)* hacer ejercicio; **it works out to 5 each** sale a 5 cada uno.
worked up *adj* **to get worked up** excitarse.
work·er trabajador, -a *mf*, *(manual)* obrero, -a *mf.*
work·force mano *f* de obra.
work·ing *adj (population, capital)* activo, -a; **w. class** clase *f* obrera; **it is in w. order** funciona.
work·man *(manual)* obrero *m.*
work·out entrenamiento *m.*
work·shop taller *m.*
work·sta·tion estación *f* de trabajo.
world 1 *n* mundo *m*; **all over the w.** en todo el mundo. **2** *adj (record, war)* mundial; **w. champion** campeón, -ona *mf* mundial; **The W. Cup** el Mundial *m.*
world·wide *adj* mundial.
worm lombriz *f.*
worn *adj* gastado, -a.
worn-out *adj (thing)* gastado, -a; *(person)* agotado, -a.
wor·ry 1 *vt* preocupar. **2** *vi* preocuparse (**about** por); **don't w.** no te preocupes. **3** *n* inquietud *f*, **my main w.** mi principal preocupación.
wor·ry·ing *adj* preocupante.
worse *adj & adv* peor; **to get w.** empeorar; **w. than ever** peor que nunca.
wors·en *vti* empeorar.
wor·ship *vt* adorar.
worst 1 *adj & adv* peor; **the w. part about it is that ...** lo peor es que ... **2** *n (person)* el/la peor, los/las peores.
worth 1 *adj* **a house w. $50,000** una casa que vale 50,000 dólares; **a book w. reading** un libro que merece la pena leer; **how much is it w.?** ¿cuánto vale?; **it's w. your while, it's w. it** vale la pena. **2** *n* valor *m*; **five dollars' w. of gas** gasolina por valor de 5 dólares.
worth·while *adj* valioso, -a, que vale la pena.
wor·thy *adj (deserving)* digno, -a (**of** de).
would *v aux (conditional)* **I w. go if I had time** iría si tuviera tiempo; **he w. have won but for that** habría ganado si no hubiera sido por eso. ▪ *(willingness)* **w. you do me a favor?** ¿quiere hacerme un favor?; **w. you like a cigarette?** ¿quiere un cigarrillo?; **the car wouldn't start** el coche no arrancaba. ▪ *(custom)* **we w. go for walks** solíamos dar paseos.
wound 1 *n* herida *f.* **2** *vt* herir.
wrap *vt* envolver.
▸**wrap up 1** *vt* envolver. **2** *vi* **w. up well!** ¡abrígate!
wrap·per *(of sweet)* envoltorio *m.*
wrap·ping pa·per papel *m* de envolver.
wreath (*pl* **wreaths**) *(of flowers)* corona *f.*
wreck 1 *n (sinking)* naufragio *m*; *(ship)* barco *m* naufragado; *(of car, plane)* restos *mpl.* **2** *vt (car, machine)* destrozar; *(holiday)* estropear.
wrench *(tool)* llave *f.*
wres·tle *vi* luchar.
wres·tler luchador, -a *mf.*
wres·tling lucha *f.*
wring* *vt (clothes)* escurrir.
wrin·kle arruga *f.*
wrist muñeca *f.*
wrist·watch reloj *m* de pulsera.
write* *vti* escribir (**about** sobre); **to w. sb** escribir a.
▸**write back** *vi* contestar.
▸**write down** *vt* poner por escrito; *(note)* apuntar.
▸**write off** *vt sep (debt)* condonar.
▸**write off for** *vt* pedir por escrito.
▸**write out** *vt (check)* extender; *(recipe)* escribir.
write-pro·tect·ed *adj* protegido, -a contra escritura.
writ·er *(by profession)* escritor, -a *mf*, *(of book, letter)* autor, -a *mf.*
writ·ing *(script)* escritura *f*, *(handwriting)* letra *f*, **in w.** por escrito.
writ·ing pa·per papel *m* de escribir.
wrong 1 *adj (erroneous)* incorrecto, -a; *(unsuitable)* inadecuado, -a; *(time)* inoportuno, -a; *(not right) (person)* equivocado, -a; *(immoral etc)* malo, -a; **my watch is w.** mi reloj anda mal; **to go the w. way** equivocarse de camino; **I was w. about that boy** me equivoqué con ese chico; **to be w.** no tener razón; **what's w. with smoking?** ¿qué tiene de malo fumar?; **what's w. with you?** ¿qué te pasa? **2** *adv* mal; **to get it w.** equivocarse; **to go w.** *(plan)* salir mal. **3** *n (evil, bad action)* mal *m*; **you were w. to hit him** hiciste mal en pegarle; **to be in the w.** tener la culpa.
wrong·ly *adv (incorrectly)* incorrectamente.

X

X·mas *abbr of* **Christmas** Navidad *f.*
X-ray 1 *n (picture)* radiografía *f*, **to have an X.** hacerse una radiografía. **2** *vt* radiografiar.

Y

yacht yate *m.*
yard[1] *(measure)* yarda *f (aprox 0,914 metros).*
yard[2] patio *m*; jardín *m*; *(of school)* patio *m* (de recreo).
yarn hilo *m.*
yawn 1 *vi* bostezar. **2** *n* bostezo *m.*
year año *m*; *(at school)* curso *m*; **I'm ten years old** tengo diez años.
year·ly *adj* anual.
yeast levadura *f.*
yell 1 *vi* gritar (**at** a). **2** *n* grito *m.*
yel·low *adj & n* amarillo, -a *(m).*
yes *adv* sí.
yes·ter·day *adv* ayer; **the day before y.** anteayer; **y. morning** ayer por la mañana.
yet 1 *adv* **not y.** todavía no; **as y.** hasta ahora; **I haven't eaten y.** no he comido todavía. ▪ *(in questions)* ya; **has he arrived y.?** ¿ha venido ya? **2** *conj (nevertheless)* sin embargo.
yo·gurt yogur *m.*
yolk yema *f.*
you *pers pron (subject) (familiar use) (sing)* tú; *(pl)* vosotros, -as; *(polite use) (sing)* usted; *(pl)* ustedes; **how are y.?** ¿cómo estás?, ¿cómo estáis? ▪ *(object) (familiar use) (sing) (before verb)* te; *(after preposition)* ti; *(pl) (before verb)* os; *(after preposition)* vosotros, -as; **I saw y.** te vi, os vi; **with y.** contigo, con vosotros, -as. ▪ *(object) (polite use) (sing) (before verb)* le; *(after preposition)* usted; *(pl) (before verb)* les; *(after preposition)* ustedes; **I saw y.** le vi, les vi; **with y.** con usted, con ustedes. ▪ *(subject) (impers use)* **y. never know** nunca se sabe.
young 1 *adj* joven; *(brother etc)* pequeño, -a. **2** *n* **the y.** los jóvenes *mpl*; *(animals)* las crías.

young·ster muchacho, -a *mf.*
your *poss adj (familiar use) (referring to one person)* tu, tus; *(referring to more than one person)* vuestro, -a, vuestros, -as. ▪ *(polite use)* su, sus. ▪ *(impers use)* **the house is on y. right** la casa queda a la derecha; **they clean y. shoes for you** te limpian los zapatos.
yours *poss pron (familiar use) (referring to one person)* el tuyo, la tuya, los tuyos, las tuyas; *(referring to more than one person)* el vuestro, la vuestra, los vuestros, las vuestras; **the house is y.** la casa es tuya. ▪ *(polite use)* el suyo, la suya; *(pl)* los suyos, las suyas; **the house is y.** la casa es suya.
your·self *(pl* **yourselves***)* **1** *pers pron (familiar use) sing* tú mismo, -a; *pl* vosotros, -as mismos, -as; **by y.** (tú) solo; **by yourselves** vosotros, -as solos, -as. ▪ *(polite use) sing* usted mismo, -a; *pl* ustedes mismos, -as; **by y.** (usted) solo, -a; **by yourselves** (ustedes) solos, -as. **2** *reflexive pron* **did you wash y.?** *(familiar use) sing* ¿te lavaste?; *pl* ¿os lavasteis?; *(polite use) sing* ¿se lavó?, *pl* ¿se lavaron?
youth juventud *f, (young man)* joven *m.*
youth club club *m* juvenil.
Yu·go·slav *adj & n* yugoslavo, -a *(mf).*

Z

ze·bra cebra *f.*
ze·ro cero *m.*
zig·zag **1** *n* zigzag *m.* **2** *vi* zigzaguear.
zip *n* z. **(fastener)** cremallera *f.*
▸**zip up** *vt* subir la cremallera de.
ZIP code código *m* postal.
Zip® drive unidad *f* Zip®.
zip·per cremallera *f.*
zit *fam (pimple)* espinilla *f.*
zone zona *f.*
zoo zoo *m.*
zuc·chi·ni calabacín *m.*